THE INDEPENDENT SCHOOLS GUIDE

2011–2012

SEVENTEENTH EDITION

THE INDEPENDENT SCHOOLS GUIDE

2011–2012

A fully comprehensive guide to independent education in the United Kingdom

The global experts in British independent education

KoganPage

LONDON   PHILADELPHIA   NEW DELHI

Publisher's note

The information supplied in this *Guide* has been published in good faith on the basis of information submitted by the schools listed. Neither Kogan Page nor Gabbitas Educational Consultants can guarantee the accuracy of the information in this *Guide* and accept no responsibility for any error or misrepresentation. All liability for loss, disappointment, negligence or other damage caused by the reliance on the information contained in this *Guide*, or in the event of bankruptcy or liquidation or cessation of trade of any company, individual or firm mentioned, is hereby excluded.

Photographs on front cover reproduced with kind permission of (top) Tring Park School for the Performing Arts, (left to right) Homefield Preparatory School, City of London School and Parkgate House School.

First published in Great Britain in 1995 by Kogan Page Limited
This seventeeth edition published in 2012

120 Pentonville Road
London N1 9JN
United Kingdom
www.koganpage.com

1518 Walnut Street, Suite 1100
Philadelphia PA 19102
USA

4737/23 Ansari Road
Daryaganj
New Delhi 110002
India

© Gabbitas and Kogan Page, 2012

British Library Cataloguing in Publication Data

A CIP record for this book is available from the British Library

ISBN   978 0 7494 6418 9
E-ISBN   978 0 7494 6419 6

Typeset by AJS DataSolutions Ltd., Huddersfield
Print production managed by Jellyfish
Printed and bound in Great Britain by Ashford Colour Press Ltd, Gosport

Contents

PART 5:
REFERENCE SECTION

Acknowledgements

The Independent Schools Guide is the result of many, many hours, weeks and indeed months of work by editors, proof-readers, designers, data administrators, publishing professionals, educationalists and friends of Gabbitas. The guide you see today is the result of generations of experience, a good helping of insight and heaps of industrious lucubration.

For those who have already glanced at the contents, the next acknowledgements will come as no surprise. Additional editorial contributions from Peter Dix, Hilary Moriarty, Sarah Belotti, James Wardrobe, Durrell Barnes, Fergus Rose, Towry Law and Dr Wendy Piatt, are all included with thanks.

Special thanks also go to the parent company of Gabbitas, Prospects Services and in particular Ray Auvray, Executive Chairman – whose support is greatly appreciated.

It would be entirely amiss not to mention the contributions from independent schools. Thanks go to Tring Park School for the Performing Arts, Homefield Preparatory School, City of London School and Parkgate House School for kind permission to reproduce photographs used in the cover design, a particular mention goes to Homefield School, as their entry won first place in this year's young photographer competition.

We must not forget all the Heads and school contacts who have so promptly provided information in the making of this new-format seventeenth edition. The many educational associations and organizations that add to the rich, characteristic idiosyncrasies of the independent sector are also owed a debt of gratitude for the useful information they provide.

Thank you.

Foreword

Welcome to the seventeenth edition of
The Independent Schools Guide

The first Gabbitas schools guide appeared in 1924 (then simply entitled 'Schools'). The modest publication with thin glossy paper, tiny print and dubiously reproduced monochrome images has been reincarnated, year on year through many an event, not least World War II, bringing invaluable information and guidance to generations of parents.

The guide has, as you will see, evolved immeasurably since the first edition and represents a great departure from more recent editions. Introductions such as full-colour, new editorial contributors and an intuitively arranged directory make for an imminently accessible, contemporary guidebook.

Independent schools have, similarly, seen many a change. There has been a conspicuous shift towards co-education, with only 20 per cent of schools now single sex. Exclusive full boarding schools are in the minority, with day boarding schools growing in number. Adapting to changing attitudes, flexi-boarding and weekly boarding are also much more widespread.

International intake is more evident than ever with as many as 23,000 overseas pupils in attendance throughout the sector. A feature addressed in 'Coming from Overseas', the section dedicated to those living outside the UK contemplating British independent schools.

The curriculum has, of course, changed since the first edition. Throughout the years we have seen the O-level, then the CSE discontinued giving way to the GCSE and the many revised versions of same. In more recent years, the IB has featured prominently and independent educationalists have established teaching of the IGCSE and Pre-U. In response to calls for greater differentiation amongst top-grade students the A* grade has appeared, first for GCSE, and more recently for A-level.

A defining characteristic of independent schools remains unmoved by trends... that is the quality of education provided. Independent senior schools, now as ever, produce some of the very best academic results. A fact that sees them frequently featured at the top of league tables - statistical methodologies allowing

As the independent sector has seen many a development, there is manifest need for an accurate record of schools and for guidance when choosing between them. *The Independent Schools Guide* in its seventeenth edition provides this and a great deal more, collated in a creatively redesigned new reference format.

About *The Independent Schools Guide*

Within the pages readers are advised by The Global Experts in British Independent Education – Gabbitas. The consultants introduce and explain all pertinent aspects of independent education and offer invaluable guidance for those preparing for and selecting independent schools.

The Independent Schools Guide provides comprehensive coverage with circa 2,000 school entries and is equally well suited to parents with nascent children, planning for day nursery and pre prep induction, as to seniors and their families preparing for boarding schools, independent sixth forms and colleges. Visit the online accompaniment to the guidebook at www.independentschoolsguide.com.

About Gabbitas

Established since 1873, Gabbitas is uniquely placed to offer independent expertise. Each year the consultants provide personal advice and guidance to thousands of parents and pupils the world over, at all stages of education. Advice and Guidance covers:

- choosing the right independent school (pre-prep, prep and senior);
- educational assessment;
- sixth form options – including A levels, IB, Cambridge Pre-U and vocational courses;
- university and degree choices, also UCAS applications;
- alternatives to university;
- careers assessment and guidance, job searching and interview technique.

Gabbitas also advises on transferring to the British education system and offers AEGIS accredited guardianship services for overseas pupils at UK boarding schools. To find out more contact us at:

GABBITAS EDUCATION
Norfolk House I 30 Charles II Street I London I SW1Y 4AE
T +44(0)20 7734 0161 **F** +44(0)20 7437 1764 **E** info@gabbitas.co.uk or visit
W www.gabbitas.co.uk

The global experts in British independent education

How to Use the Guide

About independent schools

The first part of this *Guide* offers extensive information about independent schools, examinations, fee-planning, scholarships and bursaries as well as guidance on choosing a school.

Researching individual schools

The main index at the back gives all page references for each school.

Selecting schools

If you are looking for a school in a specific area, turn to the directory section (Part Two), which is arranged geographically by town and county. Schools in London are listed under their postal areas. Each entry gives the name, postal address, telephone and fax numbers and e-mail address of the school, together with the name of the Head, details of the type and age range of pupils accepted, the number of pupils, number of boarders (where applicable) and the annual fees.

Schools which have an asterisk also appear in the School Profiles section (Part Three), where advertisers provide more detailed information. These schools also have a map reference to show their exact location.

The Schools by Category section contains a number of advertising schools listed with details of their particular charactersitics.

For further references, for example to find out whether a school offers scholarships, turn to the appropriate index at the back.

Scholarships, bursaries and reserved entrance awards

Many schools offer scholarships for children with a particular talent, bursaries where there is financial hardship or reserved entrance awards for children with a parent in a specific profession such as the clergy or HM Forces. Part Five contains a complete list of schools, by county, which offer such awards.

This section is necessarily only a brief guide to awards available. More specific information can be obtained from individual schools.

Religious affiliation

The index in Part Five provides a full list of schools under appropriate headings.

Single-sex schools

For a complete list of single-sex schools, turn to Part Five.

Boarding schools

Schools with boarding provision generally offer full, weekly or flexi-boarding options. Some Sixth Form colleges, with no residential facilities, may offer accommodation with host families. The number of boarders is shown in the entries in Part Two. For an index of boarding provision by county, see Part Five.

Dyslexia

Most schools offer help, in varying degrees, for pupils with dyslexia. A list of schools registered with CReSTeD (Council for the Registration of Schools Teaching Dyslexic Pupils) appears in Part Five.

English as a foreign language

Most independent schools offer assistance to overseas pupils who require special English language tuition. A list of schools, arranged by county, appears in Part Five.

Schools accredited by the Independent Schools Council

Part Five contains an index of schools in membership of the associations listed below, which together form the Independent Schools Council (ISC). A satisfactory inspection report by the Independent Schools Inspectorate is a requirement for any school wishing to join one of these associations and for its continued accreditation as a member. For more information on the inspection of independent schools, see Part 1.1.

- Headmasters' and Headmistresses' Conference (HMC)
- Girls' Schools Association (GSA) (including the Girls' Day School Trust GDST)
- Society of Headmasters and Headmistresses of Independent Schools (SHMIS)
- Independent Association of Prep Schools (IAPS)
- Independent Schools Association (ISA).

Other associations which are constituent members of ISC but are not covered by the index are the Association of Governing Bodies of Independent Schools (AGBIS), the Independent Schools Bursars' Association (ISBA) and the Council of British International Schools (COBIS).

The Independent Schools Guide online

Remember that you can search for schools at www.independentschoolsguide.com.

PART ONE

THE INDEPENDENT SECTOR AND INDEPENDENT SCHOOLS

The Independent Schools Guide Photography Competition 2011

2nd Prize Winner

Merchiston Castle School
Marcus Cameron

The independent sector and independent schools

Independent schools are largely self-governing and are not required to comply with all legislation covering schools maintained by the state. Under the Education Act 2002 all schools in England must be registered with the Department for Education (DfE), in Wales the Department for Children, Education, Lifelong Learning and Skills (DCELLS). In accordance with the Education Scotland Act 1980, independent schools in Scotland are registered by the Scottish government. However, independent schools throughout the UK receive little or no direct state funding and are free from much central and local government control.

Independent sector – defining terms

There is quite some discourse about the appropriate defining and descriptive language for schools in the sector. The term 'private school', although referring specifically to privately owned schools, is used to indicate schools free from government control. Although used more often in previous years, it is still relevant for today's parents.

A phrase frequently voiced by those familiar with independent education is 'fee paying schools'. This figurative saying includes reference to school fees paid *to* schools.

Another term, 'public school', is well known and generally refers to old established schools in membership of the Headmasters' and Headmistresses' Conference (HMC). As many of these date back to the days when education was a luxury chiefly provided by private tutors, the term 'public school' was used to indicate a school which the public could attend.

Gabbitas consultants tend to use the term 'independent school', which is in line with the current customs of teachers, the Department for Education and parents. As you read on you will see that it is also used throughout *The Independent Schools Guide*.

School organizational structures and management

Most independent schools are run as charitable trusts under a board of governors. Schools with charitable status are effectively non-profit-making concerns; surplus funds are allocated at the discretion of the governors. Often they are invested in new facilities or in scholarships or bursaries. A few schools are still privately owned.

The board of governors is the policy-making body for the school. It is responsible for the appointment of the head, allocation of finances and major decisions affecting the school and its development. Governors give their time voluntarily, often contributing professional expertise in education, business, finance, marketing or other areas relevant to the management of the school. The board commonly includes a number of parent-governors who have children at the school.

Day-to-day responsibility for the running of the school is delegated to the head, who is accountable to the board of governors, with support from one or more deputy heads. Other key figures include the bursar, who is responsible for the school's financial management, the director of studies, who manages the curriculum, timetable, examinations and other academic matters, and the registrar, who is responsible for admissions and arrangements for parents to visit the school. Further details of independent school staff and contacts can be found at the end of Part 1.2.

Independent sector – number of schools

Independent schools in the UK represent approximately 7 per cent of all schools. Most of the 2,000 or so independent schools are to be found in England, with a small proportion located in Scotland, Wales and Northern Ireland.

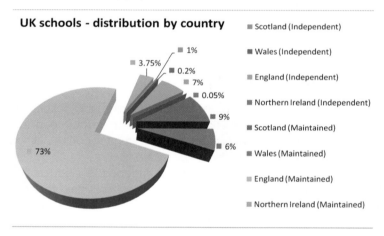

UK schools - distribution by country

- Scotland (Independent)
- Wales (Independent)
- England (Independent)
- Northern Ireland (Independent)
- Scotland (Maintained)
- Wales (Maintained)
- England (Maintained)
- Northern Ireland (Maintained)

1%
3.75%
0.2%
7%
0.05%
9%
6%
73%

Details of independent schools in each of the regions of the UK and some schools in mainland Europe are included in Parts 2 and 3.

Different schools, different styles

The independent sector includes schools of many different styles and philosophies, including both the traditional and the more liberal. Each is unique, with its own ethos and culture. Sizes can vary greatly, from small schools with less than a hundred pupils to much larger intake schools catering for up to two thousands pupils. Some are based in towns or cities, while others, including many boarding schools, are located in the countryside. Many are co-educational and others are single-sex, although it is not uncommon for boys' and girls' schools to co-educate for specific age ranges eg for pre-prep or sixth form. International pupil intake is a characteristic of some independent schools. Boarding schools, for example, tend to attract significant numbers of overseas pupils and there are a few schools (international schools and international study centres) primarily for international pupils.

Education for all

Your child's academic needs are a high priority. Independent schools are not only for the most academically gifted children, although there is always some form of selection. The most selective accept only pupils capable of keeping pace with a fast-moving curriculum but there are many others catering for a wider range of ability. Some, for example, specialize in educating those in need of more individual attention in a less academic environment. Good independent schools enable pupils, whatever their academic ability, to achieve their best. Their success in helping children to fulfil their potential is evident from the excellent examination results reported each year.

Development of strengths and interests

Pupils are encouraged to develop their strengths outside, as well as inside, the classroom, ensuring that special talents, in music, drama, art or sport, are nurtured. They provide a range of extra-curricular activities which inspire enthusiasm for a great many wider interests.

Small classes and individual attention

Small class sizes and close individual attention are prime characteristics of the sector. Generally, classes for children at the lower end of the age range have between 15 and 20 pupils. At senior school, GCSE (or IGCSE) class numbers tend to be between 12 and 18. Independent school sixth forms offer the opportunity for more attentive tuition still, with between 4 and 12 pupils in a class.

Traditional values and personal growth

Much emphasis is placed on the traditional values of tolerance and consideration for others and on personal development within a secure, disciplined environment. Pupils normally have a personal tutor who, as part of an experienced team, monitors progress and personal welfare throughout their time at school.

Excellent teachers and facilities

The independent sector often appeals to teachers at the height of their profession. Academic traditions and greater educational liberty draw those with a dedication to education and young people's learning. Many schools also offer unparalleled facilities for teaching, accommodation, sports and all aspects of school life, complementing the quality of teaching.

Following this brief introduction to the independent offering, we turn to the personal matter of selecting the right school for your child.

Choosing an independent school

Peter Dix, Former Head of Port Regis, provides advice and guidance on choosing a school for your child

Choosing the right school(s) for one's children is likely to be the most important decision parents will make for them, so it is vital to do all that is possible to get it right.

Beginning your research

If you plan to send your children locally and have some familiarity with your school options, it is never too early to engage purposefully with your research. If you are moving to a new part of the country, however, or have recently done so, you have even more work to do, so get cracking now! Often parents are torn as to whether they should find the house or the school first: my resounding advice is choose the right school and let the house follow, even if, as is so often the case, you have to rent for a while before you settle on your choice of house. The school is by far the more important consideration!

Entering schools – appropriate stages

Changing schools at 15 or 17 is not generally recommended because of the likely disruption to GCSE or A level studies, particularly if the move means a change to a different examination syllabus. If a move has to be made after age 13, it may be best to wait until after GCSEs or their equivalent have been completed.

School selection

You will, no doubt, start off by establishing your parameters: location (which, for boarding schools, will include proximity to airports, the country cottage, grandparents, and so on); fee levels; co-ed or single-sex; style (highly academic, more all-round; traditional, more contemporary; campus or urban...) and what facilities and emphasis there may be for your child's particular interests and talents. I would strongly advise you, though, not to be too exclusive in all this. You may just find, for example, that a more forward-looking co-ed school really appeals despite your assumption that traditional single-sex is what you are looking for. In other words, make sure you have a long preliminary list of possible schools that includes a few outside your template.

A vital consideration when choosing an independent school is when to register and enrol your child. The independent sector provides schooling for all age ranges. Entry stages are shown below:

Independent school entry age by school type

Entry age	School type
2–7/8	Nursery or pre-preparatory school
7/8–13	Preparatory school
11/13–16/18	Senior school
16–18	Sixth form

Sources of useful information

I am sure you will be chatting to your friends and neighbours, and may also consider using an educational consultancy, to identify target schools. You should then have a look at the websites of any contenders to make sure that each school is offering more or less what you are looking for and then phone the school – much better than writing or going via the website's 'Contact Us' link – and ask for a prospectus and the current school magazine (plus any other such material they may have available). You should also go onto the Independent Schools Inspectorate (ISI) website (www.isi.net) and read the latest inspection report of each one, and do the same on the Ofsted site (www.ofsted.gov.uk) for the pastoral reports on schools which have boarding provision (more details on schools inspections can also be found later in this guide). As the independent sector consists of uniformly good to excellent schools, expect these inspection reports to glow... but look for small points of difference, which can prove very revealing. I suspect you will then find yourself drawing up a long list of half a dozen or so schools, which, as you refine the process, you reduce to two or three for your short list.

Misleading league tables

Do *not* be over-exercised about league table positions. These tell you quite a lot about the selectivity of a school and very little about what the school will do for your child. They also indicate levels of attainment in a school (where the pupils are) but nothing about degrees of achievement (how far they have travelled to get there, or, to put it another way, the all-important 'value-added'). Remember too that more and more senior schools, including many of the most academically prestigious, are refusing to cooperate with the league-table industry (which has now been largely discredited) and that most of the best prep schools don't even do the National Curriculum tests on which their league tables are based.

Keeping your options open

You may well be looking in the first instance for a prep school, perhaps with a pre-prep and nursery attached. London day schools are often in heavy demand and you may be confronted by an entrance test of some sort, irrespective of the age of the child. Such a process can prove stressful for the parents and equally so for the child – but only if the parents let that happen. I strongly advise you *not* to tell a child that the rest of his or her life depends on the outcome! This will almost certainly lead to underperformance. If a place is not offered, don't worry; there are dozens and dozens of terrific schools available. It may all just take a little longer as you cast your net wider.

More than a purely academic consideration

You may feel, as many do, that education is about much more than merely the academic and that having a narrow focus on this is not the best way to educate children. All schools, I believe, but especially prep schools, have a responsibility to provide an education which is also moral, spiritual, emotional, physical and cultural to prepare children for what awaits them at the next stage of their education and for life in the outside world. My advice would be to look for a school that does not sell itself exclusively, or even mainly, on exam results but seeks instead to nurture rounded and civilized children who develop an attitude to work which is based on self-motivation and enthusiasm. The best schools are those which enrich children's outlook on life, encouraging critical thinking and intellectual curiosity, as well as introducing them to the history and range of language, ideas and civilizations. The appreciation of art, music, poetry and much else is an important part of what it is to be educated, and all of this should be embodied in the school's approach to education. I have always felt it important that children at school strive to engage enthusiastically with things outside the classroom and to develop the sort of considerate and decent conduct towards others that produces rounded and emotionally literate people. This general competence should sit comfortably and effectively alongside academic ability, and so I feel you should strive to find a school that has such an educational agenda.

Entry procedures

Most prep schools will have a more informal admissions process, with any entrance test not much more than a procedure for making sure the children can access the Common Entrance curriculum (which is followed by a large number of such schools) or the less demanding National Curriculum (which is also offered by state schools). Schools will also be looking for a good 'fit' of child (and parents!) to school, and so it is standard procedure for the family to visit the schools as part of the application process.

   The entry requirements for senior independent schools are often more demanding, with the better-known ones operating admissions procedures which do require (sometimes quite significant) academic potential to be proven. This may take the form of a full-blown entrance exam covering up to seven subjects, almost inevitably the 'Common Entrance' exam or a less comprehensive but equally searching assessment which usually consists of an IQ test of some sort (increasingly often taken on computer), an interview and a report from the child's current school. Parents should, of course, look into all of these options and procedures as part of their research, and the junior school heads will always be extremely helpful in the process. Candidates from overseas, who have not been following the same curriculum as their UK counterparts, will nearly always find senior schools offering a different and more appropriate form of entrance assessment. The schools will advise.

Visiting schools

And so to your all-important visit to the schools. I do have some reservations about the usefulness of open days. They are by definition rather artificial marketing exercises where schools roll out their best teachers and pupils to impress and steer parents to what they want them to see. There are also likely to be limited opportunities for one-to-one discussion with heads and other senior staff. Given the choice, I would visit on any ordinary day and get an impression of the school in action without the razzmatazz and make sure I had appointments to meet certain staff. If you can do both, however, go for it, because you will then at the very least see what the school is like when it is really making an effort and be able to make judgements from that, especially in comparison with a normal day! If you have the choice, try to visit senior schools in the first half of the Autumn or Summer terms, and avoid the second half of the Summer one when schools are in full exam (or worse, post-exam) mode. Prep schools can be visited comfortably at any time. Schools look best in good weather, but perhaps it is better to see them in the wet and gloom when you are less likely to be seduced by the look of the place!

Finding the human dimension

On any visit, please look out for the human dimension of the school. Look at the faces of the children as you walk around (are they bright-eyed and happy?); watch how the pupils interact with one another and the staff (is that the tone and style of relationship you want?); is there recent and lively work on display round the school?; is there evidence of attention to detail (notices pinned neatly on boards; little or no litter around; reasonably tidy changing-rooms. . . because negatives here can betray a rather casual attitude in general)?; how efficiently has your communication been handled? Is the atmosphere purposeful, friendly, warm, and particularly where young children are involved, is there a sense of fun? Small word; massive importance! Most of all though, does it feel right? Does the school reflect your own values and will it reinforce these in your child when you are not there? Do not sign up to any school or boarding house until you are satisfied that you (and, in most cases, your child) are happy with all this.

Touring the school

Your visit will always include a tour, and each school will have its own style of doing things. Here is your chance, whoever is showing you round, of seeing the school in action and getting a real feel for how the school manages things which you feel are important. At the heart of every school is the classroom lesson, and what happens in the classroom should be one of your main criteria in choosing a school. You should insist on visiting some classes in action and just hope it is not one of those silly schools that think prospective parents would rather see the lesson freeze to a standstill, with children suddenly standing and looking awkwardly at you (and vice versa) when you walk in. If this does happen, I suggest you say hello to the teacher and pupils and ask the teacher to carry on. . . and then watch what happens! You will have your own ideas about how lessons should be conducted, but I do not think it is good practice to have children sitting passively in front of a teacher who drones on and on without involving them in active learning. The only sound in the world to beat the purr of happy parents is the hum of children engaged enthusiastically in learning (and the former is likely to follow the latter)! A good lesson will have some traditional whole-class delivery from the teacher with hands up and the like from the children; some individual written work performed in silence by the children; but also some grouping of the children where they spark off one another. . . without undue noise and general mayhem! Good teachers teach on the edge some of the time to create excitement in their lessons and an enthusiasm for learning. Bad teachers grip their classes either so tightly that any spark is obliterated or so slackly that conflagration ensues! Your instinct and common sense will help you decide whether what is happening in a class when you visit is inspiring the children or not. You will also quickly get a feel for the teacher–pupil chemistry as well as the extent to which the environment of the classrooms is likely to be helping or hindering the pupils' learning. This is your chance to glance over children's shoulders at their books and to have a look at what is on the walls. The corridors too should be bright and covered with examples of recent work. Frown at any displays that are more than a term old. Insist too on going off-piste on your tour. Ask (courteously, of course) to peep behind doors which are closed, and make sure you stop and talk to passing pupils and teachers, who have not been specifically briefed to impress you!

Trusting your own judgement

Of course, different schools suit different children, but above all else please be guided by your gut-feeling when you are choosing a school. When buying a house, the estate agent's details about size of sitting room or type of kitchen, which you thought were so important, will often go out the window in favour of the strong intuitive sense you have when you walk into a house that just feels right – so too with schools. Do not be over-impressed by glossy prospectuses or smooth-talking staff. They may have a wonderful new music school, for example, but talk to pupils about how it is used and whether it is making a difference to the school's music. Is the head of Music dynamic and inspirational? Good facilities are not the defining feature of good schools – and any head would rather have good staff than good facilities – but the best schools have both.

The head and house staff

The head is a really key figure in any school (particularly, perhaps, in a junior school), with much of the ethos, character and style determined by him or her, and in a boarding school the housemaster/mistress is also extremely important. You may well want to know how much longer the head is likely to be at the school and how many years the housemaster/mistress has on their contract, but I would not let this be the overriding concern. The independent sector is full of talented and ambitious staff, and these good schools will always find good replacements! Details of other important independent school contacts appear later in Part 1.2.

Questions to ask the head

Ask the head searching questions about things academic and look at some pupils' books if you can, and just check that they are being marked positively and thoroughly. There will also be any number of other things you will want to ask during your interview, so be advised to make a list before you go! You should certainly enquire as to the destinations of leavers – this will give you a steer on the academic levels achieved as well as the ambitions of the schools – and you will also doubtless want to know about how well the school can sustain and develop your child's interests and talents in various things like sport, art, drama, music and technology. Ask for evidence and do not allow yourself to be fobbed off with bland assurances. You may want to know about religious observance as well as the cultural mix of the school. You will probably want to understand how inclusive the school's selection policies are: are there sports teams for everyone or just the superstars; can anyone be in the play, or is it always reserved for the thespians; will your child's artwork ever go on view; and will his enthusiastic but comparatively modest scrapings on the violin ever be heard in the recital hall?

I would turn my back on any school that was interested more in obviously talented children than in the others. Satisfy yourself that your child will not disappear between the cracks and make as sure as you possibly can that he or she will enjoy being there and will really get something out of the experience over and above certain grades at the end of the process. The child is the father of the man, and you have a golden opportunity to ensure he inherits the value of the opportunities that an independent school provides.

A word or two on boarding

There is detailed advice about boarding schools later in Part 1.2 but please allow me to say just a word or two. Whilst every school in the country, boarding or day, has a loose-limbed group or two, there tends to be much more overview of social interaction in a boarding school than is possible in a day school, where any bullying is more likely to happen outside the school gates and/or electronically. Good boarding schools can monitor the latter issue pretty effectively too, and the same applies to sex and drugs. These things are much more likely to swirl around outside school... not least at parties! Whilst there are no guarantees in these things, if you are considering a boarding school for your child, there is an excellent chance nowadays that things will work out well. . . but you do need to trust the school and *not* interfere over every minor issue. A good school will employ excellent communication with parents, especially perhaps those who live overseas, and as long as any queries or concerns you have about your child are responded to promptly and reassuringly, you should let go and thank goodness that such wonderful boarding schools are now available to people just like you.

Involving your children in the decision

One might well ask these days who is actually doing the choosing – the parents or the child? Even at the prep school stage, children are becoming more and more involved in the decision (as, one might venture, parents become more and more indulgent!). I do think children should have a say, especially when the senior school is being chosen, but I do not think they should drive the process. Too often they can, in their lack of experience, be over-impressed or otherwise swayed by relatively unimportant considerations. I was shocked (and not a little upset) a year or two ago when a parent told me they had chosen Port Regis for their son, not as a result of my scintillating sales pitch, or my wife's dazzling charm or the fabulous reputation of the rugby team, but rather because he had seen several Manchester United posters on the dormitory walls and so had insisted that this should be his school! My advice would be to make the decision yourselves but to take the child along in this with you, using your powers of persuasion to let him see that, whilst he may have preferred another, this will be the one that will suit him best. . . even if Chelsea posters predominate! Do not, however, persist with a choice towards which he is furiously hostile. It will end in tears.

An invaluable investment

Finally, the independent schools sector in the UK is full of world-class schools and it is quite properly the envy of the rest of the world. You need only look at the thousands of pupils who are sent over to the UK by their parents from almost any country you can think of to take advantage of what our schools have to offer. We are uniquely privileged to have them on our own doorstep. Yes, they can be expensive, but, if you are able to meet the costs (and the least expensive are no more than £6,000 a year, and there is also generous bursarial help available at every school), you will find you have made the most valuable investment of your life, with the dividend being repaid many times over for years and years to come. Good luck with your choice!

Hilary Moriarty, Director of the Boarding Schools' Association, explains the changing character of boarding education and what parents should now expect

Hands up if you think boarding schools are great for education but boarding itself is not likely to be great. Keep your hand up if that translates into big dormitories, possibly with the windows wide open and great draughts of cold air billowing the thin curtains between the iron beds, no privacy, communal bathrooms with 20 or more sinks, big common rooms where bullied children are ignored, bleak dining rooms serving dismal plates of unappetizing food and in general a tough, Spartan regime that no one in their right minds would contemplate for a beloved child. And – quite simply – no child in his or her right mind would agree to attend.

Now put your hand down and let me tell you a little about modern boarding, about boarding schools in 21st-century Britain, and about why, increasingly, a boarding education is the perfect choice for children and young people today.

Why and how have boarding schools changed so much?

The question of Why?

'Why?' is easy to answer: because changing the product for a changing market was essential. Change was not necessary while the old market was constant – colonial or aristocratic families, happy to send their children to the schools the parents themselves (usually Dad) had attended, pragmatic about separation, convinced of the value of a stiff upper lip in the youngest child, seeing school as a place where a child was not only educated but also toughened up for a future serving an empire. At least one boarding school to my knowledge has on its walls portraits of no fewer than seven old boys awarded VCs. That was service with honour and distinction, and under fire.

But all the certainties of a constant market collapsed in the latter half of the 20th century – we learned more about child development and psychology and fewer parents wanted prolonged separation from their children. If parents were sent abroad, they expected children to go too. And overseas, high-quality international schools sprang up to cater for such children on the spot.

The cost of running boarding schools rose and fees marched inexorably beyond the range of many families. So schools themselves had to change.

How did they change?

Many took day pupils, original all-boys schools went co-ed, boarding itself had to be better, or it would not survive at all. The best way to be better was to get closer to what parents wanted. So boarding schools moved towards more comfort and less separation. More access and less distance. Less toughening up of young children and more recognition of the value of nurturing young people. Less discipline, more happiness. More pastoral care, and more recognition that schools are actually all about pastoral care. Boarding school heads began to adopt new philosophies: an unhappy child will not thrive, children prosper if they are happy, happy schools attract more pupils. A positive, virtuous circle, with the child at the very heart of the school and all that it accomplishes, became the boarding paradigm.

Boarding schools – statistics

About 13 per cent of all independent school pupils are boarders and in the region of 700 schools, including single-sex and co-educational schools, offer boarding places. Relatively few schools are for boarders only as most also admit a significant number of day pupils.

Boarding staff – changing practices

Improvements in the quality of the pastoral care practices of those at the sharp end of residential provision have contributed to the transformation of boarding schools over the past 15 years. The Boarding Schools Association (BSA), amongst other bodies, has contributed to the development of quality care practices for children at boarding school through its Professional Development and Training. The specialist care provided by housemasters and housemistresses has come on a great deal and is a strength of the modern boarding experience – especially so for pupils who are often some distance from home.

What you see is what you get (boarding facilities)

Let's think about the home comforts first. In the past several years, independent boarding schools have spent in the region of £100 million on boarding accommodation. They have refurbished listed buildings and built new if necessary. Boarding accommodation really is comfortable now.

Bedrooms

While psychologists advise that younger boarders should share bedrooms in threes or fours so that they can forge the kind of friendships and ward off those inevitable pangs of homesickness in the early days, older pupils increasingly find that their bedrooms are singles or doubles, often with en suite facilities. Schools recognize that privacy matters – oh the bliss of your own shower – and parents and pupils alike seek the quiet study space which is more likely if your room mate is not playing heavy metal until late at night.

Common rooms and kitchens

Common rooms, and the small kitchens in which snacks are made both early and late, are comfortable spaces, probably warmer and more convivial than those their occupants will find at university halls of residence in due course.

Recreational facilities

With such facilities, schools seek to create the 'Wow!' factor. Really attractive bedrooms, warm and comfortable, are very important to pupils as well as to their mums and dads.

Schools are also competing to feature in the conversation in the car – 'But I really loved the one where...' and it might be the Olympic-sized swimming pool, or the near-professional theatre, or the really cool library created with metal mezzanine floors out of the old gym after the new sports hall had been built.

These recreational spaces, plus the courts and the pitches and the astro-turfs and now the riding schools, are a major part of marketing not just a school but boarding itself. Many day schools also have such facilities, but cater only for a day population which is trudging home by tea-time.

Increased opportunity in the boarder's day

But boarding days are long and of course it's not just about studying in a pleasant room. Boarders still have hours at their disposal – hours for supervised prep, so it is thoroughly done, but also hours for music practice and joining a choir or orchestra, for an impromptu five-aside match or a game of volley-ball. For all the things, in fact, which a modern parent would want them to be doing but may not have time to organize or transport to and from.

Day schools with boarding (day boarders)

Even when a school has a large day population and a relatively small number of boarders, many would say that boarding is at the heart of their operation. Keeping boarders occupied, engaged and interested, happy with their term-time lives, is vital even when there are relatively few of them!

At school, in touch

There was a time when a boarding school really was something of a closed and often remote world. That is infinitely less so today. British parents are increasingly likely to choose a boarding school for their child which is within an hour and a half of home. Some boarders have even grumped gently that they went to boarding school and that Mum and Dad seemed to follow! Parents make huge efforts to get to concerts, productions and matches, as well as speech days and carol services. There is also a real recognition on the part of schools that they are in a living, working partnership with parents to ensure the best for the child, and parental support is always valued.

Writing home or is that facebooking and tweeting home?

For all boarders, but of most interest to international pupils, boarding has been transformed by the online revolution. Fewer and fewer pupils actually *write* home: while it's always lovely to get a handwritten letter or card, 'snail mail' has been completely overtaken by e-mail, texts and of course by the growing range of social media websites available. And how fast and effective! A great test result can be relayed to Mum on the far side of the world at break-time; an evening e-mail (tweet or status update) can keep child and parent in touch every single day.

Schools will be mindful of their responsibility to protect children from the worst effects and possible dangers of the internet, and details will be in their policy statements for parents to inspect. Expect greater supervision of younger boarders – prep schools in particular work with parents to ensure that they are happy about their child's access to the internet and to mobile phones. But oh what a change for a child to have a phone at school – how good that the days are gone when a worried parent might call one phone on a long corridor when the child was never available.

Accessibility: a defining feature of today's boarding

Accessibility, in fact, might be the biggest difference between boarding then and boarding now: whatever the distance, a boarder now is never, really, that far away. And it's really useful to be able to e-mail a houseparent if you're worried. However, with so many means of keeping in touch with boarders available, parents should keep in mind that it can sometimes be advisable to reduce contact with children if they are having problems settling in. Although difficult, this can help by giving time and freedom for new relationships to develop.

Full, weekly and flexi-boarding options

Changing the pattern of boarding itself has been another response from schools to the needs of modern families. In many boarding schools, there is a 'mixed economy' of boarders who may be 'full', ie go home or to guardians one weekend in three, or 'weekly', ie are in school from Monday to Friday (or Sunday night to Saturday lunchtime if the school has lessons on Saturday) and go home every weekend, or 'flexi', ie stay sometimes.

Flexi-boarding

Flexi-boarding really can be as various as the parents wish and the school finds workable and is particularly popular for younger pupils: some children stay for one or two nights a week on a regular basis; others stay occasionally, perhaps for a concert or trip night, or when parents are called away unexpectedly. Flexi-boarders who find they like it often grow into weekly boarders, with both children and parents recognizing that homesickness was not, after all, the enormous problem it might have been, and school journeys can usefully disappear, with time better spent all round.

Prospective full boarders – weekend population

For international pupils or for British children with parents abroad, it is probably wise to be sure that the school of your choice has a substantial weekend population. There is more likely to be plenty to do if a lot of the boarders are still on site than if most have gone home. Ask for details at interview, such as, 'Exactly how many boarders of my daughter's age were in last weekend?'

Tell me everything! (Researching boarding options online)

The internet revolution allows parents an intimate view of any school they are considering for their child: What does their website look like? Do you like the feel of it? Does it have videos? Do these look like people you could get along with? You can learn all that from the comfort of your chair and without the school even knowing you're looking.

Boarding school inspections

Boarding at all English schools is inspected by Ofsted (although the responsibility is set to move to the ISI for independent schools' boarding inspection) and their reports are available on the Ofsted website as well – probably – as on the school's own. Check them out. They're about 12 pages long and they rate a school's boarding as Outstanding, Good, Satisfactory or Inadequate. For further details see Part 1.6 on inspections.

Things to ask when visiting a boarding school

When you visit, ask to be toured by a pupil – this is usual, so don't be afraid to ask. And ask them what it's really like: What is the worst meal of the day? What is the best thing for them about being a boarder? What goes on at weekends? On that subject, check with the head how many activities are included in the fees and how many would be pay-for extras.

Questions for prospective boarders' parents

Where is the school? How good are the transport connections?

If you're coming from overseas, where's the nearest airport? Which airlines fly into there and are flights expensive?

How much does a journey from school to airport cost if your child is flying alone? Does the school run a minibus service to airports?

If overseas, have you arranged a guardian family for your child when they can't get home? Nice to have grandparents or relatives reasonably close, but, in general, don't rely on work colleagues to be guardians – it can be quite an undertaking.

If your child will be a full boarder, not going home at weekends, how many other boarders of their age are likely to be on the premises with them?

How full a programme of activities operates at weekends, and which are included in the fees and which are paid-for extras? And is it always just shopping or cinemas?

What activities are provided in the evening? The prospectus may say there are choirs and bands and debating and Scrabble clubs, but all will depend on staff – do these activities really happen and happen regularly?

Does the school have a good counselling service? If a child is lonely or upset or homesick, who will notice, who will help?

If the child is an international pupil needing help with English language, who decides how much help, and what will it cost?

For an older pupil, how does the school arrange visits to universities so that the pupil makes an informed choice if applying to university?

How good is the food – really, every evening and every weekend? How much do pupils contribute to any debates about food?

Does the school let out its premises at weekends and does this have an impact on the boarders' lives?

Additional school selection considerations

Courses and qualifications offered

Do research the qualifications and courses available at the schools that interest you. Independent schools in England and Wales are not required to teach the National Curriculum or to use the National Tests, which are compulsory for state-maintained schools. However, since most are preparing pupils for public examinations, they generally do follow the National Curriculum, complementing it with additional options or areas of study as desired. Independent schools in Scotland are free to form their own curriculum policy, but, like maintained schools in Scotland, they are normally preparing pupils for Standard and Higher examinations. Most senior schools in England and Wales are preparing pupils for the General Certificate of Secondary Education (GCSEs) or international GCSE (IGCSE), taken at 16, the Advanced Subsidiary (AS) and Advanced GCE (A2) taken in the sixth form. In Scotland pupils are prepared for Scottish National Qualifications. Find out in advance whether the schools that interest you are offering the courses appropriate for your child. For further details see Part 1.4.

Assessment and examination

Assessments and examinations may take place for each subject as frequently as each term. Many schools operate a tutorial system under which a House tutor is assigned to each pupil to monitor social and personal development as well as academic progress. Parents receive a full report at the end of each term. In some schools, mock examinations (in preparation for GCSE, AS/A2 or Scottish equivalents) are held in the spring preceding the real examinations. These are marked internally by the school and give an indication of likely performance in the summer. To ensure your son or daughter is appropriately prepared it is a good idea to find out what form assessment takes well ahead of his or her first day. Further details about examinations can also be found in Part 1.4.

Sixth form options

There are many different decisions to make regarding sixth form studies, including whether to opt for the sixth form at the current school or to look for a place at an independent college. Seniors need to be planning for sixth form study, including course choice, before completing GCSE (or equivalent) examinations. As sixth formers need to study with greater independence, senior school pupils should be reflecting on their study skills and areas for improvement before beginning their course. More details about sixth form options can be found in Part 1.7.

Education and wider activities

Aside from academic studies, independent schools place great emphasis on wider activities. Many excel in areas such as sport, where pupils can develop their talents through fixtures against other schools as well as county or national school championships. Most schools recognize, however, that not all pupils enjoy team games. Many offer more individual sports, including, for example, squash, horse-riding, sailing and golf. Music, art and drama are also important aspects of the curriculum and extra-curricular activities. Many schools offer individual music lessons on a range of instruments and encourage pupils to play in the school orchestra, other music groups or to sing in the choir. Drama is often taught to a very high standard, with performances staged for public festivals as well as in school. Many schools offer preparation for examinations set by the Associated Board of the Royal Schools of Music and the London Academy of Music and Dramatic Art (LAMDA) and there may be regular trips to galleries, concerts, the theatre or the ballet. Many schools have long traditions in particular sports or performance arts, so make sure your school short list includes those which cater for your son or daughter's non-academic interests as well. School profiles, in Part 3, often include details about specialisms and provide insight into the whole educational experience provided.

Pastoral care and discipline

Many independent schools, whether boarding or day, operate a house system, which divides pupils into smaller communities to ensure a good staff:pupil ratio for pastoral care. Boarders are often accommodated in small groups with resident house staff. The housemaster or housemistress is in charge of pastoral care and will also go through the school report with each child at the end of term. House staff monitor overall progress, keep the head informed about each child and, in boarding schools, may be the first point of contact for parents. Many schools also allocate each pupil a personal tutor, who assists with educational guidance, keeps progress and welfare under constant review and can deal with issues arising on a day-to-day basis. All schools are legally obliged to provide a statement of the policy and system of care in place for pupils. They are also required to have a published policy on bullying.

Most schools keep rules simple, encouraging self-discipline and common sense in their pupils and giving praise for good behaviour. Sometimes children may contribute to a house points system, being awarded points for good work, thoughtful behaviour and for showing initiative or making a particular effort. Points might be deducted for bad behaviour. Other sanctions imposed might include limitations on leaving school premises or detention. A breach of school rules with regard to smoking or alcohol may mean suspension. Breaches involving illegal drugs may mean immediate permanent exclusion. Corporal punishment is illegal in all schools.

Religious affiliation

Spiritual growth is an important aspect of life in most independent schools, whatever their affiliation. The range includes Church of England, Roman Catholic, Quaker, Methodist, Jewish and others. Most adopt an inter-denominational approach and are happy to accept children of other faiths, but parents should check with individual schools the extent to which their child, if of a faith other than the majority of pupils, would be expected to participate in school worship. School profiles, in Part 2, show religious affiliation and an index of schools by religious affiliation appears in Part 5.

Educational guidance and careers assessment

The value of good educational guidance cannot be overestimated, particularly in view of the complexity and variety of options now available to school leavers and the importance of making the right choice. Some schools have a well-stocked, permanently staffed careers department and a full programme of careers guidance which includes formal assessment, talks from visiting speakers and work experience opportunities. Others may have more limited resources. For parents seeking specialist guidance, an independent provider such as Gabbitas may be a useful option. For more details of the one-to-one careers assessment services visit www.gabbitas.co.uk/uk-parents-consultancy-services.

Special educational needs

Parents of children in need of extensive individual attention, usually those with specific learning difficulties such as dyslexia, will find that there is a wide range of support available in mainstream independent schools. Some may bring in a specialist teacher to assist pupils at set times during the week. Some may have specialist teachers permanently on staff. Others may run a specially staffed department or unit. Parents interested in schools which offer provision for dyslexia in some form should look out for CReSTeD registered schools indicated in the geographic schools directory in Part 2 and school profiles in Part 3. There is also an index of CReSTeD registered schools in the reference section in Part 5. More detailed information on special needs provision and special schools is to be found in a separate Gabbitas publication, *Schools for Special Needs*.

Inspections and school standards

Independent schools must meet rigorous inspection criteria. Schools in membership of any of the associations which form the Independent Schools Council must conform to strict accreditation requirements and are regularly inspected by the Independent Schools Inspectorate. Other independent schools in England and Wales are inspected by Her Majesty's Inspectorate for Ofsted. Inspection reports can provide useful insight for parents before selecting a school. For more details please turn to Part 1.6 on independent school inspections.

Overseeing your child's progress

Once your son or daughter begins at a school there is a good deal of information available to help you monitor their progress. Every child receives a termly report which is sent home to parents. The results of any internal examinations are generally included in these reports. Parent's evenings are held at regular intervals in which parents are briefed on their child's progress. In addition the evening provides the opportunity for parents to discuss their child's education and any areas of concern. Invitations are also extended to attend school sporting, musical and theatrical events, whether or not their child is taking part, and sometimes to help with school projects such as fundraising activities.

School fees – general trends

As each independent school is very much an individual *institution*, fees can vary a great deal. It is generally the case that fees are higher the older the pupil. It is safe to expect that nurseries and pre-preps are at the lowest end of the fees scale, with prep schools being higher priced and senior and sixth form places commanding the greatest fees. Other influencing factors include accommodation type, location, gender taught, the history and reputation of a school and the bursaries and scholarships available. For further details on fees, fees planning, scholarships and bursaries please see Part 1.5.

Independent school contacts

The board of governors

The board of governors is the planning and policy-making body which controls the administration and finance of the school. Some board members may also be parents of children at the school. The governors are responsible for the appointment of the head and for all major decisions affecting the school. Governors give their time voluntarily. Many are individuals with expertise in their professional lives, for example in law or accountancy, who can contribute their knowledge for the benefit of the school.

Head

With accountability to the board of governors, the head or principal is responsible for all elements of the day-to-day management of a school. Included within this remit is appointment of staff, the administrative structure, curriculum content, and the safety and welfare of pupils. Many heads are accomplished academics who dedicate time in the week to teaching; to share their subject knowledge and to develop relationships amongst the pupil body. A good number take a lead on the marketing of their school, although more now recruit marketing directors.

Bursar

The bursar, in conjunction with the governors, is responsible for financial matters within the school. The bursar also takes charge of maintenance of the grounds, premises and buildings as well as catering arrangements.

Director of studies

Many schools have a director of studies, who is responsible for day-to-day curriculum matters, timetabling and for ensuring that staff are kept informed of new developments.

Registrar/Admissions secretary

The registrar is responsible for the admission of pupils and arrangements for parents to visit the school and meet the head. He or she also takes care of the practical aspects of registration and joining. This is the first person to contact for registration and enrolment details.

Housemaster/Housemistress

The housemaster or housemistress takes care of the welfare and overall progress of children in the house and is normally the first point of contact for parents. He or she will keep the head informed of each child's progress and may often be the first to hear of any problems. Serious issues are always referred to the head.

Subject teachers

Subject teachers are responsible for the academic progress of pupils taking their subject eg Sciences, English, Latin, Mathematics etc. They are responsible for classroom teaching and for in-class pastoral care. Subject teachers also produce a termly report for each of their students and attend parents' evenings.

Chaplain

The chaplain has a special role within school. Independent of academic or disciplinary considerations, the chaplain is responsible for the spiritual development of pupils and can often provide a sympathetic ear to children who seek guidance on issues of concern.

Matron

The matron looks after the practical aspects of boarding life, supervising and arranging laundry. Separate houses normally have their own Matron. She often knows children individually and can provide sympathy and support for those who feel homesick or upset.

Sister

The sister is a qualified nurse responsible for medical arrangements. She looks after pupils who may be admitted into the sanatorium with minor ailments and may require a few days in bed. Within a boarding school, serious medical matters are always referred to the school doctor and where necessary children will be taken to hospital.

Pupils

Independent schools encourage their pupils to take on positions of responsibility as part of school life. Senior pupils who show good sense and have contributed to the school by their achievements in academic work, musical or sporting activities, for example, may be granted suitable senior positions in recognition of their efforts. Hence an excellent sportsman may be made games captain or an outstanding chorister head of choir. Pupils with an excellent academic record or who deserve merit for other contributions may be given the post of head boy or girl. Prefects are students appointed to take responsibility for some of the daily routines in school and are encouraged to set a good example to younger pupils.

Overseas pupils and students – coming to the UK

If you live overseas, the best advice is to plan ahead as far as possible and at least a year in advance. This will give you a wider choice of school and allow you time to research all the options properly and make an informed choice. To help you, the most important aspects of coming to school in the UK are explored here.

Level of English

Most independent schools will expect your child to speak some English on arrival, although additional tuition is often available in school to improve fluency and accuracy and to ensure that your child can cope with a normal curriculum.

If your child is to board in the UK but speaks only a little or no English, he or she may benefit from a short period in one of the specialist boarding schools ('international study centres'), which prepare overseas pupils for entry into mainstream boarding schools at senior level. Detailed information on international study centres appears later in Part 1.3.

Alternatively, you may wish to arrange for your child to spend the summer at one of the UK's many language schools before joining a boarding school in September.

Academic background

If your child has been educated within the British system, it should not be difficult to join a school in the UK, although care should be taken to avoid changing schools while a pupil is in the middle of GCSE or A level studies. However, if your child has not been following a British curriculum, entry to a mainstream independent school may be less straightforward. The younger your child, the easier it is likely to be for him or her to adapt to a new school environment. Prep schools may accept overseas pupils at any stage up to the final two years, when pupils are prepared for Common Entrance exams. Senior schools, in particular, will normally look for evidence of ability and achievement comparable with pupils educated in the

British system and will probably wish to test your child in English, Maths and Science before deciding whether to offer a place. Pupils wishing to enter the sixth form will probably be tested in the subjects they wish to study. Recent reports and transcripts, in translation, should also be made available to schools.

If your child has been following the International Baccalaureate (IB) programme overseas, you will find a number of schools and colleges in the UK which offer the IB. Details of IB schools and colleges can be found in Parts 2 and 3.

For schools with a broad mix of nationalities offering international curricula (often incorporating the IB) you can select from a range of international schools. More detailed information on international schools appears later in Part 1.3.

Length of stay

If your stay is relatively short and you plan to return home afterwards, you may be able to enter your child in one of the schools in the UK specifically for nationals of other countries who are based in the UK. France, Germany, Sweden, Norway, Greece and Japan are all represented. Your own embassy in London should be able to provide further details.

Boarding schools – location

If you are looking for a boarding school, try not to focus your search too narrowly. Most schools, including those in the most beautiful and rural parts of the UK, are within easy reach of major transport links and the UK is well served by air, rail and road routes. In addition, most schools will make arrangements to have your child escorted between school and the airport and vice versa.

Visiting schools

Once you have decided on the most suitable type of school, you can obtain information on specific schools. It is essential that you visit schools before making a final choice. Try to plan your visits during term time.

Independent schools set their own holidays and term dates, making it difficult to give a definitive schedule for the year at all schools. As a general guide, the academic year is divided into three terms (autumn, spring and summer), each with a half-term holiday. A generous, six-week 'summer holiday' follows the summer term.

Term/holiday	Dates
Autumn term (half-term holiday)	22 Oct–3 Nov
Christmas holiday	15 Dec–9 Jan
Spring term (half-term holiday)	11 Feb–20 Feb
Easter holiday	1 Apr–25 Apr
Summer term (half-term holiday)	28 May–5 June
Summer holiday	2 Jul–6 Sep

Questions to ask

English language support

What level of English does the school expect? Is additional support available at school? How is this organized? Is there a qualified English language teacher?

Pupil mix

International schools naturally have pupils of many different nationalities at any one time. If you are looking to enter your child into a mainstream independent school, you may wish to find out how many other pupils of your nationality attend the school and what arrangements are made to encourage them to mix with English pupils.

Pastoral care

If your child has special dietary needs or is required to observe specific religious principles, is the school willing and able to cope? Would your child also be expected to take part in the school's normal worship?

If your child speaks little English, it can be very comforting during the early days when homesickness and minor worries arise, or in the event of an emergency, to have a member of staff on hand to whom the child can speak in his or her own language. Bear in mind, however, that fewer schools are likely to have staff who speak non-European languages.

Ask about arrangements for escorting your child to and from school at the beginning and end of term. Some schools have a minibus service to take children to railway stations and airports or will arrange a taxi where appropriate.

AEGIS accredited guardianship

Most schools insist that boarding pupils whose parents live overseas have an appointed guardian living near the school who can offer a home for 'exeats' (weekends out of school), half-term breaks and at the beginning and end of term in case flights do not coincide exactly with school dates. A guardian may be a relative or friend appointed by parents, but bear in mind that the arrangement may need to continue for some years and that guardianship is a substantial commitment.

For parents with no suitable contacts in the UK, schools may be able to assist in making arrangements. Alternatively, there are independent organizations, including Gabbitas, which specialize in the provision of guardianship services. Good guardian families should offer a 'home from home', looking after the interests and welfare of your child as they would their own, providing a separate room and space for study, attending school events and parents' evenings, involving your child in all aspects of family life and encouraging him or her to feel comfortable and relaxed while away from school. Some guardianship organizations are very experienced in selecting suitable families who will offer a safe and happy home to pupils a long way from their own parents. The range of services offered and fees charged by different providers will vary, but you should certainly look for a service which:

- personally ensures that families are visited in their homes by an experienced member of staff and that all appropriate checks are made;
- takes a genuine interest in your child's educational and social welfare and progress;

- keeps in touch with you, your child, the school and the guardian family to ensure that all is running smoothly;

- provides administrative support as required and assistance with visa and travel requirements, medical and dental checks and insurance, and any other matters such as the purchase of school uniform, sports kit and casual clothes.

Parents seeking a guardianship provider may like to contact AEGIS (Association for the Education and Guardianship of International Students), of which Gabbitas is a founder member. The purpose of AEGIS is to promote best practice in all areas of guardianship and to safeguard the welfare and happiness of overseas children attending educational institutions in the UK. AEGIS aims to provide accreditation for all reputable guardianship organizations. Applicants for membership are required to undergo assessment and inspection to ensure that they are adhering to the AEGIS Code of Practice and fulfilling the Membership Criteria before full membership can be granted. For further details contact Gabbitas Guardianship on +44 (0)20 7734 0161 or visit www.gabbitas.co.uk. For further information about AEGIS, visit the website at www.aegisuk.net.

Preparing your child to come to the UK

Coming to school in a different country is an enriching and exciting experience. You can help your child to settle in more quickly by encouraging him or her to take a positive approach and to absorb the traditions and social customs of school and family life in the UK. After the first year, most children begin to feel more confident and comfortable in their surroundings, both at school and with their guardian family. A good guardianship organization will ensure that you and your child know what to expect from life in the UK, and that you are aware of the kind of behaviour and approach which the school and guardian family will expect. They should be able to advise on visas, UK entry requirements and related matters, and provide support on a range of issues throughout your transition to the UK.

Where to go for help

You may be able to obtain information about schools from official sources in your own country. For detailed guidance and assistance in the UK you may wish to contact an independent educational consultancy such as Gabbitas which can advise you on all aspects of education in the UK and transferring into the British system.

International study centres

By Sarah Bellotti, director of King's International, The King's School Ely

International study centre (ISC) is a term used to describe a school that gives support to both the academic and linguistic needs of international pupils in an independent school setting. ISCs are usually, but not always, part of larger independent boarding schools, either existing within the school itself or separately on the same site but in a different purpose-built building.

ISCs exist to provide a supportive pastoral framework and academic environment for international pupils. For the international pupil, it is often their first experience of UK schools and the study centre serves as a bridge between a pupil's education and culture and the British educational system.

What do international study centres offer?

The ISCs have reliable methods of assessing the linguistic needs of the international pupil according to their age and ability. While a strong emphasis is placed on improving the pupil's English, there is a rigorous programme of academic study, including a range of curriculum subjects taught by teachers who have had specialist training in teaching pupils with English as a second language (ESL).

The ISC classroom experience

Class sizes are typically smaller than ordinary school classes – usually ranging from 5 up to a maximum of 12 pupils per class. The classes tend to be interactive, where the pupil is encouraged to participate and teachers focus on helping the pupils articulate their under-standing. Pupils often work in pairs or in small groups to maximize their speaking and are encouraged to verbalize as much as possible. There is often a vocabulary focus to each lesson, helping the pupils build up an academic lexis which will serve for use as they further their study.

The courses on offer

Many study centres focus on intensive one- or two-year GCSE programmes where pupils, usually between the ages of 14 and 17, can study five or more subjects depending on their needs, abilities and interests. Maths and English are compulsory. Many ISCs also offer programmes of study for junior pupils, who are younger than 14, and 'Pre-GCSE programmes' which prepare pupils for GCSE subjects. In some schools, the international pupils may integrate into the mainstream school for some subjects.

Extra-curricular activities

Like all independent schools, ISCs also provide international pupils with extra-curricular activities and clubs which take place after school or during lunch times. In these activities, the international pupil will often have the opportunity of mixing with the British pupils from the main school through, for example, the school orchestra or sports teams. ISCs also usually include some element of explicit instruction in the discipline and culture of British boarding school life and of British culture in the wider sense. Most offer a programme of events, excursions and trips which take the international pupils to see different places of cultural interest in the UK.

Pastoral care and boarding

Pastoral care is of particular importance for pupils who are far away from home and ISCs pay close attention to make sure that the international pupils' needs are well catered for. There is 24-hour residential care by responsible adults based on the boarding house model and an appropriate and age-specific leisure programme. Boarding houses have rigorous guidelines and are inspected regularly.

ISCs aim to host a wide variety of nationalities and their mission is to embrace and include the cultures of their international pupil bodies into their own academic and pastoral programmes, showing respect for diversity.

Destination of pupils

Most international pupils come to the UK as part of a longer educational journey, culminating in studying at a British university. However, some pupils wish to stay for just a year, to improve their English, and then slot back into their native education system. Many stay between one and two years and then move on to mainstream education, sometimes within the same school, for example studying GCSEs at the ISC and A levels/IB at the main school. Others move to a different school to complete their further education.

Accreditation

Many international study centres have been accredited by the British Council and once accredited are regularly inspected to ensure standards are maintained. The accreditation scheme sets overarching standards in four areas: *management, resources and environment, teaching and learning*, and *welfare and student services*. Study centres that have not been accredited by the British Council will have been accredited by other reputable accreditation boards such as the Independent Schools Council (ISC) or Council of Independent Schools (CIS). The British Association of International Schools and Colleges (BAISC) also accredits international study centres for quality assurance purposes and provides help in the form of development, training and mutual support to its members.

The international study centre pupil

Cristina Blazquez is a 13-year-old pupil from Madrid, in the Pre-GCSE group at King's International.

'Last summer I was very excited and nervous because, for the first time, I would spend a whole year studying in another country, in England.

'I am studying 11 subjects, but they are not very difficult for me because the teachers make a great effort to teach us and they spend time outside of class to help us. I also get additional help from my friends to do my homework. I have joined some clubs where I have met some British students, so I can improve my English faster.

'I am sure that when I finish this year here and go back to Spain, my English will be very good.

'I have many friends from different countries and I learn interesting things about their culture and lifestyle. This is also an opportunity to get to know about life around the world.'

Liwei Zhang is a 16-year-old girl from China. She is taking the One Year Intensive GCSE course at King's International.

'It is a totally new experience of studying in a different country with people from all over the world... The school also organizes many interesting trips to other cities in England, such as Cambridge and London, which is a great experience.

'Compared to life in China, studying here is more relaxing and exciting. The diverse ways of teaching have inspired my imagination and curiosity.'

After finishing her GCSEs at King's International, Liwei will be moving to Lancing School to study A levels.

International study centres

- Bedford School Study Centre, Bedfordshire

- Box Hill International Study Centre, Surrey

- Dover College, International Study Centre, Kent

- The International Centre, Ackworth School, West Yorkshire

- International College, Sherborne School, Dorset

- International Study Centre at Kent College, Canterbury, Kent

- International Study Centre at The Royal School, Haslemere, Surrey

- King's International Study Centre, The King's School, Ely, Cambridgeshire

- Millfield English Language School, Millfield School, Somerset

- Rossall School International Study Centre, Lancashire

- Sidcot Academic English School, Sidcot School, North Somerset

- Taunton International Study Centre, Somerset

For further details please see entries in the geographical directory in Part 2 and the school profile section in Part 3.

International schools

Fergus Rose, Senior Management Team, ACS International Schools

In a world where global mobility is increasing, the value of the international school is well understood. International schools bring together young people from many different cultures and countries, including the UK, in a motivating, educational environment where they can gain qualifications recognized the world over. As well as providing a distinctive academic experience, UK international schools enable pupils to establish lasting friendships and affinities with peers from around the world. Although a relatively small element of the UK independent education sector, international schools contribute to the diversity of schooling options available for those seeking to study in the UK.

Indubitably international

The character of an international school in the UK lies principally in its overseas pupil population, with pupils from as many as 50 different countries admitted to a particular school, and in the provision of teaching of English as an additional language. Although they share these characteristics with international study centres they offer a distinct educational option. International schools, unlike study centres, generally offer international qualifications and have no affiliation to a British Boarding school (many ISCs are based on the same premises as an independent boarding school). Moreover, international schools tend to be 'straight-through' providers catering for the full range of ages from 2 to 18 – although some do specialize in teaching specific age groups such as junior or senior pupils.

The international school experience

Being involved with people from different cultures at a young age really benefits pupils later on in adult life. The multi-cultural experience available at international schools provides pupils with the global perspective and social skills necessary to interact successfully with a wide range of people from the UK and abroad in a variety of academic and professional environments.

The international school pupil

Izabella Kaminski-Cook is a 17-year-old pupil studying at ACS Egham International School. Izabella joined ACS Egham in the 10th grade and has had experience of international education both in Bangkok where she attended an international school following the British education system for three years and in France where she studied at a bilingual school for two years.

Izabella's school day routine is in fact fairly similar to those of school pupils across the globe, with her day consisting of four lessons, each one hour and 10 minutes in length, followed by homework and recreational activities (including music tuition for the flute and football three nights a week). Yet amongst her immediate friendship group Izabella has close friends from Britain, Holland, Brazil, Australia, America and Canada. With over 500 pupils, the school itself represents 40 countries from across the world, making the cultural diversity of pupils alongside whom Izabella studies even wider.

Izabella has found that attending school with young people from a variety of different countries and cultures has enriched her knowledge in a way that simply cannot be taught in a classroom.

'Working alongside my peers of varying nationalities has increased my cultural awareness incredibly because I have direct access to first-hand accounts of different cultures. I am able to see a wide variety of different aspects of the world through my peers and their experiences and I am also able to share my own experience.

'Studying with people of different nationalities in the classroom certainly encourages the learning process and provides an excellent preparation for life in the real world, which is culturally diverse and varied.'

In addition to learning from the experiences of her peers, Izabella also learns about cultural diversity during her course of study, by following the IB Diploma.

Izabella's overall view of her international education is very positive: 'Having studied in international schools in various countries, I have found it to be a fantastic opportunity. It is both enjoyable and cultured and allows me to constantly meet new people from different backgrounds.'

Curricula and qualifications

Many schools offer a choice of US and international qualifications, and a few also offer British qualifications. English as a foreign language, native language enrichment and university preparation courses are also frequently available.

IB, American High School Diploma and Advanced Placement

The International Baccalaureate (IB) programme is most frequently offered (see Part 1.4, which follows, for more information on the IB). However, for US expatriates who plan to return to the

United States or those who wish to study in the United States in later life, many international schools offer a course based on the American High School Diploma. These pupils can also choose to meet credit requirements for graduation through regular high school courses, honours-level high school courses, Advanced Placement (AP) and/or IB courses.

Advanced Placement (AP) courses are widely available for those seeking to win places at universities around the world – especially those applying for US university places; 90 per cent of US higher education institutions and many foreign institutions accept AP credits for college applications. The course is designed to expose able and motivated high school pupils to college-level academic material. Those that perform particularly well in their AP exams can increase their chances of being awarded scholarships.

English language support

For those whose first language is not English, and who are deemed to need help with their English language skills, English as an Additional Language (EAL) support is provided. For some pupils, this means regularly scheduled, small-group sessions, offered in place of some core subjects. Pupils generally take these sessions until English proficiency commensurate with their age and grade level is achieved. Many schools also offer the opportunity to take International English Language Testing System (IELTS) examinations to provide formal recognition of their English language skills.

Native language enrichment

Non-native English-speaking pupils are often encouraged to maintain their native language and cultures by participating in native language enrichment classes, often led by teachers or parents from their native countries. This gives pupils the opportunity to maintain their own cultural identity and share their experiences with peers from their native countries, whose relocation experiences may have been similar.

Accreditation

International schools established in the UK have to be registered with the appropriate government department (Department for Education, in England), as with all independent schools. International schools can apply for membership of one of the Independent Schools Council (ISC) associations, and receive inspections carried out by the Independent Schools Inspectorate (ISI) (which is monitored by Ofsted).

However, international schools are often subject to a number of additional inspections and accreditations. Those providing further education, for pupils 16 and over, can also seek accreditation from the British Accreditation Council (BAC). This is required for institutions that wish to enrol visa pupils, as visas will only be granted to pupils who have an offer from a licensed school. A number of schools also gain accreditation from the Council of International Schools (CIS), an international organization with school members throughout the world.

International schools that offer the International Baccalaureate can seek accreditation from the governing organization, The IB. The IB makes a formal school visit every five years to 'authorize' the school curriculum, and establish that its governance and philosophy are in keeping with the values of The IB.

Destination of pupils

As might be expected with international schools, pupils often go on to attend universities and higher education institutions across the globe. Many will return to their native country to continue their education, or relocate to another country to complete their global education. However, a large number of pupils from international schools in the UK choose to remain in the country for university; a true testament to the high quality education available in the UK.

UK independent school examinations and qualifications

Active initiation and introduction of courses and qualifications lead to great diversity in assessment methods used in independent schools. The IB, IGCSE and Cambridge Pre U were, for example, initially offered only in the independent sector. Independence enables schools to offer qualifications outside the national framework, adding to the breadth of options available to pupils.

As independent schools have 'selective' entry policies, this section begins with the senior school entry examination – Common Entrance (CE). Attention then moves to senior school courses and qualifications ranging from GCSE and IGCSE to A levels and other sixth-form courses.

Common Entrance (CE)

The Common Entrance examination forms the basis of entry to many independent senior schools, although some schools set their own entrance exams. Traditionally it is taken by boys at the age of 13+ and by girls at the age of 11+. However, with the growth of co-education at senior level the divisions have become less sharply defined and the examinations are open to both boys and girls.

The Common Entrance papers are set centrally by the Independent Schools Examinations Board. The papers are marked, however, by the individual schools, which have their own marking schemes and set their own entry standards. Common Entrance is not an exam which candidates pass by reaching a national standard.

The content of the Common Entrance papers has undergone regular review and the Independent Schools Examinations Board has adapted syllabuses to bring them into line with Curriculum requirements.

Candidates are entered by their junior or preparatory schools. Parents whose children attend state schools should apply to the Independent School Examinations Board, ideally four months before the scheduled examination date. Some pupils may need additional coaching for the exam if they are not attending an independent preparatory school. To be eligible, pupils must normally have been offered a place by a senior school subject to their performance in the exam. Pupils applying for scholarships may be required to pass Common Entrance before sitting the scholarship exam. Candidates normally take the exam in their own junior or preparatory school.

At 11+ the Common Entrance exam consists of papers in English, Mathematics and Science, and is designed to be suitable for all pupils. Most pupils who take the exam at 13+ come from independent preparatory schools. Subjects are English, Mathematics, Science (these are compulsory); French, History, Geography, Religious Studies, German, Spanish, Latin and Greek (these are optional).

The examination for 13+ entry takes place in January and May/June. For entry at 11+ the exam is held in January. Further information on Common Entrance is available from Gabbitas or the ISEB:

The General Secretary
Independent Schools Examinations Board
The Pump House
16 Queen's Avenue
Christchurch BH23 1BZ
Tel: 01202 487538
Fax: 01202 473728
E-mail: enquiries@iseb.co.uk

General Certificate of Secondary Education (GCSE)

The GCSE forms the principal course for senior school pupils aged between 14 and 16 years of age. Pupils are generally required to choose GCSE subjects in year 9 before commencing their studies in year 10 at age 14. Most pupils of average ability take 9 or 10 GCSEs, including Mathematics, English and Science, although some may take 11 or more. Most GCSE courses are taught over two years but very able pupils may take some GCSE examinations after one year.

GCSE (Short Course) qualifications are also available and take only half the study time of a full GCSE. These courses are graded on the same scale as a full GCSE, covering fewer topics, and are equivalent to half. The GCSE (Short Course) can be used in various ways: to offer able pupils additional choices such as a second modern language or to offer a subject which could not otherwise be studied as a full GCSE because of other subject choices. It may also be attractive to pupils who need extra time in their studies and would be better suited to a two-year course devoted to a GCSE (Short Course) rather than a full GCSE.

All results for GCSE are graded on a scale from A* to G. Examinations generally have differentiated or tiered papers that target different ability ranges within the A*–G grade range. Many large-entry GCSE subjects are examined through a foundation tier covering grades C–G and a higher tier covering grades A*–D.

A review of the GCSE led to changes in the assessment system which affect both course work and examinations. Course work is replaced by controlled assessment in most subjects and external examination questions are revised. Controlled assessment was introduced to provide greater control in three areas: setting of tasks, task taking and task marking. Assessed task taking, for example, is carried out in a supervised environment such as the classroom to safeguard against plagiarism and undue assistance. External examinations now incorporate a number of different question styles to enable pupils to better demonstrate their knowledge, understanding and ability.

International General Certificate of Secondary Education (IGCSE)

The International General Certificate of Secondary Education (IGCSE) was originally developed for use by international schools. However, IGCSEs have since been adopted by many independent schools in the UK because they are thought to afford greater flexibility and rigour in assessment, including the capacity to stretch the more able candidates.

The IGCSE, which is marked on the same A*–G scale as the GCSE, is widely recognized by schools, universities and employers as equivalent, and provides progression to AS and A level study in the same way. There are, however, differences in the content and examination of the two qualifications, which vary by subject.

Examination for the IGCSE generally has either an optional coursework component with terminal (end of course) examination or examination-only assessment.

There are two awarding bodies for IGCSEs: University of Cambridge International Examinations (CIE), which has been awarding the qualifications for over 20 years; and Edexcel which began to award IGCSEs more recently. In addition to the differences between the IGCSE and GCSE, the content and assessment structure of the CIE and Edexcel IGCSE also vary by subject. Please contact these organizations for further information.

University of Cambridge International Examinations
1 Hills Road Cambridge CB1 2EU
United Kingdom
Tel: +44 (0) 1223 553554
Fax: +44 (0) 1223 553558

Edexcel International
One90 High Holborn
London WC1V 7BH
United Kingdom
Tel: +44 (0) 1204 770696
Fax: +44 (0) 207 190 5700

GCE A levels and GCE AS levels

Advanced and Advanced Subsidiary Levels are the post-16 qualifications most widely taught in UK sixth forms and tutorial colleges. A and AS levels, as they are commonly known, are also the most prevalent means of entry to higher education in the UK. Subjects offered include academic studies such as Mathematics, English Literature, Physics and Geography. Vocationally focused 'Applied A levels' are also available in subjects ranging from Art and Design to Business Studies (further details about vocational qualifications can be found later in Part 1.4).

A level subjects are generally taught over two years, typically with two units studied in the first year and a further two in the second (although most now have four modules – some do remain with six units). The first-year units make up an Advanced Subsidiary (AS) course. If these are followed in the second year by the appropriate number of A2 units (these are at a higher level than the AS units), the AS and A2 units combined represent a complete A Level course.

Pupils may take four or five AS level subjects in the first year, with the option of reducing the number to three or four A2 subjects in the second year. Advanced Subsidiary units focus on material appropriate for the first year of an A level course and are assessed accordingly. Second-year A2 modules are more demanding and are assessed at full A level standard.

Overall assessment is based on examinations and/or coursework and may be made at stages during the course (modular) or at the end of the course (linear). A synoptic component is also incorporated into these assessments to examine pupils' understanding of the course as a whole and the connections between its different elements.

An A level grade is reached by combining AS and A2 grades. AS and A levels also attract UCAS (University and Colleges Admission Service) tariff points for the purpose of university entry. Pupils who successfully complete the first-year units will be awarded an AS level. This is a qualification in its own right, although it is not enough to gain entry to university.

Passes at AS and A levels are initially graded on a scale of A to E, with the U grade (unclassified) indicating a fail. An A* is awarded for the achievement of an A grade overall with a score of at least 90 per cent, according to the Uniform Mark Scale, in the A2 units studied. Individual units can be retaken and the best attempts are used when certification is requested.

An optional extended project is available, which gives pupils the opportunity to undertake individual study in a subject of their own choosing in addition to their A level courses. The extended project is a single piece of work, requiring a high degree of planning, preparation, research and autonomous working. It is assessed at the same level as A level but is equivalent to half an A level. The extended project is also graded from A* to E and for university entrance attracts half the UCAS tariff points of an A level.

Vocational education and training

There are 116 awarding bodies for vocational education and training awards. Many of these are sector based and provide specific qualifications for their particular industry. However, there are also a number of key awarding bodies that provide a wide range of vocational qualifications across sectors and subjects. These include:

- Edexcel (offers BTEC qualifications);
- City & Guilds;
- Cambridge International Examinations;
- Oxford, Cambridge and RSA Examinations;
- AQA.

Many vocational qualifications come within the National Qualifications Framework, falling into one of two broad categories, namely Vocationally Related Qualifications and National Vocational Qualifications (NVQs). The latter are competence-based occupational qualifications and are generally taken while the candidate is in employment. The body responsible for the overall framework is the Qualifications and Curriculum Development Authority. In Scotland the equivalent body for the Scottish Vocational Qualifications framework (SVQ and GSVQ) is the Scottish Qualifications Authority.

Applied GCSEs

Pupils generally take Applied GCSE subjects alongside academic ones in years 10 and 11. These qualifications are designed for pupils who seek a course that gives a general introduction to a broad vocational area. Most Applied GCSEs are available as single and double awards (double awards are graded from A*A* to GG). Subjects available include: Applied Art and Design, Applied Business, Applied ICT, Applied Science, Engineering, Health and Social Care.

Applied A levels

Applied A levels are general qualifications set in the context of a broad vocational area. Subjects generally correspond to applied subjects available at GCSE such as Art and Design, ICT, Performing Arts and Business. Like traditional A levels, courses are usually taken over two years with the first year's study representing an AS level. Pupils are normally expected to have achieved at least four or five GCSEs at grades A* to C to undertake studies including Applied A levels. As with traditional A levels, the qualifications provide preparation for both higher education and employment.

In Scotland, General Scottish Vocational Qualifications (GSVQs) have been brought under the new National Qualifications framework. Applied A levels and GSVQs are recognized by universities as a basis for entry to higher education. As well as qualifications within the vocational framework, the awarding bodies offer a range of other qualifications. Further guidance may be obtained from schools, colleges and careers advisers. Alternatively, contact a reputable independent consultancy such as Gabbitas.

Scottish National Qualifications

Most schools in Scotland prepare pupils for Standard Grade examinations taken at 16. All pupils who stay on in education after Standard Grade follow a qualifications system which begins at one of five levels, depending on their examination results.

Access, Intermediate 1 and Intermediate 2 are progressive levels which a pupil might take to gain a better grounding in a subject before going on to take one of two higher levels: Higher and Advanced Higher. The lower three levels are not compulsory for pupils with aptitude, who may move straight on to study one of the higher-level courses. With the exception of Standard Grade, each National Qualification is built on units, courses and group awards:

- National Units – these are the smallest elements of a qualification and are internally assessed; most require 40 hours of study.

- Courses – National Courses are usually taken in S5 or S6 and at college. They are made up of three units each, and are assessed internally and by examination for which grades A–C are awarded.

- Scottish Group Awards (SGAs) – these are programmes of courses and units that cover 16 broad subject areas. An SGA can be obtained within one year, or worked towards over a longer period.

There are 75 subjects available, including Philosophy, Politics, Care; job-orientated subjects such as Travel and Tourism; and traditional ones such as Maths and English. All National

Qualifications have core skills embedded in them, although it is possible to take stand-alone units, for example Problem Solving, Communication, Numeracy and Information Technology.

For further information contact the Scottish Qualifications Authority – www.sqa.org.uk.

Cambridge Pre-University Diploma

The Cambridge Pre-U Diploma is a new post-16 qualification developed by University of Cambridge International Examinations in collaboration with schools and universities. The qualification is designed to prepare pupils with the skills and knowledge required for successful progression to higher education.

Recently accredited for use within the national qualifications framework, the Cambridge Pre-U is expected to be available at over 100 schools in the next two years. Schools generally offer the Cambridge Pre-U alongside A levels. Within the structure of the qualification it is possible to exchange up to two A levels for corresponding Principal Subjects.

The qualification offers opportunities for interdisciplinary study, includes independent research that builds on individual subject specialisms and is informed by an international perspective. Pupils choose from a total of 26 Principal Subjects including Mathematics, Russian, Classical Greek and Music. To qualify for the Cambridge Pre-U Diploma, pupils must achieve passes in at least three Principal Subjects, an Independent Research Report and a Global Perspectives Portfolio.

Cambridge Pre-U is underpinned by the following educational aims:

- encouraging the development of well-informed, open- and independent-minded individuals;

- promoting deep understanding through subject specialization, with a depth and rigour appropriate to progression to higher education;

- helping learners to acquire specific skills of problem-solving, critical thinking, creativity, team-working, independent learning and effective communication;

- recognizing a wide range of individual talents and interests;

- promoting an international outlook and cross-cultural awareness.

The structure of the qualification is linear, with one set of examinations at the end of the two-year course. Achievement is reported on a scale of nine grades: D1 (Distinction 1), D2, D3, M1 (Merit 1), M2, M3, P1 (Pass 1), P2, P3. The grade D1 reports achievement above the A level A* grade (see GCE A levels and GCE Advanced Subsidiary). The intention is to enable greater differentiation between pupils, especially at the higher end of the grading scale.

The Universities and Colleges Admission Service (UCAS) formally recognizes the Cambridge Pre-U Diploma for entry to higher education institutions in the UK. UCAS tariff points have now been attributed to the individual elements of the qualification, enabling university admissions staff to assess applications from diploma pupils. For more information please contact:

University of Cambridge International Examinations
1 Hills Road
Cambridge CB1 2EU
United Kingdom
Tel: 01223 553554
E-mail: international@cie.org.uk

The International Baccalaureate (information supplied by The International Baccalaureate)

The International Baccalaureate is a non-profit, international educational foundation registered in Switzerland that was established in 1968. The Diploma Programme, for which the IB is best known, was developed by a group of schools seeking to establish a common curriculum and a university-entry credential for geographically mobile pupils. They believed that an education that emphasized critical thinking and exposure to a variety of points of view would encourage inter-cultural understanding and acceptance of others by young people. They designed a comprehensive curriculum for the last two years of secondary school that could be administered in any country and that would be recognized by universities worldwide.

Today the IB offers three programmes to schools. The Diploma Programme is for pupils aged 16 to 19 in the final two years of secondary school. The Middle Years Programme, adopted in 1994, is for pupils aged 11 to 16. The Primary Years Programme, adopted in 1997, is for pupils aged 3 to 12. The IB has in the region of 2,400 authorized schools in 129 countries. This number is fairly evenly divided between state schools and private (including international) schools.

The Diploma Programme

The Diploma Programme (DP), for pupils aged 16 to 19, is a two-year course of study. Recognized internationally as a qualification for university entrance, it also allows pupils to fulfil the requirements of their national education system. Pupils share an educational experience that emphasizes critical thinking as well as inter-cultural understanding and respect for others in the global community.

The DP offers a broad and balanced curriculum in which pupils are encouraged to apply what they learn in the classroom to real-world issues and problems. Wherever possible, subjects are taught from an international perspective. In economics, for example, pupils look at economic systems from around the world. Pupils study six courses (including both the sciences and the humanities) selected from the following six subject groups:

- Group 1 language A1
- Group 2 (second language) language ab initio, language B, language A2, and classical languages
- Group 3 individuals and societies
- Group 4 experimental sciences
- Group 5 mathematics and computer science
- Group 6 the arts.

Pupils must also submit an extended essay, follow a course in theory of knowledge (TOK) and take part in activities to complete the creativity, action and service (CAS) requirement.

The assessment of pupil work in the DP is largely external. At the end of the course, pupils take examinations that are marked by external examiners who work closely with the IB. The types of questions asked in the examination papers include multiple-choice questions, essay questions, data-analysis questions and case studies. Pupils are also graded on the extended essay and on an essay and oral presentation for the TOK course.

A smaller part of the assessment of pupil work is carried out within schools by DP teachers. The work that is assessed includes oral commentaries in the languages, practical experimental work in the sciences, fieldwork and investigations in the humanities, and exhibitions and performances in the arts. Examiners check the assessment of samples of work from each school to ensure that IB standards are consistently applied. For each examination session, approximately 80 per cent of DP pupils are awarded the Diploma. The majority of pupils register for the Diploma, but pupils may also register for a limited number of Diploma subjects, for each of which they are awarded a certificate with the final grade.

The Middle Years Programme (MYP)

The Middle Years Programme (MYP), for pupils aged 11 to 16, recognizes that pupils in this age group are particularly sensitive to social and cultural influences and are struggling to define themselves and their relationships to others. The programme helps pupils develop the skills to cope with this period of uncertainty. It encourages them to think critically and independently, to work collaboratively and to take a disciplined approach to studying. The aim of the MYP is to give pupils an international perspective to help them become informed about the experiences of people and cultures throughout the world. It also fosters a commitment to help others and to act as a responsible member of the community at the local, national and international levels.

Pupils in the MYP study all the major disciplines, including languages, humanities, sciences, mathematics, arts, technology and physical education. Each of the disciplines or 'subject groups' is studied through five areas of interaction:

● approaches to learning;

● community and service;

● human ingenuity;

● environment;

● health and social education.

The framework is flexible enough to allow a school to include subjects that are not part of the MYP curriculum but that might be required by Local Authorities. While the courses provide pupils with a strong knowledge base, they emphasize the principles and concepts of the subject and approach topics from a variety of points of view, including the perspectives of other cultures.

MYP teachers use a variety of tools to assess pupil progress, including oral presentations, tests, essays and projects, and they apply the assessment criteria established by the IB to pupils' work. Schools may opt for official IB certification by asking the IB to validate their internal assessment. This is often referred to as the 'moderation system'. In this process, the IB reviews samples of the schools' assessment of pupil work and checks that schools are correctly applying the MYP assessment criteria. The IB offers guidance for teachers in the form of published examples of assessment.

The Primary Years Programme

The Primary Years Programme (PYP), for pupils aged 3 to 12, focuses on the development of the whole child, addressing social, physical, emotional and cultural needs. At the same time, it gives pupils a strong foundation in all the major areas of knowledge: mathematics, social studies, drama, language, music, visual arts, science, personal and social education, and physical education. The PYP aims to help pupils develop an international perspective – to become aware of and sensitive to the points of view of people in other parts of the world.

The PYP curriculum is organized around six themes:

- who we are;
- where we are in place and time;
- how we express ourselves;
- how the world works;
- how we organize ourselves;
- sharing the planet.

These themes are intended to help pupils make sense of themselves, of other people and of the physical environment, and to give them different ways of looking at the world. Assessment is used for two purposes: to guide teaching and to give pupils an opportunity to show, in a variety of ways, what they know and what they can do. In the PYP, assessment takes many forms. It ranges from completing checklists and monitoring progress to compiling a portfolio of a pupil's work. The IB offers schools substantial guidance for conducting assessment, including a detailed handbook and professional development workshops. Pupil portfolios and records of PYP exhibitions are reviewed on a regular basis by the IB as part of programme evaluation. For further information about the IB programmes, please contact:

International Baccalaureate Programme
Route des Morillons 15
CH-1218 Grand-Saconnex
Geneva
Switzerland
Tel: +41 22 791 7740
Fax: + 41 22 791 0277
E-mail: ibhq@ibo.org
Website: www.ibo.org

Independent school fees, fees planning, bursaries and scholarships

School fees, financial planning, scholarships and bursaries are often the first considerations for parents who have decided upon an independent education for their child. Part 1.5 explores some of the financial components of school choice. To commence with, the varying school fees to expect throughout the independent sector are explained.

Independent school fees

Fees differ widely depending on the types of school you are contemplating. As a general guide, in 2011/12 parents can expect to pay annual fees of between £4,000 and £12,000 at a preparatory day school or £12,000 to £19,000 for boarding. At senior level, fees range from about £8,000 to £17,000 at day schools, or £18,000 to £24,000+ for a boarding place.

School type	From	To
Prep day	£4,000	£12,000
Prep boarding	£12,000	£19,000
Senior day	£8,000	£17,000
Senior boarding	£18,000	£24,000+

Fees at girls, boys and co-ed schools

Fees at girls' schools tend to be marginally lower than those at boys' and co-educational schools. While day places, as you can see from the table above, tend to be less expensive than boarding places, there is quite a range. Day places at boarding schools, for instance, generally command higher fees than similar places at a day school.

Fees at independent sixth form colleges

Fees at independent sixth form colleges are usually charged per subject, with accommodation constituting a separate fee. The overall costs of tuition and accommodation for a pupil studying three subjects at A level are broadly in line with those charged at a senior boarding school.

How are fees paid?

Parents are normally asked to pay fees in three termly instalments, one at the start of each term, although some schools may offer a choice of payment methods. If you wish to move your child to another school, the present school will normally require a full term's notice in writing. If notice isn't given you may find that you are charged an additional term's fees in lieu.

Insurance policies for school fees

Many schools encourage parents to take out insurance against the risk of their child not being able to attend school, for example in the event of illness. Parents may be asked to meet additional costs during the school year for school lunches, school trips, sports kit, music lessons and similar items. So it is important to check what is and what is not included in the basic termly fee and to take account of other essentials when estimating the overall costs. Boarders will also require additional items such as bed linen and weekend wear.

Fees for international pupils

If you live overseas, bear in mind that there will be other costs associated with a boarding education in the UK. These include the costs of guardianship, travel and any specialist dental treatment, eye tests or spectacles which your child may need while he or she is in the UK. Your child will also need a regular supply of pocket money. Schools discourage pupils from carrying large amounts of cash, but your child will probably want to buy music or clothes as well as small treats.

Scholarships and bursaries

If your child is exceptionally talented in a specific area, there may well be scholarship opportunities which could reduce the fees by as much as 50 per cent or possibly more. If financial hardship is an issue, bursaries may be available to help top up the shortfall. The decision to grant a bursary will be taken according to individual circumstances. Further details of the types of scholarship and bursaries available can be found later in Part 1.5.

Towry Law Financial Services Limited – finding the fees

Your first decision is what fees you are planning to meet. Do you have a specific school or schools in mind and if so what are the fees? Hopefully you have started planning early, which means that you are unlikely to have made a final choice of school. In this case you need to work on the average or typical fees for the type of school. This can range from day preparatory to senior boarding school. If your child was born in the latter part of the year, check that you are planning for the right period, ie don't plan to provide funds a year early, leaving a gap year at the end.

Next, you need to allow for inflation. A school's major cost is teacher and other salaries, which tend to increase in line with earnings rather than prices. Historically, earnings rise faster than prices so inflation is not something you can ignore.

The distinctive feature of planning for educational costs

This lies in the fact that you are planning for a 'known commitment'. You know that at the beginning of each term or school year you will have a bill to pay and will need to draw on your investments.

This is where the 'reward–risk' spectrum comes in. At one end, asset-backed investments offer a higher potential reward but also a degree of investment risk and potential volatility. In the longer term, such investments have been the way to achieve real growth and outpace inflation (though the past is not necessarily a guide to future performance). On the other hand, you do not want to rely on such investments if it means encashing them at the worst possible time, just after a stock market setback. Remember, because of the nature of educational planning you probably do not have any choice about when you need funds to pay a bill.

At the other end of the reward–risk spectrum are deposit accounts; just about as safe as safe can be (so long as the institution is safe), but will they keep up with inflation? You do not need to plump for either extreme. The answer partly depends on the period over which you are investing. If you are starting soon after birth, asset-backed investment can play a larger role, giving greater potential for real growth. Nearer the time, your holdings can be switched on a phased basis into more secure investment vehicles to lock in any gains and from which you can draw during the schooling period.

An alternative approach is 'mix and match'. A mixture of asset-backed investments and more secure ones will allow you to draw from the former in years when their values are high. In other years, you can draw from the more secure investments.

Existing investments

Your strategy should take into account any existing investments or savings that may be suitable. These may not have been taken out with school fees in mind. For example, you may have started a mortgage endowment some years ago and changed to a repayment mortgage. This would free up the endowment, which could be used for school fees.

Tax-efficient investments

You can invest regular contributions or a lump sum into Individual Savings Accounts (ISAs). They are generally a good idea, especially for a higher-rate taxpayer, because the tax benefits should enhance returns. You can use ISAs for cash deposits, equities, fixed interest and commercial property investments. There is a limit on the contributions that can be made in each year, but both parents can take out an ISA.

Rather than investing in individual shares, investors nowadays more commonly use 'collective' investments like unit trusts (or open-ended investment companies – OEICs) or investment trusts. Collective funds give access to the benefits of equity investments without the investment risk inherent in investing in one or a small number of individual shares. Collective funds are a low-cost way of spreading risk by investing in a portfolio of shares, with the added advantage of professional fund management.

Investment services are now available that offer diversification across a wider range of asset classes than just equities and bonds. The allocation between asset classes should also be maintained to keep the investment in line with your objectives of meeting as much of the fees as possible without undue risk. Together, this very broad diversification and ongoing oversight of the investment should achieve an effective form of risk management.

Any existing ISAs could, of course, be used as part of your planning. Not everyone is aware that you can transfer existing ISAs from one manager to another if appropriate, so that they will better meet your current objectives.

Other investment options

A range of other investment options are available. For instance, if you will be over 55 when fees (or university expenses) are required, you may be eligible to contribute more to a pension and use the benefits towards the bills (although this will reduce the amount available to provide retirement income).

Once you have used your ISA entitlement, you can still invest in the same underlying funds and benefit from the manager's expertise, but without the tax advantages of an ISA.

Insurance companies also offer a number of lump-sum investment options with a range of underlying investments and risk ratings.

Expatriate parents

If you are an expatriate or offshore investor, there are offshore versions of most of the investments described above. Important considerations are your tax position while you are offshore and, if you will be returning to the UK during the schooling period, your UK tax position.

Late planning

If you have left it late to start planning, say within five years, you could consider the following:

- Check the school's terms for payment in advance (sometimes called composition fees schemes) as these can be attractive. Ask what happens if, for whatever reason, you switch to another school.

- Consider deposit-based schemes.

- Tax-efficient investments may play a part (cash ISAs).

- For other deposit accounts, consider internet or postal accounts, as they often offer better rates.

- National Savings, gilts and fixed-interest securities could also be considered.

- Loan schemes may be available whereby you arrange a 'drawdown' facility secured on your house. This assumes you have some 'free equity' (the difference between the value of the house and your mortgage) and is usually set up as a second mortgage. You can then 'draw down' from the facility as and when you need to pay fees. Hence, you do not start paying interest sooner than necessary, keeping down the total cost. However, you should think carefully before securing other debts against your home. Your home may be repossessed if you do not keep up repayments on your mortgage.

- Because of the interest payments, loan schemes are costly, so they should be regarded as a last resort and only after you have reviewed your finances to check that there is no alternative.

The need for protection

For most families, the major resource for educational expenses is the parents' earnings. Death or prolonged illness could destroy a well-laid plan and have a terrible effect on a family's standard of living and a child's education. You should therefore review your existing arrangements (whether from a company or private scheme) and make sure you are sufficiently protected.

University expenses

Although many of the same investment considerations apply, planning needs to cover living expenses and the appropriate fees. There is a system of student loans. Although university expenses are generally not as high as school fees, they have become more onerous in recent years.

Seeking advice

Whatever your circumstances, it is sensible to take professional advice to ensure you are headed in the right direction; making inappropriate investment decisions can be very costly. You should seek an independent wealth adviser, able to advise on all investment products, who is not paid solely by commissions from sales.

'Golden' rules of educational planning

- Plan as early in the child's life as possible.
- Set out what funds you need and when you need them, and plan accordingly.
- Mitigate tax on the investments wherever possible.
- Use capital if available, particularly from grandparents.
- Take professional financial advice.

This article briefly outlines some of the considerations and investment opportunities and does not make specific or individual recommendations. There is no one answer to suit everyone as solutions depend on a number of considerations. For a strategy tailored to your individual circumstances, seek professional advice.

Towry Law Financial Services Limited
Towry Law House
Western Road
Bracknell RG12 1TL
Tel: 0845 788 9933
E-mail: info@towrylaw.com
Website: www.towrylaw.com

Scholarships, bursaries and other awards

In addition to your own school fees investment planning, assistance may be available from scholarship, bursaries and other awards. Here we explore the various types of school fees support that can be found.

Scholarships

Many senior schools offer scholarship opportunities. These are awarded at the discretion of the school to pupils displaying particular ability or promise in academic subjects, as an all-rounder or in specific areas such as music or art. Candidates are normally assessed on the basis of their performance in an examination or audition. Scholarship examinations are normally held in the February or March preceding September entry. Pupils awarded scholarships in, for example, music or art may be required to sit the Common Entrance examination to ensure that they meet the normal academic requirements of the awarding school.

When and who are eligible?

Scholarships are normally offered at the usual entry stage or stages of a school (eg 11 or 13+ for senior). Some schools also offer awards for sixth form entry, for example for pupils who have performed particularly well in the GCSE examinations. These awards may be restricted to pupils already attending the school or may also be open to prospective entrants coming from other schools.

The value

Scholarships vary in value, although full-fee scholarships are now rarely available. Scholarships are generally awarded as a percentage of the full tuition fee to allow for inflation.

Prep school scholarships

Fewer scholarships are available at preparatory school level. Choristers are, however, a special category. Choir schools generally offer much reduced fees for choristers, well below the normal day fee. Help may also be available at senior schools, although in practice it is common for choristers to gain music scholarships at their senior schools. Information about other music awards at independent schools is available from the Music Masters' and Mistresses' Association (MMA) at www.mma-online.org.uk.

For a general guide to scholarships offered by individual schools, turn to the Scholarships index in Part 5.

Bursaries

Bursaries are intended primarily to ensure that children obtain provision suited to their needs and ability in cases where parents cannot afford the normal fees. They are awarded on the basis of financial hardship, rather than particular ability. All pupils applying for a bursary are required to demonstrate that they meet academic requirements, typically by passing Common Entrance or the school's own entry tests. The size of the award is entirely at the discretion of the school. An index of schools that offers bursaries is given in Part 5.

Reserved entrance awards

Some schools reserve awards for children with parents in a specific profession, for example in HM Forces, the clergy or in teaching. These are similar to bursaries in that the child must meet the normal entry requirements of the school, but eligibility for the award will be dependent upon fulfilment of one of the criteria stated above. Normally schools will reserve only a few places on this basis. Once a place for a specific award has been filled, it will not become available again until the pupil currently in receipt leaves the school. Hence the award may be available only once every five years or so.

A list of schools and brief summary of the reserved entrance awards offered by each is given in Part 5. The awards covered include those offered to children with one or both parents working in any of HM Forces, the Foreign Office, the medical profession, teaching, the clergy or as Christian missionaries.

Other awards

Schools may also offer concessions for brothers and sisters (sibling discounts) or for the children of former pupils.

If you are interested in the possibility of a scholarship or bursary or in other awards, it is a good idea to advise the schools you are interested in accordingly when you first contact them.

The GDST Scholarship and Bursary Scheme

The GDST (Girls' Day School Trust), which comprises 26 girls' schools educating over 20,000 girls, has traditionally aimed to make its schools accessible to bright, motivated girls from families who could not afford a place at a GDST school without financial assistance. It has a Scholarship and Bursary Scheme specifically designed for low-income families. Grants are only awarded at GDST schools.

Most bursaries under the scheme are awarded to girls from families with a total annual income of under £16,500, and it is unlikely that a bursary would be awarded in cases where total gross income exceeds £48,000. Bursaries are means-tested and may cover up to full fees. Scholarships, which are not means-tested, are awarded on merit and may cover up to half the fees. Most awards are available either on entry at 11 or for girls entering the sixth form. The Scheme is also designed to assist pupils already attending a GDST school whose parents face unexpected financial difficulties which could mean having to remove their daughter from the school and disrupt her education.

Awards are made at the discretion of individual school heads rather than the Trust and requests for further information should therefore be directed to the head of the school at which parents wish to apply for a place.

Other government grants

Assistance with the payment of fees is also offered to personnel employed by the Foreign and Commonwealth Office (FCO) and by the Ministry of Defence, where a boarding education may be the only feasible option for parents whose professional lives demand frequent moves or postings overseas.

The FCO termly boarding allowance is available to FCO parents on request and is reviewed annually. Parents in need of further information should contact the FCO Personnel Services Department on 020 7238 4357.

Services personnel may seek guidance from the Service Children's Education Advisory Service, which can advise on choosing a boarding school and on the Continuity of Education Allowance (formerly boarding allowance). The Continuity of Education Allowance is in the region of £4,480 per term for junior boarding pupils and £5,833 per term for senior boarding pupils. An allowance is also available for children with special educational needs. Further information may be obtained from Children's Education Advisory Service, Trenchard Lines, Upavon, Pewsey, Wiltshire SN9 6BE; Tel: 01980 618244. You may also find it helpful to visit www.army.mod.uk and www.sceschools.com.

Parents may also find it helpful to consult the list of schools offering reserved entrance awards in Part 5. Some schools may be able to supplement allowances offered by employers through a reserved entrance award offered to pupils who meet the relevant criteria, eg with a parent in HM Forces.

Grant-giving trusts

There are various educational and charitable trusts which exist to provide help with the payment of independent school fees. Usually the criteria restrict eligibility to particular groups, for example orphans, or to cases of sudden and unforeseen financial hardship. In many cases a grant may be given only to enable a child to complete the present stage of education, eg to finish a GCSE or A Level course. Applications are normally considered on an individual basis by an appointed committee. The criteria for eligibility and for the award of a grant will vary according to individual policy. In some cases several trusts may each contribute an agreed sum towards one individual case in order to make up the fees required. It should be noted that such trusts receive many more applications for grants than can possibly be issued and competition is fierce. Applications for financial help purely on the grounds that parents would like an independent education for their child but cannot afford it from their own resources will be rejected. Parents are advised to consider carefully before applying for an independent school place and entering a child for the entrance examination if they cannot meet the fees unaided and cannot demonstrate a genuine need, as defined by the criteria published by the awarding trust. Parents may find it helpful to consult the Educational Grants Directory, published by the Directory of Social Change. Charitable funding can also be sought from The Royal National Children's Foundation, Sandy Lane, Cobham, Surrey KT11 2ES; contact David Howarth or Chris Hughes on 01932 8686822.

Local Authority grants

Grants from Local Authorities are sometimes available where a need for a child to board can be demonstrated, for example where the child has special educational needs which cannot be met in a day school environment or where travel on a daily basis is not feasible. Such grants are few in number. Awards for boarding fees at an independent school may not be granted unless it can be shown that there is no boarding place available at one of the 35 state boarding schools nationwide.

Awards from Local Authorities are a complex issue. Parents wishing to find out more should contact the director of education for the Authority in which they live.

1.6

Independent school inspections

Durell Barnes, the Independent Schools Inspectorate (ISI)

Inspections undertaken by the Independent Schools Inspectorate (ISI) are for the benefit of pupils as they are designed to improve the quality and effectiveness of education and welfare. Inspections also provide objective and reliable reports that are available to parents, school associations, the government and the wider community – making schools more accountable. One of the most important roles of inspection is to help governors and teaching staff recognize and build on strengths and improve on any weaker areas. The inspection standards also encourage best practice throughout the independent sector.

Inspection of Independent Schools Council schools

ISI is the agency responsible for the inspection of schools in membership of the associations of the Independent Schools Council (ISC).

Other inspectorates

Other non-association independent schools are inspected by Ofsted (www.ofsted.gov.uk). There are also two small independent inspectorates that inspect a few non-association schools (the Bridge Schools Inspectorate (BSI) and School Inspection Services (SIS)). More information can be found on their websites (www.bridgeschoolsinspectorate.co.uk and www.schoolinspectionservice.co.uk).

The inspection process

Currently, there are two models of inspection: two-day interim inspections (the three-yearly 'health check' required by the last government) alternate with five-day standard inspections where the two-day visit is supplemented by a team visit some weeks later: this focuses on quality of provision and outcomes and improvement since the last inspection.

Changes to inspections in the future

In 2011–12, the inspection of boarding welfare in ISC schools is scheduled to transfer from Ofsted to ISI. Thereafter, schools will need to deal with only one inspectorate and parents will need to consult only a single report. The educational landscape is changing rapidly at present, not least because of the new agenda being pursued by the coalition government, and as a result the nature of inspection is likely to evolve. The shape and frequency of inspection may well also change, but the aims will remain the same.

Inspectors

The number of inspectors involved varies, from two on an interim inspection of a school with no boarding or early years, to five for each section of a large school with both junior and senior departments. Teams are led by highly trained reporting inspectors who are usually former HMI (Her Majesty's Inspectors), senior Ofsted inspectors or suitably qualified and trained heads or senior staff from independent schools. ISI operates a peer review system whereby team inspectors are usually serving heads or senior staff in ISC schools. This ensures both that current practitioners contribute to the judgements made about the schools and that the experience of inspection enables best practice to be spread throughout the sector.

Areas covered by inspection

In addition to looking at regulatory compliance, inspectors report on the fulfilment of the aims and the distinctiveness of each school, on the extent to which pupils are supported to be healthy, stay safe, enjoy school and achieve good educational standards, make a positive contribution to their own or the wider community and develop skills that will contribute to their future economic well-being.

Inspector conduct, inspection evidence and judgements

Inspectors observe a code of conduct and ensure that their judgements are first-hand, valid, comprehensive, corporate, even-handed, reliable and objective. The evidence on which their judgements are based includes the observation of lessons, scrutiny of samples of pupils' work and consultation with pupils, governors, the head and staff. Also taken into account is analysis of pre-inspection parental and pupil surveys and documentary evidence, including performance indicators and self-evaluation. The corporate findings of the team are given in the afternoon of the last day of the inspection. The report should then reach the school within four weeks and should be delivered to parents within a further two weeks.

Interim inspection reports

Interim inspection reports, written after a two-day visit, focus primarily on regulatory compliance. They begin with a section of the characteristics of the school, including its aims and distinctive features. They go on to review the success of the school in terms of: the quality of the pupils' achievements and their learning, attitudes and basic skills; the quality of the pupils' personal development; and the effectiveness of governance, leadership and management. There is then a section on action points, beginning with regulatory compliance as follows:

Regulatory requirements (covered by inspection)

Quality of education provided (curriculum)
Quality of education provided (teaching)
Spiritual, moral, social and cultural development of pupils
Welfare, health and safety of pupils
Suitability of staff, supply staff and proprietors
Premises and accommodation
Provision of information
Manner in which complaints are handled

This section ends with any recommendations for further improvement. Where appropriate, there is a section on the effectiveness of the early years foundation stage (EYFS).

Standard inspection reports

Standard inspection reports, written after two visits lasting five days altogether, include sections on the characteristics of the school, the success of the school and action points, and (where appropriate) the effectiveness of the EYFS, as above. In addition, there are sections on the quality of provision and the outcomes for pupils.

Quality of provision and outcomes for pupils (covered by inspection)

- **The quality of academic and other achievements**
- The quality of the pupils' achievements and their learning, attitudes and skills
- The contribution of curricular and extra-curricular provision (including community links of benefit to pupils
- The contribution of teaching
- **The quality of the pupils' personal development**
- The spiritual, moral, social and cultural development of the pupils
- The contribution of the arrangements for welfare, health and safety
- The quality of boarding education (where appropriate)
- **The effectiveness of governance, leadership and management**
- The quality of governance
- The quality of leadership and management
- The quality of links with parents, carers and guardians

Judgement criteria

The criteria for judgements in these areas can be found in the ISI Inspection Framework. The ISI Framework is distinct from the Ofsted Frameworks for maintained schools and for non-association independent schools and for this reason they are not directly comparable. Ofsted reports, for example, often include an overarching grade for the school. ISI reports do not have an overall grade for the school and although an overarching judgement is explicitly made at the beginning of each section, numerical grades are not given. Both inspectorates work on a four-grade scale (from excellent or outstanding to inadequate or unsatisfactory). However, apart from compliance issues, judgements for each inspectorate are based on unique criteria and in ISI, for example, inspectors will arrive at judgements by taking into account the typical, and usually more demanding, standards expected for similar ISC schools as opposed to 'national' standards. This means that the grades awarded by Ofsted and ISI are not interchangeable.

Finding ISI reports

Reports can be accessed on the ISI website (www.isi.net). Any non-compliance is found on interim inspections. Where this cannot be rectified by the second part of a standard inspection, the DfE will ask the school to produce an action plan to deal with the failings. ISI is later asked to evaluate that plan, either remotely or by a further visit to the school. Schools also produce an action plan for their association, which ISI is also consulted about. The whole process is quality assured in a variety of ways: reports are edited by expert readers and subsequently proof read; schools and inspectors complete evaluations after inspections; senior and experienced reporting inspectors are deployed to monitor inspections on behalf of the ISI; and Ofsted also monitors a proportion of ISI inspections and reports on behalf of the DfE.

Reading a school's ISI report

Parents can readily use reports to ascertain the extent of regulatory compliance in a school and the inspectors' judgements as to the quality of provision and outcomes. ISI aims to avoid all jargon in reports and they are accessible to the lay reader. As schools can develop and change very quickly it is important to appreciate that an inspection report is, like any health check or diagnosis, accurate at the time it is undertaken. Parents will want to use other information, for example from the school's website, from other parents and from visiting the school, to make their own judgements about a school. Some parents find it helpful to ask schools what has contributed to any aspect deemed excellent or outstanding and how such standards are maintained. Many ask what schools have done in terms of the recommended actions in reports to evaluate how schools have used findings to aid their ongoing self-improvement.

The sixth form and beyond – parents' guide

Pupils studying for GCSEs, IGCSEs or the equivalent, like most 15- and 16-year-olds, are probably still some way from decisions about higher education and careers. At this stage there is, of course, plenty of room for the development and discussion of ideas and interests. To reach the right decisions, it is important to have an open mind about all of the options and to begin preliminary planning well in advance. This section introduces some of the most important considerations.

Making the right choices for future plans

Choosing the right sixth form course is becoming increasingly important as the options at 18 become more complex. Pupils who have given some thought to their future plans and to their own strengths and personal qualities will find it easier to identify broad potential career areas. This in turn will enable them to choose suitable sixth form and higher education options, which allow flexibility for the development of skills and personal growth. At the same time, extra-curricular activities, relevant work experience and other activities will help to build up the essential personal and practical skills sought by today's employers.

Careers advice

Good advice is essential. Some schools have excellent careers guidance programmes and materials and may also arrange talks from visiting speakers and work experience opportunities. Others may have more limited resources. Computer-based or online careers assessments are often used in schools. Such assessments are not designed to provide all the answers but rather to highlight possibilities. They should form part of a much more extensive discussion that includes consideration of academic achievements and aspirations, attitudes, interests and any special needs. Your son or daughter may also find it helpful to speak to an independent consultant, who can offer an objective view and perhaps a wider perspective of potential careers.

Sixth form options

The main options available after GCSE are: Advanced Subsidiary GCE (AS) and Advanced GCE (A2); in Scotland, National Qualifications (Highers); the International Baccalaureate (IB);

and Applied A levels; although the Cambridge Pre-U is now available at some schools. The basic structure of these courses is covered in Part 1.4.

All can be used as a means of entry to British universities. The IB, as its name implies, is an international qualification and is also recognized for admissions purposes by many universities worldwide. Similarly, the Cambridge Pre-U is an international qualification that can be used for university entry. Unlike AS and A levels, however, these courses are not widely taught in the UK.

Subjects or areas of study

Is depth or breadth the most important factor? A levels offer a high degree of specialization. The IB is a demanding academic qualification but covers a wider range of subjects in less depth. A vocational course will probably have a relatively narrow focus on a particular career area such as Business, Leisure and Tourism, or Information Technology.

Course load

Most pupils take four AS subjects in the lower sixth form and continue three of these as A2s in the upper sixth form, thus emerging with three full A levels and one AS in a fourth subject. The equivalent of three A level passes is the core requirement for university entry. However, in some cases universities may ask for specific grades in certain subjects and in others they may seek an overall number of UCAS points. In this relatively uncertain climate, sixth formers should appreciate that quality is more important than quantity – in other words additional courses should not be taken if this would jeopardize the grades obtained in core subjects. If they are in any doubt about the combination of A/AS levels and grades which will be acceptable to a university, they should not hesitate to contact admissions staff or seek other forms of professional advice.

Availability

Is the required course available at your child's present school or, if not, at another school or independent college? Is living away from home an option?

Assessment method and course structure

Some pupils prefer regular assessment through submission of coursework or projects rather than exam-based assessment. Most A level courses, traditionally assessed through a final exam, now include coursework as part of the assessment – applied A levels tend to have a large coursework component. Cambridge Pre-U Diploma includes assessed projects and final examinations. Assessment for the IB is chiefly by examination.

Academic ability

A level courses often demand a good deal of reading and the ability to write well-argued essays. In science-based subjects, abstract thinking and in some cases strong mathematical skills are important. Pupils must reflect on their areas of strength and real subject interests when selecting courses and make realistic choices based on their academic abilities.

Future plans

Pupils aiming for a specific career should check whether their preferred sixth form options are suitable. Those still undecided should choose a programme which allows some flexibility.

Which A levels?

It is natural for pupils to want to continue with subjects they enjoy. Clearly, a high GCSE result suggests that a similar result may be expected at A level. This is important, of course, but pupils must also consider whether or not their preferred combination of subjects is suitable for their higher education or career plans. It is also possible to take certain A level courses in subjects not previously studied.

Career choice

Some careers, for example engineering, medicine and architecture, demand a specific degree. This may limit, or sometimes dictate, the choice of A level subjects and pupils must be confident that they can do well in these. If career plans are undecided, it is wise to choose subjects which will leave a number of options open.

Requirements for sixth form studies

It is advisable to have achieved at least a grade B at GCSE in any subjects being considered for A level (ideally grade A in Maths, Science and Modern Languages). Some A level subjects such as Economics can be taken without any previous knowledge, but pupils should consider what skills are required, eg numerical, analytical or essay writing, and whether or not it will suit them.

Different examining bodies may assess the same subject in different ways. If your son or daughter has concerns about a final exam-based assessment, he or she might consider a syllabus which offers a modular structure and a higher degree of assessment through coursework. Remember, however, that if all the subjects chosen are assessed on this basis, the workload and the pressure to meet deadlines during the course could be very heavy.

Interest and motivation

Genuine interest is essential if a pupil is to feel motivated throughout the two-year course and achieve high grades. Pupils in a dilemma over the choice between a subject they enjoy and a subject which they feel they ought to do might be well advised to opt for the former but should check that this is suitable for their future plans. Pupils who are thinking of taking up a new subject, for example Psychology, may find it helpful to read a few books on the subject to test their interest before making any decisions.

Which subject combinations?

If no specific combination is demanded, how can pupils ensure a suitable choice? At least two subjects should be complementary, ie two arts/social sciences or two sciences. It is quite common for pupils to combine arts and sciences. It should be remembered that even those career areas which do not demand specific degree courses may still require certain skills, which some A level subjects will develop better than others.

If a particular degree course does not require an A level in the subject, eg Psychology, it may be better to choose a different A level subject or perhaps a complementary option and so demonstrate a wider knowledge/skills base to university admissions tutors. This also avoids the risk of repeating the A level syllabus in the first year at university.

Other matters to consider include the timetabling constraints at school which may make a certain combination impossible, in which case pupils may have to compromise or change to a school or college with greater flexibility.

Where shall I study?

Staying on into the sixth form of the present school does have advantages, including continuity and familiarity with surroundings, staff and fellow pupils. It is not unusual, however, for pupils to change schools at 16. Some may be looking for a course, subjects or combination of subjects not available at their present school. Others may simply want a change of atmosphere or a different style of education.

If a change to a different school is sought, consider the school's academic pace and examination results, its university entry record, the criteria for entry to the sixth form and the availability of places. Other considerations include the size of the sixth form and of the teaching groups and, where appropriate, the opportunities to develop skills or pursue interests aside from A level studies. Independent sixth form colleges or tutorial colleges offer an alternative environment that can suit some pupils – more details on this option follow.

James Wardrobe, Council of Independent Education (CIFE), explains what independent sixth form colleges have to offer

Independent sixth form colleges in the UK, often still referred to as tutorial colleges, have a distinctive history. The earliest were established in the early 20th century to prepare students for Oxbridge and officer-level entry to the Armed Forces. Following the Second World War more tutorial colleges specializing in A level and O level teaching surfaced but they were still often derided as 'crammers'. The now fully accepted contemporary *independent sixth form colleges* are much in demand from UK and international students seeking quality in teaching and examination preparation.

Wide A level subject range

Colleges tend to offer a wider range of subjects and greater flexibility in subject combinations than traditional schools. Most allow students any combination of subjects and there are commonly over 40 AS and A level subjects to choose from! Unusual subject combinations such as Accounting, Psychology and History can be accommodated more readily and joining a college for the second year of A level (A2) is often possible. At some London colleges you will also find one-year courses (covering AS and A2 modules) and retake courses (both one-term and one-year).

Flexible GCSE courses

Although the majority of students take A levels, most colleges run equally flexible GCSE courses, usually offering more creative subjects such as Photography alongside the mainstream ones. Again, the number of subjects to choose from is generally greater than that offered by schools. One-year GCSE courses are also often available, as are standard two-year courses.

The college atmosphere and pastoral support

The college environment is famous for being more relaxed and less rules-driven than at school. There are no uniform requirements and generally held philosophy that 'students are to be treated as adults' is evident. Nevertheless, pastoral and academic support is of a high standard. Colleges tend to succeed in balancing authority with liberty by guiding students without dictating to them. This approach enables students to grow in confidence without compromising their well-being and safety.

Other qualifications available

As well as A level and GCSE courses, some institutions offer one-year University Foundation courses, designed specifically for overseas students. Scottish colleges, as you would expect, tend to offer SQA courses. Most colleges also run EFL programmes, usually leading to internationally recognized qualifications such as IELTS. Some offer preparation for SATS for US university entrance. As yet, no independent sixth form colleges offer the Cambridge Pre-U and the International Baccalaureate is not widely available. Colleges do, however, offer short courses unavailable at most schools, such as intensive Easter revision courses.

Class sizes

Small classes are the norm even at GCSE level. This is especially true in less common subjects, such as Geology, Philosophy, Italian and Classical Greek. An average of just six students per class has been noted, resulting in an atmosphere similar to that of a university tutorial where all are encouraged to debate and actively engage with course topics.

Teaching at independent sixth form colleges

As a former college principal, headmaster and ISI inspector, I have observed hundreds, if not thousands, of lessons taught in prep schools, senior schools and sixth form colleges. This gamut of lessons has ranged from unsatisfactory (occasionally) to outstanding. As far as the sixth form colleges are concerned, I have frequently seen what I believe are some of the best A level practitioners in the business, who would be equally comfortable teaching in highly selective academic schools. Of course, as all good teachers do, they display great enthusiasm and passion for their subject and communicate effectively their impressive subject knowledge. However, these college tutors seem to have two added advantages. Firstly, they are able to specialize in their subject at a particular level for a particular syllabus throughout their whole teaching timetable, thus acquiring a specific expertise; for example, one college had a Maths tutor who taught only A level Further Mathematics. Secondly, the informal, relaxed nature of the tutorial college's small-group environment enables tutors to quickly establish and maintain highly productive working relationships with students.

Teaching resources

In terms of teaching resources, as you will discover for yourself if you make a visit, all the reputable colleges have well-equipped science laboratories, IT equipment, libraries and, where such subjects are offered, art, music, drama, film and media studies facilities.

University preparation

As far as UCAS advice is concerned, in my experience, college tutors know the examination and university entrance systems inside-out and pride themselves on keeping up to date on the latest admissions requirements. Some colleges run very sophisticated and targeted programmes of support for students applying for challenging university courses. These include specialist Medical Sciences programmes, with guest lectures from medical admission tutors, and tailor-made courses for potential Oxbridge, Medical, Dental and Veterinary students. Many also offer study skills and work experience programmes.

Extra-curricular activities

Most colleges offer a wide range of sporting opportunities. If sport is important to you, college staff members encourage you to continue by joining their own teams or those of associated local clubs and leisure centres. A quick glance at college websites will give you a good idea of the range of leisure activities on offer. Schemes such as the Duke of Edinburgh's Award and the Young Enterprise programme are often available.

Why consider independent sixth form college?

Students choose sixth form colleges in the independent sector for diverse reasons, but seem united by their ambition to get the best education and the best preparation they can before moving on to university. The old image of catering largely for public school expellees and drop-outs is completely out of date and was probably never that true anyway. Often students who make a change after GCSEs feel that they have outgrown the traditional school ethos and are looking for a better transition to the less regulated environment encountered at university. In recent years there have certainly been growing numbers following traditional two-year A level courses at independent colleges. Some others want to make a fresh start for their upper sixth year after studying AS levels elsewhere (approximately 10 per cent of the annual intake of colleges are students who have spent their lower sixth year in another school). Appropriate courses are available to them, which often revitalize higher education prospects. Although only one component of their expertise, these colleges are very well equipped for those wishing to retake courses, both one-term and one-year, and the best have a remarkably consistent record for grade improvement. Some colleges have also discovered a small but growing trend for IB students to 'retake' their subjects as A levels in one year.

International students

As well as home students, you will find students from overseas who are preparing for UK universities by taking A levels, or possibly a university foundation course. They are usually very hard-working, very focused on their academic studies and contribute a great deal to sixth form life. At the annual CIFE Academic Awards Presentation, held at the House of Lords in March 2011, the Gold Award went to Xenia Dethlefs, a student from Italy who studied for 18 months at Cambridge Centre for Sixth Form Studies, achieving four A*s and one A grade in five A level subjects.

Overall, this part of the independent sector, which prides itself on getting students into higher education, is booming. This is helped, in no small part, by the increasing demand from international and domestic students aspiring to take places at ever more selective universities.

Admissions procedures

All reputable colleges will expect prospective students to visit for interview. If that's impossible, most can make assessments via reports and references etc. Interviews are not meant to be stressful – they are designed to explore what a student has done, what their hopes are and what, for them, is the best *blend* of courses. Students should take along their most recent school reports and examples of written work to give college staff an insight into their ability and attainment. Colleges generally offer places when they can provide the courses and support required.

Course fees

These independent colleges rely entirely on student fees to provide the high staffing levels required for small groups and individual attention. They are, therefore, by no means cheap. Colleges mostly charge according to the number, type and duration of courses taken, so the variety of possible combinations makes it difficult to give an accurate general fee. In terms of comparison, the annual fees for GCSE and A level courses are generally in line with those of a good senior independent school.

Financial support

Some colleges offer financial help and each college will have its own criteria for awarding bursaries and scholarships. It is likely that you will have to prove that you have exceptional academic promise and financial hardship. Timing is important and you should apply to the college of your choice as early as possible in the preceding academic year.

Accommodation

It is vital to have somewhere quiet, comfortable and safe to live while you study, particularly if you have to live away from home. The proportion of residential students varies from college to college. Some have accommodation on site or in college-managed dorms nearby. Most colleges have a team of host families with whom they have well-established relationships.

Choosing the right college

Finding the right college depends on the type of person and on the need. Each college has its own unique atmosphere and to know which one will best suit a student can only really be judged by visiting the college and meeting the staff. However, colleges of good reputation rely to a large extent on word-of-mouth referrals from previous students, so asking around amongst friends and older students who have actually been to a sixth form college is probably the best way to start research. Most colleges give detailed exam results and university entry success information on their websites and all the good ones will be happy to answer questions about grades achieved and student destinations.

Accreditation

All reputable colleges are inspected regularly by at least one of the following national bodies: the Independent Schools Inspectorate (ISI), the Office for Standards in Education (Ofsted) or the British Accreditation Council (BAC). Latest inspection reports can be found on their websites at www.isi.net, www.ofsted.gov.uk and www.the-bac.org. Many of the best colleges are members of the Conference for Independent Education (CIFE), the president of which is Baroness Perry of Southwark. For more information visit www.cife.org.uk.

Fresh starts, successful pre-university education

The sixth form colleges, once a poor relation of the independent sector, have established themselves as reliable and successful providers of pre-university education. For senior school pupils who need a fresh start, this type of college is ideal and may well offer the precise opportunity they are seeking.

The university challenge

Despite continuing pressures on graduate employment opportunities and the introduction of increased tuition fees, higher education applications are still great in number. Higher education offers a unique range of academic, career and social opportunities. However, under-preparing for university applications can prove disastrous. 'Having made the wrong choice' is often cited as the root cause by students who do not complete their degree courses – and this can be as many as one in five.

Why does your son or daughter want to go to university? Is he or she genuinely motivated and keen to study a particular subject in depth, to qualify for a specific career and to take advantage of all the benefits which university life offers? All these reasons are valid, but some pupils may apply to university largely because they feel under pressure at home and/or at school to do so. It is important to allow time to consider options – pupils who are unsure of what to study should not rush into a decision. It may be better to take a year out and to use the additional time constructively before making a choice.

Most schools encourage pupils to begin thinking seriously about higher education soon after entering the sixth form. During the spring and summer terms of the lower sixth form pupils should be researching course and university options. Information is available from reference guides, student-focused websites and university prospectuses. Most universities organize open days where pupils can visit and talk to staff and students. Pupils and their families should use all available resources to prepare for applications. Applications are due to arrive at UCAS (the Universities and Colleges Admissions Service) in January of the year of intended enrolment. Submissions must be made by the end of June to avoid clearing. Pupils applying to Oxford, Cambridge, Medicine, Veterinary Science or Dentistry should note that their applications are required earlier, by mid-October in the year preceding planned entry.

Support and guidance from school, external advisers and parents is essential throughout this period but the final choice of course and university lies with the pupil. It is important that they take an active part in the process and come to a well-reasoned decision. So what are the key points to consider?

Which course?

Is a specific degree necessary for a specific career? In some cases, typically medicine, yes. In many cases, however, including law, students have more flexibility. If there are no specific requirements, prospective employers will often take account of the quality of degree obtained and the reputation of the university as much as the subject studied, and will look for other skills and qualities which match their requirements. This means that students should take a subject in which they expect to do well rather than something which they may, perhaps wrongly, believe to be '*the right thing*'. There are differing views over the importance of taking some career-related degree subjects, for example Business Studies or Media/Communication Studies. Some employers may prefer to employ graduates with a wider education background and train them in-house. Others may prefer applicants to be able to demonstrate practical knowledge and interest. Taking the above examples, this might include work experience with a company or involvement with the university newspaper or radio station.

Sandwich courses including work experience as part of the programme are quite prevalent. They can help employment prospects, enhance practical skills and allow students to test their interest in a particular career before committing themselves. In some cases placements may turn into permanent positions with the same employer after graduation. Some students may, however, not want to delay graduation (a sandwich course usually takes an extra year), and may dislike the disruption of a year spent in a work placement.

For those who would appreciate an extra year off-campus, many universities offer Language degrees incorporating a year spent abroad. Students on a range of other courses can also find opportunities to study abroad as part of their studies.

Foundation degrees

Foundation degrees are vocationally focused intermediate qualifications, slightly below the level of an Honours degree. Foundation degrees take two years' full-time study, but they can also be studied part-time. They often combine work experience with the traditional academic structure of a degree course and are intended to equip students with the skills required by today's employers. Each Foundation degree is usually linked with at least one Honours degree in the same subject area, which means that those who wish to further their qualification can go on to a BA/BSc (Hons) qualification if they choose to do so. Entry to Foundation degrees is flexible in order to attract school leavers and those already in employment who are seeking to develop their skills.

Specialization

Students have amongst others a choice of studying one subject (single honours) or a combination (combined honours). A combined course offers more breadth and the opportunity to follow complementary studies, but almost always means a heavier workload.

For students unsure about taking a subject not studied at school or about going directly into a specialized field, for example civil engineering, a more general foundation year may be helpful.

Checking course content

Courses with the same name may be very different in content, so it is essential to read the prospectus for details. Modern language degrees, for example, vary widely in focus. Some place particular emphasis on practical language skills and an understanding of current affairs; others may have a more traditional emphasis on literature. Course titles like Communication Studies can also mean a wide variety of things.

Entry requirements

What subjects and grades does the course specify? Is the pupil likely to achieve these grades or should he or she look for a course with less stringent entry requirements? Remember that published grades are given only as a guide and may be adjusted upwards or downwards when offers are made to individual pupils. With the variety of sixth form programmes being taken, Gabbitas strongly recommends that pupils contact universities direct to find out what they may be expected to achieve. For arts A level pupils who wish to take a degree in a science-based subject such as Medicine or Engineering, one-year conversion courses are available, but pupils will be expected to have good GCSE grades in Maths and Science. Many modern language courses do not require previous knowledge, although evidence of competency in another foreign language is usually essential.

Remember too that as the A level pass rate rises, admissions tutors increasingly use AS and GCSE results as well as A level grades as an indicator of ability. The A level A* grade is now also included in offers made by some universities.

Which university?

Quality and reputation are as important for the individual course and department as for the institution as a whole. Beware of published league tables, which will not necessarily answer your questions. Find out about the career or employment destinations of recent graduates. This information may be available from the university or in one of the many published handbooks. If you have in mind a particular employer, it may be useful to contact the recruitment department to find out their views on specific universities or degree courses. If you have decided on a career area, you might similarly contact the relevant professional body. Also consider asking the university about the teaching styles, methods of assessment and the level of supervision available.

Some pupils may be attracted to a collegiate-style university such as Oxford, Cambridge or London. Others may prefer a self-contained campus where all academic, social and other facilities are available on-site. Some may prefer a big city environment; others a smaller, more rural location. Living costs are a further important, but often neglected, issue. What is the local transport like? Is a car necessary? How safe is the area after dark? How far is the campus from home? What other facilities are offered to cater for individual hobbies and interests?

There is, of course, much more to finding the right university than simply the course. Aspects such as accommodation (both on and off campus), location or availability of social activities, can generate just as much anxiety and dissatisfaction as academic worries. So it is a good idea to consider the whole offering.

The Universities and Colleges Admissions Service (UCAS) tariff point system

The UCAS tariff point system is designed to help universities and colleges set course entry requirements to select undergraduate students. Universities generally set a minimum UCAS point requirement for entry to a course or make conditional offers to pupils based on the UCAS point value of their sixth form examinations – with a certain number being required for entry. An offer will include the points accepted based on three A Levels or equivalent. Offer levels depend on the popularity of the course and can range from unconditional '0' points to '420' (three A*s) or more.

UCAS tariff points (AS and A level)

Grade	GCE A levels	AS levels
A*	140	
A	120	60
B	100	50
C	80	40
D	60	30
E	40	20

(For the UCAS point value of other qualifications such as the Cambridge Pre U and the IB please refer to UCAS.)

The UCAS tariff point system converts qualifications into UCAS points to create an objective, common currency for university admissions staff. Pupils then use the tariff to calculate their UCAS point total to find out whether they have enough to gain a place on the course of their choice. Pupils are advised that attaining the UCAS point total is not necessarily the only criterion for entry to a course.

Other things to consider when using the UCAS tariff point system

Entry requirements and conditional offers that use the UCAS tariff point system will often have certain conditions that have to be met, eg '320 points needed but with an A grade in English'.

Certain qualifications build up over different levels, with each level attracting a certain number of UCAS tariff points. The tariff point values of each level cannot be combined to create a total. Simply count the UCAS point value from the highest level attained. Examples of qualifications with levels where this applies are:

Qualifications where UCAS points are awarded at different levels

GCE Advanced Subsidiary level and GCE Advanced level
Scottish Highers and Advanced Highers
Key Skills at levels 2, 3 and 4
Speech, drama and music awards at grades 6, 7 and 8

Use of the UCAS tariff system can vary from department to department within one university or college. Therefore you should always check on the specific entry requirements for a particular course with the university or college department itself.

Not all post-16 qualifications attract tariff points and not every university or college uses the tariff when making offers. Applicants may, therefore, still be accepted onto their chosen course if their qualifications do not translate into tariff points.

Where a prospective applicant is unsure of the acceptability of a qualification, it is recommended that advice is sought from the relevant university or college before a formal application is submitted to UCAS. For pupils with overseas qualifications the government-funded body NARIC (www.naric.org.uk) can be consulted for an evaluation and to issue a comparability statement against UK qualifications.

Alternatives to university entry

Pupils who are not attracted by the idea of full-time study at university will find that there are a number of alternatives available. It is possible to study for a degree part-time by distance learning through private institutions, or if practical skills are sought there are many short courses available in areas such as business, computer skills, marketing, PR and languages.

There are also companies and other organizations which take on young people with A levels or the equivalent and offer them part-time academic training leading to relevant professional qualifications, which can be the equivalent of a first degree or postgraduate qualification. Examples include the Armed Forces and Emergency Services, the Merchant Navy, retail, hotel and catering, IT, accountancy, estate agency and certain branches of the Law.

Finding out more

There are, of course, many other options and issues which your son or daughter may want to discuss. These might include the pros and cons of taking a year out after school and how to make the best use of it, sponsorship to help finance a degree course, presenting a well-structured and effective UCAS application, interview techniques, CV writing and job applications.

Advice should be available from your child's school. Expert, independent guidance is also available from Gabbitas for seniors and current undergraduates, including: advice on university choices and applications, changing course or university and career options. For more details please visit www.gabbitas.co.uk/careers-colleges-and-universities or contact our post-16 and higher education team on tel: 020 7734 0161 or e-mail he@gabbitas.co.uk.

Dr Wendy Piatt expresses why seniors should contemplate studying at a Russell Group university

University offers the chance to learn – about a subject, about the world, about yourself. But before arriving for your first day at university you will have to make many choices. What subject should you choose? Where should you study it? Would it be better to study part-time or full-time? You will probably want to consider all sorts of factors, such as the course content, the teaching style, the entry requirements, and even where the institution is located.

Higher education options

The UK offers a very wide range of options for studying at higher education level and it is important to take the time to investigate what all these options are before deciding the best match for your interests, aspirations and abilities.

World-class educational setting

Russell Group universities are to be found in all four nations and in every major city of the UK. They offer a wide range of subjects at both undergraduate and postgraduate level, with teaching conducted in a setting where world-class, groundbreaking research is being undertaken. Students at Russell Group universities can choose internationally renowned courses across a range of subjects, from medical, biological and physical sciences to business, social sciences and the humanities.

The research endeavour

The size and success of the research endeavour in Russell Group universities enables them to offer a student experience where teaching and learning are enriched and informed by leading-edge, world-class academic exploration. Research such as that carried out by Andre Geim and Konstantin Novoselov, two physicists who forged their careers in the University of Manchester and who were jointly awarded the 2010 Nobel Prize in Physics for their creation, graphene, the thinnest and strongest material in the world hailed a 'wonder material' when the two made their discovery in 2004. And in the Department of Zoology in the University of Oxford, a novel IT application originally developed by Torsten Reil and Colm Massey in order to achieve a better understanding of animal and human motion is now incorporated in blockbuster video games such as *Grand Theft Auto IV* and *Star Wars: The Force Unleashed*.

Discovery and intellectual curiosity

There is a high ratio of staff to students in Russell Group universities and it can be thrilling to learn from award-winning academics like the pioneers and their teams mentioned above and to get involved in their research. The academic, personal and professional benefits of this sort of experience can be enormous. You learn the importance of thinking independently. The emphasis on active processes of discovery and intellectual curiosity develops not only specialist knowledge but the entrepreneurialism, analytical problem-solving and communication skills which are so vital for success in many careers. This is demonstrated by the fact that graduates of Russell Group universities are held in particularly high esteem by employers: in a recent survey of international graduate recruiters 12 Russell Group universities were ranked in the top 50 in the world.[1]

International connections

Their world-class status means that Russell Group institutions also have partners across the globe, including businesses and governments as well as other universities. These relationships mean that students are offered excellent opportunities to apply their skills to issues outside their university, whether through work placements, international exchange programmes or other activities.

Facilities

As well as first-rate academic facilities, Russell Group universities offer excellent facilities for a wide range of activities, from social and sporting activities to cultural resources including exceptional libraries, museums and galleries. With a wide range of public arts and science events, the universities make a major contribution to the cultural life of the UK.

Well-regarded university places

Given the high standards of teaching and learning resources, as well as the opportunities students are offered outside their formal studies, it is not surprising that Russell Group universities are amongst the most popular in the UK. Drop-out rates are very low indeed, particularly in comparison with universities even in the United States. Levels of student satisfaction at Russell Group universities are particularly notable, with 86 per cent of students reporting satisfaction with the quality of their course.

Competitive entry

With this excellence and popularity comes competition for entry, however. Far more people apply to Russell Group universities than these institutions can accept, and the vast majority have high grades – so competition for places is fierce. Because of this, you will need excellent results in A levels or equivalents in order to take up a place. It is advisable to be as realistic as possible during the application process and make sure that you have an 'insurance offer' or have considered other options you could pursue in the event that you don't achieve the grades you were hoping for.

Other universities

There are many other universities that are not Russell Group members. The majority tend to be more recently established, particularly after 1992 when many polytechnics became univer-

---

[1] Source: QS World Rankings – http://www.topuniversities.com/university-rankings/world-university-rankings/2010/indicator-rankings/employer-review

sities. Entry requirements tend to be lower than those at Russell Group institutions but offers vary depending on which faculty and course you are contemplating.

Choosing sixth form subjects

To maximize your chances of getting into the university and course of your choice, you should consider your choice of subjects at school very carefully. Many courses at university level build on knowledge gained while still at school, and so universities need to make sure that all the students they admit have prepared themselves in the best way to cope with their chosen course. Some university courses require you to have studied a specific subject prior to entry, though others may not.

Facilitating subjects

Some subjects are required or recommended more often than others for entry to courses at Russell Group institutions; these include: Mathematics and Further Maths, English, Physics, Biology, Chemistry, Geography, History and Languages. These are sometimes called 'facilitating subjects' and by choosing them at advanced level (A level) you will have a much wider range of options open to you at university.

Researching options

The best way to check your options is to find out the entry requirements of courses you are interested in studying at a particular university through the university prospectus or UCAS website.

Remember the 'extra' elements when making an application

Getting your post-16 subject choices right is an important first step towards university and working as hard as you can to get the best grades possible is the second. But academic achievement, while vitally important, is only one of several things universities will take into account when they consider your application.

Russell Group universities are constantly seeking to develop the most effective ways of identifying real potential. Our admissions tutors are skilled at reviewing a range of factors and information about candidates to identify those with the most talent and potential to excel on our courses whatever their social or educational background.

They will also want to select students who are clearly well motivated and passionate about their subject. The vast majority of admissions tutors use personal statements and references when assessing candidates. Some departments may interview applicants or ask them to sit additional tests, particularly for the most competitive courses like Medicine or Law.

These 'extra' elements of the admissions process are not designed to catch students out and shouldn't be seen as obstacles to get around. They are there to give candidates as many opportunities as possible to demonstrate their strengths, passion and commitment for a subject and to help the university identify a student's true potential as accurately and fairly as possible. Admissions tutors may also take into account any particular barriers a candidate may have faced during their education, such as spending time in care.

University and financial support

Over recent months there has been a considerable amount of discussion and debate about the cost of going to university in the UK, particularly in England. It is important to be aware of the financial support – usually in the form of government loans or grants and university bursaries – which is available to students entering undergraduate courses. The details of what is available to you will differ depending on whether you live in England, Scotland, Wales, Northern Ireland or elsewhere in the EU, and where your university is located.

It is really important to understand that student loans are a world away from conventional 'debt'. Graduates are only asked to start making repayments once they are have finished studying and are earning a reasonable salary. Even then, contributions are what we call 'income-contingent'; this means that graduates repay only a small proportion of their income above a certain level each month.

In addition to the loans and grants provided by the government, Russell Group universities offer a wide range of bursaries and financial aid for their students. You are strongly advised to look at the financial support pages of university websites to see what is available at different institutions. Remember, graduates, not students, are asked to make a contribution to the costs of going to university and that contribution is a sound investment. University can lead to the most satisfying careers but also offer the most amazing experiences which many people only fully appreciate once they've left.

The university experience

I relished my time at two Russell Group universities – Lincoln College, Oxford and King's College, London – so much so that I spent as long as possible being a student, first as an undergraduate and then going on to study for a Masters and a PhD! If you are contemplating going to university you are in the enviable position of embarking on one of the best experiences of your life. So make sure you find out as much as you can about what is on offer, work hard and make the most of your time when you're there, and don't forget to appreciate and enjoy the ride.

More information about the Russell Group and its member universities is available from our website (www.russellgroup.ac.uk).

PART TWO

GEOGRAPHICAL DIRECTORY

The Independent Schools Guide Photography Competition 2011

3rd Prize Winner

Aldenham School
Alan Reader

Notes on information given in the directory section

Type of school

The directory comprises schools listed within the Department for Education register of independent schools. Maintained schools, foundation schools, special schools, independent further education colleges and overseas schools are not included, unless they have a profile in Part 3.

Schools are listed by type as follows: Nursery and Pre-Prep, Preparatory, Senior, Independent Sixth Form College/Tutorial College or International Schools and International Study Centres. The highest age range admitted has been used to categorize (except in the case of International Schools and International Study Centres), eg a straight-through school of 3-18 will appear under Senior, rather than Nursery and Prep-Prep or Preparatory.

Each school is given a brief entry which provides address details, web address (where available) and age range admitted. In some cases single-sex schools take small numbers of the opposite sex within a specified age range. These are indicated where appropriate, eg: 3–18 (Girls 16–18).

Also included is colour coded information about the gender admitted, accommodation available, the presence of a 6th form, whether the IB is offered and CReSTeD registration.

Please refer to the symbol key that follows when using the directory.

Symbol Key

Gender

● Girls
● Boys
● Coed

Accommodation

♠ Boarding only
♠ Boarding and Day
♠ Day and Boarding
♠ Day Only

★ International Baccalaureate (IB)

◆ The Council for the Registration of Schools Teaching Dyslexic Pupils (CReSTeD)

▲ Has 6th Form

* The school has a profile in Part 3

2.2

England

BEDFORDSHIRE

NURSERY AND PRE-PREP

PILGRIMS PRE-PREPARATORY SCHOOL

●🏠
Brickhill Drive, Bedford,
Bedfordshire MK41 7QZ
W: www.pilgrimpreprep.org.uk

PREPARATORY

ACORN SCHOOL

●🏠
15 St Andrews Road, Bedford,
Bedfordshire MK40 2LL
W: www.acornschool.net
Age Range: 2–8

BEDFORD PREPARATORY SCHOOL

●🏠
De Parys Avenue, Bedford,
Bedfordshire MK40 2TU
W: www.bedfordschool.org.uk
Age Range: 7–13

CHILDREN'S MONTESSORI SCHOOL

●🏠
Green End, Sandy, Bedfordshire
SG19 3LB
Age Range: 4–9 (Nursery)

MOORLANDS SCHOOL

●🏠
Leagrave Hall, Luton,
Bedfordshire LU4 9LE
W: www.moorlandsschool.com
Age Range: 2–11

POLAM SCHOOL

●🏠
45 Lansdowne Road, Bedford,
Bedfordshire MK40 2BU
W: www.polamschool.co.uk
Age Range: 2–9

ST GEORGE'S

●🏠
28 Priory Road, Dunstable,
Bedfordshire LU5 4HR
Age Range: 2–11

SENIOR

BEDFORD HIGH SCHOOL FOR GIRLS

●🏠★▲
Bromham Road, Bedford,
Bedfordshire MK40 2BS
W: www.bedfordhigh.co.uk
Age Range: 7–18

BEDFORD MODERN SCHOOL

●🏠▲
Manton Lane, Bedford,
Bedfordshire MK41 7NT
W: www.bedmod.co.uk
Age Range: 7–18

BEDFORD SCHOOL

●🏠★▲
De Parys Avenue, Bedford,
Bedfordshire MK40 2TU
W: www.bedfordschool.org.uk
Age Range: 7–18

DAME ALICE HARPUR SCHOOL

Cardington Road, Bedford, Bedfordshire MK42 0BX
W: www.dahs.co.uk
Age Range: 7–18

RUSHMOOR SCHOOL

58–60 Shakespeare Road, Bedford, Bedfordshire MK40 2DL
Age Range: 4–16

ST ANDREW'S SCHOOL

78 Kimbolton Road, Bedford, Bedfordshire MK40 2PA
W: www.standrewsschoolbedford.com
Age Range: 3–16 (Boys 3–7)

SCEPTRE SCHOOL

Ridgeway Avenue, Dunstable, Bedfordshire LU5 4QL
Age Range: 11–18

INTERNATIONAL SCHOOLS AND INTERNATIONAL STUDY CENTRES

BEDFORD SCHOOL STUDY CENTRE

67 De Parys Avenue, Bedford, Bedfordshire MK40 2TR
W: www.bedfordschool.org.uk/bssc
Age Range: 10–17

BERKSHIRE

NURSERY AND PRE-PREP

BROCKHURST & MARLSTON HOUSE PRE-PREPARATORY SCHOOL

Hermitage, Thatcham, Berkshire RG18 9UL
W: www.brockmarl.org.uk
Age Range: 3–6

PREPARATORY

ALDER BRIDGE SCHOOL

Bridge House, Reading, Berkshire RG7 4JU
W: www.alderbridge.org.uk
Age Range: 3–13

THE ARK SCHOOL

School Road, Reading, Berkshire RG7 4JA
W: www.arkschool.co.uk

BROCKHURST AND MARLSTON HOUSE SCHOOLS

Hermitage, Newbury, Berkshire RG18 9UL
W: www.brockmarl.org.uk
Age Range: 3–13

THE CEDARS SCHOOL

Church Road, Aldermaston, Berkshire RG7 4LR
W: www.thecedarsschool.co.uk
Age Range: 4–11

CHEAM SCHOOL*

Headley, Newbury, Berkshire RG19 8LD
W: www.cheamschool.com
Age Range: 7–13

CHILTERN COLLEGE SCHOOL

16 Peppard Road, Reading, Berkshire RG4 8JZ
W: www.chilterncollegeschool.co.uk/
Age Range: 4–11

CLAIRES COURT SCHOOLS, RIDGEWAY

Maidenhead, Berkshire SL6 3QE
W: www.clairescourt.com
Age Range: 4–11

CROSFIELDS SCHOOL

Shinfield, Reading, Berkshire RG2 9BL
W: www.crosfields.com
Age Range: 4–13

DOLPHIN SCHOOL

Waltham Road, Reading, Berkshire RG10 0FR
W: www.dolphinschool.com
Age Range: 3–13

EAGLE HOUSE*

Crowthorne Road, Sandhurst, Berkshire GU47 8PH
W: www.eaglehouseschool.com
Age Range: 3–13

ELSTREE SCHOOL

Woolhampton, Reading, Berkshire RG7 5TD
W: www.elstreeschool.org.uk
Age Range: 3–13 (Girls 3–7)

ETON END PNEU

35 Eton Road, Slough, Berkshire SL3 9AX
W: www.etonend.org
Age Range: 3–11 (Boys 3–7)

HERRIES SCHOOL

Dean Lane, Maidenhead, Berkshire SL6 9BD
W: www.herries.ws
Age Range: 3–11

HIGHFIELD SCHOOL

2 West Road, Maidenhead,
Berkshire SL6 1PD
W: www.highfield.berks.sch.uk
Age Range: 3–11

THE HIGHLANDS SCHOOL

Wardle Avenue, Reading,
Berkshire RG31 6JR
W: www.highlandsschool.co.uk
Age Range: 2–11

HOLME GRANGE SCHOOL

Heathlands Road, Wokingham,
Berkshire RG40 3AL
W: www.holmegrange.org
Age Range: 3–13

HORRIS HILL SCHOOL

Newbury, Berkshire RG20 9DJ
W: www.horrishill.com
Age Range: 7–13

LAMBROOK SCHOOL*

Winkfield Row, Bracknell,
Berkshire RG42 6LU
W: www.lambrook.berks.sch.uk
Age Range: 3–13

LANGLEY MANOR SCHOOL

St Marys Road, Langley, Berkshire
SL3 6BZ
W: www.langleymanorschool.
co.uk
Age Range: 3–11

LUDGROVE

Wokingham, Berkshire RG40 3AB
W: www.ludgrove.net
Age Range: 8–13

THE MARIST PREPARATORY SCHOOL

Kings Road, Ascot, Berkshire
SL5 7PS
W: www.themaristschools.com
Age Range: 2–11

MEADOWBROOK MONTESSORI SCHOOL

Malt Hill, Bracknell, Berkshire
RG42 6JQ
Age Range: 3–11

NEWBOLD SCHOOL

Popeswood Road, Bracknell,
Berkshire RG42 4AH
W: www.newboldschool.co.uk
Age Range: 3–11

OUR LADY'S PREPARATORY SCHOOL

The Avenue, Crowthorne,
Berkshire RG45 6PB
W: www.ourladysprep.co.uk
Age Range: 1–11

PAPPLEWICK SCHOOL*

Windsor Road, Ascot, Berkshire
SL5 7LH
W: www.papplewick.org.uk
Age Range: 6–13

ST ANDREW'S SCHOOL

Buckhold, Reading, Berkshire
RG8 8QA
W: www.standrewspangbourne.
co.uk
Age Range: 3–13

ST BERNARD'S PREPARATORY SCHOOL

Hawtrey Close, Slough, Berkshire
SL1 1TB
W: www.st-bernards-prep.slough.
sch.uk
Age Range: 3–11

ST EDWARD'S SCHOOL

64 Tilehurst Road, Reading,
Berkshire RG30 2JH
W: www.stedwards.org.uk
Age Range: 4–13

ST GEORGE'S SCHOOL

Windsor Castle, Windsor,
Berkshire SL4 1QF
W: www.stgwindsor.co.uk
Age Range: 3–13

ST JOHN'S BEAUMONT

Priest Hill, Windsor, Berkshire
SL4 2JN
W: www.stjohnsbeaumont.org.uk
Age Range: 4–13

ST PIRAN'S PREPARATORY SCHOOL*

Gringer Hill, Maidenhead,
Berkshire SL6 7LZ
W: www.stpirans.co.uk
Age Range: 3–13

SUNNINGDALE SCHOOL

Dry Arch Road, Sunningdale,
Berkshire SL5 9PY
W: www.sunningdaleschool.co.uk
Age Range: 8–13

THORNGROVE SCHOOL

The Mount, Newbury, Berkshire
RG20 9PS
W: www.thorngroveschool.co.uk
Age Range: 2–13

UPTON HOUSE SCHOOL*

115 St Leonard's Road, Windsor,
Berkshire SL4 3DF
W: www.uptonhouse.org.uk
Age Range: 2–11

WAVERLEY SCHOOL

Waverley Way, Wokingham,
Berkshire RG40 4YD
W: www.waverley.wokingham.
sch.uk
Age Range: 3–11

WHITE HOUSE PREPARATORY SCHOOL

Finchampstead Road,
Wokingham, Berkshire RG40 3HD
W: www.whitehouse.wokingham.
sch.uk
Age Range: 2–11 (Boys 2–4)

WINBURY SCHOOL

Braywick Park, Maidenhead,
Berkshire SL6 1UU
W: www.winburyschool.co.uk
Age Range: 2–8

SENIOR

THE ABBEY SCHOOL*

● 🏠 ★ ▲

17 Kendrick Road, Reading, Berkshire RG1 5DZ
W: www.theabbey.co.uk
Age Range: 3–18

BEARWOOD COLLEGE*

● 🏠 ▲

Bearwood Road, Wokingham, Berkshire RG41 5BG
W: www.bearwoodcollege.co.uk
Age Range: 0–18 (Nursery 0–5 years, Pre-Prep 4–7 years, Prep 7–11 years, Senior (including Sixth Form) 11–18 years.)

BRADFIELD COLLEGE*

● 🏠 ▲

Bradfield, Reading, Berkshire RG7 6AU
W: www.bradfieldcollege.org.uk
Age Range: 13–18

BRIGIDINE SCHOOL WINDSOR

● 🏠 ▲

Queensmead, Windsor, Berkshire SL4 2AX
W: www.brigidine.org.uk
Age Range: 3–18 (Boys 3–7)

CLAIRES COURT SCHOOL

● 🏠

Ray Mill Road East, Maidenhead, Berkshire SL6 8TE
W: www.clairescourt.com
Age Range: 11–16 (Co-ed VIth Form)

CLAIRES COURT SCHOOLS, THE COLLEGE

● 🏠

1 College Avenue, Maidenhead, Berkshire SL6 6AW
W: www.clairescourt.com
Age Range: 3–16 (Boys 3–5, co-ed VIth Form)

DOWNE HOUSE

● 🏠 ▲

Cold Ash, Thatcham, Berkshire RG18 9JJ
W: www.downehouse.net
Age Range: 11–18

ETON COLLEGE

● 🏠 ▲

Windsor, Berkshire SL4 6DW
W: www.etoncollege.com
Age Range: 13–18

HEATHFIELD SCHOOL*

● 🏠 ▲

London Road, Ascot, Berkshire SL5 8BQ
W: www.heathfieldschool.net
Age Range: 11–18

HEMDEAN HOUSE SCHOOL

● 🏠

Hemdean Road, Reading, Berkshire RG4 7SD
W: www.hemdeanhouse.co.uk
Age Range: 3–16

HURST LODGE SCHOOL

● 🏠 ▲

Bagshot Road, Ascot, Berkshire SL5 9JU
W: www.hurstlodge.co.uk
Age Range: 3–18 (Boys and Girls 3–18)

LONG CLOSE SCHOOL

● 🏠

Upton Court Road, Slough, Berkshire SL3 7LU
W: www.longcloseschool.co.uk
Age Range: 2–16

LUCKLEY-OAKFIELD SCHOOL*

● 🏠 ▲

Luckley Road, Wokingham, Berkshire RG40 3EU
W: www.luckley.wokingham.sch.uk
Age Range: 11–18

LVS ASCOT*

● 🏠 ▲

London Road, Ascot, Berkshire SL5 8DR
W: www.lvs.ascot.sch.uk
Age Range: 4–18

THE MARIST SENIOR SCHOOL

● 🏠 ▲

Kings Road, Ascot, Berkshire SL5 7PS
W: www.themaristschools.com
Age Range: 11–18

THE ORATORY SCHOOL

● 🏠 ▲

Reading, Berkshire RG8 0PJ
W: www.oratory.co.uk
Age Range: 11–18

PANGBOURNE COLLEGE

● 🏠 ★ ▲

Pangbourne, Berkshire RG8 8LA
W: www.pangbournecollege.com
Age Range: 11–18

QUEEN ANNE'S SCHOOL

● 🏠 ▲

Henley Road, Berkshire RG4 6DX
W: www.qas.org.uk
Age Range: 11–18

READING BLUE COAT SCHOOL*

● 🏠 ▲

Holme Park, Sonning-on-Thames, Reading, Berkshire RG4 6SU
W: www.rbcs.org.uk
Age Range: 11–18 (Co-ed VIth Form)

READING SCHOOL

● 🏠 ★ ▲

Erleigh Road, Reading, Berkshire RG1 5LW
W: www.readingschool.reading.sch.uk
Age Range: 11–18

REDROOFS THEATRE SCHOOL

● 🏠

26 Bath Road, Maidenhead, Berkshire SL6 34JT
W: www.redroofs.co.uk
Age Range: 9–16

ST GABRIEL'S

● 🏠 ▲

Sandleford Priory, Berkshire RG20 9BD
W: www.stgabriels.co.uk
Age Range: 3–18 (Girls 3–18 Boys 3–7)

ST GEORGE'S SCHOOL

● 🏠 ▲

Ascot, Berkshire SL5 7DZ
W: www.stgeorges-ascot.org.uk
Age Range: 11–18

ST JOSEPH'S COLLEGE

Upper Redlands Road, Reading, Berkshire RG1 5JT
W: www.stjosephscollege.co.uk
Age Range: 3–18

ST MARY'S SCHOOL, ASCOT*

St Mary's Road, Ascot, Berkshire SL5 9JF
W: www.st-marys-ascot.co.uk
Age Range: 11–18

ST MICHAELS SCHOOL

Harts Lane, Newbury, Berkshire RG20 9JW
Age Range: 7–18 (Single-sex ed 13–18)

WELLINGTON COLLEGE*

Duke's Ride, Crowthorne, Berkshire RG45 7PU
W: www.wellingtoncollege.org.uk
Age Range: 13–18

INDEPENDENT SIXTH FORM COLLEGE / TUTORIAL COLLEGE

PADWORTH COLLEGE

Padworth, Reading, Berkshire RG7 4NR
W: www.padworth.com
Age Range: 13–19

INTERNATIONAL SCHOOLS AND INTERNATIONAL STUDY CENTRES

ARDMORE LANGUAGE SCHOOLS

Berkshire College, Maidenhead, Berkshire SL6 6QR
W: http://www.ardmore-language-schools.com/

NEWBURY HALL INTERNATIONAL SCHOOL

Enborne Road, Newbury, Berkshire RG14 6AD
W: www.newburyhall.com
Age Range: 13–17 (We cater for International students only.)

PADWORTH INTERNATIONAL COLLEGE

Padworth, Reading, Berkshire RG7 4NR

BRISTOL

NURSERY AND PRE-PREP

CLIFTON COLLEGE PRE-PREP – BUTCOMBE

Guthrie Road, Bristol BS8 3EZ
W: www.cliftoncollegeuk.com
Age Range: 3–8

PREPARATORY

BRISTOL STEINER SCHOOL

Redland Hill House, Bristol BS6 6UX
W: www.steiner.bristol.sch.uk
Age Range: 3–14

CLEVE HOUSE SCHOOL

254 Wells Road, Bristol BS4 2PN
W: www.clevehouseschool.co.uk
Age Range: 3–11

CLIFTON COLLEGE PREPARATORY SCHOOL

The Avenue, Bristol BS8 3HE
W: www.cliftoncollegeuk.com
Age Range: 8–13

COLSTON'S LOWER SCHOOL

Park Road, Bristol BS16 1BA
Age Range: 3–11

THE DOWNS SCHOOL

Wraxall, Bristol BS48 1PF
W: www.thedownsschool.co.uk
Age Range: 4–13

FAIRFIELD SCHOOL

Fairfield Way, Backwell, Bristol BS48 3PD
W: www.fairfieldschool.org.uk
Age Range: 3–11

GRACEFIELD PREPARATORY SCHOOL

266 Overndale Road, Fishponds, Bristol BS16 2RG
W: www.gracefieldschool.co.uk
Age Range: 4–11

OVERNDALE SCHOOL

Chapel Lane, Old Sodbury, Bristol BS37 6NQ
W: www.overndaleschool.co.uk
Age Range: 1–11

TOCKINGTON MANOR SCHOOL

Tockington, Bristol BS32 4NY
W: tockington.bristol.sch.uk
Age Range: 2–14

TORWOOD HOUSE SCHOOL

27–29 Durdham Park, Redland,
Bristol BS6 6XE
W: www.torwoodhousebristol.
sch.uk

SENIOR

BADMINTON SCHOOL*

Westbury Road, Westbury-on-
Trym, Bristol BS9 3BA
W: www.badminton.bristol.sch.uk
Age Range: 3–18

BRISTOL CATHEDRAL SCHOOL

College Square, Bristol BS1 5TS
W: www.bristolcathedral.bristol.
sch.uk
Age Range: 10–18 (Co-ed VIth
Form)

BRISTOL GRAMMAR SCHOOL*

University Road, Bristol BS8 1SR
W: www.bristolgrammarschool.
co.uk
Age Range: 4–18

CARMEL CHRISTIAN SCHOOL

817A Bath Road, Bristol BS4 5NL
W: www.carmelcentre.org
Age Range: 4–17

CLIFTON COLLEGE*

32 College Road, Clifton, Bristol
BS8 3JH
W: www.cliftoncollegeuk.com
Age Range: 3–18

CLIFTON HIGH SCHOOL

College Road, Bristol BS8 3JD
W: www.cliftonhigh.bristol.sch.uk
Age Range: 3–18

COLSTON'S COLLEGIATE SCHOOL

Stapleton, Bristol BS16 1BJ
W: www.colstons.bristol.sch.uk
Age Range: 3–18

PROSPECT SCHOOL

1 Tramway Road, Bristol BS4 3DS
Age Range: 11–17

QUEEN ELIZABETH'S HOSPITAL

Berkeley Place, Bristol BS8 1JX
W: www.qehbristol.co.uk
Age Range: 7–18 (Sixth Form
International students are
welcome on a Guardianship basis)

THE RED MAIDS' SCHOOL

Westbury-on-Trym, Bristol
BS9 3AW
W: www.redmaids.co.uk
Age Range: 11–18

REDLAND HIGH SCHOOL FOR GIRLS

Redland Court, Bristol BS6 7EF
W: www.redlandhigh.com
Age Range: 3–18

ST URSULA'S HIGH SCHOOL

Brecon Road, Westbury-on-Trym,
Bristol BS9 4DT
W: www.st-ursulas.bristol.sch.uk
Age Range: 3–16

INDEPENDENT SIXTH FORM COLLEGE / TUTORIAL COLLEGE

ST BRENDAN'S VITH FORM COLLEGE

●

Broomhill Road, Bristol BS4 5RQ
W: www.stbrn.ac.uk

BUCKINGHAMSHIRE

NURSERY AND PRE-PREP

KINGSCOTE PRE-PREPARATORY SCHOOL

Oval Way, Gerrards Cross,
Buckinghamshire SL9 8PZ
W: www.kingscoteschool.info
Age Range: 3–7

PREPARATORY

AKELEY WOOD LOWER SCHOOL

Lillingstone Dayrell, Buckingham,
Buckinghamshire MK18 5AN
W: www.akeleywoodschool.co.uk
Age Range: 9–11

ASHFOLD SCHOOL

Aylesbury, Buckinghamshire
HP18 9NG
W: www.ashfoldschool.co.uk
Age Range: 3–13

THE BEACON SCHOOL

Amersham Road, Amersham,
Buckinghamshire HP6 5PF
W: www.beaconschool.co.uk
Age Range: 3–13

BROUGHTON MANOR PREPARATORY SCHOOL

Newport Road, Broughton,
Buckinghamshire MK10 9AA
W: www.bmprep.co.uk

CALDICOTT SCHOOL

Crown Lane, Farnham Royal,
Buckinghamshire SL2 3SL
W: www.caldicott.com
Age Range: 7–13

CHESHAM PREPARATORY SCHOOL

Two Dells Lane, Chesham,
Buckinghamshire HP5 3QF
W: www.cheshamprep.co.uk
Age Range: 3–13

CROWN HOUSE SCHOOL

19 London Road, High Wycombe,
Buckinghamshire HP11 1BJ
W: www.crownhouseschool.co.uk
Age Range: 4–11

DAIR HOUSE SCHOOL TRUST LTD

Bishops Blake, Farnham Royal,
Buckinghamshire SL2 3BY
W: www.dairhouse.co.uk
Age Range: 3–11

DAVENIES SCHOOL

73 Station Road, Beaconsfield,
Buckinghamshire HP9 1AA
W: www.davenies.co.uk
Age Range: 4–13

FILGRAVE SCHOOL

Filgrave, Newport Pagnell,
Buckinghamshire MK16 9ET
W: www.filgraveschool.org.uk
Age Range: 3–9

GATEWAY SCHOOL

1 High Street, Great Missenden,
Buckinghamshire HP16 9AA
Age Range: 2–12

GAYHURST SCHOOL

Bull Lane, Gerrards Cross,
Buckinghamshire SL9 8RJ
W: www.gayhurstschool.eu
Age Range: 3–13

GODSTOWE PREPARATORY SCHOOL

Shrubbery Road, High Wycombe,
Buckinghamshire HP13 6PR
W: www.godstowe.org
Age Range: 3–13 (Boys 3–8)

GROVE INDEPENDENT SCHOOL

Redland Drive, Milton Keynes,
Buckinghamshire MK5 8HD
W: www.groveindependentschool.
co.uk
Age Range: 2–13

HEATHERTON HOUSE SCHOOL

Copperkins Lane, Amersham,
Buckinghamshire HP6 5QB
W: www.heathertonhouse.co.uk
Age Range: 3–11 (Girls can start
in Early Years from the age of 2.5)

HIGH MARCH SCHOOL

23 Ledborough Lane,
Beaconsfield, Buckinghamshire
HP9 2PZ
W: www.highmarch.co.uk
Age Range: 3–11 (Boys are only
admitted into our Upper Nursery
class)

LADYMEDE

Little Kimble, Aylesbury,
Buckinghamshire HP17 0XP
W: www.ladymedeschool.bucks.
sch.uk
Age Range: 3–11

MALTMAN'S GREEN SCHOOL

Maltmans Lane, Gerrards Cross,
Buckinghamshire SL9 8RR
W: www.maltmansgreen.com
Age Range: 3–11

MILTON KEYNES PREPARATORY SCHOOL

Tattenhoe Lane, Milton Keynes,
Buckinghamshire MK3 7EG
W: www.mkps.co.uk

ST TERESA'S CATHOLIC INDEPENDENT & NURSERY SCHOOL

Aylesbury Road, Princes
Risborough, Buckinghamshire
HP27 0JW
W: www.st-teresas.bucks.sch.uk
Age Range: 3–11

SWANBOURNE HOUSE SCHOOL*

Swanbourne, Milton Keynes,
Buckinghamshire MK17 0HZ
W: www.swanbourne.org
Age Range: 3–13

SENIOR

AKELEY WOOD SCHOOL

Akeley Wood, Buckingham,
Buckinghamshire MK18 5AE
W: www.akeleywoodschool.co.uk
Age Range: 3–18

BURY LAWN SCHOOL

Soskin Drive, Milton Keynes,
Buckinghamshire MK14 6DP
W: www.burylawnschool.co.uk
Age Range: 2–18

PIPERS CORNER SCHOOL*

Pipers Lane, Great Kingshill, High
Wycombe, Buckinghamshire
HP15 6LP
W: www.piperscorner.co.uk
Age Range: 3–18

ST MARY'S SCHOOL*

94 Packhorse Road, Gerrards
Cross, Buckinghamshire SL9 8JQ
W: www.stmarysschool.co.uk
Age Range: 3–18

SEFTON PARK SCHOOL

School Lane, Stoke Poges,
Buckinghamshire SL2 4QA
Age Range: 11–18

STOWE SCHOOL

Stowe, Buckingham,
Buckinghamshire MK18 5EH
W: www.stowe.co.uk
Age Range: 13–18

THORNTON COLLEGE CONVENT OF JESUS AND MARY

Thornton, Milton Keynes,
Buckinghamshire MK17 0HJ
W: www.thorntoncollege.com
Age Range: 2–16 (Boys 2–4)

THORPE HOUSE SCHOOL

Oval Way, Gerrards Cross,
Buckinghamshire SL9 8QA
W: www.thorpehouse.co.uk
Age Range: 3–16

WYCOMBE ABBEY SCHOOL

High Wycombe, Buckinghamshire
HP11 1PE
W: www.wycombeabbey.com
Age Range: 11–18

CAMBRIDGESHIRE

NURSERY AND PRE-PREP

MADINGLEY PRE-PREPARATORY SCHOOL

Cambridge Road, Cambridge,
Cambridgeshire CB23 8AH
W: www.madingleyschool.co.uk
Age Range: 3–8

PREPARATORY

ST FAITH'S

Trumpington Road, Cambridge,
Cambridgeshire CB2 8AG
W: www.stfaiths.co.uk
Age Range: 4–13

ST JOHN'S COLLEGE SCHOOL

73 Grange Road, Cambridge,
Cambridgeshire CB3 9AB
W: www.sjcs.co.uk
Age Range: 4–13

ST MARY'S JUNIOR SCHOOL

2 Brookside, Cambridge,
Cambridgeshire CB2 1JE
W: www.stmaryscambridge.co.uk
Age Range: 4–11

WHITEHALL SCHOOL

117 High Street, Huntingdon,
Cambridgeshire PE28 3EH
W: www.whitehallschool.com
Age Range: 3–11

SENIOR

CAMBRIDGE INTERNATIONAL SCHOOL

Cherry Hinton Hall, Cambridge,
Cambridgeshire CB1 8DW
Age Range: 4–16

KIMBOLTON SCHOOL

Kimbolton, Huntingdon,
Cambridgeshire PE28 0EA
W: www.kimbolton.cambs.sch.uk
Age Range: 4–18 (Boarders from 11)

THE KING'S SCHOOL ELY

Ely, Cambridgeshire CB7 4DB
W: www.kingsschoolely.co.uk
Age Range: 2–18

THE LEYS SCHOOL*

Trumpington Road, Cambridge,
Cambridgeshire CB2 7AD
W: www.theleys.net
Age Range: 11–18

THE PERSE SCHOOL

Hills Road, Cambridge,
Cambridgeshire CB2 8QF
W: www.perse.co.uk
Age Range: 11–18

THE PERSE SCHOOL FOR GIRLS

Union Road, Cambridge,
Cambridgeshire CB2 1HF
W: www.perse.cambs.sch.uk
Age Range: 7–18

THE PETERBOROUGH SCHOOL*

Thorpe Road, Peterborough,
Cambridgeshire PE3 6AP
W: www.thepeterboroughschool.
co.uk
Age Range: 4–18

ST MARY'S SCHOOL, CAMBRIDGE*

Bateman Street, Cambridge,
Cambridgeshire CB2 1LY
W: www.stmaryscambridge.co.uk
Age Range: 4–18

SANCTON WOOD SCHOOL

2 St Paul's Road, Cambridge,
Cambridgeshire CB1 2EZ
W: www.sanctonwood.co.uk
Age Range: 1–16

WISBECH GRAMMAR SCHOOL

Wisbech, Cambridgeshire
PE13 1JX
W: www.wgs.cambs.sch.uk
Age Range: 4–18

INDEPENDENT SIXTH FORM COLLEGE / TUTORIAL COLLEGE

BELLERBYS COLLEGE & EMBASSY CES CAMBRIDGE

Queens Campus, Cambridge,
Cambridgeshire CB2 1LU
W: www.bellerbys.com
Age Range: 14–25

CAMBRIDGE CENTRE FOR SIXTH-FORM STUDIES

1 Salisbury Villas, Cambridge,
Cambridgeshire CB1 2JF
W: www.ccss.co.uk
Age Range: 15–21

CATS COLLEGE CAMBRIDGE

13–14 Round Church Street,
Cambridge, Cambridgeshire
CB5 8AD
W: www.catscollege.com/
cambridge
Age Range: 15–21

MPW (MANDER PORTMAN WOODWARD)

3/4 Brookside, Cambridge,
Cambridgeshire CB2 1JE
W: www.mpw.co.uk
Age Range: 15–21

ST ANDREW'S

13 Station Road, Cambridge,
Cambridgeshire CB1 2JB
W: www.standrewscambridge.
co.uk
Age Range: 14–18

INTERNATIONAL SCHOOLS AND INTERNATIONAL STUDY CENTRES

KING'S INTERNATIONAL*

The King's School Ely,
Cambridge, Cambridgeshire
CB7 4DB
W: www.kingsschoolely.co.uk
Age Range: 9–17

CHANNEL ISLANDS

PREPARATORY

FCJ PRIMARY SCHOOL

Deloraine Road, Jersey, Channel
Islands JE2 7XB
W: www.fcj.sch.je
Age Range: 4–11

ORMER HOUSE PREPARATORY SCHOOL

La Vallee, Alderney, Channel
Islands GY9 3XA
W: www.ormerhouse.com
Age Range: 2–13

ST GEORGE'S PREPARATORY SCHOOL

La Hague Manor, Jersey, Channel
Islands JE3 7DB
W: www.stgeorgesprep.co.uk
Age Range: 3–13

ST MICHAEL'S PREPARATORY SCHOOL

La Rue de la Houguette, Jersey,
Channel Islands JE2 7UG
W: www.stmichaelsschool.je
Age Range: 3–13

VICTORIA COLLEGE PREPARATORY SCHOOL

Pleasant Street, Jersey, Channel
Islands
W: www.vcp.sch.je
Age Range: 7–11

SENIOR

BEAULIEU CONVENT SCHOOL

Wellington Road, Jersey, Channel
Islands JE2 4RJ
Age Range: 4–18

ELIZABETH COLLEGE

Guernsey, Channel Islands
GY1 2PY
W: www.elizcoll.org
Age Range: 2–18 (Co-ed Pre-prep
and Prep School. Joint Co-ed
Sixth Form with local girls' school)

THE LADIES' COLLEGE

Les Gravees, Guernsey, Channel
Islands GY1 1RW
W: www.ladiescollege.sch.gg
Age Range: 4–18

VICTORIA COLLEGE

Jersey, Channel Islands JE1 4HT
W: www.victoriacollege.je
Age Range: 11–19

CHESHIRE

PREPARATORY

ABBEY GATE SCHOOL

Clare Avenue, Chester, Cheshire
CH2 3HR
W: www.abbeygateschool.org.uk
Age Range: 3–11

ALTRINCHAM PREPARATORY SCHOOL

Marlborough Road, Altrincham,
Cheshire WA14 2RR
W: www.altprep.co.uk
Age Range: 3–11

BOWDON PREPARATORY SCHOOL FOR GIRLS

48 Stamford Road, Altrincham,
Cheshire WA14 2JP
Age Range: 2–12

BRABYNS SCHOOL

34–36 Arkwright Road, Stockport,
Cheshire SK6 7DB
W: www.brabynsprepschool.
co.uk
Age Range: 2–11

THE FIRS SCHOOL

45 Newton Lane, Chester,
Cheshire CH2 2HJ
W: www.firsschool.net
Age Range: 4–11

FOREST PARK SCHOOL
Lauriston House, Sale, Cheshire
M33 6NB
W: www.forestparkschool.co.uk
Age Range: 3–11

FOREST SCHOOL
Moss Lane, Altrincham, Cheshire
WA15 6LJ
W: www.forestschool.co.uk
Age Range: 2–11

GREENBANK PREPARATORY SCHOOL

Heathbank Road, Cheadle,
Cheshire SK8 6HU
W: www.greenbankschool.co.uk
Age Range: 3–11

HALE PREPARATORY SCHOOL

Broomfield Lane, Altrincham,
Cheshire WA15 9AS
Age Range: 4–11

HULME HALL SCHOOLS (JUNIOR SCHOOL)

75 Hulme Hall Road, Cheadle,
Cheshire SK8 6LA
W: www.hulmehallschool.org
Age Range: 3–11

LADY BARN HOUSE SCHOOL

Langlands, Cheadle, Cheshire
SK8 1JE
W: www.ladybarnhouse.stockport.
sch.uk
Age Range: 3–11

LORETO PREPARATORY SCHOOL

Dunham Road, Altrincham,
Cheshire WA14 4GZ
W: www.loretoprep.co.uk
Age Range: 3–11 (Boys 4–7)

MERTON HOUSE

Abbot's Park, Chester, Cheshire
CH1 4BD
W: mertonhousechester.co.uk
Age Range: 3–11

NORFOLK HOUSE PREPARATORY & KIDS CORNER NURSERY

Norfolk House, Sandbach,
Cheshire CW11 1HF
W: www.norfolkhouse.net

POWNALL HALL SCHOOL

Carrwood Road, Wilmslow,
Cheshire SK9 5DW
W: www.pownallhall.cheshire.
sch.uk
Age Range: 2–11

RAMILLIES HALL SCHOOL

Ramillies Avenue, Cheadle,
Cheshire SK8 7AJ
W: www.ramillieshall.co.uk

THE RYLEYS

Ryleys Lane, Alderley Edge,
Cheshire SK9 7UY
W: www.theryleys.cheshire.sch.uk
Age Range: 3–13

ST AMBROSE PREPARATORY SCHOOL

Hale Barns, Altrincham, Cheshire
WA15 0HE
W: www.st-ambrose-prep.
trafford.sch.uk
Age Range: 3–11

ST CATHERINE'S PREPARATORY SCHOOL

Hollins Lane, Stockport, Cheshire
SK6 5BB
W: www.stcatherinesprep.
stockport.sch.uk
Age Range: 3–11

STELLA MARIS JUNIOR SCHOOL

St John's Road, Stockport,
Cheshire SK4 3BR
W: www.stellamarisschool.co.uk
Age Range: 3–11

TERRA NOVA SCHOOL

Holmes Chapel, Cheshire
CW4 8BT
W: www.terranovaschool.co.uk
Age Range: 3–13

England – Cheshire

WILMSLOW PREPARATORY SCHOOL

Grove Avenue, Wilmslow, Cheshire SK9 5EG
W: www.wilmslowprep.co.uk
Age Range: 2–11

YORSTON LODGE SCHOOL

18 St John's Road, Knutsford, Cheshire WA16 0DP
W: www.yorstonlodge.com
Age Range: 3–11

SENIOR

ABBEY GATE COLLEGE

Saighton Grange, Chester, Cheshire CH3 6EN
W: www.abbeygatecollege.org
Age Range: 4–18

ALDERLEY EDGE SCHOOL FOR GIRLS

Wilmslow Road, Alderley Edge, Cheshire SK9 7QE
Age Range: 3–18

BEECH HALL SCHOOL

Beech Hall Drive, Macclesfield, Cheshire SK10 2EG
W: www.beechallschool.org
Age Range: 4–16 (Kindergarten 1–5)

CHEADLE HULME SCHOOL

Claremont Road, Cheadle, Cheshire SK8 6EF
W: www.cheadlehulmeschool.co.uk
Age Range: 4–18

CRANSLEY SCHOOL

Belmont Hall, Northwich, Cheshire CW9 6HN
W: www.cransleyschool.co.uk
Age Range: 3–16 (Boys 3–11)

CULCHETH HALL

Ashley Road, Altrincham, Cheshire WA14 2LT
W: www.culcheth-hall.org.uk
Age Range: 3–16 (Boys 2–4)

THE GRANGE SCHOOL

Bradburns Lane, Northwich, Cheshire CW8 1LU
W: www.grange.org.uk
Age Range: 4–18

HAMMOND SCHOOL

Hoole Bank House, Chester, Cheshire CH2 4ES
W: www.thehammondschool.co.uk
Age Range: 11–18

HILLCREST GRAMMAR SCHOOL

Beech Avenue, Stockport, Cheshire SK3 8HB
W: www.hillcrest.stockport.sch.uk
Age Range: 3–16

HULME HALL SCHOOLS

75 Hulme Hall Road, Cheadle, Cheshire SK8 6LA
W: www.hulmehallschool.org
Age Range: 2–16

THE KING'S SCHOOL

Wrexham Road, Chester, Cheshire CH4 7QL
W: www.kingschester.co.uk
Age Range: 7–18

THE KING'S SCHOOL

Macclesfield, Cheshire SK10 1DA
W: www.kingsmac.co.uk
Age Range: 3–18 (Single-sex ed 11–16)

NORTH CESTRIAN GRAMMAR SCHOOL

Dunham Road, Altrincham, Cheshire WA14 4AJ
W: www.ncgs.co.uk
Age Range: 11–18

THE QUEEN'S SCHOOL

City Walls Road, Chester, Cheshire CH1 2NN
W: www.queens.cheshire.sch.uk
Age Range: 4–18

STOCKPORT GRAMMAR SCHOOL

Buxton Road, Stockport, Cheshire SK2 7AF
W: www.stockportgrammar.co.uk
Age Range: 3–18

TRINITY SCHOOL

Birbeck Street, Stalybridge, Cheshire SK15 1SH
W: www.trinityschool.org.uk
Age Range: 4–18

CORNWALL

PREPARATORY

POLWHELE HOUSE SCHOOL

Newquay Road, Truro, Cornwall
TR4 9AE
W: www.polwhelehouse.co.uk
Age Range: 3–13

ROSELYON

St Blazey Road, Par, Cornwall
PL24 2HZ
W: www.roselyon.cornwall.sch.uk
Age Range: 2–11

ST IA SCHOOL
St Ives Road, St Ives, Cornwall
TR26 2SF
W: www.st-ia.cornwall.sch.uk
Age Range: 4–11

ST PETROC'S SCHOOL
Ocean View Road, Bude, Cornwall
EX23 8NJ
W: www.stpetrocs.com
Age Range: 3–11 (Nursery from 3
mths)

TRURO SCHOOL PREPARATORY SCHOOL

Highertown, Truro, Cornwall
TR1 3QN
W: www.truroprep.com
Age Range: 3–11

SENIOR

GEMS BOLITHO SCHOOL
Polwithen Road, Penzance,
Cornwall TR18 4JR
W: www.bolithoschool.co.uk
Age Range: 4–18

HIGHFIELDS PRIVATE SCHOOL
Lower Cardrew Lane, Redruth,
Cornwall TR15 1SY
W: highfields-school.com
Age Range: 4–16

ST JOSEPH'S SCHOOL

St Stephen's Hill, Launceston,
Cornwall PL15 8HN
W: www.st-josephs.cornwall.
sch.uk
Age Range: 3–16 (Boys 3–11)

ST PIRAN'S SCHOOL

14 Trelissick Road, Hayle,
Cornwall TR27 4HY
W: www.stpirans.net
Age Range: 3–16

TRURO HIGH SCHOOL

Falmouth Road, Truro, Cornwall
TR1 2HU
W: www.trurohigh.co.uk
Age Range: 3–18 (Boys 3–5)

TRURO SCHOOL
Trennick Lane, Truro, Cornwall
TR1 1TH
W: www.truroschool.com
Age Range: 11–18

CUMBRIA

PREPARATORY

HOLME PARK SCHOOL

Hill Top, Kendal, Cumbria LA8 0AE
W: www.holme-park-school.com
Age Range: 2–12

HUNTER HALL SCHOOL

Frenchfield, Penrith, Cumbria
CA11 8UA
Age Range: 3–11

ST URSULAS CONVENT SCHOOL
Burnfoot, Wigton, Cumbria
CA7 9HL
W: www.stursulas.co.uk
Age Range: 2–11

SEDBERGH JUNIOR SCHOOL
Danson House, Sedbergh,
Cumbria LA10 5HG
W: www.sedberghjuniorschool.
org
Age Range: 4–13

SENIOR

AUSTIN FRIARS ST MONICA'S SCHOOL

Etterby Scaur, Carlisle, Cumbria
CA3 9PB
W: www.austinfriars.cumbria.
sch.uk
Age Range: 3–18

CASTERTON SCHOOL

Kirkby Lonsdale, Cumbria
LA6 2SG
W: www.castertonschool.co.uk
Age Range: 3–18 (Day boys 3–11)

CHETWYNDE SCHOOL

Croslands, Barrow-in-Furness, Cumbria LA13 0NY
W: www.chetwynde.cumbria.
sch.uk
Age Range: 3–18

DALLAM SCHOOL

Milnthorpe, Cumbria LA7 7DD
W: www.dallam.eu
Age Range: 11–18

KESWICK SCHOOL

Vicarage Hill, Keswick, Cumbria
CA12 5QE
W: www.keswick.cumbria.sch.uk
Age Range: 11–18

LIME HOUSE SCHOOL

Holm Hill, Carlisle, Cumbria
CA5 7BX
W: www.limehouseschool.co.uk
Age Range: 4–18

ST BEES SCHOOL

St Bees, Cumbria CA27 0DS
W: www.st-bees-school.org
Age Range: 4–18

SEDBERGH SCHOOL

Sedbergh, Cumbria LA10 5HG
W: www.sedberghschool.org
Age Range: 14–18

WINDERMERE SCHOOL

Windermere, Cumbria LA23 1NW
W: www.windermereschool.co.uk
Age Range: 2–18

DERBYSHIRE

PREPARATORY

BARLBOROUGH HALL SCHOOL*

Barlborough, Chesterfield,
Derbyshire S43 4TJ
W: www.barlboroughhallschool.
co.uk
Age Range: 3–11

EMMANUEL SCHOOL

Juniper Lodge, Derby, Derbyshire
DE22 1FP
Age Range: 3–14

FOREMARKE HALL

Derby, Derbyshire DE65 6EJ
W: www.foremarke.org.uk
Age Range: 3–13

GATEWAY CHRISTIAN SCHOOL

Moor Lane, Ilkeston, Derbyshire
DE7 4PP
W: www.gatewayschool.org.uk
Age Range: 3–11

MORLEY HALL PREPARATORY SCHOOL

Hill House, Derby, Derbyshire
DE21 4QZ
W: www.morleyhallschool.co.uk
Age Range: 3–11

THE OLD VICARAGE SCHOOL

11 Church Lane, Derby,
Derbyshire DE22 1EW
W: www.oldvicarageschool.co.uk
Age Range: 3–11

S. ANSELM'S SCHOOL

Bakewell, Derbyshire DE45 1DP
W: www.sanselms.co.uk
Age Range: 3–13

ST JOSEPH'S CONVENT

42 Newbold Road, Chesterfield,
Derbyshire S41 7PL
W: www.st-josephs-convent-sch.
org.uk
Age Range: 2–11

ST PETER & ST PAUL SCHOOL

Brambling House, Chesterfield,
Derbyshire S41 0EF
W: www.spsp.org.uk
Age Range: 4–11

ST WYSTAN'S SCHOOL

High Street, Repton, Derbyshire
DE65 6GE
W: www.stwystans.org.uk
Age Range: 2–11

SENIOR

DERBY GRAMMAR SCHOOL

Rykneld Road, Derby, Derbyshire
DE23 4BX
W: www.derbygrammar.co.uk
Age Range: 7–18

DERBY HIGH SCHOOL

Hillsway, Derby, Derbyshire
DE23 3DT
W: www.derbyhigh.derby.sch.uk
Age Range: 3–18

MICHAEL HOUSE STEINER SCHOOL

The Field, Heanor, Derbyshire
DE75 7JH
W: www.michaelhouseschool.
co.uk; www.steinerwaldorf.org.uk
Age Range: 4–16

MOUNT ST MARY'S COLLEGE*

Spinkhill, Derbyshire S21 3YL
W: www.msmcollege.com
Age Range: 11–18 (Boarders are accepted into Barlborough Hall at age 10.)

OCKBROOK SCHOOL

The Settlement, Derby, Derbyshire DE72 3RJ
W: www.ockbrook.derby.sch.uk
Age Range: 3–18

REPTON SCHOOL

Repton, Derby, Derbyshire DE65 6FH
W: www.repton.org.uk
Age Range: 13–18

DEVON

PREPARATORY

THE ABBEY SCHOOL

Hampton Court, Torquay, Devon TQ1 4PR
W: www.abbeyschool.co.uk

ABBOTSBURY SCHOOL

Newton Abbot, Devon TQ12 2JD
Age Range: 2–7

BENDARROCH SCHOOL

Exeter, Devon EX5 2BY
W: www.bendarroch.co.uk
Age Range: 5–13

BLUNDELL'S PREPARATORY SCHOOL

Milestones House, Tiverton, Devon EX16 4NA
W: www.blundells.org
Age Range: 3–11

THE DOLPHIN SCHOOL

Raddenstile Lane, Exmouth, Devon EX8 2JH
W: www.dolphin-school.org.uk
Age Range: 3–11

EXETER CATHEDRAL SCHOOL

The Chantry, Exeter, Devon EX1 1HX
W: www.exetercs.org
Age Range: 3–13

EXETER JUNIOR SCHOOL

Victoria Park Road, Exeter, Devon EX2 4NS
W: www.exeterschool.org.uk
Age Range: 7–11

FLETEWOOD SCHOOL

88 North Road East, Plymouth, Devon PL4 6AN
W: www.fletewoodschool.co.uk
Age Range: 3–11

KELLY COLLEGE PREPARATORY SCHOOL

Hazeldon House, Tavistock, Devon PL19 0JS
W: www.kellycollegeprep.com
Age Range: 2–11

KING'S SCHOOL

Hartley Road, Plymouth, Devon PL3 5LW
W: www.kingsschool-plymouth.co.uk
Age Range: 3–11

MARIA MONTESSORI SCHOOL

3 St Leonards Place, Exeter, Devon EX2 4LZ
W: www.exeter-montessori.com
Age Range: 3–7

MOUNT HOUSE SCHOOL

Tavistock, Devon PL19 9JL
W: www.mounthouse.devon.sch.uk
Age Range: 3–13

NEW SCHOOL

The Avenue, Exeter, Devon EX6 8AT
W: www.thenewschool.supanet.com
Age Range: 3–8

PARK SCHOOL

Park Road, Totnes, Devon TQ9 6EQ
W: www.park-school.org.uk
Age Range: 3–11

PLYMOUTH COLLEGE PREPRATORY SCHOOL

St Dunstan's Abbey, Plymouth, Devon PL1 3JL
W: www.plymouthcollege.com
Age Range: 3–11 (We have only just begun to offer boarding to Years 5 & 6. We do not have a Prep Boarding House but pupils reside in the Boarding House at our Senior School site).

ST CHRISTOPHERS SCHOOL

Mount Barton, Totnes, Devon TQ9 6PF
W: www.st-christophers.devon.sch.uk
Age Range: 3–11

ST MICHAEL'S

Tawstock Court, Barnstaple, Devon EX31 3HY

ST PETER'S SCHOOL

Exmouth, Devon EX8 5AU
W: www.stpetersprep.co.uk
Age Range: 3–13

WEST BUCKLAND PREPARATORY SCHOOL

Barnstaple, Devon EX32 0SX
W: www.westbuckland.devon.
sch.uk
Age Range: 3–11

SENIOR

BLUNDELL'S SCHOOL*

Tiverton, Devon EX16 4DN
W: www.blundells.org
Age Range: 11–18

BRAMDEAN SCHOOL

Richmond Lodge, Exeter, Devon EX1 2QR
W: www.bramdeanschool.co.uk
Age Range: 3–18

EDGEHILL COLLEGE

Northdown Road, Bideford, Devon EX39 3LY
W: www.edgehill.devon.sch.uk
Age Range: 2–18

EXETER SCHOOL

Victoria Park Road, Exeter, Devon EX2 4NS
W: www.exeterschool.org.uk
Age Range: 7–18

KELLY COLLEGE

Parkwood Road, Tavistock, Devon PL19 0HZ
W: www.kellycollege.com
Age Range: 11–18

KINGSLEY SCHOOL

Kingsley School, Bideford, Devon EX39 3LY
W: www.kingsleyschoolbideford.
co.uk
Age Range: 11–18

MAGDALEN COURT SCHOOL

Mulberry House, Exeter, Devon EX2 4NU
W: www.magdalencourtschool.
co.uk
Age Range: 2–18

THE MAYNARD SCHOOL

Denmark Road, Exeter, Devon EX1 1SJ
W: www.maynard.co.uk
Age Range: 7–18 (A selective independent day school for girls aged 7–17.)

PLYMOUTH COLLEGE

Ford Park, Plymouth, Devon PL4 6RN
W: www.plymouthcollege.com
Age Range: 11–18

ST MARGARET'S SCHOOL

147 Magdalen Road, Exeter, Devon EX2 4TS
W: www.stmargarets-school.co.uk
Age Range: 7–18

ST WILFRID'S SCHOOL

29 St David's Hill, Exeter, Devon EX4 4DA
W: www.stwilfrids.devon.sch.uk
Age Range: 5–16

SANDS SCHOOL

Greylands, Ashburton, Devon TQ13 7AX
W: www.sands-school.co.uk
Age Range: 11–17

SHEBBEAR COLLEGE

Beaworthy, Devon EX21 5HJ
W: www.shebbearcollege.co.uk
Age Range: 5–18

THE SMALL SCHOOL

Fore Street, Bideford, Devon EX39 6AB
W: www.thesmallschool.org.uk
Age Range: 11–16

SOUTH DEVON STEINER SCHOOL

Hood Manor, Dartington, Devon TQ9 6AB
W: steiner-south-devon.org
Age Range: 3–16

STOODLEY KNOWLE SCHOOL

Ansteys Cove Road, Torquay, Devon TQ1 2JB
W: www.stoodleyknowle.devon.
sch.uk
Age Range: 2–18

STOVER SCHOOL

Stover, Newton Abbot, Devon TQ12 6QG
W: www.stover.co.uk
Age Range: 3–18

TOWER HOUSE SCHOOL

Fisher Street, Paignton, Devon TQ4 5EW
Age Range: 2–16

TRINITY SCHOOL

Buckeridge Road, Teignmouth, Devon TQ14 8LY
W: www.trinityschool.co.uk
Age Range: 4–20

WEST BUCKLAND SCHOOL

Barnstaple, Devon EX32 0SX
W: www.westbuckland.devon.
sch.uk
Age Range: 3–18

INDEPENDENT SIXTH FORM COLLEGE / TUTORIAL COLLEGE

EXETER TUTORIAL COLLEGE

●🏠

44/46 Magdalen Road, Exeter, Devon EX2 4TE
W: www.tutorialcollege.com

INTERNATIONAL SCHOOLS AND INTERNATIONAL STUDY CENTRES

SIDMOUTH INTERNATIONAL SCHOOL

●

May Cottage, Sidmouth, Devon EX10 8EN

DORSET

PREPARATORY

BOURNEMOUTH COLLEGIATE PREP SCHOOL

●🏠

40 St Osmund's Road, Poole, Dorset BH14 9JY
W: www.
bournemouthcollegiateschool.co.uk
Age Range: 3–11

BUCKHOLME TOWERS

●🏠

18 Commercial Road, Poole, Dorset BH14 0JW
W: www.buckholmetowers.com
Age Range: 3–12

CASTLE COURT PREPARATORY SCHOOL

●🏠

The Knoll House, Wimborne, Dorset BH21 3RF
W: www.castlecourt.com
Age Range: 3–13

CLAYESMORE PREPARATORY SCHOOL

●🏠◆

Iwerne Minster, Blandford Forum, Dorset DT11 8PH
W: www.clayesmore.com
Age Range: 3–13 (The age of entry into the Pre-Prep of the school is 'rising 3'.)

DUMPTON SCHOOL

●🏠

Deans Grove House, Wimborne, Dorset BH21 7AF
W: www.dumpton.com
Age Range: 2–13

KNIGHTON HOUSE

●🏠

Durweston, Blandford Forum, Dorset DT11 0PY
W: www.knightonhouse.dorset.sch.uk
Age Range: (Day boys 4–7)

THE PARK SCHOOL

●🏠

Queen's Park South Drive, Bournemouth, Dorset BH8 9BJ
Age Range: 4–11

PORT REGIS PREPARATORY SCHOOL

●🏠

Motcombe Park, Shaftesbury, Dorset SP7 9QA
W: www.portregis.com
Age Range: 3–13

ST MARTIN'S SCHOOL

●🏠

15 Stokewood Road, Bournemouth, Dorset BH3 7NA
W: www.stmartinsschool.co.uk
Age Range: 4–12

ST THOMAS GARNET'S SCHOOL

●🏠

Parkwood Road, Bournemouth, Dorset BH5 2BH
W: www.stg.web-page.net

SUNNINGHILL PREPARATORY SCHOOL

●🏠

South Court, Dorchester, Dorset DT1 1EB
W: www.sunninghillprep.co.uk
Age Range: 3–13

TALBOT HOUSE PREPARATORY SCHOOL

●🏠

8 Firs Glen Road, Bournemouth, Dorset BH9 2LR
Age Range: 3–12

THORNLOW PREPARATORY SCHOOL

●🏠

Weymouth, Dorset DT4 0SA
W: www.thornlow.co.uk
Age Range: 3–13

YARRELLS SCHOOL

●🏠

Yarrells House, Poole, Dorset BH16 5EU
W: www.yarrells.co.uk
Age Range: 2–13

SENIOR

BOURNEMOUTH COLLEGIATE SCHOOL

●🏠▲

College Road, Bournemouth, Dorset BH5 2DY
W: www.
bournemouthcollegiateschool.co.uk
Age Range: 11–18

BRYANSTON SCHOOL*

Blandford Forum, Dorset DT11 0PX
W: www.bryanston.co.uk
Age Range: 13–18

CANFORD SCHOOL

Wimborne, Dorset BH21 3AD
W: www.canford.com
Age Range: 13–18

CLAYESMORE

Iwerne Minster, Blandford Forum, Dorset DT11 8LL
W: www.clayesmore.com
Age Range: 3–18 (Boys and girls in the Pre-Prep join the school as 'rising' 3 year olds.)

LEWESTON SCHOOL

Sherborne, Dorset DT9 6EN
W: www.leweston.co.uk
Age Range: 2–18 (Boys 2–11)

MILTON ABBEY SCHOOL*
Blandford Forum, Dorset DT11 0BZ
W: www.miltonabbey.co.uk
Age Range: 13–18[†]

ST MARY'S SCHOOL, DORSET

Shaftesbury, Dorset SP7 9LP
W: www.st-marys-shaftesbury.co.uk
Age Range: 9–18

SHERBORNE GIRLS

Bradford Road, Sherborne, Dorset DT9 3QN
W: www.sherborne.com
Age Range: 11–18

SHERBORNE SCHOOL

Abbey Road, Sherborne, Dorset DT9 3AP
W: www.sherborne.org
Age Range: 13–18

TALBOT HEATH

Rothesay Road, Bournemouth, Dorset BH4 9NJ
W: www.talbotheath.org.uk
Age Range: 3–18 (Boys 3–7)

INDEPENDENT SIXTH FORM COLLEGE / TUTORIAL COLLEGE

INTERNATIONAL COLLEGE, SHERBORNE SCHOOL*

Newell Grange, Sherborne, Dorset DT9 4EZ
W: www.sherborne-ic.net
Age Range: 11–17

COUNTY DURHAM

PREPARATORY

THE CHORISTER SCHOOL

The College, Durham, County Durham DH1 3EL
W: www.choristers.durham.sch.uk
Age Range: 4–13

HURWORTH HOUSE SCHOOL

The Green, Darlington, County Durham DL2 2AD
W: www.hurworthhouse.co.uk
Age Range: 3–18

YARM AT RAVENTHORPE SCHOOL

96 Carmel Road North, Darlington, County Durham DL3 8JB
W: www.yarmschool.org
Age Range: 3–11

SENIOR

BARNARD CASTLE SCHOOL
Barnard Castle, County Durham DL12 8UN
W: www.barnardcastleschool.org.uk
Age Range: 4–18

DURHAM HIGH SCHOOL FOR GIRLS
Farewell Hall, Durham, County Durham DH1 3TB
W: www.dhsfg.org.uk
Age Range: 3–18

DURHAM SCHOOL
Quarryheads Lane, Durham, County Durham DH1 4SZ
W: www.durhamschool.co.uk/prospectus.htm
Age Range: 3–18

POLAM HALL
Grange Road, Darlington, County Durham DL1 5PA
W: www.polamhall.com
Age Range: 2–18 (Co-educational Junior School from age 2 to Year 4. Separate teaching Year 5 to Year 11. Co-educational Sixth Form)

ESSEX

PREPARATORY

ALLEYN COURT PREPARATORY SCHOOL

Wakering Road, Southend-on-Sea, Essex SS3 0PW
W: www.alleyn-court.co.uk
Age Range: 2–11

AVON HOUSE

490 High Road, Woodford Green, Essex IG8 0PN
W: www.avonhouse.org.uk
Age Range: 3–11

BEEHIVE PREPARATORY SCHOOL

233 Beehive Lane, Ilford, Essex IG4 5ED
Age Range: 4–11

COLLEGE SAINT-PIERRE

16 Leigh Road, Leigh-on-Sea, Essex SS9 1LE
W: www.saintpierreschool.com
Age Range: 2–11

COOPERSALE HALL SCHOOL

Flux's Lane, Epping, Essex CM16 7PE
W: www.coopersalehallschool.co.uk
Age Range: 3–11

CROWSTONE PREPARATORY SCHOOL

121–123 Crowstone Road, Westcliff-on-Sea, Essex SS0 8LH
W: crowstoneprepschool.com
Age Range: 2–11

THE DAIGLEN SCHOOL

68 Palmerston Road, Buckhurst Hill, Essex IG9 5LG
W: www.daiglenschool.co.uk
Age Range: 3–11

DAME BRADBURY'S SCHOOL

Ashdon Road, Saffron Walden, Essex CB10 2AL
W: www.damebradburys.com
Age Range: 3–11

EASTCOURT INDEPENDENT SCHOOL

1 Eastwood Road, Ilford, Essex IG3 8UW
Age Range: 4–11

ELM GREEN PREPARATORY SCHOOL

Parsonage Lane, Chelmsford, Essex CM3 4SU
W: www.elmgreen.essex.sch.uk
Age Range: 4–11

GIDEA PARK COLLEGE

Balgores House, Romford, Essex RM2 5JR
W: www.gideaparkcollege.co.uk
Age Range: 2–11

GLENARM COLLEGE

20 Coventry Road, Ilford, Essex IG1 4QR
W: www.glenarmcollege.com
Age Range: 3–11

GOODRINGTON SCHOOL

17 Walden Road, Hornchurch, Essex RM11 2JT
W: www.goodrington.org
Age Range: 3–11

HEATHCOTE SCHOOL

Eves Corner, Chelmsford, Essex CM3 4QB
W: www.heathcoteschool.co.uk
Age Range: 2–11

HERINGTON HOUSE SCHOOL

Mount Avenue, Brentwood, Essex CM13 2NS
W: www.heringtonhouseschool.co.uk
Age Range: 3–11

HOLMWOOD HOUSE

Chitts Hill, Colchester, Essex CO3 9ST
W: www.holmwood.essex.sch.uk
Age Range: 4–13

ILFORD PREPARATORY SCHOOL

Carnegie Buildings, Ilford, Essex IG3 8RW
W: www.ilfordprep.co.uk
Age Range: 3–11

ILFORD URSULINE PREPARATORY SCHOOL

2–4 Coventry Road, Ilford, Essex IG1 4QR
W: www.ilfordursuline-prep.org.uk
Age Range: 3–11

LITTLEGARTH SCHOOL

Horkesley Park, Colchester, Essex CO6 4JR
W: www.littlegarth.essex.sch.uk
Age Range: 2–11

LOYOLA PREPARATORY SCHOOL

103 Palmerston Road, Buckhurst Hill, Essex IG9 5NH
W: www.loyola.essex.sch.uk
Age Range: 3–11

MALDON COURT PREPARATORY SCHOOL

Silver Street, Maldon, Essex CM9 4QE
W: www.maldoncourtschool.org
Age Range: 3–11

OAKFIELDS MONTESSORI SCHOOLS LTD

Harwood Hall, Upminster, Essex RM14 2YG
W: www.oakfieldsmontessorischool.org.uk
Age Range: 2–11

OAKLANDS SCHOOL

8 Albion Hill, Loughton, Essex IG10 4RA
W: www.oaklandsschool.co.uk
Age Range: 2–11

OXFORD HOUSE SCHOOL

2 Lexden Road, Colchester, Essex CO3 3NE
W: www.oxfordhouseschool.net
Age Range: 2–11

ST ANNE'S PREPARATORY SCHOOL

154 New London Road, Chelmsford, Essex CM2 0AW
W: www.stannesprep.essex.sch.uk
Age Range: 3–11

ST AUBYN'S SCHOOL

Bunces Lane, Woodford Green, Essex IG8 9DU
W: www.staubyns.com
Age Range: 3–13

ST CEDD'S SCHOOL

Maltese Road, Chelmsford, Essex CM1 2PB
W: www.stcedds.org.uk
Age Range: 4–11

ST MARGARET'S SCHOOL

Gosfield Hall Park, Halstead, Essex CO9 1SE
Age Range: 2–11

ST MARY'S HARE PARK SCHOOL

South Drive, Romford, Essex RM2 6HH
W: www.smhp.ik.org
Age Range: 2–11

ST MICHAEL'S SCHOOL

198 Hadleigh Road, Leigh-on-Sea, Essex SS9 2LP
W: www.stmichaelsschool.com
Age Range: 3–11

ST PHILIP'S PRIORY SCHOOL

178 New London Road, Chelmsford, Essex CM2 0AR
Age Range: 4–11

ST PHILOMENA'S PREPARATORY SCHOOL

Hadleigh Road, Frinton-on-Sea, Essex CO13 9HQ
W: www.stphilomenas.com
Age Range: 3–11

URSULINE PREPARATORY SCHOOL

Old Great Ropers, Brentwood, Essex CM13 3HR
W: www.ursulineprepwarley.co.uk
Age Range: 3–11

WIDFORD LODGE

Widford Road, Chelmsford, Essex CM2 9AN
W: www.widfordlodge.co.uk
Age Range: 2–11

WOODFORD GREEN PREPARATORY SCHOOL

Glengall Road, Woodford Green, Essex IG8 0BZ
W: www.woodfordgreenprep.co.uk
Age Range: 3–11

WOODLANDS SCHOOLS

Warley Street, Brentwood, Essex CM13 3LA
W: www.woodlandsschools.co.uk
Age Range: 3–11

SENIOR

BANCROFT'S SCHOOL

Woodford Green, Essex IG8 0RF
W: www.bancrofts.org
Age Range: 7–18

BRAESIDE SCHOOL FOR GIRLS

130 High Road, Buckhurst Hill, Essex IG9 5SD
W: www.braesideschool.co.uk
Age Range: 3–16 (Independent day school for girls aged 3 to 16 years)

BRENTWOOD SCHOOL

Ingrave Road, Brentwood, Essex CM15 8AS
W: www.brentwoodschool.co.uk
Age Range: 3–18 (Single-sex Education aged 11–16)

CHIGWELL SCHOOL

High Road, Chigwell, Essex IG7 6QF
W: www.chigwell-school.org
Age Range: 7–18

COLCHESTER HIGH SCHOOL

Wellesley Road, Colchester, Essex CO3 3HD
W: www.colchesterhighschool.co.uk
Age Range: 3–16

CRANBROOK

34 Mansfield Road, Ilford, Essex IG1 3BD
W: www.cranbrook-school.co.uk
Age Range: 3–16

FELSTED SCHOOL

Felsted, Essex CM6 3LL
W: www.felsted.org
Age Range: 13–18 (Felsted Prep School accepts day and boarding boys and girls from ages 4–12. Pupils are able to board from age 8.)

FRIENDS' SCHOOL

Mount Pleasant Road, Saffron Walden, Essex CB11 3EB
W: www.friends.org.uk
Age Range: 3–18

GOSFIELD SCHOOL*

Halstead Road, Gosfield,
Halstead, Essex CO9 1PF
W: www.gosfieldschool.org.uk
Age Range: 4–18

IMMANUEL SCHOOL

Havering Grange Centre,
Romford, Essex RM1 4HR
W: www.immanuelministries.
org.uk
Age Range: 3–16

NEW HALL SCHOOL

The Avenue, Chelmsford, Essex
CM3 3HS
W: www.newhallschool.co.uk
Age Range: 3–18 (Co-ed
Preparatory School (3–11)
Boys' Division (11–16)
Girls' Division (11–16)
Co-ed Sixth Form)

PARK SCHOOL FOR GIRLS

20–22 Park Avenue, Ilford, Essex
IG1 4RS
W: www.parkschool.org.uk
Age Range: 3–16

RAPHAEL INDEPENDENT SCHOOL

Park Lane, Hornchurch, Essex
RM11 1XY
W: www.raphaelschool.com
Age Range: 4–16

ST HILDA'S SCHOOL

15 Imperial Avenue, Westcliff-on-
Sea, Essex SS0 8NE
W: www.sthildasschool.co.uk
Age Range: 2–16 (Boys 2–7)

ST JOHN'S SCHOOL

Stock Road, Billericay, Essex
CM12 0AR
W: www.stjohnsschool.net
Age Range: 3–16

ST MARY'S SCHOOL

91 Lexden Road, Colchester,
Essex CO3 3RB
W: www.stmarysschool.org.uk
Age Range: 4–16

ST NICHOLAS SCHOOL

Hillingdon House, Harlow, Essex
CM17 0NJ
W: www.saintnicholasschool.net
Age Range: 4–16

THORPE HALL SCHOOL

Wakering Road, Southend-on-
Sea, Essex SS1 3RD
W: www.thorpehall.southend.
sch.uk
Age Range: 2–16

GLOUCESTERSHIRE

PREPARATORY

AIRTHRIE SCHOOL

27–29 Christchurch Road,
Cheltenham, Gloucestershire
GL50 2NY
W: www.airthrie-school.co.uk
Age Range: 3–11

BEAUDESERT PARK SCHOOL

Stroud, Gloucestershire GL6 9AF
W: www.beaudesert.gloucs.
sch.uk
Age Range: 4–13

BERKHAMPSTEAD SCHOOL

Pittville Circus Road, Cheltenham,
Gloucestershire GL52 2QA
W: www.berkhampsteadschool.
co.uk
Age Range: 3–11

CHELTENHAM COLLEGE JUNIOR SCHOOL

Thirlestaine Road, Cheltenham,
Gloucestershire GL53 7AB
W: www.cheltcoll.gloucs.sch.uk
Age Range: 3–13

DEAN CLOSE PREPARATORY SCHOOL

Lansdown Road, Cheltenham,
Gloucestershire GL51 6QS
W: www.deanclose.org.uk
Age Range: 3–13

THE DORMER HOUSE PNEU SCHOOL

High Street, Moreton-in-Marsh,
Gloucestershire GL56 0AD
W: www.dormerhouse.co.uk
Age Range: 2–11

HATHEROP CASTLE SCHOOL

Hatherop, Cirencester,
Gloucestershire GL7 3NB
W: www.hatheropcastle.co.uk
Age Range: 2–13

HOPELANDS SCHOOL

38 Regent Street, Stonehouse,
Gloucestershire GL10 2AD
W: www.hopelands.org.uk
Age Range: 3–11

THE RICHARD PATE SCHOOL

Southern Road, Cheltenham,
Gloucestershire GL53 9RP
W: www.richardpate.co.uk
Age Range: 3–11

ROSE HILL SCHOOL

Alderley, Wotton-under-Edge,
Gloucestershire GL12 7QT
W: www.rosehillschool.com
Age Range: 3–13

ROSE HILL WESTONBIRT SCHOOL

Tetbury, Gloucestershire GL8 8QG
W: www.querns.gloucs.sch.uk
Age Range: 3–13

ST ANTHONYS SCHOOL

93 Bellevue Road, Cinderford,
Gloucestershire GL14 2AA
W: www.stanthonysconvent.
gloucs.sch.uk
Age Range: 3–11

WYCLIFFE PREPARATORY SCHOOL

Ryeford Hall, Stonehouse,
Gloucestershire GL10 2LD
W: www.wycliffe.co.uk
Age Range: 2–13

SENIOR

THE ACORN SCHOOL

Church Street, Nailsworth,
Gloucestershire GL6 0BP
W: www.theacornschool.com
Age Range: 6–19

BREDON SCHOOL*

Pull Court, Bushley, Tewkesbury,
Gloucestershire GL20 6AH
W: www.bredonschool.org
Age Range: 5–18[†]

CHELTENHAM COLLEGE

Bath Road, Cheltenham,
Gloucestershire GL53 7LD
W: www.cheltenhamcollege.org
Age Range: 13–18

CHELTENHAM LADIES' COLLEGE

Bayshill Road, Cheltenham,
Gloucestershire GL50 3EP
W: www.cheltladiescollege.org
Age Range: 11–18

DEAN CLOSE SCHOOL

Shelburne Road, Cheltenham,
Gloucestershire GL51 6HE
W: www.deanclose.org.uk
Age Range: 13–18

GLOUCESTERSHIRE ISLAMIC SECONDARY SCHOOL FOR GIRLS

Sinope Street, Gloucester,
Gloucestershire GL1 4AW
Age Range: 11–16

THE KING'S SCHOOL

Gloucester, Gloucestershire
GL1 2BG
W: www.thekingsschool.co.uk
Age Range: 3–18

RENDCOMB COLLEGE*

Rendcomb, Cirencester,
Gloucestershire GL7 7HA
W: www.rendcombcollege.org.uk
Age Range: 3–18

ST EDWARD'S SCHOOL CHELTENHAM

Cirencester Road, Cheltenham,
Gloucestershire GL53 8EY
W: www.stedwards.co.uk
Age Range: 11–18

THE SCHOOL OF THE LION

Beauchamp House, Gloucester,
Gloucestershire GL2 8AA
W: www.schoolofthelion.org.uk
Age Range: 4–18

WESTONBIRT SCHOOL

Tetbury, Gloucestershire GL8 8QG
W: www.westonbirt.gloucs.sch.uk
Age Range: 11–18

WYCLIFFE COLLEGE

Bath Road, Stonehouse,
Gloucestershire GL10 2JQ
W: www.wycliffe.co.uk
Age Range: 2–18

WYNSTONES SCHOOL

Church Lane, Gloucester,
Gloucestershire GL4 0UF
W: www.wynstones.com
Age Range: 3–19

SOUTH GLOUCESTERSHIRE

PREPARATORY

SILVERHILL SCHOOL

Swan Lane, Winterbourne, South
Gloucestershire BS36 1RL
W: www.silverhillschool.co.uk
Age Range: 2–11

HAMPSHIRE

NURSERY AND PRE-PREP

CHERUBS PRE – SCHOOL

13 Milvil Road, Lee-on-the-Solent,
Hampshire PO13 9LU
Age Range: 2–8

STOCKTON HOUSE SCHOOL

Stockton Avenue, Fleet,
Hampshire GU51 4NS
W: www.stocktonhouseschool.
co.uk
Age Range: 2–4

PREPARATORY

BALLARD SCHOOL

Fernhill Lane, New Milton,
Hampshire BH25 5SU
W: www.ballardschool.co.uk
Age Range: 2–16

BOUNDARY OAK SCHOOL

Roche Court, Fareham,
Hampshire PO17 5BL
W: www.boundaryoak.co.uk
Age Range: 3–13

CHURCHERS COLLEGE JUNIOR SCHOOL

Midhurst Road, Liphook,
Hampshire GU30 7HT
W: www.churcherscollege.com
Age Range: 4–11

DANESHILL SCHOOL

Stratfield Turgis, Basingstoke,
Hampshire RG27 0AR
W: www.daneshillprepschool.com
Age Range: 2–13

DUNHURST (BEDALES JUNIOR SCHOOL)*

Alton Road, Petersfield,
Hampshire GU32 2DP
W: www.bedales.org.uk
Age Range: 8–13

DURLSTON COURT

Becton Lane, New Milton,
Hampshire BH25 7AQ
W: www.durlstoncourt.co.uk
Age Range: 2–13

FARLEIGH SCHOOL

Red Rice, Andover, Hampshire
SP11 7PW
W: www.farleighschool.com
Age Range: 3–13

FORRES SANDLE MANOR

Station Road, Fordingbridge,
Hampshire SP6 1NS
W: www.fsmschool.com
Age Range: 3–13

GLENHURST SCHOOL

16 Beechworth Road, Havant,
Hampshire PO9 1AX
W: www.glenhurstschool.co.uk
Age Range: 2–9

GREY HOUSE PREPARATORY SCHOOL

Mount Pleasant Road, Hook,
Hampshire RG27 8PW
W: www.greyhouseschool.com
Age Range: 4–11

HIGHFIELD SCHOOL

Highfield Lane, Liphook,
Hampshire GU30 7LQ
W: www.highfieldschool.org.uk
Age Range: 8–13

HORDLE WALHAMPTON SCHOOL

Lymington, Hampshire SO41 5ZG
W: www.hordlewalhampton.co.uk
Age Range: 2–13

KINGS PRIMARY SCHOOL

26 Quob Lane, Southampton,
Hampshire SO30 3HN
Age Range: 5–11

KINGSCOURT SCHOOL

Catherington House,
Catherington, Hampshire PO8 9NJ
W: www.kingscourt.org.uk
Age Range: 2–11

MARYCOURT SCHOOL

27 Crescent Road, Gosport,
Hampshire PO12 2DJ
Age Range: 2–9

THE PILGRIMS' SCHOOL

3 The Close, Winchester,
Hampshire SO23 9LT
W: www.pilgrims-school.co.uk
Age Range: 7–13

PRINCE'S MEAD SCHOOL

Winchester, Hampshire SO21 1AN
W: www.princesmeadschool.
org.uk
Age Range: 3–11

ROOKESBURY PARK SCHOOL

Southwick Road, Portsmouth,
Hampshire PO17 6HT
W: www.rookesburypark.co.uk
Age Range: 3–13

ST NEOT'S SCHOOL

St Neots Road, Hook, Hampshire
RG27 0PN
W: www.st-neots-prep.co.uk
Age Range: 1–13

ST SWITHUN'S JUNIOR SCHOOL

Alresford Road, Winchester,
Hampshire SO21 1HA
W: www.stswithuns.com
Age Range: 3–11 (Accepts
Boys 3–7)

ST WINIFRED'S SCHOOL

17–19 Winn Road, Southampton,
Hampshire SO17 1EJ
W: www.stwinifreds.southampton.
sch.uk
Age Range: 2–11

SHERBORNE HOUSE SCHOOL

Lakewood Road, Eastleigh,
Hampshire SO53 1EU
W: www.sherbornehouse.co.uk
Age Range: 3–11

THE STROUD SCHOOL

Highwood House, Romsey,
Hampshire SO51 9ZH
W: www.stroud-romsey.com
Age Range: 3–13

TWYFORD SCHOOL

Twyford, Winchester, Hampshire
SO21 1NW
W: www.twyfordschool.com
Age Range: 3–13

WOODHILL PREPARATORY SCHOOL

Brook Lane, Southampton,
Hampshire SO30 2ER
W: www.woodhill.hants.sch.uk
Age Range: 3–11

WOODHILL SCHOOL

61 Brownhill Road, Chandler's
Ford, Hampshire SO53 2EH
W: www.woodhill.hants.sch.uk
Age Range: 3–11

YATELEY MANOR PREPARATORY SCHOOL

51 Reading Road, Yateley,
Hampshire GU46 7UQ
W: www.yateleymanor.com
Age Range: 3–13

SENIOR

ALTON CONVENT SCHOOL

Anstey Lane, Alton, Hampshire
GU34 2NG
W: www.alton-convent.hants.
sch.uk
Age Range: 2–18 (Co-ed 2–11)

BEDALES SCHOOL*

Petersfield, Hampshire GU32 2DG
W: www.bedales.org.uk
Age Range: 13–18

BROCKWOOD PARK SCHOOL

Bramdean, Hampshire SO24 0LQ
W: www.brockwood.org.uk
Age Range: 14–19

DITCHAM PARK SCHOOL

Ditcham Park, Petersfield,
Hampshire GU31 5RN
W: www.ditchampark.com
Age Range: 4–16

FARNBOROUGH HILL

Farnborough Road, Farnborough,
Hampshire GU14 8AT
W: www.farnborough-hill.org.uk
Age Range: 11–18

THE GREGG SCHOOL

Townhill Park House,
Southampton, Hampshire
SO18 2GF
W: www.gregg.southampton.
sch.uk
Age Range: 11–16

HAMPSHIRE COLLEGIATE SCHOOL, UCST*

Embley Park, Romsey, Hampshire
SO51 6ZE
W: www.hampshirecs.org.uk
Age Range: 2$^{1}/_{2}$–18

KING EDWARD VI SCHOOL

Wilton Road, Southampton,
Hampshire SO15 5UQ
W: www.kes.hants.sch.uk
Age Range: 11–18

THE KING'S SCHOOL

Basingstoke Community Church, Basingstoke, Hampshire RG21 8SR
Age Range: 7–16

THE KING'S SCHOOL SENIOR

Lakesmere House, Eastleigh, Hampshire SO50 7DB
W: www.kingssenior.hants.sch.uk
Age Range: 11–16

LORD WANDSWORTH COLLEGE*

Long Sutton, Hook, Hampshire RG29 1TB
W: www.lordwandsworth.org
Age Range: 11–18

MAYVILLE HIGH SCHOOL

35 St Simon's Road, Southsea, Hampshire PO5 2PE
W: www.mayvilleschool.com

MEONCROSS SCHOOL

Burnt House Lane, Fareham, Hampshire PO14 2EF
W: www.meoncross.co.uk
Age Range: 3–16

MOYLES COURT SCHOOL

Moyles Court, Ringwood, Hampshire BH24 3NF
W: www.moylescourt.co.uk
Age Range: 3–16

THE PORTSMOUTH GRAMMAR SCHOOL

High Street, Portsmouth, Hampshire PO1 2LN
W: www.pgs.org.uk
Age Range: 2–18

PORTSMOUTH HIGH SCHOOL GDST

Kent Road, Southsea, Hampshire PO5 3EQ
W: www.portsmouthhigh.co.uk
Age Range: 3–18

RAMSHILL SCHOOL

Petersfield, Hampshire GU31 4AS
W: www.churcherscollege.com
Age Range: 4–18

RINGWOOD WALDORF SCHOOL

Folly Farm Lane, Ringwood, Hampshire BH24 2NN
W: www.ringwoodwaldorfschool. org.uk
Age Range: 3–17 (Ages 3–17)

ROOKWOOD SCHOOL

Weyhill Road, Andover, Hampshire SP10 3AL
W: www.rookwood.hants.sch.uk
Age Range: 3–16 (Boy boarders from age 8)

ST JOHN'S COLLEGE

Grove Road South, Southsea, Hampshire PO5 3QW
W: www.stjohnscollege.co.uk
Age Range: 2–18

ST MARY'S COLLEGE

57 Midanbury Lane, Southampton, Hampshire SO18 4DJ
W: www.stmaryscollegesoton. bizland.com
Age Range: 3–18

ST NICHOLAS' SCHOOL*

Redfields House, Redfields Lane, Church Crookham, Fleet, Hampshire GU52 0RF
W: www.st-nicholas.hants.sch.uk
Age Range: 3–16 (Boys 3–7)

ST SWITHUN'S SCHOOL

Alresford Road, Winchester, Hampshire SO21 1HA
W: www.stswithuns.com
Age Range: 11–18

SALESIAN COLLEGE

Reading Road, Farnborough, Hampshire GU14 6PA
W: www.salesiancollege.com
Age Range: 11–18

SHERFIELD SCHOOL

Reading Road, Hook, Hampshire RG27 0HT
W: www.sherfieldschool.co.uk
Age Range: 2–18 (Pupils enter baby Gems between ages 2 months and 2 years. The upper age of the school has recently increased to 18.)

WINCHESTER COLLEGE

College Street, Winchester, Hampshire SO23 9NA
W: www.winchestercollege.org
Age Range: 13–18

WYKEHAM HOUSE SCHOOL

East Street, Fareham, Hampshire PO16 0BW
W: www.wykehamhouse.com
Age Range: 2–16

INDEPENDENT SIXTH FORM COLLEGE / TUTORIAL COLLEGE

ALTON COLLEGE

Old Odiham Road, Alton, Hampshire GU34 2LX
W: www.altoncollege.ac.uk
Age Range: 16–19

HEREFORDSHIRE

PREPARATORY

THE HEREFORD CATHEDRAL JUNIOR SCHOOL

28 Castle Street, Hereford,
Herefordshire HR1 2NW
W: www.hcjs.org
Age Range: 3–11

ST RICHARD'S

Bredenbury Court, Bromyard,
Herefordshire HR7 4TD
W: www.st-richards.org.uk
Age Range: 3–13

SENIOR

HEREFORD CATHEDRAL SCHOOL

Old Deanery, Hereford,
Herefordshire HR1 2NG
W: www.herefordcs.com
Age Range: 11–18

LUCTON SCHOOL

Lucton, Leominster, Herefordshire
HR6 9PN
W: www.luctonschool.org

HERTFORDSHIRE

NURSERY AND PRE-PREP

NORFOLK LODGE MONTESSORI NURSERY

Dancers Hill Road, Barnet,
Hertfordshire EN5 4RP
W: www.norfolklodgeschool.co.uk
Age Range: 1–4

PREPARATORY

ALDWICKBURY SCHOOL

Wheathampstead Road,
Harpenden, Hertfordshire AL5 1AD
W: www.aldwickbury.org.uk
Age Range: 4–13

BEECHWOOD PARK SCHOOL

St Albans, Hertfordshire AL3 8AW
W: www.beechwoodpark.herts.
sch.uk
Age Range: 2–13

BERKHAMSTED SCHOOL

Kings Road, Berkhamsted,
Hertfordshire HP4 3YP
W: www.
berkhamstedcollegiateschool.org.uk
Age Range: 3–11

BISHOP'S STORTFORD COLLEGE JUNIOR SCHOOL

Maze Green Road, Bishop's
Stortford, Hertfordshire CM23 2PH
W: www.bishops-stortford-
college.herts.sch.uk
Age Range: 4–13

DUNCOMBE SCHOOL

4 Warren Park Road, Hertford,
Hertfordshire SG14 3JA
W: www.duncombe-school.co.uk
Age Range: 2–11

EDGE GROVE*

Aldenham Village, Hertfordshire
WD25 8NL
W: www.edgegrove.com
Age Range: 3–13

FRANCIS HOUSE PREPARATORY SCHOOL

Aylesbury Road, Tring,
Hertfordshire HP23 4DL
W: www.francishouseschool.co.uk
Age Range: 2–11

HARESFOOT PREPARATORY SCHOOL

Chesham Road, Berkhamsted,
Hertfordshire HP4 2SZ
W: www.haresfoot.herts.sch.uk
Age Range: (Children may join
from 5 months of age into our Day
Nursery.)

HEATH MOUNT SCHOOL

Woodhall Park, Hertford,
Hertfordshire SG14 3NG
W: www.heathmount.org
Age Range: 3–13

HIGH ELMS MANOR SCHOOL

High Elms Lane, Watford,
Hertfordshire WD25 0JX
W: http://www.
highelmsmanorschool.com

HOMEWOOD PRE-PREPARATORY SCHOOL

Hazel Road, St Albans, Hertfordshire AL2 2AH
Age Range: 3–8

HOWE GREEN HOUSE SCHOOL

Bishop's Stortford, Hertfordshire CM22 7UF
W: www.howegreenhouseschool. co.uk
Age Range: 2–11

THE JUNIOR SCHOOL, BISHOP'S STORTFORD COLLEGE

Maze Green Road, Bishop's Stortford, Hertfordshire CM23 2PH
W: www.bishops-stortford-college.herts.sch.uk
Age Range: 4–13

KINGSHOTT SCHOOL

Hitchin, Hertfordshire SG4 7JX
W: www.kingshottschool.co.uk
Age Range: 4–13

LITTLE ACORNS MONTESSORI SCHOOL

Lincolnsfields Centre, Bushey, Hertfordshire WD2 2ER
W: www.littleacorns-montessori. org
Age Range: 2–7

LOCKERS PARK

Lockers Park Lane, Hemel Hempstead, Hertfordshire HP1 1TL
W: www.lockerspark.herts.sch.uk
Age Range: 5–13

LONGWOOD SCHOOL

Bushey Hall Drive, Bushey, Hertfordshire WD23 2QG
W: www.longwoodschool.co.uk
Age Range: (Day nursery accepts children from 3 months to 4 years. School accepts children from 3 years to 11 years.)

LYONSDOWN SCHOOL TRUST LTD

3 Richmond Road, Barnet, Hertfordshire EN5 1SA
W: www.lyonsdownschool.co.uk
Age Range: 3–11

MANOR LODGE SCHOOL

Rectory Lane, Shenley, Hertfordshire WD7 9BG
W: www.manorlodgeschool.com
Age Range: 3–11

NORTHWOOD PREPARATORY SCHOOL

Moor Farm, Rickmansworth, Hertfordshire WD3 1LW
W: www.northwoodprep.co.uk
Age Range: 3–13 (Girls 3–4)

RADLETT PREPARATORY SCHOOL

Kendal Hall, Radlett, Hertfordshire WD7 7LY
W: www.radlett-prep.herts.sch.uk
Age Range: 4–11

RICKMANSWORTH PNEU SCHOOL

88 The Drive, Rickmansworth, Hertfordshire WD3 4DU
W: www.rickmansworthpneu. co.uk
Age Range: 3–11

ST HILDA'S SCHOOL

High Street, Bushey, Hertfordshire WD23 3DA
W: www.sthildas-school.co.uk
Age Range: 3–11 (Boys 3–5)

ST. HILDA'S SCHOOL

28 Douglas Road, Harpenden, Hertfordshire AL5 2ES
W: www.sthildasharpenden.co.uk
Age Range: 2–11

ST JOHN'S PREPARATORY SCHOOL

Brownlowes, Potters Bar, Hertfordshire EN6 5QT
W: www.stjohnsprepschool.co.uk
Age Range: 4–11

ST JOSEPH'S IN THE PARK

St Mary's Lane, Hertford, Hertfordshire SG14 2LX
W: www.stjosephsinthepark.co.uk
Age Range: 3–11

STORMONT

The Causeway, Potters Bar, Hertfordshire EN6 5HA
W: www.stormont.herts.sch.uk
Age Range: 4–11

WESTBROOK HAY PREPARATORY SCHOOL

Hemel Hempstead, Hertfordshire HP1 2RF
W: www.westbrookhay.co.uk
Age Range: 2–13

YORK HOUSE SCHOOL

Sarratt Road, Hertfordshire WD3 4LW
W: www.york-house.com
Age Range: 3–13 (Co-ed 2–5)

SENIOR

ABBOT'S HILL SCHOOL*

Bunkers Lane, Hemel Hempstead, Hertfordshire HP3 8RP
W: www.abbotshill.herts.sch.uk
Age Range: 3–16 (Boys 3–5)

ALDENHAM SCHOOL*

Elstree, Hertfordshire WD6 3AJ
W: www.aldenham.com
Age Range: 3–18

BERKHAMSTED SCHOOL

Castle Street, Berkhamsted, Hertfordshire HP4 2BB
W: www. berkhamstedcollegiateschool.org.uk
Age Range: 11–18 (Single-sex ed 11–16)

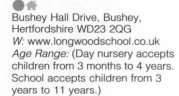

BISHOP'S STORTFORD COLLEGE

Maze Green Road, Bishop's Stortford, Hertfordshire CM23 2PJ
W: www.bishops-stortford-college.herts.sch.uk
Age Range: 13–18

HABERDASHERS' ASKE'S BOYS' SCHOOL

Butterfly Lane, Elstree, Hertfordshire WD6 3AF
W: www.habsboys.org.uk
Age Range: 5–18

HABERDASHERS' ASKE'S SCHOOL FOR GIRLS

Aldenham Road, Elstree, Hertfordshire WD6 3BT
W: www.habsgirls.org.uk
Age Range: 4–18

HAILEYBURY*

Hertford, Hertfordshire SG13 7NU
W: www.haileybury.com
Age Range: 11–18

IMMANUEL COLLEGE

87/91 Elstree Road, Bushey, Hertfordshire WD23 4EB
W: www.immanuelcollege.co.uk
Age Range: 4–18

THE KING'S SCHOOL

Elmfield, Harpenden, Hertfordshire AL5 4DU
W: www.thekingsschool.com
Age Range: 4–16

THE PURCELL SCHOOL

Aldenham Road, Bushey, Hertfordshire WD23 2TS
W: www.purcell-school.org
Age Range: 8–18

QUEENSWOOD

Shepherds Way, Hatfield, Hertfordshire AL9 6NS
W: www.queenswood.org
Age Range: 11–18

REDEMPTION ACADEMY

PO Box 352, Stevenage, Hertfordshire SG1 9AG
W: www.redemption-academy.org
Age Range: 3–18

THE ROYAL MASONIC SCHOOL FOR GIRLS*

Rickmansworth Park, Rickmansworth, Hertfordshire WD3 4HF
W: www.royalmasonic.herts.sch.uk
Age Range: 2–19 (Pre School opened in January 2010 for boys and girls aged 2–4.)

ST ALBANS HIGH SCHOOL FOR GIRLS

1–3 Townsend Avenue, St Albans, Hertfordshire AL1 3SJ
W: www.stahs.org.uk
Age Range: 4–18

ST ALBANS SCHOOL*

Abbey Gateway, St Albans, Hertfordshire AL3 4HB
W: www.st-albans.herts.sch.uk
Age Range: 17–18 (Co-ed VIth Form)

ST CHRISTOPHER SCHOOL

Barrington Road, Letchworth Garden City, Hertfordshire SG6 3JZ
W: www.stchris.co.uk
Age Range: 2–18

ST COLUMBA'S COLLEGE*

King Harry Lane, St Albans, Hertfordshire AL3 4AW
W: www.stcolumbascollege.org
Age Range: 4–18

ST EDMUND'S COLLEGE AND PREP SCHOOL*

Old Hall Green, Ware, Hertfordshire SG11 1DS
W: www.stedmundscollege.org
Age Range: 3–18

ST FRANCIS' COLLEGE

The Broadway, Letchworth Garden City, Hertfordshire SG6 3PJ
W: www.st-francis.herts.sch.uk
Age Range: 3–18

ST MARGARET'S SCHOOL*

Merry Hill Road, Bushey, Hertfordshire WD23 1DT
W: www.stmargaretsbushey.org.uk
Age Range: 4–18

ST MARTHA'S SENIOR SCHOOL

Camlet Way, Barnet, Hertfordshire EN4 0NJ
W: www.st-marthas.org.uk
Age Range: 11–18

STANBOROUGH SCHOOL

Watford, Hertfordshire WD25 9JT
W: www.stanboroughpark.herts.sch.uk
Age Range: 3–16

SHERRARDSWOOD SCHOOL

Lockleys, Welwyn, Hertfordshire AL6 0BJ
W: www.sherrardswood.herts.sch.uk
Age Range: 2–18

SUSI EARNSHAW THEATRE SCHOOL

The Bull Theatre, Barnet, Hertfordshire EN5 5SJ
W: www.susiearnshaw.co.uk
Age Range: 11–16

TRING PARK SCHOOL FOR THE PERFORMING ARTS*

Tring Park, Tring, Hertfordshire HP23 5LX
W: www.tringpark.com
Age Range: 8–19

WATFORD GRAMMAR SCHOOL FOR GIRLS

Lady's Close, Watford,
Hertfordshire WD1 8AE
W: www.
watfordgrammarschoolforgirls.org.uk
Age Range: 11–18

INDEPENDENT SIXTH FORM COLLEGE / TUTORIAL COLLEGE

JUSTIN CRAIG EDUCATION

Kinetic Centre, Hertfordshire
WD6 4PJ
W: www.justincraig.ac.uk
Age Range: 15–19

ST ALBANS TUTORS

●

69 London Road, St Albans,
Hertfordshire AL1 1LN
W: www.stalbanstutors.org.uk

ISLE OF MAN

PREPARATORY

THE BUCHAN SCHOOL

Arbory Road, Castletown, Isle of
Man IM9 1RD
W: www.buchan.sch.im
Age Range: 4–11

SENIOR

KING WILLIAM'S COLLEGE

Castletown, Isle of Man IM9 1TP
W: www.kwc.sch.im
Age Range: 11–18

ISLE OF WIGHT

SENIOR

PRIORY SCHOOL

Alverstone Manor, Shanklin, Isle of
Wight PO37 7JB
W: www.prioryschool.org.uk
Age Range: 2–18

RYDE SCHOOL

Queen's Road, Ryde, Isle of Wight
PO33 3BE
W: www.rydeschool.org.uk
Age Range: 3–18

KENT

NURSERY AND PRE-PREP

SOMERHILL PRE-PREPARATORY SCHOOL

Tonbridge, Kent TN11 0NJ
W: www.schoolsatsomerhill.com
Age Range: 3–7

PREPARATORY

ASHGROVE SCHOOL

116 Widmore Road, Bromley, Kent
BR1 3BE
W: www.ashgrove.org.uk
Age Range: 3–11

BENEDICT HOUSE PREPARATORY SCHOOL

●

1–5 Victoria Road, Sidcup, Kent
DA15 7HD
W: www.
BenedictHousePrepSchool.co.uk
Age Range: 3–11

BICKLEY PARK SCHOOL*

14/24 Page Heath Lane, Bickley, Bromley, Kent BR1 2DS
W: www.bickleyparkschool.co.uk
Age Range: 3–13

BREASIDE PREPARATORY SCHOOL

41 Orchard Road, Bromley, Kent BR1 2PR
W: www.breaside.co.uk
Age Range: 2–11

BRONTE SCHOOL

7 Pelham Road, Gravesend, Kent DA11 0HN
W: www.bronteschool.co.uk
Age Range: 4–11

BRYONY SCHOOL

Marshall Road, Gillingham, Kent ME8 0AJ
Age Range: 2–11

CHARTFIELD SCHOOL

45 Minster Road, Westgate-on-Sea, Kent CT8 8DA
Age Range: 4–11

CONVENT PREPARATORY SCHOOL

46 Old Road East, Gravesend, Kent DA12 1NR
W: www.sjcps.org
Age Range: 3–11

DERWENT LODGE SCHOOL FOR GIRLS

Tonbridge, Kent TN11 0NJ
W: www.schoolsatsomerhill.com
Age Range: 7–11

DULWICH PREPARATORY SCHOOL, CRANBROOK

Coursehorn, Cranbrook, Kent TN17 3NP
W: www.dcpskent.org
Age Range: 3–13

ELLIOTT PARK SCHOOL

18–20 Marina Drive, Sheerness, Kent ME12 2DP
Age Range: 4–11

FOSSE BANK SCHOOL

Mountains Country House, Tonbridge, Kent TN11 8ND
W: www.fossebankschool.co.uk
Age Range: 3–11

THE GRANVILLE SCHOOL

2 Bradbourne Park Road, Sevenoaks, Kent TN13 3LJ
W: www.granville-school.com
Age Range: 3–11 (Boys 3–5)

HADDON DENE SCHOOL

57 Gladstone Road, Broadstairs, Kent CT10 2HY
W: www.haddondene.co.uk
Age Range: 3–11

HARENC SCHOOL TRUST

167 Rectory Lane, Sidcup, Kent DA14 5BU
W: www.harencschool.co.uk
Age Range: 3–11

HILDEN GRANGE SCHOOL

62 Dry Hill Park Road, Tonbridge, Kent TN10 3BX
W: www.hildengrange.gdst.net
Age Range: 3–13

HILDEN OAKS SCHOOL

38 Dry Hill Park Road, Tonbridge, Kent TN10 3BU
W: www.hildenoaks.co.uk

HOLMEWOOD HOUSE*

Barrow Lane, Langton Green, Tunbridge Wells, Kent TN3 0EB
W: www.holmewood.kent.sch.uk
Age Range: 3–13

JUNIOR KING'S CANTERBURY*

Milner Court, Sturry, Canterbury, Kent CT2 0AY
W: www.junior-kings.co.uk
Age Range: 3–13

KENT COLLEGE INFANT & JUNIOR SCHOOL

Vernon Holme, Canterbury, Kent CT2 9AQ
W: www.kentcollege.com/junior
Age Range: 3–11

KING'S PREPARATORY SCHOOL

King Edward Road, Rochester, Kent ME1 1UB
W: www.kings-school-rochester.co.uk
Age Range: 8–13

LORENDEN PREPARATORY SCHOOL

Painter's Forstal, Faversham, Kent ME13 0EN
W: www.lorenden.org.uk
Age Range: 3–11

MARLBOROUGH HOUSE SCHOOL

High Street, Hawkhurst, Kent TN18 4PY
W: www.marlboroughhouseschool.co.uk
Age Range: 3–13

THE MEAD SCHOOL

16 Frant Road, Tunbridge Wells, Kent TN2 5SN
W: www.meadschool.info
Age Range: 3–11

MERTON COURT PREPARATORY SCHOOL

38 Knoll Road, Sidcup, Kent DA14 4QU
W: www.mertoncourt.kent.sch.uk
Age Range: 2–11

THE NEW BEACON

Brittains Lane, Sevenoaks, Kent TN13 2PB
W: www.newbeacon.kent.org.uk
Age Range: 4–13

NORTHBOURNE PARK SCHOOL

Betteshanger, Deal, Kent
CT14 0NW
W: www.northbournepark.com
Age Range: 3–13

RUSSELL HOUSE SCHOOL

Station Road, Sevenoaks, Kent
TN14 5QU
W: www.russellhouseschool.co.uk
Age Range: 2–11

ST ANDREW'S SCHOOL

24–28 Watts Avenue, Rochester,
Kent ME1 1SA
W: www.st-andrews.rochester.
sch.uk
Age Range: 3–11

ST CHRISTOPHER'S SCHOOL

New Dover Road, Canterbury,
Kent CT1 3DT
W: www.stchristopherschool.
co.uk
Age Range: 3–11

ST CHRISTOPHER'S SCHOOL

49 Bromley Road, Beckenham,
Kent BR3 5PA
W: www.stchristophersthehall.
co.uk
Age Range: 3–11

ST DAVID'S COLLEGE

Justin Hall, West Wickham, Kent
BR4 0QS
W: www.stdavidscollege.com
Age Range: 4–11

ST EDMUNDS JUNIOR SCHOOL

St Thomas Hill, Canterbury, Kent
CT2 8HU
W: www.stedmunds.org.uk
Age Range: 7–13

ST FAITH'S AT ASH SCHOOL

5 The Street, Canterbury, Kent
CT3 2HH
Age Range: 3–11

ST JOSEPH'S CONVENT PREPARATORY SCHOOL*

46 Old Road East, Gravesend,
Kent DA12 1NR
W: www.sjcps.org
Age Range: 3–11

ST LAWRENCE COLLEGE JUNIOR SCHOOL

College Road, Ramsgate, Kent
CT11 7AF
W: www.slcuk.com
Age Range: 3–11

ST MICHAEL'S SCHOOL

Otford Court, Sevenoaks, Kent
TN14 5SA
W: www.stmichaels-otford.co.uk
Age Range: 2–13

SHERNOLD SCHOOL

Hill Place, Maidstone, Kent
ME16 0ER
W: www.shernoldschool.co.uk
Age Range: 3–11

SOLEFIELD SCHOOL

Solefields Road, Sevenoaks, Kent
TN13 1PH
W: www.solefieldschool.org
Age Range: 4–13

SPRING GROVE SCHOOL

Harville Road, Ashford, Kent
TN25 5EZ
W: www.springgroveschool.co.uk
Age Range: 2–13

STEEPHILL INDEPENDENT SCHOOL*

Castle Hill, Fawkham, Longfield,
Kent DA3 7BG
W: www.steephill.co.uk
Age Range: 3–11

SUTTON VALENCE PREPARATORY SCHOOL

Church Road, Maidstone, Kent
ME17 3RF
W: www.svs.org.uk
Age Range: 3–11

WEST LODGE PREPARATORY SCHOOL

36 Station Road, Sidcup, Kent
DA15 7DU
W: www.westlodge.org.uk
Age Range: 3–11

YARDLEY COURT PREPARATORY SCHOOL

Somerhill, Tonbridge, Kent
TN11 0NJ
W: www.schoolsatsomerhill.com
Age Range: 7–13

SENIOR

ASHFORD SCHOOL

Ashford, Kent TN24 8PB
W: www.ashfordschool.co.uk
Age Range: 3–18 (Co-ed 3–11)

BABINGTON HOUSE SCHOOL

Grange Drive, Chislehurst, Kent
BR7 5ES
W: www.babingtonhouse.com
Age Range: 3–16 (Boys 3–7)

BEECHWOOD SACRED HEART SCHOOL

Pembury Road, Tunbridge Wells,
Kent TN2 3QD
W: www.beechwood.org.uk
Age Range: 3–18 (Boarding for
Girls only
Boys may stay with host families.)

BENENDEN SCHOOL

Cranbrook, Kent TN17 4AA
W: www.benenden.kent.sch.uk
Age Range: 11–18

BETHANY SCHOOL

Curtisden Green, Cranbrook, Kent
TN17 1LB
W: www.bethanyschool.org.uk
Age Range: 11–18

BISHOP CHALLONER RC SCHOOL*

228 Bromley Road, Shortlands, Bromley, Kent BR2 0BS
W: www.bishopchallonerschool.com
Age Range: 3–18

BROMLEY HIGH SCHOOL GDST

Blackbrook Lane, Bromley, Kent BR1 2TW
W: www.gdst.net/bromleyhigh
Age Range: 4–18

CANTERBURY STEINER SCHOOL

Garlinge Green, Canterbury, Kent CT4 5RU
Age Range: 4–17

COBHAM HALL*

Cobham, Gravesend, Kent DA12 3BL
W: www.cobhamhall.com
Age Range: 11–18

COMBE BANK SCHOOL

Combe Bank Drive, Sevenoaks, Kent TN14 6AE
W: www.combebank.kent.sch.uk
Age Range: 3–18

CRANBROOK SCHOOL*

Cranbrook, Kent TN17 3JD
W: www.cranbrookschool.co.uk
Age Range: 13–18

DARUL ULOOM LONDON

Foxbury Avenue, Chislehurst, Kent BR7 6SD
W: www.darululoomlondon.co.uk
Age Range: 11–18

DOVER COLLEGE

Effingham Crescent, Dover, Kent CT17 9RH
W: www.dovercollege.org.uk
Age Range: 3–18

DUKE OF YORK'S ROYAL MILITARY SCHOOL

Dover, Kent CT15 5EQ
W: www.doyrms.mod.uk
Age Range: 11–18

FARRINGTONS SCHOOL*

Perry Street, Chislehurst, Kent BR7 6LR
W: www.farringtons.org.uk
Age Range: 3–19

GAD'S HILL SCHOOL

Higham, Rochester, Kent ME3 7PA
W: www.gadshill.org
Age Range: 3–16

KENT COLLEGE

Whitstable Road, Canterbury, Kent CT2 9DT
W: www.kentcollege.com
Age Range: 3–18

KENT COLLEGE PEMBURY

Old Church Road, Tunbridge Wells, Kent TN2 4AX
W: www.kent-college.co.uk
Age Range: 3–18

KING'S ROCHESTER

Satis House, Rochester, Kent ME1 1TE
W: www.kings-rochester.co.uk
Age Range: 3–18

THE KING'S SCHOOL

Canterbury, Kent CT1 2ES
W: www.kings-school.co.uk
Age Range: 13–18

ST EDMUND'S SCHOOL CANTERBURY

St Thomas Hill, Canterbury, Kent CT2 8HU
W: www.stedmunds.org.uk
Age Range: 3–18

ST LAWRENCE COLLEGE*

College Road, Ramsgate, Kent CT11 7AE
W: www.slcuk.com
Age Range: 3–18

SACKVILLE SCHOOL

Tonbridge Road, Tonbridge, Kent TN11 9HN
W: www.sackvilleschool.co.uk
Age Range: 11–18

SEVENOAKS SCHOOL

High Street, Sevenoaks, Kent TN13 1HU
W: www.sevenoaksschool.org
Age Range: 11–18

SUTTON VALENCE SCHOOL

Sutton Valence, Sutton Valence, Kent ME17 3HL
W: www.svs.org.uk
Age Range: 3–18

TONBRIDGE SCHOOL*

Tonbridge, Kent TN9 1JP
W: www.tonbridge-school.co.uk
Age Range: 13–18

WALTHAMSTOW HALL

Hollybush Lane, Sevenoaks, Kent TN13 3UL
W: www.walthamstow-hall.co.uk
Age Range: 2–18

WICKHAM COURT SCHOOL

West Wickham, Kent BR4 9HW
W: www.wickhamcourt.org.uk
Age Range: 2–16

INDEPENDENT SIXTH FORM COLLEGE / TUTORIAL COLLEGE

CATS COLLEGE CANTERBURY

68 New Dover Road, Canterbury, Kent CT1 3LQ
W: www.catscollege.com/canterbury
Age Range: 15–21

ROCHESTER INDEPENDENT COLLEGE

Star Hill, Rochester, Kent ME1 1XF
W: www.rochester-college.org
Age Range: 11–18

INTERNATIONAL SCHOOLS AND INTERNATIONAL STUDY CENTRES

STAFFORD HOUSE SCHOOL OF ENGLISH

●

19 New Dover Road, Canterbury,
Kent CT1 3AH
W: www.staffordhouseelt.com

LANCASHIRE

PREPARATORY

ASHBRIDGE INDEPENDENT SCHOOL

●🏠

Lindle Lane, Preston, Lancashire
PR4 4AQ
Age Range: 2–11

THE BENNETT HOUSE SCHOOL

●🏠

332 Eaves Lane, Chorley,
Lancashire PR6 0DX
W: www.bennetthouse.lancs.
sch.uk

BURY CATHOLIC PREPARATORY SCHOOL

●🏠

Arden House, Bury, Lancashire
BL9 9BH
W: www.burycatholicprepschool.
co.uk
Age Range: 3–11

CLEVELANDS PREPARATORY SCHOOL

●🏠

Chorley New Road, Bolton,
Lancashire BL1 5DH
W: www.clevelandsprepschool.
co.uk
Age Range: 2–11

FARROWDALE HOUSE PREPARATORY SCHOOL

●🏠

Farrow Street, Oldham,
Lancashire OL2 7AD
W: www.farrowdale.co.uk
Age Range: 3–11

FIRWOOD MANOR PREP SCHOOL

●🏠

Broadway, Oldham, Lancashire
OL9 0AD
W: www.firwoodmanor.org.uk
Age Range: 2–11

GRASSCROFT INDEPENDENT SCHOOL

●🏠

Lydgate Parish Hall, Oldham,
Lancashire OL4 4JJ
Age Range: 2–7

HIGHFIELD PRIORY SCHOOL

●🏠

Fulwood Row, Preston, Lancashire
PR2 6SL
W: www.highfieldpriory.co.uk
Age Range: 2–11

LANCASTER STEINER SCHOOL

●🏠

Lune Road, Lancaster, Lancashire
LA1 5QU
W: www.lancastersteiner.org.uk
Age Range: 5–14

LANGDALE PREPARATORY SCHOOL

●🏠

95 Warbreck Drive, Blackpool,
Lancashire FY2 9RZ
W: www.langdaleprepschool.
co.uk
Age Range: 3–11

OLDHAM HULME KINDERGARTEN

●🏠

Plum Street, Oldham, Lancashire
OL8 1TJ
W: www.hulmegrammar.oldham.
sch.uk
Age Range: 3–7

THE POTTERS HOUSE SCHOOL

●🏠

6 Arley Avenue, Bury, Lancashire
BL9 5HD
Age Range: 5–10

ROSSALL SCHOOL

●🏠

Fleetwood, Lancashire FY7 8JW
W: www.rossallschool.org.uk
Age Range: 2–11

ST JOSEPH'S SCHOOL, PARK HILL

●🏠

Park Hill, Burnley, Lancashire
BB12 6TG
W: www.parkhillschool.co.uk
Age Range: 3–11

ST MARY'S HALL

Clitheroe, Lancashire BB7 9PU
W: www.stonyhurst.ac.uk
Age Range: 3–13

ST PIUS X PREPARATORY SCHOOL

200 Garstang Road, Preston,
Lancashire PR2 8RD
W: www.stpiusx.co.uk
Age Range: 2–11

SADDLEWORTH PREPARATORY SCHOOL

Huddersfield Road, Oldham,
Lancashire OL4 4AG
W: www.
saddleworthpreparatoryschool.
org.uk
Age Range: 4–7

STONEHOUSE NURSERY SCHOOL

90 School Lane, Leyland,
Lancashire PR25 2TU
W: stonehousenurseryandprimaryschool.
com

TASHBAR SCHOOL

20 Upper Park Road, Salford,
Lancashire M7 4HL
Age Range: 2–11

SENIOR

AL-ISLAH SCHOOL

108 Audley Range, Blackburn,
Lancashire BB1 1TF
Age Range: 5–16

ARNOLD SCHOOL

Lytham Road, Blackpool,
Lancashire FY4 1JG
W: www.arnoldschool.com
Age Range: 2–18

BEECH HOUSE SCHOOL

184 Manchester Road, Rochdale,
Lancashire OL11 4JQ
W: www.beechhouseschool.co.uk
Age Range: 2–16

BOLTON MUSLIM GIRLS SCHOOL

Swan Lane, Bolton, Lancashire
BL3 6TQ
Age Range: 11–16

BOLTON SCHOOL (BOYS' DIVISION)

Chorley New Road, Bolton,
Lancashire BL1 4PA
W: http://www.boltonschool.org
Age Range: 7–18

BOLTON SCHOOL (GIRLS' DIVISION)

Chorley New Road, Bolton,
Lancashire BL1 4PB
W: www.boltonschool.org/
seniorgirls
Age Range: 4–18 (Boys 4–7
before they move into Bolton
School Boys' Division)

BURY GRAMMAR SCHOOL BOYS

Tenterden Street, Bury,
Lancashire BL9 0HN
W: www.bgsboys.co.uk
Age Range: 7–18

BURY GRAMMAR SCHOOL GIRLS

Bridge Road, Bury, Lancashire
BL9 0HH
W: www.bgsg.bury.sch.uk
Age Range: 3–18 (Boys 4–7)

HEATHLAND COLLEGE

Broadoak, Accrington, Lancashire
BB5 2AN
W: www.heathlandschool.co.uk
Age Range: 1–16

THE HULME GRAMMAR SCHOOL FOR GIRLS

Chamber Road, Oldham,
Lancashire OL8 4BX
W: www.hulme-grammar.oldham.
sch.uk
Age Range: 3–18

ISLAMIYAH SCHOOL

Willow Street, Blackburn,
Lancashire BB1 5NQ
Age Range: 11–16

JAMEA AL KAUTHAR

Ashton Road, Lancaster,
Lancashire LA1 5AJ
W: www.jamea.co.uk
Age Range: 11–19

KING EDWARD VII AND QUEEN MARY SCHOOL

Clifton Drive South, Lytham St
Annes, Lancashire FY8 1DT
W: www.keqms.co.uk
Age Range: 2–18

KINGSWOOD COLLEGE TRUST

Scarisbrick Hall, Ormskirk,
Lancashire L40 9RQ
W: www.kingswoodcollege.co.uk
Age Range: 2–19

KIRKHAM GRAMMAR SCHOOL

Ribby Road, Preston, Lancashire
PR4 2BH
W: www.kirkhamgrammar.co.uk
Age Range: 3–18

LORD'S COLLEGE

53 Manchester Road, Bolton,
Lancashire BL2 1ES
Age Range: 10–17

MAHARISHI SCHOOL

Ashtons Farm, Ormskirk,
Lancashire L40 6JJ
W: www.maharishischool.com
Age Range: 4–16

MARKAZUL ULOOM

Park Lee Road, Blackburn,
Lancashire BB2 3NY
Age Range: 11–19 (No Boarding
for girls)

MOORLAND SCHOOL

Ribblesdale Avenue, Clitheroe,
Lancashire BB7 2JA
W: www.moorlandschool.co.uk
Age Range: 1–16

OAKHILL COLLEGE

Wiswell Lane, Clitheroe,
Lancashire BB7 9AF
W: www.oakhillcollege.co.uk
Age Range: 2–16

THE OLDHAM HULME GRAMMAR SCHOOLS

Chamber Road, Oldham,
Lancashire OL8 4BX
W: www.hulme-grammar.oldham.
sch.uk
Age Range: 3–18

QUEEN ELIZABETH'S GRAMMAR SCHOOL

West Park Road, Blackburn,
Lancashire BB2 6DF
W: www.qegs.blackburn.sch.uk
Age Range: 3–18 (Girls and boys
admitted at all ages, 3 to 18.)

RIVINGTON PARK INDEPENDENT SCHOOL

Knowle House, Horwich,
Lancashire BL6 7RX
W: www.rivingtonparkschool.
co.uk
Age Range: 1–16

ROCHDALE GIRLS SCHOOL

36 Taylor Street, Rochdale,
Lancashire OL12 0HX
Age Range: 11–16

ROSSALL SCHOOL

Fleetwood, Lancashire FY7 8JW
W: www.rossallschool.org.uk
Age Range: 11–18

ST ANNE'S COLLEGE GRAMMAR SCHOOL

293 Clifton Drive South, Lytham St
Annes, Lancashire FY8 1HN
W: www.collgram.u-net.com
Age Range: 3–18

STONYHURST COLLEGE

Clitheroe, Lancashire BB7 9PZ
W: www.stonyhurst.ac.uk
Age Range: 13–18

TAUHEEDUL ISLAM GIRLS HIGH SCHOOL

31 Bicknell Street, Blackburn,
Lancashire BB1 7EY
W: www.tauheedulislam.com
Age Range: 11–16

WESTHOLME SCHOOL

Wilmar Lodge, Blackburn,
Lancashire BB2 6QU
W: www.westholmeschool.com
Age Range: 3–18 (Boys 3–7)

INTERNATIONAL SCHOOLS AND INTERNATIONAL STUDY CENTRES

ROSSALL SCHOOL INTERNATIONAL STUDY CENTRE

Rossall School, Fleetwood,
Lancashire FY7 8JW
W: www.rossallschool.org.uk
Age Range: 11–16

LEICESTERSHIRE

PREPARATORY

AL-AQSA PRIMARY SCHOOL

The Wayne Way, Leicester,
Leicestershire LE5 4PP
Age Range: 3–11

FAIRFIELD PREPARATORY SCHOOL

Leicester Road, Loughborough,
Leicestershire LE11 2AE
W: www.lesfairfield.org
Age Range: 4–11

GRACE DIEU MANOR SCHOOL

Grace Dieu, Leicester,
Leicestershire LE67 5UG
W: www.gracedieu.com
Age Range: 3–13

LEICESTER GRAMMAR JUNIOR SCHOOL

Evington Hall, Leicester,
Leicestershire LE5 6HN
W: www.leicestergrammar.org
Age Range: 3–11

STONEYGATE COLLEGE

2 Albert Road, Leicester,
Leicestershire LE2 2AA
W: www.stoneygate-college.co.uk
Age Range: 3–11

STONEYGATE SCHOOL

London Road, Leicester,
Leicestershire LE8 9DJ
W: www.stoneygateschool.co.uk
Age Range: 3–13

SENIOR

THE DIXIE GRAMMAR SCHOOL

●🏠▲

Station Road, Market Bosworth,
Leicestershire CV13 0LE
W: www.dixie.org.uk
Age Range: 3–18

LEICESTER GRAMMAR SCHOOL

●🏠▲

London Road, Leicester,
Leicestershire LE8 9FL
W: www.leicestergrammar.org.uk
Age Range: 3–18

LEICESTER HIGH SCHOOL FOR GIRLS

●🏠▲

454 London Road, Leicester,
Leicestershire LE2 2PP
W: www.leicesterhigh.co.uk
Age Range: 3–18

LEICESTER MONTESSORI GRAMMAR SCHOOL

●🏠▲

58 Stoneygate Road, Leicester,
Leicestershire LE2 2BN
Age Range: 3–18

LEICESTER MONTESSORI SCHOOL

●🏠▲

194 London Road, Leicester,
Leicestershire LE1 1ND
W: www.montessorigroup.com

LOUGHBOROUGH GRAMMAR SCHOOL

●🏠▲

Burton Walks, Loughborough,
Leicestershire LE11 2DU
W: www.lesgrammar.org
Age Range: 10–18

LOUGHBOROUGH HIGH SCHOOL

●🏠▲

Burton Walks, Loughborough,
Leicestershire LE11 2DU
W: www.leshigh.org
Age Range: 11–18

MANOR HOUSE SCHOOL

●🏠

South Street, Ashby-de-la-Zouch,
Leicestershire LE65 1BR
W: www.manorhouseashby.co.uk
Age Range: 4–16

OUR LADY'S CONVENT SCHOOL

●🏠◆▲

Gray Street, Loughborough,
Leicestershire LE11 2DZ
W: www.olcs.leics.sch.uk
Age Range: 3–18

RATCLIFFE COLLEGE

●🏠▲

Fosse Way, Leicester,
Leicestershire LE7 4SG
W: www.ratcliffe-college.co.uk
Age Range: 3–18

ST CRISPIN'S SCHOOL

●🏠◆

6 St Mary's Road, Leicester,
Leicestershire LE2 1XA
W: members.aol.com/bharrild/
stcrispins
Age Range: 3–16

INDEPENDENT SIXTH FORM COLLEGE / TUTORIAL COLLEGE

BROOKE HOUSE COLLEGE*

●🏠▲

12 Leicester Road, Market
Harborough, Leicestershire
LE16 7AU
W: www.brookehouse.com
Age Range: 14–20

LINCOLNSHIRE

PREPARATORY

AYSCOUGHFEE HALL SCHOOL

●🏠

Welland Hall, Spalding,
Lincolnshire PE11 2TE
W: www.ahs.me.uk
Age Range: 3–11

BICKER PREPARATORY SCHOOL

●🏠

School Lane, Boston, Lincolnshire
PE20 3DW
W: www.bickerprep.co.uk
Age Range: 3–11

COPTHILL SCHOOL

●🏠

Barnack Road, Stamford,
Lincolnshire PE9 4TD
W: www.copthill.com
Age Range: 2–11

DUDLEY HOUSE SCHOOL

●🏠

1 Dudley Road, Grantham,
Lincolnshire NG31 9AA
W: www.dudleyhouseschool.
co.uk
Age Range: 3–11 (All faiths
welcome)

EXCELL INTERNATIONAL SCHOOL

●🏠

Tunnard Street, Boston,
Lincolnshire PE21 6PL
W: www.xl1884.co.uk
Age Range: 2–11

THE GRANTHAM PREPARATORY SCHOOL

●🏠

Gorse Lane, Grantham,
Lincolnshire NG31 7UF
W: www.tgps.co.uk
Age Range: 3–11

GREENWICH HOUSE INDEPENDENT SCHOOL

106 High Holme Road, Louth, Lincolnshire LN11 0HE

HANDEL HOUSE PREPARATORY SCHOOL

Northolme, Gainsborough, Lincolnshire DN21 2JB
Age Range: 2–11

ST HUGH'S SCHOOL

Cromwell Avenue, Woodhall Spa, Lincolnshire LN10 6TQ
W: www.st-hughs.lincs.sch.uk
Age Range: 2–13

ST MARY'S PREPARATORY SCHOOL

5 Pottergate, Lincoln, Lincolnshire LN2 1PH
W: www.stmarysprep.co.uk
Age Range: 2–11

STAMFORD JUNIOR SCHOOL

Stamford, Lincolnshire PE9 2LR
W: www.ses.lincs.sch.uk
Age Range: 2–11

VIKING SCHOOL

140 Church Road North, Skegness, Lincolnshire PE25 2QJ
Age Range: 2–11

WITHAM HALL

Witham-on-the-Hill, Bourne, Lincolnshire PE10 0JJ
W: www.withamhall.com
Age Range: 4–13

SENIOR

KING EDWARD VI SCHOOL

Edwards Street, Louth, Lincolnshire LN11 9LL
W: www.kevigs.lincs.sch.uk
Age Range: 14–18

KIRKSTONE HOUSE SCHOOL

Main Street, Bourne, Lincolnshire PE6 9PA
W: www.kirkstonehouseschool.co.uk
Age Range: 4–16

LOCKSLEY CHRISTIAN SCHOOL

Bilney Block, Manby, Lincolnshire LN11 8UT
W: www.locksley.org
Age Range: 3–19

MAYPOLE HOUSE SCHOOL

Alford, Lincolnshire LN13 0ET
W: www.maypolehouseschool.co.uk
Age Range: 3–16

STAMFORD HIGH SCHOOL

St Martin's, Stamford, Lincolnshire PE9 2LL
W: www.ses.lincs.sch.uk
Age Range: 11–18

STAMFORD SCHOOL

Southfield's House, Stamford, Lincolnshire PE9 2BQ
W: www.ses.lincs.sch.uk
Age Range: 11–18

NORTH EAST LINCOLNSHIRE

PREPARATORY

ST MARTIN'S PREPARATORY SCHOOL

63 Bargate, Grimsby, North East Lincolnshire DN34 5AA
W: www.stmartinsprep.com
Age Range: 3–11

SENIOR

ST JAMES' SCHOOL

22 Bargate, Grimsby, North East Lincolnshire DN34 4SY
W: www.saintjamesschool.co.uk
Age Range: 2–18

NORTH LINCOLNSHIRE

PREPARATORY

TRENTVALE PREPARATORY SCHOOL

Trentside, Keadby, North
Lincolnshire DN17 3EF
W: www.trentvaleprep.co.uk
Age Range: 4–11

LONDON

West

NURSERY AND PRE-PREP

CHEPSTOW HOUSE SCHOOL

19 Pembridge Villas, London
W11 3EP
Age Range: 3–7

FULHAM PREP SCHOOL (PRE-PREP)

47A Fulham High Street, London
SW6 3JJ
W: www.fulhamprep.co.uk
Age Range: 4–7

GREAT BEGINNINGS MONTESSORI SCHOOL

39 Brendon Street, London
W1H 5JE
Age Range: 2–6

HOLLAND PARK PRE-PREPARATORY SCHOOL

5 & 9 Holland Road, London
W14 8HJ
W: www.hpps.co.uk

L'ECOLE DES PETITS

2 Hazlebury Road, London
SW6 2NB
W: www.lecoledespetits.co.uk
Age Range: 2–6 (Bilingual)

LE HERISSON

c/o The Methodist Church, London
W6 9JT
W: www.leherissonschool.co.uk
Age Range: 2–6

PAINT POTS MONTESSORI SCHOOL BAYSWATER

Bayswater United Reformed
Church, London W2 5LS
W: www.paint-pots.co.uk
Age Range: 2–5

PAINT POTS MONTESSORI SCHOOL CHELSEA

Chelsea Community Church,
London SW10 0LB
W: www.paint-pots.co.uk
Age Range: 2–5

PAINT POTS MONTESSORI SCHOOL HYDE PARK

St John's Parish Hall, Hyde Park
Crescent, London W2 2QD
W: www.paint-pots.co.uk
Age Range: 2–5

PICASSO HOUSE MONTESSORI SCHOOL IN CHELSEA

Chelsea Community Church,
London SW10 0LB
W: www.paint-pots.co.uk
Age Range: 2–8

RAVENSTONE DAY NURSERY AND NURSERY SCHOOL

St George's Fields, London
W2 2AX
W: www.ravenstoneschoolslondon.
com

THOMAS'S KINDERGARTEN

14 Ranelagh Grove, London
SW1W 8PD
Age Range: 2–4

PREPARATORY

AL-MUNTADA ISLAMIC SCHOOL

●🏠

7 Bridges Place, London
SW6 4HW
Age Range: 4–11

ASTON HOUSE SCHOOL

●🏠

1 Aston Road, London W5 2RL
W: www.happychild.co.uk
Age Range: 2–11

AVENUE HOUSE SCHOOL

●🏠

70 The Avenue, London W13 8LS
W: www.avenuehouse.org
Age Range: 3–11

BASSETT HOUSE SCHOOL*

●

60 Bassett Road, London W10 6JP
W: www.bassetths.org.uk
Age Range: 3–11

BUTE HOUSE PREPARATORY SCHOOL FOR GIRLS

●🏠

Luxemburg Gardens, London
W6 7EA
W: www.butehouse.co.uk
Age Range: 4–11

CAMERON HOUSE SCHOOL*

●🏠◆

4 The Vale, Chelsea, London
SW3 6AH
W: www.cameronhouseschool.org
Age Range: 4–11

CHISWICK AND BEDFORD PARK PREPARATORY SCHOOL

●🏠

Priory House, London W4 1TX
W: www.cbppschool.co.uk
Age Range: 4–11

CLIFTON LODGE PREPARATORY SCHOOL

●🏠

8 Mattock Lane, London W5 5BG
W: www.cliftonlodgeschool.co.uk
Age Range: 4–13

CONNAUGHT HOUSE

●🏠

47 Connaught Square, London
W2 2HL
W: www.connaughthouseschool.
co.uk
Age Range: 4–11

DURSTON HOUSE

●🏠

12–14 & 26 Castlebar Road,
London W5 2DR
W: www.durstonhouse.org
Age Range: 4–13

EATON HOUSE BELGRAVIA

●🏠

3 -5 Eaton Gate, London
SW1W 9BA
W: www.eatonhouseschools.com
Age Range: 4–8

EATON HOUSE THE VALE

●🏠

2 Elvaston Place, London
SW7 5QH
W: www.eatonhouseschools.com
Age Range: 4–11

EATON SQUARE SCHOOL

●🏠

79 Eccleston Square, London
SW1V 1PP
Age Range: 2–13

ECOLE FRANCAISE JACQUES PREVERT

●🏠

59 Brook Green, London W6 7BE
W: www.ecoleprevert.org.uk
Age Range: 4–11

ERIDGE HOUSE PREPARATORY

●🏠

1 Fulham Park Road, London
SW6 4LJ
W: www.eridgehouse.co.uk
Age Range: 3–11

THE FALCONS SCHOOL FOR BOYS

●🏠

2 Burnaby Gardens, London
W4 3DT
W: www.falconschool.com
Age Range: 3–8

THE FALCONS SCHOOL FOR GIRLS*

●🏠

15 Gunnersbury Avenue, Ealing,
London W5 3XD
W: www.falconschool.com
Age Range: 3–11

FALKNER HOUSE

●🏠

19 Brechin Place, London
SW7 4QB
W: www.falknerhouse.co.uk
Age Range: 3–11 (Co-ed 3–4)

FULHAM PREP SCHOOL*

●🏠

Prep Department, 200 Greyhound
Road, London W14 9SD
W: www.fulhamprep.co.uk
Age Range: 4–13

GARDEN HOUSE SCHOOL

●🏠

Turks Row, London SW3 4TW
W: www.gardenhouseschool.
co.uk
Age Range: 3–11 (Co-ed nursery)

GEMS HAMPSHIRE SCHOOL

●🏠

Main School, London SW3 6NB
W: www.ths.westminster.sch.uk
Age Range: 3–13

GLENDOWER PREPARATORY SCHOOL*

●🏠

86/87 Queen's Gate, South
Kensington, London SW7 5JX
W: www.glendowerprep.org
Age Range: 4–11

HAWKESDOWN HOUSE SCHOOL

●🏠

27 Edge Street, London W8 7PN
W: www.hawkesdown.co.uk
Age Range: 3–8

HEATHFIELD HOUSE SCHOOL

●🏠

Turnham Green Church Hall,
London W4 4JU
W: www.heathfieldhouse.co.uk
Age Range: 4–11

England – London – West

HILL HOUSE INTERNATIONAL JUNIOR SCHOOL

17 Hans Place, London SW1X 0EP
W: www.hillhouseschool.co.uk
Age Range: 4–13

KENSINGTON PREP SCHOOL

596 Fulham Road, London
SW6 5PA
W: www.gdst.net/kensingtonprep
Age Range: 4–11

KNIGHTSBRIDGE SCHOOL

67 Pont Street, London SW1X 0BD
W: www.knightsbridgeschool.com
Age Range: 3–13 (Nursery Class
for Siblings only–other entry from 4
(Reception class upwards))

LATYMER PREP SCHOOL

36 Upper Mall, London W6 9TA
W: www.latymerprep.org
Age Range: 7–11

THE LLOYD WILLIAMSON SCHOOL

12 Telford Road, London W10 5SH
W: www.lloydwilliamsonschools.
co.uk

NORLAND PLACE SCHOOL

162–166 Holland Park Avenue,
London W11 4UH
W: www.norlandplace.com
Age Range: 4–11

NOTTING HILL PREPARATORY SCHOOL

95 Lancaster Road, London
W11 1QQ
W: www.nottinghillprep.com
Age Range: 4–13

ORCHARD HOUSE SCHOOL*

16 Newton Grove, Bedford Park,
London W4 1LB
W: www.orchardhs.org.uk
Age Range: 3–11

PEMBRIDGE HALL

18 Pembridge Square, London
W2 4EH
W: www.pembridgehall.co.uk
Age Range: 4–11

QUEEN'S COLLEGE PREP SCHOOL

61 Portland Place, London
W1B 1QP
W: www.qcps.org.uk
Age Range: 4–11

RAVENSCOURT PARK PREPARATORY SCHOOL*

16 Ravenscourt Avenue,
Hammersmith, London W6 0SL
W: www.rpps.co.uk
Age Range: 4–11

REDCLIFFE SCHOOL*

47 Redcliffe Gardens, London
SW10 9JH
W: www.redcliffeschool.com
Age Range: 2–11

ST BENEDICT'S JUNIOR SCHOOL

5 Montpelier Avenue, London
W5 2XP
W: www.stbenedictsealing.org.uk
Age Range: 3–11

ST JAMES JUNIOR SCHOOL

Earsby Street, London W14 8SH
W: www.stjamesjuniors.co.uk
Age Range: 4–11

ST PHILIP'S SCHOOL

6 Wetherby Place, London
SW7 4ND
W: www.stphilipschool.co.uk
Age Range: 7–13

SINCLAIR HOUSE SCHOOL

159 Munster Road, London
SW6 6AD
W: www.sinclairhouseschool.
co.uk
Age Range: 2–8

SUSSEX HOUSE SCHOOL

68 Cadogan Square, London
SW1X 0EA
Age Range: 8–13

THOMAS'S FULHAM

Hugon Road, London SW6 3ES
W: www.thomas-s.co.uk
Age Range: 4–11

THOMAS'S PREPARATORY SCHOOL

17–19 Cottesmore Gardens,
London W8 5PR
W: www.thomas-s.co.uk
Age Range: 4–11

WESTMINSTER ABBEY CHOIR SCHOOL

Dean's Yard, London SW1P 3NY
W: www.westminster-abbey.org
Age Range: 8–13

WESTMINSTER CATHEDRAL CHOIR SCHOOL

Ambrosden Avenue, London
SW1P 1QH
W: www.choirschool.com
Age Range: 7–13

WESTMINSTER UNDER SCHOOL

Adrian House, London SW1P 2NN
W: www.westminsterunder.org.uk
Age Range: 7–13

WETHERBY PREPARATORY SCHOOL

48 Bryanstan Square, London
W1H 2EA
W: www.wetherbyprep.co.uk
Age Range: 8–13

WETHERBY SCHOOL

11 Pembridge Square, London
W2 4ED
W: www.alphaplusgroup.co.uk
Age Range: 4–8

SENIOR

ARTS EDUCATIONAL SCHOOLS LONDON*

Cone Ripman House, 14 Bath Road, Chiswick, London W4 1LY
W: www.artsed.co.uk
Age Range: 11–16

ASHBOURNE MIDDLE SCHOOL

17 Old Court Place, London W8 4PL
W: www.ashbournecollege.co.uk
Age Range: 12–16

BARBARA SPEAKE STAGE SCHOOL

East Acton Lane, London W3 7EG
W: www.barbaraspeake.com
Age Range: 3–16

EALING COLLEGE UPPER SCHOOL

83 The Avenue, London W13 8JS
Age Range: 11–18 (Co-ed VIth Form)

FRANCIS HOLLAND SCHOOL, SLOANE SQUARE SW1*

39 Graham Terrace, London SW1W 8JF
W: www.fhs-sw1.org.uk
Age Range: 4–18

THE GODOLPHIN AND LATYMER SCHOOL

Iffley Road, London W6 0PG
W: www.godolphinandlatymer.com
Age Range: 11–18

HARVINGTON SCHOOL

20 Castlebar Road, London W5 2DS
W: harvingtonschool.com
Age Range: 3–16 (Boys 3–5)

INSTITUTO ESPANOL VICENTE CANADA BLANCH

317 Portobello Road, London W10 5SY
Age Range: 4–19

JAMAHIRIYA SCHOOL

Glebe Place, London SW3 5JP
Age Range: 5–17

THE JAPANESE SCHOOL

87 Creffield Road, London W3 9PU
W: www.thejapaneseschool.ltd.uk
Age Range: 6–15

KING FAHAD ACADEMY

Bromyard Avenue, London W3 7HD
W: www.thekfa.org.uk
Age Range: 5–18

LATYMER UPPER SCHOOL*

King Street, Hammersmith, London W6 9LR
W: www.latymer-upper.org
Age Range: 11–18

LYCEE FRANCAIS CHARLES DE GAULLE

35 Cromwell Road, London SW7 2DG
W: www.lyceefrancais.org.uk
Age Range: 4–19

MANDER PORTMAN WOODWARD

90–92 Queen's Gate, London SW7 5AB
W: www.mpw.co.uk
Age Range: 14–19

NOTTING HILL AND EALING HIGH SCHOOL GDST

2 Cleveland Road, London W13 8AX
W: www.gdst.net/nhehs
Age Range: 4–18

PORTLAND PLACE SCHOOL

56–58 Portland Place, London W1B 1NJ
W: www.portland-place.co.uk
Age Range: 10–18

QUEEN'S GATE SCHOOL*

133 Queen's Gate, London SW7 5LE
W: www.queensgate.org.uk
Age Range: 4–18

ST AUGUSTINE'S PRIORY

Hillcrest Road, Ealing, London W5 2JL
W: www.saintaugustinespriory.org.uk
Age Range: 4–18

ST BENEDICT'S SCHOOL*

54 Eaton Rise, Ealing, London W5 2ES
W: www.stbenedicts.org.uk
Age Range: 3–18

ST JAMES SENIOR GIRLS' SCHOOL

Earsby Street, London W14 8SH
W: www.stjamesgirls.co.uk
Age Range: 10–18

ST PAUL'S GIRLS' SCHOOL

Brook Green, London W6 7BS
W: www.spgs.org
Age Range: 11–18

SOUTHBANK INTERNATIONAL SCHOOL, WESTMINSTER

63–65 Portland Place, London W1B 1QR
W: www.southbank.org
Age Range: 11–18

TABERNACLE SCHOOL

32 St Ann's Villas, London W11 4RS
Age Range: 3–16

England – London – West

THE WALMER ROAD SCHOOL

221 Walmer Road, London W11 4EY
W: www.rugbyportobello.org.uk
Age Range: 14–16

WESTMINSTER SCHOOL*

17 Dean's Yard, Westminster, London SW1P 3PB
W: www.westminster.org.uk
Age Range: 13–18

INDEPENDENT SIXTH FORM COLLEGE / TUTORIAL COLLEGE

ABBEY COLLEGE

22 Grosvenor Gardens, London SW1W 0DH
W: www.abbeycolleges.co.uk

ALBEMARLE INDEPENDENT COLLEGE

18 Dunraven Street, London W1K 7FE
W: www.albemarle.org.uk
Age Range: 14–21

ARTS EDUCATIONAL SCHOOLS LONDON – SIXTH FORM*

Cone Ripman House, 14 Bath Road, Chiswick, London W4 1LY
W: www.artsed.co.uk
Age Range: 16–18

BALES COLLEGE

742 Harrow Road, London W10 4AA
W: www.balescollege.co.uk
Age Range: 11–19

CHELSEA INDEPENDENT COLLEGE*

517–523 Fulham Road, London SW6 1HD
W: www.cic.ac
Age Range: 14–19

COLLINGHAM INDEPENDENT GCSE AND SIXTH FORM COLLEGE*

23 Collingham Gardens, London SW5 0HL
W: www.collingham.co.uk
Age Range: 14–20

DAVID GAME COLLEGE

69 Notting Hill Gate, London W11 3JS
W: www.davidgame-group.com
Age Range: 15–19

DLD COLLEGE (DAVIES LAING AND DICK)*

100 Marylebone Lane, London W1U 2QB
W: www.dldcollege.org
Age Range: 14–24[†]

DUFF MILLER

59 Queen's Gate, London SW7 5JP
W: www.duffmiller.com
Age Range: 14–19

EALING INDEPENDENT COLLEGE

83 New Broadway, Ealing, London W5 5AL
W: www.ealingindependentcollege.com
Age Range: 13–20

LANSDOWNE COLLEGE

40–44 Bark Place, London W2 4AT
W: www.lansdownecollege.com
Age Range: 14–19 (Lansdowne is an independent Sixth Form College with a GCSE Department from Year 10.)

MANDER PORTMAN WOODWARD

90–92 Queen's Gate, London SW7 5AB
W: www.mpw.co.uk
Age Range: 14–19

WESTMINSTER TUTORS*

86 Old Brompton Road, London SW7 3LQ
W: www.westminstertutors.co.uk
Age Range: 11–25

INTERNATIONAL SCHOOLS AND INTERNATIONAL STUDY CENTRES

INTERNATIONAL SCHOOL OF LONDON*

139 Gunnersbury Avenue, London W3 8LG
W: www.ISLondon.com
Age Range: 3–19

SOUTHBANK INTERNATIONAL SCHOOL, KENSINGTON

36–38 Kensington Park Road, London W11 3BU
W: www.southbank.org
Age Range: 3–11

North West London

NURSERY AND PRE-PREP

BROADHURST SCHOOL

●🏠
19 Greencroft Gardens, London
NW6 3LP
W: www.broadhurstschool.com
Age Range: 2–5

HAMPSTEAD HILL PRE-PREPARATORY & NURSERY SCHOOL

●🏠
St Stephen's Hall, London
NW3 2PP
W: www.hampsteadhillschool.
co.uk
Age Range: 2–8

NORTH BRIDGE HOUSE NURSERY SCHOOL

●🏠
33 Fitzjohn's Avenue, London
NW3 5JY
W: www.northbridgehouse.com
Age Range: 3–6

ST JOHNS WOOD PRE-PREPARATORY SCHOOL

●🏠
St Johns Hall, London NW8 7NE
W: www.sjwpre-prep.org.uk
Age Range: 3–7

PREPARATORY

ABERCORN SCHOOL

●🏠
28 Abercorn Place, London
NW8 9XP
W: www.abercornschool.com
Age Range: 2–13

THE ACADEMY SCHOOL

●🏠
2 Pilgrims Place, Hampstead,
London NW3 1NG
Age Range: 6–12

ARNOLD HOUSE SCHOOL

●🏠
1 Loudoun Road, London
NW8 0LH
W: www.arnoldhouse.co.uk
Age Range: 5–13

BELMONT (MILL HILL PREPARATORY SCHOOL)

●🏠
The Ridgeway, London NW7 4ED
W: www.belmontschool.com
Age Range: 7–13 (7–13)

THE CAVENDISH SCHOOL*

●🏠
31 Inverness Street, London
NW1 7HB
W: www.cavendishschool.co.uk
Age Range: 3–11

DEVONSHIRE HOUSE PREPARATORY SCHOOL*

●🏠
2 Arkwright Road, Hampstead,
London NW3 6AE
W: www.devonshirehouseschool.
co.uk
Age Range: 2^1/$_2$–13

GOLDERS HILL SCHOOL

●🏠
666 Finchley Road, London
NW11 7NT
Age Range: 2–7

GOODWYN SCHOOL

●🏠
Hammers Lane, London NW7 4DB
W: www.goodwyn-school.co.uk
Age Range: 3–11

GOWER HOUSE SCHOOL

●🏠
Blackbird Hill, London NW9 8RR
W: www.gowerhouseschool.co.uk
Age Range: 2–11

THE HALL SCHOOL

●🏠
23 Crossfield Road, London
NW3 4NU
W: www.hallschool.co.uk
Age Range: 4–13

HEATHSIDE PREPARATORY SCHOOL

●🏠
16 New End, Hampstead, London
NW3 1JA
W: www.heathside.net
Age Range: 3–11

HENDON PREPARATORY SCHOOL

●🏠
20 Tenterden Grove, Hendon,
London NW4 1TD
W: www.hendonprep.co.uk
Age Range: 2–13

HEREWARD HOUSE SCHOOL

●🏠
14 Strathray Gardens, London
NW3 4NY
W: www.herewardhouse.co.uk
Age Range: 4–13

L'ILE AUX ENFANTS

●🏠
22 Vicar's Road, London NW5 4NL
W: www.ileauxenfants.co.uk
Age Range: 3–11

LYNDHURST HOUSE PREPARATORY SCHOOL*

●🏠
24 Lyndhurst Gardens,
Hampstead, London NW3 5NW
W: www.lyndhursthouse.co.uk
Age Range: 4–13

MAPLE WALK SCHOOL

●
62A Crownhill Road, London
NW10 4EB
W: www.newmodelschool.co.uk
Age Range: 4–11

MARIA MONTESSORI SCHOOL HAMPSTEAD

●🏠
26 Lyndhurst Gardens, London
NW3 5NW
W: www.mariamontessorischools.
co.uk
Age Range: 2–11

THE MULBERRY HOUSE SCHOOL*

7 Minster Road, West Hampstead, London NW2 3SD
W: www.mulberryhouseschool. com
Age Range: 2–8

NAIMA JEWISH PREPARATORY SCHOOL

21 Andover Place, London NW6 5ED
W: www.naimajps.co.uk
Age Range: 3–11

NORTH BRIDGE HOUSE JUNIOR SCHOOL

8 Netherhall Gardens, London NW3 5RR
W: www.northbridgehouse.com
Age Range: 6–8

NORTH BRIDGE HOUSE LOWER PREP SCHOOL

1 Gloucester Avenue, London NW1 7AB
W: www.northbridgehouse.com
Age Range: 8–11

NORTH BRIDGE HOUSE UPPER PREP SCHOOL

1 Gloucester Avenue, London NW1 7AB
W: www.northbridgehouse.com
Age Range: 10–13

OYH PRIMARY SCHOOL

Finchley Lane, London NW4 1DJ
Age Range: 3–11

THE PHOENIX SCHOOL

36 College Crescent, London NW3 5LF
W: www.ucs.org.uk
Age Range: 3–7

RAINBOW MONTESSORI JUNIOR SCHOOL

13 Woodchurch Road, London NW6 3PL
W: www.rainbowmontessori.co.uk
Age Range: 5–12

ST ANTHONY'S PREPARATORY SCHOOL

90 Fitzjohns Avenue, London NW3 6NP
W: www.stanthonysprep.org.uk
Age Range: 5–13

ST CHRISTINA'S RC PREPARATORY SCHOOL

25 St Edmunds Terrace, London NW8 7PY
W: www.saintchristinas.org.uk
Age Range: 3–11 (Boys 3–7)

ST CHRISTOPHER'S SCHOOL

32 Belsize Lane, London NW3 5AE
W: www.st-christophers.hampstead. sch.uk
Age Range: 4–11

ST MARTIN'S

22 Goodwyn Avenue, London NW7 3RG
W: www.stmartinsmillhill.co.uk
Age Range: 3–11

ST MARY'S SCHOOL HAMPSTEAD

47 Fitzjohn's Avenue, London NW3 6PG
W: www.stmh.co.uk
Age Range: 2–11 (Boys 2–7)

ST NICHOLAS SCHOOL

22 Salmon Street, London NW9 8PN
W: www.happychild.co.uk
Age Range: 2–11

SARUM HALL

15 Eton Avenue, London NW3 3EL
W: www.sarumhallschool.co.uk
Age Range: 3–11

SOUTHBANK INTERNATIONAL SCHOOL, HAMPSTEAD

16 Netherhall Gardens, London NW3 5TH
W: www.southbank.org
Age Range: 3–11

TREVOR ROBERTS SCHOOL

57 Eton Avenue, London NW3 3ET
Age Range: 5–13

UNIVERSITY COLLEGE SCHOOL JUNIOR BRANCH

11 Holly Hill, London NW3 6QN
W: www.ucs.org.uk
Age Range: 7–11

THE VILLAGE SCHOOL

2 Parkhill Road, London NW3 2YN
W: www.thevillageschool.co.uk
Age Range: 3–11

WELSH SCHOOL OF LONDON

Welsh School of London, London NW10 8NG
W: www.llundain.freeserve.co.uk
Age Range: 3–11

SENIOR

AL-SADIQ AND AL-ZAHRA SCHOOLS

134 Salusbury Road, London NW6 6PF
W: www.al-sadiqal-zahraschools. co.uk
Age Range: 4–16

BEIS HAMEDRASH ELYON

211 Golders Green Rd, London NW11 9BY
Age Range: 11–14

BETH JACOB GRAMMAR FOR GIRLS

Stratford Road, London NW4 2AT
Age Range: 10–16

BRONDESBURY COLLEGE FOR BOYS

8 Brondesbury Park, London NW6 7BT
W: www.bcbcollege.com
Age Range: 11–16

FINE ARTS COLLEGE*

24 Lambolle Place, Hampstead,
London NW3 4PG
W: www.hampsteadfinearts.com
Age Range: 14–19

FRANCIS HOLLAND SCHOOL, REGENT'S PARK NW1*

Clarence Gate, Ivor Place, London
NW1 6XR
W: www.francisholland.org.uk
Age Range: 11–18

ISLAMIA GIRLS' SCHOOL

129 Salusbury Road, London
NW6 6PE
W: www.islamiagirlsschool.com
Age Range: 11–16

THE KING ALFRED SCHOOL

149 North End Road, London
NW11 7HY
W: www.kingalfred.org.uk
Age Range: 4–18

LONDON JEWISH GIRLS' HIGH SCHOOL

18 Raleigh Close, London
NW4 2TA
Age Range: 11–16

MILL HILL SCHOOL

The Ridgeway, London NW7 1QS
W: www.millhill.org.uk
Age Range: 13–18

THE MOUNT SCHOOL

Milespit Hill, London NW7 2RX
W: www.mountschool.com
Age Range: 4–18

NORTH BRIDGE HOUSE SENIOR SCHOOL*

1 Gloucester Avenue, London
NW1 7AB
W: www.northbridgehouse.com;
www.nbhseniorschool.co.uk
Age Range: 2^1/$_2$–16

THE ROYAL SCHOOL, HAMPSTEAD

65 Rosslyn Hill, London NW3 5UD
W: www.royalschoolhampstead.
net
Age Range: 3–16

ST MARGARET'S SCHOOL

18 Kidderpore Gardens, London
NW3 7SR
W: www.st-margarets.co.uk
Age Range: 4–16

SOUTH HAMPSTEAD HIGH SCHOOL

3 Maresfield Gardens, London
NW3 5SS
W: www.shhs.gdst.net
Age Range: 4–18

SYLVIA YOUNG THEATRE SCHOOL

Rossmore Road, London NW1 6NJ
W: www.sylviayoungtheatreschool.
co.uk
Age Range: 10–16

UNIVERSITY COLLEGE SCHOOL

Frognal, London NW3 6XH
W: www.ucs.org.uk
Age Range: 11–18 (Boys aged
11–18
Girls aged 16–18 (Co-educational
Sixth Form only))

INDEPENDENT SIXTH FORM COLLEGE / TUTORIAL COLLEGE

BRAMPTON COLLEGE

Lodge House, London NW4 4DQ
W: www.bramptoncollege.com
Age Range: 15–19

INTERNATIONAL SCHOOLS AND INTERNATIONAL STUDY CENTRES

THE AMERICAN SCHOOL IN LONDON*

1 Waverley Place, London
NW8 0NP
W: www.asl.org
Age Range: 4–18

INTERNATIONAL COMMUNITY SCHOOL*

ICS Primary School: 4 York
Terrace East, Regent's Park,
London NW1 4PT
ICS Secondary School: 21 Star
Street, London W2 1QB
W: www.icschool.co.uk
Age Range: 3–19

North London

NURSERY AND PRE-PREP

ANNEMOUNT SCHOOL

18 Holne Chase, London N2 0QN
W: www.annemount.co.uk
Age Range: 3–7 (Pupils are admitted from 2 years 9 months.)

THE MONTESSORI HOUSE

5 Princes Avenue, London N10 3LS
W: www.montessori-house.co.uk
Age Range: 1–5

PREPARATORY

CHANNING JUNIOR SCHOOL

Fairseat, London N6 5JR
W: www.channing.co.uk
Age Range: 4–11

EXCEL PREPARATORY SCHOOL

The Annex, Selby Centre, London N17 8JL
Age Range: 2–12

EXCELSIOR COLLEGE

Selby Centre, London N17 8JN
W: www.excelsiorcollege.co.uk
Age Range: 3–11

GRANGE PARK PREPARATORY SCHOOL

13 The Chine, London N21 2EA
W: www.gpps.org.uk
Age Range: 4–11

HOLLY PARK MONTESSORI SCHOOL

The Holly Park, London N4 4BY
W: www.mariamontessorischools.co.uk
Age Range: 2–7

ISLAMIC SHAKHSIYAH FOUNDATION

1st Floor {Suffolk Road Entrance}, London N15 5RG
Age Range: 5–11

KEBLE PREPARATORY SCHOOL

Wades Hill, London N21 1BG
W: www.kebleprep.co.uk
Age Range: 4–13

KEREM SCHOOL

London N2 0RE
W: www.kerem.org.uk
Age Range: 4–11

NORFOLK HOUSE SCHOOL

10 Muswell Avenue, London N10 2EG
W: www.norfolkhouseschool.org
Age Range: 4–11

PARKSIDE PREPARATORY SCHOOL

Church Lane, London N17 7AA
Age Range: 3–11

PRIMROSE INDEPENDENT SCHOOL

Congregational Church, London N5 2TE
Age Range: 2–11

SALCOMBE PREPARATORY SCHOOL

224–226 Chase Side, London N14 4PL
W: www.salcombeprep.co.uk
Age Range: 4–11

TALMUD TORAH BOBOV PRIMARY SCHOOL

87 Egerton Road, London N16 6UE
Age Range: 2–13

VITA ET PAX PREPARATORY SCHOOL

6A Priory Close, London N14 4AT
W: www.vitaetpax.co.uk
Age Range: 3–11

YETEV LEV DAY SCHOOL FOR BOYS

111–115 Cazenove Road, London N16 6AX
Age Range: 3–11

SENIOR

BEIS CHINUCH LEBANOS GIRLS SCHOOL

Woodberry Down Centre, London N4 2SH
Age Range: 2–16

BEIS ROCHEL D'SATMAR GIRLS SCHOOL

51–57 Amhurst Park, London N16 5DL
Age Range: 2–17

CHANNING SCHOOL*

Highgate, London N6 5HF
W: www.channing.co.uk
Age Range: 4–18

HIGHGATE SCHOOL

North Road, London N6 4AY
W: www.highgateschool.org.uk
Age Range: 3–18

LUBAVITCH HOUSE SENIOR SCHOOL FOR GIRLS

107–115 Stamford Hill, London N16 5RP
W: lubavitchseniorgirls.com
Age Range: 11–18

MECHINAH LIYESHIVAH ZICHRON MOSHE

86 Amhurst Park, London N16 5AR
Age Range: 11–16

PALMERS GREEN HIGH SCHOOL

104 Hoppers Road, London
N21 3LJ
W: www.pghs.co.uk
Age Range: 3–16

PARDES GRAMMAR BOYS' SCHOOL

Hendon Lane, London N3 1SA
Age Range: 11–17

TAWHID BOYS SCHOOL, TAWHID EDUCATIONAL TRUST

21 Cazenove Road, London
N16 6PA
Age Range: 9–16

TAYYIBAH GIRLS SCHOOL

88 Filey Avenue, London N16 6JJ
Age Range: 5–18

YESODEY HATORAH JEWISH SCHOOL

2–4 Amhurst Park, London
N16 5AE
Age Range: 3–16

INTERNATIONAL SCHOOLS AND INTERNATIONAL STUDY CENTRES

THE NORTH LONDON INTERNATIONAL SCHOOL*

6 Friern Barnet Lane, London
N11 3LX
W: www.nlis.org
Age Range: 2–19†

London City

PREPARATORY

CHARTERHOUSE SQUARE SCHOOL

40 Charterhouse Square, London
EC1M 6EA
W: www.
charterhousesquareschool.co.uk
Age Range: 3–11

DALLINGTON SCHOOL

8 Dallington Street, London
EC1V 0BW
W: www.dallingtonschool.co.uk
Age Range: 3–11

THE LYCEUM

6 Paul Street, London EC2A 4JH
W: www.lyceumschool.org
Age Range: 3–11

ST PAUL'S CATHEDRAL SCHOOL*

2 New Change, London EC4M 9AD
W: www.spcs.london.sch.uk
Age Range: 4–13

SENIOR

CITY OF LONDON SCHOOL FOR GIRLS

St Giles' Terrace, London
EC2Y 8BB
W: www.clsg.org.uk
Age Range: 7–18

CITY OF LONDON SCHOOL*

Queen Victoria Street, London
EC4V 3AL
W: www.clsb.org.uk
Age Range: 10–18

THE ITALIA CONTI ACADEMY OF THEATRE ARTS

23 Goswell Road, London
EC1M 7AJ
W: www.italiaconti-acting.co.uk
Age Range: 9–21

ROYAL BALLET SCHOOL

46 Floral Street, London
WC2E 9DA
W: www.royal-ballet-school.org.uk
Age Range: 11–18

THE URDANG ACADEMY OF BALLET

The Old Finsbury Town Hall,
London EC1R 4RP
W: www.theurdangacademy.com
Age Range: 16–23

INDEPENDENT SIXTH FORM COLLEGE / TUTORIAL COLLEGE

CATS COLLEGE LONDON

43–45 Bloomsbury Square,
London WC1A 2RA
W: www.catscollege.com/london
Age Range: 15–21

East London

PREPARATORY

FARADAY SCHOOL

●

Trinity Buoy Wharf, London
E14 0JW
W: www.newmodelschool.co.uk
Age Range: 4–11

GATEHOUSE SCHOOL*

●🏠

Sewardstone Road, Victoria Park,
London E2 9JG
W: www.gatehouseschool.co.uk
Age Range: 3–11

GRANGEWOOD INDEPENDENT SCHOOL

●🏠

Chester Road, London E7 8QT
W: www.grangewoodschool.com
Age Range: 3–11

GREEN GABLES MONTESSORI PRIMARY SCHOOL

●🏠

The Institute, London E1W 3DH
W: www.greengables.org.uk

HYLAND HOUSE

●🏠

896 Forest Road, London E17 4AE
Age Range: 3–11

JAMIAH MADANIYAH PRIMARY SCHOOL

●🏠

80–82 Stafford Road, London
E7 8NN
Age Range: 3–8

LUBAVITCH HOUSE SCHOOL (JUNIOR BOYS)

●🏠

135 Clapton Common, London
E5 9AE
W: www.lubavitchuk.com
Age Range: 5–13

NOOR UL ISLAM PRIMARY SCHOOL

●🏠

135 Dawlish Road, London
E10 6QW
W: www.noorulislam.co.uk
Age Range: 4–11

PARAGON CHRISTIAN ACADEMY

●🏠

233–241 Glyn Road, London
E5 0JP
Age Range: 3–11

QUWWATT UL ISLAM GIRLS SCHOOL

●🏠

16 Chaucer Road, London E7 9NB
W: www.quwwatulislam.com
Age Range: 4–13

RIVER HOUSE MONTESSORI SCHOOL

●🏠

Unit C Great Eastern Enterprise,
London E14 9XP
W: www.river-house.co.uk
Age Range: 3–11

ST JOSEPH'S CONVENT SCHOOL

●🏠

59 Cambridge Park, London
E11 2PR
Age Range: 3–11

SNARESBROOK COLLEGE PREPARATORY SCHOOL

●🏠

75 Woodford Road, London
E18 2EA
Age Range: 3–11

WALTHAMSTOW MONTESSORI SCHOOL

●🏠

Penryhn Hall, London E17 5DA
W: www.walthamstowmontessori.
com
Age Range: 3–11

SENIOR

AL-MIZAN PRIMARY & LONDON EAST ACADEMY SECONDARY & SIXTH FORM

●🏠▲

82–92 Whitechapel Road, London
E1 1JX
W: www.leacademy.com
Age Range: 7–18

DARUL HADIS LATIFIAH

●🏠▲

1 Cornwall Avenue, London
E2 0HW
Age Range: 11–19

EAST LONDON CHRISTIAN CHOIR SCHOOL

●🏠

St. Mark's Community Halls,
London E8 2NL
W: www.elccs.org.uk
Age Range: 3–16

FOREST SCHOOL*

●🏠▲

College Place, Snaresbrook,
London E17 3PY
W: www.forest.org.uk
Age Range: 4–18

LONDON ISLAMIC SCHOOL

●🏠

18–22 Damien Street, London
E1 2HX
Age Range: 11–16

MADNI GIRLS SCHOOL

●🏠▲

Myrdle Street, London E1 1HL
Age Range: 12–18

NORMANHURST SCHOOL

●🏠

68/74 Station Road, London
E4 7BA
W: www.normanhurstschool.co.uk
Age Range: 3–16

South East London

NURSERY AND PRE-PREP

BLACKHEATH PREPARATORY SCHOOL

●🏠

4 St Germans Place, London SE3 0NJ
W: www.blackheathprepschool.com
Age Range: 3–11

THE VILLA PRE-PREPARATORY SCHOOL

●🏠

54 Lyndhurst Grove, London SE15 5AH
W: www.thevillaschoolandnursery.com
Age Range: 4–7

PREPARATORY

DULWICH COLLEGE PREPARATORY SCHOOL

●🏠

42 Alleyn Park, London SE21 7AA
W: www.dcpslondon.org
Age Range: 3–13 (Girls 3–5)

HEATH HOUSE PREPARATORY SCHOOL

●🏠

37 Wemyss Road, London SE3 0TG
W: www.heathhouseprepschool.com
Age Range: 4–11

HERNE HILL SCHOOL

●🏠

The Old Vicarage, London SE24 9LY
W: www.hernehillschool.co.uk
Age Range: 3–7

JAMES ALLEN'S PREPARATORY SCHOOL

●🏠

East Dulwich Grove, London SE22 8TE
W: www.jags.org.uk/japs
Age Range: 4–11

OAKFIELD PREPARATORY SCHOOL

●🏠

125–128 Thurlow Park Road, London SE21 8HP
W: www.oakfield.dulwich.sch.uk
Age Range: 2–11

THE POINTER SCHOOL

●🏠

19 Stratheden Road, London SE3 7TH
W: www.pointers-school.co.uk
Age Range: 3–11

ROSEMEAD PREPARATORY SCHOOL

●🏠

70 Thurlow Park Road, London SE21 8HZ
W: www.rosemeadprepschool.org.uk
Age Range: 3–11

ST OLAVE'S PREPARATORY SCHOOL

●🏠

106–110 Southwood Road, London SE9 3QS
W: www.stolaves.org.uk
Age Range: 3–11

SPRINGFIELD CHRISTIAN SCHOOL

●🏠

145 Perry Hill, London SE6 4LP
W: www.springfieldsch.co.uk

THEODORE MCLEARY PRIMARY SCHOOL

●🏠

31 East Dulwich Grove, Clapham, London SE22 8PW
Age Range: 5–10

VIRGO FIDELIS

●🏠

147 Central Hill, London SE19 1RS
Age Range: 3–11

SENIOR

ALLEYN'S SCHOOL

●🏠▲

Townley Road, London SE22 8SU
W: www.alleyns.org.uk
Age Range: 4–18

BLACKHEATH HIGH SCHOOL GDST

●🏠▲

Vanbrugh Park, London SE3 7AG
W: www.blackheathhighschool.gdst.net
Age Range: 3–18

COLFE'S SCHOOL

●🏠▲

Horn Park Lane, London SE12 8AW
W: www.colfes.com
Age Range: 3–18

DULWICH COLLEGE

●🏠▲

Dulwich Common, London SE21 7LD
W: www.dulwich.org.uk
Age Range: 7–18

ELTHAM COLLEGE

●🏠▲

Grove Park Road, London SE9 4QF
W: www.eltham-college.org.uk
Age Range: 7–18

JAMES ALLEN'S GIRLS' SCHOOL

●🏠▲

East Dulwich Grove, London SE22 8TE
W: www.jags.org.uk
Age Range: 4–18

RIVERSTON SCHOOL

●🏠

63–69 Eltham Road, London SE12 8UF
W: www.riverston.greenwich.sch.uk
Age Range: 1–16

ST DUNSTAN'S COLLEGE

Stanstead Road, London SE6 4TY
W: www.stdunstans.org.uk
Age Range: 3–18

SYDENHAM HIGH SCHOOL GDST

19 Westwood Hill, London SE26 6BL
W: www.gdst.net/sydenhamhigh/
Age Range: 4–18

INDEPENDENT SIXTH FORM COLLEGE / TUTORIAL COLLEGE

HOLBORN COLLEGE

Woolwich Road, London SE7 8LN
W: www.holborncollege.ac.uk

South West London

NURSERY AND PRE-PREP

EATON HOUSE THE MANOR PRE-PREPARATORY

58 Clapham Common Northside, London SW4 9RU
W: www.eatonhouseschools.com
Age Range: 4–8

THOMAS'S KINDERGARTEN, BATTERSEA

The Crypt, London SW11 3NA
W: www.thomas-s.co.uk
Age Range: 2–5

PREPARATORY

BALHAM PREPARATORY SCHOOL

47a Balham High Road, London SW12 9AW
Age Range: 3–16

BROOMWOOD HALL SCHOOL

68–74 Nightingale Lane, London SW12 8NR
W: www.broomwood.co.uk
Age Range: 4–13

COLET COURT

St Paul's Preparatory School, London SW13 9JT
W: www.coletcourt.org.uk
Age Range: 7–13

DOLPHIN SCHOOL (INCLUDING NOAH'S ARK NURSERY SCHOOL)*

106 Northcote Road, Battersea, London SW11 6QW
W: www.dolphinschool.org.uk
Age Range: 2–11

THE DOMINIE

55 Warriner Gardens, London SW11 4DX
W: www.thedominie.co.uk
Age Range: 6–12

DONHEAD PREP SCHOOL

33 Edge Hill, London SW19 4NP
W: www.donhead.org.uk
Age Range: 4–11

EATON HOUSE THE MANOR PREPARATORY

58 Clapham Common Northside, London SW4 9RU
W: www.eatonhouseschools.com
Age Range: 3–13

EVELINE DAY SCHOOL

14 Trinity Crescent, London SW17 7AE
W: www.evelinedayschool.com
Age Range: 3–11

FINTON HOUSE SCHOOL

171 Trinity Road, London SW17 7HL
W: www.fintonhouse.org.uk
Age Range: 4–11

HALL SCHOOL WIMBLEDON (JUNIOR SCHOOL)

Stroud Crescent, London SW15 3EQ
W: www.hsw.co.uk
Age Range: 4–11

HORNSBY HOUSE SCHOOL

Hearnville Road, London SW12 8RS
W: www.hornsby-house.co.uk
Age Range: 4–11

THE HURLINGHAM SCHOOL

122 Putney Bridge Road, London SW15 2NQ
W: www.hurlinghamschool.co.uk
Age Range: 4–11

KING'S COLLEGE JUNIOR SCHOOL

Southside, London SW19 4TT
W: www.kcs.org.uk
Age Range: 7–13

LION HOUSE SCHOOL

The Old Methodist Hall, London SW15 6EH
W: www.lionhouseschool.co.uk
Age Range: 3–8

THE MERLIN SCHOOL

4 Carlton Drive, London SW15 2BZ
Age Range: 4–8

NEWTON PREP

149 Battersea Park Road, London SW8 4BX
W: www.newtonprepschool.co.uk
Age Range: 3–13

NORTHCOTE LODGE SCHOOL

26 Bolingbroke Grove, London SW11 6EL
W: www.northcotelodge.co.uk
Age Range: 8–13

PARKGATE HOUSE SCHOOL*

80 Clapham Common North Side, London SW4 9SD
W: www.parkgate-school.co.uk
Age Range: 2–11

PROSPECT HOUSE SCHOOL*

75 Putney Hill, London SW15 3NT
W: www.prospecths.org.uk
Age Range: 3–11

THE ROCHE SCHOOL

11 Frogmore, London SW18 1HW
W: www.therocheschool.co.uk
Age Range: 2–11

THE ROWANS SCHOOL

19 Drax Avenue, London SW20 0EG
W: www.kcs.org.uk
Age Range: 3–8

THE STUDY PREPARATORY SCHOOL

Wilberforce House, London SW19 4UN
W: www.thestudyprep.co.uk
Age Range: 4–11

THOMAS'S PREPARATORY SCHOOL

28–40 Battersea High Street, London SW11 3JB
W: www.thomas-s.co.uk
Age Range: 4–13

THOMAS'S PREPARATORY SCHOOL CLAPHAM

Broomwood Road, London SW11 6JZ
W: www.thomas-s.co.uk
Age Range: 4–13

TOWER HOUSE SCHOOL

188 Sheen Lane, London SW14 8LF
W: http://www.thsboys.org.uk/
Age Range: 4–13

URSULINE PREPARATORY SCHOOL

18 The Downs, London SW20 8HR
W: www.ursuline-prep.merton. sch.uk
Age Range: 3–11 (Boys 3–7)

WALDORF SCHOOL OF SOUTH WEST LONDON

Woodfields, London SW16 1AP
W: www.waldorf-swlondon.org
Age Range: 4–14

THE WHITE HOUSE PREP & WOODENTOPS KINDERGARTEN

24 Thornton Road, London SW12 0LF
W: www.whitehouseschool.com
Age Range: 2–11

WILLINGTON SCHOOL

Worcester Road, London SW19 7QQ
W: www.willingtonschool.co.uk
Age Range: 4–13

WIMBLEDON COMMON PREPARATORY SCHOOL

113 Ridgway, London SW19 4TA
W: www.wimbledoncommonprep. co.uk
Age Range: 4–8

SENIOR

EMANUEL SCHOOL

Battersea Rise, London SW11 1HS
W: www.emanuel.org.uk
Age Range: 10–18

HALL SCHOOL WIMBLEDON (SENIOR SCHOOL)

17 The Downs, London SW20 8HF
W: www.hsw.co.uk
Age Range: 11–16

THE HARRODIAN

Lonsdale Road, London SW13 9QN
W: www.harrodian.com
Age Range: 5–18

IBSTOCK PLACE SCHOOL

Clarence Lane, London SW15 5PY
W: www.ibstockplaceschool.co.uk
Age Range: 3–18

KING'S COLLEGE SCHOOL

London SW19 4TT
W: www.kcs.org.uk
Age Range: 13–18

MORE HOUSE SCHOOL*

22–24 Pont Street, Knightsbridge, London SW1X 0AA
W: www.morehouse.org.uk
Age Range: 11–18

THE NORWEGIAN SCHOOL

28 Arterberry Road, London SW20 8AH
Age Range: 3–16

PUTNEY HIGH SCHOOL GDST

35 Putney Hill, London SW15 6BH
W: www.gdst.net/putneyhigh
Age Range: 4–18

PUTNEY PARK SCHOOL*

11 Woodborough Road, Putney, London SW15 6PY
W: www.putneypark.london. sch.uk
Age Range: 4–16

ST PAUL'S SCHOOL

●🏠▲

Lonsdale Road, London SW13 9JT
W: www.stpaulsschool.org.uk
Age Range: 13–18

STREATHAM & CLAPHAM HIGH SCHOOL

●🏠▲

42 Abbotswood Road, London
SW16 1AW
W: www.gdst.net/streathamhigh
Age Range: 3–18 (Boys 3–5)

THAMES CHRISTIAN COLLEGE

●🏠◆

Wye Street, London SW11 2HB
W: www.thameschristiancollege.
org.uk
Age Range: 11–16

WIMBLEDON HIGH SCHOOL GDST

●🏠▲

Mansel Road, London SW19 4AB
W: www.wimbledonhigh.gdst.net
Age Range: 4–18

GREATER MANCHESTER

PREPARATORY

ABBOTSFORD PREPARATORY SCHOOL

211 Flixton Road, Manchester,
Greater Manchester M41 5PR
W: www.abbotsfordprepschool.
co.uk
Age Range: 3–11

BRANWOOD PREPARATORY SCHOOL

Stafford Road, Eccles, Greater
Manchester M30 9HN
Age Range: 3–11

CLARENDON COTTAGE SCHOOL

Ivy Bank House, Eccles, Greater
Manchester M30 9BJ
W: www.clarendoncottage.com
Age Range: 1–11

LIGHTHOUSE CHRISTIAN SCHOOL

193 Ashley Lane, Manchester,
Greater Manchester M9 4NQ
W: www.lighthousechristianschool.
co.uk
Age Range: 2–14

MANCHESTER MUSLIM PREPARATORY SCHOOL

551 Wilmslow Road, Manchester,
Greater Manchester M20 4BA
Age Range: 3–11

MONTON PREP SCHOOL WITH MONTESSORI NURSERIES

The School House, Eccles,
Greater Manchester M30 9PR
W: www.montonvillageschool.com
Age Range: 2–13

MOOR ALLERTON SCHOOL

131 Barlow Moor Road,
Manchester, Greater Manchester
M20 2PW
W: www.moorallertonschool.com
Age Range: 3–11

PRESTWICH PREPARATORY SCHOOL

400 Bury Old Road, Prestwich,
Greater Manchester M25 1PZ
Age Range: 2–11

SENIOR

AL JAMIAH AL ISLAMIYYAH

Hospital Road, Bolton, Greater
Manchester BL7 9PY
W: www.al-jamiah-al-islamiyyah.
org.uk
Age Range: 13–16

BRIDGEWATER SCHOOL

●🏠▲

Drywood Hall, Manchester,
Greater Manchester M28 2WQ
W: www.bridgewater-school.co.uk
Age Range: 3–18

CHETHAM'S SCHOOL OF MUSIC

●🏠▲

Long Millgate, Manchester,
Greater Manchester M3 1SB
W: www.chethams.com
Age Range: 8–18

KASSIM DARWISH GRAMMAR SCHOOL FOR BOYS

●🏠

Hartley Hall, Manchester, Greater
Manchester M16 8NH
Age Range: 11–16

KING OF KINGS SCHOOL

●🏠

142 Dantzic Street, Manchester,
Greater Manchester M4 4DN
Age Range: 3–16

THE MANCHESTER GRAMMAR SCHOOL

Old Hall Lane, Manchester,
Greater Manchester M13 0XT
W: www.mgs.org
Age Range: 9–18

MANCHESTER HIGH SCHOOL FOR GIRLS

Grangethorpe Road, Manchester,
Greater Manchester M14 6HS
W: www.manchesterhigh.co.uk
Age Range: 4–18

MANCHESTER ISLAMIC HIGH SCHOOL

55 High Lane, Manchester,
Greater Manchester M21 9FA
Age Range: 11–16

ST BEDE'S COLLEGE

Alexandra Park, Manchester,
Greater Manchester M16 8HX
W: www.stbedescollege.co.uk
Age Range: 4–18

WITHINGTON GIRLS' SCHOOL

100, Wellington Road,
Manchester, Greater Manchester
M14 6BL
W: www.withington.manchester.
sch.uk
Age Range: 7–18

INDEPENDENT SIXTH FORM COLLEGE / TUTORIAL COLLEGE

ABBEY COLLEGE

Cheapside, Manchester, Greater
Manchester M2 4WG
W: www.abbeymanchester.co.uk
Age Range: 14–19

MERSEYSIDE

PREPARATORY

ATHERTON HOUSE SCHOOL

6 Alexandra Road, Liverpool,
Merseyside L23 7TF
W: www.athertonhouse.ndo.co.uk
Age Range: 2–11

AVALON PREPARATORY SCHOOL

Caldy Road, Wirral, Merseyside
CH48 2HE
W: www.avalon-school.co.uk
Age Range: 2–11

BEECHENHURST PREPARATORY SCHOOL

145 Menlove Avenue, Liverpool,
Merseyside L18 3EE
W: www.beechenhurst-school.
org.uk
Age Range: 3–11

CARLETON HOUSE PREPARATORY SCHOOL

Lyndhurst Road, Liverpool,
Merseyside L18 8AQ
W: www.carletonhouse.co.uk
Age Range: 4–11

NEWTON BANK SCHOOL

34 High Street, Newton-Le-
Willows, Merseyside WA12 9SN
Age Range: 2–10

PRENTON PREPARATORY SCHOOL

Mount Pleasant, Wirral,
Merseyside
W: www.prentonprep.co.uk
Age Range: 2–11

REDCOURT – ST ANSELMS

7 Devonshire Place, Prenton,
Merseyside CH43 1TX
W: www.redcourtstanselms.com
Age Range: 3–11

RUNNYMEDE ST EDWARD'S SCHOOL

North Drive, Liverpool, Merseyside
L12 1LE
W: www.runnymede-school.org.uk
Age Range: 3–11

SUNNYMEDE SCHOOL

4 Westcliffe Road, Southport,
Merseyside PR8 2BN
W: www.sunnymedeschool.org
Age Range: 3–11

SENIOR

ARDEN COLLEGE

40 Derby Road, Southport,
Merseyside PR9 0TZ
W: www.ardencollege.ac.uk
Age Range: 16–25

AUCKLAND COLLEGE

65–67 Parkfield Road, Liverpool,
Merseyside L17 4LE
W: www.aucklandcollege.com
Age Range: 7–18

BIRKENHEAD SCHOOL

58 Beresford Road, Wirral,
Merseyside CH43 2JD
W: www.birkenheadschool.co.uk
Age Range: 3–18

HIGHFIELD SCHOOL

96 Bidston Road, Birkenhead,
Merseyside CH43 6TW
W: www.btinternet.com/
highfield.school
Age Range: 2–16

KINGSMEAD SCHOOL

Bertram Drive, Wirral, Merseyside
CH47 0LL
W: www.kingsmeadschool.com
Age Range: 2–16

LIVERPOOL COLLEGE

Queens's Drive, Liverpool,
Merseyside L18 8BG
W: www.liverpoolcollege.org.uk
Age Range: 3–18

MERCHANT TAYLORS' BOYS' SCHOOLS

Liverpool Road, Liverpool,
Merseyside L23 0QP
W: www.merchanttaylors.com
Age Range: 4–18

MERCHANT TAYLORS' GIRLS' SCHOOL

Liverpool Road, Liverpool,
Merseyside L23 5SP
W: www.merchanttaylors.com
Age Range: 4–18 (Infant Boys 4–7)

ST MARY'S COLLEGE

Liverpool, Merseyside L23 5TW
W: www.stmarys.ac

STREATHAM HOUSE SCHOOL

Victoria Road West, Liverpool,
Merseyside L23 8UQ
W: www.streathamhouse.co.uk
Age Range: 2–16 (Boys 2–11)

TOWER COLLEGE

Mill Lane, Prescot, Merseyside
L35 6NE
W: www.towercollege.com
Age Range: 3–16

MIDDLESEX

NURSERY AND PRE-PREP

JACK AND JILL SCHOOL

30 Nightingale Road, Hampton,
Middlesex TW12 3HX
W: www.jackandjillschool.co.uk
Age Range: 2–7 (Boys 3–5)

PREPARATORY

ALPHA PREPARATORY SCHOOL

21 Hindes Road, Harrow,
Middlesex HA1 1SH
W: www.alpha.harrow.sch.uk
Age Range: 4–11

ASHTON HOUSE SCHOOL

50/52 Eversley Crescent,
Isleworth, Middlesex TW7 4LW
W: www.ashtonhouse.com
Age Range: 3–11

ATHELSTAN HOUSE SCHOOL

36 Percy Road, Hampton,
Middlesex TW12 2LA
W: www.athelstanhouseschool.
co.uk
Age Range: 3–7

BUCKINGHAM COLLEGE PREPARATORY SCHOOL

458 Rayners Lane, Pinner,
Middlesex HA5 5DT
W: www.buckprep.org
Age Range: 4–11

BUXLOW PREPARATORY SCHOOL

5/6 Castleton Gardens, Wembley,
Middlesex HA9 7QJ
W: www.buxlowschool.com
Age Range: 4–11

DENMEAD SCHOOL

41–43 Wensleydale Road,
Hampton, Middlesex TW12 2LP
W: www.denmead.richmond.
sch.uk
Age Range: 3–11 (Girls 3–7)

HOLLAND HOUSE

1 Broadhurst Avenue, Edgware,
Middlesex HA8 8TP
W: www.hollandhouse.org.uk
Age Range: 4–11

INNELLAN HOUSE SCHOOL

44 Love Lane, Pinner, Middlesex
HA5 3EX
Age Range: 3–7

THE MALL SCHOOL

185 Hampton Road, Twickenham,
Middlesex TW2 5NQ
W: www.mall.richmond.sch.uk
Age Range: 4–13

NEWLAND HOUSE SCHOOL

Waldegrave Park, Twickenham,
Middlesex TW1 4TQ
W: www.newlandhouse.co.uk
Age Range: 4–13

ORLEY FARM SCHOOL

●🏠

South Hill Avenue, Harrow,
Middlesex HA1 3NU
Age Range: 4–13

QUAINTON HALL SCHOOL

●🏠

91 Hindes Road, Harrow,
Middlesex HA1 1RX
W: www.quaintonhall.org.uk
Age Range: 4–13

REDDIFORD

●🏠

36–38 Cecil Park, Pinner,
Middlesex HA5 5HH
W: www.reddiford.org.uk
Age Range: 2–11

ROXETH MEAD SCHOOL

●🏠

Buckholt House, Harrow on the
Hill, Middlesex HA2 0HW
W: www.roxethmead.com
Age Range: 3–7

ST CHRISTOPHER'S SCHOOL

●🏠

71 Wembley Park Drive, Wembley,
Middlesex HA9 8HE
W: www.happychildschools.co.uk
Age Range: 4–11

ST HELEN'S COLLEGE

●🏠

Parkway, Hillingdon, Middlesex
UB10 9JX
W: sthelenscollege.com
Age Range: 3–11

ST JOHN'S NORTHWOOD

●🏠

Potter Street Hill, Northwood,
Middlesex HA6 3QY
W: www.st-johns.org.uk
Age Range: 3–13

ST MARTIN'S SCHOOL

●🏠

40 Moor Park Road, Northwood,
Middlesex HA6 2DJ
W: www.stmartins.org.uk
Age Range: 3–13

STAINES PREPARATORY SCHOOL

●🏠

3 Gresham Road, Staines,
Middlesex TW18 2BT
W: www.stainesprep.co.uk
Age Range: 3–11 (The earliest we
can accept pupils is in the term
they are rising three years of age.)

TWICKENHAM PREPARATORY SCHOOL

●🏠

Beveree, Hampton, Middlesex
TW12 2SA
W: www.twickenhamprep.co.uk
Age Range: 4–13

SENIOR

BUCKINGHAM COLLEGE SCHOOL

●🏠▲

11–17 Hindes Road, Harrow,
Middlesex HA1 1SH
W: www.buckcoll.org
Age Range: 11–18 (Co-ed VIth
Form, but currently boys only.)

HALLIFORD SCHOOL

●🏠▲

Russell Road, Shepperton,
Middlesex TW17 9HX
W: www.hallifordschool.co.uk
Age Range: 11–18 (Co-ed VIth
Form)

HAMPTON SCHOOL

●🏠▲

Hanworth Road, Hampton,
Middlesex TW12 3HD
W: www.hamptonschool.org.uk
Age Range: 11–18

HARROW SCHOOL

●🏠▲

1 High Street, Harrow on the Hill,
Middlesex HA1 3HT
W: www.harrowschool.org.uk
Age Range: 13–18

HEATHFIELD SCHOOL

●🏠▲

Beaulieu Drive, Pinner, Middlesex
HA5 1NB
W: www.heathfield.gdst.net
Age Range: 3–18

THE JOHN LYON SCHOOL

●🏠▲

Middle Road, Harrow, Middlesex
HA2 0HN
W: www.johnlyon.org
Age Range: 11–18

THE LADY ELEANOR HOLLES SCHOOL

●🏠▲

102 Hanworth Road, Hampton,
Middlesex TW12 3HF
W: www.lehs.org.uk
Age Range: 7–18

LITTLE EDEN & EDEN HIGH SDA

●🏠

St George's Hall, Brentford,
Middlesex TW8 0EN
W: www.theedenschool.com
Age Range: 3–16

MERCHANT TAYLORS' SCHOOL

●🏠▲

Sandy Lodge, Northwood,
Middlesex HA6 2HT
W: www.mtsn.org.uk
Age Range: 11–18

NORTH LONDON COLLEGIATE

●🏠★▲

Canons Drive, Edgware,
Middlesex HA8 7RJ
W: www.nlcs.org.uk
Age Range: 4–18

NORTHWOOD COLLEGE*

●🏠▲

Maxwell Road, Northwood,
Middlesex HA6 2YE
W: www.northwoodcollege.co.uk
Age Range: 3–18

PETERBOROUGH & ST MARGARET'S SCHOOL

●🏠

Common Road, Stanmore,
Middlesex HA7 3JB
W: www.psmschool.org
Age Range: 4–16

RAVENSCOURT THEATRE SCHOOL

●🏠

3 Thameside Centre, Middlesex
TW8 0HF
W: www.ravenscourt.net
Age Range: 8–16

ST CATHERINE'S SCHOOL*

Cross Deep, Twickenham,
Middlesex TW1 4QJ
W: www.stcatherineschool.co.uk
Age Range: 3–18

ST HELEN'S SCHOOL*

Eastbury Road, Northwood,
Middlesex HA6 3AS
W: www.sthn.co.uk
Age Range: 3–18

ST JOHN'S SENIOR SCHOOL

North Lodge, Enfield, Middlesex
EN2 8BE
W: www.stjohnsseniorschool.com
Age Range: 10–18

INDEPENDENT SIXTH FORM COLLEGE / TUTORIAL COLLEGE

ACORN INDEPENDENT COLLEGE

39–47 High Street, Southall,
Middlesex UB1 3HF
W: www.acorn-college.co.uk
Age Range: 13–20

INTERNATIONAL SCHOOLS AND INTERNATIONAL STUDY CENTRES

ACS HILLINGDON INTERNATIONAL SCHOOL*

Hillingdon Court, 108 Vine Lane,
Hillingdon, Middlesex UB10 0BE
W: www.acs-schools.com
Age Range: 4–18

NORFOLK

NURSERY AND PRE-PREP

STRETTON SCHOOL

1 Albemarle Road, Norwich,
Norfolk NR2 2DF
W: www.stretton-school.co.uk
Age Range: 1–8

PREPARATORY

BEESTON HALL SCHOOL

Cromer, Norfolk NR27 9NQ
W: www.beestonhall.co.uk
Age Range: 7–13

DOWNHAM PREP SCHOOL AND MONTESSORI NURSERY

The Old Rectory, Kings Lynn,
Norfolk PE34 3HT
W: www.dpsmn.norfolk.sch.uk
Age Range: 2–11

GLEBE HOUSE SCHOOL

2 Cromer Road, Hunstanton,
Norfolk PE36 6HW
W: www.glebehouseschool.co.uk
Age Range: 4–13

LANGLEY PREPARATORY SCHOOL & NURSERY

Beech Hill, Norwich, Norfolk
NR7 0EA
W: www.langleyprep.norfolk.
sch.uk
Age Range: 2–11

NOTRE DAME PREPARATORY SCHOOL

147 Dereham Road, Norwich,
Norfolk NR2 3TA
W: www.notredameprepschool.
co.uk
Age Range: 3–11

RIDDLESWORTH HALL

Diss, Norfolk IP22 2TA
W: www.riddlesworthhall.com
Age Range: 2–13 (Coeducational
boarding)

ST CHRISTOPHER'S SCHOOL

George Hill, Norwich, Norfolk
NR6 7DE
W: www.stchristophersnorwich.
co.uk
Age Range: 2–8

ST NICHOLAS HOUSE KINDERGARTEN & PREP SCHOOL

North Walsham, Norfolk NR28 9AT
W: www.stnicholashouse.com
Age Range: 3–11

TAVERHAM HALL PREPARATORY SCHOOL

Taverham Park, Norwich, Norfolk
NR8 6HU
W: www.taverhamhall.co.uk
Age Range: 1–13

TOWN CLOSE HOUSE PREPARATORY SCHOOL

14 Ipswich Road, Norwich, Norfolk
NR2 2LR
W: www.townclose.com
Age Range: 3–13

SENIOR

ALL SAINTS SCHOOL

School Road, Norwich, Norfolk
NR12 0DJ
W: www.allsaintslessingham.co.uk
Age Range: 2–16

GRESHAM'S SCHOOL

Cromer Road, Holt, Norfolk
NR25 6EA
W: www.greshams.com
Age Range: 13–18

HETHERSETT OLD HALL SCHOOL

Norwich Road, Norwich, Norfolk
NR9 3DW
W: www.hohs.co.uk
Age Range: 4–18 (Day boys
admitted aged 4–11
Day girls admitted aged 4–18
Boarding girls admitted aged
9–18
No boys boarding)

LANGLEY SCHOOL

Langley Park, Norwich, Norfolk
NR14 6BJ
W: www.langleyschool.co.uk
Age Range: 10–18

THE NEW ECCLES HALL SCHOOL

Norwich, Norfolk NR16 2NZ
W: www.neweccleshall.com
Age Range: 4–16

NORWICH HIGH SCHOOL FOR GIRLS GDST

Eaton Grove, Norwich, Norfolk
NR2 2HU
W: www.gdst.net/norwich
Age Range: 3–18

NORWICH SCHOOL

70 The Close, Norwich, Norfolk
NR1 4DD
W: www.norwich-school.org.uk
Age Range: 7–18 (Co-ed VIth
Form)

SACRED HEART SCHOOL

17 Mangate Street, Swaffham,
Norfolk PE37 7QW
W: www.sacredheart.norfolk.
sch.uk
Age Range: 3–16

THETFORD GRAMMAR SCHOOL

Bridge Street, Thetford, Norfolk
IP24 3AF
W: www.thetgram.norfolk.sch.uk
Age Range: 3–18

THORPE HOUSE SCHOOL

7 Yarmouth Road, Norwich,
Norfolk NR7 0EA
W: www.thorpehouseschool.com
Age Range: 3–16

WOOD DENE SCHOOL

Aylmerton Hall, Norwich, Norfolk
NR11 8QA
W: www.wood-dene.co.uk
Age Range: 2–16

NORTHAMPTONSHIRE

NURSERY AND PRE-PREP

SLAPTON PRE-PREPARATORY SCHOOL

Chapel Lane, Towcester,
Northamptonshire NN12 8PE
W: www.slaptonpreprep.org
Age Range: 4–8

PREPARATORY

BEACHBOROUGH SCHOOL

Westbury, Brackley,
Northamptonshire NN13 5LB
W: www.beachborough.com
Age Range: 2–13

GREAT HOUGHTON PREPARATORY SCHOOL

Great Houghton Hall,
Northampton, Northamptonshire
NN4 7AG
W: www.ghps.co.uk
Age Range: 1–13

LAXTON JUNIOR SCHOOL*

East Road, Oundle, Nr
Peterborough, Northamptonshire
PE8 4BX
W: www.laxtonjunior.org.uk
Age Range: 4–11

MAIDWELL HALL SCHOOL

Maidwell, Northamptonshire
NN6 9JG
W: www.maidwellhall.co.uk
Age Range: 7–13 (The school is
accepting girls for the first time in
September 2010.)

ST MATTHEWS SCHOOL

100 Park Avenue North,
Northampton, Northamptonshire
NN3 2JB
Age Range: 2–9

ST PETER'S SCHOOL

52 Headlands, Kettering,
Northamptonshire NN15 6DJ
W: www.st-peters.org.uk
Age Range: 2–11

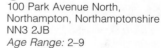

SPRATTON HALL

Smith Street, Northampton,
Northamptonshire NN6 8HP
W: www.sprattonhall.com
Age Range: 4–13

WINCHESTER HOUSE SCHOOL

Brackley, Northamptonshire
NN13 7AZ
W: www.winchester-house.org
Age Range: 3–13

SENIOR

NORTHAMPTON HIGH SCHOOL

Newport Pagnell Road,
Northampton, Northamptonshire
NN4 6UU
W: www.gdst.net/
northamptonhigh
Age Range: 3–18

NORTHAMPTONSHIRE GRAMMAR SCHOOL

Pitsford Hall, Pitsford,
Northamptonshire NN6 9AX
W: www.ngs-school.com
Age Range: 4–18

OUNDLE SCHOOL

The Great Hall, Nr Peterborough,
Northamptonshire PE8 4GH
W: www.oundleschool.org.uk
Age Range: 11–19

QUINTON HOUSE SCHOOL

Upton Hall, Northampton,
Northamptonshire NN5 4UX
W: www.quintonhouseschool.
co.uk
Age Range: 2–18

ST PETER'S INDEPENDENT SCHOOL

Lingswood Park, Blackthorn,
Northamptonshire NN3 8TA
W: www.
stpetersindependentschool.co.uk
Age Range: 4–18

WELLINGBOROUGH SCHOOL

Wellingborough,
Northamptonshire NN8 2BX
W: www.wellingboroughschool.
org
Age Range: 3–18

INDEPENDENT SIXTH FORM COLLEGE / TUTORIAL COLLEGE

BOSWORTH INDEPENDENT COLLEGE

Nazareth House, Northampton,
Northamptonshire NN2 6AF
W: www.bosworthcollege.com
Age Range: 14–21

NORTHUMBERLAND

PREPARATORY

MOWDEN HALL SCHOOL

Stocksfield, Northumberland
NE43 7TP
W: www.mowdenhall.co.uk
Age Range: 3–13

ROCK HALL SCHOOL

Rock, Alnwick, Northumberland
NE66 3SB
W: www.rockhallschool.com
Age Range: 3–13

SENIOR

LONGRIDGE TOWERS SCHOOL

Berwick-upon-Tweed,
Northumberland TD15 2XQ
W: www.lts.org.uk
Age Range: 4–18

ST OSWALD'S SCHOOL

Spring Gardens, Alnwick,
Northumberland NE66 2NU
W: www.st-oswalds.
northumberland.sch.uk
Age Range: 3–16

NOTTINGHAMSHIRE

PREPARATORY

ARLEY HOUSE SCHOOL

8 Station Road, East Leake,
Nottinghamshire LE12 6LQ
W: www.arley-pneu.eastleake.
sch.uk
Age Range: 3–11

COTESWOOD HOUSE SCHOOL

19 Thackeray's Lane, Nottingham,
Nottinghamshire NG5 4HT
Age Range: 3–11

GREENHOLME SCHOOL

392 Derby Road, Nottingham,
Nottinghamshire NG7 2DX
W: www.greenholmeschool.co.uk
Age Range: 3–11

GROSVENOR SCHOOL

Edwalton Grange, Nottingham,
Nottinghamshire NG12 4BS
W: www.grosvenorschool.co.uk
Age Range: 1–13

HAZEL HURST SCHOOL

400 Westdale Lane, Nottingham,
Nottinghamshire NG3 6DG
W: www.hazelhurstschool.co.uk
Age Range: 2–8

HIGHFIELDS SCHOOL

London Road, Newark,
Nottinghamshire NG24 3AL
W: www.highfieldsschool.co.uk
Age Range: 3–11

MOUNTFORD HOUSE SCHOOL

373 Mansfield Road, Nottingham,
Nottinghamshire NG5 2DA
Age Range: 3–11

NOTTINGHAM HIGH JUNIOR SCHOOL

Waverley Mount, Nottingham,
Nottinghamshire NG7 4ED
W: www.nottinghamhigh.co.uk
Age Range: 7–11

PLUMTREE SCHOOL

Church Hill, Nottingham,
Nottinghamshire NG12 5ND
W: www.plumtreeschool.co.uk
Age Range: 3–11

RANBY HOUSE SCHOOL

Retford, Nottinghamshire
DN22 8HX
W: www.ranbyhouseschool.co.uk
Age Range: 3–13

ST JOSEPH'S SCHOOL

33 Derby Road, Nottingham,
Nottinghamshire NG1 5AW
W: www.st-josephs.nottingham.
sch.uk
Age Range: 1–11

SALTERFORD HOUSE SCHOOL

Salterford Lane, Nottingham,
Nottinghamshire NG14 6NZ
W: www.salterfordhouseschool.
co.uk
Age Range: 2–11

SAVILLE HOUSE SCHOOL

11 Church Street, Mansfield,
Nottinghamshire NG19 8AH
W: www.savillehouse.co.uk
Age Range: 3–11

WELLOW HOUSE SCHOOL

Newark, Nottinghamshire
NG22 0EA
W: www.wellowhouse.notts.sch.uk
Age Range: 3–13

SENIOR

AL KARAM SECONDARY SCHOOL

Eaton Hall, Retford,
Nottinghamshire DN22 0PR
W: www.alkaram.org
Age Range: 11–16

DAGFA HOUSE SCHOOL

57 Broadgate, Nottingham,
Nottinghamshire NG9 2FU
W: www.dagfahouse.notts.sch.uk
Age Range: 2–16

THE KING'S SCHOOL

Green Street, Nottingham,
Nottinghamshire NG2 2LA
W: www.thekingsschool.info
Age Range: 3–16

LAMMAS SCHOOL

Lammas Road, Sutton in Ashfield,
Nottinghamshire NG17 2AD
W: www.lammas-school.co.uk.
Age Range: 4–16

NOTTINGHAM HIGH SCHOOL FOR GIRLS GDST

9 Arboretum Street, Nottingham,
Nottinghamshire NG1 4JB
W: www.gdst.net/
nottinghamgirlshigh
Age Range: 4–18

TRENT COLLEGE & THE ELMS

Long Eaton, Nottingham,
Nottinghamshire NG10 4AD
W: www.trentcollege.net
Age Range: 3–18

WORKSOP COLLEGE

Worksop, Nottinghamshire
S80 3AP
W: www.worksopcollege.notts.
sch.uk
Age Range: 13–18

England – Oxfordshire

OXFORDSHIRE

PREPARATORY

ABINGDON PREPARATORY SCHOOL

Josca's House, Abingdon, Oxfordshire OX13 5NX
W: www.abingdon.org.uk/prep
Age Range: 4–13 (Girls 4–7)

THE CARRDUS SCHOOL

Overthorpe Hall, Banbury, Oxfordshire OX17 2BS
W: www.carrdusschool.co.uk
Age Range: 3–11 (Boys 3–8)

CHANDLINGS MANOR SCHOOL

Bagley Wood, Oxford, Oxfordshire OX1 5ND
W: www.chandlings.com
Age Range: 4–11

CHRIST CHURCH CATHEDRAL SCHOOL

3 Brewer Street, Oxford, Oxfordshire OX1 1QW
W: www.cccs.org.uk
Age Range: 3–13 (Girls 2–4)

COTHILL HOUSE PREPARATORY SCHOOL

Cothill, Abingdon, Oxfordshire OX13 6JL
W: www.cothill.net
Age Range: 8–13

DRAGON SCHOOL
Bardwell Road, Oxford, Oxfordshire OX2 6SS
W: www.dragonschool.org
Age Range: 4–13

EMMANUEL CHRISTIAN SCHOOL
Sandford Road, Oxford, Oxfordshire OX4 4PU
W: www.ecschool.co.uk
Age Range: 3–11

FERNDALE PREPARATORY SCHOOL

5–7 Bromsgrove, Faringdon, Oxfordshire SN7 7JF
W: www.ferndaleschool.co.uk
Age Range: 3–11

THE KING'S SCHOOL, PRIMARY

New Yatt Road, Witney, Oxfordshire OX29 6TA
W: www.occ.org.uk/tks/
Age Range: 5–11

THE MANOR PREPARATORY SCHOOL

Faringdon Road, Abingdon, Oxfordshire OX13 6LN
W: www.manorprep.org
Age Range: 2–11

MOULSFORD PREPARATORY SCHOOL

Wallingford, Oxfordshire OX10 9HR
W: www.moulsford.com
Age Range: 4–13

NEW COLLEGE SCHOOL

2 Savile Road, Oxford, Oxfordshire OX1 3UA
W: www.newcollegeschool.org
Age Range: 4–13

THE ORATORY PREPARATORY SCHOOL

Goring Heath, Reading, Oxfordshire RG8 7SF
W: www.oratoryprep.org.uk
Age Range: 3–13

OUR LADY'S ABINGDON JUNIOR SCHOOL

St John's Road, Abingdon, Oxfordshire OX14 2HB
W: www.olab.org.uk
Age Range: 3–11

OXFORD MONTESSORI SCHOOLS

Forest Farm, Oxford, Oxfordshire OX3 9UW
W: www.oxfordmontessori.co.uk
Age Range: 2–12

RUPERT HOUSE

90 Bell Street, Henley-on-Thames, Oxfordshire RG9 2BN
W: www.ruperthouse.org
Age Range: 4–11

ST ANDREW'S

Wallingford Street, Wantage, Oxfordshire OX12 8AZ
W: www.standrewswantage.org.uk
Age Range: 3–11

ST HUGH'S SCHOOL

Carswell Manor, Faringdon, Oxfordshire SN7 8PT
W: www.st-hughs.co.uk
Age Range: 3–13

ST JOHN'S PRIORY SCHOOL

St John's Road, Banbury, Oxfordshire OX16 5HX
W: www.stjohnspriory.com
Age Range: 2–11

ST MARY'S SCHOOL
13 St Andrew's Road, Henley-on-Thames, Oxfordshire RG9 1HS
W: www.cognitaschools.co.uk
Age Range: 3–11

SUMMER FIELDS

Mayfield Road, Oxford, Oxfordshire OX2 7EN
W: www.summerfields.oxon.sch.uk
Age Range: 7–13

WINDRUSH VALLEY SCHOOL

The Green, Chipping Norton,
Oxfordshire OX7 6AN
W: www.windrushvalley@aol.com
Age Range: 3–11

SENIOR

ABINGDON SCHOOL

Park Road, Abingdon, Oxfordshire
OX14 IDE
W: www.abingdon.org.uk
Age Range: 11–18

ASH-SHIFA SCHOOL

Merton Street, Banbury,
Oxfordshire OX16 8RU
W: www.ash-shifa.org.uk
Age Range: 11–16

COKETHORPE SCHOOL

Witney, Oxfordshire OX29 7PU
W: www.cokethorpe.org.uk
Age Range: 4–18

CRANFORD HOUSE SCHOOL

Wallingford, Oxfordshire OX10 9HT
W: www.cranford-house.org
Age Range: 3–16 (Boys 3–7)

HEADINGTON SCHOOL

Oxford, Oxfordshire OX3 7TD
W: www.headington.org
Age Range: 3–18 (Co-ed 3–4)

IQRA SCHOOL

Lawn Upton House, Oxford,
Oxfordshire OX4 4PU
W: www.iqraschool.org.uk
Age Range: 10–16

LECKFORD PLACE SCHOOL

Leckford Road, Oxford,
Oxfordshire OX2 6HX
W: www.leckfordplace.com
Age Range: 11–16

MAGDALEN COLLEGE SCHOOL

Cowley Place, Oxford, Oxfordshire
OX4 1DZ
W: www.mcsoxford.org
Age Range: 7–18

OUR LADY'S ABINGDON SCHOOL

Radley Road, Abingdon,
Oxfordshire OX14 3PS
W: www.olab.org.uk
Age Range: 3–18 (Co-ed Junior
school. Boys admitted to Senior
school in Yr 7 & 6th form. Fully co-
ed in 2013.)

OXFORD HIGH SCHOOL GDST

Belbroughton Road, Oxford,
Oxfordshire OX2 6XA
W: www.oxfordhigh.gdst.net
Age Range: 3–18 (Boys 4 -6)

RADLEY COLLEGE

Abingdon, Oxfordshire OX14 2HR
W: www.radley.org.uk
Age Range: 13–18

ST CLARE'S, OXFORD*

139 Banbury Road, Oxford,
Oxfordshire OX2 7AL
W: www.stclares.ac.uk
Age Range: 15–19

ST EDWARD'S SCHOOL*

Woodstock Road, Oxford,
Oxfordshire OX2 7NN
W: www.stedwards.oxon.sch.uk
Age Range: 13–18

ST HELEN & ST KATHARINE

Faringdon Road, Abingdon,
Oxfordshire OX14 1BE
W: www.shsk.org.uk
Age Range: 9–18

SHIPLAKE COLLEGE

Henley-on-Thames, Oxfordshire
RG9 4BW
W: www.shiplake.org.uk
Age Range: 11–18 (Day girls
16–18)

SIBFORD SCHOOL

Sibford Ferris, Banbury,
Oxfordshire OX15 5QL
W: www.sibford.oxon.sch.uk
Age Range: 4–18

TUDOR HALL SCHOOL*

Wykham Park, Banbury,
Oxfordshire OX16 9UR
W: www.tudorhallschool.com
Age Range: 11–18

WYCHWOOD SCHOOL

74 Banbury Road, Oxford,
Oxfordshire OX2 6JR
W: www.wychwood-school.org.uk
Age Range: 11–18

INDEPENDENT SIXTH FORM COLLEGE / TUTORIAL COLLEGE

ABACUS COLLEGE

Threeways House, Oxford,
Oxfordshire OX1 2BT
W: www.abacuscollege.co.uk
Age Range: 16–21

CHERWELL COLLEGE

Greyfriars, Oxford, Oxfordshire
OX1 1LD
W: www.cherwell-college.co.uk
Age Range: (Focus on A-levels
with the addition of A-level retake
and final year GCSE, 16–19)

GREENE'S TUTORIAL COLLEGE

45 Pembroke Street, Oxford,
Oxfordshire OX1 1BP
W: www.greenes.org.uk
Age Range: 6–75 (Boarding (host
families))

THE HENLEY COLLEGE

Deanfield Avenue, Henley-On-
Thames, Oxfordshire RG9 1UH
W: www.henleycol.ac.uk

OXFORD TUTORIAL COLLEGE*

12 King Edward Street, Oxford, Oxfordshire OX1 4HT
W: www.otc.ac.uk
Age Range: (16+)

INTERNATIONAL SCHOOLS AND INTERNATIONAL STUDY CENTRES

D'OVERBROECK'S COLLEGE OXFORD*

The Swan Building, 111 Banbury Road, Oxford, Oxfordshire OX2 6JX
W: www.doverbroecks.com
Age Range: 11–19 (Many students join for sixth form from other schools.)

ST CLARE'S OXFORD

18 Bardwell Road, Oxford, Oxfordshire OX2 6SP
W: www.stclares.ac.uk

ST CLARES, OXFORD*

139 Banbury Road, Oxford, Oxfordshire OX2 7AL
W: www.stclares.ac.uk
Age Range: 15–19; boarders from 15

RUTLAND

PREPARATORY

BROOKE PRIORY SCHOOL

Station Approach, Oakham, Rutland LE15 6QW
W: www.brooke.rutland.sch.uk
Age Range: 2–11

SENIOR

OAKHAM SCHOOL

Chapel Close, Oakham, Rutland LE15 6DT
W: www.oakham.rutland.sch.uk
Age Range: 10–18

UPPINGHAM SCHOOL

Uppingham, Rutland LE15 9QE
W: www.uppingham.co.uk
Age Range: 13–18 (Year 9–Fourth Form
Year 10–Lower Fifth
Year 11–Upper Fifth
Year 12–Lower VI
Year 13–Upper VI)

SHROPSHIRE

PREPARATORY

CASTLE HOUSE SCHOOL

Newport, Shropshire TF10 7JE
W: www.castlehouseschool.co.uk
Age Range: 2–11

DOWER HOUSE SCHOOL

Quatt, Bridgnorth, Shropshire WV15 6QW
W: www.dowerhouseschool.co.uk
Age Range: 2–11

KINGSLAND GRANGE

Old Roman Road, Shrewsbury, Shropshire SY3 9AH
W: www.kingslandgrange.com
Age Range: 4–13

MOOR PARK SCHOOL

Moor Park, Ludlow, Shropshire SY8 4DZ
W: www.moorpark.org.uk
Age Range: 3–13

THE OLD HALL SCHOOL

Stanley Road, Telford, Shropshire TF1 3LB
W: www.oldhall.co.uk
Age Range: 4–11

OSWESTRY SCHOOL BELLAN HOUSE

Bellan House, Oswestry, Shropshire SY11 2ST
W: www.oswestryschool.org.uk
Age Range: 2–9

PACKWOOD HAUGH SCHOOL

Ruyton XI Towns, Shrewsbury, Shropshire SY4 1HX
W: www.packwood-haugh.co.uk
Age Range: 4–13

PRESTFELDE PREPARATORY SCHOOL

London Road, Shrewsbury, Shropshire SY2 6NZ
W: www.prestfelde.co.uk
Age Range: 3–13

ST WINEFRIDE'S CONVENT SCHOOL

Belmont, Shrewsbury, Shropshire SY1 1TE
Age Range: 3–11

WHITE HOUSE SCHOOL

Heath Road, Whitchurch, Shropshire SY13 2AA
Age Range: 3–11

SENIOR

ADCOTE SCHOOL FOR GIRLS

Little Ness, Shrewsbury, Shropshire SY4 2JY
W: www.adcoteschool.co.uk
Age Range: 4–18

BEDSTONE COLLEGE

Bucknell, Shropshire SY7 0BG
W: www.bedstone.org
Age Range: 3–18

ELLESMERE COLLEGE

Ellesmere, Shropshire SY12 9AB
W: www.ellesmere.com
Age Range: 7–18

MORETON HALL SCHOOL*

Weston Rhyn, Oswestry, Shropshire SY11 3EW
W: www.moretonhall.org
Age Range: 3–18 (Boys 3–11)

OSWESTRY SCHOOL*

Upper Brook Street, Oswestry, Shropshire SY11 2TL
W: www.oswestryschool.org.uk

SHREWSBURY HIGH SCHOOL GDST

32 Town Walls, Shrewsbury, Shropshire SY1 1TN
W: www.shrewsburyhigh.gdst.net
Age Range: 3–18

SHREWSBURY SCHOOL

The Schools, Shrewsbury, Shropshire SY3 7BA
W: www.shrewsbury.org.uk
Age Range: 13–18 (Boys are admitted at 13[†] and 14[†], and boys and girls at 16[†] into the Sixth Form.)

WREKIN COLLEGE

Wellington, Shropshire TF1 3BH
W: www.wrekincollege.ac.uk
Age Range: 11–19

INDEPENDENT SIXTH FORM COLLEGE / TUTORIAL COLLEGE

CONCORD COLLEGE

Acton Burnell Hall, Shrewsbury, Shropshire SY5 7PF
W: www.concordcollegeuk.com
Age Range: 13–19

SOMERSET

PREPARATORY

ALL HALLOWS

Shepton Mallet, Somerset BA4 4SF
W: www.allhallowsschool.co.uk
Age Range: 4–13

CHARD SCHOOL

Fore Street, Chard, Somerset TA20 1QA
W: www.chardschool.ik.org
Age Range: 2–11

HAZLEGROVE*

Sparkford, Yeovil, Somerset BA22 7JA
W: www.hazlegrove.co.uk
Age Range: 2–13

KING'S HALL

Taunton, Somerset TA2 8AA
W: www.kingshalltaunton.co.uk
Age Range: 3–13

MILLFIELD PREPARATORY SCHOOL

Edgarley Hall, Glastonbury, Somerset BA6 8LD
W: www.millfieldprep.com
Age Range: 2–13

PERROTT HILL SCHOOL

North Perrott, Crewkerne, Somerset TA18 7SL
W: www.perrotthill.com
Age Range: 3–13

QUEEN'S COLLEGE JUNIOR, PRE-PREP & NURSERY SCHOOLS

Trull Road, Taunton, Somerset
TA1 4QP
W: www.queenscollege.org.uk
Age Range: 3–11

SOUTHLEIGH KINDERGARTEN

11 Rectory Road, Burnham-on-Sea, Somerset TA8 2BY
W: www.southleigh.org.uk
Age Range: 2–7

TAUNTON PREPARATORY SCHOOL

Staplegrove Road, Taunton,
Somerset TA2 6AE
W: www.tauntonschool.co.uk
Age Range: 2–13

WELLS CATHEDRAL JUNIOR SCHOOL

8 New Street, Wells, Somerset
BA5 2LQ
W: marketing@wellscs.somerset.sch.uk
Age Range: 3–11

SENIOR

BRUTON SCHOOL FOR GIRLS

Sunny Hill, Bruton, Somerset
BA10 0NT
W: www.brutonschool.co.uk
Age Range: 2–18 (Boys aged 2–7)

CHILTON CANTELO SCHOOL

Chilton Cantelo, Yeovil, Somerset
BA22 8BG
Age Range: 7–16

DOWNSIDE SCHOOL

Bath, Somerset BA3 4RJ
W: www.downside.co.uk
Age Range: 11–18

KING'S COLLEGE

South Road, Taunton, Somerset
TA1 3LA
W: www.kings-taunton.co.uk
Age Range: 13–18

MILLFIELD SCHOOL

Butleigh Road, Street, Somerset
BA16 0YD
W: www.millfieldschool.com
Age Range: 13–18

THE PARK SCHOOL

The Park, Yeovil, Somerset
BA20 1DH
W: www.parkschool.com
Age Range: 3–19

QUEEN'S COLLEGE

Trull Road, Taunton, Somerset
TA1 4QS
W: www.queenscollege.org.uk
Age Range: 3–18

TAUNTON SCHOOL SENIOR

Staplegrove Road, Taunton,
Somerset TA2 6AD
W: www.tauntonschool.co.uk
Age Range: 13–18

WELLINGTON SCHOOL

South Street, Wellington, Somerset
TA21 8NT
W: www.wellington-school.org.uk
Age Range: 10–18

WELLS CATHEDRAL SCHOOL

The Liberty, Wells, Somerset
BA5 2ST
W: www.wells-cathedral-school.com
Age Range: 3–18

INDEPENDENT SIXTH FORM COLLEGE / TUTORIAL COLLEGE

BATH ACADEMY

27 Queen Square, Bath, Somerset
BA1 2HX
W: www.bathacademy.co.uk
Age Range: 16–20

BRIDGWATER COLLEGE

Bath Road, Bridgwater, Somerset
TA6 4PZ
W: www.bridgwater.ac.uk

INTERNATIONAL SCHOOLS AND INTERNATIONAL STUDY CENTRES

TAUNTON SCHOOL INTERNATIONAL

Taunton School, Taunton,
Somerset TA2 6AD
W: www.tauntoninternational.co.uk
Age Range: 14–17

BATH & NORTH EAST SOMERSET

NURSERY AND PRE-PREP

KING EDWARD'S PRE-PREP SCHOOL

● 🏠

Weston Lane, Bath, Bath & North East Somerset BA1 4AQ
Age Range: 3–7

PREPARATORY

KING EDWARD'S JUNIOR SCHOOL

● 🏠

North Road, Bath, Bath & North East Somerset BA2 6JA
W: www.kesbath.com
Age Range: 7–11

KINGSWOOD PREPARATORY SCHOOL

● 🏠

College Road, Bath, Bath & North East Somerset BA1 5SD
W: www.kingswood.bath.sch.uk
Age Range: 3–11

PARAGON SCHOOL, PRIOR PARK COLLEGE JUNIOR

● 🏠

Lyncombe House, Bath, Bath & North East Somerset BA2 4LT
W: www.paragonschool.co.uk
Age Range: 3–11

SENIOR

BEECHEN CLIFF SCHOOL

● 🏠 ★ ▲

Alexandra Park, Bath, Bath & North East Somerset BA2 4RE
W: www.beechencliff.org.uk
Age Range: 11–18

KING EDWARD'S SCHOOL, BATH*

North Road, Bath, Bath & North East Somerset BA2 6HU
W: www.kesbath.com.uk
Age Range: 3–18

KINGSWOOD SCHOOL*

Lansdown, Bath, Bath & North East Somerset BA1 5RG
W: www.kingswood.bath.sch.uk
Age Range: 3–18

PRIOR PARK COLLEGE

Ralph Allen Drive, Bath, Bath & North East Somerset BA2 5AH
W: www.thepriorfoundation.com
Age Range: 11–18 (Boarding from 13)

THE ROYAL HIGH SCHOOL, BATH*

● 🏠 ★ ▲

Lansdown Road, Bath, Bath & North East Somerset BA1 5SZ
W: www.royalhighbath.gdst.net
Age Range: (Day) girls 3–18; girls boarding 10–18

NORTH SOMERSET

PREPARATORY

ASHBROOKE HOUSE

● 🏠

9 Ellenborough Park North, Weston-Super-Mare, North Somerset BS23 1XH
Age Range: 3–11

LANCASTER HOUSE SCHOOL

● 🏠

38 Hill Road, Weston-Super-Mare, North Somerset BS23 2RY
W: www.lhslhs.co.uk
Age Range: 4–11

SENIOR

SIDCOT SCHOOL*

● 🏠 ★ ◆ ▲

Oakridge Lane, Winscombe, North Somerset BS25 1PD
W: www.sidcot.org.uk
Age Range: 3–18†

STAFFORDSHIRE

PREPARATORY

BROOKLANDS SCHOOL & LITTLE BROOKLANDS NURSERY

●🏠

167 Eccleshall Road, Stafford, Staffordshire ST16 1PD
W: www.brooklandsschool.com
Age Range: (0–3 year old children in Day Nursery total 63 in addition to main School total of 110.)

EDENHURST SCHOOL

●🏠

Westlands Avenue, Newcastle-under-Lyme, Staffordshire ST5 2PU
W: www.edenhurst.co.uk
Age Range: 3–14

ST DOMINIC'S INDEPENDENT JUNIOR SCHOOL

●🏠

Hartshill Road, Stoke-on-Trent, Staffordshire ST4 7LY
W: www.stdominicsstoke.co.uk
Age Range: 3–11

ST JOSEPH'S PREPARATORY SCHOOL

●🏠

Rookery Lane, Stoke-on-Trent, Staffordshire ST4 5RF
W: www.stjosephsprepschool.co.uk
Age Range: 3–11

SMALLWOOD MANOR PREPARATORY SCHOOL

●🏠

Uttoxeter, Staffordshire ST14 8NS
W: www.smallwoodmanor.co.uk
Age Range: 2–11

VERNON LODGE PREPARATORY SCHOOL

●🏠

School Lane, Brewood, Staffordshire ST19 9LJ
W: www.vernonlodge.co.uk
Age Range: 2–11

YARLET SCHOOL

●🏠

Yarlet, Stafford, Staffordshire ST18 9SU
W: www.yarletschool.co.uk
Age Range: 2–13

THE YARLET SCHOOLS

●🏠

Yarlet, Stafford, Staffordshire ST18 9SU
W: www.yarletschool.org
Age Range: 3–13

SENIOR

ABBOTS BROMLEY SCHOOL FOR GIRLS

●🏠▲

Abbots Bromley, Staffordshire WS15 3BW
W: www.abbotsbromley.staffs.sch.uk
Age Range: 3–18

ABBOTSHOLME SCHOOL*

●🏠▲

Rocester, Uttoxeter, Staffordshire ST14 5BS
W: www.abbotsholme.co.uk
Age Range: 4–18

CHASE ACADEMY

●🏠▲

Lyncroft House, Cannock, Staffordshire WS11 0UR
W: www.chaseacademy.com
Age Range: 3–18 (3–18 years Boys and Girls)

DENSTONE COLLEGE

●🏠▲

Uttoxeter, Staffordshire ST14 5HN
W: www.denstonecollege.org
Age Range: 11–18

LICHFIELD CATHEDRAL SCHOOL

●🏠

The Close, Lichfield, Staffordshire WS13 7LH
W: www.lichfieldcathedralschool.com
Age Range: 3–16

NEWCASTLE-UNDER-LYME SCHOOL

●🏠▲

Mount Pleasant, Newcastle-under-Lyme, Staffordshire ST5 1DB
W: www.nuls.org.uk
Age Range: 3–18

ST DOMINIC'S PRIORY SCHOOL

●🏠▲

21 Station Road, Stone, Staffordshire ST15 8EN
W: www.stdominicspriory.co.uk
Age Range: 2–18 (Boys 2–11)

ST DOMINIC'S SCHOOL

●🏠▲

32 Bargate Street, Stafford, Staffordshire ST19 9BA
W: www.stdominicsschool.co.uk
Age Range: 2–18 (Co-ed 2–7)

STAFFORD GRAMMAR SCHOOL

●🏠▲

Burton Manor, Stafford, Staffordshire ST18 9AT
W: www.staffordgrammar.staffs.sch.uk
Age Range: 11–18

STOCKTON-ON-TEES

SENIOR

RED HOUSE SCHOOL

36 The Green, Norton, Stockton-on-Tees TS20 1DX
W: www.redhouseschool.co.uk
Age Range: 3–16

TEESSIDE HIGH SCHOOL

The Avenue, Eaglescliffe, Stockton-on-Tees TS16 9AT
W: www.teessidehigh.co.uk
Age Range: 3–18

YARM SCHOOL

The Friarage, Yarm, Stockton-on-Tees TS15 9EJ
W: www.yarmschool.org
Age Range: 3–18

SUFFOLK

PREPARATORY

THE ABBEY

The Prep School for Woodbridge School, Woodbridge, Suffolk IP12 1DS
W: www.woodbridge.suffolk.sch.uk/the_abbey
Age Range: 4–11

ARBOR PREPARATORY

Flempton Road, Bury St Edmunds, Suffolk IP28 6QJ
W: www.arborschool.co.uk

BARNARDISTON HALL PREPARATORY SCHOOL

Haverhill, Suffolk CB9 7TG
W: www.barnardiston-hall.co.uk
Age Range: 2–13

BRANDESTON HALL, THE PREPARATORY SCHOOL FOR FRAMLINGHAM COLLEGE

Brandeston Hall, Brandeston, Suffolk IP13 7AH
W: www.framlinghamcollege.co.uk
Age Range: 3–13

FAIRSTEAD HOUSE SCHOOL

Fordham Road, Newmarket, Suffolk CB8 7AA
W: www.fairsteadhouse.co.uk
Age Range: 3–11

IPSWICH PREPARATORY SCHOOL

3 Ivry Street, Ipswich, Suffolk IP1 3QW
W: www.ipswich.suffolk.sch.uk
Age Range: 3–11

MORETON HALL PREPARATORY SCHOOL

Mount Road, Bury St Edmunds, Suffolk IP32 7BJ
W: www.moretonhall.net
Age Range: 2–13

OLD BUCKENHAM HALL SCHOOL

Brettenham Park, Ipswich, Suffolk IP7 7PH
W: www.obh.co.uk
Age Range: 2–13

THE OLD SCHOOL

Beccles, Suffolk NR34 7LG
Age Range: 4–11

ORWELL PARK

Ipswich, Suffolk IP10 0ER
W: www.orwellpark.co.uk
Age Range: 3–13

ST GEORGE'S SCHOOL

Southwold, Suffolk IP18 6SD
Age Range: 2–11

SOUTH LEE PREPARATORY SCHOOL

Nowton Road, Bury St Edmunds, Suffolk IP33 2BT
W: www.southlee.co.uk
Age Range: 2–13

SENIOR

AMBERFIELD SCHOOL

Nacton, Ipswich, Suffolk IP10 0HL
W: www.amberfield.suffolk.sch.uk
Age Range: 2–16 (Boys 2–7)

CULFORD SCHOOL*

Bury St Edmunds, Suffolk IP28 6TX
W: www.culford.co.uk
Age Range: 3–18

FINBOROUGH SCHOOL

The Hall, Stowmarket, Suffolk IP14 3EF
W: www.finborough.suffolk.sch.uk
Age Range: 2–18

England – Surrey

FRAMLINGHAM COLLEGE*

Framlingham, Woodbridge,
Suffolk IP13 9EY
W: www.framlinghamcollege.
co.uk
Age Range: 13–18

IPSWICH HIGH SCHOOL GDST

Woolverstone, Ipswich, Suffolk
IP9 1AZ
W: www.ipswichhigh.gdst.net
Age Range: 3–18

IPSWICH SCHOOL

Henley Road, Ipswich, Suffolk
IP1 3SG
W: www.ipswich.suffolk.sch.uk
Age Range: 11–18

THE ROYAL HOSPITAL SCHOOL

Holbrook, Ipswich, Suffolk IP9 2RX
W: www.royalhospitalschool.org
Age Range: 11–18

ST JOSEPH'S COLLEGE

Belstead Road, Ipswich, Suffolk
IP2 9DR
W: www.stjos.co.uk
Age Range: 2–18

SAINT FELIX SCHOOL

Halesworth Road, Southwold,
Suffolk IP18 6SD
W: www.stfelix.co.uk
Age Range: 1–18 (Boarding (girls
only) 11†)

STOKE COLLEGE

Sudbury, Suffolk CO10 8JE
W: www.stokecollege.co.uk
Age Range: 3–16

WOODBRIDGE SCHOOL

Burkitt Road, Woodbridge, Suffolk
IP12 4JH
W: www.woodbridge.suffolk.
sch.uk
Age Range: 11–18

INTERNATIONAL SCHOOLS AND INTERNATIONAL STUDY CENTRES

ALEXANDERS INTERNATIONAL SCHOOL*

Bawdsey Manor, Bawdsey,
Woodbridge, Suffolk IP12 3AZ
W: www.alexandersschool.com
Age Range: 11–17

FELIXSTOWE INTERNATIONAL COLLEGE

Maybush House, Felixstowe,
Suffolk IP11 7NA
Age Range: 9–17

SUMMERHILL SCHOOL

Westward Ho, Leiston, Suffolk
IP16 4HY
W: www.summerhillschool.co.uk
Age Range: 5–17

SURREY

NURSERY AND PRE-PREP

DOWNSEND SCHOOL–ASHTEAD LODGE

22 Oakfield Road, Ashtead, Surrey
KT21 2RE
W: www.downsend.co.uk
Age Range: 2–6

DOWNSEND SCHOOL–EPSOM LODGE

6 Norman Avenue, Epsom, Surrey
KT17 3AB
W: www.downsend.co.uk
Age Range: 2–6

PARK HILL SCHOOL

8 Queens Road, Kingston-upon-
Thames, Surrey KT2 7SH
W: www.parkhillschool.com
Age Range: 3–8

PREPARATORY

ABERDOUR SCHOOL

Brighton Road, Tadworth, Surrey
KT20 6AJ
W: www.aberdourschool.co.uk
Age Range: 2–13

ALDRO SCHOOL

Lombard Street, Godalming,
Surrey GU8 6AS
W: www.aldro.org
Age Range: 7–13

AMESBURY

Hazel Grove, Hindhead, Surrey
GU26 6BL
W: www.amesburyschool.co.uk
Age Range: 3–13

BARFIELD SCHOOL AND NURSERY

Guildford Road, Farnham, Surrey
GU10 1PB
W: www.barfieldschool.com
Age Range: 3–13

BARROW HILLS SCHOOL

Roke Lane, Godalming, Surrey
GU8 5NY
W: www.barrowhills.org.uk
Age Range: 3–13

BISHOPSGATE SCHOOL

Englefield Green, Egham, Surrey
TW20 0YJ
W: www.bishopsgate.surrey.
sch.uk
Age Range: 2–13

BRAMLEY SCHOOL

Chequers Lane, Tadworth, Surrey
KT20 7ST
W: www.bramleyschool.co.uk
Age Range: 3–11

BROOMFIELD HOUSE
SCHOOL

10 Broomfield Road, Richmond,
Surrey TW9 3HS
W: www.broomfieldhouse.com
Age Range: 3–11

CATERHAM PREPARATORY
SCHOOL

Caterham, Surrey CR3 6YB
W: www.caterhamschool.co.uk
Age Range: 3–11

CHINTHURST SCHOOL

Tadworth Street, Tadworth, Surrey
KT20 5QZ
W: www.chinthurstschool.co.uk
Age Range: 3–13

COLLINGWOOD SCHOOL

3 Springfield Road, Wallington,
Surrey SM6 0BD
W: www.collingwood.sutton.
sch.uk
Age Range: 2–11

COWORTH-FLEXLANDS
SCHOOL

Valley End, Woking, Surrey
GU24 8TE
W: www.coworthflexlands.co.uk
Age Range: 3–11

CRANLEIGH PREPARATORY
SCHOOL

Horseshoe Lane, Cranleigh,
Surrey GU68 8QH
W: www.cranleigh.org
Age Range: 7–13

CRANMORE SCHOOL

Leatherhead, Surrey KT24 6AT
W: www.cranmoreprep.co.uk
Age Range: 3–13

CUMNOR HOUSE SCHOOL

168 Pampisford Road, South
Croydon, Surrey CR2 6DA
W: www.cumnorhouse.com
Age Range: 4–13

CUMNOR HOUSE SCHOOL

1 Woodcote Lane, Purley, Surrey
CR8 3HB
W: www.cumnorhouse.com.
Age Range: 4–13

DANES HILL SCHOOL

Leatherhead Road, Leatherhead,
Surrey KT22 0JG
W: www.daneshillschool.co.uk
Age Range: 3–13

DANESFIELD MANOR
SCHOOL

Rydens Avenue, Walton-on-
Thames, Surrey KT12 3JB
W: www.danesfieldmanorschool.
co.uk
Age Range: 1–11

DATE VALLEY SCHOOL

9–11 Commonside East, Mitcham,
Surrey CR4 2QA
W: www.datevalley.com
Age Range: 2–11

DOWNSEND SCHOOL

1 Leatherhead Road,
Leatherhead, Surrey KT22 8TJ
W: www.downsend.co.uk
Age Range: 2–13 (Children age
2–6 attend one of our three
Nursery & Pre-Preparatory
Departments or Lodges, based in
Ashtead, Epsom & Leatherhead.)

DRAYTON HOUSE SCHOOL

35 Austen Road, Guildford, Surrey
GU1 3NP
W: www.draytonhouse.co.uk
Age Range: 3–8 (Nursery 1–3)

EDGEBOROUGH

Frensham, Farnham, Surrey
GU10 3AH
W: www.edgeborough.co.uk
Age Range: 2–13

EDUCARE SMALL SCHOOL

12 Cowleaze Road, Kingston-
upon-Thames, Surrey KT2 6DZ
W: educaresmallschool.org.uk
Age Range: 3–11

ELMHURST SCHOOL

44–48 South Park Hill Road, South
Croydon, Surrey CR2 7DW
W: www.elmhurstschool.net
Age Range: 4–11

EMBERHURST

94 Ember Lane, Esher, Surrey
KT10 8EN
W: www.emberhurst-school.com
Age Range: 2–8

ESSENDENE LODGE
SCHOOL

Essendene Road, Caterham,
Surrey CR3 5PB
W: www.essendenelodge.surrey.
sch.uk
Age Range: 2–11

FELTONFLEET SCHOOL

Cobham, Surrey KT11 1DR
W: www.feltonfleet.co.uk
Age Range: 3–13

GLENESK SCHOOL

Ockham Road North,
Leatherhead, Surrey KT24 6NS
W: www.glenesk.co.uk
Age Range: 2–7

GRANTCHESTER HOUSE

5 Hinchley Way, Esher, Surrey
KT10 0BD
W: www.grantchesterhouseschool.
com
Age Range: 3–7

GREENFIELD SCHOOL

Brooklyn Road, Woking, Surrey
GU22 7TP
W: www.greenfield.surrey.sch.uk
Age Range: 3–11

HALL GROVE SCHOOL

Bagshot, Surrey GU19 5HZ
W: www.hallgrove.co.uk
Age Range: 4–13

HALSTEAD PREPARATORY SCHOOL

Woodham Rise, Woking, Surrey
GU21 4EE
W: www.halstead-school.org.uk
Age Range: 2–11

HASLEMERE PREPARATORY SCHOOL

The Heights, Haslemere, Surrey
GU27 2JP
W: www.haslemere-prep.co.uk
Age Range: 2–14

THE HAWTHORNS SCHOOL

Pendell Court, Redhill, Surrey
RH1 4QJ
W: www.hawthorns.com
Age Range: 2–13

HOE BRIDGE SCHOOL*

Hoe Place, Old Woking Road,
Woking, Surrey GU22 8JE
W: www.hoebridgeschool.co.uk
Age Range: 2–13

HOLY CROSS PREPARATORY SCHOOL

Kingston upon Thames, Surrey
KT2 7NU
W: www.holycrossprepschool.
co.uk
Age Range: 4–11

HOMEFIELD PREPARATORY SCHOOL*

Western Road, Sutton, Surrey
SM1 2TE
W: www.homefield.sutton.sch.uk
Age Range: 3–13

KEW COLLEGE

24/26 Cumberland Road,
Richmond, Surrey TW9 3HQ
W: www.kewcollege.com
Age Range: 3–11

KEW GREEN PREPARATORY SCHOOL*

Layton House, Ferry lane,
Richmond, Surrey TW9 3AF
W: www.kgps.co.uk
Age Range: 4–11

KING'S HOUSE SCHOOL

68 Kings Road, Richmond, Surrey
TW10 6ES
W: www.kingshouse.richmond.
sch.uk
Age Range: 4–13

KINGSWOOD HOUSE SCHOOL

56 West Hill, Epsom, Surrey
KT19 8LG
W: www.kingswoodhouse.org
Age Range: 3–13

LALEHAM LEA SCHOOL

29 Peaks Hill, Purley, Surrey
CR8 3JJ
W: www.lalehamlea.co.uk
Age Range: 3–11

LANESBOROUGH

Maori Road, Guildford, Surrey
GU1 2EL
W: www.lanesborough.surrey.
sch.uk
Age Range: 3–13

LINLEY HOUSE

6 Berrylands Road, Surbiton,
Surrey KT5 8RA
W: www.linleyhouseschool.com
Age Range: 3–7

LONGACRE SCHOOL

Hullbrook Lane, Guildford, Surrey
GU5 0NQ
W: www.longacre.surrey.sch.uk
Age Range: 2–11

LYNDHURST SCHOOL

36 The Avenue, Camberley,
Surrey GU15 3NE
W: www.lyndhurstschool.co.uk
Age Range: 2–12

MICKLEFIELD SCHOOL

10 Somers Road, Reigate, Surrey
RH2 9DU
W: www.micklefieldschool.co.uk
Age Range: 3–11

MILBOURNE LODGE SCHOOL

43 Arbrook Lane, Esher, Surrey
KT10 9EG
W: www.milbournelodge.co.uk
Age Range: 4–13

NEW LIFE CHRISTIAN SCHOOL

Cairo New Road, Croydon, Surrey
CR0 1XP
W: www.newlifecroydon/
nlcs.co.uk
Age Range: 4–11

NOTRE DAME PREPARATORY SCHOOL

Burwood House, Cobham, Surrey
KT11 1HA
W: www.notredame.co.uk
Age Range: 2–11 (Boys 2–5)

OAKHYRST GRANGE SCHOOL

160 Stanstead Road, Caterham,
Surrey CR3 6AF
W: www.oakhyrstgrangeschool.
co.uk
Age Range: 4–11

OAKWOOD SCHOOL & NURSERY

Godstone Road, Purley, Surrey
CR8 2AN
W: www.oakwoodschool.org.uk
Age Range: 2–11

OLD VICARAGE SCHOOL

48 Richmond Hill, Richmond,
Surrey TW10 6QX
Age Range: 4–11

PARKSIDE SCHOOL

The Manor, Cobham, Surrey
KT11 3PX
W: www.parkside-school.co.uk
Age Range: 2–13 (Co-ed 2–4)

PEASLAKE SCHOOL

Colmans Hill, Guildford, Surrey
GU5 9ST
W: peaslake.surrey.sch.uk
Age Range: 3–7

PRIORY PREPARATORY SCHOOL*

Bolters Lane, Banstead, Surrey
SM7 2AJ
W: www.prioryprep.co.uk
Age Range: 2–13

REDEHALL PREPARATORY SCHOOL

Redehall Road, Horley, Surrey
RH6 9QA
W: www.redehallschool.com
Age Range: 3–11

REIGATE ST MARY'S PREPARATORY AND CHOIR SCHOOL

Chart Lane, Reigate, Surrey
RH2 7RN
W: www.reigatestmarys.org
Age Range: 3–11 (Rising 3 year
olds to 11 year olds)

RIPLEY COURT SCHOOL

Rose Lane, Woking, Surrey
GU23 6NE
W: www.ripleycourt.co.uk
Age Range: 3–13

ROKEBY SCHOOL

George Road, Kingston-upon-
Thames, Surrey KT2 7PB
W: www.rokebyschool.co.uk
Age Range: 4–13

ROWAN PREPARATORY SCHOOL

6 Fitzalan Road, Esher, Surrey
KT10 0LX
W: www.rowan.surrey.sch.uk
Age Range: 2–11

RYDES HILL PREPARATORY SCHOOL

Aldershot Road, Guildford, Surrey
GU2 8BP
W: www.rydeshill.com
Age Range: 3–11

ST. ANDREW'S (WOKING) SCHOOL TRUST

Church Hill House, Woking, Surrey
GU21 4QW
W: www.st-andrews.woking.
sch.uk
Age Range: 3–13

ST CHRISTOPHER'S SCHOOL

6 Downs Road, Epsom, Surrey
KT18 5HE
W: www.st-christophers.surrey.
sch.uk
Age Range: 3–7

ST DAVID'S SCHOOL

23 Woodcote Valley Road, Purley,
Surrey CR8 3AL
W: www.st-davidsschool.co.uk
Age Range: 3–11

ST EDMUND'S SCHOOL

Portsmouth Road, Hindhead,
Surrey GU26 6BH
W: www.saintedmunds.co.uk
Age Range: 2–13

ST GEORGE'S COLLEGE JUNIOR SCHOOL

Thames Street, Weybridge, Surrey
KT13 8NL
W: www.st-georges-college.co.uk
Age Range: 3–11

ST HILARY'S SCHOOL

Holloway Hill, Godalming, Surrey
GU7 1RZ
W: www.sthilarysschool.com
Age Range: 1–11

ST IVES SCHOOL

Three Gates Lane, Haslemere,
Surrey GU27 2ES
W: www.stiveshaslemere.com
Age Range: 3–11 (Boys 3–5)

ST TERESA'S PREPARATORY SCHOOL

Grove House, Effingham, Surrey
KT24 5QA
W: www.stteresasschool.com
Age Range: 2–11

SEATON HOUSE SCHOOL

67 Banstead Road South, Sutton,
Surrey SM2 5LH
W: www.seatonhouse.sutton.
sch.uk
Age Range: 3–11 (Boys 3–5
Girls 3–11)

SHREWSBURY HOUSE SCHOOL

107 Ditton Road, Surbiton, Surrey
KT6 6RL
W: www.shrewburyhouse.net
Age Range: 7–13

THE STUDY SCHOOL

57 Thetford Road, New Malden,
Surrey KT3 5DP
W: www.thestudyschool.co.uk
Age Range: 3–11

SURBITON PREPARATORY SCHOOL

3 Avenue Elmers, Surbiton, Surrey
KT6 4SP
W: www.surbitonhigh.com
Age Range: 4–11

UNICORN SCHOOL

238 Kew Road, Richmond, Surrey
TW9 3JX
W: www.unicornschool.org.uk
Age Range: 3–11

WARLINGHAM PARK SCHOOL

Chelsham Common, Croydon,
Surrey CR6 9PB
W: www.warlinghamparkschool.
com
Age Range: 2–11

WEST DENE SCHOOL

167 Brighton Road, Purley, Surrey
CR8 4HE
Age Range: 2–11

England – Surrey

WESTBURY HOUSE SCHOOL

80 Westbury Road, New Malden,
Surrey KT3 5AS
W: westburyhouse.surrey.sch.uk
Age Range: 3–11

WESTON GREEN SCHOOL

Weston Green Road, Thames
Ditton, Surrey KT7 0JN
W: www.westongreenschool.
org.uk
Age Range: 2–8

WESTWARD PREPARATORY SCHOOL

47 Hersham Road, Walton-on-
Thames, Surrey KT12 1LE
Age Range: 3–11

WOODCOTE HOUSE SCHOOL

Snow's Ride, Windlesham, Surrey
GU20 6PF
W: www.woodcotehouseschool.
co.uk
Age Range: 7–14

SENIOR

BOX HILL SCHOOL*

Old London Road, Mickleham,
Dorking, Surrey RH5 6EA
W: www.boxhillschool.com
Age Range: 11–18

CANBURY SCHOOL

Kingston Hill, Kingston-upon-
Thames, Surrey KT2 7LN
W: www.canburyschool.org.uk
Age Range: 10–16

CHARTERHOUSE

Godalming, Surrey GU7 2DX
W: www.charterhouse.org.uk
Age Range: 13–18 (Co-ed Sixth
Form)

CITY OF LONDON FREEMEN'S SCHOOL

Ashtead Park, Ashtead, Surrey
KT21 1ET
W: www.clfs.surrey.sch.uk
Age Range: 7–18

CLAREMONT FAN COURT SCHOOL*

Claremont Drive, Esher, Surrey
KT10 9LY
W: www.claremont-school.co.uk
Age Range: 3–18

CRANLEIGH SCHOOL

Horseshoe Lane, Cranleigh,
Surrey GU6 8QQ
W: www.cranleigh.org
Age Range: 13–18

CROYDON HIGH SCHOOL GDST

Old Farleigh Road, South
Croydon, Surrey CR2 8YB
W: www.croydonhigh.gdst.net
Age Range: 3–18

DUKE OF KENT SCHOOL

Peaslake Road, Guildford, Surrey
GU6 7NS
W: www.dukeofkentschool.org.uk
Age Range: 3–16

DUNOTTAR SCHOOL

High Trees Road, Reigate, Surrey
RH2 7EL
W: www.dunottarschool.com
Age Range: 3–18

EPSOM COLLEGE

College Road, Epsom, Surrey
KT17 4JQ
W: www.epsomcollege.org.uk
Age Range: 13–18

EWELL CASTLE SCHOOL

Church Street, Epsom, Surrey
KT17 2AW
W: www.ewellcastle.co.uk
Age Range: 3–18 (Girls 3–11)

FRENSHAM HEIGHTS SCHOOL

Rowledge, Farnham, Surrey
GU10 4EA
W: www.frensham-heights.org.uk
Age Range: 3–18

THE GERMAN SCHOOL

Douglas House, Richmond, Surrey
TW10 7AH
W: www.dslondon.org.uk
Age Range: 5–19

GREENACRE SCHOOL FOR GIRLS

Sutton Lane, Banstead, Surrey
SM7 3RA
W: www.greenacre.surrey.sch.uk
Age Range: 3–18

GUILDFORD HIGH SCHOOL

Guildford, Surrey GU1 1SJ
W: www.guildfordhigh.surrey.
sch.uk
Age Range: 4–18

HAMPTON COURT HOUSE

Hampton Court Road, East
Molesey, Surrey KT8 9BS
W: www.hamptoncourthouse.
co.uk
Age Range: 3–17

HAWLEY PLACE SCHOOL

Fernhill Road, Camberley, Surrey
GU17 9HU
W: www.hawleyplace.com
Age Range: 2–16

HURTWOOD HOUSE*

Holmbury St Mary, Dorking, Surrey
RH5 6NU
W: www.hurtwoodhouse.com
Age Range: 16–18

KING EDWARD'S SCHOOL WITLEY

Petworth Road, Godalming,
Surrey GU8 5SG
W: www.kesw.org
Age Range: 11–18

KINGSTON GRAMMAR SCHOOL

London Road, Kingston-upon-
Thames, Surrey KT2 6PY
W: www.kgs.org.uk
Age Range: 10–18

LINGFIELD NOTRE DAME SCHOOL

St Piers Lane, Lingfield, Surrey
RH7 6PH
W: www.lingfieldnotredame.co.uk
Age Range: 2–18

MANOR HOUSE SCHOOL

Manor House Lane, Leatherhead,
Surrey KT23 4EN
W: www.manorhouseschool.org
Age Range: 2–16

MARYMOUNT INTERNATIONAL SCHOOL*

George Road, Kingston-upon-
Thames, Surrey KT2 7PE
W: www.marymountlondon.com
Age Range: 11–18

NOTRE DAME SENIOR SCHOOL

Burwood House, Cobham, Surrey
KT11 1HA
W: www.notredame.co.uk
Age Range: 11–18

OAKFIELD SCHOOL

Coldharbour Road, Woking,
Surrey GU22 8SJ
W: www.oakfieldschool.co.uk
Age Range: 3–16

OLD PALACE OF JOHN WHITGIFT SCHOOL*

Old Palace Road, Croydon, Surrey
CR0 1AX
W: www.oldpalaceofjohnwhitgift.
org
Age Range: 1–19

PRIOR'S FIELD SCHOOL

Priorsfield Road, Godalming,
Surrey GU7 2RH
W: www.priorsfieldschool.com
Age Range: 11–18

REED'S SCHOOL

Sandy Lane, Cobham, Surrey
KT11 2ES
W: www.reeds.surrey.sch.uk
Age Range: 11–18 (Co-ed VIth
Form)

REIGATE GRAMMAR SCHOOL

Reigate Road, Reigate, Surrey
RH2 0QS
W: www.reigategrammar.org
Age Range: 11–18

ROYAL ALEXANDRA AND ALBERT SCHOOL*

Gatton Park, Reigate, Surrey
RH2 0TD
W: www.raa-school.co.uk
Age Range: 7–18

ROYAL BALLET SCHOOL

White Lodge, Richmond, Surrey
TW10 5HR
Age Range: 11–16

ROYAL GRAMMAR SCHOOL

High Street, Guildford, Surrey
GU1 3BB
W: www.rgs-guildford.co.uk
Age Range: 11–18

ROYAL RUSSELL SCHOOL

Coombe Lane, Croydon, Surrey
CR9 5BX
W: www.royalrussell.co.uk
Age Range: 3–18

THE ROYAL SCHOOL

Farnham Lane, Haslemere, Surrey
GU27 1HQ
W: www.royal-school.org
Age Range: 6–18 (Boys 2–4)

THE ROYAL SCHOOL FOR GIRLS

Farnham Lane, Haslemere, Surrey
GU27 1HQ
W: www.royal.surrey.sch.uk
Age Range: 11–18

ST CATHERINE'S SCHOOL

Station Road, Guildford, Surrey
GU5 0DF
W: www.stcatherines.info
Age Range: 4–18

ST GEORGE'S COLLEGE

Weybridge Road, Weybridge,
Surrey KT15 2QS
W: www.st-georges-college.co.uk
Age Range: 11–18

ST JAMES INDEPENDENT SCHOOL FOR BOYS (SENIOR)

Church Road, Ashford, Surrey
TW15 3DZ
W: www.stjamesboys.co.uk
Age Range: 10–18

ST JOHN'S SCHOOL

Epsom Road, Leatherhead, Surrey
KT22 8SP
W: www.stjohnsleatherhead.co.uk
Age Range: 13–18 (Co-ed VIth
Form)

ST TERESA'S SCHOOL*

Effingham Hill, Dorking, Surrey
RH5 6ST
W: www.stteresasschool.com
Age Range: 11–18

SIR WILLIAM PERKINS'S SCHOOL

Guildford Road, Chertsey, Surrey
KT16 9BN
W: www.swps.org.uk
Age Range: 11–18

SURBITON HIGH SCHOOL*

Surbiton Crescent, Kingston-
upon-Thames, Surrey KT1 2JT
W: www.surbitonhigh.com
Age Range: 4–18 (Boys 4–11)

SUTTON HIGH SCHOOL GDST

55 Cheam Road, Sutton, Surrey
SM1 2AX
W: www.gdst.net/suttonhigh
Age Range: 3–18

TORMEAD SCHOOL

27 Cranley Road, Guildford,
Surrey GUI 2JD
W: www.tormeadschool.org.uk
Age Range: 4–18

England – East Sussex

TRINITY SCHOOL*

 Shirley Park, Croydon, Surrey
CR9 7AT
W: www.trinity-school.org
Age Range: 10–18 (Boys 10–18
Girls 16–18)

WHITGIFT SCHOOL

 Haling Park, South Croydon,
Surrey CR2 6YT
W: www.whitgift.co.uk
Age Range: 10–18

YEHUDI MENUHIN SCHOOL

 Stoke D'Abernon, Cobham, Surrey
KT11 3QQ
W: www.yehudimenuhinschool.
co.uk
Age Range: 8–18

INDEPENDENT SIXTH FORM COLLEGE / TUTORIAL COLLEGE

CAMBRIDGE TUTORS COLLEGE

 Water Tower Hill, Croydon, Surrey
CR0 5SX
W: www.ctc.ac.uk
Age Range: 15–22

INTERNATIONAL SCHOOLS AND INTERNATIONAL STUDY CENTRES

ACS COBHAM INTERNATIONAL SCHOOL*

 Heywood, Portsmouth Road,
Cobham, Surrey KT11 1BL
W: www.acs-schools.com
Age Range: 2–18

ACS EGHAM INTERNATIONAL SCHOOL*

Woodlee, London Road (A30),
Egham, Surrey TW20 0HS
W: www.acs-schools.com
Age Range: 2–18

TASIS THE AMERICAN SCHOOL IN ENGLAND*

Coldharbour Lane, Thorpe, Surrey
TW20 8TE
W: www.tasisengland.org
Age Range: 3–18

EAST SUSSEX

PREPARATORY

ASHDOWN HOUSE SCHOOL

 Forest Row, East Sussex RH18 5JY
W: www.ashdownhouse.co.uk
Age Range: 8–13

BODIAM MANOR SCHOOL

Bodiam, Robertsbridge, East
Sussex TN32 5UJ
W: www.bodiammanorschool.
co.uk
Age Range: 2–13

BRICKLEHURST MANOR PREPARATORY

 Bardown Road, Wadhurst, East
Sussex TN5 7EL
W: www.bricklehurst.co.uk
Age Range: 3–11

BRIGHTON COLLEGE PRE-PREPARATORY SCHOOL

 Sutherland Road, Brighton, East
Sussex BN2 0EQ
W: www.brightoncollege.org.uk
Age Range: 3–8

BRIGHTON COLLEGE PREP SCHOOL

Walpole Lodge, Brighton, East
Sussex BN2 0EU
W: www.brightoncollege.org.uk
Age Range: 8–13

CLAREMONT SCHOOL

 Baldslow, St Leonards-on-Sea,
East Sussex TN37 7PW
W: www.Claremontschool.co.uk
Age Range: 1–14

DEEPDENE SCHOOL

 Hove, East Sussex BN3 4ED
W: www.deepdeneschool.com
Age Range: 1–8

DHARMA SCHOOL

 White House, Brighton, East
Sussex BN1 8TB
W: www.dharmaschool.co.uk
Age Range: 3–11

THE FOLD SCHOOL

 201 New Church Road, Hove, East
Sussex BN3 4ED
Age Range: 3–11

LANCING COLLEGE PREPARATORY SCHOOL AT MOWDEN

The Droveway, Hove, East Sussex BN3 6LU
W: www.lancingprep.co.uk
Age Range: 3–13

ST ANDREW'S SCHOOL

Meads, Eastbourne, East Sussex BN20 7RP
W: www.androvian.co.uk
Age Range: 2–13

ST AUBYNS SCHOOL

76 High Street, Brighton, East Sussex BN2 7JN
W: www.staubynsschoolbrighton.co.uk
Age Range: 3–13

ST BEDE'S PREP SCHOOL

Duke's Drive, Eastbourne, East Sussex BN20 7XL
W: www.stbedesschool.org
Age Range: 2–13

SACRED HEART R.C. PRIMARY SCHOOL

Mayfield Lane, Wadhurst, East Sussex TN5 6DQ
W: www.sacredheartwadhurst.org.uk
Age Range: 3–11

SKIPPERS HILL MANOR PREPARATORY SCHOOL

Five Ashes, Mayfield, East Sussex TN20 6HR
W: www.skippershill.com
Age Range: 3–13

VINEHALL SCHOOL

Robertsbridge, East Sussex TN32 5JL
W: www.vinehallschool.com
Age Range: 2–13

SENIOR

BATTLE ABBEY SCHOOL

High Street, Battle, East Sussex TN33 0AD
W: www.battleabbeyschool.com
Age Range: 2–18

BRIGHTON AND HOVE HIGH SCHOOL GDST

Montpelier Road, Brighton, East Sussex BN1 3AT
Age Range: 3–18

BRIGHTON COLLEGE

Eastern Road, Brighton, East Sussex BN2 0AL
W: www.brightoncollege.net
Age Range: 11–18

BRIGHTON STEINER SCHOOL LIMITED

Roedean Road, Brighton, East Sussex BN2 5RA
W: www.brightonsteinerschool.org.uk
Age Range: 2–16

DARVELL SCHOOL

Darvell Bruderhof, Robertsbridge, East Sussex TN32 5DR
Age Range: 4–16

THE DRIVE PREP SCHOOL

101 The Drive, Hove, East Sussex BN3 6GE
W: www.driveprep.co.uk
Age Range: 3–16

EASTBOURNE COLLEGE*

Old Wish Road, Eastbourne, East Sussex BN21 4JY
W: www.eastbourne-college.co.uk
Age Range: 13–18 (50% boarding / 50% day 58% boys / 42% girls)

GREENFIELDS SCHOOL

Priory Road, Forest Row, East Sussex RH18 5JD
W: www.greenfieldsschool.com
Age Range: 3–19

LEWES OLD GRAMMAR SCHOOL

140 High Street, Lewes, East Sussex BN7 1XS
W: www.oldgrammar.e-sussex.sch.uk
Age Range: 3–18

MICHAEL HALL (STEINER WALDORF SCHOOL)

Kidbrooke Park, Forest Row, East Sussex RH18 5JA
W: www.michaelhall.co.uk

MOIRA HOUSE GIRLS SCHOOL*

Upper Carlisle Road, Eastbourne, East Sussex BN20 7TE
W: www.moirahouse.co.uk
Age Range: 2–18

NEWLANDS SCHOOL

Eastbourne Road, Seaford, East Sussex BN25 4NP
W: www.newlands-school.com
Age Range: 2–18 (nursery & pre-prep)

ROEDEAN SCHOOL

Roedean Way, Brighton, East Sussex BN2 5RQ
W: www.roedean.co.uk
Age Range: 11–18

ST BEDE'S SCHOOL

Upper Dicker, Hailsham, East Sussex BN27 3QH
W: www.stbedesschool.org
Age Range: 13–19

ST LEONARDS-MAYFIELD SCHOOL

The Old Palace, Mayfield, East Sussex TN20 6PH
W: www.mayfieldgirls.org
Age Range: 11–19

STONELANDS SCHOOL OF BALLET & THEATRE ARTS

Hove, East Sussex BN3 2DJ
W: www.stonelandsschool.co.uk
Age Range: 5–16

INDEPENDENT SIXTH FORM COLLEGE / TUTORIAL COLLEGE

BARTHOLOMEWS TUTORIAL COLLEGE

22–23 Prince Albert Street, Brighton, East Sussex BN1 1HF
W: www.bartscollege.co.uk

BELLERBYS COLLEGE

Manor Campus, Hove, East Sussex BN3 3ER
W: www.bellerbys.com

INTERNATIONAL SCHOOLS AND INTERNATIONAL STUDY CENTRES

BUCKSWOOD SCHOOL*

Guestling, Hastings, East Sussex TN35 4LT
W: www.buckswood.co.uk
Age Range: 10–19

WEST SUSSEX

PREPARATORY

ARDINGLY COLLEGE JUNIOR SCHOOL

Haywards Heath, West Sussex RH17 6SQ
W: www.ardingly.com
Age Range: 7–13 (and pre-prep)

BROADWATER MANOR SCHOOL

Broadwater Road, Worthing, West Sussex BN14 8HU
W: www.broadwatermanor.com
Age Range: 2–13

CONIFERS SCHOOL

Egmont Road, Midhurst, West Sussex GU29 9BG
W: www.conifersschool.com
Age Range: 3–11

COPTHORNE PREP SCHOOL

Effingham Lane, Copthorne, West Sussex RH10 3HR
W: www.copthorneprep.co.uk
Age Range: 2–13

COTTESMORE SCHOOL

Buchan Hill, Pease Pottage, West Sussex RH11 9AU
W: www.cottesmoreschool.com
Age Range: 7–13

DORSET HOUSE SCHOOL

The Manor, Pulborough, West Sussex RH20 1PB
W: www.dorsethouseschool.com
Age Range: 3–13

FONTHILL LODGE

Coombe Hill Road, East Grinstead, West Sussex RH19 4LY
W: www.fonthill-lodge.co.uk
Age Range: 2–11 (Single-sex ed 8–11)

GREAT BALLARD SCHOOL

Eartham, Chichester, West Sussex PO18 0LR
W: www.greatballard.co.uk
Age Range: 2–13

GREAT WALSTEAD

East Mascalls Lane, Haywards Heath, West Sussex RH16 2QL
W: www.greatwalstead.co.uk
Age Range: 2–13

HANDCROSS PARK SCHOOL

Handcross, Haywards Heath, West Sussex RH17 6HF
W: www.handcrossparkschool.co.uk
Age Range: 2–13

OAKWOOD SCHOOL

Chichester, West Sussex PO18 9AN
W: www.oakwoodschool.co.uk
Age Range: 2–11

PENNTHORPE SCHOOL

Church Street, Horsham, West Sussex RH12 3HJ
W: www.pennthorpe.com
Age Range: 2–14

THE PREBENDAL SCHOOL

54 West Street, Chichester, West Sussex PO19 1RT
W: www.prebendalschool.org.uk
Age Range: 3–14

PREBENDAL SCHOOL (NORTHGATE HOUSE)

38 North Street, Chichester, West Sussex PO19 1LX
Age Range: 3–7

ST MARGARET'S SCHOOL

Petersfield Road, Midhurst, West Sussex GU29 9JN
W: www.conventofmercy.org
Age Range: 2–11

SOMPTING ABBOTTS SCHOOL

Church Lane, Sompting, West Sussex BN15 0AZ
W: www.somptingabbotts.com
Age Range: 3–13

TAVISTOCK & SUMMERHILL SCHOOL

Summerhill Lane, Haywards Heath, West Sussex RH16 1RP
W: www.tavistockandsummerhill.co.uk
Age Range: 3–13

WESTBOURNE HOUSE SCHOOL

Coach Road, Chichester, West Sussex PO20 2BH
W: www.westbournehouse.org
Age Range: 2–13

WILLOW TREE MONTESSORI SCHOOL

Charlwood House, Crawley, West Sussex RH11 0QA
W: www.wt-montessori-school.co.uk
Age Range: 1–8

WINDLESHAM HOUSE SCHOOL

Washington, Pulborough, West Sussex RH20 4AY
W: www.windlesham.com
Age Range: 4–13

SENIOR

ARDINGLY COLLEGE

Haywards Heath, West Sussex RH17 6SQ
W: www.ardingly.com
Age Range: 3–17

BURGESS HILL SCHOOL FOR GIRLS*

Keymer Road, Burgess Hill, West Sussex RH15 0EG
W: www.burgesshill-school.com
Age Range: 2–18

CHRIST'S HOSPITAL

Horsham, West Sussex RH13 0YP
W: www.christs-hospital.org.uk
Age Range: 11–18

FARLINGTON SCHOOL

Strood Park, Horsham, West Sussex RH12 3PN
W: www.farlingtonschool.net
Age Range: 3–18

HURSTPIERPOINT COLLEGE

College Lane, Hurstpierpoint, West Sussex BN6 9JS
W: www.hppc.co.uk
Age Range: 7–18

OUR LADY OF SION SCHOOL

Gratwicke Road, Worthing, West Sussex BN11 4BL
W: www.sionschool.org.uk
Age Range: 2–18

SEAFORD COLLEGE*

Lavington Park, Petworth, West Sussex GU28 0NB
W: www.seaford.org
Age Range: 7–18

SHOREHAM COLLEGE

St Julian's Lane, Shoreham-by-Sea, West Sussex BN43 6YW
W: www.shorehamcollege.co.uk
Age Range: 3–16

SLINDON COLLEGE

Arundel, West Sussex BN18 0RH
W: www.slindoncollege.co.uk
Age Range: 8–16

THE TOWERS CONVENT SCHOOL

Henfield Road, Steyning, West Sussex BN44 3TF
W: www.towers.w-sussex.sch.uk
Age Range: 3–16 (Boys 3–11)

WORTH SCHOOL

Paddockhurst Road, Turners Hill, West Sussex RH10 4SD
W: www.worthschool.co.uk
Age Range: 11–18 (Co-ed Sixth Form at present, welcoming day girls into Year 7 (age 11) and day and boarding girls into Year 9 (age 13)

INDEPENDENT SIXTH FORM COLLEGE / TUTORIAL COLLEGE

CHICHESTER COLLEGE

Westgate Fields, Chichester, West Sussex PO19 1SB
W: www.chichester.ac.uk

England – Tyne and Wear

TYNE AND WEAR

PREPARATORY

DAME ALLAN'S JUNIOR SCHOOL

72 Station Road, Newcastle upon Tyne, Tyne and Wear NE12 9BQ
W: www.dameallans.co.uk
Age Range: 3–11

NEWCASTLE PREPARATORY SCHOOL

6 Eslington Road, Newcastle upon Tyne, Tyne and Wear NE2 4RH
W: www.newcastleprepschool.org.uk
Age Range: 3–11

SENIOR

ARGYLE HOUSE SCHOOL

19/20 Thornhill Park, Sunderland, Tyne and Wear SR2 7LA
W: www.argylehouseschool.co.uk
Age Range: 3–16

CENTRAL NEWCASTLE HIGH SCHOOL GDST

Eskdale Terrace, Newcastle upon Tyne, Tyne and Wear NE2 4DS
W: newcastlehigh.gdst.net
Age Range: 3–18

CHURCH HIGH SCHOOL, NEWCASTLE UPON TYNE

Tankerville Terrace, Newcastle upon Tyne, Tyne and Wear NE2 3BA
W: www.churchhigh.com
Age Range: 3–18 (Pre School Nursery on site and Sixth Form.)

DAME ALLAN'S BOYS SCHOOL

Fowberry Crescent, Newcastle upon Tyne, Tyne and Wear NE4 9YJ
W: www.dameallans.co.uk
Age Range: 8–18 (Co-ed VIth Form)

DAME ALLAN'S GIRLS SCHOOL

Fowberry Crescent, Newcastle upon Tyne, Tyne and Wear NE4 9YJ
W: www.dameallans.co.uk
Age Range: 8–18 (Co-ed VIth Form)

GRINDON HALL CHRISTIAN SCHOOL

Sunderland, Tyne and Wear SR4 8PG
W: www.grindonhall.com
Age Range: 3–18

THE KING'S SCHOOL

Huntington Place, Tynemouth, Tyne and Wear NE30 4RF
W: www.kings-tynemouth.org
Age Range: 4–18

NEWCASTLE SCHOOL FOR BOYS

34 The Grove, Newcastle upon Tyne, Tyne and Wear NE3 1NH
W: www.newcastleschool.co.uk
Age Range: 3–18

ROYAL GRAMMAR SCHOOL

Eskdale Terrace, Newcastle upon Tyne, Tyne and Wear NE2 4DX
W: www.rgs.newcastle.sch.uk
Age Range: 8–18 (Co-ed VIth form)

SUNDERLAND HIGH SCHOOL

Mowbray Road, Sunderland, Tyne and Wear SR2 8HY
W: www.sunderlandhigh.co.uk
Age Range: 2–18

WESTFIELD SCHOOL

Newcastle upon Tyne, Tyne and Wear NE3 4HS
W: www.westfield.newcastle.sch.uk
Age Range: 3–18

WARWICKSHIRE

PREPARATORY

ARNOLD LODGE SCHOOL

Kenilworth Road, Leamington Spa, Warwickshire CV32 5TW
Age Range: 3–13

BILTON GRANGE

Rugby Road, Rugby, Warwickshire CV22 6QU
W: www.biltongrange.co.uk
Age Range: 4–13

CRACKLEY HALL SCHOOL

St Joseph's Park, Kenilworth, Warwickshire CV8 2FT
W: www.crackleyhall.co.uk
Age Range: 2–11

THE CRESCENT SCHOOL

Bawnmore Road, Rugby,
Warwickshire CV22 7QH
W: www.crescentschool.co.uk
Age Range: 3–11

THE CROFT PREPARATORY SCHOOL

Alveston Hill, Stratford-upon-Avon,
Warwickshire CV37 7RL
W: www.croftschool.co.uk
Age Range: 2–11

THE DIXIE GRAMMAR JUNIOR SCHOOL

Temple Hall, Nuneaton,
Warwickshire CV13 6PA
W: www.pipemedia.net/dixie
Age Range: 3–10

EMSCOTE HOUSE SCHOOL AND NURSERY

46 Warwick Place, Leamington
Spa, Warwickshire CV32 5DE
W: www.emscotehouseschool.
co.uk
Age Range: 2–8

MILVERTON HOUSE SCHOOL

Holman Way, Nuneaton,
Warwickshire CV11 4NS
W: www.milvertonschool.com

STRATFORD PREPARATORY SCHOOL

Church House, Stratford-upon-
Avon, Warwickshire CV37 6BG
W: www.stratfordprep.co.uk
Age Range: 2–11

THE TERRACE SCHOOL

54 High Street, Leamington Spa,
Warwickshire CV31 1LW
Age Range: 2–13

WARWICK PREPARATORY SCHOOL

Bridge Field, Warwick,
Warwickshire CV34 6PL
W: www.warwickprep.com
Age Range: 3–11

SENIOR

KING'S HIGH SCHOOL, WARWICK

Smith Street, Warwick,
Warwickshire CV34 4HJ
W: kingshighwarwick.co.uk
Age Range: 10–18

THE KINGSLEY SCHOOL

Beauchamp Avenue, Leamington
Spa, Warwickshire CV32 5RD
W: www.thekingsleyschool.com
Age Range: 3–18 (Boys 2–7)

PRINCETHORPE COLLEGE

Leamington Road, Rugby,
Warwickshire CV23 9PX
W: www.princethorpe.co.uk
Age Range: 11–18

RUGBY SCHOOL

School House, Rugby,
Warwickshire CV22 5EH
W: www.rugbyschool.net
Age Range: 11–18

TWYCROSS HOUSE SCHOOL

Atherstone, Warwickshire CV9 3PL
W: www.twycrosshouseschool.
org.uk
Age Range: 8–19

WARWICK SCHOOL

Myton Road, Warwick,
Warwickshire CV34 6PP
W: www.warwickschool.org
Age Range: 7–18

WEST MIDLANDS

PREPARATORY

AL HIJRAH SCHOOL

Cherrywood Centre, Birmingham,
West Midlands B9 4US
W: www.alhijrahschool.co.uk
Age Range: 4–11

BABLAKE JUNIOR SCHOOL

Coundon Road, Coventry, West
Midlands CV1 4AU
W: www.bablakejs.co.uk
Age Range: 7–11

BIRCHFIELD SCHOOL

Wolverhampton, West Midlands
WV7 3AF
W: www.birchfieldschool.co.uk
Age Range: 4–13

THE BLUE COAT SCHOOL

Somerset Road, Birmingham,
West Midlands B17 0HR
W: www.bluecoat.bham.sch.uk
Age Range: 2–11

CHESHUNT PRE-PREPARATORY SCHOOL

8 Park Road, Coventry, West
Midlands CV1 2LH
W: www.bablakeschools.com
Age Range: 3–8

COVENTRY PREP SCHOOL

Kenilworth Road, Coventry, West
Midlands CV3 6PT
W: www.coventryprep.co.uk
Age Range: 3–11

England – West Midlands

DAVENPORT LODGE SCHOOL

●🏠

21 Davenport Road, Coventry, West Midlands CV5 6QA
W: www.davenportlodge.coventry. sch.uk

THE DRIVE PREPARATORY SCHOOL

●🏠

Wood Road, Wolverhampton, West Midlands WV6 8RX
W: www.tettcoll.co.uk
Age Range: 2–7

EVERSFIELD PREPARATORY SCHOOL

●🏠

Warwick Road, Solihull, West Midlands B91 1AT
W: www.eversfield.co.uk
Age Range: 3–11

HALLFIELD SCHOOL

●🏠

48 Church Road, Birmingham, West Midlands B15 3SJ
W: www.hallfieldschool.co.uk
Age Range: 2–11

HARPER BELL SCHOOL

●🏠

29 Ravenhurst Street, Birmingham, West Midlands B2 0EP
Age Range: 2–11

KINGSWOOD SCHOOL

●🏠

St James Place, Solihull, West Midlands B90 2BA
W: www.kingswoodschool.co.uk
Age Range: 2–11

LAMBS CHRISTIAN SCHOOL

●🏠

86–95 Bacchus Road, Birmingham, West Midlands B18 4QY
W: www.christian-education.org
Age Range: 4–11

MAYFIELD PREPARATORY SCHOOL

●🏠

Sutton Road, Walsall, West Midlands WS1 2PD
W: www.mayfieldprep.co.uk
Age Range: 3–11

NEWBRIDGE PREPARATORY SCHOOL

●🏠

51 Newbridge Crescent, Wolverhampton, West Midlands WV6 0LH
Age Range: 3–11

NORFOLK HOUSE SCHOOL

●🏠

4 Norfolk Road, Birmingham, West Midlands B15 3PS
Age Range: 3–11

RATHVILLY SCHOOL

●🏠

119 Bunbury Road, Birmingham, West Midlands B31 2NB
Age Range: 3–11

ROSSLYN SCHOOL

●🏠

1597 Stratford Road, Birmingham, West Midlands B28 9JB
W: www.rosslynschool.co.uk
Age Range: 2–11

THE ROYAL WOLVERHAMPTON JUNIOR SCHOOL

●🏠

Penn Road, Wolverhampton, West Midlands WV3 0EF
W: www.theroyalschool.co.uk
Age Range: 2–11

RUCKLEIGH SCHOOL

●🏠

17 Lode Lane, Solihull, West Midlands B91 2AB
W: www.ruckleigh.co.uk
Age Range: 3–11

THE SHRUBBERY SCHOOL

●🏠

Walmley Ash Road, Sutton Coldfield, West Midlands B76 1HY
W: www.shrubberyschool.co.uk
Age Range: 3–11

WEST HOUSE SCHOOL

●🏠

24 St James's Road, Birmingham, West Midlands B15 2NX
W: www.westhouse.bham.sch.uk
Age Range: 1–11 (Girls 1–4)

WOODSTOCK GIRLS' SCHOOL

●🏠

11–15 Woodstock Road, Birmingham, West Midlands B13 9BB
Age Range: 11–15

SENIOR

ABU BAKR INDEPENDENT SCHOOL

●🏠

154–160 Wednesbury Road, Walsall, West Midlands WS1 4JJ
W: www.abubakrtrust.org
Age Range: 11–16

AL-BURHAN GRAMMAR SCHOOL

●🏠

28A George Street, Birmingham, West Midlands B12 9RG
W: www.alburhan.org.uk
Age Range: 11–16

BABLAKE SCHOOL

●🏠▲

Coundon Road, Coventry, West Midlands CV1 4AU
W: www.bablake.com
Age Range: 11–19

BIRCHFIELD INDEPENDENT GIRLS SCHOOL

●🏠

Beacon House, Birmingham, West Midlands B6 6JU
W: www.bigs.org.uk
Age Range: 11–16

COVENTRY MUSLIM SCHOOL

●🏠

643 Foleshill Road, Coventry, West Midlands CV6 5JQ
W: www.coventrymuslimschool. com
Age Range: 4–16

EDGBASTON HIGH SCHOOL FOR GIRLS

●🏠▲

Westbourne Road, Birmingham, West Midlands B15 3TS
W: www.edgbastonhigh.co.uk
Age Range: 3–18

ELMHURST SCHOOL FOR DANCE

247–249 Bristol Road,
Birmingham, West Midlands
B5 7UH
W: www.elmhurstdance.co.uk
Age Range: 11–19

EMMANUEL SCHOOL

Bath Street Centre, Walsall, West
Midlands WS1 3DB
W: www.emmanuel.walsall.sch.uk
Age Range: 3–16

HIGHCLARE SCHOOL

10 Sutton Road, Birmingham,
West Midlands B23 6QL
W: www.highclareschool.co.uk
Age Range: 1–18 (Boys 1–12 &
16–18
(Boys are being accepted into
Senior School from September
2011 from Year 7))

HYDESVILLE TOWER SCHOOL

25 Broadway North, Walsall, West
Midlands WS1 2QG
W: www.hydesville.com
Age Range: 3–16

KING EDWARD VI HIGH SCHOOL FOR GIRLS

Edgbaston Park Road,
Birmingham, West Midlands
B15 2UB
W: www.kehs.org.uk
Age Range: 11–18

KING HENRY VIII SCHOOL

Coventry, West Midlands CV3 6AQ
W: www.khviii.com
Age Range: 7–18

PATTISON COLLEGE

90 Binley Road, Coventry, West
Midlands CV3 1FQ
W: www.pattisons.co.uk
Age Range: 3–16

PRIORY SCHOOL

39 Sir Harry's Road, Birmingham,
West Midlands B15 2UR
W: www.prioryschool.net
Age Range: (Co-ed 1–11)

ST GEORGE'S SCHOOL, EDGBASTON

31 Calthorpe Road, Birmingham,
West Midlands B15 1RX
W: www.sgse.co.uk
Age Range: 3–18

SAINT MARTIN'S SCHOOL

Malvern Hall, Solihull, West
Midlands B91 3EN
W: www.saintmartins-school.com
Age Range: 3–18 (Girls may join
the school from 2 years 9 months.)

SOLIHULL SCHOOL

Warwick Road, Solihull, West
Midlands B91 3DJ
W: www.solsch.org.uk
Age Range: 7–18

TETTENHALL COLLEGE

Wood Road, Wolverhampton,
West Midlands WV6 8QX
W: www.tettenhallcollege.co.uk
Age Range: 2–18

WOLVERHAMPTON GRAMMAR SCHOOL

Compton Road, Wolverhampton,
West Midlands WV3 9RB
W: www.wgs.org.uk
Age Range: 10–18

INDEPENDENT SIXTH FORM COLLEGE / TUTORIAL COLLEGE

ABBEY COLLEGE

10 St Pauls Square, Birmingham,
West Midlands B3 1QU
W: www.abbeybirmingham.co.uk

MANDER PORTMAN WOODWARD

17–18 Greenfield Crescent,
Birmingham, West Midlands
B15 3AU
W: www.mpw.co.uk

WILTSHIRE

NURSERY AND PRE-PREP

STEPPING STONES NURSERY AND PRE-PREPARATORY SCHOOL

Oakhill Farm, Marlborough, Wiltshire SN8 3JT
W: www.steppingstonesschool.org.uk
Age Range: 2–8

PREPARATORY

AVONDALE SCHOOL

High Street, Salisbury, Wiltshire SP4 9DR
Age Range: 3–11

CHAFYN GROVE SCHOOL*

Bourne Avenue, Salisbury, Wiltshire SP1 1LR
W: www.chafyngrove.co.uk
Age Range: 3–13

GODOLPHIN PREPARATORY SCHOOL

Laverstock Road, Salisbury, Wiltshire SP1 2RB
W: www.godolphinprep.org
Age Range: 3–11

HEYWOOD PREPARATORY SCHOOL

The Priory, Corsham, Wiltshire SN13 0AP
W: www.heywoodprep.com
Age Range: 2–11

LEADEN HALL SCHOOL

70 The Close, Salisbury, Wiltshire SP1 2EP
W: www.leaden-hall.com
Age Range: 3–11 (Boys 3–4)

MEADOWPARK SCHOOL AND NURSERY

Calcutt Street, Cricklade, Wiltshire SN6 6BA
W: www.meadowparkschool.co.uk

THE MILL SCHOOL

Whistley Road, Devizes, Wiltshire SN10 5TE
W: www.mill.wilts.sch.uk
Age Range: 3–11

NORMAN COURT PREPARATORY SCHOOL*

West Tytherley, Salisbury, Wiltshire SP5 1NH
W: www.normancourt.co.uk.
Age Range: 3–13

PINEWOOD SCHOOL

Shrivenham, Wiltshire SN6 8HZ
W: www.pinewoodschool.co.uk
Age Range: 3–13

PRIOR PARK PREPARATORY SCHOOL

Calcutt Street, Cricklade, Wiltshire SN6 6BB
W: www.priorparkschools.co.uk
Age Range: 4–13

ROUNDSTONE PREPARATORY SCHOOL

Courtfield House, Trowbridge, Wiltshire BA14 7EG
W: www.roundstone.ik.org
Age Range: 4–11

ST FRANCIS SCHOOL

Marlborough Road, Pewsey, Wiltshire SN9 5NT
W: www.st-francis.wilts.sch.uk
Age Range: 2–13

ST MARGARET'S PREPARATORY SCHOOL

Curzon Street, Calne, Wiltshire SN11 0DF
W: www.stmargaretsprep.org.uk
Age Range: 3–11

SALISBURY CATHEDRAL SCHOOL

1 The Close, Salisbury, Wiltshire SP1 2EQ
W: www.salisburycathedralschool.com
Age Range: 3–13

SANDROYD SCHOOL

Rushmore, Salisbury, Wiltshire SP5 5QD
W: www.sandroyd.org
Age Range: 7–13 (The Walled Garden pre prep ages 2 1/2–7 years
Sandroyd 7–13 years)

SOUTH HILLS SCHOOL

Home Farm Road, Salisbury, Wiltshire SP2 8PJ
W: www.southhillsschool.com

SENIOR

DAUNTSEY'S SCHOOL*

High Street, West Lavington, Devizes, Wiltshire SN10 4HE
W: www.dauntseys.org
Age Range: 11–18

EMMAUS SCHOOL

School Lane, Trowbridge, Wiltshire BA14 6NZ
W: www.emmaus-school.org.uk
Age Range: 5–16

THE GODOLPHIN SCHOOL

Milford Hill, Salisbury, Wiltshire SP1 2RA
W: www.godolphin.org
Age Range: 11–18

GRITTLETON HOUSE SCHOOL*

Grittleton, Chippenham, Wiltshire SN14 6AP
W: www.grittletonhouseschool.org
Age Range: 2–16

LEEHURST SWAN

Campbell Road, Salisbury, Wiltshire SP1 3BQ
W: www.leehurstswan.org.uk
Age Range: 2–16

MARANATHA CHRISTIAN SCHOOL

Queenlaines Farm, Swindon, Wiltshire SN6 7SQ
W: www.christian-education.org
Age Range: 3–18

MARLBOROUGH COLLEGE

Marlborough, Wiltshire SN8 1PA
W: www.marlboroughcollege.org
Age Range: 13–18

ST MARY'S CALNE*

Curzon Street, Calne, Wiltshire SN11 0DF
W: www.stmaryscalne.org
Age Range: 11–18

STONAR SCHOOL

Cottles Park, Melksham, Wiltshire SN12 8NT
W: www.stonarschool.com
Age Range: 2–18

WARMINSTER SCHOOL

Church Street, Warminster, Wiltshire BA12 8PJ
W: www.warminsterschool.org.uk
Age Range: 3–19

INTERNATIONAL SCHOOLS AND INTERNATIONAL STUDY CENTRES

BISHOPSTROW COLLEGE

Bishopstrow, Wiltshire BA12 9HU
W: www.bishopstrow.com
Age Range: 8–17

WORCESTERSHIRE

NURSERY AND PRE-PREP

BROMSGROVE PRE-PREPARATORY AND NURSERY SCHOOL

Avoncroft House, Bromsgrove, Worcestershire B60 4JS
W: www.bromsgrove-school.co.uk
Age Range: 2–7

PREPARATORY

ABBERLEY HALL

Abberley Hall, Worcester, Worcestershire WR6 6DD
W: www.abberleyhall.co.uk
Age Range: 2–13

BROMSGROVE PREPARATORY SCHOOL

Old Station Road, Bromsgrove, Worcestershire B60 2BU
W: www.bromsgrove-school.co.uk
Age Range: 7–13

THE DOWNS, MALVERN

Brockhill Road, Malvern, Worcestershire WR13 6EY
W: www.thedowns.malcol.org
Age Range: 3–13

THE ELMS

Colwall, Malvern, Worcestershire WR13 6EF
W: www.elmsschool.co.uk
Age Range: 3–13

KING'S HAWFORD

Hawford Lock Lane, Worcester, Worcestershire WR3 7SD
W: www.ksw.org.uk
Age Range: 2–11

THE KNOLL SCHOOL

33 Manor Avenue, Kidderminster, Worcestershire DY11 6EA
W: www.knoll.worcs.sch.uk
Age Range: 2–11

MADRESFIELD EARLY YEARS CENTRE

Hayswood Farm, Malvern, Worcestershire WR13 5AA
Age Range: 1–8

MOFFATS SCHOOL

Kinlet Hall, Bewdley, Worcestershire DY12 3AY
W: www.moffats.co.uk
Age Range: 4–13

RGS THE GRANGE

Grange Lane, Worcester, Worcestershire WR3 7RR
W: www.rgsao.org
Age Range: 2–11

WINTERFOLD HOUSE

Kidderminster, Worcestershire DY10 4PW
W: www.winterfoldhouse.co.uk
Age Range: 2–13

SENIOR

BOWBROOK HOUSE SCHOOL

Peopleton, Pershore,
Worcestershire WR10 2EE
W: www.bowbrookhouseschool.
co.uk
Age Range: 3–16

BROMSGROVE SCHOOL*

Worcester Road, Bromsgrove,
Worcestershire B61 7DU
W: www.bromsgrove-school.co.uk
Age Range: 13–18

DODDERHILL SCHOOL

Droitwich Spa, Worcestershire
WR9 0BE
W: www.dodderhill.co.uk
Age Range: 3–16 (Boys 3–9)

GREEN HILL SCHOOL

Evesham, Worcestershire
WR11 4NG
W: www.greenhillschool.co.uk
Age Range: 3–13

HEATHFIELD SCHOOL

Wolverley, Kidderminster,
Worcestershire DY10 3QE
W: www.heathfieldschool.co.uk
Age Range: 3–16

HOLY TRINITY SCHOOL

Birmingham Road, Kidderminster,
Worcestershire DY10 2BY
W: www.holytrinity.co.uk

THE KING'S SCHOOL

5 College Green, Worcester,
Worcestershire WR1 2LL
W: www.ksw.org.uk
Age Range: 3–18

MALVERN ST JAMES*

15 Avenue Road, Great Malvern,
Worcestershire WR14 3BA
W: www.malvernstjames.co.uk
Age Range: 4–18[†]

RGS WORCESTER & THE ALICE OTTLEY SCHOOL

Upper Tything, Worcester,
Worcestershire WR1 1HP
W: www.rgsao.org
Age Range: 11–18

RIVER SCHOOL

Oakfield House, Worcester,
Worcestershire WR3 7ST
W: www.riverschool.co.uk
Age Range: 5–16

ST MARY'S

Worcester, Worcestershire
WR5 2HP
W: www.stmarys.org.uk
Age Range: 2–18 (Boys 2–8)

SAINT MICHAEL'S COLLEGE

Oldwood Road, Tenbury Wells,
Worcestershire WR15 8PH
W: www.st-michaels.uk.com
Age Range: 14–19

SPRINGFIELD SCHOOL

Britannia Square, Worcester,
Worcestershire WR1 3DL
W: www.rgso.org
Age Range: 2–11

INDEPENDENT SIXTH FORM COLLEGE / TUTORIAL COLLEGE

THE ABBEY COLLEGE

253 Wells Road, Malvern Wells,
Worcestershire WR14 4JF
W: www.abbeycollege.co.uk
Age Range: 14–23 (English
Courses (12[†])
Vacation Courses (8[†])
Academic Courses (14[†]))

EAST RIDING OF YORKSHIRE

PREPARATORY

FROEBEL HOUSE SCHOOL

5 Marlborough Avenue, Hull, East
Riding of Yorkshire HU5 3JP
W: www.the-village.co.uk/
froebelhouse
Age Range: 4–11

HESSLE MOUNT SCHOOL

Jenny Brough Lane, Hessle, East
Riding of Yorkshire HU13 0JX
W: www.hesslemountschool.
org.uk
Age Range: 3–8

POCKLINGTON MONTESSORI SCHOOL

Carr Lane, Pocklington, East
Riding of Yorkshire YO42 1NT
W: www.pocklingtonmontessori.
com

SENIOR

HULL COLLEGIATE SCHOOL

Tranby Croft, Anlaby, East Riding
of Yorkshire HU10 7EH
W: www.hullcollegiateschool.
co.uk
Age Range: 3–18

HYMERS COLLEGE

Hymers Avenue, Hull, East Riding of Yorkshire HU3 1LW
W: www.hymerscollege.co.uk
Age Range: 8–18

POCKLINGTON SCHOOL

West Green, Pocklington, East Riding of Yorkshire YO42 2NJ
W: www.pocklingtonschool.com
Age Range: 7–18

NORTH YORKSHIRE

PREPARATORY

AYSGARTH PREPARATORY SCHOOL*

Newton-Le-Willows, Bedale, North Yorkshire DL8 1TF
W: www.aysgarthschool.com
Age Range: 3–13 (Co-ed day 3–8)

BELMONT GROSVENOR SCHOOL

Swarcliffe Hall, Harrogate, North Yorkshire HG3 2JG
W: www.belmontgrosvenor.co.uk
Age Range: 2–11

BOOTHAM JUNIOR SCHOOL

Rawcliffe Lane, York, North Yorkshire YO30 6NP
W: www.boothamschool.com
Age Range: 3–11

BOTTON VILLAGE SCHOOL

Danby, Whitby, North Yorkshire YO21 2NJ
Age Range: 4–14

BRACKENFIELD SCHOOL

128 Duchy Road, Harrogate, North Yorkshire HG1 2HE
W: www.brackenfieldschool.co.uk
Age Range: 2–11

BRAMCOTE SCHOOL

Filey Road, Scarborough, North Yorkshire YO11 2TT
W: www.bramcoteschool.com
Age Range: 3–13

CUNDALL MANOR SCHOOL

York, North Yorkshire YO61 2RW
W: www.cundallmanor.n-yorks.sch.uk
Age Range: 2–13

GIGGLESWICK JUNIOR SCHOOL

Giggleswick, Settle, North Yorkshire BD24 0DG
W: www.giggleswick.org.uk
Age Range: 3–11

HIGHFIELD PREPARATORY SCHOOL (HLC Prep School)

Clarence Drive, Harrogate, North Yorkshire HG1 2QG
W: www.highfieldprep.org.uk
Age Range: 4–11

LISVANE, SCARBOROUGH COLLEGE JUNIOR SCHOOL

Filey Road, Scarborough, North Yorkshire YO11 3BA
W: www.scarboroughcollege.co.uk
Age Range: 3–11

MALSIS SCHOOL

Near Skipton, North Yorkshire BD20 8DT
W: www.malsis.com
Age Range: 4–13

THE MINSTER SCHOOL

York, North Yorkshire YO1 7JA
W: www.minster.york.sch.uk
Age Range: 3–13

RIPON CATHEDRAL CHOIR SCHOOL

Whitcliffe Lane, Ripon, North Yorkshire HG4 2LA
W: www.cathedralchoirschool.co.uk
Age Range: 3–13

ST MARTIN'S AMPLEFORTH

Gilling Castle, York, North Yorkshire YO62 4HP
W: www.stmartins.ampleforth.org.uk
Age Range: 3–13

TERRINGTON HALL

York, North Yorkshire YO60 6PR
W: www.terringtonhall.com
Age Range: 3–13

TREGELLES

The Mount Junior School, York, North Yorkshire YO24 4DD
W: www.mount.n-yorks.sch.uk
Age Range: 3–11

WOODLEIGH SCHOOL

Malton, North Yorkshire YO17 9QN
W: www.woodleighschool.com
Age Range: 3–13

SENIOR

AMPLEFORTH COLLEGE

York, North Yorkshire YO62 4ER
W: www.college.ampleforth.org.uk
Age Range: 13–18

ASHVILLE COLLEGE

Green Lane, Harrogate, North Yorkshire HG2 9JP
W: www.ashville.co.uk
Age Range: 4–18

BOOTHAM SCHOOL

York, North Yorkshire YO30 7BU
W: www.boothamschool.com
Age Range: 11–18

FYLING HALL SCHOOL

Robin Hood's Bay, Whitby, North Yorkshire YO22 4QD
W: www.fylinghall.org
Age Range: 4–19

GIGGLESWICK SCHOOL

Giggleswick, Settle, North Yorkshire BD24 0DE
W: www.giggleswick.org.uk
Age Range: 4–18

HARROGATE LADIES' COLLEGE

Clarence Drive, Harrogate, North Yorkshire HG1 2QG
W: www.hlc.org.uk
Age Range: 11–18

THE MOUNT SCHOOL

Dalton Terrace, York, North Yorkshire YO24 4DD
W: www.mountschoolyork.co.uk
Age Range: 3–18

QUEEN ETHELBURGA'S COLLEGE

Thorpe Underwood Hall, York, North Yorkshire YO26 9SS
W: www.queenethelburgas.edu
Age Range: 3–20

QUEEN MARY'S SCHOOL

Baldersby Park, Thirsk, North Yorkshire YO7 3BZ
W: www.queenmarys.org
Age Range: 2–16 (Boys 3–7)

READ SCHOOL

Selby, North Yorkshire YO8 8NL
W: www.readschool.co.uk
Age Range: 4–18

ST PETER'S SCHOOL

York, North Yorkshire YO30 6AB
W: www.st-peters.york.sch.uk
Age Range: 13–18

SCARBOROUGH COLLEGE & LISVANE SCHOOL

Filey Road, Scarborough, North Yorkshire YO11 3BA
W: www.scarboroughcollege.co.uk
Age Range: 3–18

INDEPENDENT SIXTH FORM COLLEGE / TUTORIAL COLLEGE

HARROGATE TUTORIAL COLLEGE

2 The Oval, Harrogate, North Yorkshire HG2 9BA
W: www.htcuk.org
Age Range: 15–20

INTERNATIONAL SCHOOLS AND INTERNATIONAL STUDY CENTRES

HARROGATE LANGUAGE ACADEMY

8a Royal Parade, Harrogate, North Yorkshire HG1 2SZ
W: www.hla.co.uk

SOUTH YORKSHIRE

PREPARATORY

ASHDELL PREPARATORY SCHOOL

266 Fulwood Road, Sheffield, South Yorkshire S10 3BL
W: www.ashdellprep.co.uk
Age Range: 3–11 (Co-educational Pre-School for rising threes in association with Birkdale School)

MYLNHURST PREPARATORY SCHOOL & NURSERY

Button Hill, Sheffield, South Yorkshire S11 9HJ
W: www.mylnhurst.co.uk
Age Range: 3–11

RUDSTON PREPARATORY SCHOOL

59–63 Broom Road, Rotherham, South Yorkshire S60 2SW
W: www.rudstonschool.com
Age Range: 2–11

SYCAMORE HALL PREPARATORY SCHOOL

1 Hall Flat Lane, Doncaster, South Yorkshire DN4 8PT
Age Range: 3–11

SENIOR

BARNSLEY CHRISTIAN SCHOOL

Hope House, Barnsley, South Yorkshire S70 1AP
W: www.barnsleychristianschool.
org.uk
Age Range: 5–16

BIRKDALE SCHOOL

Oakholme Road, Sheffield, South Yorkshire S10 3DH
W: www.birkdaleschool.org.uk
Age Range: 4–18 (Co-ed VIth Form)

HANDSWORTH CHRISTIAN SCHOOL

231 Handsworth Road, Sheffield, South Yorkshire S13 9BJ
W: www.
handsworthchristianschool.co.uk
Age Range: 4–16

HILL HOUSE SCHOOL

Sixth Avenue, Doncaster, South Yorkshire DN9 3GG
W: www.hillhousestmarys.co.uk
Age Range: 2–16

SHEFFIELD HIGH SCHOOL GDST

10 Rutland Park, Sheffield, South Yorkshire S10 2PE
W: www.sheffieldhighschool.
org.uk
Age Range: 4–18

WESTBOURNE SCHOOL

60 Westbourne Road, Sheffield, South Yorkshire S10 2QT
W: www.westbourneschool.co.uk
Age Range: 4–16

WEST YORKSHIRE

PREPARATORY

BRONTE HOUSE SCHOOL

Apperley Bridge, Bradford, West Yorkshire BD10 0PQ
W: www.woodhousegrove.co.uk
Age Range: 3–11

DALE HOUSE SCHOOL

Ruby Street, Batley, West Yorkshire WF17 8HL
W: www.dhschool.co.uk
Age Range: 2–11

THE FROEBELIAN SCHOOL

Clarence Road, Leeds, West Yorkshire LS18 4LB
W: www.froebelian.co.uk
Age Range: 3–11

GHYLL ROYD SCHOOL

Greystone Manor, Ilkley, West Yorkshire LS29 7HW
W: www.ghyllroydschool.co.uk
Age Range: 3–11

THE GLEDDINGS PREPARATORY SCHOOL

Birdcage Lane, Halifax, West Yorkshire HX3 0JB
W: www.thegleddings.co.uk
Age Range: 3–11

GLEN HOUSE MONTESSORI SCHOOL

Cragg Vale, Hebden Bridge, West Yorkshire HX7 5SQ
W: www.glenhousemontessori.
calderdale.sch.uk
Age Range: 3–15

INGLEBROOK SCHOOL

Northgate Close, Pontefract, West Yorkshire WF8 1HJ
Age Range: 2–11

LADY LANE PARK SCHOOL

Lady Lane, Bingley, West Yorkshire BD16 4AP
W: www.ladylanepark.bradford.
sch.uk
Age Range: 2–11

MOORFIELD SCHOOL

Wharfedale Lodge, Ilkley, West Yorkshire LS29 8RL
W: www.moorfieldschool.co.uk
Age Range: 2–11

MOORLANDS SCHOOL

Foxhill Drive, Leeds, West Yorkshire LS16 5PF
W: www.moorlands-school.co.uk
Age Range: 2–13

MOUNT SCHOOL

3 Binham Road, Huddersfield, West Yorkshire HD2 2AP
W: www.themount.org.uk
Age Range: 3–11

MOUNTJOY HOUSE SCHOOL

63 New North Road, Huddersfield, West Yorkshire HD1 5ND
Age Range: 3–11

NETHERLEIGH AND ROSSEFIELD SCHOOL

Parsons Road, Bradford, West Yorkshire BD9 4AY
Age Range: 3–11

THE PREPARATORY SCHOOL LIGHTCLIFFE

Wakefield Road, Halifax, West
Yorkshire HX3 8AQ
W: www.hgsf.org.uk
Age Range: 2–11

THE RASTRICK INDEPENDENT SCHOOL

Ogden Lane, Brighouse, West
Yorkshire HD6 3HF
W: www.rastrickschool.co.uk
Age Range: (Day Pupils from Birth
to Sixteen years of age.)

RICHMOND HOUSE SCHOOL

170 Otley Road, Leeds, West
Yorkshire LS16 5LG
W: www.rhschool.org
Age Range: 3–11

ST AGNES PNEU SCHOOL

25 Burton Crescent, Leeds, West
Yorkshire LS6 4DN
W: www.st-agnes.demon.co.uk
Age Range: 2–7

ST HILDA'S SCHOOL

Wakefield, West Yorkshire
WF4 6BB
W: www.silcoates.wakefield.
sch.uk
Age Range: 3–11

SUNNY HILL HOUSE SCHOOL

Wrenthorpe Lane, Wakefield, West
Yorkshire WF2 0QB
W: www.silcoates.wakefield.
sch.uk/sunnyhillhouse.html
Age Range: 2–7

WAKEFIELD TUTORIAL PREPARATORY SCHOOL

Commercial Street, Leeds, West
Yorkshire LS27 8HY
W: www.wtschool.co.uk
Age Range: 4–11

WESTVILLE HOUSE PREPARATORY SCHOOL

Carter's Lane, Ilkley, West
Yorkshire LS29 0DQ
W: www.westvilleschool.co.uk
Age Range: 3–11

SENIOR

ACKWORTH SCHOOL

Pontefract, West Yorkshire
WF7 7LT
W: www.ackworthschool.com
Age Range: 2–18

BATLEY GRAMMAR SCHOOL

Batley, West Yorkshire WF17 0AD
W: www.batleygrammar.co.uk
Age Range: 2–18

BRADFORD CHRISTIAN SCHOOL

Livingstone Road, Bradford, West
Yorkshire BD2 1BT
W: www.bradfordchristianschool.
com
Age Range: 4–16

BRADFORD GIRLS' GRAMMAR SCHOOL

Squire Lane, Bradford, West
Yorkshire BD9 6RB
W: www.bggs.com
Age Range: 2–18

BRADFORD GRAMMAR SCHOOL

Keighley Road, Bradford, West
Yorkshire BD9 4JP
W: www.bradfordgrammar.com
Age Range: 6–18

THE BRANCH CHRISTIAN SCHOOL

8–10 Thomas Street,
Heckmondwike, West Yorkshire
WF16 0NW
Age Range: 3–17

BROWNBERRIE SCHOOL

173–179 New Road Side, Leeds,
West Yorkshire LS18 4DR
Age Range: 11–17

FULNECK SCHOOL

Fulneck, Leeds, West Yorkshire
LS28 8DS
W: www.fulneckschool.co.uk
Age Range: 3–18

GATEWAYS SCHOOL

Harewood, Leeds, West Yorkshire
LS17 9LE
W: www.gatewaysschool.co.uk
Age Range: 3–18 (Boys 3–7)

THE GRAMMAR SCHOOL AT LEEDS

Alwoodley Gates, Leeds, West
Yorkshire LS17 8GS
W: www.gsal.org.uk
Age Range: 3–18

HIPPERHOLME GRAMMAR SCHOOL

Bramley Lane, Halifax, West
Yorkshire HX3 8JE
W: www.hipperholmegrammar.
calderdale.co.uk
Age Range: 11–18

HUDDERSFIELD GRAMMAR SCHOOL

Royds Mount, Huddersfield, West
Yorkshire HD1 4QX
W: www.huddersfield-grammar.
co.uk
Age Range: 3–16

ISLAMIA GIRLS HIGH SCHOOL

Thornton Lodge Road,
Huddersfield, West Yorkshire
HD1 3JQ
Age Range: 11–16

NEW HORIZON COMMUNITY SCHOOL

Newton Hill House, Leeds, West
Yorkshire LS7 4JE
W: nhss.org.uk
Age Range: 11–16

OLIVE SECONDARY

8 Cunliffe Villas, Bradford, West
Yorkshire BD8 7AN
W: www.olivesecondary.org.uk
Age Range: 11–18

QUEEN ELIZABETH GRAMMAR SCHOOL

154 Northgate, Wakefield, West
Yorkshire WF1 3QX
W: www.wgsf.org.uk
Age Range: 7–18

RATHBONE CHOICES

8–10 Highfields Road,
Huddersfield, West Yorkshire
HD1 5LP
W: www.rathboneuk.org
Age Range: 14–16

RISHWORTH SCHOOL

Rishworth, West Yorkshire
HX6 4QA
W: www.rishworth-school.co.uk
Age Range: 3–18

SILCOATES SCHOOL

Wrenthorpe, Wakefield, West
Yorkshire WF2 0PD
W: www.silcoates.co.uk
Age Range: 7–18

WAKEFIELD GIRLS' HIGH SCHOOL

Wentworth Street, Wakefield, West
Yorkshire WF1 2QS
W: www.wgsf.org.uk
Age Range: 11–18

WAKEFIELD INDEPENDENT SCHOOL

The Nostell Centre, Wakefield,
West Yorkshire WF4 1QG
W: www.
wakefieldindependentschool.org.uk
Age Range: 3–16

WOODHOUSE GROVE SCHOOL

Apperley Bridge, West Yorkshire
BD10 0NR
W: www.woodhousegrove.co.uk
Age Range: 11–18

2.3

Northern Ireland

COUNTY ANTRIM

PREPARATORY

CABIN HILL SCHOOL

●🏠

562–594 Upper Newtownards
Road, Belfast, County Antrim
BT4 3HJ
W: www.cabinhill.org.uk
Age Range: 3–13 (Co-ed
kindergarten)

SENIOR

BELFAST ROYAL ACADEMY

●🏠▲

Belfast, County Antrim BT14 6JL
W: www.belfastroyalacademy.
com
Age Range: 4–19

CAMPBELL COLLEGE

●🏠▲

Belmont Road, Belfast, County
Antrim BT4 2ND
W: www.campbellcollege.co.uk
Age Range: 11–18

METHODIST COLLEGE

●🏠▲

1 Malone Road, Belfast, County
Antrim BT9 6BY
W: www.rmplc.co.uk/eduweb/
sites/mcb
Age Range: 4–19

**ROYAL BELFAST
ACADEMICAL INSTITUTION**

●🏠▲

College Square East, Belfast,
County Antrim BT1 6DL
W: www.rbai.org.uk
Age Range: 4–18

**VICTORIA COLLEGE
BELFAST**

●🏠▲

Cranmore Park, Belfast, County
Antrim BT9 6JA
W: www.victoriacollege.org.uk
Age Range: 4–18

COUNTY ARMAGH

SENIOR

THE ROYAL SCHOOL ARMAGH

College Hill, Armagh, County
Armagh BT61 9DH
W: www.royalschoolarmagh.com
Age Range: 4–19

COUNTY DOWN

SENIOR

BANGOR GRAMMAR SCHOOL

13 College Avenue, Bangor,
County Down BT20 5HJ
W: www.bangorgrammarschool.
org.uk
Age Range: 11–18

BANGOR INDEPENDENT CHRISTIAN SCHOOL

277A Clandeboye Road, Bangor,
County Down BT19 1AA
W: www.freepres.org/schools
Age Range: 4–16

THE HOLYWOOD RUDOLF STEINER SCHOOL

The Highlands, Holywood, County
Down BT18 0PR
W: www.holywood-steiner.co.uk
Age Range: 4–17

ROCKPORT SCHOOL

15 Rockport Road, Holywood,
County Down BT18 0DD
W: www.rockportschool.com
Age Range: 3–16 (Boarding 7–13)

COUNTY FERMANAGH

SENIOR

PORTORA ROYAL SCHOOL

Enniskillen, County Fermanagh
BT74 7HA
W: www.portoraroyal.co.uk
Age Range: 11–19

COUNTY TYRONE

SENIOR

**THE ROYAL SCHOOL
DUNGANNON**

1 Ranfurly Road, Dungannon,
County Tyrone BT71 6EG
W: www.royaldungannon.com
Age Range: 11–19

2.4

Scotland

ABERDEENSHIRE

PREPARATORY

THE HAMILTON SCHOOL

●🏠

55–57 Queens Road, Aberdeen,
Aberdeenshire AB15 4YP
W: www.thehamilton.aberdeen.
sch.uk
Age Range: 2–12

SENIOR

**ABERDEEN WALDORF
SCHOOL**

●🏠

Craigton Road, Aberdeen,
Aberdeenshire AB15 9QD
W: www.aberdeen waldorf.co.uk
Age Range: 3–16

ALBYN SCHOOL

●🏠▲

17–23 Queen's Road, Aberdeen,
Aberdeenshire AB15 4PB
W: www.albynschool.co.uk
Age Range: 1–18

**ROBERT GORDON'S
COLLEGE**

●🏠▲

Schoolhill, Aberdeen,
Aberdeenshire AB10 1FE
W: www.rgc.aberdeen.sch.uk
Age Range: 4–18

**ST MARGARET'S SCHOOL
FOR GIRLS**

●🏠▲

17 Albyn Place, Aberdeen,
Aberdeenshire AB10 1RU
W: www.stmargaret.aberdeen.
sch.uk
Age Range: 3–18 (Boys 3–5)

INTERNATIONAL SCHOOLS AND INTERNATIONAL STUDY CENTRES

**INTERNATIONAL SCHOOL OF
ABERDEEN**

●🏠▲

'Fairgirth', Aberdeen,
Aberdeenshire AB13 OAB
W: www.isa.aberdeen.sch.uk
Age Range: 3–18

ANGUS

SENIOR

HIGH SCHOOL OF DUNDEE

Euclid Crescent, Dundee, Angus
DD1 1HU
W: www.highschoolofdundee.
org.uk
Age Range: 5–18

LATHALLAN SCHOOL

●🏠▲

Brotherton Castle, Montrose,
Angus DD10 0HN
W: www.lathallan.org.uk
Age Range: 5–19

ARGYLL AND BUTE

SENIOR

LOMOND SCHOOL

10 Stafford Street, Helensburgh,
Argyll and Bute G84 9JX
W: www.lomond-school.org
Age Range: 3–18

SOUTH AYRSHIRE

SENIOR

WELLINGTON SCHOOL

●🏠▲

Carleton Turrets, Ayr, South
Ayrshire KA7 2XH
W: www.wellingtonschool.org
Age Range: 3–18

CLACKMANNANSHIRE

SENIOR

DOLLAR ACADEMY

Dollar, Clackmannanshire
FK14 7DU
W: www.dollaracademy.org.uk
Age Range: 5–18

FIFE

SENIOR

ST LEONARDS SCHOOL
● ♠ ★ ▲
South Street, St Andrews, Fife
KY16 9QJ
W: www.stleonards-fife.org
Age Range: 4–19

GLASGOW

PREPARATORY

THE GLASGOW ACADEMY DAIRSIE

54 Newlands Road, Glasgow
G43 2JG
W: www.theglasgowacademy.
org.uk
Age Range: 3–9

GLASGOW STEINER SCHOOL

52 Lumsden Street, Glasgow
G3 8RH
W: www.glasgowsteinerschool.
org.uk
Age Range: 3–14

ST ALOYSIUS JUNIOR SCHOOL

56–58 Hill Street, Glasgow G3 6RH
W: www.staloysius.org
Age Range: 5–12

SENIOR

CRAIGHOLME SCHOOL
● ♠ ▲
72 St Andrew's Drive, Glasgow
G41 4HS
W: www.craigholme.co.uk
Age Range: 3–18 (Boys 3–5 in
Nursery only)

THE GLASGOW ACADEMY

Colebrooke Street, Glasgow
G12 8HE
W: www.theglasgowacademy.
org.uk
Age Range: 3–18

THE HIGH SCHOOL OF GLASGOW

637 Crow Road, Glasgow G13 1PL
W: www.glasgowhigh.com
Age Range: 3–18

HUTCHESONS' GRAMMAR SCHOOL
● ♠ ▲
21 Beaton Road, Glasgow
G41 4NW
W: www.hutchesons.org
Age Range: 5–18

KELVINSIDE ACADEMY
● ♠ ▲
33 Kirklee Road, Glasgow
G12 0SW
W: www.kelvinsideacademy.
org.uk
Age Range: 3–18

ST ALOYSIUS' COLLEGE
● ♠ ▲
45 Hill Street, Glasgow G3 6RJ
W: www.staloysius.org
Age Range: 3–18

INVERCLYDE

PREPARATORY

CEDARS SCHOOL OF EXCELLENCE

31 Ardgowan Square, Greenock,
Inverclyde PA16 8NJ
W: www.cedars.inverclyde.sch.uk
Age Range: 5–14

SENIOR

ST COLUMBA'S SCHOOL
● ♠ ▲
Duchal Road, Kilmacolm,
Inverclyde PA13 4AU
W: www.st-columbas.org
Age Range: 3–18

LANARKSHIRE

SENIOR

HAMILTON COLLEGE

Bothwell Road, Hamilton,
Lanarkshire ML3 0AY
W: www.hamiltoncollege.co.uk
Age Range: 3–18

SOUTH LANARKSHIRE

SENIOR

FERNHILL SCHOOL

Fernbrae Avenue, Glasgow, South
Lanarkshire G73 4SG
W: www.fernhillschool.co.uk
Age Range: 3–18 (Boys 4–11)

LOTHIAN

PREPARATORY

BELHAVEN HILL

Dunbar, Lothian EH42 1NN
W: www.belhavenhill.com
Age Range: 7–13

CARGILFIELD

Barnton Avenue West, Edinburgh,
Lothian EH4 6HU
W: www.cargilfield.com
Age Range: 3–13

THE COMPASS SCHOOL

West Road, Haddington, Lothian
EH41 3RD
W: www.thecompassschool.co.uk
Age Range: 4–12

LORETTO JUNIOR SCHOOL

North Esk Lodge, Musselburgh,
Lothian EH21 6JA
W: www.loretto.com
Age Range: 3–12

MANNAFIELDS CHRISTIAN SCHOOL

170 Easter Road, Edinburgh,
Lothian EH7 5QE
W: www.mannafields.org.uk
Age Range: 5–14

REGIUS CHRISTIAN SCHOOL

41a South Clerk Street, Edinburgh,
Lothian EH8 8NZ
W: www.regius.edin.sch.uk

SENIOR

CLIFTON HALL SCHOOL

Edinburgh, Lothian EH28 8LQ
W: www.cliftonhall.org.uk
Age Range: 3–18

DUNEDIN SCHOOL

Liberton Bank House, Edinburgh,
Lothian EH16 5TY
W: www.dunedin.edin.sch.uk
Age Range: 10–17

THE EDINBURGH ACADEMY

42 Henderson Row, Edinburgh,
Lothian EH3 5BL
W: www.edinburghacademy.
org.uk
Age Range: 5–18 (Co-ed VIth
Form)

THE EDINBURGH RUDOLF STEINER SCHOOL

60 Spylaw Road, Edinburgh, Lothian EH10 5BR
W: www.members.aol.com/ERSschool/
Age Range: 3–18

FETTES COLLEGE

Carrington Road, Edinburgh, Lothian EH4 1QX
W: www.fettes.com
Age Range: 7–18

GEORGE HERIOT'S SCHOOL

Lauriston Place, Edinburgh, Lothian EH3 9EQ
W: www.george-heriots.com
Age Range: 3–18

GEORGE WATSON'S COLLEGE

67–71 Colinton Road, Edinburgh, Lothian EH10 5EG
W: www.gwc.org.uk
Age Range: 3–18

LORETTO SCHOOL

Linkfield Road, Musselburgh, Lothian EH21 7RE
W: www.lorettoschool.co.uk
Age Range: 3–18

THE MARY ERSKINE SCHOOL

Edinburgh, Lothian EH4 3NT
W: www.esms.edin.sch.uk
Age Range: 12–18 (Co-ed VIth Form)

MERCHISTON CASTLE SCHOOL*

Colinton, Edinburgh, Lothian EH13 0PU
W: www.merchiston.co.uk
Age Range: 8–18

ST GEORGE'S SCHOOL FOR GIRLS*

Garscube Terrace, Edinburgh, Lothian EH12 6BG
W: www.st-georges.edin.sch.uk
Age Range: (Girls) 18 months–18, (Boys) 18 months–5

ST MARY'S MUSIC SCHOOL

Coates Hall, Edinburgh, Lothian EH12 5EL
W: www.st-marys-music-school.co.uk
Age Range: 9–19

ST SERF'S SCHOOL

5 Wester Coates Gardens, Edinburgh, Lothian EH12 5LT
W: www.st-serfs.edin.sch.uk
Age Range: 5–18

STEWART'S MELVILLE COLLEGE

Queensferry Road, Edinburgh, Lothian EH4 3EZ
W: www.esms.edin.sch.uk
Age Range: 12–18 (Co-ed VIth Form)

INDEPENDENT SIXTH FORM COLLEGE / TUTORIAL COLLEGE

BASIL PATERSON TUTORIAL COLLEGE

66 Queen Street, Edinburgh, Lothian EH2 4NA
W: www.basilpaterson.co.uk
Age Range: 16–20

WALLACE COLLEGE

12 George IV Bridge, Edinburgh, Lothian EH1 1EE
W: www.wallacecollege.co.uk
Age Range: 15–21

MORAYSHIRE

PREPARATORY

ROSEBRAE SCHOOL

Spynie, Elgin, Morayshire IV30 8XT
W: www.rosebrae.moray.sch.uk
Age Range: 2–8

SENIOR

GORDONSTOUN SCHOOL*

Elgin, Morayshire IV30 5RF
W: www.gordonstoun.org.uk
Age Range: 8–18

PERTH AND KINROSS

PREPARATORY

ARDVRECK SCHOOL

Gwydyr Road, Crieff, Perth and
Kinross PH7 4EX
W: www.ardvreckschool.co.uk
Age Range: 3–13

CRAIGCLOWAN PREPARATORY SCHOOL

Edinburgh Road, Perth, Perth and
Kinross PH2 8PS
W: www.craigclowan-school.co.uk
Age Range: 3–13

SENIOR

GLENALMOND COLLEGE*

Perth, Perth and Kinross PH1 3RY
W: www.glenalmondcollege.co.uk
Age Range: 12–18

KILGRASTON

Perth, Perth and Kinross PH2 9BQ
W: www.kilgraston.com
Age Range: 2–18 (Boys day 2–9)

MORRISON'S ACADEMY

Ferntower Road, Crieff, Perth and
Kinross PH7 3AN
W: www.morrisonsacademy.org
Age Range: 3–18

QUEEN VICTORIA SCHOOL

Dunblane, Perth and Kinross
FK15 0JY
W: www.qvs.org.uk
Age Range: 11–18

STRATHALLAN SCHOOL*

Forgandenny, Perth, Perth and
Kinross PH2 9EG
W: www.strathallan.co.uk
Age Range: 9–18 (Junior aged 9
to 13, Senior aged 13 to 18)

RENFREWSHIRE

SENIOR

BELMONT HOUSE

Sandringham Avenue, Newton
Mearns, Renfrewshire G77 5DU
W: www.belmontschool.co.uk
Age Range: 3–18

ROXBURGHSHIRE

PREPARATORY

ST MARY'S PREPARATORY SCHOOL

Abbey Park, Melrose,
Roxburghshire TD6 9LN
W: www.stmarysmelrose.org.uk
Age Range: 2–13

STIRLING

PREPARATORY

BEACONHURST SCHOOL

52 Kenilworth Road, Stirling
FK9 4RR
W: www.beaconhurst.com
Age Range: 3–18

2.5

Wales

ANGLESEY

PREPARATORY

TREFFOS SCHOOL

Llansadwrn, Menai Bridge,
Anglesey LL59 5SL
W: www.treffos.org.uk

BRIDGEND

SENIOR

ST CLARE'S SCHOOL

Porthcawl, Bridgend CF36 5NR
W: www.stclares-school.co.uk
Age Range: 3–18

ST JOHN'S SCHOOL

Church Street, Porthcawl,
Bridgend CF36 5NP
W: www.stjohnsschool-porthcawl.
com
Age Range: 3–16

CAERPHILLY

PREPARATORY

WYCLIF INDEPENDENT CHRISTIAN SCHOOL

Ebenezer Baptist Chapel,
Machen, Caerphilly CF83 8PU
W: www.wyclifchristianschool.org
Age Range: 4–16

CARDIFF

PREPARATORY

THE CATHEDRAL SCHOOL

Cardiff Road, Cardiff CF5 2YH
W: www.cathedral-school.co.uk
Age Range: 3–16

ST JOHN'S COLLEGE

College Green, Cardiff CF3 5YX
W: www.stjohnscollegecardiff.
co.uk
Age Range: 3–18

SENIOR

HOWELL'S SCHOOL, LLANDAFF GDST

Cardiff Road, Cardiff CF5 2YD
W: www.howells-cardiff.gdst.net
Age Range: 3–18

KINGS MONKTON SCHOOL

Cardiff CF24 3XL
W: www.kingsmonkton.org.uk
Age Range: 2–18

UWC ATLANTIC COLLEGE

St Donat's Castle, Llantwit Major,
Cardiff CF61 1WF
W: www.atlanticcollege.org
Age Range: 16–19

WESTBOURNE SCHOOL

Hickman Road, Cardiff CF64 2AJ
W: www.westbourneschool.com
Age Range: 3–18

INDEPENDENT SIXTH FORM COLLEGE / TUTORIAL COLLEGE

THE CARDIFF ACADEMY

40–41 The Parade, Cardiff
CF24 3AB
W: www.cardiffacademy.co.uk
Age Range: 14–18

UNITED WORLD COLLEGE OF THE ATLANTIC

●

St Donat's Castle, Llantwit Major,
Cardiff CF6 9WF
W: www.atlanticcollege.org

CARMARTHENSHIRE

SENIOR

LLANDOVERY COLLEGE

Llandovery, Carmarthenshire
SA20 0EE
W: www.llandoverycollege.com
Age Range: 3–18

ST MICHAEL'S SCHOOL

Llanelli, Carmarthenshire
SA14 9TU
W: www.stmikes.co.uk
Age Range: 3–18

CONWY

SENIOR

ST DAVID'S COLLEGE

Llandudno, Conwy LL30 1RD
W: www.stdavidscollege.co.uk
Age Range: 11–18

DENBIGHSHIRE

PREPARATORY

FAIRHOLME PREPARATORY SCHOOL

Mount Road, St Asaph,
Denbighshire LL17 0DH
W: www.fairholmeschool.com
Age Range: 3–11

SENIOR

HOWELL'S SCHOOL*

Park Street, Denbigh,
Denbighshire LL16 3EN
W: www.howells.org
Age Range: 2–18

RUTHIN SCHOOL

Mold Road, Ruthin, Denbighshire
LL15 1EE
W: www.ruthinschool.co.uk
Age Range: 11–20

GWYNEDD

SENIOR

HILLGROVE SCHOOL

Ffriddoedd Road, Bangor,
Gwynedd LL57 2TW
W: hillgrove.gwynedd.sch.uk
Age Range: 3–16

ST GERARD'S SCHOOL

Ffriddoedd Road, Bangor,
Gwynedd LL57 2EL
Age Range: 3–18

MONMOUTHSHIRE

PREPARATORY

LLANGATTOCK SCHOOL

Llangattock-Vibon-Avel,
Monmouth, Monmouthshire
NP25 5NG
W: llangattockschool.co.uk
Age Range: 2–12

ST JOHN'S-ON-THE-HILL

Castleford Hill, Chepstow,
Monmouthshire NP16 7LE
W: www.stjohnsonthehill.co.uk
Age Range: (Nursery from 3
months)

SENIOR

HABERDASHERS' MONMOUTH SCHOOL FOR GIRLS

Hereford Road, Monmouth,
Monmouthshire NP25 5XT
W: www.habs-monmouth.org
Age Range: 7–18

MONMOUTH SCHOOL

Almshouse Street, Monmouth,
Monmouthshire NP25 3XP
W: www.habs-monmouth.org
Age Range: 7–18 (Boarding
11–18)

NEWPORT

SENIOR

ROUGEMONT SCHOOL

Llantarnam Hall, Newport
NP20 6QB
W: www.rougemontschool.co.uk
Age Range: 3–18

POWYS

SENIOR

CHRIST COLLEGE

Brecon, Powys LD3 8AF
W: www.christcollegebrecon.com
Age Range: 11–18

SWANSEA

PREPARATORY

CRAIG-Y-NOS SCHOOL

Clyne Common, Bishoptston,
Swansea SA3 3JB
W: www.craigynos.com
Age Range: 2–11

OAKLEIGH HOUSE SCHOOL

38 Penlan Crescent, Swansea
SA2 0RL
W: www.oakleighhouseschool.
co.uk
Age Range: 3–11

SENIOR

FFYNONE HOUSE SCHOOL

36 St James' Crescent, Swansea
SA1 6DR
W: www.ffynonehouseschool.
co.uk
Age Range: 9–18

PART THREE

SCHOOL PROFILES

COUNTIES OF ENGLAND, SCOTLAND AND WALES

SCOTLAND

Moray

Highland

Aberdeenshire

Aberdeen City

Perth and Kinross

Angus

Argyll and Bute

Stirling

Fife

East Dunbartonshire

South Lanarkshire

Borders

South Ayrshire

Dumfries and Galloway

1. Inverclyde
2. North Ayrshire
3. Renfrewshire
4. West Dunbartonshire
5. East Dunbartonshire
6. North Lanarkshire
7. Falkirk
8. Clackmannanshire
9. West Lothian
10. City of Edinburgh
11. Midlothian
12. East Lothian

NORTHERN ENGLAND

Northumberland

Newcastle upon Tyne
Hartlepool
Stockton-on-Tees
Middlesbrough

Cumbria

Durham

North Yorkshire

York

Isle of Man

Lancashire

West Yorkshire

East Riding of Yorkshire

North Lincolnshire

North East Lincolnshire

Merseyside

G. M.

South Yorkshire

EASTERN ENGLAND

Cheshire

Derbyshire

Nottinghamshire

Lincolnshire

Rutland

WALES

Denbighshire

Flintshire

Wrexham

Stafford-shire

Leicester-shire

Norfolk

Northampton-shire

Cambridge-shire

1. Monmouthshire
2. Torfean
3. Newport
4. Blaenau Gwent
5. Caerphilly
6. Cardiff
7. Merthyr Tydfil
8. Cynon Taff
9. Vale of Glamorgan
10. Bridgend
11. Neath Port Talbot
12. Swansea

Conwy

Gwynedd

Shropshire

W.M

Suffolk

Ceredigion

Powys

Worcester-shire

Warwick-shire

Hereford-shire

Bedford-shire

Buckingham-shire

HOME COUNTIES (North)

Carmarthenshire

Gloucester-shire

Oxford-shire

Hertford-shire

Essex

Pembrokeshire

Berkshire

Greater London

LONDON

CENTRAL ENGLAND

13. South Gloucestershire
14. Bath and North East Somerset
15. City of Bristol
16. North Somerset

Surrey

Kent

Wiltshire

West Sussex

East Sussex

Somerset

Hampshire

HOME COUNTIES (South)

Devon

Dorset

Isle of Wight

Cornwall

SOUTH WEST ENGLAND

3.1

England

England

MAP OF NORTHERN ENGLAND

Berwick upon Tweed

A1

A68

Stanton

A69

A69

Newcastle upon Tyne

Carlisle

A69

A596

Penrith

A66

Durham

Teesside Airport

Middlesbrough

Keswick

A66

A1(M)

A595

A591

Kendal

M6

A171

Whitby

Scarborough

A65

A1

Thirsk

4

Ripon

A64

ISLE OF MAN

Lancaster

A59

Harrogate

York

A165

Blackpool

M6

Leeds Airport

Leeds

Kingston upon Hull

Preston

Blackburn

A1

M62

M6

M62

Huddersfield

Scunthorpe

Liverpool

Manchester

Manchester Airport

M1

A1(M)

Humberside Airport

Sheffield

2

Macclesfield

1

A49

M6

M1

Stoke on Trent

3

Derby

A1

M6

Nottingham

PROFILED SCHOOLS IN NORTHERN ENGLAND

(Incorporating the counties of Cheshire, Cumbria, Derbyshire, Durham, Hartlepool, Lancashire, North East Lincolnshire, North Lincolnshire, Greater Manchester, Merseyside, Middlesbrough, Northumberland, Nottinghamshire, Staffordshire, Stockton-on-Tees, East Riding of Yorkshire, North Yorkshire, South Yorkshire, West Yorkshire)

Barlborough Hall School

Barlborough, Chesterfield, Derbyshire S43 4TJ **T**: (01246) 810511 **F**: (01246) 570605
E: barlborough.hall@virgin.net **W**: www.barlboroughhallschool.co.uk

Headteacher Mrs W E Parkinson BEd
Founded 1939
School status Co-educational day only
Religious denomination Roman Catholic
Member of HMC, IAPS
Accredited by HMC, ISC
Age range 3–11; *Nursery* 30; *Pre-prep* 85; *Prep* 141
Teacher:pupil ratio 1:7
Average class size 11
Fees per annum *(day)* £5,985–£7,985

Barlborough Hall School, preparatory school to Mount St Mary's College, is seen as one of the premier independent Catholic schools in the South Yorkshire/Derbyshire area, welcoming pupils of all denominations. Set in 300 acres of beautiful surroundings, small classes, well-motivated teachers and exceptional specialist facilities, including a technology centre, science laboratory, art studio, IT suite, theatre and indoor heated pool, ensure that our pupils receive the very best educational opportunities. The school has an excellent nursery provision (from 3 years) in a secure and safe environment with facilities second to none. A regular minibus service and an 'out of school club', with a full range of activities and run by qualified staff until 6 pm, ensure the flexibility and peace of mind required by many working parents.

Mount St Mary's College

Spinkhill, Derbyshire S21 3YL **T**: (01246) 433388 **F**: (01246) 435511 **E**: info@msmcollege.com
W: www.msmcollege.com
Admissions 01246 432872/439317

Headmaster Mr L McKell MA MEd
Founded 1842
College status Co-educational independent boarding and day Boarders are accepted into Barlborough Hall at age 10.
Religious denomination Roman Catholic
Member of BSA, CIS, HMC **Accredited by** HMC, ISC
Age range 11–18 (Boarders are accepted into Barlborough Hall at age 10.); *boarders from* 10
No of pupils 410; *(boarding)* 90; *(full boarding)* 80; *(weekly boarding)* 18; *Senior* 410
Sixth Form 98; *Girls* 161; *Boys* 249
Teacher:pupil ratio 1:8 **Average class size** 20
Fees per annum *(full boarding)* £17,262–£23,000; *(weekly)* £14,382–£18,573; *(day)* £9,672–£11,113

Mount St Mary's College welcomes children of all denominations. In beautiful surroundings close to junction 30 of the M1, with minibus services to local areas, the school is also popular with local, national and international boarders. Proudly non-academically selective, the school achieves success for pupils at all levels; with many pupils going onto chosen universities. Emphasis is placed on developing the whole person, with a wide range of extra-curricular activities rated outstanding by a recent Independent Schools Inspection. Sport, drama and music are particularly strong. The new international-standard athletics facility has attracted much interest. The jazz band, several choirs, ensembles and orchestra provide many opportunities for music-making.

Abbotsholme School

Rocester, Uttoxeter, Staffordshire ST14 5BS **T**: (01889) 594 265 **F**: (01889) 591001
E: admissions@abbotsholme.co.uk **W**: www.abbotsholme.co.uk
For more information please contact the admissions coordinator Miss Jessica Ash on +44 (0) 1889 594 265.

Headmaster Mr Steve Fairclough BSc MSc
Founded 1889
School status Co-educational independent boarding and day
Religious denomination Inter-denominational
Member of BHS, BSA, ISC, Round Square, SHMIS **Accredited by** British
Council, ISC, SHMIS
Age range 4–18; *boarders from* 10
No of pupils 318; *(boarding)* 125; *(full boarding)* 54; *(weekly boarding)* 71;
Prep 50; *Senior* 268; *Sixth Form* 74; *Girls* 122; *Boys* 196
Average class size 15
Fees per annum *(full boarding)* £7,960–£9,225; *(weekly)* £6,115–£7,730; *(day)* £2,800–£6,285

Abbotsholme is a small, warm and inclusive school providing a modern, progressive education based on cooperation rather than competition, a compassion for others, and respect for the environment. Located within 140 acres on the banks of the River Dove on the Staffordshire/Derbyshire border we are easily accessible by road, rail and air. Abbotsholme provides a flexible and caring second home for boarding pupils. Each evening or weekend the children are happily involved in the community, be it on our working farm or in our equestrian centre, playing sport, doing homework or signing up for the numerous outdoor education trips and excursions on offer. www.abbotsholme.co.uk

Aysgarth Preparatory School

Newton-Le-Willows, Bedale, North Yorkshire DL8 1TF **T**: (01677) 450240 **F**: (01677) 450736
E: lfoster@aysgarthschool.co.uk **W**: www.aysgarthschool.com

Head Mr Anthony Goddard MA (Cantab)
Founded 1877
School status Boys' boarding and day Co-ed 3–8
Religious denomination Church of England
Member of AGBIS, BSA, IAPS, ISBA, ISC, NAHT, SATIPS
Accredited by IAPS, ISC
Age range 3–13 (co-ed day 3–8); *boarders from* 8
No of pupils 205; *(boarding)* 118; *(full boarding)* 101;
(weekly boarding) 17; *(day)* 25; *Nursery* 15; *Pre-prep* 47;
Girls 29; *Boys* 176
Teacher:pupil ratio 1:7
Average class size 12
Fees per annum *(full boarding)* £19,470; *(weekly)* £19,470; *(day)* £14,970

Where boys can be boys! Aysgarth School, set in the foothills of the Yorkshire Dales, is the only all-boys boarding and day prep school in the North of England. It is one of the leading preparatory schools in the country and in the North has an unmatched record of sending boys to Eton, Harrow, Radley, Shrewsbury, Stowe, Uppingham and Winchester as well as Ampleforth and Sedbergh closer by. Staff at Aysgarth are passionate about the benefits that boarding provides. Boys are introduced to a wide range of opportunities and become happy, confident, courteous and independent.

MAP OF EASTERN ENGLAND

PROFILED SCHOOLS IN EASTERN ENGLAND

(Incorporating the counties of Cambridgeshire, Leicestershire, Lincolnshire, Norfolk, Northamptonshire, Suffolk)

King's International

The King's School Ely, Cambridge, Cambridgeshire CB7 4DB **T**: (01353) 660757 **F**: (01353) 667485
E: kisc@kingsinternational.co.uk **W**: www.kingsschoolely.co.uk

● 🏠

Director Mr P J Harris
School status Co-educational boarding only
Age range 9–17

The King's School Ely brings a thousand years of tradition and achievement to its pupils. King's International is the bridge that enables children from international cultures to access the very best of independent British education.

Years of experience have enabled us to perfect an approach which instils confidence, enthusiasm and a sense of security in our students.

English is central to the curriculum and students are prepared for English GCSEs, enabling them to continue in the British educational system. Class sizes are small and groups are organised by ability, age and need. One-to-one tutoring ensures that academic progress is closely monitored but also provides the very best in pastoral care. A full range of sports, recreational activities and educational visits are also enjoyed by all.

Students are actively encouraged to continue with Sixth Form studies at King's, and others successfully make the transition to other UK independent schools.

The Leys School

Trumpington Road, Cambridge, Cambridgeshire CB2 7AD **T**: (01223) 5078904 **F**: (01223) 505303
E: admissions@theleys.net **W**: www.theleys.net

● 🏠 ▲

Headmaster Mr Mark Slater MA
Founded 1875
School status Co-educational boarding and day
Religious denomination Inter-denominational
Member of HMC **Accredited by** British Council, HMC
Age range 11–18
No of pupils 557; *(boarding)* 273; *(full boarding)* 273;
Girls 229; *Boys* 328
Teacher:pupil ratio 1:1
Average class size 1
Fees per annum *(full boarding)* £17,775–£24,660; *(day)* £11,595–£16,260

The Leys is one of East Anglia's finest co-educational boarding and day schools for 11–18-year-olds, situated in the thriving hub that is Cambridge, in a 50-acre campus. Made famous by the novel *Goodbye Mr Chips*, the author James Hilton was an old boy of the school, which has kept true to its original ethos and values with pastoral care a major selling point. Current-day Leys' pupils enjoy a myriad of extra-curricular activities, the finest sports facilities and coaches, music in the state-of-the-art music school and drama that is the envy of most – life at the school is full. The Leys is primarily a boarding school and headmaster Mark Slater places great importance on providing a caring, friendly and secure environment for all its pupils.

The Peterborough School

Thorpe Road, Peterborough, Cambridgeshire PE3 6AP **T**: (01733) 343357 **F**: (01733) 355710
E: admin@thepeterboroughschool.co.uk **W**: www.thepeterboroughschool.co.uk
Peterborough's only independent school with nursery for boys and girls from 6 weeks to 18 years

●♠▲

Headmaster Mr A D Meadows BSc (Hons) NPQH
Founded 1895
School status Co-educational independent
Religious denomination Church of England
Member of ISC, SHMIS, Woodard Schools
Accredited by ISC, SHMIS
Age range 4–18; *boarders from* 8
No of pupils 355; *(boarding)* 25; *(full boarding)* 15;
(weekly boarding) 10; *Nursery* 56; *Prep* 160; *Senior* 180
Sixth Form 50; *Girls* 255; *Boys* 100
Teacher:pupil ratio 1:15
Average class size 15
Fees per annum *(full boarding)* £20,580–£22,260; *(weekly)* £18,108–£19,215; *(day)* £8,454–£11,958

The Peterborough School is the city's only independent school with nursery for boys and girls from 6 weeks to 18 years. Despite the expansion of the school to admit boys into the senior school from September 2010, the school continues to focus on providing excellent care and support for the individual through its small class sizes and strong pastoral system. A new sports facility is being built ready for September 2012.

St Mary's School, Cambridge

Bateman Street, Cambridge, Cambridgeshire CB2 1LY **T**: (01223) 353253 **F**: (01223) 357451
E: enquiries@stmaryscambridge.co.uk **W**: www.stmaryscambridge.co.uk
St Mary's Junior School, 6 Chaucer Road, Cambridge CB2 7EB: Tel: 01223 311666; Fax: 01223 472168

●♠▲

Headmistress Miss C Avery MA (Oxon) PGCE NPQH
Founded 1898
School status Girls' independent day and boarding
Religious denomination Roman Catholic
Member of GSA **Accredited by** GSA
Age range 4–18; *boarders from* 13; *(boarding)* 86;
(full boarding) 78; *(weekly boarding)* 8
Teacher:pupil ratio 1:6
Average class size 20
Fees per annum *(full boarding)* £27,330; *(weekly)* £23,520; *(day)* £12,690

St Mary's Cambridge is a Catholic school with a long tradition of welcoming girls from all faiths, backgrounds and nationalities. Our girls are renowned for the way they care for each other. Their happy, friendly self-confidence is evident and their achievements, whether academic, sporting or cultural, are impressive. We are situated in the centre of the beautiful university city of Cambridge, close to the railway station, 50 miles from London and within easy reach of four major airports. Both St Mary's senior and junior schools offer an excellent academic education and a strong tradition of superlative pastoral care. In the senior school, there is a lively programme of extra-curricular activities: rowing, yoga and a thriving Duke of Edinburgh's Award Scheme.

Brooke House College

12 Leicester Road, Market Harborough, Leicestershire LE16 7AU **T**: (01858) 462452 **F**: (01858) 462487
E: enquiries@brookehouse.com **W**: www.brookehouse.com

●⌂▲

Principal Mr G E I Williams MA (Oxon)
Founded 1967
College status Co-educational independent boarding and day
Religious denomination Non-denominational
Member of CIFE **Accredited by** BAC
Learning difficulties MLD
Age range 14–20; *boarders from* 14
No of pupils 240; *(boarding)* 210; *(full boarding)* 210; *Senior* 50
Sixth Form 190; *Girls* 120; *Boys* 120
Teacher:pupil ratio 1:6
Average class size 8
Fees per annum *(full boarding)* £23,250; *(day)* £13,950

Situated in the heart of rural England in the historic town of Market Harborough, Brooke House is a fully residential, international college, offering GCSE, A level and pre-university foundation courses in intensive, small classes. The college possesses excellent academic facilities, including science laboratories, an art and design studio and two recently developed IT suites. The academic and social welfare of pupils is paramount and is safeguarded by a system of personal tutors and by a secure and friendly learning environment. The college's full-time universities admissions adviser gives advice and guidance, and Brooke House has an enviable tradition of assisting international and UK pupils to gain places at the most prestigious of universities in the UK and the United States.

Laxton Junior School

East Road, Oundle, Nr Peterborough, Northamptonshire PE8 4BX **T**: (01832) 277159 **F**: (01832) 277271
E: admissions@laxtonjunior.org.uk **W**: www.laxtonjunior.org.uk

●⌂

Head Mr Mark Potter BEd (Hons) (Liverpool)
Founded 1973
School status Co-educational independent day only
Religious denomination Church of England
Member of IAPS **Accredited by** IAPS
Age range 4–11
No of pupils 271; *Pre-prep* 120; *Prep* 151; *Girls* 137; *Boys* 134
Teacher:pupil ratio 1:12 **Average class size** 19
Fees per annum *(day)* £8,370–£9,180

Founded in September 1973 and moved to new purpose-built premises in 2002, Laxton Junior acts as a preparatory school for Oundle School but also prepares children for many other schools. Our primary aim is to find the right school for your child. We can take 280 boys and girls from 4–11 years. Your child will receive personal attention in classes containing no more than 20 pupils and our staff makes every effort to help each individual realize their full potential. There are 25 fully qualified teachers plus 7 specialist teachers who all work as a team in a concerted effort to help your child become a happy, self-confident individual with an academic foundation that will prepare them for the future. We do our utmost to combine the best of both traditional and modern methods of education using National Curriculum guidelines as a foundation and your child learns to acquire excellent skills in reading, English, maths and science supplemented by art and design, computer studies, French, geography, history, performing arts, religious education and sport. Why not visit on a school day, as you will have many questions relating to your child's education and the only way to have them satisfied is by talking to us and seeing the school in action.

Alexanders International School

Bawdsey Manor, Bawdsey, Woodbridge, Suffolk IP12 3AZ **T**: (01394) 411633 **F**: (01394) 411357
E: marketing@skola.co.uk **W**: www.alexandersschool.com

● ♠

Head Mr A Laidlaw Cert Ed Dip TEFL
Founded 1975
School status Co-educational independent boarding only
Religious denomination Inter-denominational
Member of EUK **Accredited by** British Council
Age range 11–17; *boarders from* 11
No of pupils 90; *(boarding)* 90; *(full boarding)* 90; *Girls* 32; *Boys* 58
Teacher:pupil ratio 1:10
Average class size 8
Fees per annum *(full boarding)* £23,850–£23,850

Alexanders International School (AIS) is a founder member of the SKOLA Group of Schools established over 35 years ago and comprising five British Council accredited centres. AIS is situated on a 120-acre campus on the Suffolk coast which has pupil residences, classrooms, sports and recreational facilities and its own watersports centre. The School Foundation Course is a one-year course preparing pupils who wish to enter a UK boarding school. Pupils may join at any time of the year for one, two or three terms. As we are wholly independent we can advise and support pupils in their applications for their chosen school. AIS pupils have gone on to schools such as Lancing College, Roedean School, Merchiston Castle School and Wellington College. English language classes at all levels, from beginners to advanced, run throughout the academic year. I/GCSEs in English language, maths, art, business studies and IT are available as well as GCSE combined science. Pupils can be entered for UCLES examinations (KET, PET, FCE and IELTS) or I/GCSE English Language.

Culford School

Bury St Edmunds, Suffolk IP28 6TX **T**: (01284) 385308 **F**: (01284) 729146 **E**: admissions@culford.co.uk
W: www.culford.co.uk

● ♠ ▲

Headmaster Mr J F Johnson-Munday MA MBA
Founded 1881
School status Co-educational independent boarding and day
Religious denomination Methodist
Member of AGBIS, BSA, HMC, IAPS, ISC **Accredited by** HMC, IAPS
Age range 3–18; *boarders from* 7
No of pupils 665; *(boarding)* 210; *(full boarding)* 210; *Nursery* 20;
Pre-prep 75; *Prep* 220; *Senior* 350
Sixth Form 130; *Girls* 320; *Boys* 345
Teacher:pupil ratio 1:9
Average class size 18
Fees per annum *(full boarding)* £18,030–£25,665; *(weekly)* £18,030–£25,665; *(day)* £7,650–£15,885

Culford is set in 480 acres of beautiful Suffolk parkland, located 40 minutes from Cambridge and 90 minutes from London. Culford is a friendly, caring school with superb sporting and academic facilities and aims to educate the whole person. We offer a rich after-school and weekend activities programme, from art, music and drama through to the Combined Cadet Force and the Duke of Edinburgh's Award Scheme. Academic facilities include new ICT suites; a dedicated centre for art and design technology; and superb facilities in the William Miller Science Centre. Music and drama are well catered for in the new studio theatre and redevelopment of the Music School in Culford Hall. The sports centre boasts impressive facilities, including an indoor climbing wall, 25-metre pool and a new championship-standard indoor tennis centre.

England

Framlingham College

Framlingham, Woodbridge, Suffolk IP13 9EY **T**: (01728) 723789 **F**: (01728) 724546
E: admissions@framcollege.co.uk **W**: www.framlinghamcollege.co.uk

●🏠▲

Headmaster Mr P B Taylor BA (Hons)
College status Co-educational independent senior
Religious denomination Church of England
Member of HMC, IAPS, ISC **Accredited by** HMC, IAPS, ISC
Age range 13–18; *boarders from* 13
No of pupils 680; *(boarding)* 265; *(full boarding)* 200; *(weekly boarding)* 65;
Girls 290; *Boys* 390
Teacher:pupil ratio 1:8
Average class size 18
Fees per annum *(full boarding)* £18,693–£23,706; *(weekly)* £18,693–£23,706; *(day)* £11,625–£15,237

Situated close to the Suffolk Heritage coast and within easy reach of London, Cambridge and Norwich, Framlingham College is a centre of all-round excellence and enjoys a magnificent site with unparalleled views over the Mere to the famous 12th-century castle. The college has a fine record in stretching the most able, with an excellent reputation in sport, music and drama. Our 'value-added' rating for those pupils who are not automatically destined to achieve A grades at GCSE and A level stands alongside the very best in the country. The school has superb facilities on campus, including a state-of-the-art specialist theatre and music facility, an indoor swimming pool, a modern library and a dedicated centre for art and design technology.

Symbol key

Gender

● Girls
● Boys
● Coed

Accommodation

🏠 Boarding only
🏠 Boarding and Day
🏠 Day and Boarding
🏠 Day only

International Bacc.

★ School offers IB

CReSTeD

◆ CReSTeD Registered

Has 6th Form

▲ Has 6th Form

MAP OF CENTRAL ENGLAND

PROFILED SCHOOLS IN CENTRAL ENGLAND

(Incorporating the counties of Gloucestershire, Herefordshire, Oxfordshire, West Midlands, Shropshire, Warwickshire, Worcestershire)

Bredon School

Pull Court, Bushley, Tewkesbury, Gloucestershire GL20 6AH **T**: (01684) 293156 **F**: (01684) 276392
E: enquiries@bredonschool.co.uk **W**: www.bredonschool.org

●♠◆▲

Headmaster Mr J Hewitt MBA BA
Founded 1962
School status Co-educational independent boarding and day
Religious denomination Church of England
Member of BDA, BSA, CReSTeD, ISA, ISBA, ISC, SHA, SHMIS
Accredited by ISA, ISC, SHMIS
Age range 5–18; *boarders from* 9
No of pupils 245; *(boarding)* 105; *(full boarding)* 70;
(weekly boarding) 35; *Prep* 29; *Senior* 187
Sixth Form 29; *Girls* 60; *Boys* 185
Teacher:pupil ratio 1:7 **Average class size** 10
Fees per annum *(full boarding)* £17,565–£24,870; *(weekly)* £17,115–£24,405; *(day)* £5,835–£15,855

Bredon is a co-educational independent school for 245 pupils with full boarders, weekly boarders and day pupils. The school stands in attractive rural surroundings near the River Severn, on the Worcestershire and Gloucestershire border in an estate of 85 acres, which includes a school farm. Bredon follows the National Curriculum at all Key Stages through to GCSE and A level. In addition Bredon offers extensive vocational programmes at Foundation, Intermediate and Advanced levels (levels I, II and III). Pupils are able to benefit from the experience of the access centre and its team of highly qualified learning support staff. The school is CReSTeD registered. Excellent facilities exist in sport, art, design and technology, and computer studies, with a farm unit providing the basis for agricultural studies.

Rendcomb College

Rendcomb, Cirencester, Gloucestershire GL7 7HA **T**: (01285) 831213 **F**: (01285) 831121
E: HoldenL@Rendcomb.gloucs.sch.uk **W**: www.rendcombcollege.org.uk

●♠▲

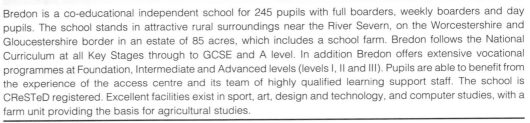

Headmaster Mr Gerry Holden MA (St Andrews) PGCE FRSA
Headmaster Junior School Mr Martin Watson MA BEd (Hons)
Founded 1920
College status Co-educational boarding and day
Religious denomination Church of England
Member of AGBIS, BHS, BSA, HMC, ISBA, SHMIS
Accredited by British Council, HMC, SHMIS
Age range 3–18
No of pupils 424; *(boarding)* 145; *(full boarding)* 115;
(weekly boarding) 30; *Nursery* 23; *Pre-prep* 52; *Prep* 74; *Senior* 179
Sixth Form 73; *Girls* 209; *Boys* 215
Teacher:pupil ratio 1:7 **Average class size** 14
Fees per annum *(full boarding)* £18,159–£23,554; *(weekly)* £18,159–£23,554; *(day)* £13,011–£17,559

Set in over 200 acres of beautiful Cotswold countryside, Rendcomb College and Junior School combines the friendliness of a small school with a long tradition of outstanding academic achievement. Committed to nurturing the individual; small class sizes and a regular academic grading system ensure that every pupil achieves their full potential. Boarding accommodation is superb and every pupil from the fourth form upwards has a single, spacious study bedroom. Nearly every sixth form pupil goes to university, including Oxbridge. Rendcomb has excellent facilities for sport, drama, music, art and ICT, and the extensive choice of extra-curricular activities, from riding to shooting, cookery to expedition training, develops pupils' self-confidence and motivation. Rendcomb is conveniently situated for the M4 and M5 and most major airports.

d'Overbroeck's College Oxford

The Swan Building, 111 Banbury Road, Oxford, Oxfordshire OX2 6JX **T**: (01865) 310000 **F**: (01865) 552296
E: mail@doverbroecks.com **W**: www.doverbroecks.com

●♠▲

Principal Mr Sami Cohen BA
Founded 1977
College status Co-educational independent
Religious denomination Non-denominational
Member of BSA, ISA, ISC, SHMIS
Accredited by British Council, ISA, ISC, SHMIS
Age range 11–19 (With many pupils joining for sixth form from other schools)
No of pupils 446; *(boarding)* 165; *Senior* 206
Sixth Form 240; *Girls* 198; *Boys* 248
Teacher:pupil ratio 1:7
Average class size 7
Fees per annum *(boarding)* £26,190–£32,775; *(day)* £12,675–£18,525

The College's approach is characterized by small classes, maximum of 10 in the sixth form and 15 up to GCSE, with a very high level of support and encouragement that makes learning enjoyable as well as highly effective. Pastoral support is excellent. Outside lessons there is a busy programme of sports, activities, arts, drama and music. Last year 59 per cent of our entries gained A* or A grade at A level. On average around 10 per cent of our upper sixth gain a place at Oxford or Cambridge. A range of scholarships are available for entry at 11, 13 and 16.

Oxford Tutorial College

12 King Edward Street, Oxford, Oxfordshire OX1 4HT **T**: (01865) 793333 **F**: (01865) 793233 **E**: info@otc.ac.uk
W: www.otc.ac.uk

●♠▲

The Principal Mr Joel Roderick MA (Oxon)
Founded 1985
College status Co-educational independent Sixth Form college senior 16+
Religious denomination Non-denominational
Member of CIFE **Accredited by** BAC
Age range (16+)
No of pupils 185
Sixth Form 150; *Girls* 95; *Boys* 90
Teacher:pupil ratio 1:1
Average class size 1–6
Fees per annum *(day)* £3,000–£23,000

Oxford Tutorial College is a leading independent college specializing in A-Level and GCSE tuition for those intending to go on to higher education at a good British university. There is a well established sixth form for students taking A-Levels for the first time. The college also has many years successful experience of running retake courses. OTC offers an environment quite different from that of a traditional school. The teaching approach is refreshingly interactive and informal. The emphasis on small group work and one-to-one tutorials enables a clear focus on individual needs and learning styles and a variation of pace and emphasis, which helps students to approach their work calmly and objectively. The full range of A-level subjects is available. OTC also provides Easter Revision Courses. Please contact us to discuss your specific requirements.

St Clare's, Oxford

139 Banbury Road, Oxford, Oxfordshire OX2 7AL **T**: (01865) 552031 **F**: (01865) 513359
E: admissions@stclares.ac.uk **W**: www.stclares.ac.uk

●♠★▲

Principal Mrs P Holloway MSc (Oxon) BSc PGCE Dip PM
Founded 1953
School status Co-educational boarding and day independent
Sixth Form college senior
Religious denomination Non-denominational
Member of CASE, CIS, IBO, ISA, LISA
Accredited by British Council, ISA
Age range 15–19; *boarders from* 15
No of pupils 225; *(boarding)* 248; *(full boarding)* 238;
(weekly boarding) 10
Sixth Form 255; *Girls* 118; *Boys* 107
Teacher:pupil ratio 1:7
Average class size 9
Fees per annum *(full boarding)* £26,449; *(weekly)* £26,134
    (day) £16,355

St Clare's is an international college founded in 1953 with a mission 'to advance international education and understanding' – something it has been doing successfully ever since.

The college embraces internationalism and academic excellence as core values. It is a co-educational day and residential college that has been offering the International Baccalaureate Diploma for over 30 years, longer than any other school or college in England.

Students from over 40 countries study at St Clare's, including British students. The atmosphere is informal and friendly, with an equal emphasis on hard work and developing personal responsibility. Each student has a personal tutor who overseas welfare and progress. Most students are enrolled for the full IB Diploma. St Clare's has an especially wide range of subjects on offer at higher and standard level and, in addition, currently teaches 28 different languages. The college takes a small number of transfer students each year.

For students not ready to take the IB Diploma, a one-year Pre-IB course is offered, with additional entry points throughout the year.

There is an extensive programme of social, cultural and sporting activities and students are encouraged to take full advantage of the opportunities that Oxford provides. The college also runs a highly successful IB Institute providing introductory, refresher and revision courses for students.

St Clare's is also authorized to run IB workshops for both new and experienced teachers in cooperation with the IBO.

St Clare's is located in the beautiful North Oxford Conservation Area. It occupies 27 large Victorian and Edwardian houses to which purpose-built facilities have been added. These include a beautiful library building with over 35,000 volumes, an IT suite and a careers and higher education information centre, four science laboratories, art and music studios, dining room and the popular Sugar House Café.

Students live in college houses close to the central campus, under the care of residential staff. The college welcomes applications from students irrespective of gender, race, colour, religious belief or national origin. Entry is based on previous academic results and interview. There is a competitive scholarship and bursary programme awarded by examination, interview and group exercises.

St Clare's highly successful ISI inspections reports can be accessed via the college website, as can the college's excellent examination results and impressive university destinations.

St Edward's School

Woodstock Road, Oxford, Oxfordshire OX2 7NN **T**: (01865) 319200 **F**: (01865) 319202
E: registrar@stedwards.oxon.sch.uk **W**: www.stedwards.oxon.sch.uk

●♠★▲

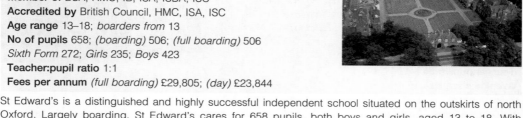

Warden Stephen Jones
Founded 1863
School status Co-educational independent boarding and day senior
Religious denomination Church of England
Member of BSA, HMC, IB, ISA, ISBA, ISC
Accredited by British Council, HMC, ISA, ISC
Age range 13–18; *boarders from* 13
No of pupils 658; *(boarding)* 506; *(full boarding)* 506
Sixth Form 272; *Girls* 235; *Boys* 423
Teacher:pupil ratio 1:1
Fees per annum *(full boarding)* £29,805; *(day)* £23,844

St Edward's is a distinguished and highly successful independent school situated on the outskirts of north Oxford. Largely boarding, St Edward's cares for 658 pupils, both boys and girls, aged 13 to 18. With approximately 100 academic scholars and exhibitioners, St Edward's offers a challenging environment where every pupil has a chance to be a leader. Academic rigour is the cornerstone of the development of the school. It has a one in eight teacher:pupil ratio and in the past five years 54 St Edward's pupils have won places to Oxbridge. An excellent 'all round' school and a safe and reliable first choice.

Tudor Hall School

Wykham Park, Banbury, Oxfordshire OX16 9UR **T**: (01295) 263434 **F**: (01295) 253264
E: admissions@tudorhallschool.com **W**: www.tudorhallschool.com

●♠▲

Headmistress Miss W Griffiths BSc PGCE
Founded 1850
School status girls' independent boarding and day
Religious denomination Church of England
Age range 11–18; *boarders from* 11
No of pupils 324; *(boarding)* 249; *(full boarding)* 249
Senior 224; *Sixth Form* 101; *Girls* 324
Teacher:pupil ratio 1:16
Fees per annum *(full boarding)* £26,700; *(day)* £17,175

Tudor Hall is a boarding and day school, set in 48 acres of rolling parkland just south of Banbury. Girls enter the school at 11 and 13 through interview and Common Entrance, and at 16 through interview, GCSE results and school references. We pride ourselves on encouraging girls to meet a wide range of challenges; physical, intellectual and social, while preparing them for a future of possibilities. All girls are involved in a broad spectrum of extra-curricular activities, including ACF, Duke of Edinburgh Awards and Mock United Nations. We encourage and develop cooperation, social skills and the sense of responsibility to a wider community, as featured in the school motto *Habeo ut Dem*, 'I have that I may give'. Academic results speak for themselves: in 2010, 96 per cent of A level pupils achieved grades A* to C and 99 per cent of GCSE grades were A* to C.

Moreton Hall School

Weston Rhyn, Oswestry, Shropshire SY11 3EW **T**: (01691) 773671 **F**: (01691) 778552
E: admin@moretonhall.com **W**: www.moretonhall.org

●⌂▲

Principal Mr J Forster BA
Founded 1913
School status Girls' independent boarding and day Boys 3–11
Religious denomination Non-denominational
Physical and medical conditions IT SM TW WA3/HEA
Age range 3–18 (boys 3–11); *boarders from* 8
No of pupils 385; *(boarding)* 213; *(full boarding)* 213; *Nursery* 29;
Pre-prep 29; *Prep* 67; *Senior* 308
Sixth Form 93; *Girls* 375; *Boys* 10
Teacher:pupil ratio 1:12
Average class size 15
Fees per annum *(full boarding)* £17,730–£27,345; *(day)* £7,710–£22,395

Going well beyond the National Curriculum, some 20 subjects are available at GCSE, ranging from the traditional academic subjects such as Latin and the sciences, to practical subjects such as drama, dance and physical education. Modern languages available include French, German, Spanish and also Mandarin. A levels in history of art, human biology, business studies and theatre studies extend the range of the curriculum. Information technology is a compulsory subject up to sixth form, optional thereafter.

Boarding starts at the age of 8. Younger girls are housed under the supervision of resident housemistresses, resident tutors and matrons. As pupils progress up the school, the dormitories are gradually replaced by double and single study-bedrooms. The introduction of the latest sixth form boarding house, Rylands, means that all sixth formers are housed in modern study rooms, complete with private en-suites. Moreton Hall has recently completed an ambitious building and refurbishment programme. The new laboratories, information technology rooms and art design centre are housed within a short distance of the central classroom, careers and library complex. An exceptionally well-equipped sports centre comprising a sports hall and floodlit tennis courts and all-weather surface, along with heated, indoor swimming pool, nine-hole golf course and playing fields, is set in 100 acres of beautiful parkland at the foot of the Berwyn Hills. The school offers a wide range of sporting options, including lacrosse, netball, hockey, cricket, tennis and athletics. Sailing and riding are also popular. Moreton Enterprises, a sixth form managed group of companies, offers the girls real business experience. Girls are admitted to the senior school, normally in September, at the age of 11.

Moreton is currently ranked as the Number 1 school in the UK by Durham University for value added on academic results. As well as a proven record of academic excellence, Moreton also stretches students with an accelerated Oxbridge programme and a unique cultural and academic enrichment programme for all, including specific learning programmes for those wishing to study medicine, dentistry and veterinary courses at university. 90 per cent of Moreton students enter top UK universities. This, in addition to an enhanced weekend activity programme, and an emphasis on target weekends, when all girls are expected to remain in the school, will help ensure that Moreton remains, as Tatler Magazine's Good Schools Guide put it, "a cracking school, trouncing local and national rivals on all fronts" – *Tatler's Schools Guide, 2011.*

"In all things, Moreton punches above its weight" – *Good Schools Guide*
"Outstanding pastoral care" – Ofsted

Oswestry School

Upper Brook Street, Oswestry, Shropshire SY11 2TL **T**: (01691) 655711 **F**: (01691) 662726
E: admissions@oswestryschool.org.uk **W**: www.oswestryschool.org.uk

●♯▲

Headmaster Mr Douglas Robb MA MEd   **Founded** 1407
School status Co-educational independent
Religious denomination Non-denominational
Member of SHMIS **Accredited by** ISC
No of pupils 459; *(boarding)* 113; *(full boarding)* 89;
(weekly boarding) 24; *Prep* 92; *Girls* 222; *Boys* 237
Average class size 15
Fees per annum *(full boarding)* £5,600–£7,380 per term; *(day)* £2,435–£4,240 per term

Oswestry School is an independent, co-educational day and boarding school on the border of England and Wales for boys and girls between the ages of 4 and 18.

The school does not focus on any one particular discipline but encourages pupils, whatever their level of talent, to make the most of their abilities.

A combination of the school's size and a high teacher-per-student ratio allows it to give a high level of individual care and attention, and to monitor and motivate pupils as they make academic and personal progress.

The school is extremely proud of the excellent academic results achieved given its non-selective admission process. A-levels for the last two years have had a 97–100 per cent pass rate and around 90 per cent of GCSE grades were A–C.

Away from the classroom there is a wide variety of sports, the school enjoys a proud tradition of music and drama, and art has always been a popular pastime. A wealth of activities, trips and expeditions play a central role in broadening pupils' experience.

Bellan House is the school's prep department and this excellent school offers small classes and specialist teaching in all areas, ensuring very high standards.

Bromsgrove School

Worcester Road, Bromsgrove, Worcestershire B61 7DU **T**: (01527) 579679 **F**: (01527) 576177
E: admissions@bromsgrove-school.co.uk **W**: www.bromsgrove-school.co.uk

●♯▲

Headmaster Mr C Edwards MA (Oxon)
Founded 1553
School status Co-educational independent boarding and day senior
Religious denomination Church of England
Member of BSA, HMC, IAPS **Accredited by** HMC, IAPS, ISC
Age range 13–18; *boarders from* 7
No of pupils 910; *(full boarding)* 407; *Girls* 399; *Boys* 284
Teacher:pupil ratio 1:9
Average class size 20
Fees per annum *(boarding)* £25,185–£28,155; *(day)* £12,855

Bromsgrove School, a self-contained campus near the town of Bromsgrove, is easily accessible from the national motorway network; Birmingham International airport is 35 minutes away and London Heathrow just two hours by car. The school is opportunity oriented and provides a very wide range of academic, extra-curricular and sporting activities. Bromsgrove School, though unashamedly academic, is not as selective at 13 as its very high league table position suggests. Entry between ages 7 and 11 is based on assessment tests and at 13 on interview and tests, or Common Entrance. Entry into the sixth form is dependent on results at GCSE.

England

Malvern St James

15 Avenue Road, Great Malvern, Worcestershire WR14 3BA **T**: (01684) 584624 **F**: (01684) 566204
E: registrar@malvernstjames.co.uk **W**: www.malvernstjames.co.uk

●🏠◆▲

Headmistress Mrs P Woodhouse BMus (Hons)
Founded 1890
School status Girls' independent boarding and day
Religious denomination Church of England
Member of BSA, CReSTeD, GSA, ISBA, NAHT, SHA
Accredited by GSA
Age range 4–18; *boarders from* 7
No of pupils 400; *(boarding)* 197; *(full boarding)* 184; *(weekly boarding)* 13;
Prep 50; *Senior* 200
Sixth Form 150; *Girls* 400
Teacher:pupil ratio 1:7
Average class size 15
Fees per annum *(full boarding)* £15,960–£28,935; *(weekly)* £14,355–£26,040; *(day)* £6,705–£14,790

Malvern St James is a leading boarding and day school which presents an imaginative vision of education for girls from the age of 4 through to 18, taught within a positive, purposeful atmosphere. MSJ fosters creativity and bold thinking, and every girl is challenged and encouraged to extend her personal horizons and realize her full potential. The school is home to a warm and welcoming community with a buoyant atmosphere of shared celebration, extolling personal success in every field of endeavour.

Expectations at the school are high: girls are equipped to think independently, discover their own interests and become intellectually curious.

Small classes, led by dedicated and dynamic teachers provide a first class education tailored to the individual. Our teaching facilities include a state-of-the-art science centre, multimedia language centre and new sports centre with fitness suite, all of which provide the best in 21st Century teaching facilities.

Our academic results are first class. Last summer, over 50 per cent of all GCSE grades were A* or A. At A level, 81.6 per cent of grades awarded were A*–B, with a fantastic 26 per cent at the coveted A* grade.

Girls take full advantage of the enviable setting and superb facilities, which inspire a wonderfully rich and imaginative extra-curricular life.

The impressive site offers girls a secure footing and liberating space to develop and grow. Girls enjoy boarding on a full, weekly or flexi-basis allowing parents and daughters to choose the option that's right for them. We offer a busy and varied weekend programme of activities to suit all interests, including watersports, rock climbing, abseiling, music, drama, Model United Nations and expeditions leading to the Duke of Edinburgh's Award. Girls leave Malvern St James as poised, self-assured and articulate young women who are able to meet and greet, with integrity, the challenges and risks of our modern world.

Following an Ofsted boarding inspection in November 2009, the school was classified as 'Outstanding' and praised for its exceptionally high quality of pastoral care. The report states that girls' 'self-knowledge, self-esteem and self-confidence is excellent because they are valued within the school community and their contributions and efforts are noticed and rewarded. Boarders benefit from excellent support provided by the staff, external professions and peers.'

Malvern St James is situated at the foot of the beautiful Malvern Hills in the heart of Worcestershire. InterCity trains run from Great Malvern, the M5 and M50 are nearby and London, Birmingham and Manchester airports are within easy reach.

Admission is through the school's own examination, or through Common Entrance examination. The school offers academic entrance scholarships and exhibitions, as well as scholarships in art, music, drama, riding and physical education.

Image courtesy of St Edward's School, Oxford

Gabbitas Education

The global experts in British independent education

Tailor-made services across the independent schools sector

- Personal advice on day and boarding school choices

- Advice on schools within specific locations for parents moving from London to the countryside, foreign nationals buying investment property in London or expats returning to the UK from overseas

- Advice on independent schools in Europe, Canada and the U.S.A.

- Sixth form and tutorial college options: A Level, IB, Cambridge PreU

- Assessment and guidance on schools with special needs provision

- Education planning prenatal to 18

- Practice interviews and exam technique for senior school pre-assessment and 13+ entry

- School prospectus libraries at all of our offices, providing a valuable information resource for parents

- Publications: The Independent Schools Guide and The Complete Guide to Schools for Special Needs

- Our team of expert consultants regularly travel to locations across the world to advise parents on independent education

+44 (0)20 7734 0161

agc@gabbitas.co.uk

www.gabbitas.co.uk

MAP OF THE HOME COUNTIES (NORTH)

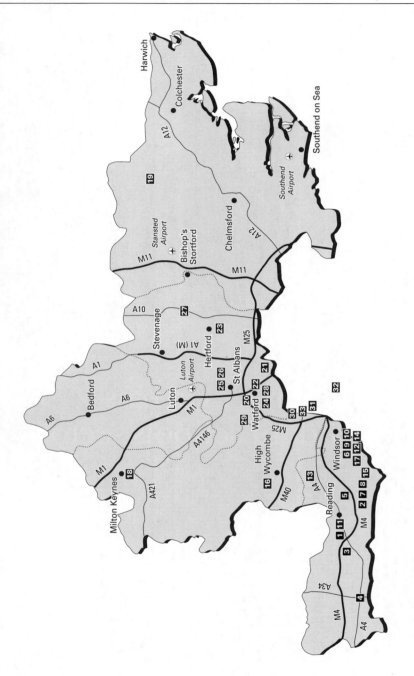

PROFILED SCHOOLS IN THE HOME COUNTIES (NORTH)

(Incorporating the counties of Bedfordshire, Berkshire, Buckinghamshire, Essex, Hertfordshire, Middlesex)

England

The Abbey School

17 Kendrick Road, Reading, Berkshire RG1 5DZ **T**: (0118) 987 2256 **F**: (0118) 987 1478
E: schooloffice@theabbey.co.uk **W**: www.theabbey.co.uk

●👫★▲

Head Mistress Mrs B E Stanley BA (Hons) PGCE FRGS
Founded 1887
School status Girls' independent day only
Religious denomination Church of England
Member of CASE, GSA, IB, ISA, ISBA, ISC
Accredited by GSA, ISA, ISC
Age range 3–18
No of pupils 1,062; *Junior* 360; *Senior* 523
Sixth Form 179
Fees per annum *(day)* £7,950–£12,600

The Abbey School in Reading, Berkshire is one of the leading academic schools in the country, offering an outstanding education for 1,050 girls between the ages of 3 and 18. The junior school provides a first-class foundation with many enrichment workshops and trips. Girls become confident, articulate and independent learners in a caring, friendly environment. The senior school has an impressive tradition and newly enhanced facilities. Girls obtain excellent results and enjoy an exceptionally wide extra-curricular programme and strong pastoral care. In the vibrant sixth form, pupils can choose between the International Baccalaureate and A levels. They gain entry to the universities of their choice, with many going to top destinations such as Oxbridge, University College and Bristol. There is an extensive Abbey coach service. Enquiries to registrar, Mrs Jackie Miles, tel: 0118 987 2256 or e-mail: registrar@theabbey.co.uk, or visit www.theabbey.co.uk.

Bearwood College

Bearwood Road, Wokingham, Berkshire RG41 5BG **T**: (0118) 974 8300 **F**: (0118) 977 3186
E: registrar@bearwoodcollege.co.uk **W**: www.bearwoodcollege.co.uk

●👫▲

Headmaster Mr S Aiano MA (Cantab) PGCE FRSA
Founded 1827
College status Co-educational independent boarding and day
Religious denomination Church of England
Member of BSA, ISBA, SHMIS **Accredited by** British Council, ISC
Age range 0–18 (Nursery 0–5 years, Pre-Prep 4–7 years, Prep 7–11
years, Senior (including sixth form) 11–18 years.); *boarders from* 11
No of pupils 494; *(boarding)* 72; *(full boarding)* 62;
(weekly boarding) 10; *Nursery* 119; *Prep* 52; *Senior* 323
Sixth Form 65; *Girls* 148; *Boys* 346
Teacher:pupil ratio 1:8
Average class size 18
Fees per annum *(full boarding)* £24,360–£28,080; *(weekly)* £24,360–£28,080; *(day)* £8,349–£16,365

Bearwood provides the best in care and education for pupils aged 3 months to 18 years old through dedicated nursery, pre-prep, prep and senior school departments. We welcome day pupils at all stages and boarders from 11. All pupils are encouraged to achieve their best, both academically and outside the classroom. Pastoral care and a supportive academic environment facilitate personal development and warm friendships. Pupils participate in an exciting programme of extra-curricular activities and outdoor pursuits. We are close to the M3 and M4, within easy reach of Heathrow and Gatwick airports, and 45 minutes from London by train.

Bradfield College

Bradfield, Reading, Berkshire RG7 6AU **T**: (0118) 964 4510 **F**: (0118) 964 4513
E: headmaster@bradfieldcollege.org.uk **W**: www.bradfieldcollege.org.uk

Head Mr S C Henderson MA (Oxon)
Founded 1850
College status Co-educational independent senior boarding
and day
Religious denomination Church of England
Member of BSA, HMC **Accredited by** HMC
Age range 13–18; *boarders from* 13
No of pupils 734; *(boarding)* 619
Sixth Form 299; *Girls* 251; *Boys* 483
Teacher:pupil ratio 1:9
Average class size 16
Fees per annum *(full boarding)* £29,535; *(day)* £23,628

Bradfield College offers a wide selection of subjects in both the Junior and Senior schools, providing challenge and choice for all through personalized programmes of study inspired by passionate and engaging teaching. Learning extends beyond the classroom through the Athena General Studies lectures and tutorial programme including Minerva seminars for scholars. Academic and Music Scholarships, Dr Gray all-rounder Exhibitions, Sports, Art, DT and Drama Awards are available at 13+ with entrance by the Common Academic Scholarship, the Bradfield College Scholarship, Common Entrance or the Bradfield College Entrance Examinations. Academic and Music Scholarships, Dr Gray all-rounder Exhibitions, Art, Sports and Performing Arts Awards are available at 16+ with entrance on attainment of a minimum of 6 B grades at GCSE, assessment at Bradfield and Headteacher's reference if transferring from elsewhere into the large and vibrant Sixth Form. The College delivers an outstanding academic education for all, unparalleled pastoral care and a diverse range of extra-curricular activities, enabling every individual to find his or her niche.

Cheam School

Headley, Newbury, Berkshire RG19 8LD **T**: (01635) 268381 **F**: (020) 7437 1764 **E**: office@cheamschool.co.uk
W: www.cheamschool.com

Head Master Mr Mark Johnson BEd
School status Co-educational boarding and day prep prep and senior
Religious denomination Church of England
Age range 7–13
No of pupils 299; *(boarding)* 85; *(full boarding)* 85; *Nursery* 24
Pre-prep 100; *Prep* 300; *Girls* 141; *Boys* 158
Average class size 18
Fees per annum *(full boarding)* £7,330; *(day)* £3,105–£5,425

Curriculum: Children are prepared in small classes (maximum 18) for Common Entrance and scholarships to all major public schools. The syllabus covers and exceeds National Curriculum requirements. Those with special needs are well catered for. Entry requirements: By interview. One bursary awarded annually at headmaster's discretion. Academic and leisure facilities set in a stimulating yet secure 80-acre estate. New classroom block, music school and refurbished chapel, completed September 2001. Modern science block; dedicated IT, art and design departments; new indoor sports centre opened 2003 and sporting facilities include squash court and nine-hole golf course. Pastoral care and boarding facilities: Each child is under the watchful eye of two house tutors and a form teacher; resident staff and matrons supervise boarders in comfortable dormitories. Separate girls' boarding accommodation. Nursery and pre-prep on site.

Eagle House

Crowthorne Road, Sandhurst, Berkshire GU47 8PH **T**: (01344) 772134 **F**: (01344) 779039
E: info@eaglehouseschool.com **W**: www.eaglehouseschool.com

● 🏠

SUBLIMIORA PETAMUS

Headmaster Mr Andrew Barnard BA (Hons) PGCE
Founded 1820
School status Co-educational independent
Religious denomination Church of England
Member of BSA, IAPS, NAHT, SATIPS **Accredited by** IAPS, ISC
Age range 3–13; *boarders from* 8
No of pupils 360; *(boarding)* 50; *(full boarding)* 20; *(weekly boarding)* 30;
Nursery 27; *Pre-prep* 100; *Prep* 283; *Girls* 142; *Boys* 218
Teacher:pupil ratio 1:8
Average class size 14
Fees per annum *(full boarding)* £19,050; *(weekly)* £19,050; *(day)* £8,880–£14,220

At Eagle House every child is unique. From 3 to 13, girls and boys develop in a friendly, creative and expressive environment. Working closely with parents, Eagle House nurtures the individual talents of every child, so that they grow in self-esteem and confidence through their success in academic subjects, sports, art, music and drama. The school believes in rewards and praise for good work and exemplary behaviour to encourage high standards and good citizenship. Eagle House benefits from superb facilities and small class sizes, and dedicated staff ensure that all children have the best academic start possible. The high sporting achievements of the pupils are testament to the opportunities and coaching offered by the school. A diverse activities programme, called Golden Eagle, is enjoyed by all pupils, helping to give them an all-round education. With boarding opportunities from Year 3 and late-stay facilities for all children, Eagle House caters for the busy lives families lead.

Heathfield School

London Road, Ascot, Berkshire SL5 8BQ **T**: (01344) 898343 **F**: (01344) 890689
E: registrar@heathfieldschool.net **W**: www.heathfieldschool.net

● 🏠 ▲

Headmistress Mrs J Heywood BSc (Hons) (Kingston) PGCE (Kingston)
Founded 1899
School status Girls' independent full boarding
Religious denomination Christian
Member of BSA, GSA, IAPS, SHA **Accredited by** GSA, IAPS, ISC
Age range 11–18; *boarders from* 11
No of pupils 200; *(boarding)* 200; *(full boarding)* 200; *Senior* 200
Sixth Form 70; *Girls* 200
Teacher:pupil ratio 1:6 **Average class size** 12
Fees per annum *(full boarding)* £27,450–£28,950

Heathfield encourages academic success but also prepares girls for the realities of the outside world. Our philosophy is to focus on the needs of individuals, nurturing both academic and personal development to help every girl achieve her potential. Modern teaching, sporting and leisure facilities make education a positive, exciting experience. Boarding accommodation is excellent, two-thirds of the pupils having single bedrooms. We have a new performing arts centre and plans for future refurbishments. Set in spacious surroundings on the outskirts of Ascot, the school is 45 minutes from London and 30 minutes from London Heathrow. A series of Open Mornings are run throughout the year; please contact Rebecca Farha, Registrar, for more details, registrar@heathfieldschool.net, 01344 898 342.

Lambrook School

Winkfield Row, Bracknell, Berkshire RG42 6LU **T**: (01344) 882717 **F**: (01344) 891114
E: info@lambrook.berks.sch.uk **W**: www.lambrook.berks.sch.uk

Headmaster Jonathan Perry BA PGCE
School status Co-educational boarding and day
Religious denomination Church of England
Member of AGBIS, BSA, IAPS, ISA, ISBA, ISC
Age range 3–13
No of pupils 450 day and boarding; *Girls* 155; *Boys* 295
Fees per term *(full boarding)* £5,611–£6,003; *(day)* £3,157–£5,060

The school was established in 1860. It has an impressive history of academic success and is proud of the excellent education it provides. The strength of the school is to be found in the enthusiasm and commitment of its accomplished staff and the support of the parents and children, underpinned by the strong leadership of the governors and headmaster. The 40 acres of grounds provide a tranquil setting conducive to learning and a wonderful space to enjoy the rewards of teamwork, the thrill of competing and the delight of success. Lambrook provides a high-quality education which is enduring and will serve a lifetime.

Luckley-Oakfield School

Luckley Road, Wokingham, Berkshire RG40 3EU **T**: (0118) 978 4175 **F**: (0118) 977 0305
E: registrar@luckley.wokingham.sch.uk **W**: www.luckley.wokingham.sch.uk

Headmistress Miss V A Davis BSc (Hons) ARCS
Founded 1918
School status Girls' independent boarding and day
Religious denomination Christian
Member of AGBIS, BSA, GSA **Accredited by** GSA
Age range 11–18; *boarders from* 11
No of pupils 273; *(boarding)* 37; *(full boarding)* 31; *(weekly boarding)* 6; *Senior* 161
Sixth Form 61; *Girls* 273
Teacher:pupil ratio 1:8
Average class size 18
Fees per annum *(full boarding)* £23,586; *(weekly)* £21,858; *(day)* £13,476

Luckley-Oakfield encourages high aspirations, independent thinking and community spirit. Each pupil experiences a truly holistic education developing her academic, cultural, creative, physical and ethical dimensions. The school has high expectations for all its pupils and achieves excellent academic results. Pupils encounter rich and varied opportunities both inside and outside the classroom. Flexi, weekly and full boarding provide a wonderful 'home from home'. Luckley-Oakfield is set in beautiful Berkshire countryside, with outstanding facilities and grounds. Generous Forces discounts are available.

LVS Ascot

London Road, Ascot, Berkshire SL5 8DR **T**: (01344) 882770 **F**: (01344) 890648 **E**: registrar@lvs.ascot.sch.uk
W: www.lvs.ascot.sch.uk

Head of Senior School Mrs Christine Cunniffe BA (Hons) MMus
Head of Junior School Mrs Helen Donnelly BA BEd (Hons)
Founded 1803
School status Co-educational independent boarding and day
Religious denomination Non-denominational
Member of AGBIS, ISA, SHMIS **Accredited by** British Council

Age range 4–18; *boarders from 8*
No of pupils 930; *(boarding)* 200; *(full boarding)* 200; *Infants and Junior* 200; *Senior* 570
Sixth Form 160; *Girls* 420; *Boys* 510
Teacher:pupil ratio 1:9 **Average class size** 16
Fees per annum *(full boarding)* £20,460–£24,240; *(day)* £7,995–£13,800

LVS Ascot is a non-selective, co-educational, independent day and boarding school for students aged 4 to 18. Situated in Ascot, just 20 miles from London, close to the historic town of Windsor, the school is within easy reach of the M4, M40 and M25 motorways and all London airports.

Set in 25 acres of landscaped gardens and playing fields, the purpose built, modern campus provides excellent facilities in a safe and stimulating environment, including an indoor swimming pool, sports hall, dance studio, medical centre, 300 seat theatre and a music suite with recording studio. The Sixth Form and Learning Resources Centres provide additional areas for independent study and extended learning.

LVS Ascot provides a broad and stimulating curriculum with an extensive choice of GCSE and A level options. These, alongside a wide range of challenging extra-curricular activities, develop individual student's skills, talents and strengths. The 2011 ISI inspection said: "The school is highly successful in achieving its aim to develop caring, confident citizens for the future."

Papplewick School

Windsor Road, Ascot, Berkshire SL5 7LH **T**: (01344) 621488 **F**: (01344) 874639 **E**: hm@papplewick.org.uk
W: www.papplewick.org.uk
Enquiries to registrar, Mrs Sarah Tysoe, at registrar@papplewick.org.uk

Head Mr T W Bunbury BA (Hons) PGCE
Founded 1947
School status Boys' independent boarding and day
Religious denomination Church of England
Member of BSA, IAPS, ISC, SATIPS
Accredited by IAPS, ISC
Age range 6–13; *boarders from 7*
No of pupils 190; *(boarding)* 126; *(full boarding)* 55;
(weekly boarding) 71; *Boys* 190
Teacher:pupil ratio 1:8
Average class size 13
Fees per annum *(full boarding)* £23,310; *(day)* £13,350–£17,895

Papplewick provides an atmosphere where boys can be boys and individuality is celebrated. Academic achievement is at the highest level and feeds UK top senior schools (three scholarships gained in the last three years, including four to Eton). Day, weekly and full boarding are offered in a family-friendly atmosphere. A new Year 2 class has been introduced. Situated in 15 acres of land opposite Ascot racecourse in Berkshire, Papplewick enjoys easy access to the M4, M3, M25, Heathrow and Gatwick. The broad range of academic and extra-curricular activities includes the popular snake club and rocket-making. The school has strong traditions of art and music. Our facilities include a sports hall, music school, IT department and covered swimming pool. Entry is by parental choice and interview, followed by a placement test.

Reading Blue Coat School

Holme Park, Sonning-on-Thames, Reading, Berkshire RG4 6SU **T**: (0118) 944 1005 **F**: (0118) 944 2690
E: admissions@rbcs.org.uk **W**: www.rbcs.org.uk

● ⌂ ▲

Headmaster Mr M J Windsor MA, BA, PGCE
Founded 1646
School status Boys' day only 11–18; Co-ed VIth form
Religious denomination Church of England
Member of AGBIS, HMC, SHMIS
Age range 11–18 (co–ed VIth form)
No of pupils 677; *Senior* 456
Sixth Form 221; *Girls* 61; *Boys* 616

Set in 46 acres of attractive parkland including a boathouse and direct access to the Thames, Blue Coat provides a stimulating and friendly atmosphere in which pupils can realize their full intellectual, physical and creative potential. To enable pupils to reach attainable goals the school provides close attention to their progress, ensuring good teaching and careful assessment. The school sets great store by the philosophy that a good education is much more than a formal academic training and consequently, while academic excellence is our goal, co-curricular activities play an important part in Blue Coat life. A wide range of sports are offered while CCF, the Duke of Edinburgh Awards, Sports Leadership Award and public speaking are some of the many activities that thrive at school. Music and drama have a strong tradition, with concerts and drama productions being staged regularly. Over a third of pupils play musical instruments.

St Mary's School Ascot

St Mary's Road, Ascot, Berkshire SL5 9JF **T**: (01344) 623721 **F**: (01344) 873281
E: admissions@st-marys-ascot.co.uk **W**: www.st-marys-ascot.co.uk

● ⌂ ▲

Headmistress Mrs M Breen MSc BSc
Founded 1885
School status Girls' independent boarding and day
Religious denomination Roman Catholic
Member of BSA, GSA **Accredited by** GSA
Age range 11–18; *boarders from* 11
No of pupils 380; *(boarding)* 367; *(day)* 13; *Senior* 295
Sixth Form 119; *Girls* 380
Teacher:pupil ratio 1:10
Average class size 16
Fees per annum *(full boarding)* £29,220; *(day)* £20,790

St Mary's School Ascot is a Roman Catholic boarding school for girls aged 11–18 years. Entry at 11+, 13+ and 16+ is subject to the school's own entry procedure. Facilities are excellent, as is our record in public examinations. We are a friendly, stable and caring community, proud of our academic, sporting and musical achievements and dedicated to bringing out the full potential of each of our pupils. We are committed to full boarding, with spaces for a few day pupils living nearby. We offer a stimulating range of extra-curricular activities which take place in the evenings and throughout the weekend.

St Piran's Preparatory School

Gringer Hill, Maidenhead, Berkshire SL6 7LZ **T**: (01628) 594302 **F**: (01628) 594301 **E**: registrar@stpirans.co.uk
W: www.stpirans.co.uk

Head Master Mr J Carroll BA (Hons) BPhilEd PGCE
Founded 1805
School status Co-educational independent day only
Religious denomination Christian
Member of IAPS, ISBA, ISC, NAHT, SATIPS
Accredited by IAPS
Age range 3–13
No of pupils 344; *Nursery* 54; *Pre-prep* 112; *Prep* 159; *Senior* 19;
Girls 129; *Boys* 215
Teacher:pupil ratio 1:8 **Average class size** 18
Fees per annum *(day)* £2,970–£11,040

Curriculum: National Curriculum subjects up to Year 8. French is offered from Reception to Year 8. Latin and Spanish are options for seniors. Sport: A comprehensive range for all pupils. Facilities are excellent and include a sports hall, indoor swimming pool, all-weather pitch, dance studio, music room, ICT suite and a learning resource centre. Fully networked ICT department, PCs and interactive whiteboards in classrooms. We have specialist teachers for those who need additional support. Trampolining, drama, games and crafts, among others, are activities for Year 5 to Year 8 at the end of the day. Entry requirements: Entry is by interview, school report and, where necessary, a short assessment if entry is higher up in the school.

Upton House School

115 St Leonard's Road, Windsor, Berkshire SL4 3DF **T**: (01753) 862610 **F**: (01753) 621950
E: info@uptonhouse.org.uk **W**: www.uptonhouse.org.uk

Headmistress Mrs M Collins BA (Hons) PGCE
Founded 1936
School status Co-educational independent day only
Religious denomination Church of England
Member of AHIS, IAPS, ISA **Accredited by** IAPS, ISC
Age range 2–11
No of pupils 250; *Nursery* 60; *Pre-prep* 110; *Prep* 80; *Girls* 170; *Boys* 80
Teacher:pupil ratio 1:10
Average class size 19
Fees per annum *(day)* £4,605–£11,985

Upton House, set in the heart of Windsor, is a happy and successful school with 250 children and 45 members of staff. It combines a dynamic learning environment with a caring ethos dedicated to allowing each child to develop his or her individual talents and, at the same time, to learn the importance of generosity to others in the wider world. A very full syllabus is offered and we take particular pride in making the whole learning process fun – with a range of extra-curricular activities, off-site visits, after-school clubs, dramatic productions, summer camps, etc. For further information or a copy of our prospectus, please contact the registrar, Mrs Jill Gilmour, on (01753) 862610 or at registrar@uptonhouse.org.uk or www.uptonhouse.org.uk.

Wellington College

Duke's Ride, Crowthorne, Berkshire RG45 7PU **T**: (01344) 444013 **F**: (01344) 444115
E: admissions@wellingtoncollege.org.uk **W**: www.wellingtoncollege.org.uk

●♟★▲

Headmaster Dr A F Seldon MA PhD FRSA MBA FRHisS
Founded 1853
College status Co-educational independent boarding and day senior
Religious denomination Church of England
Member of AGBIS, BSA, HMC, IB, ISBA, Round Square
Accredited by HMC
Age range 13–18; *boarders from* 13
No of pupils 1,020; *(boarding)* 794; *(full boarding)* 794; *Senior* 1,020
Sixth Form 463; *Girls* 392; *Boys* 628
Teacher:pupil ratio 1:9
Average class size 16
Fees per annum *(full boarding)* £30,075; *(day)* £22,545–£25,545

Wellington College is one of the country's leading independent schools. It stands in an attractive 400-acre woodland estate, 40 minutes from London and Heathrow. A sensible priority is given to academic study (98 per cent of leavers go on to degree courses), but the highest standards are also achieved in other aspects of school life, including sport, art, technology, writing, music and drama. Extra-curricular activities are important, as they develop self-confidence and provide experience in teamwork, initiative and leadership. Wellington provides a well-disciplined framework within which pupils have a wide range of opportunities to fulfil their personal potential.

Pipers Corner School

Pipers Lane, Great Kingshill, High Wycombe, Buckinghamshire HP15 6LP **T**: (01494) 718255
F: (01494) 719806 **E**: theschool@piperscorner.co.uk **W**: www.piperscorner.co.uk

●♟▲

Headmistress Mrs H J Ness-Gifford BA (Hons) PGCE
Founded 1930
School status Girls' independent
Religious denomination Church of England
Member of AGBIS, AHIS, BSA, GSA, ISBA
Accredited by GSA, ISC
Age range 3–18; *boarders from* 8
No of pupils 523; *(boarding)* 28; *(full boarding)* 14; *(weekly boarding)* 14;
Pre-prep 39; *Prep* 91; *Senior* 331
Sixth Form 62; *Girls* 523
Teacher:pupil ratio 1:12
Average class size 20
Fees per annum *(full boarding)* £18,270–£22,200; *(weekly)* £18,030–£21,960; *(day)* £6,945–£13,470

At Pipers Corner there is a focus on academic excellence as girls are supported and challenged to achieve their full potential. In addition to providing a stimulating learning environment we also encourage girls to cultivate any sporting or creative talents they have through a wide range of lunchtime and after-school clubs and activities. Girls enjoy the use of our excellent facilities, including swimming pool, sports hall and dance and drama studios. Academically successful, our girls progress to further study at Oxbridge and other top universities or specialist dance, drama and music colleges. The Pipers boarding community offers flexibility, freedom and peace of mind to both girls and their parents. Our safe and secure accommodation, together with our experienced house staff, provides a 'second home' environment at the heart of the school.

St Mary's School

94 Packhorse Road, Gerrards Cross, Buckinghamshire SL9 8JQ **T**: (01753) 883370 **F**: (01753) 890966
E: registrar@st-marys.bucks.sch.uk **W**: www.stmarysschool.co.uk
Registrar – Mrs Pearcey

Headmistress Mrs J A Ross BA (Hons) NPQH
Founded 1872
School status girls' independent day only
Religious denomination Church of England
Member of AGBIS, GSA, ISC **Accredited by** GSA, ISC
Age range 3–18
No of pupils 325; *Senior* 180
Sixth Form 40; *Girls* 325
Fees per annum *(day)* £3,300–£11,820

St Mary's is a vibrant independent day school for girls aged from 3 to 18 years. The small classes, outstanding teachers and an especially warm and happy atmosphere combine to generate a very positive environment for success. Academic results are excellent, with a 95 per cent pass rate at A level and GCSE. Scholarships and bursaries are available. There is a wide range of extra-curricular activities, from kick boxing, streetdance and internet radio to netball, orchestra and chess. The Sportsmark and Activemark awards recognize our commitment that all girls take part in high-quality PE activities every week. To read more, visit www.stmarysschool.co.uk. Visitor days take place every Thursday in term time.

Swanbourne House School

Swanbourne, Milton Keynes, Buckinghamshire MK17 0HZ **T**: (01296) 720264 **F**: (01296) 728089
E: office@swanbourne.org **W**: www.swanbourne.org

Joint Head Mrs S D Goodhart BEd (Hons)
Joint Head Mrs J S Goodhart BEd Cert Ed
Founded 1920
School status Co-educational independent boarding and day
Religious denomination Church of England
Member of BSA, IAPS, ISBA, SATIPS **Accredited by** IAPS
Age range 3–13; *boarders from* 7
No of pupils 440; *(boarding)* 92; *(full boarding)* 36; *(weekly boarding)* 56; *Nursery* 36; *Pre-prep* 132; *Prep* 272; *Girls* 197; *Boys* 243
Average class size 16
Fees per annum *(full boarding)* £16,785; *(weekly)* £16,785; *(day)* £3,600–£13,620

Swanbourne House is a successful IAPS preparatory school from which academic scholarships and awards in arts/sport and music are won every year. There are many opportunities for personal development through activities, sport, the arts, holiday clubs and trips abroad. Pastoral care is our beacon and our leadership training is renowned. We have excellent facilities. London parents say we have the 'wow' factor. Come and visit, you can be assured of a warm welcome. Entry is by a familiarization day and short assessment test. Our latest inspections describe the school, boarding, spirituality, pastoral care, organization and management as outstanding.

Gosfield School

Halstead Road, Gosfield, Halstead, Essex CO9 1PF **T**: (+44(0)1787) 474040 **F**: (+44(0)1787) 478228
E: principal@gosfieldschool.org.uk **W**: www.gosfieldschool.org.uk

Principal Dr Sarah Welch BA (Hons), PGCE, MA, PhD
Founded 1929
School status Co-educational independent
Religious denomination Inter-denominational
Member of AGBIS, BSA, HAS, ISA, ISC **Accredited by** ISA
Age range 4–18; *boarders from* 11
No of pupils 182; *(boarding)* 15; *(weekly boarding)* 15; *Prep* 68;
Senior 114
Sixth Form 9; *Girls* 86; *Boys* 96
Teacher:pupil ratio 1:6 **Average class size** 18
Fees per annum *(full boarding)* £16,275–£20,385; *(weekly)* £13,890–£15,090; *(day)* £7,020–£11,823

'Gosfield School offers a rich and fulfilling education to pupils of all ages from 4 -18.' – *The Independent Schools Inspectorate*.

Gosfield School is a family oriented co-educational school offering a warm, caring and secure environment where children will be closely supported. Our class sizes are small with no more than 20 students and we offer a broad curriculum and outstanding extra curricular activities. We have a strong learning support and extension structure and excellent pastoral care. We offer superb facilities to support our broad curriculum including an outstanding sports hall, new technologies classrooms and science laboratory, outdoor all weather playing surface and over 100 acres of playing fields. Our boarding house is a small family based environment with very comfortable shared rooms. We achieve superb results at all levels for a non-selective school. We offer EFL to overseas students from year 7. Following the previous inspection, ISI reported: 'The quality of pupils' learning remains high. The way in which pupils in all years mix and assist each other is excellent.'

Abbot's Hill School

Bunkers Lane, Hemel Hempstead, Hertfordshire HP3 8RP **T**: (01442) 240333 **F**: (01442) 269981
E: registrar@abbotshill.herts.sch.uk **W**: www.abbotshill.herts.sch.uk

Headmistress Mrs K Lewis
Founded 1912
School status Girls' independent day only
pre-prep Boys 3–5
Religious denomination Church of England
Member of AHIS, GSA **Accredited by** GSA, ISC
Age range 3–16 (boys 3–5)
No of pupils 450; *Girls* 450
Average class size 12–18
Fees per annum *(day)* £8,205–£14,640

A thriving, vibrant, high-achieving school, Abbot's Hill is set in 76 acres of parkland on the edge of Hemel Hempstead, Hertfordshire. We are justly proud of our academic record but never stray from our prime objective: to educate the whole person, to achieve his or her highest personal, social and educational potential. Every pupil benefits from being known personally by the headmistress and teaching staff in a warm and enabling environment. The school and its dedicated staff offer excellent facilities and a wide range of subjects and extra-curricular activities.

Aldenham School

Elstree, Hertfordshire WD6 3AJ **T**: (01923) 858122 **F**: (01923) 854410 **E**: enquiries@aldenham.com
W: www.aldenham.com
Contact the admissions coordinator, Ms Masters, for details of the entrance procedure.

●🏠▲

Headmaster Mr J C Fowler MA
Founded 1597
School status Co-educational independent boarding and day
Religious denomination Church of England
Member of AGBIS, BSA, CASE, HMC, IAPS, ISA, ISBA,
ISC **Accredited by** HMC, IAPS, ISA, ISC
Age range 3–18; *boarders from* 11
No of pupils 700; *(boarding)* 122; *(full boarding)* 122; *Nursery* 44;
Pre-prep 62; *Prep* 84; *Senior* 352
Sixth Form 158; *Girls* 185; *Boys* 515
Teacher:pupil ratio 1:8
Average class size 20
Fees per annum *(full boarding)* £19,101–£26,580; *(day)* £12,750–£18,249

Aldenham stands in a beautiful site of more than 110 acres, with modern state-of-the-art facilities. The curriculum includes the arts, sciences and humanities, music technology, business studies, drama and physical education. Personal tutors are provided. An extensive games and activities programme includes football, hockey, netball, basketball, squash, sailing and cricket. Strong music and drama departments stage regular productions. The Learning Support department encourages able pupils with dyslexia and dyscalculia and provides specialist English lessons for overseas pupils (EAL). Awards for academic potential, sport, music, art and technology are available.

Edge Grove

Aldenham Village, Hertfordshire WD25 8NL **T**: (01923) 855724 **F**: (01923) 859920
E: admissions@edgegrove.com **W**: www.edgegrove.com

●🏠

Headmaster I Elliott
Founded 1935
School status Co-educational independent boarding and day
Religious denomination Church of England
Member of IAPS **Accredited by** IAPS
Age range 3–13; *boarders from* 7
No of pupils 340; *(boarding)* 59; *(full boarding)* 17; *(weekly boarding)* 6;
(flexi boarding) 36
Teacher:pupil ratio 1:8
Average class size 14
Fees per annum *(full boarding)* £14,700–£18,285; *(weekly)* £14,700–£18,285; *(day)* £4,575–£13,395

Outstanding support is available for the academic, extra-curricular and personal developmental crucial for progression to senior school.

Pupils are prepared for Common Entrance at 11+/13 before moving on to a variety of senior schools throughout the country. Over 60 scholarships have been awarded to Edge Grove pupils in the last 4 years, many for places at top public schools.

The quality of care is a high priority and all staff members are sensitive to pupils in need of pastoral support. Sport and the arts feature highly amongst extra-curricular activities with many sporting fixtures and visits in the year.

"Pupils enjoy their learning and are proud of their achievements" – Recent ISI Report

Haileybury

Hertford, Hertfordshire SG13 7NU **T**: (01992) 706353 **F**: (01992) 470663 **E**: registrar@haileybury.com
W: www.haileybury.com

● 🏠 ★ ▲

Headmaster Mr J S Davies MA (Cantab)
Founded 1862
School status Co-educational independent boarding and day
Religious denomination Church of England
Member of BSA, HMC, IBO **Accredited by** HMC, ISC
Age range 11–18; *boarders from* 11
No of pupils 734; *(boarding)* 455; *(full boarding)* 455; *Senior* 629
Sixth Form 296; *Girls* 292; *Boys* 442
Teacher:pupil ratio 1:1
Average class size 16
Fees per annum *(full boarding)* £17,397–£27,384
   (day) £13,667–£20,565

Boys and girls, mostly boarding, admitted at 11 into the lower school, at 13 into the main school, and also at 16 into the sixth form. Magnificent classical buildings are complemented by modern, state-of-the-art developments. Set in 500 rural acres and situated 20 miles north of central London, Haileybury combines high academic standards with broad-ranging excellence in art, music, drama and sport. The school is pleased to offer the International Baccalaureate Diploma Programme alongside A levels. Please contact the registrar for further details.

The Royal Masonic School for Girls

Rickmansworth Park, Rickmansworth, Hertfordshire WD3 4HF **T**: (01923) 773168 **F**: (01923) 896729
E: admissions@royalmasonic.herts.sch.uk **W**: www.royalmasonic.herts.sch.uk
For further details about the school, please contact Mrs G Braiden, Admissions Secretary.

● 🏠 ▲

Headmistress Mrs D Rose MA (Cantab)
Founded 1788
School status Girls' independent
Religious denomination Non-denominational
Member of BSA, GSA, ISBA, SHA **Accredited by** GSA, ISC
Age range 2–19 (Pre School opened in January 2010 for boys
and girls aged 2–4.); *boarders from* 7
No of pupils 889; *Pre-school* 64; *Pre-prep to sixth form* 818;
(full boarding) 112; *(weekly boarding)* 36; *Pre-prep* 47; *Prep* 130;
Senior 457; *Sixth Form* 187; *Girls* 872; *Boys* 17
Teacher:pupil ratio 1:10 **Average class size** 20
Fees per annum *(full boarding)* £14,250–£23,190; *(weekly)* £14,010–£22,620; *(day)* £8,010–£14,190;
Pre-school fees on request

RMS offers an exceptionally wide-ranging curriculum in a supportive and friendly environment, where the highest standards prevail. The school has outstanding facilities and occupies a stunning 200-acre site, only 30 minutes from central London by Underground. An impressive sports hall, indoor swimming pool, squash, tennis and netball courts, and hockey pitches maintain sporting excellence. Rickmansworth is close to the M25, with easy access to London and its airports. Boarding pupils are cared for in well-appointed and spacious houses, with experienced, caring residential staff. Our boarding community is made up of British and overseas boarders and is well balanced. Admission is by the school's own entrance examination and interview. A number of generous scholarships and bursaries are available.

St Albans School

Abbey Gateway, St Albans, Hertfordshire AL3 4HB **T**: (01727) 855521 **F**: (01727) 843447
E: hm@st-albans-school.org.uk **W**: www.st-albans.herts.sch.uk

●♠▲

Headmaster Mr Andrew Grant MA PGCE FRSA
Founded 948
School status Boys' independent day only senior Co-ed VIth form
Religious denomination Inter-denominational
Member of AGBIS, HMC **Accredited by** HMC
Age range 17–18 (co-ed VIth form)
No of pupils 833; *Senior* 498
Sixth Form 281; *Girls* 54; *Boys* 779
Teacher:pupil ratio 1:10
Fees per annum *(day)* £13,794

The school is able to offer some assistance with fees, in certain circumstances of proven need, from its own endowed bursary fund. All bursaries are means-tested. A variable number of academic scholarships worth up to 50 per cent of the annual fees are awarded on academic merit at 11+, 13+ and 16+. Choral scholarships are offered at 11+ and scholarships for music and art at 13+. A music scholarship is awarded on the basis of an annual competition for Year 8 pupils already in the school. Further details of all awards are available from the head. The school is a registered charity and aims to provide an excellent education, enabling pupils to achieve the highest standard of academic success according to ability, and to develop their character and personality so as to become caring and self-disciplined adults.

St Columba's College

King Harry Lane, St Albans, Hertfordshire AL3 4AW **T**: (01727) 855185 **F**: (01727) 892024
E: admissions@st-columbas.herts.sch.uk **W**: www.stcolumbascollege.org

●♠▲

Head Mr D Buxton BA MTh MA
Founded 1939
College status Boys' day only
Religious denomination Roman Catholic
Member of HMC, IAPS, SHMIS **Accredited by** HMC, IAPS, ISC
Age range 4–18
No of pupils 850; *Pre-prep* 75; *Prep* 170; *Senior* 465
Sixth Form 140; *Boys* 850
Teacher:pupil ratio 1:10
Average class size 20
Fees per annum *(day)* £8,550–£10,884

St Columba's College is unique as the only Brothers of the Sacred Heart School in the country, originally opened in 1939. The college has progressively grown over the years to its current roll of 850. We offer a broad, progressive education to boys from 4 to 18, including a sixth form of over 160 and no fewer than 20 subjects offered at A level. Our ethos and values are rooted within the Catholic educational tradition but our community encompasses many pupils of other traditions and backgrounds. Academic standards are consistently high throughout the college, but it is the 'value added' rather than the league table position from which we derive the greater pride. We aim for every pupil to achieve his own best standard.

St Edmund's College and Prep School

Old Hall Green, Ware, Hertfordshire SG11 1DS **T**: (01920) 821504 **F**: (01920) 823011
E: admissions@stedmundscollege.org **W**: www.stedmundscollege.org

●♠▲

Headmaster Mr C P Long BA
Founded 1568
College status Co-educational independent
Religious denomination Roman Catholic
Member of BSA, EUK, HMC, ISC **Accredited by** British Council, HMC, ISC
Age range 3–18; *boarders from* 11
No of pupils 801; *(boarding)* 121; *(full boarding)* 96; *(weekly boarding)* 16; *(flexi boarding)* 9,
(Nursery to Pre-prep 61; *Prep* 99; *Senior* 641; *Sixth Form* 148; *Girls* 333; *Boys* 468
Teacher:pupil ratio 1:9
Average class size 20
Fees per annum *(full boarding)* £21,015–£24,030; *(weekly)* £19,065–£21,705; *(day)* £13,380–£14,580
Prep fees per annum *Nursery* £3,900–£7,920; *Pre-prep* £9,105; *Prep* £11,595

St Edmund's College is England's oldest Catholic school, founded in 1568. One of the key aspects of St Edmund's is its unique style and atmosphere, which values academic excellence and the achievement of a personal best, right through from St Edmund's, the prep school, to sixth form and beyond. In addition, all pupils are supported by a high level of pastoral care, based on a successful house system. Facilities include state-of-the-art IT suites, art and design technology workshops, tennis courts and an indoor swimming pool.

St Margaret's School

Merry Hill Road, Bushey, Hertfordshire WD23 1DT **T**: (020) 416 4408 **F**: (020) 416 4401
E: admissions@stmargarets.herts.sch.uk **W**: www.stmargaretsbushey.org.uk
Visitors welcome; please contact the admissions secretary for an appointment.

●♠▲

Headteacher Mrs Lynne Crighton BA (Hons)
Founded 1749
School status girls' independent boarding and day
Religious denomination Church of England
Member of BSA, GSA **Accredited by** GSA
Age range 4–18; *boarders from* 11
No of pupils 418; *(boarding)* 70; *(full boarding)* 60;
(weekly boarding) 10; *Pre-prep* 36; *Prep* 68; *Senior* 244
Sixth Form 70; *Girls* 418
Teacher:pupil ratio 1:7
Average class size 15
Fees per annum *(full boarding)* £25,050; *(weekly)* £21,330; *(day)* £8,940–£13,500

St Margaret's educates girls aged 4 to 18 years. The school is set in over 70 acres of parkland yet is less than an hour from Marble Arch and Heathrow. We provide a first-class education that delivers an enviable record of success at all public examinations within a supportive, caring community that encourages lasting friendships. The original buildings have been extended and upgraded considerably in the past decade, including a £3 million sports centre.

Tring Park School for the Performing Arts

Tring Park, Tring, Hertfordshire HP23 5LX **T**: (01442) 824255 **F**: (01442) 891069 **E**: info@tringpark.com
W: www.tringpark.com

●♠▲

Principal Mr S Anderson MA (Cantab) BMus ARCM
Founded 1919
School status Co-educational independent boarding and day
Religious denomination Inter-denominational
Member of BSA, ISA, ISC, SHA, SHMIS **Accredited by** ISA, SHMIS
Age range 8–19; *boarders from* 9
No of pupils 300; *Girls* 222; *Boys* 78
Teacher:pupil ratio 1:15
Average class size 15
Fees per annum *(full boarding)* £19,485–£27,525; *(day)* £12,600–£19,710

Tring Park offers exciting educational opportunities for pupils who show talent in one or more of the performing arts and we are committed to ensuring that all pupils fulfil their potential.

The school is set in 17 acres of attractive and secluded parkland and the main house was formerly a Rothschild mansion. The school accommodates 208 boarders and 92 day pupils and aims to provide an environment ideally suited to the teaching of the performing arts, combined with academic study to GCSE, A level and BTEC.

Tring Park is part of the Music and Dance Scheme, funded and administered by the DfE, and places are awarded annually under this scheme for talented classical dancers. A number of dance and drama awards are available for the sixth form dance course.

Up to age 14 all pupils study dance, music and drama combined with a full and vigorous academic curriculum. The pupils all study eight or nine GCSE subjects combined with the Dance or Performance foundation course. In the sixth form pupils may study up to three or four A levels or the BTEC in Performing Arts combined with the Dance, Musical Theatre or Drama Course. Academic study receives equal emphasis and the department provides a broad and balanced curriculum for all pupils.

Following success in their sixth form examinations, many of our pupils proceed to higher vocational or academic studies at universities and colleges. For others, the opportunity to perform becomes a reality immediately.

For those entering the dance course, we believe in training the whole dancer in body, mind and in artistic understanding. Dancers are encouraged to fulfil their own individual potential and each pupil's progress is monitored carefully.

Sixth form pupils joining the drama course will undertake an intensive and wide-ranging preparation for either direct entry into the theatre, further training at drama school or, with appropriate A levels, higher education on a relevant degree course. The Musical Theatre course for sixth form pupils is designed to extend the skills of the all-round performer and to focus them in this popular entertainment area.

Throughout the school, pupils have frequent opportunities to present work in the Markova Theatre and there are regular public shows given by junior and senior pupils. The range of work undertaken provides pupils with the opportunity to become versatile and able to communicate skilfully, whatever the chosen field.

Individual appointments are made to visit the school and auditions are held on a regular basis.

ACS Hillingdon International School

Hillingdon Court, 108 Vine Lane, Hillingdon, Middlesex UB10 0BE **T**: (01895) 818402 **F**: (01895) 818404
E: hillingdonadmissions@acs-schools.com **W**: www.acs-schools.com

● ★ ▲

Head of School Mrs G Apple
Founded 1967
School status Co-educational independent day only
Religious denomination Non-denominational
Member of CIS, IB, IBSCA, ISA, LISA **Accredited by** NEASC
Age range 4–18
No of pupils 602; *Girls* 283; *Boys* 319
Teacher:pupil ratio 1:8 **Average class size** 15
Fees per annum *(day)* £9,170–£19,490

ACS Hillingdon International School offers both the International Baccalaureate (IB) Middle Years programme and IB Diploma as well as the American Advanced Placement (AP). Its students have consistently achieved diploma scores well above international results, which have led to placements in top universities in America and around the world. In the UK placements have been to London School of Economics, Oxford, Imperial College London, University College London, University of Warwick, the School of Oriental and African Studies and the Royal Academy of Music. Occupying an 11-acre site, ACS Hillingdon is situated in a Grade II listed stately mansion with a modern wing accommodating classrooms, computer labs, an integrated IT network, libraries, cafeteria, a gymnasium and an auditorium. The school also has separate early-childhood pavilions and a new music technology centre with a digital recording studio, rehearsal rooms, practice studios and a computer lab. The school is approximately 30 minutes' drive from central London and has an extensive busing service (door-to-door and shuttle) including central London, making the campus widely accessible.

Northwood College

Maxwell Road, Northwood, Middlesex HA6 2YE **T**: (01923) 825446 **F**: (01923) 836526
E: admissions@northwoodcollege.co.uk **W**: www.northwoodcollege.co.uk

● 🏠 ▲

Head Mistress Miss J Pain MA MBA
Founded 1878
College status Girls' independent day only
Religious denomination Non-denominational
Member of AGBIS, GSA, IAPS, ISBA, ISC **Accredited by** GSA,
IAPS, ISC
Age range 3–18
No of pupils 800; *Nursery* 30; *Pre-prep* 125; *Prep* 168; *Senior* 372
Sixth Form 125; *Girls* 800
Average class size 22
Fees per annum *(day)* £8,250–£13,050

Northwood College is an Independent Day School for girls aged 3 to 18 years with two very special features at its heart. Our unique 'Thinking Skills' programme enables girls to develop independent and creative thinking that takes them far beyond an exam curriculum. Our emphasis on pastoral care meanwhile rests on the premise that a happy girl will always achieve her best. Put the two together and you have a school that buzzes with life, where pupils achieve outstanding results.

Our Thinking Skills programme is integrated into the curriculum and runs from Nursery through to Sixth Form. Over the years the girls build up their reasoning skills, improve their creativity and acquire strategies for tackling complex problems and decisions. They become self-sufficient learners – autonomous, inquisitive and brave. It gives the girls a life skill that will be as useful at university and in the workplace as it is now.

England

St Catherine's School

Cross Deep, Twickenham, Middlesex TW1 4QJ **T**: (020) 8891 2898 **F**: (020) 8744 9629
E: info@st-catherines-twickenham.org.uk **W**: www.stcatherineschool.co.uk

● 🏠 ▲

Headmistress Sister P Thomas BEd (Hons) MA
Founded 1914
School status Girls' independent day only
Religious denomination Roman Catholic
Member of GSA, ISA, ISC **Accredited by** GSA, CISC
Age range 3–18
No of pupils 390; *Prep* 100; *Senior* 290; *Sixth Form* 15
Average class size 18
Fees per annum *(day)* £7,950–£11,115

St Catherine's, Twickenham: Focus on the individual. St Catherine's combines nearly 100 years' experience of Catholic independent education with a modern curriculum that prepares all pupils for success in the 21st century. We are a Catholic school in the ecumenical tradition, where every pupil is a valued member of a happy community. Emphasis is placed on providing a broad education and on responsibility and the importance of respect for others. We are a school with a strong community spirit and as such are able to focus on the individual and help every child achieve high value added scroes and her personal academic best.

St Helen's School

Eastbury Road, Northwood, Middlesex HA6 3AS **T**: (01923) 843210 **F**: (01923) 843211 **E**: enquiries@sthn.co.uk
W: www.sthn.co.uk

● 🏠 ★ ▲

Headmistress Dr M Short BA (London) PhD (Cantab)
Founded 1899
School status Girls' independent day only
Religious denomination Christian
Member of GSA, IBO, ISC **Accredited by** GSA, ISC
Age range 3–18
No of pupils 1122; *Nursery* 47; *Pre-prep* 175; *Prep* 246; *Senior* 494
Sixth Form 160; *Girls* 1122
Average class size 20
Fees per annum *(day)* £9,171–£13,329

St Helen's is a highly academic school and pupils consistently achieve outstanding results, going on to prestigious universities of their first choice. In the sixth form, girls can study A levels or the International Baccalaureate Diploma. Staff are subject specialists who inspire and encourage pupils to learn independently in a friendly, secure and disciplined environment. In senior school, girls study two modern foreign languages together with Latin, and science is taught throughout as three separate subjects. We offer excellent facilities, including our new state-of-the-art sports centre; specialist facilities for science, design and technology, art, drama, music and ICT; a digital, multi-media language laboratory; an excellent library housing an extensive collection of books, ICT facilities, newspapers and periodicals; and well-equipped teaching rooms.

Image courtesy of St Edward's School, Oxford

Gabbitas Education

The global experts in British independent education

Tailor-made services across the independent schools sector

- Personal advice on day and boarding school choices

- Advice on schools within specific locations for parents moving from London to the countryside, foreign nationals buying investment property in London or expats returning to the UK from overseas

- Advice on independent schools in Europe, Canada and the U.S.A.

- Sixth form and tutorial college options: A Level, IB, Cambridge PreU

- Assessment and guidance on schools with special needs provision

- Education planning prenatal to 18

- Practice interviews and exam technique for senior school pre-assessment and 13+ entry

- School prospectus libraries at all of our offices, providing a valuable information resource for parents

- Publications: The Independent Schools Guide and The Complete Guide to Schools for Special Needs

- Our team of expert consultants regularly travel to locations across the world to advise parents on independent education

The information was concise, professional, informative, especially useful for me as I'm based overseas. Your choices were definitely appropriate to my son's needs. A most impressive service.

Mrs M, HK

+44 (0)20 7734 0161

agc@gabbitas.co.uk

www.gabbitas.co.uk

MAP OF LONDON

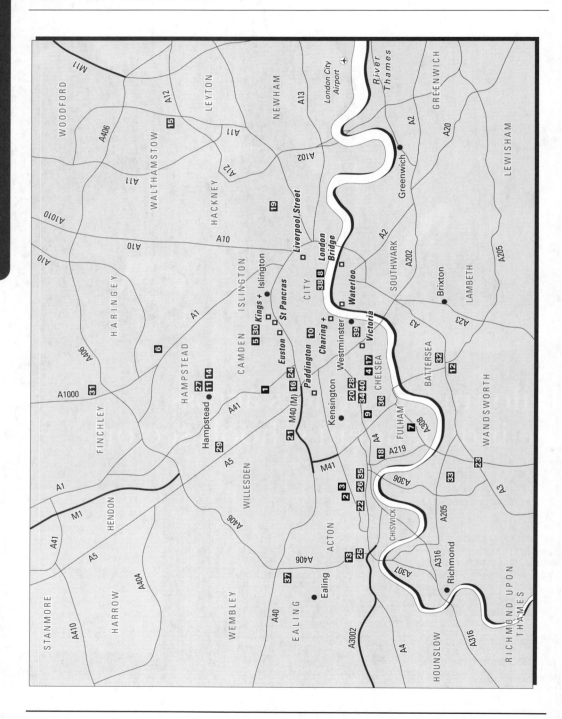

PROFILED SCHOOLS IN LONDON

The American School in London

1 Waverley Place, London NW8 0NP **T**: (020) 7449 1200 **F**: (020) 7449 1350 **E**: admissions@asl.org
W: www.asl.org

●⚜▲

Head of School Mrs C R Hester
Founded 1951
School status Co-educational independent day only
Religious denomination Non-denominational
Member of CASE, CIS, NAIS **Accredited by** CIS, MSA
Age range 4–18
No of pupils 1,350; *Girls* 670; *Boys* 680
Teacher:pupil ratio 1:9
Fees per annum *(day)* £19,350–£22,550

The American School in London is a co-educational, non-profit institution which offers an outstanding American education. The curriculum leads to an American High School Diploma, and a strong Advanced Placement programme enables pupils to enter the top universities in the United States, the UK and other countries. The core curriculum of English, maths, science and social studies is enriched with courses in modern languages, computing, fine arts and physical education. Small classes allow teachers to focus on individuals; pupils are encouraged to take an active role in learning to develop the skills necessary for independent critical thinking and expression. Many extra-curricular activities, including sports, music, drama and community service, are available for pupils of all ages. The American School in London welcomes pupils of all nationalities, including non-English speakers below the age of 10, who meet the scholastic standards. Entry is at any time throughout the year.

Symbol key

Gender

● Girls
● Boys
● Coed

Accommodation

⚜ Boarding only
⚜ Boarding and Day
⚜ Day and Boarding
⚜ Day only

International Bacc.

★ School offers IB

CReSTeD

◆ CReSTeD Registered

Has 6th Form

▲ Has 6th Form

Arts Educational Schools London

Cone Ripman House, 14 Bath Road, Chiswick, London W4 1LY **T**: (020) 8987 6600 **F**: (020) 8987 6601
E: pupils@artsed.co.uk **W**: www.artsed.co.uk
Near Turnham Green tube station – an easy two-minute walk without the need to cross major roads.

 🏠 ▲

Headmaster Mr Greg Beavis **Founded** 1919
School status Co-educational independent day only
Religious denomination Inter-denominational
Member of ISA, SHA **Accredited by** ISA, ISC
Age range 11–16 **No of pupils** 115; *Sixth Form* 71; *Girls* 142; *Boys* 62
Teacher:pupil ratio 1:8 **Average class size** 19
Fees per annum *(day)* £12,052

Excellent report from the Independent Schools Inspectorate (ISI) January 2011. The full report can be viewed at www.artsed.co.uk. ArtsEd provides an environment where the creativity of students is nurtured through the performing arts and the academic curriculum in equal measure. Specializing in dance or drama, each pupil has the opportunity to achieve at his/her highest standard through a delicately balanced academic, vocational, cultural and social curriculum. President: Lord Andrew Lloyd Webber

Headteacher's philosophy The school provides a caring, supportive and happy environment, where the students have the opportunity to maximize their talents. Academic development is given as high a priority as the vocational work, in order to ensure the success and progress of students.

The curriculum The academic curriculum is well rounded, allowing pupils a rich and stimulating educational experience. In Key Stage 3 (Years 7 to 9) pupils opt to join the acting or the dance course (making up about 30 per cent of their curriculum time). Academic classes are wideranging, comprising English, mathematics, science, French, history, geography, music and art. Students also take classes in citizenship, personal, health and social education (PHSE) and studies that aim to develop independent thinking and study skills. In the interests of the most effective learning, pupils are taught in ability groups for some subjects. In Years 10 and 11 the core academic curriculum is made up of English language, English literature, maths, biology and expressive arts (an examination subject where the relationship between two different art forms is examined in a practical study). Pupils then choose a selection from the following: art, chemistry, drama, dance, French, geography, history, media studies, music, photography and physics. ArtsEd is acutely aware of the effective ways in which new media technologies allow pupils to investigate and engage with subject matter. The school therefore encourages pupils to exploit the use of modern computer technology as an integral part of their learning. For further information visit: www.artsed.co.uk.

Arts Educational Schools London – Sixth Form

Cone Ripman House, 14 Bath Road, Chiswick, London W4 1LY **T**: (020) 8987 6600 **F**: (020) 8987 6601
E: pupils@artsed.co.uk **W**: www.artsed.co.uk

 🏠 ▲

Head Teacher Mr Greg Beavis **Founded** 1919
School status Co-educational independent day only senior
Religious denomination Non-denominational
Member of ISA **Accredited by** ISA
Age range 16–18
Fees per annum *(day)* £12,052

Excellent report from the Independent Schools Inspectorate (ISI) January 2011. The full report can be viewed at www.artsed.co.uk. Students in the sixth form study in far greater depth those subjects in which they hold the greatest interest, while complementing this experience with the – equally important – study and development of performance skills. Arts Educational Schools London is a unique and exciting establishment. We pride ourselves on balancing high academic achievement with outstanding teaching and achievement in the performing arts.

Headteacher's philosophy Artsed provides a caring, supportive and happy environment, where the students have the opportunity to maximize their talents. The sixth form has a dedicated team of tutors who are strongly committed to the success and wellbeing of students, and there is a closely structured programme of pastoral care.

The curriculum

The four A level course In Year 12, most students study four AS level subjects. These are chosen from: dance, drama, music, art and design, photography, English literature, philosophy, media studies, history, history of art, maths, French and music technology. Students also study a range of vocational studies, which are rooted in the performing arts. In Year 13 students complete the second half of their A level courses. Classes are small and results are excellent. Careful assessment and individual monitoring ensure that each student enjoys the best possible chance of achieving at the absolute highest level that he/she is capable of. The number of students achieving A grades at A level has increased significantly.

BTEC Extended Diploma in Performing Arts This two-year course provides students, on completion, with a qualification equivalent to three A levels. Students choosing this programme also take one or two A levels from a choice of subjects. The course is assessed continuously, with students taking classes in acting, jazz dance, ballet and singing and being required to undertake various assignments. Students are required to keep 'diaries' and to demonstrate their learning further by practical performances. There are no written examinations, but students produce coursework that reflects their level of understanding with regard to the historical context of their work. The coursework also demonstrates students' ability to research and develop their own ideas.

Cameron House School

4 The Vale, Chelsea, London SW3 6AH **T**: (020) 7352 4040 **F**: (020) 7352 2349 **E**: info@cameronhouseschool.org
W: www.cameronhouseschool.org

Headmistress Mrs Lucie Moore BEd (Hons) **Founded** 1980
School status Co-educational independent
Religious denomination Non-denominational
Member of CReSTeD, IAPS, NAHT, SATIPS
Accredited by IAPS, ISC **Age range** 4–11
No of pupils 114; *Pre-prep* 62; *Prep* 52; *Girls* 62; *Boys* 52
Teacher:pupil ratio 1:11 **Average class size** 18
Fees per annum *(day)* £14,025

The Curriculum

"The school fully meets its aim of maintaining high academic standards and helping each pupil to do their best." (ISI Inspection 2010).

Our academic curriculum prepares all our children for Common Entrance exams. The children study a comprehensive range of subjects using techniques that encourage them to explore, work co-operatively and be creative. High staff:pupil ratios allow the dedicated, highly-qualified teachers to provide the children with a stimulating, tailored learning environment. While emphasis is placed on the core curriculum, the school's teaching goes far beyond. French is taught from Reception, music, singing, speech and drama are popular, as is debating. The IT room, Interactive Whiteboards in every classroom and bank of laptops, provide access to online learning, and each class has its own library. A varied and dynamic sports program gives the children opportunities to take part in lessons, matches and tournaments several times a week. Numerous after school clubs foster interests including: fencing, drama, karate, ballet, orchestra, chess, choir and Latin to name just a few. Both boys and girls are thoroughly prepared for entrance exams and scholarships at 11 for prestigious London day and boarding schools.

Setup and Atmosphere

Cameron House has a nurturing environment that gives children a strong sense of belonging and purpose. With the guidance of the highly qualified staff, children of all abilities achieve excellent standards.

Pastoral Care

We encourage all our children to consider and care for others. "Exemplary pastoral care is a strong feature of the school and staff are united in their approach to the promotion of pupils' well-being and development." (ISI Inspection 2010).

Outstanding Characteristics

Cameron House is a vibrant school well-known for maintaining high academic standards while encouraging individual creativity. Children leave Cameron House as independent thinkers, brimming with intellectual curiosity. "The headteacher is highly skilled at moulding the staff into a unified team who work with a shared goal of a positive and caring approach towards each individual pupil, that has produced the outstanding response in the attitudes of pupils towards learning and to school." (ISI Report, 2010).

Next Steps

Pupils leave Cameron House to go on to a variety of London day and country boarding schools. The school is dedicated to finding the right senior school for each child. Children from Cameron House are always well prepared and confident when they take their senior school examinations and scholarships and are therefore very successful. In recent years our pupils have moved to join the following schools:

Girls: St Paul's Girls' School, Godolphin & Latymer, City of London School for Girls, Putney High School, JAGs, Queen's Gate, Francis Holland, Wycombe Abbey, Woldingham, Cheltenham Ladies' College, Downe House, St. Mary's Ascot and many more.

Boys: City of London School for Boys, Dulwich College, Colet Court, St Paul's, King's College Wimbledon, Westminster Under School, Westminster Cathedral Choir School, Sussex House, Ludgrove and many more.

Co-Educational: Latymer Upper, Alleyn's, Emanuel, Ibstock Place, The Harrodian, St. Benedict's, Hampton Court House, Northbridge House, Portland Place, The Dragon, Brighton College and many more.

Headmistress: Mrs. Lucie Moore

"The school benefits from outstanding governance" – (ISI Report). Lucie is a dynamic educator who has over 19 years experience teaching in the UK, Thailand and Italy. Her verve and enthusiasm, as well as her breadth of experience and leadership teaching 3–13 year olds, enables her to maintain and develop Cameron House's very high standards.

The Cavendish School

31 Inverness Street, London NW1 7HB **T**: (020) 7485 1958 **F**: (020) 7267 0098
E: admissions@cavendish-school.co.uk **W**: www.cavendishschool.co.uk
For all enquiries please contact the admissions secretary, Mrs Frances Jones, as above

Headmistress Mrs T Dunbar BSc (Hons) Dip
Founded 1875
School status girls' independent day only pre-prep
Religious denomination Christian
Member of AGBIS, IAPS, ISBA, NAHT, SATIPS **Accredited by** ISC
Age range 3–11
No of pupils 221; *Nursery* 24; *Pre-prep* 66; *Prep* 155; *Girls* 212; *Boys* 9
Teacher:pupil ratio 1:10
Average class size 17
Fees per annum *(day)* £5,745–£11,550

The Cavendish is a friendly school situated near Regent's Park, in the heart of Camden Town with its excellent public transport links, and is academically non-selective at entry. With strong yet informal links between home, school and the local community, we pride ourselves on the high level of our pastoral care and attention to each child's individual needs. We maintain manageable class sizes and low teacher:pupil ratios so that the foundations of a good education and effective study habits are laid from the beginning. Through a combination of a creative, broad and balanced curriculum, personalized learning and much specialized teaching our pupils flourish and gain entry, frequently with scholarships, to top senior schools at 11+. Our strength in music, drama, dance and art is reflected in our Artsmark Gold Award and sport is also given a high priority.

Channing School

Highgate, London N6 5HF **T**: (020) 8340 2328 **F**: (020) 8341 5698 **E**: info@channing.co.uk
W: www.channing.co.uk

Head Mrs Barbara Elliott
Founded 1885
School status girls' independent day only
Religious denomination Inter-denominational
Member of AHIS, GSA, ISA **Accredited by** GSA
Age range 4–18
No of pupils 604; *Prep* 184; *Senior* 340
Sixth Form 80; *Girls* 604
Average class size 20
Fees per annum *(day)* £11,430–£12,390

Channing is a leading London day school for girls aged 4–18, situated in beautiful grounds in Highgate. Teaching groups are small, allowing friendly, caring relationships. A level choices include Ancient Greek, ICT and drama. The elegant home of the former Lord Mayor of London houses our junior school and is notable for its happy and secure atmosphere. Art, drama, music and sport are all strong. ICT and library facilities are superb, and there is a new sixth form centre and performance area. Entry is by test and interview at 4, 11 and 16 and is subject to a satisfactory report from the applicant's current school. There are occasional chance vacancies.

Chelsea Independent College

517–523 Fulham Road, London SW6 1HD **T**: (020) 7610 1114 **F**: (020) 7610 3404 **E**: admissions@cic.ac
W: www.cic.ac

Principal Mr Paul Fear
College status Co-educational independent day only senior
Religious denomination Non-denominational
Member of CIFE **Accredited by** OFSTED
Age range 14–19
No of pupils 140; *Senior* 40
Sixth Form 100; *Girls* 70; *Boys* 70
Teacher:pupil ratio 1:6 **Average class size** 6
Fees per annum *(day)* £3,075–£16,035

Chelsea Independent College benefits from modern, well-resourced buildings in the heart of London. It has developed an enviable reputation for excellent teaching in a supportive, caring environment. Many of the staff are graduates of Oxford, Cambridge and colleges of the University of London, and are chosen for their ability to relate to young people. Our small size encourages a warm and supportive atmosphere in which pupils can benefit from a high standard of pastoral care coupled with a strong sense of academic discipline. The college curriculum encompasses traditional GCSE and A levels, in addition to a number of courses aimed specifically at international pupils, with every effort being made to teach according to pupils' abilities and to stretch the ablest well beyond the demands of the syllabus.

City of London School

Queen Victoria Street, London EC4V 3AL **T**: (020) 7489 0291 **F**: (020) 7329 6887 **E**: headmaster@clsb.org.uk
W: www.clsb.org.uk

Headmaster Mr David Levin BEcon MA FRSA
Founded 1442
School status Boys' independent day only
Religious denomination Non-denominational
Member of HMC
Age range 10–18
No of pupils 920
Sixth Form 250; *Boys* 920
Teacher:pupil ratio 1:10 **Average class size** 22
Fees per annum *(day)* £13,050

The ethos of the school fosters good relationships between members of the staff and the pupils. Bullying, harassment, victimization and discrimination will not be tolerated. The school and its staff will act fairly in relation to the pupils and parents and we expect the same of pupils and parents in relation to the school. The City of London School aims to welcome talented boys from a diversity of backgrounds into a tolerant, harmonious community in which they achieve the highest academic standards, make full use of their potential and develop towards responsible adulthood. Academic achievement is very high. In 2010, 90 per cent of GCSE entries were passed at A* or A grade. At A level, 93.1 per cent of entries were passed at A* to B, with 30.5 per cent at A*. For a central London school, this is a sporty place and the school plays 12 sports competitively. There is an on-site swimming pool, sports hall and fitness suite, and a beautiful 20-acre sports ground 30 minutes' coach drive away.

Collingham Independent GCSE and Sixth Form College

23 Collingham Gardens, London SW5 0HL **T**: (020) 7244 7414 **F**: (020) 7370 7312 **E**: london@collingham.co.uk
W: www.collingham.co.uk

Principal Mr G Hattee
Founded 1975
College status Co-educational day only independent Sixth Form college
Religious denomination Non-denominational
Member of CIFE **Accredited by** BAC
Age range 14–20
No of pupils 180
Sixth Form 160; *Girls* 85; *Boys* 95
Teacher:pupil ratio 1:5
Average class size 5
Fees per annum *(day)* £17,100

- Supportive environment
- Expert tuition
- Rigorous academic standards
- Individual learning programmes
- Small class size

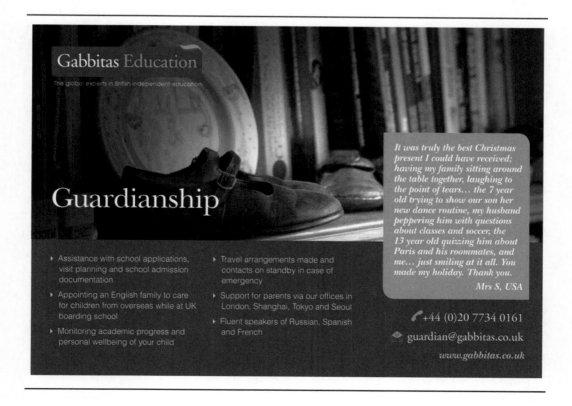

DLD College (Davies Laing and Dick)

100 Marylebone Lane, London W1U 2QB **T**: (020) 7935 8411 **F**: (020) 7935 0755 **E**: dld@dld.org
W: www.dldcollege.org
Visitors' entrance: 9 Bulstrode Street, London W1U 2JD

●⋔▲

Principal Mr David Lowe (Cantab) FRSA
Founded 1931
College status Co-educational independent fifth and sixth form
Religious denomination Non-denominational
Member of ISA, CIFE **Accredited by** ISI, Crested
Age range 14–24; *boarders from* 16
No of pupils 312; *Girls* 148; *Boys* 164
Teacher:pupil ratio 1:5
Average class size 7
Fees per annum *(day)* £2,226–£7,200

Davies Laing and Dick (DLD) College was founded in 1931 to provide tutoring for Oxbridge and Colonial Service entrance exams. Over the years the College's reputation has grown and today DLD is a leading independent fifth and sixth form college with 330 students. Our aims are:

- to help our students to achieve high academic standards;
- to offer an environment where the individual is valued and respected and where confidence is built;
- to prepare young people for university and their future career.

The College offers superb learning accommodation and facilities in a prestigious and safe central London location. There are three laboratories, two IT classrooms, a library for private study with an IT annexe, a GCSE study area, and an eighty-seat theatre, which is also used to screen films. There is a recording studio and a film edit suite. All classrooms are equipped with interactive white boards. Students are taught in small groups, enabling studies to be highly focused and progress to be clearly evaluated. Parents receive five reports a year with regular interim test results emailed on a fortnightly basis.

The student day is a stimulating mix of traditional classes, study periods and breaks, with room for a variety of extra-curricular activities; sporting, social and cultural. A new enrichment programme encourages all students to participate in one or more of our range of extra-curricular activities, drawn from the creative arts, sport, debating and the Extended Project Qualification. This participation is important for students both as an opportunity for recreation and as an effective way to improve the quality of their UCAS personal statement and CV in the future.

In a society which is ever-increasingly competitive, academic excellence alone may not guarantee success. University admission officers and employers are particularly interested in students' activities outside the classroom.

Our e-learning platform allows remote access to a range of online resources, providing an exciting new dimension to the learning process. Above all, DLD is a learning community where the right attitudes to study are encouraged. Hannah Abraham, one of our recent graduates, said in a recent interview "I have grown in confidence whilst being at DLD. I am now never afraid to ask questions or be curious about something. I am never afraid to admit that I don't understand."

DLD offers international students accommodation in Urbanest student boarding and in homestays across London. Urbanest boarding provides students with a studio en-suite bedroom on one of DLD's three secure floors, all rooms are equipped with a study space with internet access and telephone, a sofa and TV, an en-suite shower room, and a kitchen. Each floor has a live-in houseparent who offers 24-hour support to our students. Breakfast is provided daily and students have a private kitchen to prepare their evening meals. Students are able to choose additional services such as laundry, cleaning, and school buses, and can take part in our social calendar which includes weekend events and activities, cooking lessons and sports teams.

Devonshire House Preparatory School

2 Arkwright Road, Hampstead, London NW3 6AE **T**: (020) 7435 1916 **F**: (020) 7431 4787
E: enquiries@devonshirehouseprepschool.co.uk **W**: www.devonshirehouseschool.co.uk

●🏠

Headmistress Mrs S Alexander BA (Hons) PGCE
Founded 1989
School status Co-educational independent day only
Religious denomination Non-denominational
Member of IAPS, ISC, SATIPS **Accredited by** IAPS, ISC
Age range 2^1/$_2$–13
No of pupils 580; *Girls* 261; *Boys* 319
Teacher:pupil ratio 1:9
Average class size 18
Fees per annum *(day)* £7,365–£14,010

Curriculum

Early literacy and numeracy are very important and the traditional academic subjects form the core curriculum. The combined sciences form an increasingly important part of the timetable as the children grow older, and the use of computers is introduced from an early age.

Expression in all forms of communication is encouraged, with classes having lessons in art, music, drama and French. Physical exercise and games are also part of the curriculum.

Much encouragement is given to pupils to help to widen their horizons and broaden their interests. The school fosters a sense of responsibility amongst the pupils, and individuality and personal attention for each pupil are considered most important.

Entry requirements

The junior school:

For children entering the junior school from the ages of three to five, places are offered on the basis of an assessment made at the school. From the age of six, places are usually subject to a written test taken at the school.

At eight, children normally transfer directly into the upper school. Parents and their children are welcome to visit for interview and to see around the school. The school has its own nursery, The Oak Tree Nursery, which takes children from 2½ years of age.

The upper school:

Entry to the upper school is principally from the junior school. For pupils seeking to join the school from elsewhere, places are normally subject to a written entrance test.

Academic and leisure facilities

The school is situated in fine premises in the heart of Hampstead with their own walled grounds.

The aim is to achieve high academic standards whilst developing enthusiasm and initiative throughout a wide range of interests. It is considered essential to encourage pupils to develop their own individual personalities and a good sense of personal responsibility.

Dolphin School (including Noah's Ark Nursery School)

106 Northcote Road, Battersea, London SW11 6QW **T**: (020) 7924 3472 **F**: (020) 8265 8700
E: admissions@dolphinschool.org.uk **W**: www.dolphinschool.org.uk

Principal Mrs J Glen BA (Hons)
School status Co-educational independent day only
Religious denomination Christian
Age range 2–11
No of pupils 234; *Nursery* 112; *Pre-prep* 60; *Prep* 62; *Girls* 109; *Boys* 125
Teacher:pupil ratio 1:10
Average class size 15
Fees per annum *(day)* £4,290–£8,070

Our aim at Dolphin School is to help your child become the best they can possibly be. School is a training ground and our small classes enable us to focus on each individual. We train children academically, giving priority to English and maths and adding hands-on science, colourful geography, history and whole-school Spanish. We train pupils in the arts with fantastic specialist teaching and in a wide range of sports through dynamic coaching and a superb fixture list. Our Christian foundation gives us the impetus to develop children's character, teaching them the priority of good relationships throughout life.

The Falcons School for Girls

15 Gunnersbury Avenue, Ealing, London W5 3XD **T**: (020) 8992 5189 **F**: (020) 8752 1635
E: admin@falconsgirls.co.uk **W**: www.falconschool.com

Headteacher Miss J McGillewie
School status girls' day only
Religious denomination Non-denominational
Member of IAPS, ISA, ISC, NAHT
Accredited by ISA, ISC
Age range 3–11
No of pupils 120; *Nursery* 18; *Pre-prep* 102; *Girls* 120
Teacher:pupil ratio 1:16
Average class size 18
Fees per annum *(day)* £7,825

The Falcons School for Girls has a growing reputation as 'West London's Most Creative Preparatory School'. Traditional subjects and the '3Rs' are – and always will be – at the heart of what we do, but we know that new technology enables talented teachers to develop new and exciting ways of learning. "The quality of the teaching in the Early Years is truly outstanding" (ISI Inspection Report May/June 2011) – and it sets the tone for the approach to learning throughout the school.

The Headteacher, Miss Joan McGillewie, is always pleased to take parents on an individual tour of the school, and to share some of the exciting and innovative practices designed to bring out the best in your daughter.

Fine Arts College

24 Lambolle Place, Hampstead, London NW3 4PG **T**: (020) 7586 0312 **F**: (020) 7483 0355
E: mail@hampsteadfinearts.com **W**: www.hampsteadfinearts.com
For admissions enquiries please contact Georgina White-Aldworth on mail@hampsteadfinearts.com

Principal Mr N Cochrane CFA (Oxon)
Principal Ms C Cave CFA (Oxon)
Founded 1978
College status Co-educational independent day only senior
Religious denomination Non-denominational
Age range 14–19 **No of pupils** 120; *Senior* 120
Sixth Form 100; *Girls* 65; *Boys* 55
Teacher:pupil ratio 1:5 **Average class size** 7
Fees per annum *(day)* £5,700–£14,850

Fine Arts College was founded in 1978 by Candida Cave and Nicholas Cochrane as a specialist college for the study of arts and humanities. The college is situated in a delightful part of Belsize Park in North London. The main site is situated in a quiet, secluded courtyard, away from the bustle of the street. The light and airy college buildings, originally a Victorian dairy, contain specialist studios for art, music and drama. The Art department has specialist facilities for painting, photography, printmaking, computer graphics, and textiles. In addition, there are music technology, film and media studies studios nearby. Each department is well resourced with an extensive library. We encourage a close working relationship with pupils and parents and hold open days and parents' evenings each term. We also host social evenings where pupils' artistic and academic work can be seen. Our music, drama and film pupils regularly put on productions to which parents and friends are invited. The college consistently achieves excellent results, with pupils achieving high examination passes, university and art school acceptance and success in professional careers. We are pleased to show our pupils' published achievements on request.

Forest School

College Place, Snaresbrook, London E17 3PY **T**: (020) 8520 1744 **F**: (020) 8520 3656 **E**: info@forest.org.uk
W: www.forest.org.uk

Head Mrs S J Kerr-Dineen MA   **Founded** 1834
School status Co-educational independent day only
Single-sex ed 7–16
Religious denomination Church of England
Age range 4–18
No of pupils 1250; *Girls* 600; *Boys* 600
Fees per annum *(day)* £2,825–£4,298

Forest School is a large, vibrant school, with more than 1,250 pupils from the ages of 4 to 18.
    Forest School follows a unique diamond structure. When children first enter Forest School in the Pre-Prep they are taught in small mixed classes, moving onto single-sex classes within the Prep School from the age of 7. Single-sex teaching continues when they join either the Boys' School or the Girls' School, until the Sixth Form when classes are once again mixed.
    Co-curricular activities are mixed throughout, however, so the pupils have the best of all worlds.
    Pupils can join the school at most stages between 4 and 18, but almost all parents recognize the benefits of the continuous education and their child stays at Forest from Pre Prep until Sixth Form.
    Our school house structure means that each pupil is treated as an individual, of whom staff have the highest expectations, but the size of the school enables it to offer breadth and depth of opportunity through art, drama and varied sporting activities including the use of leisure facilities at the Sylvestrian Centre. Forest School puts the individual child at the centre of all it does and promotes a clear set of values, both educational and ethical.
    A humane, open minded school, where pupils' personal development is outstanding and academic attainment high. Forest is, above all, a happy school which understands the relationship between the curricular, the co-curricular and the pastoral.

Francis Holland School, Regent's Park NW1

Clarence Gate, Ivor Place, London NW1 6XR **T**: (020) 7723 0176 **F**: (020) 7706 1522
E: registrar@fhs-nw1.org.uk **W**: www.francisholland.org.uk
To enquire about admissions please contact the registrar, Mrs Jane Ruthuer.

Headmistress Mrs V M Durham
Founded 1878
School status Girls' independent day only
Religious denomination Church of England
Member of GSA, IAPS, ISA, SHA
Accredited by GSA, IAPS, ISA
Age range 11–18
No of pupils 440; *Girls* 440
Average class size 20
Fees per annum £14,400

Francis Holland, Regent's Park, is a happy, academic day school for girls aged 11 to 18. Within a friendly and supportive atmosphere, pupils achieve excellent examination results. All pupils transfer to universities, including Oxford and Cambridge. Sixth formers attend weekly lectures from visiting guest speakers. Sport, art, drama and music contribute strongly to the school's lively extra-curricular schedule. The school has its own swimming pool and uses Regent's Park for tennis, hockey, rounders and netball. The Gloucester Wing provides additional classrooms, a fourth art studio and a performance area. There are two school orchestras, several choirs and a jazz band. The school runs more than 70 clubs and societies, such as history and politics, ju jitsu, cookery, water polo, Mandarin Chinese, gymnastics and yoga. Charitable initiatives include funding of a summer activity camp for local children.

Francis Holland School, Sloane Square SW1

39 Graham Terrace, London SW1W 8JF **T**: (020) 7730 2971 **F**: (020) 7823 4066 **E**: education@fhs-sw1.org.uk
W: www.fhs-sw1.org.uk
To enquire about admissions, please contact the registrar, Mrs Jane Ruthen.

Headmistress Miss S Pattenden BSc
School status Girls' day only
Religious denomination Church of England
Member of GSA, ISC
Age range 4–18
No of pupils 450; *Girls* 450
Teacher:pupil ratio 1:9
Fees per annum *(day)* £12,630–£14,640

A 450-strong day school for girls aged 4 to 18, with high academic standards and excellent pastoral care. There is a happy and purposeful atmosphere and pupils are respected as individuals. With a challenging curriculum, the school generates an enthusiasm for learning, intellectual curiosity and creativity. This approach leads pupils to consistently high levels of academic achievement. The constant upgrading of facilities enables the school to offer an extensive extra-curricular programme, including music, art, drama and sport. Recently acquired premises next door, provide a new performance area and specialist music facility in Autumn 2010. Charity fundraising is strong, as are links with the local community. Conveniently located near Sloane Square, the school takes full advantage of its location with frequent trips to museums, galleries and theatres.

Fulham Prep School

Prep Department, 200 Greyhound Road, London W14 9SD **T**: (020) 7386 2444 **F**: (020) 7386 2449
E: prepadmin@fulhamprep.co.uk **W**: www.fulhamprep.co.uk
Pre-Prep (4–7+) based at 47A Fulham High Street, London SW6 3JJ

Principal & Head of Prep School Mrs J Emmett
Founded 1996
School status Co-educational independent day only
Religious denomination Non-denominational
Member of SATIPS
Age range 4–13
No of pupils 580; *Pre-prep* 244; *Prep* 336; *Girls* 234
   Boys 346
Teacher:pupil ratio 1:8 **Average class size** 16
Fees per annum *(day)* £12,825–£14,250

Curriculum: In the pre-prep school, the curriculum, though broadly based, lays particular emphasis on the early acquisition of the traditional basic skills of reading, writing and numeracy. We do not prepare children for 7+ and 8+ exams. The curriculum in the prep school is based on the demands of the 11+ and 13+ Common Entrance exams. **Entry requirements:** The school is non-selective at the Reception stage, while entry into other years is by assessment in maths and English. Siblings of current pupils are given priority. **Academic and extra curricula:** Academic achievement is strong but we also put a lot of emphasis on all-round development, providing an extensive range of activities featuring sport, music, art and drama. The school has two choirs and an orchestra. A wide range of lunchtime and after-school clubs is offered each term.

Gatehouse School

Sewardstone Road, Victoria Park, London E2 9JG **T**: (020) 8980 2978 **F**: (020) 8983 1642
E: admin@gatehouseschool.co.uk **W**: www.gatehouseschool.co.uk

Headmistress Mrs Belinda Canham JP BA (Hons) PGCE (Froebel)
Founded 1948
School status Co-educational independent day only
Religious denomination Christian
Member of AGBIS, ISA
Age range 3–11
No of pupils 320; *Nursery* 50; *Pre-prep* 130; *Prep* 140; *Girls* 158; *Boys* 162
Average class size 18
Fees per annum *(day)* £6,300–£7,740

Founded in May 1948 by Phyllis Wallbank, a pioneer of educational development, in the gatehouse of St Bartholomew of the Great Priory Church, West Smithfield. The school was then a pioneer of much that is now generally accepted in education. Gatehouse's policy is: Children of any race, colour, creed, background and intellect shall be accepted as pupils and work side by side without streaming or any kind of segregation with the aim that each child shall get to know and love God, and to develop their own uniqueness of personality to enable them to appreciate the world and the world to appreciate them. Gatehouse is now located in Sewardstone Road, close to Victoria Park, where it continues to follow the education philosophy of Phyllis Wallbank.

Glendower Preparatory School

86/87 Queen's Gate, South Kensington, London SW7 5JX **T**: (020) 7370 1927 **F**: (020) 7835 2849
E: office@glendower.kensington.sch.uk **W**: www.glendowerprep.org

● 🏠

Head Mistress Mrs R Bowman BA PGCE
Founded 1895
School status Girls' independent day only
Religious denomination Non-denominational
Member of ISC
Age range 4–11
No of pupils 210; *Girls* 210
Average class size 16
Fees per annum *(day)* £14,280

Why choose Glendower for your daughter? Our school is small in numbers; 210 pupils, aged between 4 and 11, but high in expectation and achievement. We aim to provide a stimulating environment in which each girl is valued and can enjoy developing her particular talents to the full, whether in art, music, sport, drama or other social activities. In the family atmosphere of Glendower, girls acquire the confidence to develop their talents to the utmost of their ability and gain the solid academic foundations necessary for competitive entry into a leading London day school or boarding school. We are a happy school! For further details please contact the school office.

Symbol key

Gender

● Girls
● Boys
● Coed

Accommodation

🏠 Boarding only
🏠 Boarding and Day
🏠 Day and Boarding
🏠 Day only

International Bacc.

★ School offers IB

CReSTeD

◆ CReSTeD Registered

Has 6th Form

▲ Has 6th Form

Bassett House School

60 Bassett Road, London W10 6JP **T**: (020) 8969 0313 **F**: (020) 8960 9624 **E**: info@bassetths.org.uk
W: www.bassetths.org.uk

Head Mrs A Harris BEd(Lond) CEPLF(Caen)   **Founded** 1947
School status Co-educational independent
Religious denomination Non-denominational
Member of IAPS **Accredited by** IAPS
Age range 3–11
No of pupils 180+; *Nursery* 20; *Pre-prep* 40; *Prep* 120
Teacher:pupil ratio 1:1 **Average class size** 18
Fees per annum *(day)* £6,660–£13,905

Bassett House School is a member of House Schools Group and has sister schools at Orchard House School in Chiswick and Prospect House School in Putney. Located in North Kensington, it was recently rebuilt to very high standards. Children are prepared for senior school examinations at 11+. The school is equipped with a science and IT lab, gym/theatre and school hall, music room and art room.

Orchard House School

16 Newton Grove, Bedford Park, London W4 1LB **T**: (020) 8742 8544 **F**: (020) 8742 8522 **E**: info@orchardhs.org.uk
W: www.orchardhs.org.uk

Headmistress Mrs S A B Hobbs BA(Hons)(Exeter) PGCE MontDip
Founded 1993
School status Co-educational independent
Religious denomination Non-denominational
Member of IAPS, ISBA **Accredited by** IAPS
Age range 3–11
No of pupils 260; *Nursery* 20; *Pre-prep* 40; *Prep* 200
Teacher:pupil ratio 1:7 **Average class size** 18
Fees per annum *(day)* £6,660–£13,905

Orchard House School is a member of House Schools Group and has sister schools at Bassett House School in Kensington and Prospect House School in Putney. Girls and boys are prepared for senior school examinations at 11+. The school has its own sports area and is equipped with a science and IT lab, music room and art room. Academic results have been strong.

Prospect House School

75 Putney Hill, London SW15 3NT **T**: (020) 8780 0456 **F**: (020) 8780 3010 **E**: info@prospecths.org.uk
W: www.prospecths.org.uk

Headmistress Mrs D Barratt MEd (Newcastle)
Founded 1991
School status Co-educational
Religious denomination Non-denominational
Member of IAPS **Accredited by** IAPS
Age range 3–11
No of pupils 200; *Girls* 100; *Boys* 100
Teacher:pupil ratio 1:7 **Average class size** 18–20
Fees per annum *(day)* £6,405–£13,290

Prospect House School is a member of House Schools Group and has sister schools at Bassett House School in Kensington and Orchard House School in Chiswick. Boys and girls are prepared for examinations at senior school at 11+. The school enjoys a large garden and all-weather sports area and many other facilities. Academic results have been strong.

International Community School

ICS Primary School: 4 York Terrace East, Regent's Park, London NW1 4PT **T**: +44 (0) 20 7935 1206
ICS Secondary School: 21 Star Street, London W2 1QB. **T:** +44 (0) 20 7402 0416
E: admissions@ics.uk.net **W:** www.icschool.co.uk

●♠★▲

Head of School Mr P Hurd BSc PGCSE
Founded 1979
School status Co-educational independent
Religious denomination Non-denominational
Member of CIS, EUK, IB, ISA, LISA
Accredited by British Council, IB World School
Age range 3–19; *boarders from* 11
No of pupils 230; *(boarding)* 4; *(full boarding)* 4; *Girls* 100
   Boys 130
Teacher:pupil ratio 1:10 **Average class size** 17
Fees per annum *(day)* £13,500–£18,450

ICS is a friendly central London school for pupils aged 3 to 18 years. We are a co-educational, inclusive school, specializing in teaching to different ability groups. We offer the International Baccalaureate Curriculum at all levels – IB Primary Years, IB Middle Years and IB Diploma. We also provide year-round English language courses. ICS has a strong pastoral care/welfare reputation and classes are kept to a maximum of 18 pupils. A large team of assistants and specialists support class teachers. Children and faculty are from 45 countries and form a dynamic learning community. We have an extensive Travel and Learn Programme giving students the opportunity to visit many different parts of the world and our own outdoor education centre in Suffolk. The admissions team welcomes year-round applications.

International School of London

139 Gunnersbury Avenue, London W3 8LG **T**: (020) 8992 5823 **F**: (020) 8993 7012 **E**: mail@islondon.com
W: www.ISLondon.com

●♠★▲

Head of School Mr Huw Davies
Founded 1972
School status Co-educational independent day only
Religious denomination Non-denominational
Member of CIS, IBO, IBSCA, LISA **Accredited by** CIS
Age range 3–19
No of pupils 337; *Girls* 151; *Boys* 186
Average class size 12
Fees per annum *(day)* £15,000–£20,500

The International School of London (ISL) welcomes pupils of all nationalities from pre-school age up to the International Baccalaureate Diploma. ISL is fully authorized to offer the IB Primary Years Programme (PYP) throughout all the primary classes, from Early childhood (3 years old) to Year 6 (10 years old). Using the PYP we provide pupils with an international curriculum which focuses on developing the whole child. The secondary curriculum follows the IB Middle Years Programme and the full IB Diploma. Comprehensive and integrated English as a Second Language programmes are available at all ages. Pupils can also follow courses in 20 home languages, including Arabic, Danish, Dutch, German, Icelandic, Italian, Japanese, Portuguese and Spanish. To join, ISL parents will need to provide the admissions office with a completed application form and previous school records. Most pupils join ISL in September, but we admit pupils throughout the year, provided that we have places available. We offer door-to-door transport covering west, central and south London.

Latymer Upper School

King Street, Hammersmith, London W6 9LR **T**: (0845) 638 5800 **F**: (020) 8748 5212
E: registrar@latymer-upper.org **W**: www.latymer-upper.org
● ⌂ ▲

Head Mr P J Winter MA (Oxon)
Founded 1624
School status Co-educational independent day only
Religious denomination Non-denominational
Member of HMC **Accredited by** HMC
Age range 11–18
No of pupils 1,140
Sixth Form 350; *Girls* 540; *Boys* 600
Teacher:pupil ratio 1:10
Average class size 22
Fees per annum *(day)* £14,955

Latymer Upper School has been providing education for local children since its foundation in 1624. Located in King Street, Hammersmith, Latymer is now an independent co-educational day school. Facilities include a state-of-the-art performing arts centre recently built, and a new science block and library building, opened in 2010. Means-tested scholarships, which can be up to the value of 100 per cent of the fees, are available for entry at 11+ and 16+. These are awarded on the basis of academic excellence and family circumstances. Academic scholarships, which are not means-tested, are also available. Music scholarships, up to the value of 40 per cent of fees, are awarded at 11, 13 and 16+ entry. Awards in sport, art and drama can also be offered at 16.

Lyndhurst House Preparatory School

24 Lyndhurst Gardens, Hampstead, London NW3 5NW **T**: (020) 7435 4936 **E**: pmg@lyndhursthouse.co.uk
W: www.lyndhursthouse.co.uk
A large detached Victorian red-brick building with its own playground in a quiet leafy side street.
● ⌂

Headmaster Mr Andrew Reid MA (Oxon) PGCE
Founded 1952
School status Boys' independent day only
Religious denomination Non-denominational
Member of IAPS, NAHT, SATIPS **Accredited by** IAPS, ISC
Age range 4–13
No of pupils 150; *Pre-prep* 45; *Prep* 105; *Boys* 150
Teacher:pupil ratio 1:7
Average class size 18
Fees per annum *(day)* £12,660–£14,160

Lyndhurst is a friendly and lively traditional boys' school, with its own special atmosphere and character. The environment is warm and friendly, small and familiar in feel, yet full of bustle, activity and purpose, in which every boy can find opportunities for engagement and fulfilment. Limited bursary support is available to boys already attending the school.

More House School

22–24 Pont Street, Knightsbridge, London SW1X 0AA **T**: (020) 7235 2855 **F**: (020) 7259 6782
E: office@morehouse.org.uk **W**: www.morehouse.org.uk

Head Master Mr R Carlysle BA MBA PGCE CertDys&Lit AKC MCoIP
Founded 1953
School status Girls' independent day only
Religious denomination Roman Catholic
Member of GSA, HMC **Accredited by** GSA, HMC
Age range 11–18
No of pupils 200; *Girls* 200
Teacher:pupil ratio 1:15 **Average class size** 15
Fees per annum *(day)* £13,497

More House was founded in 1953 at the request of parents wanting a central London Catholic day school for their daughters. The school is a Catholic Foundation, which accepts pupils of all faiths. It is an educational trust with a board of governors drawn partly from present and past parents. Despite our smaller size, we offer a full range of academic subjects up to GCSE and A level. Girls go on to a range of prestigious universities to follow courses including medicine, law, history, art, modern languages, drama, mathematics, classics, economics and biochemistry. Extra-curricular activities include running, swimming, fencing, choirs, orchestra, art, drama, photography, mathematics competition, public speaking and dance. Girls are encouraged to become involved in a range of activities, although the younger girls also benefit from supervised homework after school. Two full scholarships and smaller awards are made on entry to Year 7 and sixth form for academic and musical excellence. Occasional scholarships may be awarded at other levels of entry on academic grounds.

The Mulberry House School

7 Minster Road, West Hampstead, London NW2 3SD **T**: (020) 8452 7340 **F**: (020) 8830 7015
E: info@mulberryhouseschool.com **W**: www.mulberryhouseschool.com

Headteacher Julie Kirwan
School status Co-educational independent day only
Religious denomination Non-denominational
Member of ISA **Accredited by** ISA
Age range 2–8
Fees per annum *(day)* £7,050–£13,160

The Mulberry House School is an established independent school for two- to eight-year-olds, offering a stimulating and caring environment that meets the needs of individuals, while preparing them for the next stage of their schooling at 4+ or 7+. Extended day, full- and part-time places available. For brochures and details of open evenings, please telephone 020 8452 7340.

North Bridge House Senior School

1 Gloucester Avenue, London NW1 7AB **T**: (020) 7267 6266 **F**: (020) 7284 2508
E: prep@northbridgehouse.com; seniorschool@northbridgehouse.com **W**: www.northbridgehouse.com;
www.nbhseniorschool.co.uk

Head of Nursery and Junior School Mrs R Allsopp
Head of Prep School Mr B Bibby
Head of Senior School Ms A Ayre
School status Co-educational day nursery, junior, prep and senior
Religious denomination Non-denominational
Age range 2½–16
No of pupils 891
Fees per term *(day)* £4,355

North Bridge House School provides a complete education for children aged 2½ to 16 years. The school comprises two Victorian villas in Hampstead and one large site on Gloucester Avenue by Regent's Park. All buildings benefit from close proximity to local amenities, public transport links and road access.

At North Bridge House we aim to ensure that every child realizes their full potential. Alongside successful academic, sporting, artistic and pastoral achievement, we emphasize an environment that encourages good manners, tolerance, consideration for others and a strong sense of social responsibility.

Nursery:

The nursery is accommodated in a spacious Victorian villa containing bright, attractive classrooms and a large modern gym. It backs onto two large, safely enclosed playgrounds which offer plenty of opportunities for play and exercise.

Junior school:

Most children attend the junior school for three years before moving up to the prep school. The children participate enthusiastically in a wide range of activities both inside and outside the classroom. They continue to develop academic skills, as well as their creative and sporting abilities, in a nurturing environment which prepares them for their further education.

Prep school:

Children enter the lower prep at Year 4. All classes are taught by form teachers with specialists for music, French, PE and IT. At age 10, girls are prepared for the 11+ examination, while boys move to the upper prep for Years 6–8 to prepare for the Common Entrance. North Bridge House prep school has an outstanding record of success with many children annually entering senior schools such as St Paul's, Westminster, UCS, Highgate, City of London, South Hampstead and North London Collegiate.

Senior school:

The senior school has long been achieving excellent results at GCSE, with 97 per cent of of all GCSE grades awarded being between A* and C. Our pupils graduate to sixth forms in many schools in London, including Westminster, UCS, Highgate, City of London, South Hampstead, North London Collegiate, Channing and Francis Holland.

The North London International School

6 Friern Barnet Lane, London N11 3LX **T**: (020) 8920 0600 **F**: (020) 8211 4605 **E**: admissions@wpis.org
W: www.nlis.org

Head Mr D P Rose MA (Ed) BA Cert Ed LPSH
School status Co-educational day only
Religious denomination Non-denominational
Member of CReSTeD, IBO, LISA
Accredited by CIS, IAPS, ISA, ISC
Age range 2–19; *boarders from* 16
No of pupils 405; *Girls* 144; *Boys* 261
Fees per annum *(day)* £3,126–£14,970

North London International School provides a unique school environment where all areas of achievement are celebrated and where our pupils take pride in being members of a thriving school community. It is an accredited International Baccalaureate World School authorized to teach all three of the IB Programmes – Primary Years Programme (PYP), Middle Years Programme (MYP) and the Diploma Programme. It combines the very best features of a traditional curriculum with opportunities for discovery, inquiry and extended learning. Children are challenged to think, learn, take risks and discover new things in a happy and caring environment. The school also encourages and enables pupils to become responsible and successful members of a diverse world community. With an emphasis on individual progress and talent, the school prepares pupils well for life beyond school: higher education, business, family, society; wherever in the world the pupil might be now, or might choose to go.

Parkgate House School

80 Clapham Common North Side, London SW4 9SD **T**: (020) 7350 2461 **F**: (020) 7738 1633
E: admissions@parkgate-school.co.uk **W**: www.parkgate-school.co.uk

Principal C Shanley
Founded 1987
School status Co-educational day only
Religious denomination Non-denominational
Member of SATIPS
Age range 2–11
No of pupils 230; *Girls* 120; *Boys* 110
Teacher:pupil ratio 1:5 **Average class size** 18
Fees per annum *(day)* £4,080–£11,250

Parkgate House School is an independent school educating over 200 children aged from 2 to 11 years. Residing in an historic Georgian Grade II listed building overlooking Clapham Common, the school is supported by an impressive staff of over 40 teaching professionals. Children receive focused attention in one of three specialized areas: the Montessori nursery for two- to four-year-olds; the pre-preparatory department for those aged four to seven and the preparatory department for the 7 to 11 age range. At any age, children enjoy an expansive, high-quality curriculum, which is further enhanced by an established after-school programme including choir, IT, drama, French, sport and horse-riding. A recent Ofsted report praised Parkgate House as 'a very good school with a friendly and welcoming atmosphere and an attractive learning environment'.

Putney Park School

11 Woodborough Road, Putney, London SW15 6PY **T**: (020) 8788 8316 **F**: (020) 8780 2376
E: office@putneypark.london.sch.uk **W**: www.putneypark.london.sch.uk

Headmistress Miss Sarah Mostyn
Founded 1953
School status Co-educational independent day only
Religious denomination Church of England
Member of ISA **Accredited by** ISA, ISC
Age range 4–16
No of pupils 220; *Prep* 120; *Senior* 100; *Girls* 180; *Boys* 40
Teacher:pupil ratio 1:10
Average class size 12
Fees per annum *(day)* £10,281–£11,745

Putney Park School, established in 1953 and now in the second generation of the Tweedie-Smith family ownership, is situated in a conservation area and consists of four delightful Edwardian houses with a welcoming, family atmosphere. The aim of the school is personal success and academic achievement in a happy environment. Pupils are offered a varied curriculum to enable them to develop their creativity and individual talents to their full potential. Pupils thrive in the caring and supportive environment. The school prepares boys for entry to other schools, including Colet Court and King's College, Wimbledon, at 7+ and 8+. Girls are prepared for entry to other schools, particularly Putney High, Bute House and Wimbledon High, at 7+ and 11+.

Queen's Gate School

133 Queen's Gate, Kensington, London SW7 5LE **T**: (020) 7589 3587 **F**: (020) 7584 7691
E: registrar@queensgate.org.uk **W**: www.queensgate.org.uk
The Registrar, Miss Micklewright, can be contacted on her direct line, 0207 594 4982.

Principal Mrs R M Kamaryc BA MSc PGCE
Founded 1891
School status Girls' independent day only
Religious denomination Non-denominational
Member of AGBIS, GSA **Accredited by** GSA, ISC
Age range 4–18; *Pre-prep* 22; *Prep* 121; *Senior* 261; *Sixth Form* 60
Teacher:pupil ratio 1:6
Average class size 24
Fees per annum *(day)* £13,000–£15,300

The curriculum is rich, varied, well balanced and as wide as possible during the years leading to the GCSE examinations, and is frequently reviewed to take into account new approaches. All girls sit GCSE examinations in English language, English literature, Mathematics, a Modern Language and a Science, and have the option of taking additional subjects. Junior School: Girls enter the preliminary form aged 4 after assessment. Girls wishing to enter after this take tests in maths and English. Girls in Year 6 are required to pass the North London Independent Girls Day Schools' Consortium 11+ Examination before moving up into the senior school. Senior school: Girls sit the London Day Schools Consortium Examination at 11+ and the school's own entrance examinations at 12+, 13+ and 16+. Girls entering the Sixth Form are required to have at least six GCSE passes at Grade A, with an A grade in those subjects they wish to pursue to A2. They are expected to study 4–5 A/S levels and to continue 3 of those subjects to A2. Scholarships: One 7+ scholarship (internal), two internal sixth form scholarships, and two 11+ scholarships.

Ravenscourt Park Preparatory School

16 Ravenscourt Avenue, Hammersmith, London W6 0SL **T**: (020) 8846 9153 **F**: (020) 8846 9413
E: secretary@rpps.co.uk **W**: www.rpps.co.uk

Headmaster Mr R Relton
Founded 1991
School status Co-educational independent day only
Religious denomination Non-denominational
Member of IAPS **Accredited by** IAPS, ISC
Age range 4–11
No of pupils 340; *Girls* 170; *Boys* 170
Teacher:pupil ratio 1:7 **Average class size** 18
Fees per annum *(day)* £13,305

Ravenscourt Park Preparatory School is a co-educational independent school for children aged 4 to 11. The school provides an education of the highest quality, preparing children for transfer to the best and most selective independent schools. Parents seeking places in state or independent secondary schools at transfer age can be confident that their child will develop a range of skills and knowledge on which further specialized learning can be based. The school ethos is quite simply to ensure that each child is happy while at school – children who are content learn well. In order to achieve this we have developed a relaxed and attractive environment where a structured programme is designed to meet the needs of each individual. We are also fortunate to have a dedicated and talented teaching staff that is prepared to go that 'extra mile'. Finally, we understand that this is a partnership and we work closely with parents to create a trusting relationship based on mutual respect. 'I can assure parents that neither my staff nor I will spare any effort in order to make your child's years at this school happy, fulfilling and successful' – Robert Relton, Headmaster RPPS.

Redcliffe School

47 Redcliffe Gardens, London SW10 9JH **T**: (020) 7352 9247 **F**: (020) 7352 6936
E: admissions@redcliffeschool.com **W**: www.redcliffeschool.com

Headmistress Mrs Susan Bourne BSc (Hons) PGCE
Founded 1948
School status Co-educational independent day only
Religious denomination Christian
Member of AGBIS, IAPS **Accredited by** IAPS
Age range 2–11; *Nursery* 27; *Prep* 135
Average class size 15
Fees per annum *(day)* £12,030

Redcliffe School, founded in 1948, is an established and growing nursery and preparatory school situated in Chelsea and easily accessible from all parts of central and west London.

Redcliffe is an outstanding Prep School representing the best educational opportunities for children in South West London. Our commitment to providing the best facilities, curriculum and teaching show the school's dedication to growing excellence in all aspects of the educational experience at Redcliffe. Our children are happy, motivated learners who care for one another and have a lively interest in the many opportunities Redcliffe School has to offer.

St Benedict's School

54 Eaton Rise, Ealing, London W5 2ES **T**: (020) 8862 2254 **F**: (020) 8862 2199 **E**: enquiries@stbenedicts.org.uk
W: www.stbenedicts.org.uk
Junior School contact: 5 Montpelier Avenue, Ealing, London W5 2XP; Tel: 020 8862 2054

Headmaster Mr C J Cleugh MSc BSc
Founded 1902
School status Co-educational independent day only
Religious denomination Roman Catholic
Member of HMC, IAPS
Age range 3–18
No of pupils 1,035; *Nursery* 19; *Pre-prep* 113; *Prep* 172; *Senior* 529
Sixth Form 202; *Girls* 244; *Boys* 791
Teacher:pupil ratio 1:9
Average class size 18
Fees per annum *(day)* £10,860–£12,360

St Benedict's is proud of its uniqueness. Our mission, 'Teaching a way of living', defines us as a Benedictine school. Come and join us and experience our dynamic educational environment. We will have high expectations of you in everything that you do. We will equip you to deal with the challenges that life in the 21st century presents, teaching you the joys of learning while enabling you to retain a moral and spiritual sensibility. The £6.2 million Cloisters complex demonstrates the school's commitment to providing the best possible facilities for pupils and staff. We invite you to come to visit our school. You can be sure of a warm Benedictine welcome.

St Paul's Cathedral School

2 New Change, London EC4M 9AD **T**: (020) 7248 5156 **F**: (020) 7329 6568
E: admissions@spcs.london.sch.uk **W**: www.spcs.london.sch.uk

Head Master Mr N R Chippington MA FRCO
Founded 1123
School status Co-educational independent boarding and day
Religious denomination Church of England
Member of IAPS, ISBA, NAHT **Accredited by** IAPS, ISA, ISC
Age range 4–13; *boarders from* 7
No of pupils 247; *(boarding)* 29; *(full boarding)* 29; *Pre-prep* 62;
Prep 185; *Girls* 89; *Boys* 158
Average class size 18
Fees per annum *(full boarding)* £7,194; *(day)* £11,550–£12,435

Governed by the Dean and Chapter, the original residential choir school now includes non-chorister day boys and girls aged 4–13. Curriculum: A broad curriculum leads to scholarship and Common Entrance examinations at 13 and the school has an excellent record in placing pupils in senior schools of their choice, many with scholarships. A wide variety of sport and musical instrument tuition is offered. Choristers receive an outstanding choral training as members of the renowned St Paul's Cathedral Choir. Facilities: The refurbishment of the school's facilities has provided a separate Pre-preparatory department, improved classrooms and new boarding facilities for the choristers. Admission: Children are interviewed and tested before September entry at 4+ or 7+ years old. Voice trials and tests for choristers are held three times a year for boys of nearly 7 years and upwards.

Westminster School

17 Dean's Yard, Westminster, London SW1P 3PB **T**: (020) 7963 1003 **F**: (020) 7963 1002
E: registrar@westminster.org.uk **W**: www.westminster.org.uk

Head Master Dr S Spurr
School status Co-educational boarding and day senior
Religious denomination Church of England
Age range 13–18; *boarders from* 13
No of pupils 747; *(boarding)* 162; *(full boarding)* 1;
(weekly boarding) 161; *Girls* 132; *Boys* 615
Teacher:pupil ratio 1:7
Fees per annum *(full boarding)* £19,626–£21,282; *(weekly)* £27,516;
(day) £19,056–£20,664

Situated in the heart of London next to Westminster Abbey and the Houses of Parliament, Westminster is one of the country's leading academic schools. Most A level passes are grades A or B and many leavers go on to Oxford or Cambridge. Approximately 25 per cent of pupils board and day pupils also benefit from the school's boarding ethos. For more information or to arrange a tour call 020 7963 1003.

Westminster Tutors

86 Old Brompton Road, London SW7 3LQ **T**: (020) 7584 1288 **F**: (020) 7584 2637
E: info@westminstertutors.co.uk **W**: www.westminstertutors.co.uk

Principal V H Q L Maguire BA MLitt
Founded 1934
School status Co-educational independent day only
Religious denomination Unknown
Age range 11–25
No of pupils 40; *Senior* 5
Sixth Form 35; *Girls* 20; *Boys* 20
Teacher:pupil ratio 1:1
Average class size 2
Fees per annum *(day)* £15,000–£18,600

Westminster Tutors has been providing top-flight tuition since its establishment in 1934. The college has a friendly atmosphere and excellent examination results in a wide range of subjects. Small teaching groups allow tutors to pay attention to the individual needs of pupils, and classes combine hard work with lively discussion. Pupils have access to computers, a study room and a cheerful common room. We offer regular and intensive A level and GCSE courses, and preparation for Common Entrance. Private tuition at all levels is available throughout the year. We have been successfully preparing pupils for entrance to top universities, including Oxford and Cambridge, for over 75 years and we offer preparation for all university admissions tests.

Image courtesy of St Edward's School, Oxford

Tailor-made services across the independent schools sector

- ▸ Personal advice on day and boarding school choices

- ▸ Advice on schools within specific locations for parents moving from London to the countryside, foreign nationals buying investment property in London or expats returning to the UK from overseas

- ▸ Advice on independent schools in Europe, Canada and the U.S.A.

- ▸ Sixth form and tutorial college options: A Level, IB, Cambridge PreU

- ▸ Assessment and guidance on schools with special needs provision

- ▸ Education planning prenatal to 18

- ▸ Practice interviews and exam technique for senior school pre-assessment and 13+ entry

- ▸ School prospectus libraries at all of our offices, providing a valuable information resource for parents

- ▸ Publications: The Independent Schools Guide and The Complete Guide to Schools for Special Needs

- ▸ Our team of expert consultants regularly travel to locations across the world to advise parents on independent education

The information was concise, professional, informative, especially useful for me as I'm based overseas. Your choices were definitely appropriate to my son's needs. A most impressive service.

Mrs M, HK

☏ +44 (0)20 7734 0161

✉ agc@gabbitas.co.uk

MAP OF THE HOME COUNTIES (SOUTH)

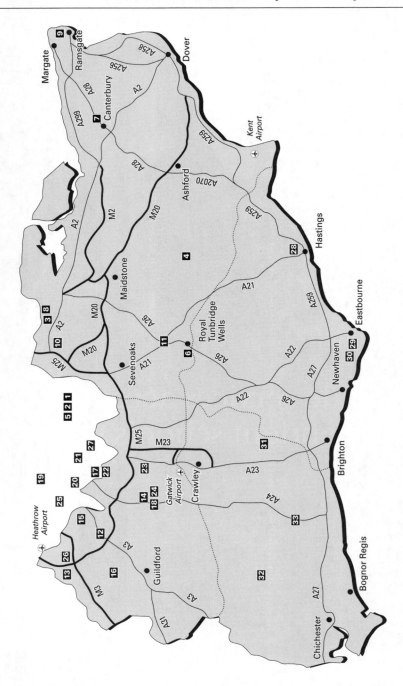

PROFILED SCHOOLS IN THE HOME COUNTIES (SOUTH)

(Incorporating the counties of Kent, Surrey, East Sussex, West Sussex)

Bickley Park School

14/24 Page Heath Lane, Bickley, Bromley, Kent BR1 2DS **T**: (020) 8460 9800 **F**: (020) 8325 5511
E: info@bickleyparkschool.co.uk **W**: www.bickleyparkschool.co.uk

●🏠

Headmaster Mr P Ashley MBA BA Cert Ed
Founded 1918
School status Boys' independent day only
Religious denomination Non-denominational
Member of IAPS, ISA, ISBA, ISC
Accredited by IAPS, ISA, ISC
Age range 3–13
No of pupils 380; *Nursery* 80; *Pre-prep* 130; *Prep* 170
Average class size 16
Fees per annum *(day)* £4,530–£12,345

At Bickley Park your son will find himself part of a safe, structured community where he can experience a wide range of opportunities, supported by excellent facilities and an encouraging, motivating environment. Dynamic teaching is underpinned by an effective pastoral care system that identifies and focuses on individual needs. Small classes, specialist teachers and a stimulating atmosphere will help your son to move confidently on to his chosen senior school. Our broad curriculum, which includes regular sport, music and drama, encourages boys to discover their abilities and to realize their potential. Good schools need good facilities and we are fortunate enough to be able to combine attractive listed buildings with first-rate modern facilities, including our own six-acre playing fields.

Bishop Challoner RC School

228 Bromley Road, Shortlands, Bromley, Kent BR2 0BS **T**: (020) 8460 3546 **F**: (020) 8466 8885
E: admissions@bishopchallonerschool.com **W**: www.bishopchallonerschool.com

●🏠▲

Headteacher Ms Karen Barry
School status Co-educational independent day only
Religious denomination Roman Catholic
Member of ISA, ISBA, NAHT **Accredited by** ISA, ISC
Age range 3–18
No of pupils 413; *Nursery* 47; *Pre-prep* 52; *Prep* 73; *Senior* 212
Sixth Form 33; *Girls* 126; *Boys* 287
Teacher:pupil ratio 1:9
Average class size 22
Fees per annum *(day)* £6,519–£9,036

At Bishop Challoner your child will learn within a caring, happy and secure environment. We are committed to 'outstanding pastoral care' and the highest level of academic achievement. As a Catholic, independent, co-educational day school, all our pupils from 3 to 18 are able to grow to their full potential so that they may become confident, responsible and caring members of society. Our ethos is one that nurtures individual talent, respects all faiths and creates a learning partnership for all. We are proud of our pupils, who flourish in a community where individual support and attention are second to none. We achieve excellent results at GCSE and A level, representing a lot of hard work and dedication. Our motto challenges each and every pupil to 'dare to do their very best'. We are recognized for outstanding success in fencing at local and national level. We look forward to extending a very warm welcome to you and your child at Bishop Challoner School.

Cobham Hall

Cobham, Gravesend, Kent DA12 3BL **T**: (01474) 823371 **F**: (01474) 825906 **E**: enquiries@cobhamhall.com
W: www.cobhamhall.com

●🏠★◆▲

Headmaster Mr P A Mitchell BSc
Founded 1962
School status Girls' independent boarding and day
Religious denomination Inter-denominational
Member of BSA, CReSTeD, GSA, IB, ISA, ISBA, ISC, Round Square
Accredited by British Council, GSA, ISC
Age range 11–18; *boarders from* 11
No of pupils 200; *(boarding)* 110; *(full boarding)* 90; *(weekly boarding)* 20; *Senior* 200
Sixth Form 60; *Girls* 200
Teacher:pupil ratio 1:7
Average class size 15
Fees per annum *(full boarding)* £21,300–£26,850; *(weekly)* £21,300–£26,850; *(day)* £14,100–£17,850

One of Britain's leading girls' schools, Cobham Hall promotes excellence in all subjects. Pre-IB and IB offered in sixth form. The majority of pupils proceed to higher education. Specialist help is provided for dyslexic pupils and our EFL department offers English language support. The school is housed in an outstanding 16th-century mansion set in 150 acres with purpose-built classroom block, modern boarding houses, an indoor swimming pool and sports centre. Membership of Round Square provides the opportunity for international exchanges and education outside the classroom. Cobham Hall is situated 25 miles from central London (17 minutes by fast train from Ebbsfleet International Station), with easy access to international airports and the Continent.

Cranbrook School

Cranbrook, Kent TN17 3JD **T**: (01580) 711800 **F**: (01580) 711828 **E**: registrar@cranbrook.kent.sch.uk
W: www.cranbrookschool.co.uk

●🏠▲

Headteacher Mrs A S Daly MA
Founded 1518
School status Co-educational voluntary aided senior
Religious denomination Non-denominational
Member of BSA, ISBA
Age range 13–18; *boarders from* 13
No of pupils 756
Sixth Form 320; *Girls* 354; *Boys* 402
Average class size 30
Fees per annum *(full boarding)* £8,850–£9,525

Cranbrook is a selective co-educational boarding and day school offering a superb all-round education at a very reasonable cost. It has a wide range of extra-curricular activities and high academic standards of 99 per cent A–C grades at GCSE and 100 per cent pass rate (67 per cent A/B grades) at A level. Music, art and drama thrive. Many productions for music and drama are held in the theatre. Cranbrook has fine facilities for the creative arts, including a performing arts centre, a sixth form centre and a design/technology centre. Team and individual sports are important and the school has playing fields, a swimming pool, a sports hall and astro-turf pitches. Teams play at the highest levels locally and nationally. Entry at 13+ is competitive and by examination. Entry at 16+ is competitive and based on school reference and GCSE grades. Boarding candidates at both 13+ and 16+ are interviewed to ensure suitability for boarding. Details from the registrar, Cranbrook School. Cranbrook School (VA) exists to promote education in Cranbrook.

Farringtons School

Perry Street, Chislehurst, Kent BR7 6LR **T**: (020) 8467 0256 **F**: (020) 8467 5442
E: admissions@farringtons.kent.sch.uk **W**: www.farringtons.org.uk
Farringtons is now co-educational in the senior school, as well as the junior school.

Headmistress Mrs C E James MA
Founded 1911
School status Co-educational independent
Religious denomination Methodist
Member of BSA **Accredited by** British Council, ISC, SHIMS
Age range 3–19; *boarders from* 11
No of pupils 600; *(boarding)* 70; *(full boarding)* 68; *(weekly boarding)* 2;
Prep 238; *Senior* 330
Sixth Form 67; *Girls* 470; *Boys* 40
Teacher:pupil ratio 1:10
Average class size 20
Fees per annum *(full boarding)* £22,500; *(weekly)* £21,150; *(day)* £8,760–£11,760

Farringtons School has a wide ability intake and a commitment to stretch every pupil to the very best of his or her ability. We are proud of the way we educate our pupils, combining traditional values with the skills required for the 21st century. We have a range of facilities, including a new computer suite, impressive sports hall with dance studio and weights room, a technology centre and a swimming pool. Our boarding facilities have just been refurbished, giving students comfortable study-bedrooms all freshly decorated with new carpets, curtains and modern furniture. Farringtons School is situated on a beautiful 25 acre site in a peaceful Kent village; yet it is a mere 12 miles from central London. It is also ideally located close to airports and the M25.

Holmewood House

Barrow Lane, Langton Green, Tunbridge Wells, Kent TN3 0EB **T**: (01892) 860006 **F**: (01892) 863970
E: registrar@holmewood.kent.sch.uk **W**: www.holmewood.kent.sch.uk

Headmaster Mr J D B Marjoribanks BEd (Hons)
Founded 1945
School status Co-educational independent
Religious denomination Inter-denominational
Member of BSA, IAPS, ISBA, ISC **Accredited by** IAPS, ISC
Age range 3–13; *boarders from* 9
No of pupils 430; *Nursery* 35; *Pre-prep* 128; *Prep* 267;
Girls 175; *Boys* 255
Teacher:pupil ratio 1:8
Average class size 15
Fees per annum *(weekly)* £17,910; *(day)* £5,340–£15,660

Set in 30 acres of beautiful grounds, Holmewood House School is a happy, busy place, where every child is considered unique and will be inspired to learn. The breadth of curriculum, specialist teaching in all subjects resulting in excellent academic results, superb facilities, a vast range of afternoon activities, in an 'outstanding family atmosphere' all combine to make Holmewood one of the leading prep schools in the country. Holmewood is 'a happy community where pupils are confident and articulate, enthusiastic and motivated, friendly and courteous'. Holmewood pupils 'clearly enjoy coming to school and revel in the opportunities the school provides'. Visit us in Tunbridge Wells to see what an inspiring place for children Holmewood truly is.

Junior King's Canterbury

Milner Court, Sturry, Canterbury, Kent CT2 0AY **T**: +44 (0) 1227 714000 **F**: +44 (0) 1227 713171
E: office@junior-kings.co.uk **W**: www.junior-kings.co.uk
For information about entry, please contact the registrar: Mrs Vivienne Wells (01227 714 000;
vwells@junior-kings.co.uk).

Headmaster Mr Peter Wells BEd (Hons)
Founded 1879
School status Co-educational independent, preparatory, boarding and day
Religious denomination Church of England
Member of BSA, IAPS, SATIPS **Accredited by** AEGIS, IAPS, ISI, Ofsted
Age range 3–13; *boarders from* 8
No of pupils 350; *(boarding)* 70; *Nursery and Pre-prep* 90
Teacher:pupil ratio 1:7 **Average class size** 15
Fees per annum *(boarding)* £20,370, *(day)* £8,850–£15,015

Junior King's is situated in 80 acres of stunning grounds with superb historic and modern facilities, just two miles
from Canterbury.

The school has a reputation for outstanding achievement at Common Entrance with pupils progressing onto
King's and other leading public schools. The broad and balanced curriculum also ensures that pupils excel in
music, creative and performing arts, while at sport, boys and girls compete at county and national level.

The vibrant boarding community is at the heart of school life with boys and girls from London, across the South
of England and overseas. It is just under an hour by train from London.

The latest ISI Inspection (February 2011) enthused that: "Pupils' achievement is outstanding in their academic
subjects and their extra-curricular activities. Across the school, pupils are consistently encouraged to make the
most of their intellectual, physical and creative talents"

St Joseph's Convent Preparatory School

46 Old Road East, Gravesend, Kent DA12 1NR **T**: (01474) 533012 **E**: secretary@sjcps.org **W**: www.sjcps.org

Head Teacher C Timney
School status Co-educational
Age range 3–11

St Joseph's Preparatory School provides a superior standard of education for children. The school has a
reputation of success and a mission to provide an infrastructure that promotes a 'School of Excellence' in
independent education.

The school offers an extensive curriculum with specialist teachers in French, music, speech and drama – and
extra-curricular clubs in Latin, Spanish, piano, violin, drums, guitar, flute, recorder, percussion, voice, swimming,
ballet, fencing and martial arts.

The School implements a discipline of high standards in order that its pupils will excel in key areas of learning,
leadership, respect, collaboration and social capability – providing them with advantages in their future
secondary and university education. We are proud in the knowledge that our professionally qualified teachers
are dedicated to the needs of our pupils.

All pupils are offered entry at 11+ and the school has consistently demonstrated the highest pass rate of all the
independent schools in the area.

The school offers non-selective entry at the age of 3 and parents are advised to register early to avoid
disappointment. The St Joseph's Nursery School is on the Government Funding programme.

St Lawrence College

College Road, Ramsgate, Kent CT11 7AE **T**: (01843) 572931 **F**: (01843) 572901 **E**: ah@slcuk.com
W: www.slcuk.com

Headmaster Rev C W M Aitken BA (Durham) Cert Theol FRSA
Founded 1879
College status Co-educational independent boarding and day
Religious denomination Christian
Member of AGBIS, BSA, HMC, IAPS, ISA, ISBA, ISC
Accredited by HMC, IAPS, ISC
Age range 3–18; *boarders from* 7
No of pupils 509; *(boarding)* 200; *(full boarding)* 200; *Nursery* 23; *Pre-prep* 60; *Prep* 96; *Senior* 328; *Sixth Form* 107; *Girls* 198; *Boys* 311
Teacher:pupil ratio 1:7
Average class size 15
Fees per annum *(full boarding)* £19,917–£26,505; *(weekly)* £19,917–£26,505; *(day)* £6,054–£15,270

Walk through the historic arch at St Lawrence College in Kent and you will immediately feel at home. The newly opened Kirby House accommodates pupils aged 11 and 12 in modern five-bedded dormitories with en-suite facilities. Senior pupils are accommodated in double and single rooms. Outstanding results are achieved by the most academic pupils who progress to many of the top universities. The school is also highly regarded as a centre of excellence for 'value added'. The school has excellent transport links to London and Europe.

Steephill Independent School

Castle Hill, Fawkham, Longfield, Kent DA3 7BG **T**: (01474) 702107 **F**: (01474) 706011
E: secretary@steephill.co.uk **W**: www.steephill.co.uk

Headteacher Mrs C Birtwell BSc MBA PGCE
Founded 1935
School status Co-educational independent day only
Religious denomination Church of England
Member of ISA **Accredited by** ISA
Age range 3–11
No of pupils 125; *Nursery* 20; *Pre-prep* 67; *Prep* 58; *Girls* 63; *Boys* 62
Teacher:pupil ratio 1:12
Average class size 14
Fees per annum *(day)* £6,735

Steephill is situated in the beautiful Fawkham Valley countryside in a quiet lane overlooking the 13th-century village church. Our small classes bring out the best in young children, who receive all the help and encouragement they need from Steephill's qualified, dedicated teachers. The high standards of care and teaching are reflected in the excellent academic results. Although a mixed ability school, all the children attain a very high standard, with typically 80 per cent of a year group gaining a grammar school place. With just a maximum of 16 pupils in a class, each child benefits from the individual attention necessary to achieve his or her full potential. Non-academic pursuits such as sport, drama and the arts also have a very high level of importance. The school has a silver Artsmark award and its choir has won the Gravesham festival two years running. As a small school the staff, parents and children all know each other and this contributes to our happy, family atmosphere.

Tonbridge School

Tonbridge, Kent TN9 1JP **T**: (01732) 304297 **F**: (01732) 363424 **E**: admissions@tonbridge-school.org
W: www.tonbridge-school.co.uk
Visitors to the school are always welcome. Please contact us to arrange an appointment.

● 合 ▲

Headmaster Mr T H P Haynes BA
Founded 1553
School status Boys' independent boarding and day
senior
Religious denomination Church of England
Member of BSA, HMC, ISC **Accredited by** ISC
Age range 13–18; *boarders from* 13
No of pupils 780; *(boarding)* 461
Sixth Form 330; *Boys* 780
Teacher:pupil ratio 1:7
Average class size 12
Fees per annum *(boarding)* £31,263; *(day)* £23,340

Tonbridge School is one of the leading boys' boarding schools in the country and highly respected internationally. Boarders and day boys of varying backgrounds are offered an education remarkable both for its breadth of opportunity and the exceptional standards routinely achieved in all areas of school life. We welcome you to visit Tonbridge to meet us and see the school. For further information or for an appointment, please contact the admissions office on 01732 304297 or e-mail admissions@tonbridge-school.org.

Symbol key

Gender

● Girls
● Boys
● Coed

Accommodation

合 Boarding only
合 Boarding and Day
合 Day and Boarding
合 Day only

International Bacc.

★ School offers IB

CReSTeD

◆ CReSTeD Registered

Has 6th Form

▲ Has 6th Form

England

ACS Cobham International School

Heywood, Portsmouth Road, Cobham, Surrey KT11 1BL **T**: (01932) 867251 **F**: (01932) 869789
E: cobhamadmissions@acs-schools.com **W**: www.acs-schools.com

●♠★▲

Head of School Mr A Eysele
Founded 1967
School status Co-educational independent boarding and day
Religious denomination Non-denominational
Member of BSA, CIS, IBO, IBSCA, ISA, LISA
Accredited by NEASC
Age range 2–18; *boarders from* 12
No of pupils 1,349; *(boarding)* 90; *(full boarding)* 60; *(weekly boarding)* 30;
Nursery 103; *Pre-prep* 377; *Prep* 371; *Senior* 498; *Girls* 585; *Boys* 764
Teacher:pupil ratio 1:9 **Average class size** 15
Fees per annum *(full boarding)* £34,590–£36,440; *(weekly)* £30,380–£32,230; *(day)* £9,240–£20,820

Offering an international curriculum including both the International Baccalaureate (IB) Diploma and American Advanced Placement (AP) courses, ACS Cobham graduates attend leading universities throughout the world. Situated on a 128-acre site, the ACS Cobham campus has excellent indoor and outdoor sports facilities, with soccer and rugby fields, softball and baseball diamonds, an Olympic-sized track, tennis courts, a six-hole golf course and a sports centre with a basketball/volleyball show court, competition-class swimming pool, dance studio, fitness suite and cafeteria. Students and teachers can interact with the world of learning through a state-of-the-art Interactive Learning Centre, with audio and video conferencing, delegate voting, and online streaming media. A co-educational boarding house provides separate-wing accommodation for 110 pupils aged between 12 and 18.

ACS Egham International School

Woodlee, London Road (A30), Egham, Surrey TW20 0HS **T**: (01784) 430800 **F**: (01784) 430626
E: eghamadmissions@acs-schools.com **W**: www.acs-schools.com

●♠★▲

Head of School Mr Jeremy Lewis
Founded 1967
School status Co-educational independent day only
Religious denomination Non-denominational
Member of CIS, IB, IBSCA, ISA, LISA **Accredited by** NEASC
Age range 2–18
No of pupils 603; *Nursery* 81; *Pre-prep* 183; *Prep* 127; *Senior* 179;
Girls 282; *Boys* 321
Teacher:pupil ratio 1:8 **Average class size** 15
Fees per annum *(day)* £9,260–£19,990

ACS Egham International School is the UK's most successful young International Baccalaureate (IB) school. Its pupils have consistently achieved 100 per cent pass rates and diploma score averages well above international results. This has led to placements in top universities worldwide. Additionally, the school is one of only four schools in the UK offering the IB Primary Years Programme (PYP), the Middle Years Programme (MYP) and the IB Diploma programme. Situated on a 20-acre site, ACS Egham has pupils from 29 nationalities speaking 19 languages, all seeking a world-class education. With a wireless network on campus, the school operates a comprehensive information technology programme supported by extensive use of laptops and individual data technology storage units. A brand new IB Diploma Centre is opening for the 2011–2012 academic year to help students achieve their goals.

Box Hill School

Old London Road, Mickleham, Dorking, Surrey RH5 6EA **T**: (01372) 373382 **F**: (01372) 363942
E: enquiries@boxhillschool.org.uk **W**: www.boxhillschool.com

● ♠ ★ ▲

Headmaster Mr M Eagers MA (Cantab) MA (Bath)
Founded 1959
School status Co-educational independent boarding and day
Religious denomination Non-denominational
Member of AGBIS, BSA, IB, ISA, ISBA, ISC, NAGC, Round
Square, SHA, SHMIS **Accredited by** British Council, ISC, SHMIS
Age range 11–18; *boarders from* 11
No of pupils 425; *(boarding)* 159; *(full boarding)* 130;
(weekly boarding) 29; *Senior* 425
Sixth Form 97; *Girls* 142; *Boys* 283
Teacher:pupil ratio 1:9 **Average class size** 18
Fees per annum *(full boarding)* £25,500–£30,600; *(weekly)* £21,465–£22,500; *(day)* £14,100–£15,600

Box Hill School is based around the ideals of pupil responsibility, service to others, outdoor adventure and international understanding. Whilst placing academic work at the heart of the school, we stress the importance of education as an all-round preparation for life. We pride ourselves on small classes, good tutoring and a flexible curriculum. All pupils are allocated to a house with a supportive family ethos, as well as a personal tutor to support their academic and pastoral development. Parents can monitor their child's progress via our 'Parents in Touch' website. Numerous activities and opportunities to represent the school are available, and our Round Square membership gives unique opportunities for international exchanges and projects in adventurous parts of the world.

Claremont Fan Court School

Claremont Drive, Esher, Surrey KT10 9LY **T**: (01372) 467841 **F**: (01372) 471109
E: seniorschoolenquiries@claremont.surrey.sch.uk **W**: www.claremont-school.co.uk
Junior School: juniorschoolenquiries@claremont.surrey.sch.uk

● ♠ ▲

Principal Mrs A Stanley-Dervin MA BA
Headmaster Mr Jonathan Insall-Reid
Founded 1922
School status Co-educational independent day only
Religious denomination Christian
Member of SHMIS
Age range 3–18
No of pupils 680; *Girls* 340; *Boys* 340
Fees per annum *(day)* £4,080–£13,650

Claremont Fan Court School is a co-educational school for pupils aged 3–18 years. The school is situated on the Claremont Estate, one of the premier historic sites in the country. In 1930 the school acquired the mansion and now owns 96 acres of peaceful parkland. The School consists of the Lower Juniors for pupils aged 3–7 years, the Upper Juniors for pupils aged 7–11 years and the Senior School for pupils from 11–18 years. Our aim is to provide each pupil with a breadth of educational, cultural, social and sporting opportunities, through which the full potential of each individual may be realized. Moral integrity and character education, together with high academic expectations, are established and developed within small classes in our happy, positive environment.

Hoe Bridge School

Hoe Place, Old Woking Road, Woking, Surrey GU22 8JE **T**: (01483) 760018 **F**: (01483) 757560
E: enquiriesprep@hoebridgeschool.co.uk **W**: www.hoebridgeschool.co.uk

Headmaster Mr N M H Arkell BSc
Founded 1987
School status Co-educational independent day only
Religious denomination Non-denominational
Member of AGBIS, IAPS, ISBA **Accredited by** IAPS
Age range 2–13
No of pupils 460; *Nursery* 45; *Pre-prep* 176; *Prep* 238;
Girls 131; *Boys* 329
Teacher:pupil ratio 1:10
Average class size 19
Fees per annum *(day)* £1,740–£12,405

The pre-prep department is for children aged 2½ to 7. It is an attractive purpose-built school with its own play areas in landscaped grounds and with its own nursery unit. The prep school prepares boys and girls between the ages of 7 and 14 for scholarship and Common Entrance requirements of all senior independent schools. The curriculum includes those subjects, games and activities necessary for a child's development. The grounds afford facilities for all games and outdoor pursuits, including rugby, football, hockey, netball, basketball, cricket, athletics, tennis and swimming. It also has four all-weather tennis courts providing ample space for all sports. A 17th-century mansion forms the heart of the school but extensive architect-designed buildings have been added. These include new laboratories, changing rooms, classrooms and a multi-purpose sports hall. The design and music centre set in a restored tower and stable block provides superb facilities for art, design technology, information technology and music. ICT is networked throughout the school.

Homefield Preparatory School

Western Road, Sutton, Surrey SM1 2TE **T**: (020) 8642 0965 **F**: (020) 8661 8039
E: administration@homefield.sutton.sch.uk **W**: www.homefield.sutton.sch.uk

Head Master Mr P R Mowbray MA (Cant)
Deputy Head Mr M Till BA PGCE
Founded 1870
School status Boys' independent day only
Religious denomination Non-denominational
Member of IAPS **Accredited by** IAPS, ISC
Age range 3–13
No of pupils 400; *EYU* 70; *junior department* 130;
Senior department 200
Teacher:pupil ratio 1:9
Average class size 17
Fees per annum *(day)* £4,390–£9,975

Homefield is a preparatory school housed in an extensive purpose-built complex complemented by a two-acre adjoining playing field. A new £1.8 million development comprising two science laboratories, a music suite, an art and DT suite and a learning resources centre was opened in September 2008. Rated by *The Sunday Times* Parent Power as 'Amongst the best performing schools in Greater London', Homefield is renowned for its family atmosphere, small class sizes, the fulfilment of individual potential, the openness of communication, the provision of specialist teaching at the earliest opportunity and its all-round academic, musical, dramatic and sporting achievements. Minibus service from Wimbledon available.

Hurtwood House

Holmbury St Mary, Dorking, Surrey RH5 6NU **T**: (01483) 279000 **F**: (01483) 267586 **E**: info@hurtwood.net
W: www.hurtwoodhouse.com

Headmaster Mr CM Jackson BEd
Founded 1970
School status Co-educational boarding and day independent Sixth Form
college senior
Religious denomination Non-denominational
Member of BSA, ISA **Accredited by** BAC, British Council, ISA, ISC
Age range 16–18; *boarders from* 16
No of pupils 300; *(boarding)* 600; *(full boarding)* 300; *(weekly boarding)* 300
Sixth Form 295; *Girls* 155; *Boys* 145
Teacher:pupil ratio 1:6
Average class size 10
Fees per annum *(full boarding)* £33,600; *(weekly)* £33,600; *(day)* £22,400

Hurtwood House has the biggest and best drama and media departments in England, with superb professional facilities. It is also hugely successful academically and we're top of the league tables two out of the last four years as the best co-educational predominantly boarding school in the UK. Uniquely, our 300 boarding pupils join us after GCSE, when they are ready for the fresh challenge of a sixth form where life is as exciting and stimulating as it is at university. Structured and secure, innovative and dynamic, Hurtwood House is one of England's most successful and exciting schools.

Kew Green Preparatory School

Layton House, Ferry Lane, Richmond, Surrey TW9 3AF **T**: (020) 8948 5999 **F**: (020) 8948 4774
E: secretary@kgps.co.uk **W**: www.kgps.co.uk

Head Mr Jem Peck BSc, PGCE
Founded 2004
School status Co-educational independent day only
Religious denomination Non-denominational
Member of IAPS, ISA, ISBA **Accredited by** IAPS, ISC
Age range 4–11
No of pupils 260; *Prep* 260; *Girls* 130; *Boys* 130
Teacher:pupil ratio 1:7
Average class size 20
Fees per annum *(day)* £13,305

Kew Green Preparatory School provides an education of the highest quality. Unlike many private schools, LPS Ltd is owned by fully qualified and experienced teachers who understand that effective learning is achieved without pressure in a warm and nurturing environment. We are committed to co-education, opposed to 'cramming', and work on the basis of keeping pupils from age 4 to secondary transfer at 11 years. Within this timescale we are able to allow children to develop at their own pace whilst providing a rich curriculum. We strive to inculcate in our pupils a proper self-esteem and respect for others. Above all, we want our children to be clamouring at our gates every morning and to show a marked reluctance to leave at the end of the day!

Marymount International School

George Road, Kingston-upon-Thames, Surrey KT2 7PE **T**: (020) 8949 0571 **F**: (020) 8336 2485
E: admissions@marymountlondon.com **W**: www.marymountlondon.com

●🏠★▲

Headmistress Ms Sarah Gallagher
Founded 1955
School status Girls' independent
Religious denomination Catholic (all faiths welcome)
Member of CIS, GSA, IB, IBO, LISA, SHA **Accredited by** CIS,
GSA, ISC, MSA
Age range 11–18; *boarders from* 11
No of pupils 245; *(boarding)* 105; *(full boarding)* 80;
(weekly boarding) 15; *Sixth Form* 100; *Girls* 245
Teacher:pupil ratio 1:5
Average class size 12
Fees per annum *(full boarding)* £29,460–£31,830; *(weekly)* £28,110–£30,480; *(day)* £16,509–£18,960

Curriculum: Marymount has taught International Baccalaureate for 31 years and has consistently been ranked within the top five per cent globally. Students go on to top universities worldwide. Marymount offers the pre-IB Middle Years Programmes: stretching students without the need for incessant testing. The school has a strong community spirit and achieves a shared purpose for girls of over 40 nationalities.

Old Palace of John Whitgift School

Old Palace Road, Croydon, Surrey CR0 1AX **T**: (020) 8688 2027 **F**: (020) 8680 5877
E: schooloffice@oldpalace.croydon.sch.uk **W**: www.oldpalaceofjohnwhitgift.org

●🏠▲

Head Mrs Carol Jewell
Founded 1889
School status Girls' day only
Religious denomination Church of England
Age range 1–19
No of pupils 823
Fees per annum *(day)* £7,914–£10,584

Old Palace offers an exciting world of exploration and discovery, building upon every child's natural curiosity. We are renowned as a vibrant community of individuals, celebrating diversity with a passion for excellence and achievement. Our team of dedicated and talented staff prioritize our pupils' well-being and happiness whilst inspiring a love of learning and creativity. We are proud of the outstanding academic, cultural and sporting successes attained in our friendly and stimulating environment as identified in our Inspection reports. An extensive, stimulating and challenging programme of learning together with an enhanced co-curricular programme of activities and sport is available at every stage of Old Palace.

Priory Preparatory School

Bolters Lane, Banstead, Surrey SM7 2AJ **T**: (01737) 366920 **F**: (01737) 366921 **E**: office@prioryprep.co.uk
W: www.prioryprep.co.uk

Headmaster Mr G D Malcolm BEd MA FRSA
Founded 1921
School status Boys' independent day only
Religious denomination Inter-denominational
Member of IAPS, NAHT, SATIPS **Accredited by** IAPS
Age range 2–13
No of pupils 200; *Boys* 200
Teacher:pupil ratio 1:11
Average class size 16
Fees per annum *(day)* £4,050–£9,450

Founded in 1921, Priory School is a preparatory school for boys aged from 2 to 13 years. We have approximately 200 pupils, with one class per age group. As well as being highly successful in preparing boys for top senior independent schools, we strive to provide an environment where each boy is valued and encouraged in all aspects of his life. We believe that happy children learn and grow successfully, so we provide a secure, caring and supportive community where boys can enjoy their childhood while preparing for the future. Priory School provides quality teaching by experienced and motivated staff. Our pupils enjoy a broad curriculum and a wide variety of extra-curricular activities that help them develop into well-rounded, enthusiastic and successful individuals.

Royal Alexandra and Albert School

Gatton Park, Reigate, Surrey RH2 0TD **T**: (01737) 649001 **F**: (01737) 649002
E: admissions@gatton-park.org.uk **W**: www.raa-school.co.uk

Headmaster Mr Paul D Spencer Ellis BA MPhil NPQH
Founded 1758
School status Co-educational boarding and day
voluntary aided
Religious denomination Church of England
Member of BHS, BSA, HMC, SHA **Accredited by** HMC
Age range 7–18; *boarders from 7*
No of pupils 910; *(boarding)* 420; *(day)* 490; *Prep* 150
Senior 610; *Sixth Form* 150; *Girls* 440; *Boys* 470
Average class size 26
Fees per annum *(full boarding)* £12,630
    (day) £3,435–£4,695

This is a true boarding school in the sense that the majority of pupils are boarders. We have Saturday morning lessons and longer holidays, and run a vast range of sporting and other activities in the afternoons, evenings and at weekends. Admission is by confidential reference from the current school and interview but is restricted to citizens of the UK and other EU countries and those with the right of residence in the UK. Set in 260 acres of parkland yet close to London, we have an excellent range of facilities, including a sports hall, riding school, indoor swimming pool, drama studio, chapel, new music centre and nine boarding houses.

St Teresa's School

Effingham Hill, Dorking, Surrey RH5 6ST **T**: (01372) 452037 **F**: (01372) 450311 **E**: info@stteresas.surrey.sch.uk
W: www.stteresasschool.com

●🏠▲

Acting Head (Senior) Mrs J Elburn
Head (Prep) Mrs M Arnal
Founded 1928
School status Girls' independent boarding and day
Religious denomination Roman Catholic
Member of BSA, GSA **Accredited by** GSA, ISC
Age range 2–18; *boarders from* 7
No of pupils 410; *(boarding)* 70; *(full boarding)* 60; *(weekly boarding)* 10
Senior 320; *Sixth Form* 80; *Girls* 410
Teacher:pupil ratio 1:10
Average class size 20
Fees per annum *(full boarding)* £18,675–£22,875; *(weekly)* £16,965–£21,165; *(day)* £6,750–£13,440

St Teresa's is a thriving girls' school situated in 48 acres of beautiful parkland in the Surrey hills, with good road and rail links to London and 30 minutes from both Heathrow and Gatwick airports.

Since its establishment in 1928, the school facilities have been continually expanded and updated to high contemporary standards. A magnificent indoor swimming pool complex opened in 2004 and a £3 million performing arts theatre hall in 2005. A brand new state-of-the-art prep and nursery opened in 2009.

St Teresa's is a community of over 400 girls, including around 70 boarders who enjoy first-class care in a flexible boarding system with a programme of weekend activities.

The school receives outstanding Boarding Inspection reports. Although a Catholic foundation, St Teresa's welcomes girls of all denominations and everyone is encouraged to respect one another in a happy, caring Christian environment. The school is particularly sensitive to the differing needs and latent talents of each individual girl and adopts a 'can do' attitude, stimulating, supporting and developing each girl's interests and talents.

Girls in the preparatory school benefit from specialist subject teachers and assume responsibility in their last year through a school council. They can take advantage of an extended day, including breakfast and homework supervision and the 19 extra-curricular activities and clubs on offer. In January 2009 they moved into brand-new purpose-built premises on the means-tested senior school site.

Entrance to the senior school is at 11+, but girls are also warmly welcomed at 12+ and 13+. Scholarships are available at all these entry points and in the sixth form. Three assisted places per year are available in the senior school and in the prep.

There are 60+ extra-curricular activities on offer and girls are encouraged to develop their life skills through the Duke of Edinburgh's Award Scheme, the Young Enterprise Scheme, World Challenge and work experience.

St Teresa's offers a very broad curriculum with 29 subjects at A level. All girls go on to higher education: many to first-rank universities, including Oxbridge, others to the best art schools, drama schools and music colleges.

Surbiton High School

Surbiton Crescent, Kingston-upon-Thames, Surrey KT1 2JT **T**: (020) 8439 1309 **F**: (020) 8547 0026
E: surbiton.high@church-schools.com **W**: www.surbitonhigh.com
●♠▲

Principal Miss A Haydon BSc (Hons) PGCE NPQH
School status Girls' independent day only Boys 4–11
Religious denomination Church of England
Member of GSA, HMC **Accredited by** GSA, HMC, IAPS
Age range 4–18 (boys 4–11)
No of pupils 1234; *Prep* 233; *Senior* 668
Sixth Form 200; *Girls* 1101; *Boys* 133
Fees per annum *(day)* £6,555–£11,163

Surbiton High School provides an exemplary independent education for girls aged from 4 to 18 and, as part of our family of three schools, Surbiton Boys' Preparatory School provides a first-rate education for boys aged from 4 to 11. We lay the foundations of our pupils' learning by creating a happy, caring atmosphere where every child is valued and encouraged. Major redevelopments of our main school site provide additional purpose-built classrooms. Our extensive sports grounds at Hinchley Wood include a pavilion, all-weather tennis and netball courts and an all-weather hockey pitch. Recently, Ann Haydon was appointed as the new head of Surbiton High School, replacing Dr Jennifer Longhurst. Ann was previously deputy headmistress at Guildford High School, Surbiton's sister school in the United Church School Trust.

TASIS The American School in England

Coldharbour Lane, Thorpe, Surrey TW20 8TE **T**: (01932) 565252 **F**: (01932) 564644
E: ukadmissions@tasisengland.org **W**: www.tasisengland.org
●♠★▲

Headmaster Mr Michael McBrien BA MEd
Founded 1976
School status Co-educational independent boarding and day
Religious denomination Non-denominational
Member of CASE, CIS, IBO, IBSCA, LISA, NAIS, NE/SA
Accredited by CIS,NEASC
Age range 3–18; *boarders from* 14
No of pupils 730; *(boarding)* 180; *Nursery* 25; *Pre-prep* 70
Prep 240; *Senior* 155
Sixth Form 240; *Girls* 360; *Boys* 370
Teacher:pupil ratio 1:8 **Average class size** 15
Fees per annum *(full boarding)* £32,130; *(day)* £5,925–£19,210

TASIS

THE AMERICAN SCHOOL IN ENGLAND

TASIS The American School in England prepares young people from over 50 nations to meet the challenges of a demanding world. Small classes and an excellent academic programme, including the International Baccalaureate Diploma and Advanced Placement courses, give TASIS its valued reputation both in England and abroad. Each year graduates are offered places at some of the finest universities in the UK, United States, Canada, Europe and worldwide. While academics are emphasized, extra-curricular activities, community service and cultural excursions are essential to the school's mission of ensuring a balanced education. Its beautiful 43-acre campus 18 miles southwest of London combines historic buildings with new well-equipped facilities for science, art, drama, music, computers and sports. TASIS England's summer programmes for day and boarding pupils (ages 11–18) include ESL, TOEFL and SAT Review, academic and enrichment courses, sports activities and travel opportunities.

Trinity School

Shirley Park, Croydon, Surrey CR9 7AT **T**: (020) 8656 9541 **F**: (020) 8655 0522
E: admissions@trinity.croydon.sch.uk **W**: www.trinity-school.org

Headmaster Mr M J Bishop MA MBA
Founded 1592
School status Boys' independent day only senior Boys 10–18
Girls 16–18
Religious denomination Christian
Member of HMC
Age range 10–18 (Boys 10–18 Girls 16–18)
No of pupils 900; *Senior* 900
Sixth Form 199; *Boys* 900
Teacher:pupil ratio 1:9 **Average class size** 22
Fees per annum *(day)* £11,604

Trinity School is part of the Whitgift Foundation which allows more than half of parents to benefit from some form of financial assistance with fees. Boys are drawn from a wide catchment area, with entry at 10, 11, 13 and 16. Academic results are consistently strong at GCSE and A level, with many boys gaining places at Oxbridge and other leading universities. There is a broad and balanced curriculum offering a wide choice of subjects. Trinity's choirs and orchestras enjoy an international reputation, with regular performances around the UK as well as professional engagements overseas. Outstanding sports facilities and top-level coaches, current and ex-professionals have enabled an impressive number of pupils to be selected to compete at national and international level. The extra-curricular provision is one of Trinity's distinctive strengths, with around 100 clubs and activities on offer.

Buckswood School

Guestling, Hastings, East Sussex TN35 4LT **T**: (+44 (0)142) 813813 **F**: (+44 (0)142) 812100
E: achieve@buckswood.co.uk **W**: www.buckswood.co.uk
For overseas admissions please contact Mr David Whitehill: admissions@buckswood.co.uk

Director Mr Giles Sutton
Founded 1933
School status Co-educational independent
Religious denomination Non-denominational
Accredited by British Council, CIS, COBIS
Age range 10–19; *boarders from* 10
No of pupils 380; *(full boarding)* 210
Sixth Form 90; *Girls* 140; *Boys* 240
Teacher:pupil ratio 1:14 **Average class size** 16
Fees per annum *(full boarding)* £22,680–£25,200; *(day)* £10,425

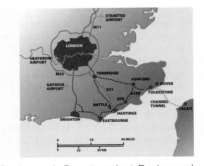

A truly international educational environment awaits your child at Buckswood. Parents select Buckswood because they know it is a school that contributes something special to their children's education. Its size allows the school to preserve a more home-like atmosphere, where the care and welfare of pupils are a priority. Buckswood follows the British curriculum, and small classes for GCSE, IB and A levels ensure pupils receive more individual attention. We have a large campus near the seaside town of Hastings, just 90 minutes from central London by direct train. On-campus facilities include: indoor heated swimming pool, stables and riding school, football academy with all-weather synthetic pitch, tennis courts, basketball courts, indoor sports hall and extensive sports grounds.

Eastbourne College

Old Wish Road, Eastbourne, East Sussex BN21 4JY **T**: (01323) 452323 **F**: (01323) 452327
E: admissions@eastbourne-college.co.uk **W**: www.eastbourne-college.co.uk
50% boarding/50% day; 60% boys/40% girls

● 🏠 ▲

Headmaster Mr S P Davies MA
Founded 1867
College status Co-educational independent boarding and day senior
50% boarding/50% day; 60% boys/40% girls
Religious denomination Church of England
Member of BSA, HMC, ISA, ISBA, ISC
Accredited by HMC
Age range 13–18 (50% boarding/50% day; 58% boys/42% girls)
No of pupils 630; *(boarding)* 306; *(full boarding)* 306; *Senior* 630
Sixth Form 280; *Girls* 265; *Boys* 365
Average class size 15
Fees per annum *(full boarding)* £27,315; *(day)* £17,985

"All schools go to great lengths to celebrate their pupils' achievements. At Eastbourne College we also work hard to develop in every pupil values that we deem to be fundamental to success at every level" says the Headmaster, Simon Davies. With 630 pupils in the school, it is a community in which every child is extremely well known. Boys and girls, day pupils and boarders are totally involved in a school that believes wholeheartedly in full co-education and full boarding and prides itself in giving its pupils the best possible grounding for a successful life at school and beyond.

Moira House Girls School

Upper Carlisle Road, Eastbourne, East Sussex BN20 7TE **T**: (01323) 644144 **F**: (01323) 649720
E: info@moirahouse.co.uk **W**: www.moirahouse.co.uk

● 🏠

Head Mrs L Watson
Founded 1875
School status Girls' independent
Religious denomination Inter-denominational
Age range 2–18
No of pupils 360; *(full boarding)* 100
Fees per annum *(full boarding)* £19,155–£24,555;
(weekly) £17,805–£17,805; *(day)* £6,000–£13,950

Moira House Girls School, in Eastbourne, is a well-established, independent day and boarding school for girls aged from 2 to 18. Every girl is treated as an individual. The 'family' atmosphere of the School helps to nurture confident and articulate students within a safe, attractive environment.

Year on year, our students consistently achieve outstanding results at both GCSE and A-Level. On average, over 95 per cent go on to University. Girls also excel in other non-academic areas from the broad curriculum of subjects and activities available such as music, drama and sport.

The School provides some wonderful opportunities for music or drama enthusiasts to perform in local Eastbourne theatres or on a tour overseas. Our brand new state of the art music recording studio enables students to compose and record their own music.

Our superb, new look Pre-Prep facility provides a spacious and modern learning environment for our younger pupils.

Moira House provides an excellent all-round education, encouraging each individual pupil to attain her highest academic, artistic, musical, social and sporting potential in a nurturing and friendly environment.

Burgess Hill School for Girls

Keymer Road, Burgess Hill, West Sussex RH15 0EG **T**: (01444) 241050 **F**: (01444) 870314
E: registrar@burgesshill-school.com **W**: www.burgesshill-school.com
For the Junior School, please telephone 01444 233167.

Headmistress Mrs Ann Aughwane BSc (Hons) Cert Ed NPQH
Founded 1906
School status girls' independent boarding and day
Religious denomination Inter-denominational
Member of BSA, GSA **Accredited by** GSA
Age range 2–18; *boarders from* 11
No of pupils 688; *(boarding)* 54; *(full boarding)* 54
Nursery 100; *Prep* 196; *Senior* 304
Sixth Form 88; *Girls* 638; *Boys* 50
Teacher:pupil ratio 1:1
Average class size 20
Fees per annum *(full boarding)* £23,910; *(day)* £6,465–£13,560

Burgess Hill School for Girls has a happy, challenging, supportive atmosphere, which encourages young people to use their initiative, be inquisitive and creative, and develop responsibility and independence. Ours is a school in which girls flourish. The focus is firmly on girls and the way they learn. They develop self-esteem and confidence and go on to make positive contribution in their chosen professions. Burgess Hill School for Girls is constantly highly ranked nationally and regularly leads the field in Sussex. We believe that education for life involves much more than academic success alone. We do not specialize in any one area.

Seaford College

Lavington Park, Petworth, West Sussex GU28 0NB **T**: (01798) 867392 **F**: (01798) 867606 **E**: seaford@clara.co.uk **W**: www.seaford.org

● ♠ ▲

Headmaster Mr T J Mullins BA MBA
Founded 1884
College status Co-educational independent boarding and day
Religious denomination Church of England
Member of HMC, SHMIS **Accredited by** HMC, SHMIS
Age range 7–18; *boarders from* 10
No of pupils 602; *(boarding)* 226; *(full boarding)* 123;
(weekly boarding) 103; *Prep* 173; *Senior* 429
Sixth Form 128; *Girls* 203; *Boys* 399
Teacher:pupil ratio 1:9
Average class size 15

Fees per annum *(full boarding)* £18,030–£24,075; *(weekly)* £15,900–£20,400; *(day)* £6,858–£15,600

Seaford College is a fully co-educational school for boarding and day pupils aged 10–18. Situated within 400 acres at the foot of the South Downs, the college is close to the historic town of Petworth and seven miles from the closest railway station. Heathrow and Gatwick airports are within an hour's drive.

Pupils may board flexi, 4-day (Mon–Fri), weekly or full-time and a bus service collects day pupils from a wide area.

Curriculum

A wide range of subjects is offered at GCSE and A level. Ninety-six per cent of leavers go on to university.

Entry requirements and procedures

Entrance to the junior house at 10+ and 11+ is based on a trial day and ability test. Entrance to the senior school at 13+ is based on similar lines, along with Common Entrance examination results. Sixth form entry is dependent on GCSE results (minimum requirement is 45 points, A* = 8, A = 7, B = 6 etc) and an interview. Overseas pupils must pass an English exam set by the college and past academic achievements will also be taken into account.

Academic and leisure facilities

The college boasts an impressive and successful art, design and technology centre. Outstanding sports facilities, including six rugby pitches, an all-weather hockey pitch and a new nine-hole golf course and driving range, along with staff who have coached at international level, have helped the college gain an excellent sporting record. The hockey and rugby teams have toured Argentina, Barbados, South Africa, Australia, Canada and New Zealand and our pupils have played at county and national level. Music and drama feature strongly in the life of the college and the chapel choir enjoys an international reputation.

Scholarships

Scholarships are offered for academic, design and technology, music (instrumental or choral), sport or art but must be accompanied by a good all-round academic standard. Value: £500. Parents who require further discount from the fees may apply for a bursary.

Bursaries

Bursaries are available to Forces' families and siblings.

Boarding facilities

Boys aged 13–18 are divided between two houses with separate boarding and day accommodation. The older boys have individual studies and the younger boys sleep in rooms of two or three. Second-year A level pupils are accommodated in a separate house, offering more privileges and responsibility and helping with the transition from the protection of school life to the relative freedom of university. The girls' boarding house, comprising dormitories for pre-GCSE girls and single and twin rooms for lower sixth, is located in the mansion house. Dormitory facilities are provided in the junior house for girls and boys aged 10–13.

For further information and a prospectus please contact the admissions secretary on 01798 867456 or e-mail jmackay@seaford.org.

Windlesham House School

Washington, Pulborough, West Sussex RH20 4AY **T**: (01903) 874700 **F**: (01903) 874702
E: office@windlesham.com **W**: www.windlesham.com

Headmaster Mr R Foster BEd (Hons)
Founded 1837
School status Co-educational independent boarding and day
Religious denomination Church of England
Member of BSA, IAPS, ISBA, SATIPS **Accredited by** IAPS
Age range 4–13; *boarders from* 7
No of pupils 336; *(boarding)* 226; *(full boarding)* 226; *Pre-prep*
53; *Prep* 313; *Girls* 154; *Boys* 212
Teacher:pupil ratio 1:7
Average class size 16
Fees per annum *(full boarding)* £20,730–£21,075; *(day)* £7,635–£18,075

Windlesham is one of the country's leading (and oldest) IAPS co-educational prep boarding and day schools, and has a history of being in the forefront of educational development. Whilst academic excellence and success is a high priority Windlesham provides a warm, secure, caring and very happy family atmosphere. The Headmaster, Richard Foster – and his wife Rachel – put every effort into getting to know each and every child well, and derive enormous pleasure in seeing children flourish in what is a wonderful environment and an unrivalled setting.

Windlesham has had an amazing 12 months: following on from the success of Odyssey in July 2010 it received an 'Outstanding' Ofsted report in October 2010 and in May 2011 a glowing ISI Inspection report. In the summer 15 children gained scholarships to senior schools including Wellington, Marlborough, Hurstpierpoint and Lancing. Sport has also blossomed with Windlesham winning their own Rugby 7s Tournament for the first time in 27 years and in June they were crowned champions at the 2011 IAPS Golf Tournament.

Symbol key

Gender

● Girls
● Boys
● Coed

Accommodation

🏠 Boarding only
🏠 Boarding and Day
🏠 Day and Boarding
🏠 Day only

International Bacc.

★ School offers IB

CReSTeD

◆ CReSTeD Registered

Has 6th Form

▲ Has 6th Form

GEORGE CROWTHER

geocrowther@hotmail.com

Consultant Educational Psychologist
Clinical & Developmental Psychologist
Education & Child Care Consultant

- Dyslexia
- Learning Difficulties
- Pre-school assessment
- Sensory or physical difficulties
- Autism/Asperger's/ASD
- Emotional & Behavioural Difficulties
- Deficits of Attention, Motor Control & Persistence (DAMP)
- Special Educational Needs Assessment
- Grammar School Selection
- Which School
- Vocational & Careers Guidance
- International Commissions
- Connexions

- Able, Gifted + Talented
- Dyspraxia/DCD
- Speech and Language Delay/Disorder
- Attention Deficit Hyperactivity Disorder (AD/HD)
- Pervasive Developmental Disorder (PDD)
- Poor School Report
- Poor SATS Results
- Special Educational Needs + Disablity Tribunal (SENDIST)
- Common Entrance
- Home Visits
- Counselling/Personal Matters
- Inclusion

Independent Professional Educational Advice

Little Hill, Colley Manor Drive, Reigate, Surrey RH2 9JS
Telephone & Fax: Reigate (+44) 01737 243286 Mobile: 07710 214349
Email: geocrowther@hotmail.com Website www.georgecrowther.co.uk

Director of Education Law Association (ELAS)
Member of Independent Tribunal Service
Single Joint Expert (SJE) Witness- The Law Society
Member of the Association for Child and Adolescent Mental Health (ACAMH)
Member of the Association of Educational Psychologists (AEP)
Member of the National Association for Gifted Children (NAGC)
Member of the National Association for Special Educational Needs (NASEN)
Member of Young Minds
Fellow of the Royal Institution of Great Britain
Registered with the Health Professions Council (HPC)

MAP OF SOUTH WEST ENGLAND

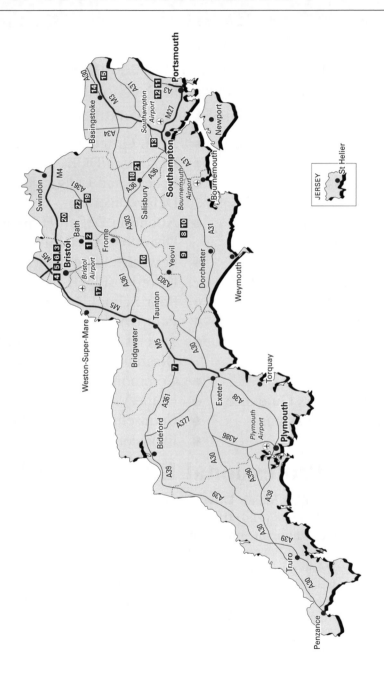

PROFILED SCHOOLS IN SOUTH WEST ENGLAND

(Incorporating the counties of Bath and North East Somerset, City of Bristol, Cornwall, Devon, Dorset, South Gloucestershire, Hampshire, Isle of Wight, Somerset, North Somerset, Wiltshire)

King Edward's School, Bath

North Road, Bath, Bath & North East Somerset BA2 6HU **T**: (01225) 464313 **F**: (01225) 481363
E: headmaster@kesbath.com **W**: www.kesbath.com.uk

Head Mr Martin Boden
Founded 1552
School status Co-educational day only
Religious denomination Non-denominational
Member of HMC, IAPS, ISBA, ISC **Accredited by** HMC, ISA
Age range 3–18
No of pupils 970; *Nursery* 30; *Pre-prep* 60; *Junior* 180; *Senior* 250

Sixth Form 180; *Girls* 380; *Boys* 590
Fees per annum *(nursery)* £6,435; *(pre-prep)* £7,830; *(junior)* £8,670 *(senior)* £10,965 *(sixth form)* £11,091
Fees per term *(nursery)* £2,145; *(pre-prep)* £2,610; *(junior)* £2,890; *(senior)* £3,655; *(sixth form)* £3,697

King Edward's School, Bath is an independent girls' and boys' day school with a Senior School (ages 11–18), Junior School (ages 7–10) and Pre-Prep School (ages 3–6). Founded in 1552 by King Edward VI; today King Edward's School is one of the country's leading independent schools.

King Edward's Senior School is situated on a 14 acre site on the southeastern edge of Bath with extensive views of the beautiful Georgian City of Bath and surrounding hills. The campus comprises an elegant Victorian manor house and architect-designed modern facilities including the award winning Junior School building; the art, design and technology complex, modern sports hall, the Wroughton theatre, new drama studio, music school, science laboratories, Sixth Form study centre, modern languages laboratory and library. The Pre-Prep School is situated in an elegant Victorian House on the edge of Weston Village.

Academic performance: One of the strengths of King Edward's School is its excellent track record of academic success. The results at A-Level, AS-Level and GCSE have put the School in the premier tier of schools in the country and pupils go on to the top universities and successful careers.

Pastoral care: Pastoral care is at the heart of School Life. A recent ISI report judged the School's pastoral care to be 'outstanding'.

Sports: King Edward's has a strong reputation for sporting excellence. The facilities are first rate; with a modern Sports Hall, all weather pitches, fitness suite and 16 acres of playing fields at Bathampton. In the Autumn term the main sports are hockey, netball and rugby; in the Spring and Summer terms, pupils enjoy cricket, tennis, rugby, hockey, rounders, athletics and football. Pupils train with highly skilled coaches and they gain valuable experience in their sport playing a programme of fixtures against other schools and on sport tours.

Creative arts: The Arts are a real strength at King Edward's. Pupils have the opportunity to play an instrument or sing in a choir. There are a number of ensembles who regularly perform at events both at the School and in the wider community. Art and photography are extremely popular. Pupils enjoy a diverse and stimulating arts education with the opportunity to try a variety of mediums. Every year there are a number of dramatic productions at the Pre-Prep, Junior and Senior School ensuring that all pupils have the opportunity of benefiting from their involvement in the performing arts.

Enriched curriculum: King Edward's School offers pupils a multitude of activities which enhance and support the academic, creative, sporting, social and cultural life of the School.

The School ensures that when each pupil leaves to proceed to the next stage of their education or career, they will be responsible, confident and adaptable. These qualities combined with excellent examination results prepare them for a fulfilling life ahead. Please come and meet us to see how King Edward's can help your child reach their full potential.

Kingswood School

Lansdown, Bath, Bath & North East Somerset BA1 5RG **T**: (01225) 734210 **F**: (01225) 734305
E: enquiries@kingswood.bath.sch.uk **W**: www.kingswood.bath.sch.uk
Contact our admissions office for information about scholarships and bursaries.

●🏠▲

Head Master Mr S Morris MA
Founded 1748
School status Co-educational boarding and day
Religious denomination Methodist
Member of BSA, HMC, IAPS, ISBA **Accredited by** British Council,
HMC, IAPS, ISC
Age range 3–18; *boarders from* 7
No of pupils 965; *(full boarding)* 147; *(weekly boarding)* 28; *Nursery* 41;
Pre-prep 138; *Prep* 173; *Senior* 645
Sixth Form 205; *Girls* 419; *Boys* 546
Teacher:pupil ratio 1:1
Average class size 22
Fees per annum *(full boarding)* £20,796–£24,909; *(weekly)* £18,165–£22,506; *(day)* £11,559

Kingswood School is set within 215 acres of beautiful parkland overlooking the World Heritage city of Bath. At inspection, it has been praised for its exceptional pastoral care, and has high academic standards. Over 100 extra-curricular activities are offered, in addition to a lively and dynamic curriculum. Scholarships, special talent awards, HM Forces remissions and some bursaries are available. Christian values permeate Kingswood's philosophy and ethos and all members of the school community are encouraged to behave in a way that creates a love of life and learning in all its pupils.

The Royal High School, Bath

Lansdown Road, Bath, Bath & North East Somerset BA1 5SZ **T**: (01225) 313877 **F**: (01225) 465446
E: royalhigh@bat.gdst.net **W**: www.royalhighbath.gdst.net
For admissions, scholarship and bursary details, HM Forces discounts or to arrange a private visit,
please contact our registrar, Lynda Bevan: l.bevan@bat.gdst.net

●🏠★▲

Headmistress Mrs Rebecca Dougall BA MA   **Founded** 1864
School status Girls' independent boarding and day.
Religious denomination Non-denominational
Member of GDST, GSA, IB
Age range *(day)* girls 3–18 *(boarding)* girls 10–18
No of pupils 770; *(boarding)* 140; *(full boarding)* 130; *(weekly boarding)* 10;
Nursery 24; *Pre-prep* 52; *Prep* 152; *Senior* 375; *Sixth Form* 160; *Girls* 770
Teacher:pupil ratio 1:10 **Average class size** 22
Fees per annum *(full boarding)* £17,445; *(weekly)* £15,486; *(day)* £8,898

We're a caring, creative, international academic community – empowering, enriching and enabling every girl to achieve her best.

Fast becoming a school of choice for boarding and day girls aged 3 to 18 and recognized for outstanding educational achievements, excellent facilities and enriching extra-curricular activities, we focus on individual care and value achievement beyond the classroom, inspiring girls to make the most of their unique talents. From Nursery, through Junior School, Senior School and Sixth Form College, offering the International Baccalaureate as well as A Levels, our girls are equally at home brandishing blowtorches, rowing for gold and climbing mountains, as they are re-living Shakespeare and unravelling algebraic equations. This all-through, all-round, all-girls education develops the confidence, capabilities and character needed to underpin success at university, throughout careers and in achieving aspirations in every aspect of life. Please contact our Registrar: l.bevan@bat.gdst.net to arrange a private visit. You are welcome at anytime.

Badminton School

Westbury Road, Westbury-on-Trym, Bristol BS9 3BA **T**: (0117) 905 5271 **F**: (0117) 962 3049
E: admissions@badminton.bristol.sch.uk **W**: www.badminton.bristol.sch.uk

Headmistress Mrs J Scarrow BA
Founded 1858
School status girls' independent boarding and day
Religious denomination Non-denominational
Member of BSA, GSA, IAPS, ISA, ISBA, ISC
Accredited by British Council, GSA, IAPS, ISA, ISC
Age range 3–18; *boarders from* 9
No of pupils 440; *(boarding)* 190; *(full boarding)* 180;
(weekly boarding) 15; *Nursery* 12; *Prep* 108; *Senior* 210
Sixth Form 110; *Girls* 440
Teacher:pupil ratio 1:7
Average class size 16
Fees per annum *(full boarding)* £18,840–£29,640; *(weekly)* £18,840–£29,640; *(day)* £7,050–£15,810

Badminton School is an independent boarding, weekly boarding and day school, located on a 20-acre campus in the heart of the attractive university city of Bristol. The school is ranked highly in the national league table and around 15 per cent of girls go on to Oxford and Cambridge. The community spirit of the school encourages girls to develop as individuals and enables them to realize their potential. By the time they leave school, the girls are confident and caring team players.

Bristol Grammar School

University Road, Bristol BS8 1SR **T**: (0117) 973 6006 **F**: (0117) 946 7485 **E**: recruitment@bgs.bristol.sch.uk
W: www.bristolgrammarschool.co.uk

Head Master Mr R I MacKinnon BSc
Founded 1532
School status Co-educational independent day only
Religious denomination non-denominational
Member of AGBIS, HMC, IAPS, ISBA
Age range 4–18
No of pupils 1,210 *Infants* 80; *Juniors* 180; *Senior* 650;
Sixth Form 300; *Girls* 475; *Boys* 735
Fees per annum *(day)* £5,993.25–£11,134.50

Bristol Grammar School aims high and is proud to do so, inspiring a love of learning, self-confidence and a sense of adventure among its pupils. Founded almost 500 years ago, BGS is an independent, co-educational day school for pupils aged 4 to 18 and considered one of the leading academic schools in the Southwest. BGS provides an excellent education, developing independence of thought through high-quality teaching of a broad curriculum and wide-ranging intellectual, physical and cultural pursuits. An exceptional pastoral care system, based around six houses, gives every pupil a sense of belonging and the security and confidence to make the most of the many opportunities offered. Prospective pupils and their families are most welcome to visit, with tours available throughout the year.

Clifton College

32 College Road, Clifton, Bristol BS8 3JH **T**: (0117) 315 7000 **F**: (0117) 315 7101
E: admissions@clifton-college.avon.sch.uk **W**: www.cliftoncollegeuk.com

Head Master Mr Mark Moore MA
Founded 1862
College status Independent boarding and day school
for girls and boys
Religious denomination Church of England
Member of HMC, IAPS
Age range 3–18
No of pupils Upper 710; the Pre 400; Butcombe 220
Teacher:pupil ratio 1:8
Average class size 15
Fees per annum (full boarding) £21,465–£27,250; (day) £12,825–£27,370

Clifton offers a broad and flexible curriculum with an unusually large number of subjects on offer. Entry at 13+ is by Common Entrance or ability tests. Scholarships are available at 11 (prep school), 13 and 16 for academic, art, music, sport and all-round abilities. The School occupies a superb site in what has been described as 'the handsomest suburb in Europe'.

Blundell's School

Tiverton, Devon EX16 4DN **T**: (01884) 252543 **F**: (01884) 243232 **E**: registrars@blundells.org
W: www.blundells.org

Head Master Mr I R Davenport BA
Founded 1604
School status Co-educational independent boarding and day
Religious denomination Church of England
Member of AGBIS, BSA, HMC, ISBA, ISC **Accredited by** HMC, ISC
Age range 11–18; boarders from 11
No of pupils 569; (boarding) 358; (full boarding) 118; (weekly boarding) 240; Senior 445
Sixth Form 180; Girls 233; Boys 336
Teacher:pupil ratio 1:9 **Average class size** 14
Fees per annum (full boarding) £17,580–£26,070; (weekly) £15,900–£22,935; (day) £10,485–£16,815

Blundell's, a key West Country school, combines balance, excellence, space and tradition to provide a unique package for 11–18-year-old day and boarding pupils. All traditional subjects are offered at A level, plus theatre studies, music, art, business studies, psychology, photography and sports science. Supplementary courses and lectures are also provided at all levels. A level entry requires a minimum of five GCSEs, interview and report from present school. At 11+ and 13+ pupils must sit Blundell's entrance test or Common Entrance. Examinations offered: GCSE, A level, music. Scholarships: 11+, 13+ and sixth form: academic, sport, music, art and all-rounder. Boarders are supported by a strong house structure and live in a family environment guided by their houseparents and tutors.

Bryanston School

Blandford Forum, Dorset DT11 0PX **T**: (01258) 452411 **F**: (01258) 484661 **E**: admissions@bryanston.co.uk
W: www.bryanston.co.uk

Head S J Thomas
School status Co-educational independent boarding and day senior
Religious denomination Church of England
Age range 13–18
No of pupils 677; *(boarding)* 573; *(full boarding)* 573; *Girls* 295; *Boys* 382
Teacher:pupil ratio 1:9
Fees per annum *(full boarding)* £29,970; *(day)* £24,576

Bryanston is a school which rejoices in its motto: *et nova et vetera*. We're a young enough school to have a crystal clear vision of our direction and values, much of them described by our founder in 1928, and these imbue all we do here. We are proud to teach pupils to learn, rather than treating them as so many empty vessels to be passively filled with facts. We're also clear on what are the important traditions for a school: at Bryanston they are those which encourage independence, individuality and thinking, as well as being able to learn from living in a loving community which fast becomes, and remains, a family. Set in 400 acres of beautiful north Dorset countryside, Bryanston provides an inspiring environment in which to grow up.

International College, Sherborne School

Newell Grange, Sherborne, Dorset DT9 4EZ **T**: (01935) 814743 **F**: (01935) 816863
E: reception@sherborne-ic.net **W**: www.sherborne-ic.net
Registrar: Mrs Anne-Marie Slack

● 🏠

Principal Dr C J Greenfield
Founded 1977
College status Co-educational independent boarding only
Religious denomination Non-denominational
Member of BSA, COBIS, ISA, ISC
Accredited by British Council, ISA, ISC
Age range 11–17
No of pupils 150; *(boarding)* 150; *(full boarding)* 150; *Senior* 150; *Girls* 50;
Boys 100
Teacher:pupil ratio 1:6
Average class size 6
Fees per annum *(full boarding)* £14,100–£19,275

The International College is unique. It was established in 1977 (as the International Study Centre) to prepare boys, and later girls, from non-British educational backgrounds so that they could function successfully in traditional British boarding schools. Typically these boys and girls spend one year at the International College before moving on to a traditional British boarding school where the majority of pupils are British.

Those pupils who join in Year 10 (usually around 14 or 15 years old) and start a two-year course leading towards GCSE examinations must stay at the school for the duration of the course. The college has three major tasks:

- concentrated improvement in spoken and written English;
- academic preparation in English in the full range of curriculum subjects;
- a good introduction to British educational procedures and the British way of life.

The arrangements of the college are designed to achieve these tasks. Classes are small, usually between six and eight pupils to each teacher. All teachers are not only experienced specialists in their own subject, but also have additional training in teaching the English language.

Characteristics: The teaching facilities at the International College include modern classrooms, eight science laboratories, an art studio, a computer centre and a library with internet access. The college uses the extensive sporting, musical and theatre facilities at Sherborne School, including a 25-metre indoor swimming pool.

The International College has gained an unrivalled reputation for providing the very best start to British independent education for children from overseas. Through a carefully supervised programme of study, pupils gain a sound working knowledge of the main British curriculum subjects such as mathematics, the sciences and humanities.

The college has high standards of discipline and pastoral care. Most weekends there is a busy programme that ensures pupils are fully occupied on Saturday and Sunday.

Milton Abbey School

Blandford Forum, Dorset DT11 0BZ **T**: (01258) 880484 **F**: (01258) 881194 **E**: info@miltonabbey.co.uk
W: www.miltonabbey.co.uk

Headmaster Mr G E Doodes MA
Founded 1954
School status Co-educational independent boarding
and day senior
Religious denomination Church of England
Member of BSA, CReSTeD, SHMIS
Accredited by SHMIS
Age range 13–18; *boarders from* 13
No of pupils 221; *(boarding)* 210
Sixth Form 104; *Girls* 20; *Boys* 84
Average class size 10
Fees per annum *(full boarding)* £9,780; *(day)* £7,350

Milton Abbey is a very personal place – a school in which everybody genuinely knows everybody. We have achieved what other schools strive in vain to achieve: an intimate community in which achievement in any area of life is never rated more highly than quality of character. No one is overlooked. Everyone is famous.

Bedales School

Petersfield, Hampshire GU32 2DG **T**: (01730) 300100 **F**: (01730) 300500 **E**: admissions@bedales.org.uk
W: www.bedales.org.uk
Contact for admissions: Janie Jarman, Registrar (direct line 01730 711733; jjarman@bedales.org.uk)

Headmaster Mr K Budge
Founded 1893
School status Co-educational independent boarding and day senior
Religious denomination Non-denominational
Member of HMC
Age range 13–18; *boarders from* 13
No of pupils 469; *(boarding)* 336; *(full boarding)* 336; *Senior* 469
Sixth Form 189; *Girls* 255; *Boys* 214
Teacher:pupil ratio 1:7
Average class size 22
Fees per annum *(full boarding)* £29,955; *(day)* £23,550

Bedales was founded as the alternative to Victorian authoritarianism. There is no uniform, everyone is on first-name terms and our pupils take the lead in organizing their own time and methods of study, but yes – we do have rules, a timetable and a curriculum. In effect, we start preparing pupils for university well before GCSE, or the unique and more demanding Bedales Assessed Courses that have replaced some of the duller GCSEs. Bedales' pupils characteristically develop very strong relationships with their teachers, develop a mind of their own and are happy with who they are – so they go into the world with confidence.

Dunhurst (Bedales Junior School)

Alton Road, Petersfield, Hampshire GU32 2DP **T**: (01730) 711733 **F**: (01730) 711820 **E**: jjarman@bedales.org.uk
W: www.bedales.org.uk
General enquiries: 01730 300200 or e-mail dunhurst@bedales.org.uk

●

Head Jane Grubb
Founded 1902
School status Co-educational independent boarding
and day prep prep and senior
Religious denomination Non-denominational
Member of HMC **Accredited by** IAPS
Age range 8–13; *boarders from 8*
No of pupils 196; *(boarding) 102; (full boarding) 51;*
(weekly boarding) 51; Prep 193; Girls 111; Boys 85
Teacher:pupil ratio 1:7
Average class size 20
Fees per annum *(full boarding)* £20,580; *(day)* £16,110

Dunhurst School follows J H Badley's vision of focusing on all aspects of a child's life: head, hand and heart. We believe education should empower children through opportunity and experience. Much learning takes place through making and doing. Children are encouraged to find their own voice: moreover, our reputation for supporting their needs is outstanding. Confidence grows as the children grow and with it their desire to question and discuss. Our distinctive approach to learning helps children excel academically. The curriculum is broad as well as deep. We are not bound by the Common Entrance syllabus; although guided by the National Curriculum, we are not locked into it. As children move up the school they learn to take responsibility for themselves and organize their own time. Pupils are expected to work hard on the academic curriculum, the creative and performing arts, sport, and the diverse wealth of activities on offer.

Hampshire Collegiate School, UCST

Embley Park, Romsey, Hampshire SO51 6ZE **T**: (01794) 512206 **F**: (01794) 518737 **E**: info@hampshirecs.org.uk
W: www.hampshirecs.org.uk

● ♠ ▲

Principal Mr H S MacDonald
Head of Sixth Form Mr Matthew Laverty
Founded 2005
School status Co-educational independent boarding and day
Religious denomination Church of England
Member of AGBIS, BSA, IAPS, SHA, SHMIS
Age range 2$^1/_2$–18; *boarders from 11*
No of pupils 720; *(boarding) 76; (full boarding) 55;*
(weekly boarding) 21
Sixth Form 95; Girls 340; Boys 380
Teacher:pupil ratio 1:15
Average class size 18
Fees per annum *(full boarding)* £22,035–£24,483; *(day)* £8,247–£13,449

HCS is a 2$^1/_2$–18 school set in 130 acres of outstanding natural beauty. ISI noted, 'Rising academic standards and very good pastoral care. Many strengths and no weaknesses'. The senior school sets its own entry test. At GCSE a core curriculum is offered together with a choice of three separate sciences, three modern languages, humanities, creative and practical subjects. At A level 22 subjects are offered. New facilities include a new junior school, purpose-built science and maths suites and astro-turf pitches. Scholarships available; also bursaries (HM Forces, clergy, teachers, single parents, and hardship cases).

England

Lord Wandsworth College

Long Sutton, Hook, Hampshire RG29 1TB **T**: (01256) 862201 **F**: (01256) 860363 **E**: info@lordwandsworth.org
W: www.lordwandsworth.org

Headmaster Mr F Q Livingstone MA
Founded 1922
College status Co-educational independent boarding and day
Religious denomination Non-denominational
Member of BSA, HMC, SHMIS **Accredited by** HMC, ISC, SHMIS
Age range 11–18; *boarders from* 11
No of pupils 535; *(boarding)* 206; *(full boarding)* 68;
(weekly boarding) 138; *Senior* 372
Sixth Form 163; *Girls* 159; *Boys* 376
Teacher:pupil ratio 1:1
Average class size 19
Fees per annum *(full boarding)* £23,730–£26,310; *(weekly)* £23,730–£225,044; *(day)* £17,718–£18,660

Lord Wandsworth College offers:

- a safe and secure environment;
- a high level of pastoral care;
- excellent exam results which consistently exceed individual expectations;
- outstanding facilities for both academic and co-curricular activities;
- an unpretentious, caring and happy relaxed atmosphere;
- a broad, balanced education.

St Nicholas' School

Redfields House, Redfields Lane, Church Crookham, Fleet, Hampshire GU52 0RF **T**: (01252) 850121
F: (01252) 850718 **E**: registrar@st-nicholas.hants.sch.uk **W**: www.st-nicholas.hants.sch.uk

Headmistress Mrs A V Whatmough BA (Hons) Cert Ed
Founded 1935
School status Girls' independent day only pre-prep Boys 3–7
Religious denomination Church of England
Member of GSA **Accredited by** GSA, ISC
Age range 3–16 (boys 3–7)
No of pupils 363; *Infants* 80; *Juniors* 85; *Senior* 194
Teacher:pupil ratio 1:12
Average class size 15
Fees per annum *(day)* £3,696–£10,038

At St Nicholas' School we believe that the best education is a partnership between teachers, pupils and parents. By creating a supportive environment, the personal and academic potential of each pupil can be developed. Classes are small and facilities are excellent. The personal and academic progress of each individual is monitored carefully and should any help be needed, it is available. The secure base laid at St Nicholas' gives pupils a wide range of choice for the next stage of their education. The fact that they are welcome wherever they go is a tribute to the work of the school.

Hazlegrove

Sparkford, Yeovil, Somerset BA22 7JA **T**: (01963) (440314) **F**: (01963) (440569) **E**: office@hazlegrove.co.uk
W: www.hazlegrove.co.uk   Admissions OfficeTel: 01963 442606 Email: admissions@hazlegrove.co.uk

The Headmaster Mr R Fenwick MA Bed
School status Co-educational independent pre-prep prep
Religious denomination Church of England
Member of BSA, CReSTeD, IAPS, ISC
Accredited by IAPS
Age range 2–13; *boarders from 7*
No of pupils 378; *(boarding)* 94; *(full boarding)* 94; *Nursery* 17; *Pre-prep*
60; *Prep* 301; *Girls* 178; *Boys* 200
Average class size 15
Fees per term *(full boarding)* £5,310–£6,775; *(weekly)* £5,310–£6,775; *(day)* £2,347–£4,757

Parkland setting with excellent facilities

Hazlegrove is an independent boarding and day preparatory school for 370 boys and girls aged 2–13. The
School is set within 200 acres of parkland in Somerset, with direct access to the A303. Excellent facilities include
a newly developed flood-lit sports area, indoor swimming pool, sports hall, squash courts, mini golf course,
theatre, music school, design and art centre and a mini farm. A purpose-built, self-contained pre-prep and
nursery gives pupils the ideal start to school life.

Opportunity from an early age

In today's rapidly changing and demanding world, it is important that children have a breadth of opportunity to
develop their abilities and potential, while enjoying the benefit of a caring, structured and secure environment.
We provide this at Hazlegrove. Children are encouraged to seek high standards in academic, creative, sporting
and many other areas of School life. At the same time, we are a family school and regard the happiness of the
individual child, at whatever level of achievement, as of vital importance to their personal progress.

Outstanding boarding

The boarding was rated "Outstanding" by Ofsted 2010/11 and pupils can board from age 7 when they join the
Prep School. The full programme of evening and weekend activities, together with the large number of boarders
staying in at weekends, ensures that there is always plenty to do.

Building self-esteem

Music and drama play a significant role in developing personal confidence with all pupils being involved in a
major production every year. Pupils have regular opportunities to perform in informal concerts and to join one or
more of the large number of ensembles. Outdoor education is part of the curriculum allowing children to develop
the skills to work as part of a team and confidence is built upon by pushing personal boundaries. Our aim is for
pupils to leave Hazlegrove with a self-esteem which is intact, prepared to face the unknown challenges which lie
ahead.

A clear vision and an exciting future

Hazlegrove is a splash of colour in an increasingly grey and conformist world. It is a school that delights in
children being children, it encourages individuality, and it values determination, perseverance and passion. The
School has retained all that is best from the past, but, at the same time, is ready to respond to contemporary
educational initiatives and to explore new technologies. Hazlegrove has a clear vision and an exciting future.

Sidcot School

Oakridge Lane, Winscombe, North Somerset BS25 1PD **T**: (01934) 843102 **F**: (01934) 844181
E: admissions@sidcot.org.uk **W**: www.sidcot.org.uk

●♠★◆▲

Headmaster Mr J Walmsley BSc
Founded 1699
School status Co-educational independent boarding and day
Religious denomination Quaker
Member of BSA, CReSTeD, IB, IBO, ISBA, ISC, SHMIS
Accredited by ISC, SHMIS
Age range 3–18
No of pupils 520; *(boarding)* 173; *(full boarding)* 163;
(weekly boarding) 10; *Nursery* 10; *Pre-prep* 62; *Prep* 115; *Senior* 188
Sixth Form 145; *Girls* 245; *Boys* 275
Teacher:pupil ratio 1:15 **Average class size** 15
Fees per annum *(full boarding)* £22,050–£27,750; *(weekly)* £21,750–£23,100; *(day)* £6,150–£14,250

Sidcot School is a thriving independent co-educational day and boarding school situated in 160 acres. Sidcot offers a blend of excellent traditional and state-of-the-art facilities. It is well equipped, with academic facilities, a new performing and creative arts centre, learning resource and sixth form centre, sports hall complex with heated swimming pool, extensive playing fields and a riding centre. Our Quaker philosophy means that we value all children whatever their abilities. Pupils gain excellent exam results but also develop as caring and confident individuals. Happy children learn, and small classes and good working relationships make for a positive and inclusive atmosphere. Scholarships are available. Quaker bursaries are available for members of the Society of Friends. We welcome pupils of all faiths or none.

Chafyn Grove School

33 Bourne Avenue, Salisbury, Wiltshire SP1 1LR **T**: (01722) 333423 **F**: (01722) 323114
E: office@chafyngrove.co.uk **W**: www.chafyngrove.co.uk

●♠

Headmaster Mr Eddy Newton BA (Hons) PGCE MA (Cantab)
Founded 1916
School status Co-educational independent boarding and day
Religious denomination Church of England
Member of BSA, IAPS, ISBA **Accredited by** IAPS
Age range 3–13; *boarders from* 7
No of pupils 301; *(boarding)* 48; *(full boarding)* 48; *Nursery* 15; *Pre-prep* 75;
Prep 226; *Girls* 91; *Boys* 210
Teacher:pupil ratio 1:9
Average class size 15
Fees per annum *(full boarding)* £15,330–£18,675; *(day)* £6,930–£13,755

High standards in a relaxed environment is our goal! At Chafyn Grove we offer a warm and welcoming setting where your child's learning experience can be nurtured in small class sizes. We aim to help each child to have high academic expectations of themselves relative to their own ability, and to take advantage of the many opportunities on offer outside the classroom. Our aim is to enable your child to thrive in the happy atmosphere that is created by a mixture of caring pastoral support, good discipline, clear traditional values and a team of talented and committed teachers. The most recent ISI inspection indicates our success: "Pupils' excellent personal development enables them to grow into confident and friendly young people who enjoy responsibility. Relationships are excellent. . . ."

Dauntsey's School

High Street, West Lavington, Devizes, Wiltshire SN10 4HE **T**: (01380) 814500 **F**: (01380) 814501
E: sagersjh@dauntseys.wilts.sch.uk **W**: www.dauntseys.org
● ♠ ▲

Head Master Mr S B Roberts MA
Founded 1542
School status Co-educational independent boarding and day
Religious denomination Inter-denominational
Member of BSA, HMC **Accredited by** HMC, ISC
Age range 11–18; *boarders from* 11
No of pupils 786; *(boarding)* 320; *(full boarding)* 320; *Senior* 786
Sixth Form 272; *Girls* 346; *Boys* 440
Teacher:pupil ratio 1:9 **Average class size** 14
Fees per annum *(full boarding)* £26,265–£29,490; *(day)* £15,585

Dauntsey's is a leading co-educational boarding and day school for 11–18-year-olds set in an estate of 150 acres of idyllic countryside on the northern edge of Salisbury Plain. The school ranks very high in the league tables for both GCSE and A levels. However, all pupils discover a breadth and depth of education that takes them beyond academic achievement. Drama, music, art and sport all flourish and the rural surroundings provide an ideal setting for many outdoor activities, which include sailing on the school's very own Tall Ship, the famous 56ft gaff cutter, the *Jolie Brise*. All information about Dauntsey's can be found on the school's regularly updated and informative website.

Grittleton House School

Grittleton, Chippenham, Wiltshire SN14 6AP **T**: (01249) 782434 **F**: (01249) 782669
E: secretary@grittletonhouseschool.org **W**: www.grittletonhouseschool.org
 ● ♠

Headmaster Mr N Dawes
Founded 1951
School status Co-educational independent day only
Religious denomination Non-denominational
Age range 2–16
No of pupils 283; *Nursery* 15; *Pre-prep* 39; *Prep* 113; *Senior* 170;
Girls 110; *Boys* 173
Teacher:pupil ratio 1:15 **Average class size** 15
Fees per annum *(day)* £6,150–£9,270

Grittleton House is an independent co-educational day school for children aged 2–16. The school was founded in 1951, and since 1967 has occupied the impressive Victorian manor house. The nursery and infant children have their own specialized area; the older children benefit from the use of science labs, art, HE and music rooms, the ICT suite, a large sports dome and heated swimming pool and a specifically converted studio theatre. The National Curriculum forms the basis of the teaching, but a wider spread of subjects is offered; the school has a strong drama and art tradition and the children participate in a full summer and winter sporting programme. Grittleton is consistently at the top of the league tables for non-selective schools and GCSEs are available in 17 subjects. Small class sizes ensure that pupils are encouraged to accept ever more exciting challenges. 'Twilight Club' available until 17.45 pm, where they may join in the many after-school activities (which vary termly) and do their homework in a quiet, supervised environment. Many children take piano, violin or woodwind lessons, and Grittleton also boasts a singing club and rock group! Transport available from many areas.

Norman Court Preparatory School

West Tytherley, Salisbury, Wiltshire SP5 1NH **T**: (01980) 862345 **F**: (01980) 862082 **E**: office@normancourt.co.uk
W: www.normancourt.co.uk.

Head Master Mr P G Savage BA (Hons)
Founded 1881
School status Co-educational independent boarding and day
Religious denomination Church of England
Member of BSA, HMC, IAPS, ISA, ISBA, ISC **Accredited by** IAPS, ISC
Age range 3–13; *boarders from* 7
No of pupils 210; *(boarding)* 64; *(full boarding)* 24; *(weekly boarding)* 40;
Girls 78; *Boys* 132
Teacher:pupil ratio 1:8
Average class size 15
Fees per annum *(full boarding)* £6,635–£6,635; *(weekly)* £6,635–£6,635; *(day)* £2,425–£4,925

If you are considering a preparatory education for your child, I urge you to visit Norman Court on their next open day. Set in 50 acres of glorious Hampshire countryside between Winchester and Salisbury, the school offers a rare educational opportunity, combining a healthy love of the outdoors with exceptional academic standards. It is a pleasure to meet a Norman Court child. They are characteristically confident, articulate and noticeably caring. Looking after the resident pigs, horse and goats and tending the new wildlife pond imbue a sense of responsibility in these girls and boys, who are being constantly challenged to explore their own potential as well as the stunning grounds. Each leaver secured their first choice of leading senior schools in the summer and an impressive half of those won scholarships. Don't let your child miss the opportunity for such a fantastic start in life.

St Mary's Calne

Curzon Street, Calne, Wiltshire SN11 0DF **T**: (01249) 857200 **F**: (01249) 857207 **E**: office@stmaryscalne.org
W: www.stmaryscalne.org

Headmistress Dr H M Wright MA (Oxon) MA (Leics) EdD (Exeter),
PGCE (Oxon) FRSA MIoD
Founded 1873
School status girls' independent boarding and day
Religious denomination Church of England
Member of AGBIS, BSA, GSA, ISA, ISC
Accredited by British Council, GSA, ISA, ISC
Age range 11–18; *boarders from* 11
No of pupils 325; *(boarding)* 260; *(full boarding)* 260; *Senior* 325
Sixth Form 104; *Girls* 325
Teacher:pupil ratio 1:6
Average class size 15
Fees per annum *(full boarding)* £28,080–£28,950; *(day)* £20,370–£21,000

St Mary's has a cutting-edge curriculum that is continually developing in order to provide girls with an education that motivates, challenges and inspires them. Girls consistently perform well in public examinations and all go on to higher education. We look for girls who have potential and an eagerness to learn, whatever their education before joining us. Extra-curricular activity enhances and is a key part of the curriculum. Eighty per cent of the girls play musical instruments and the Chamber Choir has recently performed in London, Paris and New York. Drama productions have transferred to both the London stage, owing to our unique relationship with RADA, and the Edinburgh Festival Fringe. The school is represented nationally and at county level in sport, and the girls benefit from being in a rural location which is nonetheless only just over an hour from London by train.

3.2

Scotland

MAP OF SCOTLAND

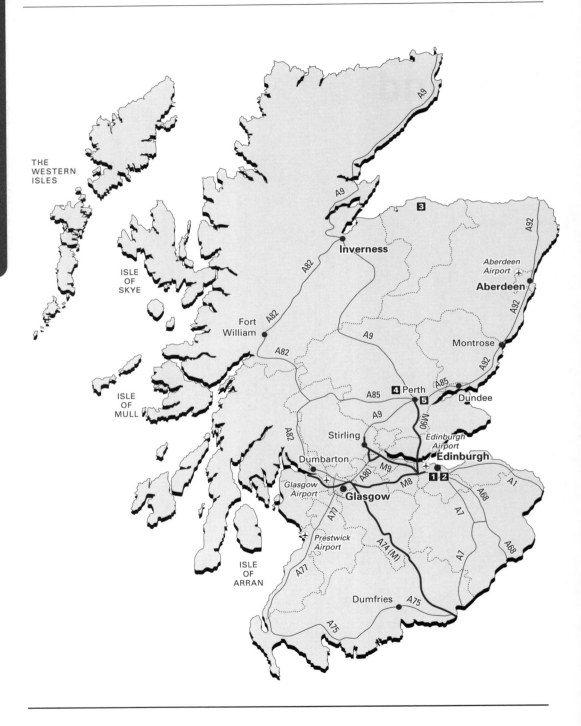

THE
WESTERN
ISLES

ISLE
OF
SKYE

ISLE
OF
MULL

ISLE
OF
ARRAN

Inverness

Fort
William

A82

A82

A82

A9

A9

A9

A9

A82

A82

A85

A85

A9

A9

3

4 Perth

5

M90

Dundee

Montrose

Aberdeen
Airport

Aberdeen

A92

A92

A92

Stirling

Dumbarton

Glasgow
Airport

Glasgow

A80

M9

M8

Edinburgh
Airport

Edinburgh

1 2

A1

A68

A68

A7

A7

A77

A77

Prestwick
Airport

A74 (M)

Dumfries

A75

A75

A75

PROFILED SCHOOLS IN SCOTLAND

(Incorporating the counties of Aberdeen City, Aberdeenshire, Angus, Argyll and Bute, East Ayrshire, North Ayrshire, South Ayrshire, Borders, City of Edinburgh, Dumfries and Galloway, East Dunbartonshire, West Dunbartonshire, Falkirk, Fife, Highland, Inverclyde, East Lothian, Midlothian, Moray, Perth and Kinross, Renfrewshire, Stirling, South Lanarkshire, West Lothian)

Merchiston Castle School

Colinton, Edinburgh, Lothian EH13 0PU **T**: (0131) 312 2200 **F**: (0131) 441 6060 **E**: admissions@merchiston.co.uk
W: www.merchiston.co.uk

●↟🏠▲

Head Mr A R Hunter BA
Founded 1833
School status Boys' independent boarding and day
Religious denomination Inter-denominational
Member of BSA, HMC, IBSCA, ISBA, SCIS
Accredited by HMC, ISC
Age range 8–18; *boarders from* 8
No of pupils 446; *(boarding)* 289; *(full boarding)* 289; *Prep* 108;
Senior 182; *Sixth Form* 156; *Boys* 446
Teacher:pupil ratio 1:9
Fees per annum *(full boarding)* £16,455–£25,755; *(day)* £11,625–£18,750

Set in 100 acres of parkland, Merchiston is a school renowned for academic and sporting excellence. Merchiston offers a full range of GCSEs and A levels with selected Highers. In 2010, 80 per cent of A level candidates gained A and B grades, while at GCSE 84 per cent of grades were awarded at A*–B; 82 per cent of pupils achieved a place at their first choice of university. Regular winners of national engineering, electronic and mathematics prizes. Sporting achievements include pupils participating at international level. Strongly featured music department with prestigious school choir and pipe band. Integral junior department (8–12 years). Strong links with two girls' schools. Junior teaching centre, refurbished science labs, modern IT suite, music school and library. Indoor pool, sports hall and new sixth form boarding house with 126 en-suite bedrooms (opened January 2009). Extensive co-curricular activities. Entry is by the school's own entrance exam; Scholarship exams or Common Entrance. Scholarships and means-tested financial assistance available.

St George's School for Girls

Garscube Terrace, Edinburgh, Lothian EH12 6BG **T**: (0131) 311 8000 **F**: (0131) 311 8120
E: admissions@st-georges.edin.sch.uk **W**: www.st-georges.edin.sch.uk

●↟🏠▲

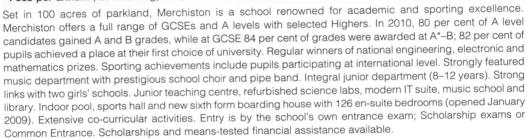

Headmistress Anne Everest BA (Hons)
Founded 1888
School status Girls' independent Boys 18 months–5 years
Religious denomination Non-denominational
Age range *(girls)* 18 months–18 years; *(boys)* 18 months–5years
No of pupils 858; *(boarding)* 60; *(full boarding)* 54; *(weekly boarding)* 6; *Girls* 850; *Boys* 8
Teacher:pupil ratio 1:18
Average class size 16
Fees per annum *(full boarding)* £22,573; *(day)* £6,765–£11,113

St George's School for Girls was founded in 1888 by a group of women who had been denied access to university education. Today the ethos of our founders remains; we put girls first by design and aim to give each one the confidence and competence to fulfil her potential. St George's provides a caring, stimulating and challenging environment in which girls learn and develop. Emphasis is placed on personal achievement, responsibility, diversity and on partnerships. Girls, staff and parents work cooperatively throughout. In partnership, we aim to ensure that the education of St George's girls meets the needs of the outside world as well as the individual. Academic excellence is valued and our examination results are outstanding, with over 98 per cent of our girls going on to university or college. Law, science, medicine, international relations, modern languages, the arts and social sciences are favoured degree courses. We welcome enquiries throughout the year and assessments are held to suit parental needs.

Gordonstoun School

Elgin, Morayshire IV30 5RF **T**: (01343) 837837 **F**: (01343) 837808 **E**: admissions@gordonstoun.org.uk
W: www.gordonstoun.org.uk

●🏠▲

Principal Mr Simon Reid
Founded 1934
School status Co-educational independent boarding and day
Religious denomination Non-denominational
Member of BSA, ISBA, SCIS **Accredited by** British Council
Age range 8–18; *boarders from* 8
No of pupils 588; *(boarding)* 486; *(full boarding)* 462; *(weekly boarding)* 24;
Prep 113; *Senior* 475
Sixth Form 251; *Girls* 241; *Boys* 347
Teacher:pupil ratio 1:7
Average class size 12
Fees per annum *(full boarding)* £17,958–£29,268; *(weekly)* £15,366; *(day)* £11,040–£21,846

Set in a magnificent estate, Gordonstoun (and its junior school, Aberlour House) lies between the sea and mountains in beautiful countryside. It is well located for easy access to international airports as well as mainline railway stations. The school's distinctive, holistic ethos is based on internationalism, challenge, responsibility and service and aims to prepare pupils to make a positive contribution to society. Offering a broad, integrated curriculum, Gordonstoun combines study for GCSE and AS/A level with sporting, creative and outdoor education, including the school's unique sail training programme, to help pupils encompass the school motto, *Plus est en Vous* (There is more in you).

Symbol key

Gender

● Girls
● Boys
● Coed

Accommodation

🏠 Boarding only
🏠 Boarding and Day
🏠 Day and Boarding
🏠 Day only

International Bacc.

★ School offers IB

CReSTeD

◆ CReSTeD Registered

Has 6th Form

▲ Has 6th Form

Glenalmond College

Perth, Perth and Kinross PH1 3RY **T**: (01738) 842056 **F**: (01738) 842063 **E**: registrar@glenalmondcollege.co.uk
W: www.glenalmondcollege.co.uk

●🏠▲

Warden Mr G Woods MA (Oxon) PGCE
Founded 1847
College status Co-educational independent boarding and day
Religious denomination Episcopalian
Member of AGBIS, BSA, HMC, ISBA, ISC, SCIS
Accredited by HMC, ISC
Age range 12–18; *boarders from* 12
No of pupils 405; *(boarding)* 355; *(full boarding)* 355; *Senior* 405
Sixth Form 174; *Girls* 166; *Boys* 239
Teacher:pupil ratio 1:10
Average class size 16
Fees per annum *(full boarding)* £20,364–£27,162; *(day)* £13,890–£18,525

Inspiring Learning

Glenalmond College stretches its pupils – academically, physically, creatively, spiritually and emotionally. The strong and supportive community helps them to develop self-belief, generosity of spirit and independence of mind, enabling them to mature into successful, confident adults.

The school is located in 300 acres of stunning countryside just outside Perth, and is an inspirational environment for the 400 boys and girls aged 12 to 18 to grow and learn.

The school has an exceptional rural setting, offering unique outdoor opportunities for pupils to develop. It is away from the distractions of the city, but only one hour from Edinburgh or Glasgow with easy transport links from the rest of the United Kingdom and overseas. Boarders and day pupils are welcomed and all benefit from the outstanding pastoral care and individual attention that are central to the school's ethos.

The full seven-days-a-week boarding environment provides the time and commitment to develop each child's potential – making the most of every pupil's talents and nurturing academic excellence. The report of the most recent HMIe inspection noted the high levels of attainment and achievement, the outstanding pastoral care and the relationships among all the members of the schools as being among Glenalmond's particular strengths.

This pursuit of excellence, with every child encouraged to make the most of their academic abilities, is fundamental to the school's commitment to its pupils and is demonstrated by the results achieved. All Glenalmond pupils study for A-Levels, and the pass rate last year was 98 per cent, with 38 per cent at A* or A grade; the GCSE pass rate was 99 per cent, with 44 per cent at A* or A. However, education at Glenalmond extends far beyond the classroom and encompasses all aspects of the individual – personality, character and intellect – as well as interests and achievements.

Academic work is balanced with an extensive range of creative, sporting, social and adventure activities, and each child is encouraged to find those areas in which they can shine. Two pipe bands, a fantastic choir, acclaimed dramatic productions, lively debating and outstanding art and design shows offer opportunities for all. Rugby, hockey, lacrosse, cross-country, sailing and horse riding are just a few of the sports on offer. The school also has its own golf course - one of the best in the United Kingdom. Many pupils gain their silver and gold Duke of Edinburgh's Award; last year 24 per cent of all the Duke of Edinburgh Gold awards achieved by pupils in Scottish independent schools were achieved by Glenalmond pupils. There is a thriving Combined Cadet Force and Glenalmond is the most significant contributor to officer training for the British Army of any Scottish school. In addition, all Glenalmond pupils work with local charities and in the community.

The atmosphere at the school is happy and friendly; the pupils work hard and bring out the best in each other, both in work and play. Pupils from Glenalmond go on to achieve great things in life; most go to their first choice of university, with a good number each year gaining places at Oxford or Cambridge universities; in 2011, five Glenalmond pupils were offered places at Oxford or Cambridge. Our alumni have made their mark in the highest ranks of the major professions, including medicine, law, finance and education.

The experience of Glenalmond is perhaps best summed up by one of the current sixth-formers, who describes the College as a place where pupils are "inspired to learn, determined to achieve." Young people make friends for life, and form part of the worldwide family of Glenalmond pupils and former pupils who support and encourage each other through their school days and beyond. Parents and children are invited to visit the school at any time – please contact the Registrar, Jeremy Poulter, on 01738 842056 or registrar@glenalmondcollege.co.uk.

Strathallan School

Forgandenny, Perth, Perth and Kinross PH2 9EG **T**: (01738) 812546 **F**: (01738) 812549
E: marketing@strathallan.co.uk **W**: www.strathallan.co.uk

●🏠▲

Headmaster Mr B K Thompson MA
Founded 1913
School status Boarding and day for boys and girls
Religious denomination Non-denominational
Accredited by British Council, HMC, ISA, ISC, SCIS
Age range 9–18 (junior aged 9 to 13; senior school aged 13 to 18);
boarders from 9
No of pupils 550; *(full boarding)* 357; *Prep* 103; *Senior* 447
Sixth Form 197; *Girls* 239; *Boys* 311
Teacher:pupil ratio 1:7
Average class size 13
Fees per annum *(full boarding)* £18,780–£26,328; *(day)* £11,721–£17,865

Strathallan's ethos is providing the opportunities for all pupils to excel, challenging them, offering support and building confidence through a range of experiences. Central to this is academic success: 82 per cent of this year's A level entries were graded A*/B. We are also committed to high standards in sport, music, theatre and a range of other activities. Our focus is very much on the individual and ensuring they get the very best education. Located in 150 acres of safe, secure countryside, our unrivalled facilities are one of the best in the country and we are proud of our reputation for outstanding pastoral care. Being a member of the Strathallan community is a wonderful experience in itself but, vitally, it is also an outstanding preparation for the future. Scholarships fee assistance / sibling discounts / Forces discounts are also available.

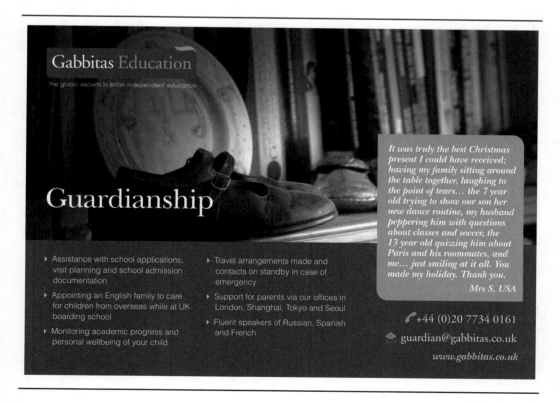

Symbol key

Gender

● Girls
● Boys
● Coed

Accommodation

🏠 Boarding only
🏠 Boarding and Day
🏠 Day and Boarding
🏠 Day only

International Bacc.

★ School offers IB

CReSTeD

◆ CReSTeD Registered

Has 6th Form

▲ Has 6th Form

3.3

Wales

MAP OF WALES

PROFILED SCHOOLS IN WALES

(Incorporating the counties of Blaenau Gwent, Bridgend, Caerphilly, Cardiff, Carmarthenshire, Ceredigion, Conwy, Cynon Taff, Denbighshire, Flintshire, Gwynedd, Merthyr, Tydfil, Monmouthshire, Neath Port Talbot, Newport, Pembrokeshire, Powys, Swansea, Torlean, Vale of Glamorgan, Wrexham)

Howell's School

Park Street, Denbigh, Denbighshire LL16 3EN **T**: (01745) 813631 **F**: (01745) 814443 **E**: enquiries@howells.org
W: www.howells.org
Contact enquiries@howells.org for queries, or to organize visits and taster days/stays.

●🏠▲

Academic Head Miss E Jones BSc (hons) PGCE MBA
Founded 1859
School status girls' independent boarding and day
Religious denomination Christian
Member of BHS, BSA, GSA, SHMIS
Accredited by GSA, SHMIS
Age range 3–18; *boarders from 7–18*
No of pupils 176
Average class size 15
Fees per annum *(full boarding)* £14,550–£20,700;
   (weekly) £14,550–£20,700; *(day)* £6,300–£11,700

Pupils at Howell's School are highly motivated and develop a very mature attitude to their school work. They feel safe, valued and settle in quickly – School Inspectorate ESTYN. Howell's School provides the perfect environment for your daughter to achieve her academic potential and to develop skills to last a lifetime and the confidence to achieve her dreams. An all-girls academic environment, with some co-educational enrichment activities. First-class range of facilities – comfortable boarding houses with WiFi and Skype, on-site equestrian centre, sports complex, performing arts weekends, watersports centre, recording studio, and vast 120-acre idyllic campus.

3.4

Schools in Continental Europe

Continental Europe

MAP OF SCHOOLS IN CONTINENTAL EUROPE

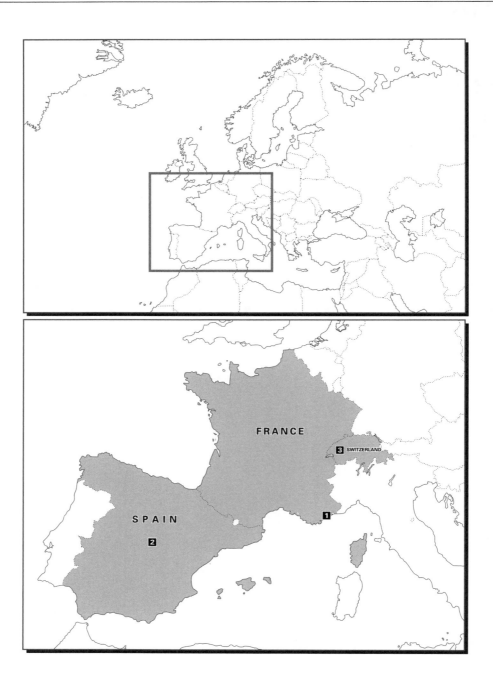

PROFILED SCHOOLS IN CONTINENTAL EUROPE

Mougins School

615 Avenue Dr Maurice Donat, Font de l'Orme, BP 401, 06251 Mougins Cedex, France **T**: (33) (0) 4 93 90 15 47
F: (33) (0) 4 93 75 31 40 **E**: information@mougins-school.com **W**: www.mougins-school.com

●🏠▲

Headmaster Mr B G Hickmore
Founded 1964
School status Co-educational independent day only
Religious denomination Non-denominational
Age range 3–18
No of pupils 454; *Nursery* 10; *Pre-prep* 20; *Prep* 130
Senior 230
Sixth Form 61; *Girls* 189; *Boys* 265
Teacher:pupil ratio 1:10
Average class size 22
Fees per annum *(day)* £4,540–£12,370

Mougins School is situated on the Côte d'Azur, north of Cannes and west of Nice, on a purpose-built campus. Facilities include a library, three science laboratories, IT centre, two art studios, music room, performing arts centre, gymnasium, all-weather football pitch and dining room. The school accepts pupils aged 3 to 18, representing over 30 nationalities. The school follows the British curriculum, modified to meet the needs of an international market with examinations in IGCSE, AS and A level. The caring family atmosphere complements the high quality of the teaching and helps to enhance the academic, cultural and physical development of our pupils. We offer a comprehensive education that produces excellent results, not only academically but also in the sporting and artistic domains, leading to entry to the world's leading universities.

Symbol key

Gender

● Girls
● Boys
● Coed

Accommodation

🏠 Boarding only
🏠 Boarding and Day
🏠 Day and Boarding
🏠 Day only

International Bacc.

★ School offers IB

CReSTeD

◆ CReSTeD Registered

Has 6th Form

▲ Has 6th Form

King's College Madrid

Paseo de los Andes, 35, 28761 Soto de Viuelas, Madrid, Spain **T**: (+34) 918 034 800 **F**: (+34) 918 036 557
E: info@kingscollege.es **W**: www.kingscollege.es
King's College School, La Moraleja

●♣🏠▲

Headmaster Mr D Johnson BEd (Hons) MSc (Oxon)
Founded 1969
College status Co-educational independent
Religious denomination Non-denominational
Member of BSA, HMC, NABSS **Accredited by** ISC
Age range 2–18; *boarders from* 13
No of pupils 1,987; *(boarding)* 20; *(full boarding)* 20; *Prep* 1250; *Senior* 571
Sixth Form 166; *Girls* 1,005; *Boys* 982
Teacher:pupil ratio 1:12
Average class size 25
Fees per annum *(full boarding)* £15,300–£16,700; *(day)* £5,000–£9,500

King's College Madrid is a co-educational day and boarding school following the English National Curriculum which prepares pupils for IGCSE and GCE A levels and offers a wide range of subjects at both levels. There are optional Spanish studies and preparation for Spanish university entrance examinations.

With almost 2,000 pupils of 48 nationalities, the school has a complement of 140 fully qualified teachers. All academic staff have British qualifications, except the Spanish teachers and some who teach modern languages.

The school has a reputation for high academic standards and excellent examination results with students going on to universities in Britain, USA, and Spain among others. An Oxbridge preparatory group works with the most able students to prepare university applications.

There are three King's College sites in Madrid: the main school in Soto de Viñuelas (Pre-nursery to Year 13), King's College School, La Moraleja (Nursery to Year 9 in September 2010) and King's Infant School, Chamartin (Nursery to Year 2).

The school has its own catering service and offers three-course midday meals. There is an optional bus service with a modern fleet of 25 vehicles covering Madrid and outlying areas for all three school sites.

The main school offers the following facilities – *Academic facilities:* Seven science laboratories, three multi-media computer centres, two libraries, two music rooms, art studio. Early Learning Centre, an auditorium with seating for 350 people and a music school for individual tuition.

Sports facilities: Gymnasium, judo room, fitness centre, 25-metre heated indoor swimming pool, 11-a-side and 5-a-side football pitches, floodlit multi-sports area, tennis courts, stables and riding school.

Boarding facilities: There are boarding facilities for boys and girls with rooms for one to two pupils over the age of 13. A brand new boarding house will open in the school grounds in September 2011. At present the residence is home to pupils from the UK, Russia, Japan as well as students from expatriate families living in Spain. Boarders enjoy access to many of the sports facilities at the weekends and after school.

There is a wide variety of optional activities including: music, ballet, handicrafts, performing arts, judo, riding, swimming and tennis.

Admission: The procedure for admission varies according to the age of the pupil. Importance is given to previous school records and from age 7 to 16 years candidates are required to sit entrance tests in mathematics and English.

Continental Europe

John F Kennedy International School

Chilchgasse 2, CH 3792 Saanen, Switzerland **T**: (0041) 33 744 1372 **F**: (0041) 33 744 8982 **E**: info@jfk.ch
W: www.jfk.ch

Director Mr Gareth Davies
Founded 1950
School status Co-educational independent boarding and day
Religious denomination Non-denominational
Member of CIS, ECIS, SGIS
Age range 5–14; *boarders from* 6
No of pupils 70; *(boarding)* 25; *(full boarding)* 25; *Pre-prep* 50; *Prep* 20
　Girls 35; *Boys* 35
Teacher:pupil ratio 1:7
Average class size 12
Fees per annum £CHF 54,000–40,0000; *(day)* £CHF 32,500–24,000

JFK was founded in 1950 in the village of Saanen, Switzerland, three kilometres from the world-famous resort of Gstaad. Features include small classes, a family-like atmosphere and well-balanced programmes emphasizing strong academic skills and good study habits. The curriculum has been especially designed for international schools and is based on a clear philosophy of international education in a time of rapid global change and endeavours to foster a 'global viewpoint'. The programme also reflects recent developments in our under-standing of how the brain works and how children learn. In addition, a conscious effort is made to take the learning process beyond the classroom through field trips, cultural activities and sports, including daily skiing in winter. Since 1973 the school has offered an outstanding summer camp for children 6 to 14.

PART FOUR

SCHOOLS BY CATEGORY

4.1

Classified listings

This section comprises schools listed alphabetically by category heading. Categories include *Boys Day School*, *Co-educational Day and Boarding School*, *Horse Riding and Mountain Biking Provision*, amongst others.

Each entry contains details, including website address and a brief description of the school's particular characteristics.

BOYS DAY & BOARDING SCHOOL

ALDWICKBURY SCHOOL
Wheathampstead Road,
Harpenden, Hertfordshire AL5 1AD
T: (01582) 713022
F: (01582) 767696
E: registrar@aldwickbury.org.uk
W: www.aldwickbury.org.uk
A day and boarding school for boys ages 4–13 in Harpenden. Aldwickbury is renowned for polite, friendly pupils who move on to a wide range of senior schools.

BOYS DAY SCHOOL

THE NEW BEACON
Brittains Lane, Sevenoaks, Kent
TN13 2PB
T: (01732) 452131
F: (01732) 459509
E: admin@newbeacon.org.uk
W: www.newbeacon.kent.org.uk
There is no doubt that a clear mission, high expectations and excellent teaching lead to achievement: they can all be found here in class, sports, performances, art, design and technology. . . .. New Beacon boys strive for personal excellence and it is our ambition to help them in this and in reaching their full potential.

CO-EDUCATIONAL DAY AND BOARDING SCHOOL

ABBERLEY HALL
Abberley Hall, Worcester,
Worcestershire WR6 6DD
T: (01299) 896275
F: (01299) 896875
E: john.walker@abberleyhall.co.uk
W: www.abberleyhall.co.uk
Abberley Hall is a co-educational full boarding school for 8–13 year olds preparing pupils for all major public schools, providing academic, sporting and social grounding required for sustained success

BATH ACADEMY
27 Queen Square, Bath, Somerset
BA1 2HX
T: (01225) 334577
F: (01225) 482414
E: principal@bathacademy.co.uk
W: www.bathacademy.co.uk
Bath Academy is an International College Offering the University Foundation Programme, GCSE, A level and International GCSE and A level (CIE). Accommodation is available in hostels or homestay.

GREAT BALLARD SCHOOL
Eartham, Chichester,
West Sussex PO18 0LR
T: (01243) 814236
F: (01243) 814586
E: office@greatballard.co.uk
W: www.greatballard.co.uk
Friendly school with small
teaching groups for children
aged 2–13. Emphasis on the
individual and a broad
curriculum. Flexi boarding is a
popular option. Extra Arts classes
on a Saturday morning.

LICHFIELD CATHEDRAL SCHOOL
The Close, Lichfield,
Staffordshire WS13 7LH
T: (01543) 306170
F: (01543) 306176
E: reception@
lichfieldcathedralschool.com
W: www.lichfieldcathedralschool.
com
We aim to provide all children
from Nursery to Secondary with a
thorough academic foundation
together with a range of
opportunities to develop
individual interests and talents.
There is strong emphasis on
pastoral care, providing a secure
and ordered framework through
which all children can develop
their self-esteem and find
success.

CO-EDUCATIONAL DAY SCHOOL

ALBEMARLE INDEPENDENT COLLEGE
18 Dunraven Street, London
W1K 7FE
T: (020) 7409 7273
F: (020) 7629 9146
E: james@eytle.com
W: www.albemarle.org.uk
Based in heart of central London
Albemarle is an independent
sixth form college offering a wide
range of GCSE and A-level
subjects, with emphasis on
producing excellent exam
results.

AUSTIN FRIARS ST MONICA'S SCHOOL
Etterby Scaur, Carlisle, Cumbria
CA3 9PB
T: (01228) 528042
F: (01228) 810327
E: office@austinfriars.cumbria.
sch.uk
W: www.austinfriars.cumbria.
sch.uk
Academic achievement
underpins all that we do, and the
outstanding results of boys and
girls from 3 -18 speak for
themselves. Music, drama,
creative and physical activity
contribute a vital part in
educating the whole student. All
are welcome in the supportive
school community, underpinned
by Christian values, and are
encouraged to share their talents
with and for others.

CHEADLE HULME SCHOOL
Claremont Road, Cheadle,
Cheshire SK8 6EF
T: (0161) 488 3330
F: (0161) 488 3344
E: registrar@chschool.co.uk
W: www.cheadlehulmeschool.
co.uk
With high academic standards,
exceptional extra-curricular
opportunities and extensive
facilities, Cheadle Hulme School
provides an outstanding
education for boys and girls aged
4 to 18.

HALLFIELD SCHOOL
48 Church Road, Birmingham,
West Midlands B15 3SJ
T: (0121) 454 1496
F: (0121) 454 9182
E: admissions@hallfield.bham.
sch.uk
W: www.hallfieldschool.co.uk
Hallfield School is an academic
school, taking children from 3
months to 11 years. Hallfield
prepares its pupils for entrance
and scholarship examinations at
11+.

KINGSTON GRAMMAR SCHOOL
London Road, Kingston-upon-
Thames, Surrey KT2 6PY
T: (020) 8546 5875
F: (020) 8547 1499
E: registar@kgs.org.uk
W: www.kgs.org.uk
Kingston Grammar School is
proud of the outstanding
achievements of its pupils
academically and in sport, music,
drama and a wide range of other
co-curricular activities.

LONGWOOD SCHOOL
Bushey Hall Drive, Bushey,
Hertfordshire WD23 2QG
T: (01923) 253715
F: (01923) 222760
E: info@longwoodschool.co.uk
W: www.longwoodschool.co.uk
Day Nursery and Primary School
offering continual education for
children from three months to
eleven years in a truly family
atmosphere. Our aim is to
provide a happy, stimulating,
healthy and safe environment
where all children can attain high
standards and develop into well-
balanced citizens. Open
weekdays between 7am and
7pm throughout the year, except
Bank Holidays.

ST MARTIN'S SCHOOL
22 Goodwyn Avenue, London
NW7 3RG
T: (020) 8959 1965
F: (020) 8959 9065
E: info@stmartinsmillhill.co.uk
W: www.stmartinsmillhill.co.uk
"If children are happy and feel
safe and secure in their
environment they will learn."
St. Martin's coed prep school
established, in its own right, for
many years has provided
generations of pupils a happy
and successful start to their
school life. We look forward to
welcoming you to our school.

CO-EDUCATIONAL PREPARATORY DAY SCHOOL

LADYMEDE
Little Kimble, Aylesbury,
Buckinghamshire HP17 0XP
T: (01844) 346154
F: (01844) 275660
E: office@ladymede.com
W: www.ladymedeschool.
  bucks.sch.uk
Ladymede is a small, friendly
school, where an opportunity for
learning is never missed, and
children received an exciting
education combined with sound
traditional values.

CO-EDUCATIONAL PREPARATORY SCHOOL

ELM GREEN PREPARATORY SCHOOL
Parsonage Lane, Chelmsford,
Essex CM3 4SU
T: (01245) 225230
F: (01245) 226008
E: admin@elmgreen.essex.sch.uk
W: www.elmgreen.essex.sch.uk
Elm Green Preparatory School is a
thriving educational community in
an idyllic woodland setting,
offering excellent academic,
sporting and musical
opportunities with outstanding
pastoral care.

COED PREP DAY AND BOARDING

FORRES SANDLE MANOR
Station Road, Fordingbridge,
Hampshire SP6 1NS
T: (01425) 653181
F: (01425) 655676
E: office@fsmschool.com
W: www.fsmschool.com
FSM is more than a school – it is an
extended family, the members of
which know and care for each
other at all times. Our aim is to
ensure that children are happy
and secure since only then can
they succeed.

DAY & NURSERY SCHOOL

QUAINTON HALL SCHOOL
91 Hindes Road, Harrow,
Middlesex HA1 1RX
T: (020) 8427 1304
F: (020) 8861 8861
E: admin@quaintonhall.org.uk
W: www.quaintonhall.org.uk
Quainton Hall School is an IAPS
day preparatory school & nursery
for children aged 2½ to 13 years
offering a very wide range of
academic, sporting and extra-
curricular opportunities.

GIRLS BOARDING & DAY SCHOOL

ABBOTS BROMLEY SCHOOL FOR GIRLS
Abbots Bromley, Staffordshire
WS15 3BW
T: (01283) 840232
F: (01283) 840988
E: registar@abbotsbromley.net
W: www.abbotsbromley.
  staffs.sch.uk
Located in a beautiful
Staffordshire village, Abbots
Bromley School for Girls provides
a high quality all-round education
for 300 girls aged 3–18.

RATHDOWN SCHOOL
Upper Glenageary Road
T: (003531) 2853133
F: (003531) 2840738
E: registrar@rathdownschool.ie
W: www.rathdownschool.ie
Rathdown girls develop the skills
and character to become life-long
learners who are successful,
responsible and active citizens of
the global community. We
welcome boarders of all
nationalities. All are encouraged to
achieve their individual potential in
all aspects of their lives;
academic, sporting, artistic and
spiritual. Academic achievements,
in particular, are outstanding.

GIRLS DAY SCHOOL

THE STUDY PREPARATORY SCHOOL
Wilberforce House, London
SW19 4UN
T: (020) 8947 6969
F: (020) 8944 5975
E: wilberforce@thestudyprep.
  co.uk
W: www.thestudyprep.co.uk
The Study is a long established,
prep school for girls aged four to
eleven, situated on the borders of
leafy Wimbledon Common.
A specialist in educating young
girls, the study feeds some of the
best senior schools in the country.
Pupils are attracted from
Wimbledon and across South
West London and Surrey. 'A very
special community that the girls
and their teachers create
together.'

HORSE RIDING AND MOUNTAIN BIKING PROVISION

BEDSTONE COLLEGE
Bucknell, Shropshire SY7 0BG
T: (01547) 530303
F: (01547) 530740
E: admissions@bedstone.org
W: www.bedstone.org
Bedstone College is South
Shropshire's leading independent,
co-educational, boarding and day
school catering for children 3 to 18
years. It enjoys a warm and
supportive family atmosphere,
where each child is encouraged to
fulfil their potential.

OUTSTANDING ACADEMIC ACHIEVEMENTS

LEIGHTON PARK SCHOOL
Shinfield Road, Reading,
Berkshire RG2 7ED
T: (0118) 987 9600
F: (0118) 987 9625
E: admissions@leightonpark.com
W: www.leightonpark.com
Founded in 1890, the school offers outstanding academic teaching and facilities, first class pastoral care, and a wealth of cultural, sporting and extra-curricular opportunities, all set in 60 acres of beautiful parkland, near Reading.

PART FIVE

Reference Section

5.1

Scholarships

The following is based on information provided by schools. The entry age, where given, is the age at which scholarships are available to pupils. Please note that for each school, not every scholarship listed is offered at all the stated entry ages. Further details of scholarships available at individual schools may be found in Part Three: School Profiles. The abbreviations are as follows:

A	Art		I	Instrumental music/Choral
AA	Academic ability		O	All-round ability
D	Drama		S	Science
G	Games		6	Sixth Form entry

ENGLAND

BEDFORDSHIRE

Bedford High School for Girls, Bedford	6 AA I O
Bedford Modern School, Bedford	
Entry age: 11+	A D G
Bedford Preparatory School, Bedford	AA
Bedford School, Bedford	
Entry age: 11, 13 and 16	6 AA G I
Moorlands School, Luton Entry age: 7+	A AA I O

BERKSHIRE

The Abbey School, Reading	
Entry age: 11+,13+,16+	6 A AA D G I O
The Ark School, Reading Entry age: 7	A AA I
Bearwood College, Wokingham	
Entry age: 11/13	6 A AA D G I O S
Bradfield College, Reading	
Entry age: 13+, 16+	6 A AA D G I O
Brigidine School Windsor, Windsor	
Entry age: 11, 16	6 A AA D G I
Brockhurst and Marlston House Schools, Newbury	A AA D G I O S
Cheam School, Newbury Entry age: Bursary Available from 8 years old	AA
Claires Court School, Maidenhead	6 A AA D G I O
Claires Court Schools, The College, Maidenhead	6 A AA D G I O

Claires Court Schools, Ridgeway, Maidenhead	A AA D G I O
Dolphin School, Reading	A AA D G I O
Downe House, Thatcham	
Entry age: 11+, 12+, 13+ and 16+	6 A AA G I
Eagle House, Sandhurst Entry age: 11	AA I
Elstree School, Reading Entry age: 7	AA
Eton College, Windsor	6 AA I
Heathfield School, Ascot	6 AA O
Hemdean House School, Reading	AA I O
Holme Grange School, Wokingham	
Entry age: 11+	AA O
Horris Hill School, Newbury	AA O
Hurst Lodge School, Ascot	
Entry age: various	6 A AA D I O
Langley Manor School, Langley	AA G I O
Long Close School, Slough Entry age: 7yrs	AA G I O
Luckley-Oakfield School, Wokingham	
Entry age: 11	6 A AA G I
LVS Ascot, Ascot	6 A AA D G I
The Marist Senior School, Ascot	
Entry age: 11	6 A AA D G I O
The Oratory School, Reading	
Entry age: 11+, 13+	6 A AA D G I O
Padworth College, Reading	
Entry age: 14, 16	6 A AA
Pangbourne College, Pangbourne	
Entry age: 11+, 13+, 16+	6 A AA D G I O S

Papplewick School, Ascot Entry age: 6–11 A AA G I O
Queen Anne's School, Reading
  Entry age: 11+, 13+, 16+   6 A AA D G I O
Reading Blue Coat School, Reading   A AA I
St Edward's School, Reading   AA O
St Gabriel's, Newbury
  Entry age: 11+, 13+, 16+   6 A AA D G I
St George's School, Ascot Entry age: 11+, 16+A AA D I
St George's School, Windsor Entry age: 7+, 9+   AA I
St Joseph's College, Reading   6 AA D G I O
St Mary's School, Ascot, Ascot Entry age: 11+, 13+ &
  16+   6 A AA G I S
St Piran's Preparatory School, Maidenhead
  Entry age: Scholarship entry – Year 3.
  Bursary applications accepted for
  any age.   A AA G I O
Sunningdale School, Sunningdale   A AA D G I O
Thorngrove School, Newbury   AA G I O
Upton House School, Windsor   A AA
Wellington College, Crowthorne   6 A AA D G I O

BRISTOL

Badminton School, Bristol
  Entry age: 11+, 13+ and 16+   6 A AA I O
Bristol Cathedral School, Bristol
  Entry age: 11+, 13+, 16+   6 AA G I
Bristol Grammar School, Bristol
  Entry age: 7, 11, 13, 16   6 A AA D G I
Clifton College, Bristol
  Entry age: 13+, 16+   6 A AA G I O
Clifton College Pre-Prep – Butcombe, Bristol   O
Clifton College Preparatory School, Bristol Entry age:
  11+   AA G I O
Clifton High School, Bristol
  Entry age: 11+, 13+, 16+   6 AA G I
Colston's Collegiate School, Bristol 6 A AA D G I O
The Downs School, Wraxall Entry age: 8+ A AA G I O
Fairfield School, Backwell   AA
Queen Elizabeth's Hospital, Bristol
  Entry age: 11, 13, 16   6 AA I S
The Red Maids' School, Bristol
  Entry age: 11+,13+, 16+   6 AA G I O
Redland High School for Girls, Bristol
  Entry age: 9, 11, 16   6 A AA G I
St Ursula's High School, Westbury-on-Trym   AA
Torwood House School, Redland   O

BUCKINGHAMSHIRE

Bury Lawn School, Milton Keynes   6
Davenies School, Beaconsfield   A AA G I O
Gateway School, Great Missenden   O
Godstowe Preparatory School, High Wycombe
  Entry age: 8, 11   AA
High March School, Beaconsfield
  Entry age: 8 and 10   AA
Ladymede, Aylesbury Entry age: 7+   AA O
Milton Keynes Preparatory School,
  Milton Keynes   A AA G I
Pipers Corner School, High Wycombe
  Entry age: 11+, 16+   6 A AA D G I O

St Mary's School, Gerrards Cross
  Entry age: 7+/11+/16+ for scholarships,
  any age for bursaries   6 AA I
Stowe School, Buckingham
  Entry age: 13, 16   6 A AA G I O
Swanbourne House School, Milton Keynes
  Entry age: 11+   AA G I
Thornton College Convent of Jesus and Mary,
  Milton Keynes Entry age: 11   AA
Thorpe House School, Gerrards Cross   AA
Wycombe Abbey School, High Wycombe
  Entry age: 11+, 13+ and sixth form entry   6 AA I

CAMBRIDGESHIRE

Bellerbys College & Embassy CES Cambridge,
  Cambridge   AA O
Cambridge Centre for Sixth-form Studies,
  Cambridge   6 AA O
CATS College Cambridge, Cambridge
  Entry age: 6th Form entry (16+)   6 AA S
Kimbolton School, Huntingdon
  Entry age: 11+, 13+, 16+   6 A AA G I O
The King's School Ely, Ely
  Entry age: 11+   6 A AA D G I
The Leys School, Cambridge
  Entry age: 11, 13, 16   6 A AA D G I O
MPW (Mander Portman Woodward),
  Cambridge   6 AA O
The Perse School, Cambridge
  Entry age: Year 7 and Year 9 – Academic Scholarship
  (based on entrance tests), Music Scholarship
  (audition).
  Sixth Form – Academic Scholarship (exam), Art
  Scholarship (interview), General Award (interview),
  Music Scholarship (audition).   6 A AA I
The Perse School for Girls, Cambridge   6 I
The Peterborough School, Peterborough
  Entry age: 11, 16   6 A AA G I O
St Faith's, Cambridge Entry age: 7+, 11+   AA
St John's College School, Cambridge   I
St Mary's School, Cambridge, Cambridge   6 AA I
Sancton Wood School, Cambridge   AA O

CHANNEL ISLANDS

Elizabeth College, Guernsey   I O
Ormer House Preparatory School, Alderney   AA
St George's Preparatory School, Jersey
  Entry age: 7+   A AA G I O S
St Michael's Preparatory School, Jersey   AA
Victoria College, Jersey   AA I S

CHESHIRE

Abbey Gate College, Chester
  Entry age: 11+, 16+   6 AA I
Abbey Gate School, Chester Entry age: 5 and 7   AA
Alderley Edge School for Girls,
  Alderley Edge   6 A AA G I
Beech Hall School, Macclesfield   O
Brabyns School, Stockport   AA

Cransley School, Northwich
Entry age: 11+   A AA G I O S
Culcheth Hall, Altrincham   AA
The Grange School, Northwich   6 AA I
Hammond School, Chester   AA D I
Hulme Hall Schools, Cheadle   AA
The King's School, Macclesfield   AA I
Merton House, Chester   AA G
The Ryleys, Alderley Edge   AA O
Stockport Grammar School, Stockport
Entry age: 11+   I
Terra Nova School, Holmes Chapel   A AA D G I O S

CORNWALL

Gems Bolitho School, Penzance
Entry age: 7+   6 A AA G I O
Polwhele House School, Truro   AA I
Roselyon, Par   AA I O
St Joseph's School, Launceston
Entry age: 7+, 11+   AA G I O
St Petroc's School, Bude
Entry age: 7+   A AA D G I O S
St Piran's School, Hayle   O
Truro High School, Truro
Entry age: 11+, 16+   6 A AA G I
Truro School, Truro   6 A AA G I

CUMBRIA

Austin Friars St Monica's School, Carlisle
Entry age: 11+   AA G I
Casterton School, Kirkby Lonsdale   6 A AA D G I O
Chetwynde School, Barrow-in-Furness   6 AA G O
Holme Park School, Kendal Entry age: 7+   AA D G O S
Lime House School, Carlisle   AA G O
St Bees School, St Bees   6 A AA G I
Sedbergh Junior School, Sedbergh
Entry age: 11   A AA D G I O
Sedbergh School, Sedbergh
Entry age: 13+, 16+, 17+   6 A AA D G I O
Windermere School, Windermere
Entry age: 11+, 13+, 16+   6 A AA D G I O

DERBYSHIRE

Derby Grammar School, Derby   6 AA G I
Derby High School, Derby
Entry age: 11/16   6 AA G I O
Foremarke Hall, Derby Entry age: 7+ and 11+
Scholarships   A AA D G I
Mount St Mary's College, Spinkhill
Entry age: 11+, 13+, 15+   6 AA G I O
Ockbrook School, Derby   A AA D G I
Repton School, Derby
Entry age: 13+, 16+   6 A AA D G I O
St Wystan's School, Repton Entry age: 7+   AA

DEVON

The Abbey School, Torquay   AA O
Blundell's School, Tiverton
Entry age: 11, 13, 16   6 A AA G I O

Bramdean School, Exeter Entry age: 7/11   AA D G I
Edgehill College, Bideford   6 A AA D G I O
Exeter Cathedral School, Exeter
Entry age: 7/12+   AA I O
Exeter Junior School, Exeter Entry age: 7+, 8+   AA
Exeter School, Exeter
Entry age: 7, 11, 12, 13   6 A AA I S
Kelly College, Tavistock
Entry age: 11, 13, 16   6 A AA G I O
Kingsley School, Bideford
Entry age: 11, 12, 13, 16+   6 A AA D G I O
The Maynard School, Exeter
Entry age: 7+, 9+, 16+   6 A AA G I O S
Mount House School, Tavistock
Entry age: Generally in the latter years of the School
eg Year 7, but all will be considered.   AA G I
Plymouth College, Plymouth
Entry age: 11, 13, 16   6 A AA G I
Plymouth College Prepratory School, Plymouth
Entry age: All scholarships are on entry to senior
school at Year 7 (aged 11 years).   A AA D G I O
St Christophers School, Totnes   O
St Margaret's School, Exeter   6 A AA D I
St Michael's, Barnstaple   A AA D G I O
St Peter's School, Exmouth   A AA G I O
St Wilfrid's School, Exeter Entry age: 7   O
Stoodley Knowle School, Torquay   6 O
Stover School, Newton Abbot
Entry age: Scholarships at 7+, 11+, 13+ & Sixth
Form.   6 A AA D G I O S
Shebbear College, Beaworthy
Entry age: 11+, 13+, 16+   6 A AA D G I O
Tower House School, Paignton
Entry age: 11   A AA D G I O S
Trinity School, Teignmouth
Entry age: Entry is considered at all times to
allow young people to get the best
education   6 A AA D G I O S
West Buckland Preparatory School, Barnstaple   AA O
West Buckland School, Barnstaple   6 AA G I O

DORSET

Bournemouth Collegiate School, Bournemouth
Entry age: Means tested bursary at 11+. Scholarships
at 11+, 12+, 13+, 16+   6 A AA D G I O
Bryanston School, Blandford Forum
Entry age: 13, 16   6 A AA G I O S
Canford School, Wimborne
Entry age: 13+ and 16+   6 A AA D G I
Castle Court Preparatory School, Wimborne   AA I
Clayesmore, Blandford Forum
Entry age: Prep School: 8 years of age
Senior School 13 years and 16 years of
age   6 A AA G I O
Clayesmore Preparatory School, Blandford Forum
Entry age: from Year 3   A AA G I O
Dumpton School, Wimborne   AA O
Knighton House, Blandford Forum   A AA D G I O
Leweston School, Sherborne
Entry age: 7–13,16   6 A AA D G I O S
Milton Abbey School, Blandford Forum
Entry age: 13 and 16   6 A AA D G I

The Park School, Bournemouth   AA I O
Port Regis Preparatory School, Shaftesbury
    Entry age: Your child needs to be aged 7 and under
    12 years of age on 1st September.   A AA G I O
St Martin's School, Bournemouth   AA G O
St Mary's School, Dorset, Shaftesbury
    Entry age: 11+, 13+, 16+   6 A AA G I
Sherborne Girls, Sherborne   6 A AA I O
Sherborne School, Sherborne
    Entry age: 13+, 16+   6 A AA D G I
Talbot Heath, Bournemouth   6 A AA D G I O
Thornlow Preparatory School, Weymouth   AA G
Yarrells School, Poole Entry age: 8+, to start
    at Year 4.   AA G I O

COUNTY DURHAM

Barnard Castle School, Barnard Castle
    Entry age: 11+ and Sixth Form   6 A AA D G I O
The Chorister School, Durham   I
Durham High School For Girls, Durham
    Entry age: 11, 16   6 A AA D G I
Durham School, Durham
    Entry age: 7, 11, 13, 16   6 A AA D G I
Hurworth House School, Darlington   AA G O
Polam Hall, Darlington
    Entry age: 7, 11, 14, 16   6 AA G I O
Yarm at Raventhorpe School, Darlington   O

ESSEX

Alleyn Court Preparatory School, Southend-on-Sea
    Entry age: 7   AA I O
Bancroft's School, Woodford Green
    Entry age: 7, 11, 13, 16   6 AA I
Brentwood School, Brentwood
    Entry age: 11, 16   6 A AA D G I O
Chigwell School, Chigwell   A AA D I O
Colchester High School, Colchester   AA
College Saint-Pierre, Leigh-on-Sea   O
Cranbrook, Ilford   A AA I O
Crowstone Preparatory School, Westcliff-on-Sea   O
The Daiglen School, Buckhurst Hill   AA
Dame Bradbury's School, Saffron Walden   I
Felsted School, Felsted
    Entry age: Ages 11, 13 and 16   6 A AA D G I O
Friends' School, Saffron Walden
    Entry age: 11, 13, 16   6 A AA G I
Gosfield School, Halstead Entry age: All   6 AA G O
Herington House School, Brentwood   D G I O
Holmwood House, Colchester   A AA G I O
Loyola Preparatory School, Buckhurst Hill   AA
New Hall School, Chelmsford
    Entry age: 3–18   6 AA D G I O
St Aubyn's School, Woodford Green   AA
St Hilda's School, Westcliff-on-Sea   O
St John's School, Billericay   O
St Margaret's School, Halstead
    Entry age: 8+   A AA G I
St Mary's School, Colchester Entry age: 11+   O

GLOUCESTERSHIRE

Berkhampstead School, Cheltenham   AA G I
Bredon School, Tewkesbury
    Entry age: 5 – 15 years   A AA G I O
Cheltenham College, Cheltenham
    Entry age: 13, 16   6 A AA D G I O S
Cheltenham College Junior School, Cheltenham
    Entry age: 11+   A AA G I
Cheltenham Ladies' College, Cheltenham
    Entry age: 11+, 12+, 13+ and 16+   6 A AA G I
Dean Close Preparatory School, Cheltenham
    Entry age: 7+, 11+ chorister awards offered
    ages 7–11   A AA G I O
Dean Close School, Cheltenham
    Entry age: 11+, 13+, 16+   6 A AA D G I O
Hatherop Castle School, Cirencester
    Entry age: 7+   AA D G I O
The King's School, Gloucester
    Entry age: 11+, 13+, 16+   6 A AA D G I O
Rendcomb College, Cirencester
    Entry age: 11, 13, 16   6 A AA D G I O
The Richard Pate School, Cheltenham
    Entry age: 7+   AA
Rose Hill School, Wotton-under-Edge   A AA D G I O
St Edward's School Cheltenham, Cheltenham
    Entry age: At Year 7 entry   6 A AA D G I O
Westonbirt School, Tetbury   6 A AA D G I O S
Wycliffe College, Stonehouse
    Entry age: 11+, 13+ and
    Sixth Form   6 A AA D G I O
Wycliffe Preparatory School, Stonehouse
    Entry age: 11   A AA D G I

HAMPSHIRE

Alton College, Alton   O
Alton Convent School, Alton Entry age: 11/16   6 AA I
Ballard School, New Milton
    Entry age: Year 3 and Year 6   A AA G I O
Bedales School, Petersfield   6 A AA I
Boundary Oak School, Fareham   AA G I
Brockwood Park School, Bramdean   O
Daneshill School, Basingstoke Entry age: Scholarship
    entries are available at Year 4 (8 years old) and Year
    7 (11 years old)   A AA D G I O S
Ditcham Park School, Petersfield Entry age: 11   AA I
Dunhurst (Bedales Junior School), Petersfield   I
Durlston Court, New Milton Entry age: Over 7 in
    September of year of entry   A AA G I
Farnborough Hill, Farnborough
    Entry age: 11+ and 16+.   6 A AA G I
The Gregg School, Southampton   A AA I
Hampshire Collegiate School, UCST,
    Romsey   6 A AA D G I O S
Highfield School, Liphook   AA
Hordle Walhampton School, Lymington   AA I O
King Edward VI School, Southampton
    Entry age: 11+, 13+, 16+   6 A AA D I S
Lord Wandsworth College, Hook
    Entry age: 11+, 13+, 16+   6 A AA D G I O
Marycourt School, Gosport Entry age: 7   O
Mayville High School, Southsea   A AA D G I
Meoncross School, Fareham Entry age: 11   AA

The Pilgrims' School, Winchester | I
The Portsmouth Grammar School,
   Portsmouth | 6 A AA D G I O S
Portsmouth High School GDST, Southsea
   Entry age: 11+, 13+, 16+ | 6 A AA D G I
Prince's Mead School, Winchester | A AA G I
Ramshill School, Petersfield | 6 AA I
Rookesbury Park School, Portsmouth | AA I
Rookwood School, Andover | AA G I
St John's College, Southsea | 6 AA G I O
St Mary's College, Southampton | AA
St Neot's School, Hook | O
St Nicholas' School, Fleet Entry age: 11, 13 | AA I O
St Swithun's School, Winchester
   Entry age: 11+, 13+, 16+ | 6 AA I
The Stroud School, Romsey | A AA D G I O
Sherborne House School, Eastleigh | A AA G I O
Sherfield School, Hook | 6 A AA D G I O S
Winchester College, Winchester
   Entry age: 13, 16 | 6 AA I
Wykeham House School, Fareham | AA
Yateley Manor Preparatory School, Yateley
   Entry age: 7+ | AA G I O

HEREFORDSHIRE

Hereford Cathedral School, Hereford
   Entry age: Years 7, 9 and Sixth Form. 6 A AA G I O
Lucton School, Leominster
   Entry age: 11, 13, 16 | 6 A AA D G I O S
St Richard's, Bromyard | AA

HERTFORDSHIRE

Abbot's Hill School, Hemel Hempstead
   Entry age: 11 | A AA G I O
Berkhamsted School, Berkhamsted | 6 A AA G I
Berkhamsted School, Berkhamsted | AA
Bishop's Stortford College, Bishop's Stortford
   Entry age: 11+, 13+, 16+ | 6 A AA I O
Bishop's Stortford College Junior School, Bishop's
   Stortford Entry age: 10+ and 11+ years | A AA I
Edge Grove, Watford
   Entry age: 7–13 yrs | AA G I O
Haberdashers' Aske's Boys' School, Elstree
   Entry age: 11, 13 | AA I
Haberdashers' Aske's School for Girls, Elstree | AA I
Haileybury, Hertford
   Entry age: 11, 13, 16 | 6 A AA G I O
Haresfoot Preparatory School, Berkhamsted
   Entry age: Year 3
   Bursaries from Reception up | A AA D I O
Heath Mount School, Hertford
   Entry age: 7+, 11+ | A AA I
High Elms Manor School, Watford | AA O
Immanuel College, Bushey
   Entry age: 4/11/16 | 6 A AA I
The Junior School, Bishop's Stortford College, Bishop's
   Stortford
   Entry age: Academic and Music scholarships
   (under 11 and 12)
   Art scholarship (under 12) | A AA I O

Lockers Park, Hemel Hempstead
   Entry age: From Year 3 (7 years) | A AA D G I O S
The Purcell School, Bushey | I
Queenswood, Hatfield | 6 AA D G I
The Royal Masonic School for Girls, Rickmansworth
   Entry age: 7, 11, 16 | 6 A AA D G I O
St Albans High School for Girls, St Albans
   Entry age: 11+ and 16+ | 6 AA I O
St Albans School, St Albans
   Entry age: 11+, 13+, 16+ | 6 A AA I
St Christopher School, Letchworth Garden City
   Entry age: ages from 11. Specific Sixth Form
   bursaries also available. | 6 AA
St Columba's College, St Albans
   Entry age: 11+/13+ | 6 AA I O
St Edmund's College and Prep School, Ware
   Entry age: 7+, 11+ and 16+ | 6 A AA G I O
St Francis' College, Letchworth
   Garden City | 6 AA D G I
St Margaret's School, Bushey | 6 A AA I O
Stanborough School, Watford | AA G I
Tring Park School for the Performing Arts, Tring
   Entry age: From 8 – 16 | D
Westbrook Hay Preparatory School, Hemel Hempstead
   Entry age: 8+ | AA G O

ISLE OF MAN

King William's College, Castletown
   Entry age: 11 and 16 | 6 AA D G I O

ISLE OF WIGHT

Ryde School, Ryde | 6 AA I

KENT

Ashford School, Ashford | 6 A AA D G I O
Babington House School, Chislehurst | AA D G I O
Beechwood Sacred Heart School, Tunbridge Wells
   Entry age: 11+, 13+, 16+ | 6 A AA D G I
Benenden School, Cranbrook
   Entry age: 11, 13, 16 | 6 A AA G I
Bethany School, Cranbrook
   Entry age: 11+, 13+, 16+ | 6 A AA D G I
Bishop Challoner RC School, Bromley
   Entry age: 11+ | AA I
Bromley High School GDST, Bromley
   Entry age: 11/16+ | 6 A AA G I
CATS College Canterbury, Canterbury
   Entry age: At 6th Form (16+) | 6 AA S
Cobham Hall, Gravesend
   Entry age: 11+, 13+, 6th Form | 6 A AA D G I O
Cranbrook School, Cranbrook | I
Darul Uloom London, Chislehurst | AA G O S
Derwent Lodge School for Girls, Tonbridge | AA
Dover College, Dover
   Entry age: 11, 13, 16 | 6 A AA G I O
Duke of York's Royal Military School,
   Dover | 6 A AA G I
Elliott Park School, Sheerness | O
Farringtons School, Chislehurst | 6 A AA D G I

Fosse Bank School, Tonbridge	G
Gad's Hill School, Rochester	
Entry age: 11	A AA D G I O
Haddon Dene School, Broadstairs	O
Hilden Grange School, Tonbridge	AA I
Holmewood House, Tunbridge Wells	
Entry age: Year 3 and above	AA
Kent College, Canterbury	
Entry age: 8, 11, 13, 16+	6 A AA D G I O
Kent College Pembury, Tunbridge Wells	
Entry age: 11, 13, 16	6 A AA D G I O
King's Preparatory School, Rochester	AA I
King's Rochester, Rochester	6 AA I
The King's School, Canterbury	6 A AA I
Merton Court Preparatory School, Sidcup	AA D G I O
Northbourne Park School, Deal	AA G I O
Rochester Independent College,	
Rochester	6 A AA D I O S
St Christopher's School, Canterbury	O
St Edmund's School Canterbury, Canterbury	
Entry age: 11+, 13+, 16+	6 A AA D G I O
St Edmunds Junior School, Canterbury	
Entry age: 11	AA G I
St Lawrence College, Ramsgate	
Entry age: 8, 11, 13, 16	6 A AA G I O
St Lawrence College Junior School, Ramsgate	
Entry age: 7.	AA G
St Michael's School, Sevenoaks	
Entry age: 7	AA G I O
Sackville School, Tonbridge	6 A AA D G I
Sevenoaks School, Sevenoaks	
Entry age: 11+, 13+, 16+	6 A AA G I
Solefield School, Sevenoaks	I
Spring Grove School, Ashford	
Entry age: 7+	A AA D G I O S
Sutton Valence School, Sutton Valence	
Entry age: 11+, 13+, 16+	6 A AA D G I
Tonbridge School, Tonbridge	
Entry age: 13+, 16+	6 A AA D G I O
Walthamstow Hall, Sevenoaks	
Entry age: 11+, 13+, 16+	6 A AA D G I
Yardley Court Preparatory School, Tonbridge	AA O

LANCASHIRE

Arnold School, Blackpool	
Entry age: 11+, 16+	6 A AA D G I O
Bury Grammar School Boys, Bury	6 AA
Bury Grammar School Girls, Bury	
Entry age: 11	6 AA
Clevelands Preparatory School, Bolton	AA O
Firwood Manor Prep School, Oldham	AA O
Heathland College, Accrington	AA I
The Hulme Grammar School for Girls, Oldham	AA
King Edward VII and Queen Mary School,	
Lytham St Annes Entry age: 11, 16	6 AA G I
Kingswood College Trust, Ormskirk	AA G I
Kirkham Grammar School, Preston	
Entry age: 11 years	
16 years	6 AA G I
Queen Elizabeth's Grammar School, Blackburn	
Entry age: 11+, 16+	6 AA S
Rossall School, Fleetwood	6 A AA G I O

Rossall School, Fleetwood	
Entry age: 11, 13, 16	6 A AA G I O S
Rossall School International Study Centre, Fleetwood	
Entry age: 11+	
16+	6 AA G I
St Anne's College Grammar School,	
Lytham St Annes	6 AA
St Joseph's School, Park Hill, Burnley	I
St Mary's Hall, Clitheroe	A AA I O
Stonyhurst College, Clitheroe	
Entry age: 13, 16	6 A AA I O
Westholme School, Blackburn	6 A AA I

LEICESTERSHIRE

Brooke House College,	
Market Harborough	6 A AA G O S
The Dixie Grammar School, Market Bosworth	
Entry age: 10, 11, 14, 16	6 A AA G I
Leicester Grammar School, Leicester	6 A AA G I O
Leicester High School For Girls, Leicester	6 AA I
Loughborough Grammar School, Loughborough	
Entry age: 10+, 11+, 13+, 16+	6 AA I
Loughborough High School, Loughborough	AA I
Ratcliffe College, Leicester	
Entry age: 11+, 13+, 16+	6 A AA D G I
St Crispin's School, Leicester	
Entry age: 7+, 11+, 13+	AA G
Stoneygate School, Leicester	AA

LINCOLNSHIRE

Copthill School, Stamford Entry age: 11	AA
The Grantham Preparatory School, Grantham	I
Kirkstone House School, Bourne	
Entry age: Various	A AA G I O
Maypole House School, Alford	AA O
Stamford High School, Stamford	6 A AA I O
Stamford School, Stamford	
Entry age: 11, 13 and 16	6 A AA I
Witham Hall, Bourne	AA O

NORTH EAST LINCOLNSHIRE

St James' School, Grimsby	6 AA G I O

LONDON

Abercorn School, London	O
Albemarle Independent College, London	
Entry age: 14+, 19+	AA
Alleyn's School, London	
Entry age: 11+, 16+	6 A AA D G I O S
Arts Educational Schools London –	
Sixth Form, London	6 A AA D O
Ashbourne Middle School, London	
Entry age: 13/16	6 A AA D O S
Barbara Speake Stage School, London	O
Belmont (Mill Hill Preparatory School), London	
Entry age: Academic and Music 11	
Bursary 10	AA I

Blackheath High School GDST, London
    Entry age: 11+/16+   6 A AA G I
Blackheath Preparatory School, London   AA
Cameron House School, Chelsea   AA
CATS College London, London
    Entry age: At Sixth Form (16+);
    also at 1 yr GCSE (15+)   6 AA S
Channing School, London
    Entry age: 11, 16   6 AA I
Chelsea Independent College,
    London   6 A AA D G I O S
City of London School, London
    Entry age: 10+, 11+, 13+, 16+   6 AA G I
City of London School for Girls, London
    Entry age: 11, 16   6 A AA D I
Colet Court, London
    Entry age: 7+, 8+ and 11+   AA I
Colfe's School, London
    Entry age: 11+, 13+ and 16+   6 A AA D G I
Connaught House, London
    Entry age: 6, 8   A AA I O
David Game College, London   AA
Davies Laing and Dick, London   6 AA O
Devonshire House Preparatory School, London   AA I
Duff Miller, London   6 AA D O S
Dulwich College, London
    Entry age: 11, 13, 16   6 A AA G I
Ealing College Upper School, London   6 AA
Ealing Independent College, Ealing   AA
Eaton House Belgravia, London Entry age: 4   O
Eaton House The Manor Pre-Preparatory,
    London   AA O
Eaton House The Manor Preparatory, London
    Entry age: 8+   A AA G I O
Eaton House The Vale, London   AA O
Eaton Square School, London   O
Eltham College, London
    Entry age: 11+, 16+   6 A AA D G I
Emanuel School, London
    Entry age: 10+, 11+, 13+. 16+   6 A AA D G I O
Eridge House Preparatory, London   A AA D
Excelsior College, London   AA
Forest School, London   6 A AA D G I S
Francis Holland School, Regent's Park NW1   6 AA I
Francis Holland School, Sloane Square SW1
    Entry age: 11+, 16+   6 AA I
GEMS Hampshire School, London   AA I O
The Godolphin and Latymer School, London   I
Hall School Wimbledon (Senior School),
    London   A AA D G I O
Hampstead Hill Pre-Preparatory & Nursery School,
    London   O
Harvington School, London   D I
Hendon Preparatory School, Hendon   AA O
Highgate School, London   6 AA I
Hill House International Junior School, London
    Entry age: 11   A I
The Hurlingham School, London
    Entry age: 7+   O
Ibstock Place School, London
    Entry age: 7+, 11+, 16+   6 A AA D G I O
International Community School, London   O
The Italia Conti Academy of Theatre Arts, London   D

James Allen's Girls' School, London
    Entry age: 11+, 16+   6 A AA G I
Keble Preparatory School, London
    Entry age: 11   AA G O
King's College Junior School, London
    Entry age: 11+ entry   AA
King's College School, London   6 A AA I
Lansdowne College, London
    Entry age: 14+, 16+   6 AA O
Latymer Prep School, London   AA
Latymer Upper School, London   6 A AA D G I
The Lloyd Williamson School, London   O
Lycee Francais Charles de Gaulle, London   6 AA
The Lyceum, London   I
Mander Portman Woodward, London   6 AA
Mill Hill School, London   6 A AA D G I O S
The Mount School, London   6 AA I
Newton Prep, London   AA
Normanhurst School, London Entry age: 11   AA
North Bridge House Lower Prep School, London   AA I
North Bridge House Senior School, London   I
The North London International School,
    London   6 A AA D G I O
Notting Hill and Ealing High School GDST, London Entry
    age: 11+, 16+   6 AA I
Orchard House School, London
    Entry age: 8+   AA
Palmers Green High School, London
    Entry age: 11+   AA I
Parkgate House School, London   AA I O
The Pointer School, London
    Entry age: 7+   AA D G O
Portland Place School, London   6 A AA D G I
Prospect House School, London
    Entry age: Year 3 (aged 7+).   AA O
Putney High School GDST, London
    Entry age: 11+, 16+   6 A AA D G I S
Queen's Gate School, London
    Entry age: 11+.   6 A AA G O
Riverston School, London   AA G I O
The Roche School, London
    Entry age: 7   AA
The Royal School, Hampstead
    Entry age: 7, 16   A AA I
St Augustine's Priory, Ealing   6 I O
St Benedict's School, Ealing
    Entry age: 11+, 16+   6 AA G I O
St Christopher's School, London
    Entry age: 4+/5+   O
St Dunstan's College, London
    Entry age: 11+ and Sixth Form   6 A AA D G I
St Margaret's School, London   AA
St Mary's School Hampstead, London   A AA G I
St Paul's Cathedral School, London   I
St Paul's Girls' School, London   6 A AA I
St Paul's School, London   6 AA I
Sinclair House School, London   O
South Hampstead High School, London
    Entry age: 11+ and 16+   6 AA I
Southbank International School, Westminster,
    London   6
Streatham & Clapham High School,
    London Entry age: 11, 16   6 A AA D G I S

Sussex House School, London	I
Sydenham High School GDST, London	
Entry age: 11/16+	6 AA I
Sylvia Young Theatre School, London	
Entry age: 10–14	D I
Thomas's Preparatory School, London	O
University College School, London	AA I
Virgo Fidelis, London Entry age: 7–11	AA
Welsh School of London, London	O
Westminster Abbey Choir School, London	I
Westminster Cathedral Choir School, London	I
Westminster School, Westminster	AA I
Westminster Tutors, London	6 AA O
Westminster Under School, London	
Entry age: 11+	I
The White House Prep & Woodentops Kindergarten, London	AA G
Willington School, London	AA
Wimbledon High School GDST, London	6 AA I S

GREATER MANCHESTER

Abbey College, Manchester	6 AA
Branwood Preparatory School, Eccles	O
Bridgewater School, Manchester	
Entry age: 11/16+	6 AA
Chetham's School of Music, Manchester	I
Manchester High School for Girls, Manchester	
Entry age: 11.	AA G I
St Bede's College, Manchester	6 AA I

MERSEYSIDE

Avalon Preparatory School, Wirral Entry age: 7	AA
Birkenhead School, Wirral	6 AA G I O
Kingsmead School, Wirral Entry age: 7/11+	AA G I
Liverpool College, Liverpool	6 A AA D G I O
Merchant Taylors' Boys' Schools, Liverpool	
Entry age: 11	6 AA G
Merchant Taylors' Girls' School, Liverpool	
Entry age: 11+ and 16+	6 AA O
Runnymede St Edward's School, Liverpool	I
St Mary's College, Liverpool	
Entry age: 11/16+	6 A AA G I
Streatham House School, Liverpool	AA
Tower College, Prescot Entry age: 7, 11	AA I

MIDDLESEX

Buckingham College Preparatory School, Pinner	AA
Buckingham College School, Harrow	6 AA
Halliford School, Shepperton	
Entry age: 11+, 13+, Sixth Form	6 A AA D G I
Hampton School, Hampton	
Entry age: 11, 13, 16	6 A AA G I O
Harrow School, Harrow on the Hill	
Entry age: 13, 16	6 A AA G I
Heathfield School, Pinner	6 AA I
The John Lyon School, Harrow	
Entry age: 11+ and 13+	A AA D G I O
The Lady Eleanor Holles School, Hampton	6 AA I
Merchant Taylors' School, Northwood	6 AA I

North London Collegiate, Edgware	6 AA I
Northwood College, Northwood	
Entry age: 11+, 16+	6 A AA G I
St Catherine's School, Twickenham	
Entry age: 11	6 A AA G I
St Helen's School, Northwood	
Entry age: Academic, art, music and sport scholarships available at 11+; academic, art, drama, music and sport scholarship available at 16+.	6 A AA D G I
Twickenham Preparatory School, Hampton	
Entry age: Bursaries together with Academic, All-Rounder, Sport and Music Awards are available for boys entering Year 7.	AA G I O

NORFOLK

All Saints School, Norwich	AA I
Glebe House School, Hunstanton	A AA G I O
Gresham's School, Holt	6 A D G I O
Hethersett Old Hall School, Norwich	
Entry age: Years 7 – 10 and Year 12.	6 A AA D G I
Langley Preparatory School & Nursery, Norwich	AA I
Langley School, Norwich	
Entry age: 11, 13, 16	6 A AA D G I O
The New Eccles Hall School, Norwich	
Entry age: 8	AA I O
Norwich High School for Girls GDST, Norwich	6 AA I
Norwich School, Norwich	
Entry age: 11+, 13+, 16+	6 A AA D G I
Sacred Heart School, Swaffham Entry age: 11+	AA
Taverham Hall Preparatory School, Norwich	
Entry age: Age 5 – 13	AA G I
Town Close House Preparatory School, Norwich	
Entry age: 7+	AA G I
Wood Dene School, Norwich	A AA D

NORTHAMPTONSHIRE

Beachborough School, Brackley	
Entry age: 8–11	AA I O
Bosworth Independent College, Northampton	AA O S
Great Houghton Preparatory School, Northampton	A AA I
Maidwell Hall School, Northampton	AA G I
Northampton High School, Northampton	
Entry age: 11, 13, 16	6 A AA D G I
Northamptonshire Grammar School, Pitsford	6 A AA D G I
Oundle School, Nr Peterborough	6 A AA D I O
Quinton House School, Northampton	6 AA O
Winchester House School, Brackley	A AA G I O

NORTHUMBERLAND

Longridge Towers School, Berwick-upon-Tweed	
Entry age: 9, 11, 13, 16	6 AA G I
Mowden Hall School, Stocksfield	AA
St Oswald's School, Alnwick	AA O

NOTTINGHAMSHIRE

Coteswood House School, Nottingham	A AA D G I O
Grosvenor School, Nottingham	
Entry age: Bursaries age 4–13	
Scholarships Yr 4 and Yr 7	AA G I O
Nottingham High School for Girls GDST, Nottingham	O
Ranby House School, Retford	
Entry age: 7+, 11+	A AA D G I O
Trent College & The Elms, Nottingham	A AA D G I O
Wellow House School, Newark	A AA G I O
Worksop College, Worksop	6 A AA G I O

OXFORDSHIRE

Abingdon Preparatory School, Abingdon	AA
Abingdon School, Abingdon	6 A AA D G I
Christ Church Cathedral School, Oxford	I
Cokethorpe School, Witney	6 A AA D G I O
Cranford House School, Wallingford	A AA D G I O
d'Overbroeck's College Oxford, Oxford	
Entry age: 16	A AA D S
Dragon School, Oxford Entry age: Yrs 4, 5, 6, 7	AA
Ferndale Preparatory School, Faringdon	AA
Headington School, Oxford	
Entry age: 11, 13, 16	6 A AA D G I
Leckford Place School, Oxford	A AA D I
Magdalen College School, Oxford	
Entry age: 11+, 13+, 16+	6 A AA G I O
New College School, Oxford Entry age: 7	I
Our Lady's Abingdon School, Abingdon	
Entry age: 5–17	6 AA I
Oxford High School GDST, Oxford	
Entry age: Year 7, Academic & Music	
Year 12, Academic, All-Rounder, Art, Drama,	
Music, Sports	
Year 7 & Year 12 entry,	
Fee Bursaries	6 A AA D G I O
Oxford Tutorial College, Oxford	AA O
Radley College, Abingdon	
Entry age: 13+	6 A AA D I O
St Clare's, Oxford, Oxford Entry age: 16+	6 AA O
St Edward's School, Oxford	
Entry age: 13+, 16+	
Bursaries for university dons	6 A AA D G I O
St Helen & St Katharine, Abingdon	6 AA I
St Hugh's School, Faringdon	AA
Shiplake College, Henley-on-Thames	
Entry age: 13+, 16+	6 A AA D G I
Sibford School, Banbury	6 A AA I
Tudor Hall School, Banbury	
Entry age: 11, 13, 16	A AA D G I
Wychwood School, Oxford	6 A AA I S

RUTLAND

Oakham School, Oakham	
Entry age: 11+, 13+ 16+	6 A AA D G I O S
Uppingham School, Uppingham	6 A AA I O

SHROPSHIRE

Adcote School for Girls, Shrewsbury	
Entry age:	6 A AA D G I O S
Bedstone College, Bucknell	6 A AA G I O
Concord College, Shrewsbury	6 AA O S
Dower House School, Bridgnorth	
Entry age: 7, 8, 9	AA O
Ellesmere College, Ellesmere	6 A AA D G I O S
Kingsland Grange, Shrewsbury	
Entry age: 7–11	AA G I
Moor Park School, Ludlow	AA O
Moreton Hall School, Oswestry	
Entry age: Junior Scholarships, 11+, 13+, 16+	6 A AA D G I O
The Old Hall School, Telford	AA I
Oswestry School, Oswestry	
Entry age: 9+, 11+, 13+, 16+	6 A AA G I O S
Oswestry School Bellan House, Oswestry	AA I O
Packwood Haugh School, Shrewsbury	A AA G I
Prestfelde Preparatory School, Shrewsbury	
Entry age: 7+, 11+	A AA G I
Shrewsbury High School GDST, Shrewsbury	6 AA I
Wrekin College, Telford	
Entry age: 11, 13, 16	6 A AA G I O

SOMERSET

All Hallows, Shepton Mallet Entry age: 11+	A I O
Bath Academy, Bath Entry age: 16+	6
Bruton School for Girls, Bruton	
Entry age: 11+, 13+, 16+	6 A AA D G I O S
Chilton Cantelo School, Yeovil	O
Downside School, Bath	6 A AA G I O
Hazlegrove Preparatory School, Yeovil	
Entry age: 7 & 11	AA G I
King's College, Taunton	6 A AA D G I O S
King's Hall, Taunton	AA G I
Millfield Preparatory School, Glastonbury	
Entry age: 7–13	A AA G I O
Millfield School, Street	
Entry age: 13, 14, 16	6 A AA G I O
The Park School, Yeovil Entry age: 8–18+	6 A AA D I
Perrott Hill School, Crewkerne	A AA D G I O
Queen's College, Taunton	
Entry age: 11+, 13+ and Sixth Form entry.	
Music also available at 10+ and	
12+ entry	6 A AA D G I O
Queen's College Junior, Pre-Prep & Nursery Schools, Taunton	
Entry age: 10+ music scholarship	A AA D G I O
Taunton Preparatory School, Taunton	
Entry age: 11+	AA G I
Taunton School International, Taunton	AA
Taunton School Senior, Taunton	6 AA G I O
Wellington School, Wellington	
Entry age: 10+, 11+, 13+, 16+	6 AA I O
Wells Cathedral Junior School, Wells	
Entry age: 8–11	AA I
Wells Cathedral School, Wells	
Entry age: 11, 13, 16	6 AA I S

BATH & NORTH EAST SOMERSET

King Edward's School, Bath, Bath
Entry age: 11–18   6 A AA D G I
Kingswood School, Bath   6 A AA D G I O
Paragon School, Prior Park College Junior,
Bath   AA G I O
Prior Park College, Bath   6 A AA D G I O
The Royal High School, Bath, Bath
Entry age: 11/16+   6 A AA D G I

NORTH SOMERSET

Sidcot School, Winscombe
Entry age: Bursary all ages
Scholarships at Year 7, 9 and
Sixth Form   6 A AA D G I O S

STAFFORDSHIRE

Abbots Bromley School for Girls, Abbots Bromley
Entry age: 11/16+   6 A AA D G I
Chase Academy, Cannock
Entry age: 3+   6 A AA G I O
Denstone College, Uttoxeter
Entry age: 11, 13, 16   6 A AA D G I O
Edenhurst School, Newcastle-under-Lyme   O
Lichfield Cathedral School, Lichfield
Entry age: 7, 9, 11   A AA D G I O
Newcastle-under-Lyme School,
Newcastle-under-Lyme   6 AA G
St Dominic's Independent Junior School,
Stoke-on-Trent Entry age: 8+   AA
St Dominic's Priory School, Stone   6 A AA D G I O
St Dominic's School, Stafford
Entry age: 11, 12   6 A AA D G I
Stafford Grammar School, Stafford   6 A AA D G I O
Vernon Lodge Preparatory School, Brewood   AA O
Yarlet School, Stafford Entry age: 11+   A AA D G I O

STOCKTON-ON-TEES

Teesside High School, Eaglescliffe   6 AA I
Yarm School, Yarm Entry age: 7+, 11+, 16+   6 AA I S

SUFFOLK

Amberfield School, Ipswich
Entry age: 11/13+   A AA G I
Arbor Preparatory, Bury St Edmunds   AA
Brandeston Hall, The Preparatory School for
Framlingham College, Brandeston
Entry age: 11+   A AA D G I
Culford School, Bury St Edmunds
Entry age: 11, 13 and 16 in a variety
of disciplines.   6 A AA D G I O S
Fairstead House School, Newmarket
Entry age: Years 4, 5 & 6   AA G I
Felixstowe International College, Felixstowe   AA O
Finborough School, Stowmarket   6 A AA G I O
Framlingham College, Woodbridge
Entry age: 11+, 13+, 16+   6 A AA D G I O S

Ipswich High School GDST, Ipswich
Entry age: 11+   6 AA I
Ipswich School, Ipswich
Entry age: 11, 13, 16   6 A AA G I O
Moreton Hall Preparatory School,
Bury St Edmunds   AA I
Orwell Park, Ipswich Entry age: 7+   A AA I O
The Royal Hospital School, Ipswich
Entry age: 11+, 13+ and 16+   6 A AA G I O
St George's School, Southwold   AA I O
St Joseph's College, Ipswich   6 A AA D G I O
Saint Felix School, Southwold
Entry age: 11, 13, 16   6 A AA D G I
Stoke College, Sudbury   AA I
South Lee Preparatory School, Bury St Edmunds
Entry age: 8+, 11+   AA O
Woodbridge School, Woodbridge
Entry age: 11+, 13+ and 16+   6 A AA D G I O

SURREY

Aberdour, Tadworth   AA
Aberdour School, Tadworth   AA
Amesbury, Hindhead   AA G I
Barfield School and Nursery, Farnham   AA G I O
Box Hill School, Dorking
Entry age: 11, 13, 16   6 A AA D G I O
Cambridge Tutors College, Croydon   6 AA
Charterhouse, Godalming
Entry age: 13+ Academic, Music, Art, All-rounder,
Sport 16+ Academic, Music, Art   6 A AA G I O
City of London Freemen's School, Ashtead
Entry age: 11+, 13+, 16+   6 AA I O
Claremont Fan Court School, Esher   6 A AA D G I
Cranleigh Preparatory School, Cranleigh   AA I
Cranleigh School, Cranleigh
Entry age: 13+, 16+   6 A AA I O
Croydon High School GDST, South Croydon
Entry age: Year 7 and 12 only   6 A AA D G I
Cumnor House School, South Croydon   AA G I
Danes Hill School, Leatherhead   AA
Danesfield Manor School, Walton-on-Thames
Entry age: Year 2 and above.   AA I S
Downsend School, Leatherhead Entry age: 7+
Scholarships for entry into Year 3.   AA
Duke of Kent School, Guildford
Entry age: 7+, 10+, 11+   AA G I
Dunottar School, Reigate
Entry age: 11, 13, 16   6 A AA G I
Edgeborough, Farnham   O
Epsom College, Epsom
Entry age: 13+, 16+   6 A AA D G I O
Essendene Lodge School, Caterham   AA O
Ewell Castle School, Epsom
Entry age: 11+, 13+, 16+   6 A AA D G I O
Feltonfleet School, Cobham   A AA I O
Frensham Heights School, Farnham   6 A AA D G I
Greenacre School for Girls, Banstead   6 A AA D G I O
Guildford High School, Guildford   6 AA I
Hampton Court House, East Molesey   AA I
Haslemere Preparatory School, Haslemere
Entry age: Entry from
Year 2 to Year 7   A AA D G I O

Hawley Place School, Camberley
  Entry age: 7, 11 — A AA D G I O
Hoe Bridge School, Woking Entry age: 7+ — AA O
Homefield Preparatory School, Sutton — A AA G I O
Hurtwood House, Dorking Entry age: 16 — 6 D O S
King Edward's School Witley, Godalming
  Entry age: 11, 13, 16 — 6 A AA D G I O S
Kingston Grammar School, Kingston-upon-Thames
  Entry age: 11+, 13+, 16+ — 6 A AA G I
Kingswood House School, Epsom — AA G
Laleham Lea School, Purley
  Entry age: Entry to Year 1 and Year 2 classes. — O
Lanesborough, Guildford Entry age: 7+ — I
Lingfield Notre Dame School, Lingfield
  Entry age: 11+ — 6 AA I O
Lyndhurst School, Camberley — AA
Manor House School, Leatherhead
  Entry age: 11+ — A AA D G I
Marymount International School,
  Kingston-upon-Thames Entry age: 11, 16 — AA O
Notre Dame Preparatory School, Cobham — O
Notre Dame Senior School, Cobham — 6 AA
Oakfield School, Woking Entry age: 7+, 11+ — AA I O
Old Palace of John Whitgift School, Croydon — AA I
Prior's Field School, Godalming
  Entry age: 11+, 13+ and 16+ — 6 A AA D G I O
Reed's School, Cobham — 6 A AA D G I O
Reigate Grammar School, Reigate — 6 AA I O
Reigate St Mary's Preparatory and Choir School,
  Reigate Entry age: 7+ — I
Ripley Court School, Woking — A AA D G I O
Rokeby School, Kingston-upon-Thames — A AA G I
Royal Grammar School, Guildford
  Entry age: 11+/13+ — A AA I
Royal Russell School, Croydon
  Entry age: 11+/16 — 6 AA D I
The Royal School, Haslemere
  Entry age: 11+, 13+, 16+ — 6 A AA D G I O
The Royal School For Girls, Haslemere — 6 AA D I O S
St Andrew's (Woking) School Trust, Woking
  Entry age: 7+ — A AA G I O
St Catherine's School, Guildford
  Entry age: 11/16+ — 6 A AA G I O
St Edmund's School, Hindhead
  Entry age: 7/8 — A AA D G I O
St George's College, Weybridge — 6 A AA I O
St Hilary's School, Godalming
  Entry age: Scholarships Years 3–6
  Bursary Year 3 — A AA D I
St Ives School, Haslemere — A AA D G I O
St James Independent School for Boys (Senior),
  Ashford — I
St John's School, Leatherhead
  Entry age: 13+, 16+ — 6 A AA G I O
St Teresa's School, Dorking — 6 A AA D G I O
Seaton House School, Sutton Entry age: Form II
  Founder's Scholarship for entry into Form III — AA
Sir William Perkins's School, Chertsey
  Entry age: Year 7 Academic, Music and Art
  Scholarship. Sixth Form Academic
  Scholarships. — 6 A AA I
Surbiton High School,
  Kingston-upon-Thames — 6 A AA G I

Sutton High School GDST, Sutton
  Entry age: 11+, 16+ — 6 A AA D G I O
Tormead School, Guildford — 6 A AA I
Trinity School, Croydon
  Entry age: 10+, 11+, 13+, 16+ — 6 A AA D G I O
West Dene School, Purley Entry age: 7 — I
Whitgift School, South Croydon
  Entry age: 10–13, 16 — 6 A AA D G I O
Woodcote House School, Windlesham — A AA G I O
Yehudi Menuhin School, Cobham — I

EAST SUSSEX

Battle Abbey School, Battle
  Entry age: 13/16+ — 6 A AA D G I O
Bellerbys College, Hove — 6 AA
Bricklehurst Manor Preparatory, Wadhurst — AA
Brighton and Hove High School GDST,
  Brighton — 6 AA
Brighton College, Brighton
  Entry age: 13+, 16+ — 6 A AA D G I O
Brighton College Prep School, Brighton
  Entry age: 11+ — A AA D G I O
Buckswood School, Hastings — AA G I
Claremont School, St Leonards-on-Sea — A AA D G I O
Eastbourne College, Eastbourne
  Entry age: Yr 9 and Yr 12. — 6 A AA D G I
The Fold School, Hove Entry age: 3+ — AA I
Lancing College Preparatory School at Mowden,
  Hove Entry age: 7+, 11+ — AA
Lewes Old Grammar School, Lewes — 6 AA I O
Moira House School, Eastbourne — O
Newlands School, Seaford — 6 A AA D G I O
Roedean School, Brighton
  Entry age: 11+, 12+, 13+, 16+ — 6 A AA D G I S
St Andrew's School, Eastbourne — A AA D G I O
St Aubyn's, Brighton — AA G O
St Aubyns School, Brighton — A AA D G I O
St Bede's Prep School, Eastbourne — A AA D G I
St Bede's School, Hailsham — 6 A AA D G I
St Leonards-Mayfield School, Mayfield
  Entry age: 11+, 13+, 16+ — 6 A AA D G I
Stonelands School of Ballet & Theatre Arts, Hove — D O
Vinehall School, Robertsbridge
  Entry age: 8+ — A AA D G I O

WEST SUSSEX

Ardingly College, Haywards Heath
  Entry age: 7+, 11+, 13+, 16+ — 6 A AA D G I O
Ardingly College Junior School, Haywards Heath
  Entry age: 11+ — A AA G I
Burgess Hill School for Girls,
  Burgess Hill — 6 A AA D G I
Conifers School, Midhurst — A AA G I O
Copthorne Prep School, Copthorne — A AA D G I
Dorset House School, Pulborough — AA I
Farlington School, Horsham — 6 A AA D G I O
Great Ballard School, Chichester
  Entry age: 7 — A AA D G I O
Great Walstead, Haywards Heath
  Entry age: 7 – 11 — AA D G I

Handcross Park School, Haywards Heath
  Entry age: 7 – 11   A AA G I O
Hurstpierpoint College, Hurstpierpoint 6 A AA D G I O
Oakwood School, Chichester   AA O
Our Lady of Sion School, Worthing
  Entry age: 11 & 16   6 AA
The Prebendal School, Chichester Entry age: 7   AA I
Shoreham College, Shoreham-by-Sea   AA G I O
Slindon College, Arundel Entry age: 10   AA O
Tavistock & Summerhill School, Haywards Heath   AA
The Towers Convent School, Steyning   AA D I O
Westbourne House School, Chichester   I
Worth School, Turners Hill
  Entry age: 11, 13, 16   6 A AA G I O

TYNE AND WEAR

Central Newcastle High School GDST,
  Newcastle upon Tyne Entry age: 11+, 16+   6 AA
Church High School, Newcastle upon Tyne,
  Newcastle upon Tyne   6 AA I
Dame Allan's Boys School,
  Newcastle upon Tyne   6 AA
Dame Allan's Girls School, Newcastle upon Tyne
  Entry age: 11   6 AA I
The King's School, Tynemouth
  Entry age: 11+   6 A AA I O
Newcastle School for Boys, Newcastle upon Tyne   AA
Sunderland High School, Sunderland   6 AA I
Westfield School, Newcastle upon Tyne 6 A AA G I O

WARWICKSHIRE

Bilton Grange, Rugby Entry age: 8+   AA
The Croft Preparatory School, Stratford-upon-Avon
  Entry age: 8   AA
King's High School, Warwick   6 AA I
The Kingsley School, Leamington Spa   6 A AA D I
Princethorpe College, Rugby
  Entry age: 11/18+   6 A AA G I O
Rugby School, Rugby   6 A AA G I
Warwick School, Warwick   6 A AA I

WEST MIDLANDS

Abbey College, Birmingham   6 AA O
Al Hijrah School, Birmingham   AA
Al-Burhan Grammar School, Birmingham
  Entry age: 11 years old   AA
Bablake Junior School, Coventry   AA
Bablake School, Coventry   6 A AA I O
Birchfield School, Wolverhampton
  Entry age: 4   A AA G I O
The Blue Coat School, Birmingham
  Entry age: 7+   AA I O
Coventry Prep School, Coventry
  Entry age: 7+   A AA I O
Edgbaston High School for Girls, Birmingham
  Entry age: 11+ 16+   6 A AA D G I
Elmhurst School for Dance, Birmingham   6
Highclare School, Birmingham
  Entry age: 11/16+   6 A AA G I O

Hydesville Tower School, Walsall   AA G I O
King Edward VI High School for Girls, Birmingham AA
King Edward's School, Birmingham
  Entry age: Academic and Music Scholarships
  available at 11+, 13+ and 16+.   6 AA I
King Henry VIII School, Coventry   6 A AA I O
Norfolk House School, Birmingham   AA
Priory School, Birmingham
  Entry age: 11, 16   6 A AA D G I
St George's School, Edgbaston, Birmingham
  Entry age: 11+   6 AA I O
Saint Martin's School, Solihull
  Entry age: 7+, 11+, 16+   6 AA G I
Solihull School, Solihull   6 A AA I S
Tettenhall College, Wolverhampton
  Entry age: 11   6 A AA D G I O
Wolverhampton Grammar School, Wolverhampton
  Entry age: 11+, 13+, 16+   6 AA I O S

WILTSHIRE

Chafyn Grove School, Salisbury
  Entry age: Bursary – all ages
  Scholarship – for entry in Years 3,
  5 and 7   A AA D G I O
Dauntsey's School, Devizes
  Entry age: 11+, 13+, 16+   6 A AA D G I O S
Godolphin Preparatory School, Salisbury   AA
The Godolphin School, Salisbury   6 A AA D G I
Grittleton House School, Chippenham   A AA D G I S
Leaden Hall School, Salisbury   AA
Leehurst Swan, Salisbury
  Entry age: 7, 11, 14   A AA G I
Marlborough College, Marlborough
  Entry age: 13+, 16+   6 A AA G I O
Norman Court Preparatory School, Salisbury
  Entry age: 7, 8, 11   A AA D G I O
Prior Park Preparatory School, Cricklade   AA
St Francis School, Pewsey
  Entry age: Scholarships – Age 7+
  Bursaries – Age 9+   A AA G I O
St Mary's Calne, Calne
  Entry age: 11+, 13+, 16+   6 A AA D G I O
Salisbury Cathedral School, Salisbury
  Entry age: 7, 10   A AA D G I
Stonar School, Melksham
  Entry age: from Year 7 through to
  Sixth Form.   6 A AA D G I O
Warminster School, Warminster
  Entry age: 7, 9, 11, 13, 16   6 A AA D G I O

WORCESTERSHIRE

The Abbey College, Malvern Wells   6 AA O S
Bromsgrove Preparatory School, Bromsgrove
  Entry age: 11+   AA I O
Bromsgrove School, Bromsgrove   6 A AA D G I O
Dodderhill School, Droitwich Spa
  Entry age: 11+   AA I
The Downs, Malvern, Malvern
  Entry age: 11+ 5   A AA D G I O

The Elms, Malvern	AA G I O
Holy Trinity School, Kidderminster	6 AA I O S
King's Hawford, Worcester Entry age: 7+, 8+	AA
The King's School, Worcester	6 AA I
The Knoll School, Kidderminster	AA
Malvern St James, Great Malvern	
Entry age: 11+, 12+, 13+, 16+	6 A AA D G I
Moffats School, Bewdley	A AA D G I O S
RGS The Grange, Worcester	AA
RGS Worcester & The Alice Ottley School,	
Worcester	A AA I
St Mary's, Worcester	
Entry age: 11+, 16+	6 A AA G I
Saint Michael's College, Tenbury Wells	6 AA O S
Winterfold House, Kidderminster	A AA G I O

EAST RIDING OF YORKSHIRE

Hull Collegiate School, Anlaby	
Entry age: 11	6 A AA G I
Pocklington School, Pocklington	6 AA I O

NORTH YORKSHIRE

Ampleforth College, York	
Entry age: 13, 16	6 A AA D G I O
Ashville College, Harrogate	
Entry age: 11–18	6 A AA D G I
Aysgarth Preparatory School, Bedale	
Entry age: Normally between 8 and	
11 years old	AA G I
Belmont Grosvenor School, Harrogate	AA
Bootham School, York	
Entry age: 11+ and 13+	AA I O
Bramcote School, Scarborough	AA G I O
Cundall Manor School, York	AA G I
Fyling Hall School, Whitby	6 AA G I O
Giggleswick Junior School, Settle	
Entry age: 10, 11	AA G I O
Giggleswick School, Settle	
Entry age: 13, 16	6 A AA D G I O
Harrogate Ladies' College, Harrogate	
Entry age: 11+, 16+	6 AA I O
Harrogate Tutorial College, Harrogate	
Entry age: 15+	6 AA O
Lisvane, Scarborough College Junior School,	
Scarborough Entry age: 7–9	AA
Malsis School, Near Skipton	
Entry age: Year 3 and above.	A AA D G I O
The Minster School, York	I
The Mount School, York	6 A AA D G I O S

Queen Ethelburga's College, York	
Entry age: 11	6 A AA D G I O S
Queen Mary's School, Thirsk	
Entry age: 11+, 12+, 13+	A AA I
Read School, Selby	
Entry age: 11+, 13+, 16+	6 AA O
Ripon Cathedral Choir School, Ripon	AA I
St Martin's Ampleforth, York	
Entry age: 7/12+	AA G I O
St Peter's School, York Entry age: 13/16+	6 AA I O
Scarborough College & Lisvane School,	
Scarborough	6 A AA I
Terrington Hall, York	A AA D G I O
Woodleigh School, Malton	A AA D G I

SOUTH YORKSHIRE

Birkdale School, Sheffield Entry age: 11, 16	6 AA I S
Hill House School, Doncaster	A AA G I
Rudston Preparatory School, Rotherham	AA
Sheffield High School GDST, Sheffield	
Entry age: 11, 16	6 AA I O
Westbourne School, Sheffield	AA G I O

WEST YORKSHIRE

Ackworth School, Pontefract	6 A AA I
Batley Grammar School, Batley	6
Bradford Girls' Grammar School, Bradford	I
Bradford Grammar School, Bradford	
Entry age: 11+	I
Bronte House School, Bradford Entry age: 9	AA
Fulneck School, Leeds	6 A AA G I O
Gateways School, Leeds Entry age: 11	6 A AA D G I
Ghyll Royd School, Ilkley Entry age: 7	AA
The Grammar School at Leeds, Leeds	
Entry age: 11+, 16+	6 AA I
Hipperholme Grammar School, Halifax	
Entry age: 16+	6 AA
Huddersfield Grammar School, Huddersfield	AA G I
Moorfield School, Ilkley	AA I
Queen Elizabeth Grammar School, Wakefield	6 AA I
The Rastrick Independent School, Brighouse	
Entry age: 11+	AA O
Richmond House School, Leeds Entry age: 7/8	AA
Rishworth School, Rishworth	
Entry age: 11, 16	6 AA D G I O
Silcoates School, Wakefield Entry age: 11	AA I
Wakefield Girls' High School, Wakefield	6 AA
Wakefield Independent School, Wakefield	AA
Wakefield Tutorial Preparatory School, Leeds	O
Woodhouse Grove School,	
Apperley Bridge	AA D G I O

NORTHERN IRELAND

COUNTY ANTRIM

Campbell College, Belfast	6 A AA G I
Methodist College, Belfast	6 I

COUNTY TYRONE

The Royal School Dungannon, Dungannon	
Entry age: 11–16	AA G I

SCOTLAND

ABERDEENSHIRE

Albyn School, Aberdeen   A AA G I
International School of Aberdeen, Aberdeen   6
Robert Gordon's College, Aberdeen   6 AA G I O

ANGUS

High School of Dundee, Dundee Entry age: 12   AA
Lathallan School, Montrose
    Entry age: Primary 7 and S5   A AA D G I O

ARGYLL AND BUTE

Lomond School, Helensburgh Entry age: 11, 16   6 I

CLACKMANNANSHIRE

Dollar Academy, Dollar   A I

FIFE

St Leonards School, St Andrews
    Entry age: Varies – please contact the Registrar for
    more information.   6 A AA D G I

GLASGOW

Craigholme School, Pollokshields
    Entry age: 11   AA
The Glasgow Academy, Glasgow
    Entry age: 11+   6 AA
The High School of Glasgow, Glasgow   AA
Kelvinside Academy, Glasgow   6 AA

LANARKSHIRE

Hamilton College, Hamilton   AA I

LOTHIAN

Cargilfield, Edinburgh   AA I O

The Edinburgh Academy, Edinburgh   6 A AA I
Fettes College, Edinburgh
    Entry age: 11+, 13+, 16+   6 A AA G I O
George Heriot's School, Edinburgh
    Entry age: 11+   6 A AA D I
George Watson's College, Edinburgh   6 AA G I S
Loretto Junior School, Musselburgh
    Entry age: 10/11   A AA D G I O
Loretto School, Musselburgh
    Entry age: on entry all age groups from
    12 years   6 A AA D G I O
The Mary Erskine School, Edinburgh   6 AA I
Merchiston Castle School, Edinburgh   6 A AA I O
St Mary's Music School, Edinburgh Entry age: 9+   I
Stewart's Melville College, Edinburgh   6 AA I

MORAYSHIRE

Gordonstoun School, Elgin Entry age: 8+ at Junior
    School Entry
    13+ at Lower School Entry
    16+ at Sixth Form Entry   6 A AA D G I O

PERTH AND KINROSS

Ardvreck School, Crieff   AA
Glenalmond College, Perth
    Entry age: 12, 13, 16   6 A AA G I O
Kilgraston, Perth   6 A AA G I O
Morrison's Academy, Crieff   6 AA
Strathallan School, Perth
    Entry age: 9, 10, 11, 12, 13 & 16   6 A AA G I O

ROXBURGHSHIRE

St Mary's Preparatory School, Melrose   G I O

STIRLING

Beaconhurst School, Bridge of Allan   AA

WALES

BRIDGEND

St John's School, Porthcawl   AA G O

CARDIFF

The Cardiff Academy, Roath   AA
The Cathedral School, Llandaff
    Entry age: 11   AA G I
Howell's School, Llandaff GDST, Llandaff
    Entry age: 11, 16   6 AA I
Kings Monkton School, Cardiff   6 A AA G I S

CARMARTHENSHIRE

Llandovery College, Llandovery
    Entry age: Year 7 to 12   6 AA D G I O
St Michael's School, Llanelli   6 AA D G I O

CONWY

St David's College, Llandudno
    Entry age: 11   6 A AA D G I O S

DENBIGHSHIRE

Howell's School, Denbigh   6 A AA D G I

Ruthin School, Ruthin
   Entry age: 11 and 16   6 A AA D G I O S

MONMOUTHSHIRE

Haberdashers' Monmouth School For Girls,
   Monmouth   6 AA I
Llangattock School, Monmouth   O
Monmouth School, Monmouth
   Entry age: 11, 13, 16   6 AA G I
St John's-on-the-Hill, Chepstow
   Entry age: External scholarships and bursaries
   available from Year 2 upwards.   A AA D G I O

CONTINENTAL EUROPE

Chavagnes International College,
   Chavagnes-En-Paillers, France   6 AA I O
King's College Madrid, Madrid, Spain   6

NEWPORT

Rougemont School, Newport   AA

POWYS

Christ College, Brecon
   Entry age: 11, 13, 16   6 A AA G I O S

SWANSEA

Ffynone House School, Swansea
   Entry age: 11   6 A AA D G I

St Columba's College, Dublin, Ireland
   Entry age: 11, 13, 16.   AA O

Bursaries and Reserved Entrance Awards

The following is compiled from information provided by schools. For further information please contact the school direct. The abbreviations used are as follows:

E	Christian Missionary or full-time worker	FO	Foreign Office
F1	The Royal Navy	H	Financial or domestic hardship
F2	The Royal Marines	M	Medical profession
F3	The Army	T	Teaching profession
F4	The Royal Air Force	+	The Clergy

ENGLAND

BEDFORDSHIRE

Bedford High School for Girls, Bedford	H
Bedford Modern School, Bedford Entry age: 11+	H
Bedford Preparatory School, Bedford	F1 F2 F4 F3 H
Dame Alice Harpur School, Bedford	H
Moorlands School, Luton Entry age: 7+	H T

BERKSHIRE

The Abbey School, Reading Entry age: 11+,13+,16+	H
The Ark School, Reading Entry age: 7	H T
Bearwood College, Wokingham Entry age: 11/13	E F1 F4 F3 H +
Brigidine School Windsor, Windsor Entry age: 11, 16	H
Brockhurst and Marlston House Schools, Newbury	E F1 F2 F4 F3 FO H M T +
Cheam School, Newbury Entry age: Bursary Available from 8 years old	H
Dolphin School, Reading	H T
Downe House, Thatcham Entry age: 11+, 12+, 13+ and 16+	H
Elstree School, Reading Entry age: 7	E H T +
Eton College, Windsor	H
Heathfield School, Ascot	F1 F2 F4 F3 FO H +
Hemdean House School, Reading	H
Highfield School, Maidenhead	H
Horris Hill School, Newbury	F1 F2 F4 F3
Hurst Lodge School, Ascot Entry age: various	F1 F2 F4 F3 H
Lambrook, Bracknell	T
Luckley-Oakfield School, Wokingham Entry age: 11	F1 F2 F4 F3 H
LVS Ascot, Ascot	F1 F2 F4 F3 H
The Oratory School, Reading Entry age: 11+, 13+	F1 F2 F4 F3 FO H T
Padworth College, Reading Entry age: 14, 16	H
Pangbourne College, Pangbourne Entry age: 11+, 13+, 16+	F1 F2 F4 F3 H
Papplewick School, Ascot Entry age: 6–11	F1 F2 F4 F3 H T
Queen Anne's School, Reading Entry age: 11+, 13+, 16+	F1 F2 F4 F3 H T +
Reading Blue Coat School, Reading	H T
St Andrew's School, Reading	+
St Gabriel's, Newbury Entry Age: 11+, 13+, 16+	H
St George's School, Ascot Entry age: 11+, 16+	H
St John's Beaumont, Windsor	H

St Joseph's College, Reading   H
St Michaels School, Newbury   H
St Piran's Preparatory School, Maidenhead   H T
Sunningdale School, Sunningdale   F1 F2 F4 F3 FO T
Upton House School, Windsor   H
Wellington College, Crowthorne   F1 F2 F4 F3 H
White House Preparatory School, Wokingham   E H +

BRISTOL

Badminton School, Bristol
    Entry Age: Scholarships are awarded at 11+, 13+
    and 16+ for academic, music, art and all
    round ability   F1 F2 F4 F3 H
Bristol Cathedral School, Bristol
    Entry Age: 11+, 13+, 16+   H
Bristol Grammar School, Bristol
    Entry Age: 7, 11, 13, 16   H
Clifton College, Bristol
    Entry Age: 13+, 16+   F1 F2 F4 F3 H T +
Clifton College Preparatory School, Bristol
    Entry Age: 11+   F1 F2 F4 F3 +
Clifton High School, Bristol
    Entry Age: 11+, 13+, 16+   H
Colston's Collegiate School, Bristol   F1 F2 F3
The Downs School, Wraxall Entry age: 8+ F1 F2 F3 H +
Fairfield School, Backwell   H
Overndale School, Old Sodbury   H
Queen Elizabeth's Hospital, Bristol
    Entry Age: 11, 13, 16   H
The Red Maids' School, Bristol
    Entry Age: 11+,13+, 16+   H
Redland High School for Girls, Bristol
    Entry Age: 9, 11, 16   F1 F2 F4 F3 H
Tockington Manor School, Tockington   T

BUCKINGHAMSHIRE

Akeley Wood School, Buckingham   H
Ashfold School, Aylesbury   E F1 F2 F4 F3 +
The Beacon School, Amersham
    Entry age: Means tested bursary from Year 3.   H
Bury Lawn School, Milton Keynes   H
Caldicott School, Farnham Royal   H T
Davenies School, Beaconsfield   H
Gayhurst School, Gerrards Cross   H +
Godstowe Preparatory School, High Wycombe
    Entry age: 8, 11   F1 F2 F4 F3 H +
High March School, Beaconsfield
    Entry age: 8 and 10   H T
Ladymede, Aylesbury Entry age: 7+   F4 H
Maltman's Green School, Gerrards Cross
    Entry age: From Year 1   H
Milton Keynes Preparatory School, Milton Keynes   H
Pipers Corner School, High Wycombe
    Entry age: 11+, 16+   F1 F2 F4 F3 H
St Mary's School, Gerrards Cross   H +
St Teresa's Catholic Independent & Nursery School,
    Princes Risborough   H
Stowe School, Buckingham Entry age: 13, 16   H
Swanbourne House School, Milton Keynes
    Entry age: 11+   F1 F2 F4 F3 FO +

Thornton College Convent of Jesus and Mary, Milton
    Keynes Entry age: 11   F1 F2 F4 F3 H
Thorpe House School, Gerrards Cross   H T
Wycombe Abbey School, High Wycombe
    Entry age: 11+, 13+ and sixth form entry   H

CAMBRIDGESHIRE

Bellerbys College & Embassy CES Cambridge,
    Cambridge   H
Cambridge Centre for Sixth-form Studies,
    Cambridge   F1 F2 F4 F3 H
CATS College Cambridge, Cambridge
    Entry age: 6th Form entry (16+)   F1 F2 F4 F3 H
Kimbolton School, Huntingdon
    Entry age: 11+, 13+, 16+   H
The King's School Ely, Ely
    Entry age: 11+   F1 F2 F4 F3 H +
The Leys School, Cambridge
    Entry age: 11, 13, 16   F1 F2 F4 F3 H +
Madingley Pre-Preparatory School, Cambridge   H
MPW (Mander Portman Woodward), Cambridge   H
The Perse School, Cambridge   H
The Perse School for Girls, Cambridge   H
The Peterborough School, Peterborough
    Entry age: 11, 16   H
St John's College School, Cambridge   H
St Mary's School, Cambridge   H
Sancton Wood School, Cambridge   H T
Wisbech Grammar School, Wisbech   H

CHANNEL ISLANDS

Ormer House Preparatory School, Alderney   H
St George's Preparatory School, Jersey
    Entry age: 7+   H T
St Michael's Preparatory School, Jersey   H +
Victoria College, Jersey   H

CHESHIRE

Abbey Gate College, Chester Entry age: 11+, 16+   H
Abbey Gate School, Chester Entry age: 5 and 7   H
Alderley Edge School for Girls, Alderley Edge   H
Beech Hall School, Macclesfield   E H T +
Cheadle Hulme School, Cheadle   H
Culcheth Hall, Altrincham   H
The Grange School, Northwich   H
Greenbank Preparatory School, Cheadle
    Entry age: Juniors Y3-Y6   H
Hillcrest Grammar School, Stockport   H
Hulme Hall Schools, Cheadle   H T
The King's School, Chester Entry age: 11/16+   H
The King's School, Macclesfield   H
North Cestrian Grammar School, Altrincham
    Entry age: 11–13 & 16   H
Pownall Hall School, Wilmslow   T
The Queen's School, Chester   H
Ramillies Hall School, Cheadle   F1 F2 F4 F3
The Ryleys, Alderley Edge   H
Stockport Grammar School, Stockport
    Entry age: 11+   H

Terra Nova School, Holmes Chapel   E F1 F2 F4 F3 H +
Wilmslow Preparatory School, Wilmslow
    Entry age: from 2.5yrs   H T

CORNWALL

Gems Bolitho School, Penzance
    Entry age: 7+   F1 F2 F4 F3 H T +
Polwhele House School, Truro   H T +
Roselyon, Par   H
St Joseph's School, Launceston Entry age: 7+, 11+ H
St Petroc's School, Bude
    Entry age: 7+   F1 F2 F4 F3 H T +
Truro High School, Truro Entry age: 11+, 16+   E H +
Truro School, Truro   H +
Truro School Preparatory School, Truro   H

CUMBRIA

Austin Friars St Monica's School, Carlisle
    Entry age: 11+   H
Casterton School, Kirkby Lonsdale   F1 F2 F4 F3 H T +
Chetwynde School, Barrow-in-Furness   H +
Hunter Hall School, Penrith   H
Lime House School, Carlisle   E F1 F2 F4 F3 FO H T
St Bees School, St Bees   F1 F2 F4 F3 H +
St Ursulas Convent School, Wigton   H
Sedbergh Junior School, Sedbergh
    Entry age: 11   F1 F2 F4 F3 H
Sedbergh School, Sedbergh
    Entry age: 13+, 16+, 17+   E F1 F2 F4 F3 H T +
Windermere School, Windermere
    Entry age: 11+, 13+, 16+   H

DERBYSHIRE

Barlborough Hall School, Chesterfield   H
Derby Grammar School, Derby   H
Derby High School, Derby Entry age: 11/16   H +
Foremarke Hall, Derby   F1 F2 F4 F3 H T
Michael House Steiner School, Heanor   H
Mount St Mary's College, Spinkhill
    Entry age: 11+, 13+, 15+   F2 F4 F3 FO H
Repton School, Derby
    Entry age: 13+, 16+   F1 F2 F4 F3 H +
S. Anselm's School, Bakewell
    Entry age: 7+   F1 F2 F4 F3 FO +
St Peter & St Paul School, Chesterfield   H
St Wystan's School, Repton Entry age: 7+   H

DEVON

Blundell's School, Tiverton
    Entry age: 11, 13, 16   F1 F2 F4 F3 FO H T
Bramdean School, Exeter Entry age: 7/11   FO H
Edgehill College, Bideford   E F1 F2 F4 F3 H +
Exeter Cathedral School, Exeter Entry age: 7/12+ H +
Exeter Junior School, Exeter Entry age: 7+, 8+   H
Exeter School, Exeter Entry age: 7, 11, 12, 13   H
Exeter Tutorial College, Exeter   H
Kelly College, Tavistock
    Entry age: 11, 13, 16   E F1 F2 F4 F3 H T

Kelly College Preparatory School, Tavistock F1 F2 F4 F3
Kingsley School, Bideford
    Entry age: 11, 12, 13, 16+   F1 F2 F4 F3 H T +
The Maynard School, Exeter
    Entry age: 7+, 9+, 16+   H
Mount House School, Tavistock
    Entry age: Generally in the latter years of the
    School eg Year 7, but all will be considered.   H T
Park School, Totnes   H
Plymouth College, Plymouth Entry age: 11, 13, 16 H
St Christophers School, Totnes   H
St Margaret's School, Exeter   E H
St Michael's, Barnstaple   F1 F2 F4 F3 H T +
St Wilfrid's School, Exeter Entry age: 7   H
Sands School, Ashburton   H
Stover School, Newton Abbot   F1 F2 F4 F3 FO H +
Shebbear College, Beaworthy
    Entry age: 11+, 13+, 16+   F1 F2 F4 F3 H +
Tower House School, Paignton Entry age: 11   H
Trinity School, Teignmouth
    Entry age: Entry is considered at all times to
    allow young people to get the best
    education   F1 F2 F4 F3 H
West Buckland Preparatory School, Barnstaple   H
West Buckland School, Barnstaple   H

DORSET

Bournemouth Collegiate Prep School, Poole   H
Bournemouth Collegiate School, Bournemouth
    Entry age: 11+.   F1 F2 F4 F3 H +
Bryanston School, Blandford Forum
    Entry age: 13, 16   H
Canford School, Wimborne Entry age: 13+ and 16+ H
Castle Court Preparatory School, Wimborne   E H +
Cla   Claremore, Blandford Forum
    Entry age: Prep School: 8 years of age
    Senior School 13 years and
    16 years of age   F1 F2 F4 F3
Claysmore Preparatory School,
    Blandford Forum   F1 F2 F4 F3 H
Dumpton School, Wimborne   H
Knighton House, Blandford Forum   F1 F2 F4 F3 H T
Leweston School, Sherborne
    Entry age: 7–13, 16   F1 F2 F4 F3 H
Milton Abbey School, Blandford Forum
    Entry age: 13 and 16   F1 F2 F4 F3 H
The Park School, Bournemouth   H
Port Regis Preparatory School, Shaftesbury
    Entry age: Your child needs to be aged 7 and under
    12 years of age on 1st September. F1 F2 F4 F3 T
St Martin's School, Bournemouth   E F1 F2 F4 F3 H T +
Sherborne Girls, Sherborne   H
Sherborne School, Sherborne
    Entry age: 13+, 16+   F1 F2 F4 F3 H T +
Talbot Heath, Bournemouth   H

COUNTY DURHAM

Barnard Castle School, Barnard Castle
    Entry age: 11+ and Sixth Form   F1 F2 F4 F3 FO H
The Chorister School, Durham   H +

Durham High School For Girls, Durham
Entry age: 11, 16   H +
Durham School, Durham
Entry age: 7, 11, 13, 16   F1 F2 F4 F3 H +
Hurworth House School, Darlington   H
Polam Hall, Darlington
Entry age: 7, 11, 14, 16   F1 F2 F4 F3 H T

ESSEX

Alleyn Court Preparatory School, Southend-on-Sea
Entry age: 7   H T +
Bancroft's School, Woodford Green
Entry age: 7, 11, 13, 16   H
Brentwood School, Brentwood Entry age: 11, 16   H T
Chigwell School, Chigwell   H T
Dame Bradbury's School, Saffron Walden
Entry age: Bursary Scheme from Year 3 for children
with a specific aptitude (ie Art, Sport, Drama) who
would benefit from the education we provide.   H
Felsted School, Felsted
Entry age: Ages 11, 13 and 16   F1 F2 F4 F3 H
Friends' School, Saffron Walden
Entry age: 11, 13, 16   F1 F4 F3
Gosfield School, Halstead Entry age: All   F3 H T
Holmwood House, Colchester   H
Littlegarth School, Colchester   H
New Hall School, Chelmsford
Entry age: 3–18   F1 F2 F4 F3 H
Park School for Girls, Ilford
Entry age: 20% bursary offered in Year 3 and Year 7
only. Means tested.   H
St Hilda's School, Westcliff-on-Sea   H
St Michael's School, Leigh-on-Sea   E T +
St Nicholas School, Harlow   H T
Thorpe Hall School, Southend-on-Sea
Entry age: 7/11   H
Woodford Green Preparatory School, Woodford Green
Entry age: 7+   H

GLOUCESTERSHIRE

Berkhampstead School, Cheltenham   H
Bredon School, Tewkesbury
Entry age: 5 – 15 years   F1 F2 F4 F3 H
Cheltenham College, Cheltenham
Entry age: 13, 16   F1 F2 F4 F3 H
Cheltenham College Junior School, Cheltenham
Entry age: 11+   F1 F2 F4 F3
Cheltenham Ladies' College, Cheltenham
Entry age: 11+, 12+, 13+ and 16+   H
Dean Close Preparatory School,
Cheltenham   E F1 F2 F4 F3 H +
Dean Close School, Cheltenham
Entry age: 11+, 13+, 16+   E F1 F2 F4 F3 H +
Hatherop Castle School, Cirencester
Entry age: 7+   F1 F2 F4 F3 H
The King's School, Gloucester   H
Rendcomb College, Cirencester
Entry age: 11, 13, 16   F1 F2 F4 F3 H
Rose Hill School, Wotton-under-Edge   F1 F2 F4 F3 H T
St Edward's School Cheltenham, Cheltenham
Entry age: At Year 7   H

The School of the Lion, Gloucester   E H
Westonbirt School, Tetbury   F1 F2 F4 F3 FO H T +
Wycliffe College, Stonehouse
Entry age: 11+, 13+ and Sixth Form F1 F2 F4 F3 H T
Wycliffe Preparatory School, Stonehouse
Entry age: 11   F1 F2 F4 F3 FO H T
Wynstones School, Gloucester   H

HAMPSHIRE

Ballard School, New Milton
Entry age: Year 3 and Year 6   H
Bedales School, Petersfield   H
Boundary Oak School, Fareham   F1 F2 F4 F3 H
Daneshill School, Basingstoke   T
Dunhurst (Bedales Junior School), Petersfield   H
Durlston Court, New Milton Entry age: Over 7 in
September of year of entry   H
Farleigh School, Andover   F1 F2 F4 F3 H
Farnborough Hill, Farnborough   H
Forres Sandle Manor, Fordingbridge   F1 F2 F4 F3
The Gregg School, Southampton   H
Hampshire Collegiate School, UCST,
Romsey   F1 F2 F4 F3 FO H T +
Highfield School, Liphook   E F1 F2 F4 F3 +
Hordle Walhampton School, Lymington   H
King Edward VI School, Southampton
Entry age: 11+, 13+, 16+   H
Mayville High School, Southsea   H T
The Pilgrims' School, Winchester   H
The Portsmouth Grammar School, Portsmouth   H T
Portsmouth High School GDST, Southsea
Entry age: 11+, 13+, 16+   H
Prince's Mead School, Winchester   H
Ramshill School, Petersfield   H
Rookesbury Park School, Portsmouth   F1 F2 F3 H
Rookwood School, Andover   H
St Neot's School, Hook   H
St Nicholas' School, Fleet Entry age: 11, 13   H
St Swithun's School, Winchester
Entry age: 11+, 13+, 16+   H
Salesian College, Farnborough   H
Stockton House School, Fleet Entry age: 2 years   H
Sherborne House School, Eastleigh   H
Winchester College, Winchester Entry age: 13, 16   H
Wykeham House School, Fareham   H

HEREFORDSHIRE

Hereford Cathedral School, Hereford   H
Lucton School, Leominster Entry age: 11, 13, 16   E H
St Richard's, Bromyard   F1 F2 F4 F3

HERTFORDSHIRE

Abbot's Hill School, Hemel Hempstead
Entry age: 11   H T
Berkhamsted School, Berkhamsted   H
Berkhamsted School, Berkhamsted   H
Bishop's Stortford College, Bishop's Stortford
Entry age: 11+, 13+, 16+   H

Bishop's Stortford College Junior School, Bishop's
Stortford
    Entry age: 10+ and 11+ years   F1 F2 F4 F3 H
Edge Grove, Aldenham village
    Entry Age: 7–13 yrs   F1 F2 F4 F3 H T +
Haberdashers' Aske's Boys' School, Elstree
    Entry age: 11, 13   H
Haberdashers' Aske's School for Girls, Elstree   H +
Haileybury, Hertford Entry age: 11, 13, 16   H
Haresfoot Preparatory School, Berkhamsted
    Entry age: from Reception up   H
High Elms Manor School, Watford   F4 H T
Immanuel College, Bushey Entry age: 4/11/16   H
The Junior School, Bishop's Stortford College,
Bishop's Stortford
    Entry age: Academic and Music scholarships
    (under 11 and 12)
    Art scholarship (under 12)   H
Lockers Park, Hemel Hempstead
    Entry age: From Year 3 (7 years)   F1 F2 F4 F3 H T
Manor Lodge School, Shenley   H
The Purcell School, Bushey   H
Queenswood, Hatfield   H
Redemption Academy, Stevenage   E H +
Rickmansworth PNEU School, Rickmansworth   H
The Royal Masonic School for Girls, Rickmansworth
    Entry age: 7, 11, 16   F1 F2 F4 F3 H
St Albans High School for Girls, St Albans
    Entry age: Fees Assistance for all entry ages from 4+
    (Reception)   H
St Albans School, St Albans Entry age: 11+, 13+, 16+ H
St Christopher School, Letchworth Garden City
    Entry age: ages from 11. Specific Sixth Form
    bursaries also available.   H
St Columba's College, St Albans
    Entry age: 11+/13+   H
St Edmund's College, Ware   F1 F2 F4 F3 H
St Edmund's College and St Hugh's School, Ware
    Entry age: 7+, 11+ and 16+   H
St Francis' College, Letchworth Garden City   H
St Hilda's School, Bushey   H
St Margaret's School, Bushey   F1 F2 F4 F3 H +
Stormont, Potters Bar   H
Tring Park School for the Performing Arts, Tring
    Entry age: From 8 – 16   F1 F2 F4 F3 H
Westbrook Hay Preparatory School, Hemel Hempstead
    Entry age: 8+   H
York House School, Rickmansworth
    Entry Age: Pre Prep onwards   H T

ISLE OF MAN

King William's College, Castletown
    Entry age: 11 and 16   F1 F2 F4 F3 H +

ISLE OF WIGHT

Ryde School, Ryde   H

KENT

Ashford School, Ashford   F1 F2 F4 F3 H +

Beechwood Sacred Heart School, Tunbridge Wells
    Entry age: 11+, 13+, 16+ E F1 F2 F4 F3 FO H M T +
Benenden School, Cranbrook Entry age: 11, 13, 16   H
Bethany School, Cranbrook
    Entry age: 11+, 13+, 16+   E F1 F2 F4 F3 H +
Bromley High School GDST, Bromley
    Entry age: 11/16+   H
CATS College Canterbury, Canterbury
    Entry age: At 6th Form (16+)   F1 F2 F4 F3
Derwent Lodge School for Girls, Tonbridge   H
Dover College, Dover
    Entry age: 11, 13, 16   F1 F2 F4 F3
Dulwich Preparatory School, Cranbrook, Cranbrook H
Elliott Park School, Sheerness   H
Farringtons School, Chislehurst   E F1 F2 F4 F3 +
Fosse Bank School, Tonbridge   H
Gad's Hill School, Rochester Entry age: 11   H
The Granville School, Sevenoaks   H
Hilden Grange School, Tonbridge   H
Hilden Oaks School, Tonbridge   H
Holmewood House, Tunbridge Wells
    Entry age: Year 3 and above   H
Kent College, Canterbury
    Entry age: 8, 11, 13, 16+   F1 F2 F4 F3 H +
Kent College Pembury, Tunbridge Wells
    Entry age: 11, 13, 16   F1 F2 F4 F3 H +
King's Preparatory School, RochesterE F1 F2 F4 F3 H +
King's Rochester, Rochester   F1 F2 F4 F3 H +
Lorenden Preparatory School, Faversham   H
Marlborough House School, Hawkhurst   H T
The Mead School, Tunbridge Wells   E H +
Merton Court Preparatory School, Sidcup   H T
Northbourne Park School, Deal   F1 F2 F4 F3 H T +
Rochester Independent College, Rochester   H
St Christopher's School, Canterbury   H
St Edmund's School Canterbury, Canterbury
    Entry age: 11+, 13+, 16+   F1 F2 F4 F3 FO H +
St Edmunds Junior School, Canterbury
    Entry age: 11   F1 F2 F4 F3 FO +
St Lawrence College, Ramsgate
    Entry age: 8, 11, 13, 16   F1 F2 F4 F3 H
St Lawrence College Junior School,
Ramsgate   F1 F2 F4 F3 H
St Michael's School, Sevenoaks Entry age: 7   H
Sackville School, Tonbridge   H
Sevenoaks School, Sevenoaks
    Entry age: 11+, 13+, 16+   H
Solefield School, Sevenoaks   H T
Sutton Valence School, Sutton Valence
    Entry age: 11+, 13+, 16+   F1 F2 F4 F3 FO H
Tonbridge School, Tonbridge
    Entry age: 13+, 16+   F1 F2 F4 F3 H
Walthamstow Hall, Sevenoaks
    Entry age: 11+, 13+, 16+   E H +
Yardley Court Preparatory School, Tonbridge   H

LANCASHIRE

Arnold School, Blackpool Entry age: 11+, 16+   H +
Beech House School, Rochdale   H
Bolton School (Boys' Division), Bolton   H
Bolton School (Girls' Division), Bolton
    Entry age: 11+, 16+   H

Bury Grammar School Boys, Bury	H
Bury Grammar School Girls, Bury Entry age: 11	H
Heathland College, Accrington	H
The Hulme Grammar School for Girls, Oldham	H
King Edward VII and Queen Mary School,	
Lytham St Annes Entry age: 11, 16	H
Kingswood College Trust, Ormskirk	H T
Kirkham Grammar School, Preston	
Entry age: 11 years, 16 years	H
Moorland School, Clitheroe	F1 F2 F4 F3
The Oldham Hulme Grammar Schools, Oldham	H
Queen Elizabeth's Grammar School, Blackburn	
Entry age: 11+, 16+	H
Rossall School, Fleetwood	F3 +
Rossall School, Fleetwood	
Entry age: 11, 13, 16	F1 F2 F3 +
Rossall School International Study Centre, Fleetwood	
Entry age: 11+, 16+	E F1 F4 F3 H +
St Anne's College Grammar School,	
Lytham St Annes	F1 F2 F4 F3 FO
St Mary's Hall, Clitheroe	H
Stonyhurst College, Clitheroe	
Entry age: 13, 16	F1 F2 F4 F3 FO H M T +

LEICESTERSHIRE

Leicester Grammar School, Leicester	H
Leicester High School For Girls, Leicester	H
Loughborough Grammar School, Loughborough	
Entry age: 10+, 11+, 13+, 16+	F1 F2 F4 F3 H +
Loughborough High School, Loughborough	H
Manor House School, Ashby-de-la-Zouch	H
Ratcliffe College, Leicester	
Entry age: 11+, 13+, 16+	F1 F2 F4 F3 H
St Crispin's School, Leicester	
Entry age: 7+, 11+, 13+	H
Stoneygate School, Leicester	E H +

LINCOLNSHIRE

The Grantham Preparatory School, Grantham	H
Kirkstone House School, Bourne Entry age: Various	H
Maypole House School, Alford	H
St Hugh's School, Woodhall Spa	F1 F2 F4 F3 T
St Mary's Preparatory School, Lincoln	F1 F2 F4 F3
Stamford High School, Stamford	H
Stamford School, Stamford Entry age: 11, 13 and 16	H
Witham Hall, Bourne	H T

NORTH EAST LINCOLNSHIRE

St James' School, Grimsby	F1 F2 F4 FO H T +

LONDON

Albemarle Independent College, London	
Entry Age: 14+, 19+	H
Alleyn's School, London	
Entry Age: 11+, 16+	H
The American School in London, London	H
Arnold House School, London	H
Arts Educational Schools London, London	H

Ashbourne Middle School, London	
Entry Age: 13/16	F4 FO H M T +
Bales College, London	H
Barbara Speake Stage School, London	H
Belmont (Mill Hill Preparatory School), London	
Entry Age: Academic and Music 11	
Bursary 10	H
Blackheath High School GDST, London	
Entry Age: 11+/16+	H
CATS College London, London	
Entry Age: At Sixth Form (16+);	
also at 1 yr GCSE (15+)	F1 F2 F4 F3 FO
The Cavendish School, London	H
Channing School, London	
Entry Age: 11, 16	H
City of London School, London	
Entry Age: 10+, 11+, 13+, 16+	H T
City of London School for Girls, London	
Entry Age: 11, 16	H
Colet Court, London Entry Age: 7+, 8+ and 11+	H
Colfe's School, London	
Entry Age: 11+, 13+ and 16+	H
Collingham Independent GCSE and Sixth Form College,	
London	FO H T
Dallington School, London	H
Davies Laing and Dick, London	H
Dolphin School (Including Noah's Ark Nursery School),	
London	E H +
Duff Miller, London	H M
Dulwich College, London	
Entry Age: 11, 13, 16	H
Dulwich College Preparatory School, London	
Entry Age: 7 or 8 years old	H
Durston House, London Entry age: 7–12 years old	H
Ealing College Upper School, London	H
Eaton House Belgravia, London Entry age: 4	H T
Eaton House The Manor Preparatory, London	
Entry Age: 8+	H T
Eltham College, London	
Entry Age: 11+, 16+	E H
Emanuel School, London	
Entry Age: 10+, 11+, 13+, 16+	H
Forest School, London	H +
Francis Holland School, Regent's Park NW1	E
Francis Holland School, Sloane Square SW1	
Entry Age: 11+, 16+	E FO H +
Garden House School, London	H
The Godolphin and Latymer School, London	H
The Hall School, London	H
Hampstead Hill Pre-Preparatory & Nursery School,	
London	H
Hereward House School, London	+
Highgate School, London	H
Hill House International Junior School, London	
Entry Age: 11	T
The Hurlingham School, London	
Entry Age: 7+	H
Ibstock Place School, London	
Entry Age: 7+, 11+, 16+	H
James Allen's Girls' School, London	
Entry Age: 11+, 16+	H
Kerem School, London	H
King Fahad Academy, London	H

King's College Junior School, London
    Entry Age: Bursary at all entry stages   H
King's College School, London   H
Knightsbridge School, London
    Entry Age: 11   H
Lansdowne College, London
    Entry Age: 14+, 16+   H
Latymer Upper School, London   H
Mander Portman Woodward, London   FO T
Mander Portman Woodward, London   H T
Mill Hill School, London   H
Naima Jewish Preparatory School, London   H
Newton Prep, London   H
The North London International School, London   H
The Norwegian School, London   F1 F2 F4 F3 FO
Notting Hill and Ealing High School GDST, London
    Entry Age: 11+, 16+   H
Palmers Green High School, London
    Entry Age: 11+   H
The Pointer School, London   E F1 F2 F4 F3 H +
Putney High School GDST, London
    Entry Age: 11+, 16+   H
Queen's Gate School, London
    Entry Age: Bursaries and Scholarships available to
    Pupils entering the Senior School from 11+.   H
Redcliffe School, London   H
Riverston School, London   H +
The Roche School, London Entry Age: 7   H
Royal Ballet School, London   H
The Royal School, Hampstead
    Entry Age: 7, 16   F1 F4 F3 H
St Augustine's Priory, Ealing   H
St Benedict's School, Ealing Entry age: 11+, 16+   H
St Dunstan's College, London
    Entry Age: 11+ and Sixth Form   H
St James Junior School, London
    Entry Age: From Reception Class where applicable H
St James Senior Girls' School, London   H
St Johns Wood Pre-Preparatory School, London   H
St Margaret's School, London Entry Age: Bursary
    applicants may apply for any age group.   H
St Mary's School Hampstead, London   H
St Paul's Cathedral School, London   H
St Paul's Girls' School, London   H
St Paul's School, London   H
Sarum Hall, London   H
Sinclair House School, London   H
South Hampstead High School, London
    Entry Age: 11+ and 16+   H
Streatham & Clapham High School, London
    Entry Age: 11, 16   H
Sussex House School, London   E T +
Sydenham High School GDST, London
    Entry Age: 11/16+   H
Sylvia Young Theatre School, London
    Entry Age: 10–14   H
Thames Christian College, London   E +
University College School, London   H
Westminster Cathedral Choir School, London   H
Westminster School, Westminster   H
Westminster Tutors, London   H
Westminster Under School, London
    Entry Age: 11+   H

The White House Prep & Woodentops Kindergarten,
    London   H
Willington School, London   H

GREATER MANCHESTER

Abbey College, Manchester   M
Bridgewater School, Manchester Entry age: 11/16+ H
The Manchester Grammar School, Manchester   H
Manchester High School for Girls, Manchester
    Entry age: Scholarships and Bursaries at 11.
    Bursaries at 16.   H
Monton Prep School with Montessori Nurseries,
    Eccles   H T
St Bede's College, Manchester   H
Withington Girls' School, Manchester
    Entry age: 11–18   H

MERSEYSIDE

Avalon Preparatory School, Wirral Entry age: 7   H
Birkenhead School, Wirral   H
Highfield School, Birkenhead   H
Kingsmead School, Wirral
    Entry age: 7/11+   E F1 F2 F4 F3 H +
Liverpool College, Liverpool   E F1 F2 F4 F3 H M +
Merchant Taylors' Boys' Schools, Liverpool
    Entry age: 11   H
Merchant Taylors' Girls' School, Liverpool
    Entry age: 11+ and 16+   H
St Mary's College, Liverpool Entry age: 11/16+   H
Streatham House School, Liverpool   H
Sunnymede School, Southport   H T
Tower College, Prescot Entry age: 7, 11   E

MIDDLESEX

Alpha Preparatory School, Harrow   T
Halliford School, Shepperton
    Entry age: 11+ 13+ Sixth Form   H
Hampton School, Hampton Entry age: 11, 13, 16 H
Harrow School, Harrow on the Hill
    Entry age: 13, 16   H +
Heathfield School, Pinner   H
The John Lyon School, Harrow
    Entry age: 11+ and 13+   H
The Lady Eleanor Holles School, Hampton   H
The Mall School, Twickenham Entry age: 7+/8+   H
Merchant Taylors' School, Northwood   H
Newland House School, Twickenham   H
North London Collegiate, Edgware   H
Northwood College, Northwood
    Entry age: 11+, 16+   H
Quainton Hall School, Harrow   H T +
St Helen's School, Northwood   F1 F2 F4 F3 H
St John's Northwood, Northwood   H
Staines Preparatory School, Staines
    Entry age: Reception through to Year 6 only.   H
Twickenham Preparatory School, Hampton
    Entry age: Year 7.   H

NORFOLK

Beeston Hall School, Cromer Entry age: All ages
  considered   F1 F2 F4 F3 H
Glebe House School, Hunstanton   T +
Gresham's School, Holt   F1 F2 F4 F3
Hethersett Old Hall School, Norwich
  Entry age: age 7–18.   F1 F4 F3 H +
Langley Preparatory School & Nursery,
  Norwich   F1 F2 F4 F3 H
Langley School, Norwich
  Entry age: 11, 13, 16   E F1 F2 F4 F3 FO H
The New Eccles Hall School, Norwich
  Entry age: 8   F1 F2 F4 F3 H +
Norwich High School for Girls GDST, Norwich   H
Norwich School, Norwich
  Entry age: 11+, 13+, 16+
Riddlesworth Hall, Diss   F1 F2 F4 F3 H
Sacred Heart School, Swaffham Entry age: 11+ E H T
Taverham Hall Preparatory School, Norwich
  Entry age: Age 5 – 13   F1 F2 F4 F3 H +
Thetford Grammar School, Thetford
  Entry age: 16+   H
Town Close House Preparatory School, Norwich
  Entry age: 7+   H
Wood Dene School, Norwich   H

NORTHAMPTONSHIRE

Beachborough School, Brackley Entry age: 8–11   H
Bosworth Independent College,
  Northampton   F1 F2 F4 F3 H
Great Houghton Preparatory School, Northampton H
Maidwell Hall School, Northampton F1 F2 F4 F3 H
Northampton High School, Northampton
  Entry age: 11, 13, 16   H
Northamptonshire Grammar School, Pitsford H +
Oundle School, Nr Peterborough   H T
Quinton House School, Northampton   H
St Peter's School, Kettering   H
Spratton Hall, Northampton Entry age: 7/8   H T +

NORTHUMBERLAND

Longridge Towers School, Berwick-upon-Tweed
  Entry age: 9, 11, 13, 16   F1 F2 F4 F3 H
Mowden Hall School, Stocksfield   F1 F2 F4 F3 H T
St Oswald's School, Alnwick   E H T

NOTTINGHAMSHIRE

Greenholme School, Nottingham   F1 F2 F4 F3 +
Grosvenor School, Nottingham
  Entry age: Bursaries age 4–13
  Scholarships Yr 4 and Yr 7   F1 F2 F4 F3 H +
The King's School, Nottingham   H
Nottingham High School for Girls GDST, Nottingham H
Ranby House School, Retford
  Entry age: 7+, 11+   F1 F2 F4 F3 H
Trent College & The Elms, Nottingham F1 F2 F4 F3 H
Wellow House School, Newark   H
Worksop College, Worksop   F1 F2 F4 F3 H +

OXFORDSHIRE

Abingdon Preparatory School, Abingdon   H
Abingdon School, Abingdon   H
The Carrdus School, Banbury Entry age: 3/11   H T
Cherwell College, Oxford   F1 F2 F3 H
Cokethorpe School, Witney   H
Cranford House School, Wallingford   H T
Dragon School, Oxford Entry age: Bursaries – Yr 4
  Scholarships – Yrs 4, 5, 6, 7   H
Emmanuel Christian School, Oxford Entry age: 5   H
Headington School, Oxford
  Entry age: 11, 13, 16   F1 F2 F4 F3 H +
Magdalen College School, Oxford
  Entry age: 11+, 13+, 16+   H
The Manor Preparatory School, Abingdon
  Entry age: All age groups
The Oratory Preparatory School,
  Reading   F1 F2 F4 F3 H
Our Lady's Abingdon School, Abingdon
  Entry age: 5–17   H
Oxford High School GDST, Oxford
  Entry age: Year 7, Academic & Music
  Year 12, Academic, All-Rounder, Art, Drama, Music,
  Sports
  Year 7 & Year 12 entry, Fee Bursaries   H
Oxford Tutorial College, Oxford   H
Radley College, Abingdon Entry age: 13+   H +
St Andrew's, Wantage   H
St Clare's, Oxford, Oxford Entry age: 16+   H
St Edward's School, Oxford Entry age: 13+, 16+
  Bursaries for university dons   +
St Helen & St Katharine, Abingdon   H
St Hugh's School, Faringdon   F1 F2 F4 F3 H
Shiplake College, Henley-on-Thames
  Entry age: 13+, 16+   H
Sibford School, Banbury   H
Wychwood School, Oxford   H

RUTLAND

Oakham School, Oakham Entry age: 11+, 13+, 16+ H
Uppingham School, Uppingham   H

SHROPSHIRE

Adcote School for Girls,
  Shrewsbury   E F1 F2 F4 F3 FO H M T +
Bedstone College, Bucknell   F1 F2 F3 H
Castle House School, Newport Entry age: Kindergarten
  (Reception) year or any age up to Year 6. Means
  tested bursaries available on application.   H
Concord College, Shrewsbury   H
Dower House School, Bridgnorth Entry age: 7, 8, 9 H
Ellesmere College, Ellesmere F1 F2 F4 F3 FO H T +
Kingsland Grange, Shrewsbury Entry age: 7–11 H T
Moor Park School, Ludlow   F1 F2 F4 F3 H
Moreton Hall School, Oswestry
  Entry age: E F1 F2 F4 F3 FO H T
Oswestry School, Oswestry
  Entry age: 9+, 11+, 13+, 16+   F1 F2 F4 F3 H T
Oswestry School Bellan House,
  Oswestry   F1 F2 F4 F3 T +

Packwood Haugh School,
Shrewsbury   F1 F2 F4 F3 H T +
Prestfelde Preparatory School, Shrewsbury
   Entry age: 7+, 11+   H T +
Shrewsbury High School GDST, Shrewsbury   H
Wrekin College, Telford
   Entry Age: 11, 13, 16   F1 F2 F4 F3 FO H T

SOMERSET

All Hallows, Shepton Mallet
   Entry age: 11+   F1 F2 F4 F3 FO H
Bruton School for Girls, Bruton
   Entry age: 11+, 13+, 16+   F1 F2 F4 F3 H
Chard School, Chard   H
Downside School, Bath   F3 H
Hazlegrove Preparatory School, Yeovil
   Entry age: 7 & 11   F1 F2 F4 F3 H
King's College, Taunton   E F1 F2 F3 H +
King's Hall, Taunton   F1 F2 F4 F3 +
Millfield Preparatory School, Glastonbury
   Entry age: 7–13   F1 F4 H
Millfield School, Street
   Entry age: 13, 14, 16   F1 F2 F4 F3 H
The Park School, Yeovil
   Entry age: 8–18+   E F1 F2 F4 F3 +
Perrott Hill School, Crewkerne F1 F2 F4 F3 FO H T +
Queen's College, Taunton   F1 F2 F4 F3 H
Queen's College Junior, Pre-Prep & Nursery Schools,
   Taunton Entry age: 10+ music scholarship   H
Taunton Preparatory School, Taunton
   Entry age: 11+   F1 F2 F4 F3 H +
Taunton School Senior, Taunton   E F1 F2 F4 F3
Wellington School, Wellington
   Entry age: 10+, 11+, 13+, 16+   F1 F2 F4 F3 H T
Wells Cathedral Junior School, Wells
   Entry age: 8–11   H +
Wells Cathedral School, Wells
   Entry age: 11, 13, 16   F1 F2 F4 F3 H

BATH & NORTH EAST SOMERSET

King Edward's School, Bath, Bath Entry age: 11–18 H
Kingswood Preparatory School, Bath
   Entry age: 7+   F1 F2 F4 F3 +
Kingswood School, Bath   E F1 F2 F4 F3 FO H +
Paragon School, Prior Park College Junior, Bath   H
Prior Park College, Bath   F1 F2 F4 F3 H
The Royal High School, Bath, Bath
   Entry age: 11/16+   F1 F2 F4 F3 H

NORTH SOMERSET

Sidcot School, Winscombe Entry age: Bursary all ages
   Scholarships at Year 7, 9 and Sixth Form   H

STAFFORDSHIRE

Abbots Bromley School for Girls, Abbots Bromley
   Entry age: 11/16+   F1 F4 F3 H +
Abbotsholme School, Uttoxeter   F1 F2 F4 F3 FO

Brooklands School & Little Brooklands Nursery, Stafford
   Entry age: Any   H
Chase Academy, Cannock Entry age: 3+ F1 F2 F4 F3 H
Denstone College, Uttoxeter
   Entry age: 11, 13, 16   F1 F2 F4 F3 H T +
Edenhurst School, Newcastle-under-Lyme   T +
Lichfield Cathedral School, Lichfield
   Entry age: 7, 9, 11   F1 F2 F4 F3 H +
Newcastle-under-Lyme School,
   Newcastle-under-Lyme   H
St Dominic's Priory School, Stone   H
St Dominic's School, Stafford Entry age: 11, 12   H
St Joseph's Preparatory School, Stoke-on-Trent
   Entry age: 3   H
Stafford Grammar School, Stafford   H
Yarlet School, Stafford Entry age: 11+   H T
The Yarlet Schools, Stafford   F1 F4 F3 T +

STOCKTON-ON-TEES

Teesside High School, Eaglescliffe   H
Yarm School, Yarm Entry age: 7+, 11+, 16+   H

SUFFOLK

Amberfield School, Ipswich Entry age: 11/13+   H
Barnardiston Hall Preparatory School,
   Haverhill   F1 F2 F4 F3 +
Brandeston Hall, The Preparatory School for
   Framlingham College, Brandeston
   Entry age: 11+   F1 F2 F4 F3 H
Culford School, Bury St Edmunds E F1 F2 F4 F3 H T +
Fairstead House School, Newmarket
   Entry age: 4, 5 & 6   H
Framlingham College, Woodbridge
   Entry age: 11+, 13+, 16+   F1 F2 F4 F3 H
Ipswich High School GDST, Ipswich
   Entry age: 11+   H
Ipswich School, Ipswich
   Entry age: 11, 13, 16   F1 F4 F3 H
Moreton Hall Preparatory School,
   Bury St Edmunds   F1 F2 F4 F3 H T
Old Buckenham Hall School, Ipswich E F1 F2 F4 F3 +
Orwell Park, Ipswich Entry age: 7+ F1 F2 F4 F3 H T
The Royal Hospital School, Ipswich
   Entry age: 11+, 13+ and 16+   F1 F2 F4 F3
St George's School, Southwold   H T
St Joseph's College, Ipswich   F1 F2 F4 F3 H
Saint Felix School, Southwold
   Entry age: 11, 13, 16   F1 F4 F3 FO H T
Stoke College, Sudbury   H
Woodbridge School, Woodbridge
   Entry age: 11+, 13+ and 16+.   H

SURREY

Aberdour, Tadworth   H
Aberdour School, Tadworth   T +
Aldro School, Godalming   E F1 F2 F4 F3 H +
Amesbury, Hindhead   T
Barfield School and Nursery, Farnham F1 F2 F4 F3 H
Barrow Hills School, Godalming   H

Bishopsgate School, Egham   H
Box Hill School, Dorking Entry age: 11, 13, 16   H
Bramley School, Tadworth Entry age: 7+   H
Cambridge Tutors College, Croydon   H
Caterham Preparatory School, Caterham   +
Charterhouse, Godalming Entry age: 13+   H
Cranleigh School, Cranleigh
    Entry age: 13+, 16+   F1 F2 F4 F3 H T +
Croydon High School GDST, South Croydon
    Entry age: Year 7 and 12 only   H
Drayton House School, Guildford   H
Duke of Kent School, Guildford
    Entry age: 7+, 10+, 11+   F1 F2 F4 F3
Dunottar School, Reigate Entry age: 11, 13, 16   H
Edgeborough, Farnham   F1 F2 F4 F3 H
Epsom College, Epsom Entry age: 13+, 16+   M
Essendene Lodge School, Caterham   H
Ewell Castle School, Epsom Entry age: 11+, 13+, 16+ H
Feltonfleet School, Cobham   H
Frensham Heights School, Farnham   H
Glenesk School, Leatherhead   H
Greenacre School for Girls, Banstead   H
Guildford High School, Guildford   H +
Halstead Preparatory School, Woking   H
Haslemere Preparatory School, Haslemere
    Entry age: Entry from Year 2 to Year 7   T
Hawley Place School, Camberley Entry age: 7, 11   H
The Hawthorns School, Redhill   H +
Hoe Bridge School, Woking Entry age: 7+   H
Homefield Preparatory School, Sutton   H
King Edward's School Witley, Godalming
    Entry age: 11, 13, 16   E F1 F2 F4 F3 H T +
King's House School, Richmond   H
Kingston Grammar School, Kingston-upon-Thames
    Entry age: 11+, 13+, 16+   H
Kingswood House School, Epsom   H T +
Laleham Lea School, Purley
    Entry age: Entry to Year 1 and Year 2 classes.   H
Lingfield Notre Dame School, Lingfield
    Entry age: 11+   H
Lyndhurst School, Camberley   H
Manor House School, Leatherhead   H
Marymount International School,
    Kingston-upon-Thames Entry age: 11, 16   H
Notre Dame Preparatory School, Cobham   H
Oakfield School, Woking Entry age: 7+, 11+   H T
Oakwood School & Nursery, Purley   H
Parkside School, Cobham   H
Prior's Field School, Godalming
    Entry age: 11+, 13+ and 16+   F1 F2 F4 F3 H T
Priory Preparatory School, Banstead   T
Redehall Preparatory School, Horley
    Entry age: Charity Bursary   H
Reed's School, Cobham   H
Reigate Grammar School, Reigate   H
Reigate St Mary's Preparatory and Choir School,
    Reigate Entry age: 7+   H
Ripley Court School, Woking   H T
Royal Alexandra and Albert School, Reigate   H +
Royal Grammar School, Guildford
    Entry age: 11+/13+   H
Royal Russell School, Croydon
    Entry age: 11+/16   F1 F2 F4 F3 H

The Royal School, Haslemere
    Entry age: 11+, 13+, 16+   F1 F2 F4 F3 H T
The Royal School For Girls, Haslemere   F1 F2 H
St. Andrew's (Woking) School Trust, Woking
    Entry age: 7+   H
St Catherine's School, Guildford Entry age: 11/16+   H
St David's School, Purley   H
St Edmund's School, Hindhead
    Entry age: 7/8   F1 F2 F4 F3 H T
St Hilary's School, Godalming Entry age: Year 3   H
St Ives School, Haslemere   H
St James Independent School for Boys (Senior),
    Ashford   H
St John's School, Leatherhead Entry age: 13+, 16+   +
St Teresa's School, Dorking   F1 F2 F4 F3 H T
Shrewsbury House School, Surbiton   T
Sir William Perkins's School, Chertsey   H
Surbiton High School, Kingston-upon-Thames   H +
Sutton High School GDST, Sutton
    Entry age: 11+, 16+   H
TASIS The American School in England, Thorpe   H
Trinity School, Croydon
    Entry age: 10+, 11+, 13+, 16+   H
Warlingham Park School, Croydon   H
Whitgift School, South Croydon
    Entry age: 10–13, 16   H
Woodcote House School, Windlesham   H T
Yehudi Menuhin School, Cobham   H

EAST SUSSEX

Ashdown House School, Forest Row   T +
Battle Abbey School, Battle
    Entry age: 13/16+   F1 F2 F4 F3 H T
Bricklehurst Manor Preparatory, Wadhurst   H
Brighton and Hove High School GDST, Brighton   H
Brighton College, Brighton
    Entry age: 13+, 16+   F3 H T +
Buckswood School, Hastings   H
Eastbourne College, Eastbourne   F1 F4 F3 FO H
The Fold School, Hove Entry age: 3+   H
Lancing College Preparatory School at Mowden, Hove
    Entry age: 7+, 11+   H +
Michael Hall (Steiner Waldorf School), Forest Row
    Entry age: On entry to Kindergarten (age 3/4)   H
Moira House School, Eastbourne   H T
Newlands School, Seaford   F1 F2 F4 F3
Roedean School, Brighton
    Entry age: 11+, 12+, 13+, 16+ F1 F2 F4 F3 FO H +
St Andrew's School, Eastbourne   F1 F2 F4 F3
St Aubyn's, Brighton   T +
St Aubyns School, Brighton   H T +
St Bede's Prep School, Eastbourne   F1 F2 F4 F3 H
St Bede's School, Hailsham   F1 F2 F4 F3 H +
St Leonards-Mayfield School, Mayfield
    Entry age: 11+, 13+, 16+   H
Sacred Heart R.C. Primary School, Wadhurst   H
Vinehall School, Robertsbridge
    Entry age: 8+   F1 F2 F4 F3 H

WEST SUSSEX

Ardingly College, Haywards Heath
  Entry age: 7+, 11+, 13+, 16+   H +
Ardingly College Junior School, Haywards Heath
  Entry age: 11+   H
Burgess Hill School for Girls, Burgess Hill   H
Christ's Hospital, Horsham   F1 F2 F4 H +
Conifers School, Midhurst   H T
Copthorne Prep School, Copthorne   H T
Cottesmore School, Pease Pottage   H
Dorset House School, Pulborough   H T +
Farlington School, Horsham   F1 F2 F3 H +
Fonthill Lodge, East Grinstead   H
Great Ballard School, Chichester
  Entry age: 7   F1 F2 F4 F3
Great Walstead, Haywards Heath
  Entry age: 7–11   E H T +
Handcross Park School, Haywards Heath
  Entry age: 7–11   H T
Our Lady of Sion School, Worthing
  Entry age: 11 & 16   H
Pennthorpe School, Horsham   H
The Prebendal School, Chichester Entry age: 7   H +
Shoreham College, Shoreham-by-Sea   H +
Slindon College, Arundel Entry age: 10   F1 F2 F4 F3 H
Sompting Abbotts School, Sompting   T
Tavistock & Summerhill School, Haywards Heath   H
The Towers Convent School, Steyning   H T

TYNE AND WEAR

Central Newcastle High School GDST,
  Newcastle upon Tyne Entry age: 11+, 16+   H
Dame Allan's Boys School, Newcastle upon Tyne   H
Dame Allan's Girls School, Newcastle upon Tyne
  Entry age: 11   H
Grindon Hall Christian School, Sunderland   E T +
The King's School, Tynemouth Entry age: 11+   E H +
Newcastle Preparatory School, Newcastle upon Tyne   H
Sunderland High School, Sunderland   E H
Westfield School, Newcastle upon Tyne   H

WARWICKSHIRE

Bilton Grange, Rugby
  Entry age: Bursary: 4+
  Scholarship: 8+   F1 F2 F4 F3 H
King's High School, Warwick, Warwick   H
The Kingsley School, Leamington Spa   H
Princethorpe College, Rugby Entry age: 11/18+   H
Rugby School, Rugby   H
Warwick School, Warwick   H

WEST MIDLANDS

Abbey College, Birmingham   H
Al-Burhan Grammar School, Birmingham
  Entry age: 11 years old   H
Bablake Junior School, Coventry   H
Bablake School, Coventry   H

Birchfield School, Wolverhampton
  Entry age: 4   F4 H T
The Blue Coat School, Birmingham
  Entry age: 7+   H
Edgbaston High School for Girls, Birmingham
  Entry age: 11+ 16+   H
Elmhurst School for Dance, Birmingham   F1 F4 F3 H
Eversfield Preparatory School, Solihull
  Entry age: 7+ entry.   H
Highclare School, Birmingham Entry age: 11/16+   H
King Edward VI High School for Girls, Birmingham   H
King Edward's School, Birmingham 11+, 13+ and 16+.
  Means-tested Assisted Places
  available at 11+ and 16+.   H
King Henry VIII School, Coventry   H +
Newbridge Preparatory School, Wolverhampton   +
Pattison College, Coventry   H
Priory School, Birmingham Entry age: 11, 16   H
The Royal Wolverhampton Junior School,
  Wolverhampton   F1 F3 H
St George's School, Edgbaston, Birmingham
  Entry age: 11+   H +
Saint Martin's School, Solihull
  Entry age: 7+, 11+, 16+   H
Solihull School, Solihull   +
Tettenhall College, Wolverhampton
  Entry age: 11   F1 F2 F4 F3 H +
West House School, Birmingham   H T
Wolverhampton Grammar School, Wolverhampton
  Entry age: 11+, 13+, 16+   H

WILTSHIRE

Chafyn Grove School, Salisbury   F1 F2 F4 F3 H T
Dauntsey's School, Devizes
  Entry age: 11+, 13+, 16+   H
Godolphin Preparatory School, Salisbury   F1 F2 F4 F3 H
The Godolphin School, Salisbury   F1 F2 F4 F3 H
Leaden Hall School, Salisbury   +
Marlborough College, Marlborough
  Entry age: 13+, 16+   +
Norman Court Preparatory School, Salisbury
  Entry age: 7, 8, 11   F1 F2 F4 F3 H
Pinewood School, Shrivenham   H
Prior Park Preparatory School, Cricklade   F1 F2 F4 F3
St Francis School, Pewsey Entry age: Age 9+   H T
St Mary's Calne, Calne
  Entry age: 11+, 13+, 16+   F1 F2 F4 F3 H
Stonar School, Melksham Entry age: Scholarships
  offered from Year 7 through to Sixth Form.
  All Bursaries available from Pre-prep School
  upwards   F1 F2 F4 F3 H
South Hills School, Salisbury   H
Warminster School, Warminster
  Entry age: 7, 9, 11, 13, 16   F1 F2 F4 F3 H

WORCESTERSHIRE

Abberley Hall, Worcester   F1 F2 F4 F3
The Abbey College, Malvern Wells   H
Bromsgrove Preparatory School, Bromsgrove
  Entry age: 11+   F1 F2 F4 F3 H

Bromsgrove School, Bromsgrove   F1 F2 F4 F3 H T
The Downs, Malvern, Malvern
    Entry age: 11+ Scholarship
    Bursarial Assistance may be applied for
    from age 5   F1 F2 F4 F3 FO H T
The Elms, Malvern   F1 F2 F4 F3 H T
King's Hawford, Worcester Entry age: 7+, 8+   +
The King's School, Worcester   H
Malvern St James, Great Malvern
    Entry age: 11+, 12+, 13+, 16+   H
Moffats School, Bewdley   E F1 F2 F4 F3 FO H M T +
RGS Worcester & The Alice Ottley School,
    Worcester   H
River School, Worcester   H
St Mary's, Worcester Entry age: 11+, 16+   H
Winterfold House, Kidderminster   H

EAST RIDING OF YORKSHIRE

Hull Collegiate School, Anlaby Entry age: 11   H
Hymers College, Hull   H
Pocklington School, Pocklington   F1 F2 F4 F3 H

NORTH YORKSHIRE

Ampleforth College, York Entry age: 13, 16   H
Ashville College, Harrogate
    Entry age: 11–18   E F1 F2 F4 F3 H T +
Aysgarth Preparatory School, Bedale
    Entry age: Normally between 8 and
    11 years old   E F1 F2 F4 F3 H T +
Belmont Grosvenor School, Harrogate   F1 F2 F4 F3 +
Bootham School, York Entry age: 11+, 13+ entry.   H
Bramcote School, Scarborough   F1 F2 F4 F3 H T
Cundall Manor School, York   F1 F2 F4 F3 FO
Fyling Hall School, Whitby   H
Gigglewick Junior School, Settle
    Entry age: 10, 11   F1 F2 F4 F3 T
Gigglewick School, Settle
    Entry age: 13, 16   F1 F2 F4 F3 H T
Harrogate Ladies' College, Harrogate
    Entry age: 11+, 16+   E F1 F2 F4 F3 H T +
Harrogate Tutorial College, Harrogate
    Entry age: 15+   F1 F2 F4 F3 FO H T
Highfield Preparatory School,
    Harrogate   E F1 F2 F4 F3 T +
Malsis School, Near Skipton
    Entry age: Scholarships and Bursaries are available
    to children in Year 3 and above. F1 F2 F4 F3 H T +
The Mount School, York   H
Queen Ethelburga's College, York
    Entry age: 11   F1 F2 F4 F3 FO M T +

Queen Mary's School, Thirsk
    Entry age: 11+, 12+, 13+   F1 F2 F4 F3 H T +
Read School, Selby Entry age: 11+, 13+, 16+   H
Ripon Cathedral Choir School, Ripon   F1 F2 F4 F3 H
St Martin's Ampleforth, York
    Entry age: 7/12+   F1 F2 F4 F3
St Peter's School, York
    Entry age: 13/16+   F1 F2 F4 F3 H +
Scarborough College & Lisvane School,
    Scarborough   F2 F4 F3 H
Terrington Hall, York   F1 F2 F4 F3 H T +
Woodleigh School, Malton   F1 F2 F3

SOUTH YORKSHIRE

Ashdell Preparatory School, Sheffield Entry age: 4+ H
Birkdale School, Sheffield Entry age: 11, 16   H +
Handsworth Christian School, Sheffield   H
Rudston Preparatory School, Rotherham   H T
Sheffield High School GDST, Sheffield
    Entry age: 11, 16   H
Westbourne School, Sheffield   H

WEST YORKSHIRE

Ackworth School, Pontefract   H
Batley Grammar School, Batley   H
Bradford Girls' Grammar School, Bradford   H
Bradford Grammar School, Bradford Entry age: 11+ H
Bronte House School, Bradford
    Entry age: 9   F1 F2 F3 H
The Froebelian School, Leeds   H
Fulneck School, Leeds   E F1 F2 F4 F3 H +
Gateways School, Leeds Entry age: 11   H
The Grammar School at Leeds, Leeds
    Entry age: 11+, 16+   H
Hipperholme Grammar School, Halifax
    Entry age: 16+   H
Huddersfield Grammar School, Huddersfield   H
Moorfield School, Ilkley Entry age: Bursary from
    Reception   H
Moorlands School, Leeds   H
Queen Elizabeth Grammar School, Wakefield   H
Richmond House School, Leeds Entry age: 7/8   H T
Rishworth School, Rishworth Entry age: 11, 16   H
Silcoates School, Wakefield Entry age: 11   +
Wakefield Girls' High School, Wakefield   H
Woodhouse Grove School,
    Apperley Bridge   F1 F2 F4 F3 H +

NORTHERN IRELAND

COUNTY ANTRIM

Cabin Hill School, Belfast   F3
Methodist College, Belfast   +
Royal Belfast Academical Institution, Belfast   H

COUNTY ARMAGH

The Royal School Armagh, Armagh   +

COUNTY DOWN

The Holywood Rudolf Steiner School, Holywood   H

COUNTY TYRONE

The Royal School Dungannon, Dungannon
    Entry age: 11–16   E F1 F2 F4 F3 +

SCOTLAND

ABERDEENSHIRE

Aberdeen Waldorf School, Aberdeen	H
International School of Aberdeen, Aberdeen	H
Robert Gordon's College, Aberdeen	H
St Margaret's School for Girls, Aberdeen	H

ANGUS

High School of Dundee, Dundee Entry age: 12	H
Lathallan School, Montrose	
Entry age: Primary 7 and S5	F1 F2 F4 F3 H

SOUTH AYRSHIRE

Wellington School, Ayr	H

FIFE

St Leonards School, St Andrews	
Entry age: Varies – please contact the	
Registrar for more information.	F1 F2 F4 F3 H

GLASGOW

Craigholme School, Glasgow	
Entry Age: 11	F1 F2 F4 F3 H +
The Glasgow Academy, Pollokshields	
Entry Age: 11+	H +
The High School of Glasgow, Glasgow	H
Hutchesons' Grammar School, Glasgow	
Entry Age: S1 (age 11/12)	H
St Aloysius' College, Glasgow	
Entry Age: Senior School only	H

INVERCLYDE

St Columba's School, Kilmacolm	H

SOUTH LANARKSHIRE

Fernhill School, Glasgow	H

LOTHIAN

Belhaven Hill, Dunbar Entry age: 8+	H T

WALES

BRIDGEND

St John's School, Porthcawl	H

CARDIFF

The Cathedral School, Llandaff	
Entry Age: 11	H
Howell's School, Llandaff GDST, Llandaff	
Entry Age: 11, 16	H

CARMARTHENSHIRE

Llandovery College, Llandovery	
Entry age: Year 7 to 12	E F1 F2 F4 F3 H +

Cargilfield, Edinburgh	F1 F2 F4 F3 T
Clifton Hall School, Edinburgh	F1 F2 F4 F3 H
The Compass School, Haddington Entry age: 9/11	H
The Edinburgh Academy, Edinburgh	H
Fettes College, Edinburgh	
Entry age: 11+, 13+, 16+	F1 F2 F4 F3 H T
George Heriot's School, Edinburgh Entry age: 11+	H
George Watson's College, Edinburgh	H
Loretto School, Musselburgh Entry age: on entry all age	
groups from 12 years	F1 F2 F4 F3 H
The Mary Erskine School, Edinburgh	H
Merchiston Castle School, Edinburgh	F1 F2 F4 F3
St George's School for Girls, Edinburgh	
Entry age: 12, 13, 16–18	H
Stewart's Melville College, Edinburgh	H

MORAYSHIRE

Gordonstoun School, Elgin	
Entry age: 8+ at Junior School Entry	
13+ at Lower School Entry	
16+ at Sixth Form Entry	H
Rosebrae School, Elgin	H

PERTH AND KINROSS

Ardvreck School, Crieff	F1 F2 F4 F3
Craigclowan Preparatory School, Perth	H T
Glenalmond College, Perth	
Entry age: 12, 13, 16	E F1 F2 F4 F3 H T +
Kilgraston, Perth	F1 F2 F4 F3 H T
Morrison's Academy, Crieff	H
Queen Victoria School, Dunblane	F1 F2 F4 F3
Strathallan School, Perth Entry age: 9, 10, 11,	
12, 13 & 16	E F1 F2 F4 F3 FO H M T +

STIRLING

Beaconhurst School, Bridge of Allan	H

St Michael's School, Llanelli	H

CONWY

St David's College, Llandudno	
Entry age: 11	E F1 F2 F4 F3 FO H +

DENBIGHSHIRE

Howell's School, Denbigh	F1 F2 F4 F3 H T +
Ruthin School, Ruthin	
Entry age: 11 and 16	F1 F2 F4 F3 H

GWYNEDD

Hillgrove School, Bangor   E

MONMOUTHSHIRE

Haberdashers' Monmouth School For Girls,
   Monmouth   F1 F2 F4 F3 H
Llangattock School, Monmouth   H
Monmouth School, Monmouth
   Entry age: 11, 13, 16   F1 F2 F4 F3 H T
St John's-on-the-Hill, Chepstow
   Entry age: External scholarships and bursaries
   available from Year 2 upwards.   F1 F2 F4 F3 H

NEWPORT

Rougemont School, Newport   H

POWYS

Christ College, Brecon
   Entry age: 11, 13, 16   F1 F4 F3 H T +

SWANSEA

Ffynone House School, Swansea
   Entry Age: 11   H
Oakleigh House School, Swansea   H

CONTINENTAL EUROPE

Chavagnes International College,
   Chavagnes-En-Paillers, France   H

St Columba's College, Dublin, Ireland
   Entry Age: 11, 13, 16.   +

Specialist Schools

Schools in the directory which specialize in the theatre, dance or music are listed below. For full details about entrance requirements and the curriculum, parents are advised to contact schools direct.

Arts Schools

Arts Educational Schools, London W4
Barbara Speake Stage School, London W3
The Italia Conti Academy of Theatre Arts, London EC1
Pattison College, Coventry
Ravenscourt Theatre School, London W6
Sylvia Young Theatre School, London NW1
Tring Park School for the Performing Arts, Tring

Dance Schools

Elmhurst School for Dance, Birmingham
Hammond School, Chester
Royal Ballet School, London WC2E
Stonelands School of Ballet & Theatre Arts, Hove
The Urdang Academy of Ballet, London WC2

Music Schools

Chetham's School of Music, Manchester
The Purcell School, Bushey
St Mary's Music School, Edinburgh
Yehudi Menuhin School, Cobham

Single-Sex Schools

For details consult the school listings in Part 2.

BOYS

ENGLAND

BEDFORDSHIRE

Bedford Preparatory School, Bedford	7–13
Bedford School, Bedford	7–18

BERKSHIRE

Claires Court School, Maidenhead	11–16 (Co-ed VIth Form)
Claires Court Schools, Ridgeway, Maidenhead	4–11
Elstree School, Reading	3–13 (Girls 3–7)
Eton College, Windsor	13–18
Horris Hill School, Newbury	7–13
Ludgrove, Wokingham	8–13
The Oratory School, Reading	11–18
Papplewick School, Ascot	6–13
Reading Blue Coat School, Reading	11–18 (Co-ed VIth Form)
Reading School, Reading	11–18
St Edward's School, Reading	4–13
St John's Beaumont, Windsor	4–13
Sunningdale School, Sunningdale	8–13

BRISTOL

Queen Elizabeth's Hospital, Bristol	7–18 (Sixth Form International students are welcome on a Guardianship basis)

BUCKINGHAMSHIRE

The Beacon School, Amersham	3–13
Caldicott School, Farnham Royal	7–13
Davenies School, Beaconsfield	4–13
Kingscote Pre-Preparatory School, Gerrards Cross	3–7
Thorpe House School, Gerrards Cross	3–16

CHANNEL ISLANDS

Victoria College, Jersey	11–19
Victoria College Preparatory School, Jersey	7–11

CHESHIRE

Altrincham Preparatory School, Altrincham	3–11
The Ryleys, Alderley Edge	3–13
St Ambrose Preparatory School, Altrincham	3–11

DORSET

Sherborne School, Sherborne	13–18

COUNTY DURHAM

Hurworth House School, Darlington	3–18

ESSEX

Loyola Preparatory School, Buckhurst Hill	3–11

HAMPSHIRE

The Pilgrims' School, Winchester	7–13
Salesian College, Farnborough	11–18
Winchester College, Winchester	13–18

HERTFORDSHIRE

Aldwickbury School, Harpenden	4–13
Haberdashers' Aske's Boys' School, Elstree	5–18
Lockers Park, Hemel Hempstead	5–13
Northwood Preparatory School, Rickmansworth (Girls 3–4)	4–13
St Albans School, St Albans	11–18 (Co-ed VIth Form)
St Columba's College, St Albans	4–18

KENT

Bickley Park School, Bromley	3–13
Darul Uloom London, Chislehurst	11–18
Harenc School Trust, Sidcup	3–11

The New Beacon, Sevenoaks	4–13
Solefield School, Sevenoaks	4–13
Tonbridge School, Tonbridge	13–18
Yardley Court Preparatory School, Tonbridge	7–13

LANCASHIRE

Bolton School (Boys' Division), Bolton	7–18
Bury Grammar School Boys, Bury	7–18
Tashbar School, Salford	2–11

LEICESTERSHIRE

Loughborough Grammar School, Loughborough	10–18

LINCOLNSHIRE

Stamford School, Stamford	11–18

LONDON

Al-Mizan Primary & London East Academy Secondary & Sixth Form, London	7–18
Arnold House School, London	5–13
Beis Hamedrash Elyon, London	11–14
Brondesbury College For Boys, London	11–16
City of London School, London	10–18
Clifton Lodge Preparatory School, London	4–13
Colet Court, London	7–13
Darul Hadis Latifiah, London	11–19
Donhead Prep School, London	4–11
Dulwich College, London	7–18
Dulwich College Preparatory School, London	3–13 (Girls 3–5)
Durston House, London	4–13
Eaton House Belgravia, London	4–8
Eaton House The Manor Pre-Preparatory, London	4–8
Eaton House The Manor Preparatory, London	3–13
The Falcons School for Boys, London	3–8
The Hall School, London	4–13
Hawkesdown House School, London	3–8
Hereward House School, London	4–13
Keble Preparatory School, London	4–13
King's College Junior School, London	7–13
King's College School, London	13–18
London Islamic School, London	11–16
Lubavitch House School (Junior Boys), London	5–13
Lyndhurst House Preparatory School, London	4–13
Mechinah Liyeshivah Zichron Moshe, London	11–16
North Bridge House Upper Prep School, London	10–13
Northcote Lodge School, London	8–13
Pardes Grammar Boys' School, London	11–17
St Anthony's Preparatory School, London	5–13
St Paul's School, London	13–18
St Philip's School, London	7–13
Sussex House School, London	8–13
Talmud Torah Bobov Primary School, London	2–13
Tawhid Boys School, Tawhid Educational Trust, London	9–16
Tower House School, London	4–13

University College School Junior Branch, London	7–11
Westminster Abbey Choir School, London	8–13
Westminster Cathedral Choir School, London	7–13
Westminster Under School, London	7–13
Wetherby Preparatory School, London	8–13
Wetherby School, London	4–8
Willington School, London	4–13
Wimbledon Common Preparatory School, London	4–8
Yetev Lev Day School for Boys, London	3–11

GREATER MANCHESTER

Al Jamiah Al Islamiyyah, Bolton	13–16
Kassim Darwish Grammar School for Boys, Manchester	11–16
The Manchester Grammar School, Manchester	9–18

MERSEYSIDE

Merchant Taylors' Boys' Schools, Liverpool	4–18

MIDDLESEX

Buckingham College Preparatory School, Pinner	4–11
Buckingham College School, Harrow	11–18 (Co-ed VIth Form, but currently boys only.)
Denmead School, Hampton	3–11 (Girls 3–7)
Halliford School, Shepperton	11–18 (Co-ed VIth Form)
Hampton School, Hampton	11–18
Harrow School, Harrow on the Hill	13–18
The John Lyon School, Harrow	11–18
The Mall School, Twickenham	4–13
Merchant Taylors' School, Northwood	11–18
St John's Northwood, Northwood	3–13
St Martin's School, Northwood	3–13

NOTTINGHAMSHIRE

Al Karam Secondary School, Retford	11–16
Nottingham High Junior School, Nottingham	7–11

OXFORDSHIRE

Abingdon School, Abingdon	11–18
Christ Church Cathedral School, Oxford	3–13 (Girls 2–4)
Cothill House Preparatory School, Abingdon	8–13
Moulsford Preparatory School, Wallingford	4–13
New College School, Oxford	4–13
Radley College, Abingdon	13–18
Summer Fields, Oxford	7–13

SHROPSHIRE

Kingsland Grange, Shrewsbury	4–13

BATH & NORTH EAST SOMERSET

Beechen Cliff School, Bath   11–18

SURREY

Aldro School, Godalming   7–13
Charterhouse, Godalming   13–18 (Co-ed Sixth Form)
Chinthurst School, Tadworth   3–13
Cranmore School, Leatherhead   3–13
Cumnor House School, South Croydon   4–13
Elmhurst School, South Croydon   4–11
Haslemere Preparatory School, Haslemere   2–14
Homefield Preparatory School, Sutton   2–13
King's House School, Richmond   4–13
Kingswood House School, Epsom   3–13
Lanesborough, Guildford   3–13
Parkside School, Cobham   2–13 (Co-ed 2–4)
Priory Preparatory School, Banstead   2–13
Reed's School, Cobham   11–18 (Co-ed VIth Form)
Rokeby School, Kingston-upon-Thames   4–13
Royal Grammar School, Guildford   11–18
St James Independent School for Boys (Senior),
   Ashford   10–18
Shrewsbury House School, Surbiton   7–13
Surbiton Preparatory School, Surbiton   4–11
Trinity School,
   Croydon   10–18 (Boys 10–18, Girls 16–18)
Whitgift School, South Croydon   10–18
Woodcote House School, Windlesham   7–14

WEST SUSSEX

Slindon College, Arundel   8–16

TYNE AND WEAR

Dame Allan's Boys School,
   Newcastle upon Tyne   8–18 (Co-ed VIth Form)
Newcastle School for Boys,
   Newcastle upon Tyne   3–18
Royal Grammar School,
   Newcastle upon Tyne   8–18 (Co-ed VIth form)

WARWICKSHIRE

Warwick School, Warwick   7–18

WEST MIDLANDS

King Edward's School, Birmingham   11–18
West House School, Birmingham   1–11 (Girls 1–4)

NORTH YORKSHIRE

Aysgarth Preparatory School,
   Bedale   3–13 (Co-ed day 3–8)

SOUTH YORKSHIRE

Birkdale School, Sheffield   4–18 (Co-ed VIth Form)

WEST YORKSHIRE

Olive Secondary, Bradford   11–18
Queen Elizabeth Grammar School, Wakefield   7–18

NORTHERN IRELAND

COUNTY ANTRIM

Cabin Hill School, Belfast   3–13 (Co-ed kindergarten)
Campbell College, Belfast   11–18
Royal Belfast Academical Institution, Belfast   4–18

COUNTY DOWN

Bangor Grammar School, Bangor   11–18

COUNTY FERMANAGH

Portora Royal School, Enniskillen   11–19

SCOTLAND

LOTHIAN

The Edinburgh Academy, Edinburgh 5–18 (Co-ed VIth
   Form)

Merchiston Castle School, Edinburgh   8–18
Stewart's Melville College,
   Edinburgh   12–18 (Co-ed VIth Form)

WALES

MONMOUTHSHIRE

Monmouth School, Monmouth   7–18 (Boarding 11–18)

GIRLS

ENGLAND

BEDFORDSHIRE

Bedford High School for Girls, Bedford	7–18
Dame Alice Harpur School, Bedford	7–18
St Andrew's School, Bedford	3–9 (Boys 3–7)

BERKSHIRE

The Abbey School, Reading	3–18
Brigidine School Windsor, Windsor	3–7 (Boys 3–7)
Claires Court Schools, The College, Maidenhead	3–5
(Boys 3–5, co-ed VIth Form)	
Downe House, Thatcham	11–18
Heathfield School, Ascot	11–18
Highfield School, Maidenhead	3–5
Luckley-Oakfield School, Wokingham	11–18
The Marist Preparatory School, Ascot	2–11
The Marist Senior School, Ascot	11–18
Queen Anne's School, Reading	11–18
St Gabriel's, Newbury	3–7 (Girls 3–18, Boys 3–7)
St George's School, Ascot	11–18
St Mary's School, Ascot, Ascot	11–18

BRISTOL

Badminton School, Bristol	3–18
The Red Maids' School, Bristol	11–18
Redland High School for Girls, Bristol	3–18

BUCKINGHAMSHIRE

Godstowe Preparatory School, High Wycombe	3–8 (Boys 3–8)
Heatherton House School, Amersham	3–11 (Girls can start in Early Years from the age of 2.5)
High March School, Beaconsfield	3–4 (Boys are only admitted into our Upper Nursery class)
Maltman's Green School, Gerrards Cross	3–11
Pipers Corner School, High Wycombe	3–18
St Mary's School, Gerrards Cross	3–18
Thornton College Convent of Jesus and Mary, Milton Keynes	2–4 (Boys 2–4)
Wycombe Abbey School, High Wycombe	11–18

CAMBRIDGESHIRE

The Perse School for Girls, Cambridge	7–18
St Mary's Junior School, Cambridge	4–11
St Mary's School, Cambridge, Cambridge	4–18

CHANNEL ISLANDS

Beaulieu Convent School, Jersey	4–18
The Ladies' College, Guernsey	4–18

CHESHIRE

Alderley Edge School for Girls, Alderley Edge	3–18
Bowdon Preparatory School For Girls, Altrincham	2–12
Culcheth Hall, Altrincham	3–5 (Boys 2–4)
The Queen's School, Chester	4–18
Wilmslow Preparatory School, Wilmslow	2–11

CORNWALL

Truro High School, Truro	3–5 (Boys 3–5)

DERBYSHIRE

Ockbrook School, Derby	3–11

DEVON

The Maynard School, Exeter	7–18 (A selective independent day school for girls aged 7–17.)
St Margaret's School, Exeter	7–18
Stoodley Knowle School, Torquay	2–18

DORSET

Knighton House, Blandford Forum	2–13 (Day boys 4–7)
Leweston School, Sherborne	2–8 (Boys 2–11)
St Mary's School, Dorset, Shaftesbury	9–18
Sherborne Girls, Sherborne	11–18
Talbot Heath, Bournemouth	3–7 (Boys 3–7)

COUNTY DURHAM

Durham High School For Girls, Durham	3–18

ESSEX

Braeside School for Girls, Buckhurst Hill	3–16
(Independent day school for girls aged 3 to 16 years)	
Ilford Ursuline Preparatory School, Ilford	3–4
Park School for Girls, Ilford	3–16
St Hilda's School, Westcliff-on-Sea	2–7 (Boys 2–7)
St Mary's School, Colchester	4–16

GLOUCESTERSHIRE

Cheltenham Ladies' College, Cheltenham   11–18
Gloucestershire Islamic Secondary School For Girls,
    Gloucester   11–16
Westonbirt School, Tetbury   11–18

HAMPSHIRE

Alton Convent School, Alton   2–11 (Co-ed 2–11)
Farnborough Hill, Farnborough   11–18
Portsmouth High School GDST, Southsea   3–18
St Nicholas' School, Fleet   3–7 (Boys 3–7)
St Swithun's School, Winchester   11–18
Wykeham House School, Fareham   2–16

HERTFORDSHIRE

Abbot's Hill School, Hemel Hempstead 3–5 (Boys 3–5)
Haberdashers' Aske's School for Girls, Elstree   4–18
Queenswood, Hatfield   11–18
Rickmansworth PNEU School, Rickmansworth   3–11
The Royal Masonic School for Girls,
    Rickmansworth   2–4 (Pre School opened in January
    2010 for boys and girls aged 2–4.)
St Albans High School for Girls, St Albans   4–18
St Francis' College, Letchworth Garden City   3–18
St Hilda's School, Bushey   3–5 (Boys 3–5)
St Margaret's School, Bushey   4–18
St Martha's Senior School, Barnet   11–18
St. Hilda's School, Harpenden   2–11
Stormont, Potters Bar   4–11
Watford Grammar School For Girls, Watford   11–18

KENT

Babington House School, Chislehurst   3–7 (Boys 3–7)
Benenden School, Cranbrook   11–18
Bromley High School GDST, Bromley   4–18
Cobham Hall, Gravesend   11–18
Combe Bank School, Sevenoaks   3–5
Derwent Lodge School for Girls, Tonbridge   7–11
The Granville School, Sevenoaks   3–5 (Boys 3–5)
Kent College Pembury, Tunbridge Wells   3–18
Walthamstow Hall, Sevenoaks   2–18

LANCASHIRE

Bolton Muslim Girls School, Bolton   11–16
Bolton School (Girls' Division), Bolton   4–7 (Boys 4–7
    before they move into Bolton School Boys' Division)
Bury Grammar School Girls, Bury   3–7 (Boys 4–7)
The Hulme Grammar School for Girls, Oldham   3–18
Islamiyah School, Blackburn   11–16
Jamea Al Kauthar, Lancaster   11–19
Rochdale Girls School, Rochdale   11–16
Tauheedul Islam Girls High School, Blackburn   11–16
Westholme School, Blackburn   3–11 (Boys 3–7)

LEICESTERSHIRE

Leicester High School For Girls, Leicester   3–18
Loughborough High School, Loughborough   11–18

LINCOLNSHIRE

Stamford High School, Stamford   11–18

LONDON

Beis Chinuch Lebanos Girls School, London   2–16
Beis Rochel D'Satmar Girls School, London   2–17
Beth Jacob Grammar for Girls, London   10–16
Blackheath High School GDST, London   3–18
Bute House Preparatory School for Girls, London   4–11
The Cavendish School, London   3–7
Channing Junior School, London   4–11
Channing School, London   4–18
City of London School for Girls, London   7–18
The Falcons School for Girls, London   3–11
Falkner House, London   3–4 (Co-ed 3–4)
Francis Holland School, Regent's Park NW1,
    London   11–18
Francis Holland School, Sloane Square SW1,
    London   4–18
Glendower Preparatory School, London   4–11
The Godolphin and Latymer School, London   11–18
Grange Park Preparatory School, London   4–11
Harvington School, London   3–5 (Boys 3–5)
Islamia Girls' School, London   11–16
James Allen's Girls' School, London   4–18
Kensington Prep School, London   4–11
London Jewish Girls' High School, London   11–16
Lubavitch House Senior School for Girls,
    London   11–18
Madni Girls School, London   12–18
The Mount School, London   4–18
Notting Hill and Ealing High School GDST,
    London   4–18
Palmers Green High School, London   3–16
Pembridge Hall, London   4–11
Putney High School GDST, London   4–18
Queen's College Prep School, London   4–11
Queen's Gate School, London   4–18
Quwwatt Ul Islam Girls School, London   4–13
The Royal School, Hampstead, London   3–16
St Augustine's Priory, Ealing   4–18
St Christopher's School, London   4–11
St James Senior Girls' School, London   10–18
St Joseph's Convent School, London   3–11
St Margaret's School, London   4–16
St Paul's Girls' School, London   11–18
Streatham & Clapham High School,
    London   3–5 (Boys 3–5)
Sarum Hall, London   3–11
The Study Preparatory School, London   4–11
South Hampstead High School, London   4–18
Sydenham High School GDST, London   4–18
Tayyibah Girls School, London   5–18
Ursuline Preparatory School, London   3–7 (Boys 3–7)
The Village School, London   3–11
Wimbledon High School GDST, London   4–18

GREATER MANCHESTER

Manchester High School for Girls, Manchester   4–18
Manchester Islamic High School, Manchester   11–16
Withington Girls' School, Manchester   7–18

MERSEYSIDE

Merchant Taylors' Girls' School, Liverpool   4–18 (Infant
    Boys 4–7)

MIDDLESEX

Heathfield School, Pinner	3–18
Jack and Jill School, Hampton	2–5 (Boys 3–5)
The Lady Eleanor Holles School, Hampton	7–18
North London Collegiate, Edgware	4–18
Northwood College, Northwood	3–18
Peterborough & St Margaret's School, Stanmore	4–16
St Catherine's School, Twickenham	3–18 (Girls 3–18)
St Helen's School, Northwood	3–18

NORFOLK

Norwich High School for Girls GDST, Norwich	3–18
Thorpe House School, Norwich	3–16

NORTHAMPTONSHIRE

Northampton High School, Northampton   3–18

NOTTINGHAMSHIRE

Nottingham High School for Girls GDST,
    Nottingham   4–18

OXFORDSHIRE

Ash-Shifa School, Banbury	11–16
The Carrdus School, Banbury	3–8 (Boys 3–8)
Headington School, Oxford	3–18 (Co-ed 3–4)
IQRA School, Oxford	10–16
Oxford High School GDST, Oxford	4–6 (Boys 4 -6)
St Helen & St Katharine, Abingdon	9–18
Tudor Hall School, Banbury	11–18
Wychwood School, Oxford	11–18

SHROPSHIRE

Adcote School for Girls, Shrewsbury	4–18
Moreton Hall School, Oswestry	3–11 (Boys 3–11)

SOMERSET

Bruton School for Girls, Bruton   2–7 (Boys aged 2–7)

BATH & NORTH EAST SOMERSET

The Royal High School, Bath,
    Bath   3–18 (Boys admitted (day only) into Sixth Form)

STAFFORDSHIRE

Abbots Bromley School for Girls, Abbots Bromley	3–18
St Dominic's School, Stafford	2–7 (Co-ed 2–7)

SUFFOLK

Amberfield School, Ipswich	2–7 (Boys 2–7)
Ipswich High School GDST, Ipswich	3–18

SURREY

Bramley School, Tadworth	3–11
Croydon High School GDST, South Croydon	3–18
Cumnor House School, Purley	4–13
Dunottar School, Reigate	3–18
Greenacre School for Girls, Banstead	3–18
Guildford High School, Guildford	4–18
Halstead Preparatory School, Woking	2–11
Holy Cross Preparatory School, Kingston upon Thames	4–11
Manor House School, Leatherhead	2–16
Marymount International School, Kingston-upon-Thames	11–18
Notre Dame Preparatory School, Cobham	2–5 (Boys 2–5)
Notre Dame Senior School, Cobham	11–18
Old Palace of John Whitgift School, Croydon	1–4
Old Vicarage School, Richmond	4–11
Prior's Field School, Godalming	11–18
Rowan Preparatory School, Esher	2–11
The Royal School, Haslemere	6–4 (Boys 2–4)
The Royal School For Girls, Haslemere	11–18
St Catherine's School, Guildford	4–18
St Ives School, Haslemere	3–5 (Boys 3–5)
St Teresa's Preparatory School, Effingham	2–11
St Teresa's School, Dorking	11–18
Seaton House School, Sutton	3–5 (Boys 3–5, Girls 3–11)
Sir William Perkins's School, Chertsey	11–18
Surbiton High School, Kingston-upon-Thames (Boys 4–11)	4–11
Sutton High School GDST, Sutton	3–18
Tormead School, Guildford	4–18

EAST SUSSEX

Brighton and Hove High School GDST, Brighton	3–18
Moira House Girls School, Eastbourne	2–4
Moira House School, Eastbourne	2–11
Roedean School, Brighton	11–18
St Leonards-Mayfield School, Mayfield	11–19

WEST SUSSEX

Burgess Hill School for Girls, Burgess Hill	2–4
Farlington School, Horsham	3–18
The Towers Convent School, Steyning	3–11 (Boys 3–11)

TYNE AND WEAR

Central Newcastle High School GDST, Newcastle upon Tyne	3–18
Church High School, Newcastle upon Tyne	3–18 (We have a Pre School Nursery on site and Sixth Form.)

Dame Allan's Girls School, Newcastle upon Tyne 8–18
    (Co-ed VIth Form)
Westfield School, Newcastle upon Tyne   3–18

WARWICKSHIRE

King's High School, Warwick, Warwick   10–18
The Kingsley School,
    Leamington Spa   3–7 (Boys 2–7)

WEST MIDLANDS

Al-Burhan Grammar School, Birmingham   11–16
Birchfield Independent Girls School,
    Birmingham   11–16
Coventry Muslim School, Coventry   4–16
Edgbaston High School for Girls, Birmingham   3–18
King Edward VI High School for Girls,
    Birmingham   11–18
Newbridge Preparatory School, Wolverhampton   3–4
Saint Martin's School, Solihull   3–18 (Girls may join the
    school from 2 years 9 months.)
Woodstock Girls' School, Birmingham   11–15

WILTSHIRE

Godolphin Preparatory School, Salisbury   3–11
The Godolphin School, Salisbury   11–18
Leaden Hall School, Salisbury   3–4 (Boys 3–4)
St Mary's Calne, Calne   11–18
Stonar School, Melksham   2–8

WORCESTERSHIRE

Dodderhill School, Droitwich Spa   3–7 (Boys 3–9)
Malvern St James, Great Malvern   4–18
St Mary's, Worcester   2–8 (Boys 2–8)

NORTH YORKSHIRE

Harrogate Ladies' College, Harrogate   11–18 (Highfield
    Prep School, part of the HLC Group of Schools is co-
    ed from age 4–11.)
Queen Mary's School, Thirsk   2–7 (Boys 3–7)

SOUTH YORKSHIRE

Ashdell Preparatory School, Sheffield   3–5 (Co-
    educational Pre-School for rising threes in association
    with Birkdale School)
Sheffield High School GDST, Sheffield   4–18

WEST YORKSHIRE

Bradford Girls' Grammar School, Bradford   2–7
Gateways School, Leeds   3–7 (Boys 3–7)
Islamia Girls High School, Huddersfield   11–16
Moorfield School, Ilkley   2–11
New Horizon Community School, Leeds   11–16
Wakefield Girls' High School, Wakefield   11–18

NORTHERN IRELAND

COUNTY ANTRIM

Victoria College Belfast, Belfast   4–18

SCOTLAND

ABERDEENSHIRE

St Margaret's School for Girls,
    Aberdeen   3–5 (Boys 3–5)

GLASGOW

Craigholme School, Pollokshields   3–5 (Boys 3–5 in
    Nursery only)

LOTHIAN

The Mary Erskine School,
    Edinburgh   16–18 (Co-ed VIth Form)
St George's School for Girls,
    Edinburgh   1–4 (Boys 2–4)

PERTH AND KINROSS

Kilgraston, Perth   2–9 (Boys day 2–9)

WALES

DENBIGHSHIRE

Howell's School, Denbigh   2–18

MONMOUTHSHIRE

Haberdashers' Monmouth School For Girls,
    Monmouth   7–18

COED

ENGLAND

BERKSHIRE

Brockhurst & Marlston House Pre-Preparatory School,
  Thatcham   3–6
Brockhurst and Marlston House Schools,
  Newbury   3–13
St Michaels School, Newbury   7–18 (Single-sex ed
  13–18)

CHESHIRE

The King's School, Macclesfield   3–18 (Single-sex ed
  11–16)

DEVON

Stover School, Newton Abbot   3–18

COUNTY DURHAM

Polam Hall, Darlington   2–18 (Co-educational Junior
  School from age 2 to Year 4. Separate teaching Year
  5 to Year 11. Co-educational Sixth Form)

ESSEX

Brentwood School, Brentwood   3–18 (Single-sex
  Education aged 11–16)
New Hall School, Chelmsford 3–18 (Co-ed Preparatory
  School (3–11), Boys' Division (11–16), Girls' Division
  (11–16), Co-ed Sixth Form, Girls and boys between
  the ages of 11–16 are educated in single-sex classes
  but with the benefit of a mixed environment)

GLOUCESTERSHIRE

Berkhampstead School, Cheltenham   3–11

HERTFORDSHIRE

Berkhamsted School, Berkhamsted   11–18 (Single-sex
  ed 11–16)
Immanuel College, Bushey   4–18

LANCASHIRE

Markazul Uloom, Blackburn   11–19 (No Boarding for
  girls)

LONDON

Al-Sadiq and Al-Zahra Schools, London   4–16
Forest School, London   4–18 (Single-sex ed 7–16)
Garden House School, London   3–11 (Co-ed nursery)
Yesodey Hatorah Jewish School, London   3–16

MIDDLESEX

St John's Senior School, Enfield   11–18

WEST SUSSEX

Fonthill Lodge,
  East Grinstead   2–11 (Single-sex ed 8–11)

WEST MIDLANDS

Al Hijrah School, Birmingham   4–11

5.5

Boarding Provision (Full, Weekly and Flexi-Boarding, Host Families)

The schools and colleges listed below offer boarding/residential accommodation. Full boarding is indicated by 'F', weekly boarding by 'W'. Many schools now offer flexi-boarding (Fl), ie pupils may board for part of the week or on an occasional basis. Please note that in some cases independent Sixth Form colleges may offer accommodation with host families (H) or in hostels. For further details please contact schools direct.

ENGLAND

BEDFORDSHIRE

Bedford High School for Girls, Bedford	F
Bedford Preparatory School, Bedford	F W Fl
Bedford School, Bedford	F W Fl
Bedford School Study Centre, Bedford	F

BERKSHIRE

Bearwood College, Wokingham	F W Fl
Bradfield College, Reading	F
Brockhurst and Marlston House Schools, Newbury	W Fl
Cheam School, Newbury	W Fl
Downe House, Thatcham	F
Eagle House, Sandhurst	F W Fl
Elstree School, Reading	F W Fl
Eton College, Windsor	F
Heathfield School, Ascot	F
Horris Hill School, Newbury	F
Hurst Lodge School, Ascot	W Fl
Lambrook, Bracknell	W Fl
Luckley-Oakfield School, Wokingham	F W Fl

Ludgrove, Wokingham	F
LVS Ascot, Ascot	F W
Newbury Hall International School, Newbury	F H
The Oratory School, Reading	F
Padworth College, Reading	F W Fl
Pangbourne College, Pangbourne	F W Fl
Papplewick School, Ascot	F W
Queen Anne's School, Reading	F W Fl
St Andrew's School, Reading	W Fl
St George's School, Ascot	F
St George's School, Windsor	F W Fl
St John's Beaumont, Windsor	F W
St Mary's School, Ascot, Ascot	F
St Michaels School, Newbury	F W Fl
Sunningdale School, Sunningdale	F
Wellington College, Crowthorne	F

BRISTOL

Badminton School, Bristol	F W Fl
Clifton College, Bristol	F Fl
Clifton College Preparatory School, Bristol	F W Fl

Clifton High School, Bristol	H
Colston's Collegiate School, Bristol	F Fl
The Downs School, Wraxall	F W Fl
Queen Elizabeth's Hospital, Bristol	H
Tockington Manor School, Tockington	F Fl

BUCKINGHAMSHIRE

Ashfold School, Aylesbury	W Fl
Caldicott School, Farnham Royal	F
Godstowe Preparatory School, High Wycombe	F W Fl
Pipers Corner School, High Wycombe	F W Fl
Stowe School, Buckingham	F
Swanbourne House School, Milton Keynes	F W Fl
Thornton College Convent of Jesus and Mary, Milton Keynes	F W Fl
Wycombe Abbey School, High Wycombe	F

CAMBRIDGESHIRE

Bellerbys College & Embassy CES Cambridge, Cambridge	F
Cambridge Centre for Sixth-form Studies, Cambridge	F W Fl
CATS College Cambridge, Cambridge	F W Fl H
Kimbolton School, Huntingdon	F Fl
The King's School Ely, Ely	F W Fl
The Leys School, Cambridge	F
MPW (Mander Portman Woodward), Cambridge	Fl
The Peterborough School, Peterborough	F W Fl
St Andrew's, Cambridge	Fl
St John's College School, Cambridge	F W Fl
St Mary's School, Cambridge, Cambridge	F W H

CHESHIRE

Hammond School, Chester	F W
Terra Nova School, Holmes Chapel	W Fl

CORNWALL

Gems Bolitho School, Penzance	F W Fl
Polwhele House School, Truro	W Fl
Truro High School, Truro	F W Fl
Truro School, Truro	F Fl

CUMBRIA

Casterton School, Kirkby Lonsdale	F Fl
Holme Park School, Kendal	Fl
Lime House School, Carlisle	F W
St Bees School, St Bees	F W Fl
Sedbergh Junior School, Sedbergh	F W Fl
Sedbergh School, Sedbergh	F
Windermere School, Windermere	F W Fl

DERBYSHIRE

Foremarke Hall, Derby	F W Fl
Mount St Mary's College, Spinkhill	F W Fl
Ockbrook School, Derby	F W Fl

Repton School, Derby	F
S. Anselm's School, Bakewell	F

DEVON

Blundell's School, Tiverton	F W Fl
Edgehill College, Bideford	F W Fl
Exeter Cathedral School, Exeter	F W Fl
Exeter Tutorial College, Exeter	Fl H
Kelly College, Tavistock	F W Fl
Kelly College Preparatory School, Tavistock	F W Fl
Kingsley School, Bideford	F W
The Maynard School, Exeter	H
Mount House School, Tavistock	F Fl
Plymouth College, Plymouth	F W
St Peter's School, Exmouth	W Fl
Stover School, Newton Abbot	F W Fl H
Shebbear College, Beaworthy	F W Fl
Trinity School, Teignmouth	F W Fl
West Buckland Preparatory School, Barnstaple	F Fl
West Buckland School, Barnstaple	F W Fl

DORSET

Bournemouth Collegiate School, Bournemouth	F W Fl
Bryanston School, Blandford Forum	F
Canford School, Wimborne	F
Claysmore, Blandford Forum	F W
Claysmore Preparatory School, Blandford Forum	F W Fl
International College, Sherborne School, Sherborne	F
Knighton House, Blandford Forum	F W Fl
Leweston School, Sherborne	F W Fl
Milton Abbey School, Blandford Forum	F
Port Regis Preparatory School, Shaftesbury	F W
St Mary's School, Dorset, Shaftesbury	F
Sherborne Girls, Sherborne	F
Sherborne School, Sherborne	F
Talbot Heath, Bournemouth	F W Fl
Thornlow Preparatory School, Weymouth	Fl

COUNTY DURHAM

Barnard Castle School, Barnard Castle	F Fl
The Chorister School, Durham	F W Fl
Durham School, Durham	F W Fl
Polam Hall, Darlington	F W Fl

ESSEX

Brentwood School, Brentwood	F W
Chigwell School, Chigwell	F W Fl
Felsted School, Felsted	F Fl
Friends' School, Saffron Walden	F W Fl
Gosfield School, Halstead	F W Fl
Holmwood House, Colchester	W Fl
New Hall School, Chelmsford	F W Fl

GLOUCESTERSHIRE

Beaudesert Park School, Stroud	W Fl
Bredon School, Tewkesbury	F W Fl
Cheltenham College, Cheltenham	F Fl
Cheltenham College Junior School, Cheltenham	F W Fl
Cheltenham Ladies' College, Cheltenham	F
Dean Close Preparatory School, Cheltenham	F Fl
Dean Close School, Cheltenham	F Fl
Hatherop Castle School, Cirencester	F W Fl
Rendcomb College, Cirencester	F W Fl
Westonbirt School, Tetbury	F W Fl
Wycliffe College, Stonehouse	F Fl H
Wycliffe Preparatory School, Stonehouse	F W
Wynstones School, Gloucester	F W Fl H

HAMPSHIRE

Bedales School, Petersfield	F
Boundary Oak School, Fareham	F W Fl H
Brockwood Park School, Bramdean	F
Dunhurst (Bedales Junior School), Petersfield	F W Fl
Farleigh School, Andover	F W Fl
Forres Sandle Manor, Fordingbridge	F W
Hampshire Collegiate School, UCST, Romsey	F W Fl
Highfield School, Liphook	F
Hordle Walhampton School, Lymington	F W
Lord Wandsworth College, Hook	F W Fl
Moyles Court School, Ringwood	F
The Pilgrims' School, Winchester	F W
Rookesbury Park School, Portsmouth	F W Fl
Rookwood School, Andover	F W Fl
St John's College, Southsea	F Fl
St Neot's School, Hook	W Fl
St Swithun's School, Winchester	F W
Twyford School, Winchester	W Fl H
Winchester College, Winchester	F

HEREFORDSHIRE

Lucton School, Leominster	F W Fl
St Richard's, Bromyard	F W Fl

HERTFORDSHIRE

Aldwickbury School, Harpenden	W Fl
Beechwood Park School, St Albans	W Fl
Berkhamsted School, Berkhamsted	F W Fl
Bishop's Stortford College, Bishop's Stortford	F W Fl
Bishop's Stortford College Junior School, Bishop's Stortford	F W Fl
Edge Grove, Aldenham Village	F W Fl
Haileybury, Hertford	F Fl
Heath Mount School, Hertford	W Fl
Lockers Park, Hemel Hempstead	F W Fl
The Purcell School, Bushey	F
Queenswood, Hatfield	F Fl
The Royal Masonic School for Girls, Rickmansworth	F W Fl
St Christopher School, Letchworth Garden City	F W Fl
St Edmund's College and St Hugh's School, Ware	F W Fl
St Francis' College, Letchworth Garden City	F W Fl
St Margaret's School, Bushey	F W Fl
Stanborough School, Watford	F W Fl
Tring Park School for the Performing Arts, Tring	F
Westbrook Hay Preparatory School, Hemel Hempstead	Fl

ISLE OF MAN

King William's College, Castletown	F W

ISLE OF WIGHT

Ryde School, Ryde	F W Fl

KENT

Ashford School, Ashford	F W Fl
Beechwood Sacred Heart School, Tunbridge Wells	F W Fl
Benenden School, Cranbrook	F
Bethany School, Cranbrook	F W
CATS College Canterbury, Canterbury	F W Fl H
Cobham Hall, Gravesend	F W Fl
Cranbrook School, Cranbrook	F
Darul Uloom London, Chislehurst	F
Dover College, Dover	F W Fl
Duke of York's Royal Military School, Dover	F
Dulwich Preparatory School, Cranbrook, Cranbrook	W Fl
Farringtons School, Chislehurst	F W Fl
Holmewood House, Tunbridge Wells	W Fl
Junior King's Canterbury, Canterbury	F W Fl
Kent College, Canterbury	F W Fl
Kent College Infant & Junior School, Canterbury	F W Fl
Kent College Pembury, Tunbridge Wells	F W Fl
King's Preparatory School, Rochester	F W Fl
King's Rochester, Rochester	F W
The King's School, Canterbury	F
Marlborough House School, Hawkhurst	Fl
The New Beacon, Sevenoaks	Fl
Northbourne Park School, Deal	F W Fl
Rochester Independent College, Rochester	F W Fl
St Edmund's School Canterbury, Canterbury	F W Fl
St Edmunds Junior School, Canterbury	F Fl
St Lawrence College, Ramsgate	F
St Lawrence College Junior School, Ramsgate	F W Fl
Sevenoaks School, Sevenoaks	F
Sutton Valence School, Sutton Valence	F W Fl
Tonbridge School, Tonbridge	F W

LANCASHIRE

Jamea Al Kauthar, Lancaster	F
Kirkham Grammar School, Preston	F W Fl
Markazul Uloom, Blackburn	F
Moorland School, Clitheroe	F W Fl
Rossall School, Fleetwood	F Fl
Rossall School, Fleetwood	F Fl
Rossall School International Study Centre, Fleetwood	F

St Anne's College Grammar School, Lytham St Annes	F W Fl H
St Mary's Hall, Clitheroe	F W Fl
Stonyhurst College, Clitheroe	F W

LEICESTERSHIRE

Brooke House College, Market Harborough	F W Fl H
Loughborough Grammar School, Loughborough	F W Fl
Ratcliffe College, Leicester	F W Fl

LINCOLNSHIRE

St Hugh's School, Woodhall Spa	F W
Stamford High School, Stamford	F W Fl
Stamford Junior School, Stamford	F W Fl
Stamford School, Stamford	F W Fl
Witham Hall, Bourne	F W Fl

NORTH EAST LINCOLNSHIRE

St James' School, Grimsby	F W Fl

LONDON

Albemarle Independent College, London	Fl
CATS College London, London	F W Fl
Chelsea Independent College, London	H
David Game College, London	Fl H
Davies Laing and Dick, London	H
Dulwich College, London	F W
Dulwich College Preparatory School, London	W
International Community School, London	F W H
Mill Hill School, London	F
The North London International School, London	H
Royal Ballet School, London	F
The Royal School, Hampstead	F W Fl
St Paul's Cathedral School, London	F
St Paul's School, London	F W Fl
Sylvia Young Theatre School, London	F W H
Walthamstow Montessori School, London	Fl
Westminster Abbey Choir School, London	F Fl
Westminster Cathedral Choir School, London	F
Westminster School, Westminster	F W
Westminster Tutors, London	Fl H

GREATER MANCHESTER

Abbey College, Manchester	Fl
Chetham's School of Music, Manchester	F
St Bede's College, Manchester	H

MERSEYSIDE

Kingsmead School, Wirral	F W Fl

MIDDLESEX

Harrow School, Harrow on the Hill	F

NORFOLK

Beeston Hall School, Cromer	F
Glebe House School, Hunstanton	W Fl
Gresham's School, Holt	F
Hethersett Old Hall School, Norwich	F W Fl
Langley Preparatory School & Nursery, Norwich	Fl
Langley School, Norwich	F W
The New Eccles Hall School, Norwich	F W Fl
Riddlesworth Hall, Diss	F W Fl
Sacred Heart School, Swaffham	F W Fl
Taverham Hall Preparatory School, Norwich	W Fl

NORTHAMPTONSHIRE

Beachborough School, Brackley	Fl
Bosworth Independent College, Northampton	F W H
Maidwell Hall School, Northampton	F W
Oundle School, Nr Peterborough	F
Quinton House School, Northampton	H
Winchester House School, Brackley	F W Fl

NORTHUMBERLAND

Longridge Towers School, Berwick-upon-Tweed	F W Fl
Mowden Hall School, Stocksfield	F W

NOTTINGHAMSHIRE

Al Karam Secondary School, Retford	F Fl
Ranby House School, Retford	F W Fl
Trent College & The Elms, Nottingham	F W Fl
Wellow House School, Newark	W Fl
Worksop College, Worksop	F W Fl

OXFORDSHIRE

Abacus College, Oxford	H
Abingdon School, Abingdon	F W
Cherwell College, Oxford	F W H
Cothill House Preparatory School, Abingdon	F
d'Overbroeck's College Oxford, Oxford	F H
Dragon School, Oxford	F
Greene's Tutorial College, Oxford	F W Fl H
Headington School, Oxford	F W Fl
Moulsford Preparatory School, Wallingford	W
The Oratory Preparatory School, Reading	F W Fl
Oxford Tutorial College, Oxford	W Fl H
Radley College, Abingdon	F
St Clare's, Oxford, Oxford	F W Fl
St Edward's School, Oxford	F
St Hugh's School, Faringdon	W Fl
Shiplake College, Henley-on-Thames	F W
Sibford School, Banbury	F W Fl
Summer Fields, Oxford	F
Tudor Hall School, Banbury	F
Wychwood School, Oxford	F W Fl

RUTLAND

Oakham School, Oakham	F Fl
Uppingham School, Uppingham	F

SHROPSHIRE

Adcote School for Girls, Shrewsbury	F W Fl H
Bedstone College, Bucknell	F Fl
Concord College, Shrewsbury	F
Ellesmere College, Ellesmere	F W Fl
Moor Park School, Ludlow	F W Fl
Moreton Hall School, Oswestry	F H
The Old Hall School, Telford	Fl
Oswestry School, Oswestry	F W Fl
Oswestry School Bellan House, Oswestry	Fl
Packwood Haugh School, Shrewsbury	F
Prestfelde Preparatory School, Shrewsbury	W Fl
Shrewsbury School, Shrewsbury	F
Wrekin College, Telford	F W Fl

SOMERSET

All Hallows, Shepton Mallet	F Fl
Bath Academy, Bath	F H
Bruton School for Girls, Bruton	F W Fl
Chilton Cantelo School, Yeovil	F Fl
Downside School, Bath	F
Hazlegrove Preparatory School, Yeovil	F W Fl
King's College, Taunton	F
King's Hall, Taunton	F W Fl
Millfield Preparatory School, Glastonbury	F
Millfield School, Street	F
The Park School, Yeovil	F W H
Perrott Hill School, Crewkerne	F W Fl
Queen's College, Taunton	F Fl
Queen's College Junior, Pre-Prep & Nursery Schools, Taunton	F
Taunton Preparatory School, Taunton	F W Fl
Taunton School International, Taunton	F H
Taunton School Senior, Taunton	F
Wellington School, Wellington	F W Fl
Wells Cathedral Junior School, Wells	F W Fl
Wells Cathedral School, Wells	F W Fl

BATH & NORTH EAST SOMERSET

Kingswood Preparatory School, Bath	F W Fl
Kingswood School, Bath	F W Fl
Prior Park College, Bath	F W Fl
The Royal High School, Bath, Bath	F W Fl

NORTH SOMERSET

Lancaster House School, Weston-Super-Mare	Fl
Sidcot School, Winscombe	F W Fl

STAFFORDSHIRE

Abbots Bromley School for Girls, Abbots Bromley	F W Fl
Abbotsholme School, Uttoxeter	F W Fl
Chase Academy, Cannock	F
Denstone College, Uttoxeter	F W Fl
Lichfield Cathedral School, Lichfield	F W Fl
Yarlet School, Stafford	Fl

SUFFOLK

Alexanders International School, Woodbridge	F
Barnardiston Hall Preparatory School, Haverhill	F W Fl
Brandeston Hall, The Preparatory School for Framlingham College, Brandeston	F W Fl
Culford School, Bury St Edmunds	F W Fl
Felixstowe International College, Felixstowe	F
Finborough School, Stowmarket	F W Fl
Framlingham College, Woodbridge	F W Fl
Ipswich School, Ipswich	F W Fl
Moreton Hall Preparatory School, Bury St Edmunds	F W Fl
Old Buckenham Hall School, Ipswich	F W
Orwell Park, Ipswich	F W Fl
The Royal Hospital School, Ipswich	F W Fl H
St George's School, Southwold	Fl
St Joseph's College, Ipswich	F W Fl H
Saint Felix School, Southwold	F W Fl
Stoke College, Sudbury	W Fl
Summerhill School, Leiston	F
Woodbridge School, Woodbridge	F W Fl

SURREY

ACS Cobham International School, Cobham	F W
Aldro School, Godalming	F W Fl
Amesbury, Hindhead	Fl
Bishopsgate School, Egham	W Fl
Box Hill School, Dorking	F W Fl
Cambridge Tutors College, Croydon	H
Charterhouse, Godalming	F
City of London Freemen's School, Ashtead	F
Cranleigh School, Cranleigh	F
Duke of Kent School, Guildford	F W Fl
Edgeborough, Farnham	W Fl
Epsom College, Epsom	F W
Feltonfleet School, Cobham	W Fl
Frensham Heights School, Farnham	F Fl
Hall Grove School, Bagshot	W Fl
Hurtwood House, Dorking	F W
King Edward's School Witley, Godalming	F W Fl
Marymount International School, Kingston-upon-Thames	F W Fl H
Prior's Field School, Godalming	F W Fl
Reed's School, Cobham	F
Royal Alexandra and Albert School, Reigate	F
Royal Russell School, Croydon	F W Fl
The Royal School, Haslemere	F W Fl
St Catherine's School, Guildford	F W Fl
St Edmund's School, Hindhead	W Fl
St James Independent School for Boys (Senior), Ashford	W
St John's School, Leatherhead	F W
St Teresa's Preparatory School, Effingham	F W Fl
St Teresa's School, Dorking	F W Fl
TASIS The American School in England, Thorpe	F
Woodcote House School, Windlesham	F
Yehudi Menuhin School, Cobham	F Fl

EAST SUSSEX

Ashdown House School, Forest Row	F
Battle Abbey School, Battle	F W Fl

Bellerbys College, Hove	F
Brighton College, Brighton	F W
Buckswood School, Hastings	F W Fl
Eastbourne College, Eastbourne	F
Greenfields School, Forest Row	F W Fl
Michael Hall (Steiner Waldorf School), Forest Row	F W Fl H
Moira House Girls School, Eastbourne	F W Fl
Moira House School, Eastbourne	F W Fl
Newlands School, Seaford	F W
Roedean School, Brighton	F Fl
St Andrew's School, Eastbourne	F W Fl
St Aubyns School, Brighton	W Fl
St Bede's Prep School, Eastbourne	F W Fl
St Bede's School, Hailsham	F W
St Leonards-Mayfield School, Mayfield	F W Fl
Stonelands School of Ballet & Theatre Arts, Hove	F Fl
Vinehall School, Robertsbridge	F Fl

WEST SUSSEX

Ardingly College, Haywards Heath	F W Fl
Ardingly College Junior School, Haywards Heath	Fl
Burgess Hill School for Girls, Burgess Hill	F Fl
Christ's Hospital, Horsham	F
Copthorne Prep School, Copthorne	W Fl
Cottesmore School, Pease Pottage	F W Fl
Dorset House School, Pulborough	W Fl
Farlington School, Horsham	F W Fl
Great Ballard School, Chichester	W Fl
Great Walstead, Haywards Heath	W Fl
Handcross Park School, Haywards Heath	W Fl
Hurstpierpoint College, Hurstpierpoint	F W Fl
The Prebendal School, Chichester	F W Fl
Seaford College, Petworth	F W Fl
Slindon College, Arundel	F W Fl
Sompting Abbotts School, Sompting	W Fl
The Towers Convent School, Steyning	F W Fl
Westbourne House School, Chichester	F Fl
Worth School, Turners Hill	F

WARWICKSHIRE

Bilton Grange, Rugby	F W Fl
Rugby School, Rugby	F
Warwick School, Warwick	F W Fl

WEST MIDLANDS

Abbey College, Birmingham	Fl
Birchfield School, Wolverhampton	W
Darul Uloom Islamic High School & College, Birmingham	F
Elmhurst School for Dance, Birmingham	F
The Royal Wolverhampton Junior School, Wolverhampton	F
Tettenhall College, Wolverhampton	F W Fl

WILTSHIRE

Bishopstrow College, Warminster	F
Chafyn Grove School, Salisbury	F Fl
Dauntsey's School, Devizes	F

The Godolphin School, Salisbury	F W Fl H
Leaden Hall School, Salisbury	F Fl
Marlborough College, Marlborough	F
Norman Court Preparatory School, Salisbury	F W Fl
Pinewood School, Shrivenham	F W Fl
Prior Park Preparatory School, Cricklade	F W Fl
St Mary's Calne, Calne	F
Salisbury Cathedral School, Salisbury	F Fl
Sandroyd School, Salisbury	F Fl
Stonar School, Melksham	F W Fl
Warminster School, Warminster	F W Fl

WORCESTERSHIRE

Abberley Hall, Worcester	F Fl
The Abbey College, Malvern Wells	Fl
Bromsgrove Preparatory School, Bromsgrove	F W Fl
Bromsgrove School, Bromsgrove	F
The Downs, Malvern, Malvern	F W Fl
The Elms, Malvern	F Fl
Malvern St James, Great Malvern	F W Fl
Moffats School, Bewdley	F W Fl
Saint Michael's College, Tenbury Wells	F H

EAST RIDING OF YORKSHIRE

Pocklington School, Pocklington	F W

NORTH YORKSHIRE

Ampleforth College, York	F
Ashville College, Harrogate	F W Fl
Aysgarth Preparatory School, Bedale	F W Fl
Bootham School, York	F W Fl
Bramcote School, Scarborough	F W Fl
Cundall Manor School, York	F
Fyling Hall School, Whitby	F W Fl
Giggleswick Junior School, Settle	F Fl
Giggleswick School, Settle	F
Harrogate Ladies' College, Harrogate	F W Fl
Harrogate Tutorial College, Harrogate	F W Fl H
Highfield Preparatory School, Harrogate	F W Fl
Lisvane, Scarborough College Junior School, Scarborough	F W
Malsis School, Near Skipton	F
The Mount School, York	F W Fl
Queen Ethelburga's College, York	F
Queen Mary's School, Thirsk	F W Fl
Read School, Selby	F W Fl
Ripon Cathedral Choir School, Ripon	F W Fl
St Martin's Ampleforth, York	F Fl
St Peter's School, York	F
Scarborough College & Lisvane School, Scarborough	F W Fl
Terrington Hall, York	F W Fl
Woodleigh School, Malton	F W Fl

WEST YORKSHIRE

Ackworth School, Pontefract	F W Fl
Bronte House School, Bradford	F W Fl
Fulneck School, Leeds	F W Fl
Rishworth School, Rishworth	F W Fl
Woodhouse Grove School, Apperley Bridge	F W Fl

NORTHERN IRELAND

COUNTY ANTRIM

Cabin Hill School, Belfast	Fl
Campbell College, Belfast	F W Fl
Methodist College, Belfast	F
Victoria College Belfast, Belfast	F W Fl

COUNTY DOWN

Rockport School, Holywood	F W Fl

COUNTY ARMAGH

The Royal School Armagh, Armagh	F W Fl

COUNTY TYRONE

The Royal School Dungannon, Dungannon	F W Fl

SCOTLAND

ANGUS

Lathallan School, Montrose	F W Fl

ARGYLL AND BUTE

Lomond School, Helensburgh	F H

CLACKMANNANSHIRE

Dollar Academy, Dollar	F W Fl

FIFE

St Leonards School, St Andrews	F W Fl

LOTHIAN

Basil Paterson Tutorial College, Edinburgh	H
Belhaven Hill, Dunbar	F
Cargilfield, Edinburgh	F W Fl
The Edinburgh Academy, Edinburgh	Fl
The Edinburgh Rudolf Steiner School, Edinburgh	Fl
Fettes College, Edinburgh	F
George Watson's College, Edinburgh	H

Loretto Junior School, Musselburgh	F W Fl
Loretto School, Musselburgh	F W Fl
The Mary Erskine School, Edinburgh	F W
Merchiston Castle School, Edinburgh	F
St George's School for Girls, Edinburgh	F W Fl
St Mary's Music School, Edinburgh	F
Stewart's Melville College, Edinburgh	F W Fl

MORAYSHIRE

Gordonstoun School, Elgin	F W

PERTH AND KINROSS

Ardvreck School, Crieff	F
Glenalmond College, Perth	F
Kilgraston, Perth	F W Fl
Queen Victoria School, Dunblane	F
Strathallan School, Perth	F

ROXBURGHSHIRE

St Mary's Preparatory School, Melrose	W Fl

WALES

CARMARTHENSHIRE

Llandovery College, Llandovery	F W Fl
St Michael's School, Llanelli	F H

CONWY

St David's College, Llandudno	F W Fl

DENBIGHSHIRE

Howell's School, Denbigh	F W Fl
Ruthin School, Ruthin	F

MONMOUTHSHIRE

Haberdashers' Monmouth School For Girls, Monmouth	F W Fl
Monmouth School, Monmouth	F W Fl
St John's-on-the-Hill, Chepstow	F W Fl

POWYS

Christ College, Brecon	F W Fl

CONTINENTAL EUROPE

Chavagnes International College, Chavagnes-En-Paillers, France	F W Fl
John F Kennedy International School, Saanen, Switzerland	F
King's College Madrid, Madrid, Spain	F
Mougins School, France	H
St Columba's College, Dublin, Ireland	F

5.6

Religious Affiliation

The following index lists all schools specifying a particular denomination. However, it should be noted that this is intended as a guide only and that many of the schools listed also welcome children of other faiths. Schools which claim to be non- or inter-denominational are not listed. Parents should check precise details with individual schools. A full list of each school's entries elsewhere in the book is given in the main index at the back.

BUDDHIST

Dharma School, Brighton
Shi-Tennoji School In UK, Bury St Edmunds

CHRISTIAN

Abbey Gate School, Chester
Abingdon Preparatory School, Abingdon
Alderley Edge School for Girls, Alderley Edge
Aldro School, Godalming
All Saints School, Norwich
Amberfield School, Ipswich
Ardvreck School, Crieff
Arnold Lodge School, Leamington Spa
Ashdell Preparatory School, Sheffield
Ashfold School, Aylesbury
Avon House, Woodford Green
Avondale School, Salisbury
Ballymoney Independent Christian School, Ballymoney
Bangor Independent Christian School, Bangor
Barn School, Much Hadham
Barnardiston Hall Preparatory School, Haverhill
Barnsley Christian School, Barnsley
Beechwood School, Whittlesord
Benedict House Preparatory School, Sidcup
Benty Heath School and Kindergarten, South Wirral
Berkhamsted School, Berkhamsted
Bethany School, Cranbrook
Blundell's Preparatory School, Tiverton
Bowbrook House School, Pershore
Bradford Christian School, Bradford
Branch Christian School, Dewsbury
Breckland Park School, Swaffham
Bromley High School GDST, Bromley
Broomwood Hall School, Wandsworth

Brownberrie School, Leeds
Bushey Place School, Norwich
Carmel Christian School, Bristol
Castle Court Preparatory School, Wimborne
Castle House School, Newport
Caterham Preparatory School, Caterham
Cedar School, London
Cedars Christian School, Rochester
Chard School, Chard
Chase Academy, Cannock
Chorcliffe School, Chorley
Christ the King School, Sale
Christian Fellowship School, Liverpool
Christian School (Takeley), Bishop's Stortford
Clifton Lodge Preparatory School, Bristol
Combe Bank School, Sevenoaks
Croham Hurst School, South Croydon
Dale House School, Batley
Dame Alice Harpur School, Bedford
Danes Hill School, Leatherhead
Danesfield Manor School, Walton-on-Thames
Darvell School, Robertsbridge
Davenies School, Beaconsfield
Dean Close School, Cheltenham
Derby Grammar School, Derby
Derwent Lodge School for Girls, Tonbridge
Ditcham Park School, Petersfield
Dolphin School (Including Noah's Ark Nursery School), London
Downham Prep School and Montessori Nursery, Kings Lynn
East London Christian Choir School, London
Edgbaston College, Birmingham
Emmanuel Christian School, Crosskeys
Emmanuel Christian School, Oxford
Emmanuel Christian School, Rochdale

Emmanuel School, Derby
Emmanuel School, Exeter
Emmanuel School, Walsall
Emmaus School, Trowbridge
Eversfield Preparatory School, Solihull
Eversley School, Southwold
Exeter Junior School, Exeter
Exeter School, Exeter
Felsted School, Felsted
Ffynone House School, Swansea
Filgrave School, Newport Pagnell
Fosse Bank School, Tonbridge
Francis House Preparatory School, Tring
Fulneck School, Leeds
Gatehouse School, London
Gateway Christian School, Ilkeston
Gems Bolitho School, Penzance
Ghyll Royd School, Ilkley
Glen Morven School, Aboyne
Glenarm College, Ilford
Godolphin Preparatory School, Salisbury
Gracefield Preparatory School, Fishponds
Grangewood Independent School, London
Great Walstead, Haywards Heath
Grey House Preparatory School, Hook
Guildford High School, Guildford
Hamilton College, Hamilton
Handsworth Christian School, Sheffield
Haslemere Preparatory School, Haslemere
Haylett Grange Preparatory School, Haverfordwest
Heath House Preparatory School, London
Heathfield School, Ascot
Hereford Cathedral School, Hereford
Herne Hill School, London
High Leas Education Centre, Lincoln
Highfield School, Liphook
Highway Christian School, London
Hill House School, Mayfield
Hillgrove School, Bangor
Holy Trinity School, Kidderminster
Honeybourne School, Birmingham
Horris Hill School, Newbury
Howell's School, Denbigh
Hydesville Tower School, Walsall
Immanuel School, Plymouth
Jack and Jill School, Hampton
Joseph Rayner Independent School, Audenshaw
King of Kings School, Manchester
King's School, Plymouth
Kingdom Christian School, Kirkcaldy
Kings Primary School, Southampton
Kingsfold Christian School, Preston
Kingsley Preparatory School, Solihull
Kingsmead School, Wirral
Kingston Grammar School, Kingston-upon-Thames
Kingsway School, Wigan
Kingsway School, East Grinstead
Knighton House, Blandford Forum
Kwabena Montessori School, Farnborough
La Sagesse School, Newcastle upon Tyne
Lady Barn House School, Cheadle
Lady Eden's School, London
Lambs Christian School, Birmingham

Langley Manor School, Slough
Lea House School, Kidderminster
Leeds Christian School, Farnley
Leehurst Swan, Salisbury
Leicester Grammar School, Leicester
Lighthouse Christian School, Manchester
Lingfield Notre Dame School, Lingfield
Lisvane, Scarborough College Junior School, Scarborough
Littlefield School, Liphook
Lochinver House School, Potters Bar
Locksley Christian School, Manby
London Christian Learning Centre, London
Lorenden Preparatory School, Faversham
Luckley-Oakfield School, Wokingham
Lucton School, Leominster
Mannafields Christian School, Edinburgh
Maranatha Christian School, Swindon
Marlin Montessori School, Berkhamsted
Mayfield Preparatory School, Walsall
Maypole House School, Alford
Meadowpark School and Nursery, Cricklade
Mereside Education Trust, Sale
Midland Oak School, Tipton
Monton Prep School with Montessori Nurseries, Eccles
Mount Lourdes Grammar School, Enniskillen
Mount Zion School, Eastville
Mountjoy House School, Huddersfield
Mourne Independent Christian School, Kilkeel
New Harvest Learning Centre, Salford
New Life Christian School, Croydon
Norfolk House Preparatory & Kids Corner Nursery, Sandbach
Norfolk House School, Birmingham
Northampton Christian School, Northampton
Northcote Lodge School, London
Norwich School, Norwich
Paragon Christian Academy, London
Perivale Study Centre, London
Phoenix School, Westoning
Plymouth College, Plymouth
Priory School, Shanklin
Promised Land Academy, London
Prospect School, Bristol
Red House School, Norton
Redcliffe School, London
Redemption Academy, Stevenage
Regius Christian School, Edinburgh
Richmond House School, Leeds
Ridgeway School, Maidenhead
River School, Worcester
Roundstone Preparatory School, Trowbridge
Sacred Heart Preparatory School, Chew Magna
Sceptre School, Dunstable
Sedbergh Junior School, Sedbergh
Sefton Park School, Stoke Poges
Shepherds Community School, London
Sherborne Preparatory School, Sherborne
Shobrooke House School, Crediton
Silchester Manor School, Taplow
Silfield School, Kings Lynn
Somerhill Pre-Preparatory School, Tonbridge
South Hills School, Salisbury

Springfield Christian School, Bell Green
St. Andrew's (Woking) School Trust, Woking
St Anne's Mixed High School, South Shields
St Aubyn's School, Woodford Green
St Christophers School, Totnes
St David's College, Llandudno
St David's School, Brecon
St Dominic's School, Stafford
St Faith's, Cambridge
St Francis' College, Letchworth Garden City
St George's School, Edgbaston, Birmingham
St Helen's College, Hillingdon
St Helen's School, Northwood
St Hilda's School, Westcliff-on-Sea
St John's Senior School, Enfield
St Joseph's College, Ipswich
St Lawrence College, Ramsgate
St Mary's Preparatory School, Lincoln
St Mary's Westbrook, Folkestone
St Matthews School, Northampton
St Michael's School, Leigh-on-Sea
St Oswald's School, Alnwick
St Peter's School, Exmouth
St Piran's Preparatory School, Maidenhead
St Swithun's Junior School, Winchester
Stanway School, Dorking
Stonefield House, Lincoln
Stonehouse Nursery School, Leyland
Stoneygate College, Leicester
Stretton House Pre-preparatory School, Knutsford
Sunflower Montessori School, Twickenham
Sunninghill Preparatory School, Dorchester
Tabernacle School, London
Thames Christian College, London
The Ark School, Reading
The Beacon School, Amersham
The Branch Christian School, Heckmondwike
The Cavendish School, London
The Cedars School, Aldermaston
The Crescent School, Rugby
The Daiglen School, Buckhurst Hill
The Dolphin School, Exmouth
The Downs, Malvern, Malvern
The Froebelian School, Leeds
The King's School, Harpenden
The King's School, Nottingham
The King's School Senior, Eastleigh
The King's School, Primary, Witney
The Lady Eleanor Holles School, Hampton
The Lyceum, London
The Mead School, Tunbridge Wells
The Octagon School, London
The Park School, Yeovil
The Pointer School, London
The Portsmouth Grammar School, Portsmouth
The Potters House School, Bury
The Preparatory School Lightcliffe, Halifax
The Rastrick Independent School, Brighouse
The Royal Hospital School, Ipswich
The School of the Lion, Gloucester
The Terrace School, Leamington Spa
Thomas's Kindergarten, London
Thorpe Hall School, Southend-on-Sea

Trent College & The Elms, Nottingham
Trinity School, Stalybridge
Trinity School, Croydon
Twickenham Preparatory School, Hampton
Victoria College, Jersey
Victory Academy, Leeds
Vine School, Southampton
Wakefield Tutorial Preparatory School, Leeds
Warlingham Park School, Croydon
Warwick Preparatory School, Warwick
Wellspring Christian School, Carlisle
West Buckland School, Barnstaple
West Hill Park School, Fareham
Westmont School, Newport
Weston Green School, Thames Ditton
Westwing School, Thornbury
Wetherby Preparatory School, London
Wharfedale Montessori School, Skipton
White House Preparatory School, Wokingham
Willowfields School, Bradford
Windmill House Preparatory School, Uppingham
Woodford Green Preparatory School, Woodford Green
Worksop College, Worksop
Wyclif Independent Christian School, Machen
Yardley Court Preparatory School, Tonbridge
Yarm School, Yarm

CHRISTIAN SCIENCE

Claremont Fan Court School, Esher
Haberdashers' Aske's School for Girls, Elstree

CHURCH IN WALES

Agincourt School, Monmouth
Christ College, Brecon
Ffynone House School, Swansea
Llandovery College, Llandovery
Lyndon School, Colwyn Bay
Monmouth School, Monmouth
The Cathedral School, Cardiff

CHURCH OF ENGLAND

Abbey Gate College, Chester
Abbot's Hill School, Hemel Hempstead
Abbots Bromley School for Girls, Abbots Bromley
Abbots Junior Hill School, Hemel Hempstead
Abbotsbury School, Newton Abbot
Aberdour School, Tadworth
Abingdon School, Abingdon
Adcote School for Girls, Shrewsbury
Airthrie School, Cheltenham
Aldenham School, Elstree
Aldwickbury School, Harpenden
Alleyn Court Preparatory School, Southend-on-Sea
Alleyn's School, London
Allhallows College, Lyme Regis
Ambleside PNEU School, Cheam
Amesbury, Hindhead
Arden Lawn, Solihull
Ardingly College, Haywards Heath

Ardingly College Junior School, Haywards Heath
Arnold House School, London
Ashdown House School, Forest Row
Aymestrey School, Worcester
Aysgarth Preparatory School, Bedale
Ballard School, New Milton
Bancroft's School, Woodford Green
Barfield School and Nursery, Farnham
Beachborough School, Brackley
Bearwood College, Wokingham
Beaudesert Park School, Stroud
Bedford Preparatory School, Bedford
Bedford School, Bedford
Bedstone College, Bucknell
Beech Hall School, Macclesfield
Beechenhurst Preparatory School, Liverpool
Beechwood Park, St Albans
Beechwood Park School, St Albans
Beeston Hall School, Cromer
Bellerbys College, Wadhurst, Wadhurst
Benenden School, Cranbrook
Berkhampstead School, Cheltenham
Bilton Grange, Rugby
Birchfield School, Wolverhampton
Bloxham School, Banbury
Blundell's School, Tiverton
Bodiam Manor School, Robertsbridge
Bow School, Durham
Bradfield College, Reading
Brambletye, East Grinstead
Bramcote Lorne School, Retford
Bramcote School, Scarborough
Brandeston Hall, The Preparatory School for
    Framlingham College, Brandeston
Bredon School, Tewkesbury
Brentwood School, Brentwood
Brigg Preparatory School, Brigg
Brighton College, Brighton
Brighton College Pre-preparatory School, Brighton
Brighton College Prep School, Brighton
Bristol Cathedral School, Bristol
Broadwater Manor School, Worthing
Brockhurst & Marlston House Pre-Preparatory School,
    Thatcham
Brockhurst and Marlston House Schools, Newbury
Bromsgrove Pre-preparatory and Nursery School,
    Bromsgrove
Bromsgrove Preparatory School, Bromsgrove
Bromsgrove School, Bromsgrove
Bronte School, Gravesend
Brookland Hall Golf Academy, Welshpool
Broomfield House School, Richmond
Bruern Abbey School, Oxford
Bryanston School, Blandford Forum
Buckingham College Preparatory School, Pinner
Cable House School, Woking
Caldicott School, Farnham Royal
Canford School, Wimborne
Casterton School, Kirkby Lonsdale
Cawston College, Norwich
Chafyn Grove School, Salisbury
Chandlings Manor School, Oxford
Charterhouse, Godalming

Cheam School, Newbury
Cheltenham College, Cheltenham
Cheltenham College Junior School, Cheltenham
Chigwell School, Chigwell
Chilton Cantelo School, Yeovil
Christ Church Cathedral School, Oxford
Christ's Hospital, Horsham
Church High School, Newcastle upon Tyne,
    Newcastle upon Tyne
Claremont School, St Leonards-on-Sea
Clayesmore, Blandford Forum
Clayesmore Preparatory School, Blandford Forum
Clifton College, Bristol
Clifton College Preparatory School, Bristol
Colet Court, London
Colfe's School, London
Colston's Collegiate School, Bristol
Conifers School, Midhurst
Coopersale Hall School, Epping
Copthorne Prep School, Copthorne
Cothill House Preparatory School, Abingdon
Cottesmore School, Pease Pottage
Coventry Prep School, Coventry
Cranford House School, Wallingford
Cranleigh Preparatory School, Cranleigh
Cranleigh School, Cranleigh
Croft House School, Blandford Forum
Croftdown House Malvern Girls' Preparatory, Malvern
Cumnor House School, South Croydon
Cumnor House School, Haywards Heath
Cundall Manor School, York
Dair House School Trust Ltd, Farnham Royal
Dame Allan's Junior School, Newcastle upon Tyne
Daneshill School, Basingstoke
Dean Close Preparatory School, Cheltenham
Deepdene School, Hove
Denmead School, Hampton
Denstone College, Uttoxeter
Derby High School, Derby
Dorset House School, Pulborough
Dover College, Dover
Downe House, Thatcham
Downside Preparatory School, Purley
Duke of York's Royal Military School, Dover
Dulwich College, London
Dulwich College Preparatory School, London
Dulwich Preparatory School, Cranbrook
Dumpton School, Wimborne
Duncombe School, Hertford
Durham High School For Girls, Durham
Durham School, Durham
Durlston Court, New Milton
Eagle House, Sandhurst
Eastbourne College, Eastbourne
Edenhurst School, Newcastle-under-Lyme
Edge Grove, Watford
Edgeborough, Farnham
Edgehill School, Newark
Elizabeth College, Guernsey
Ellesmere College, Ellesmere
Elmhurst School for Dance, Birmingham
Elmslie Girls' School, Blackpool
Elstree School, Reading

Emanuel School, London
Emanuel School, London
Emscote Lawn School, Warwick
Epsom College, Epsom
Eton College, Windsor
Eton End PNEU, Slough
Ewell Castle School, Epsom
Excell International School, Boston
Exeter Cathedral School, Exeter
Fairfield School, Backwell
Fairholme Preparatory School, St Asaph
Farlington School, Horsham
Felixstowe International College, Felixstowe
Felsted Preparatory School, Felsted
Feltonfleet School, Cobham
Fen School, Sleaford
Flexlands School, Woking
Fonthill Lodge, East Grinstead
Foremarke Hall, Derby
Forest Girls' School, London
Forest School, London
Forres Sandle Manor, Fordingbridge
Foxley Nursery School, Reading
Framlingham College, Woodbridge
Francis Holland School, Regent's Park
Francis Holland School, Sloane Square
Friern Barnet Grammar School, London
Gayhurst School, Gerrards Cross
Giggleswick School, Settle
Glebe House School, Hunstanton
Godstowe Preparatory School, High Wycombe
Great Ballard School, Chichester
Gresham's Prep School, Holt
Gresham's School, Holt
Haberdashers' Aske's Boys' School, Elstree
Haileybury, Hertford
Haileybury Junior School, Windsor
Hallfield School, Birmingham
Halstead Preparatory School, Woking
Hammond School, Chester
Hampden Manor School, Great Missenden
Hampshire Collegiate School, UCST, Romsey
Handcross Park School, Haywards Heath
Hanford School, Blandford Forum
Harrogate Ladies' College, Harrogate
Harrow School, Harrow on the Hill
Hatherop Castle School, Cirencester
Hazelwood School, Oxted
Hazlegrove Preparatory School, Yeovil
Headington School, Oxford
Heath Mount School, Hertford
Helvetia House School, Jersey
Hethersett Old Hall School, Norwich
Highfield Preparatory School, Harrogate
Highfield School, Liphook
Highgate Junior School, London
Highgate Pre-Preparatory School, London
Highgate School, London
Hilden Grange School, Tonbridge
Hilden Oaks School, Tonbridge
Hillcroft Preparatory School, Stowmarket
Hollington School, Ashford
Holme Grange School, Wokingham

Holme Park School, Kendal
Hordle House, Lymington
Hordle Walhampton School, Lymington
Hull Collegiate School, Anlaby
Hull Grammar School, Kingston-Upon-Hull
Hurstpierpoint College, Hurstpierpoint
Innellan House School, Pinner
Ipswich School, Ipswich
James Allen's Girls' School, London
James Allen's Preparatory School, London
Junior King's Canterbury, Canterbury
Kelly College, Tavistock
Kelly College Preparatory School, Tavistock
Keswick School, Keswick
King Edward's School, Birmingham
King Edward's School Witley, Godalming
King William's College, Castletown
King's Bruton Pre-Preparatory & Junior School, Yeovil
King's College, Taunton
King's College Junior School, London
King's College School, London
King's College School, Cambridge
King's Hall, Taunton
King's Hawford, Worcester
King's Preparatory School, Rochester
King's Rochester, Rochester
King's School Rochester, Rochester
Kingscote Pre-Preparatory School, Gerrards Cross
Kingshott School, Hitchin
Kingsland Grange, Shrewsbury
Knighton House, Blandford Forum
Lambrook, Bracknell
Lancing College, Lancing
Lancing College Preparatory School at Mowden, Hove
Landry School, Ingatestone
Lanesborough, Guildford
Lanherne Nursery and Junior School, Dawlish
Lavant House, Chichester
Laxton Junior School, Nr Peterborough
Laxton School, Peterborough
Leicester Grammar Junior School, Leicester
Leicester High School For Girls, Leicester
Leverets School, Stow on the Wold
Lichfield Cathedral School, Lichfield
Liverpool College, Liverpool
Lockers Park, Hemel Hempstead
Lorne House, Retford
Ludgrove, Wokingham
Magdalen College School, Oxford
Maidwell Hall School, Northampton
Malsis School, Near Skipton
Malvern College, Malvern
Malvern College Preparatory and Pre-Prep School, Malvern
Malvern St James, Great Malvern
Manor Independent School, Taunton
Mansfield Infant College, Ilford
Margaret May Schools Ltd, Sevenoaks
Marlborough College, Marlborough
Marlborough House School, Hawkhurst
Marlston House School, Newbury
Meadowbrook Montessori School, Bracknell
Merchant Taylors' School, Northwood

Merton Court Preparatory School, Sidcup
Merton House, Chester
Micklefield School, Reigate
Milbourne Lodge School, Esher
Millbrook House School, Abingdon
Milton Abbey School, Blandford Forum
Moffats School, Bewdley
Monkton Prep, Bath
Monkton Senior School, Bath
Moorland School, Clitheroe
Morley Hall Preparatory School, Derby
Moulsford Preparatory School, Wallingford
Mount House School, Tavistock
Mowden Hall School, Stocksfield
Moyles Court School, Ringwood
Netherwood School, Saundersfoot
Nevill Holt School, Market Harborough
New College School, Oxford
New Lodge School, Dorking
New School, Exeter
Norman Court Preparatory School, Salisbury
North Foreland Lodge School, Basingstoke
Northampton High School, Northampton
Northbourne Park School, Deal
Northwood Preparatory School, Rickmansworth
Oakham School, Oakham
Oakland Nursery School, Banstead
Oakwood School, Chichester
Old Buckenham Hall School, Ipswich
Old Palace of John Whitgift School, Croydon
Old Vicarage School, Richmond
Oriel Bank, Stockport
Orley Farm School, Harrow
Orley Farm School, Harrow
Oswestry School Bellan House, Oswestry
Oundle School, Nr Peterborough
Packwood Haugh School, Shrewsbury
Pangbourne College, Reading
Pangbourne College, Pangbourne
Papplewick School, Ascot
Park Hill School, Kingston-upon-Thames
Parkside School, Northampton
Parsons Mead, Ashtead
Peaslake School, Guildford
Pennthorpe School, Horsham
Perrott Hill School, Crewkerne
Peterborough & St Margaret's School, Stanmore
Pilgrims Pre-Preparatory School, Bedford
Pinewood School, Shrivenham
Pipers Corner School, High Wycombe
Plumtree School, Nottingham
Pocklington School, Pocklington
Prebendal School (Northgate House), Chichester
Prestfelde Preparatory School, Shrewsbury
Prince's Mead School, Winchester
Princess Helena College, Hitchin
Putney Park School, London
Quainton Hall School, Harrow
Queen Anne's School, Reading
Queen Ethelburga's College, York
Queen Margaret's School, York
Queen Mary's School, Thirsk
Queen's College London, London

Queen's College Prep School, London
Radley College, Abingdon
Ranby House School, Retford
Rathdown School, Dublin
Rathvilly School, Birmingham
Ravenscourt Theatre School, London
Read School, Selby
Reading Blue Coat School, Reading
Red House School, York
Reddiford, Pinner
Reed's School, Cobham
Reigate St Mary's Preparatory and Choir School, Reigate
Rendcomb College, Cirencester
Repton School, Derby
Riddlesworth Hall, Diss
Ripon Cathedral Choir School, Ripon
Rishworth School, Rishworth
Rock Hall School, Alnwick
Rodney School, Newark
Roedean School, Brighton
Rose Hill School, Wotton-under-Edge
Rose Hill Westonbirt School, Tetbury
Roselyon, Par
Rosemead School, Littlehampton
Rossall School, Fleetwood
Rosslyn School, Birmingham
Roxeth Mead School, Harrow on the Hill
Royal Alexandra and Albert School, Reigate
Royal Russell School, Croydon
Rugby School, Rugby
Runton & Sutherland School, Cromer
Rushmoor School, Bedford
Russell House School, Sevenoaks
Ryde School, Ryde
S. Anselm's School, Bakewell
Sackville School, Tonbridge
Saddleworth Preparatory School, Oldham
Saint Ronan's School, Hawkhurst
Salisbury Cathedral School, Salisbury
Sancton Wood School, Cambridge
Sanderstead Junior School, South Croydon
Sandroyd School, Salisbury
Sarum Hall, London
Seaford College, Petworth
Sedbergh School, Sedbergh
Selwyn School, Gloucester
Shaw House School, Bradford
Sherborne Girls, Sherborne
Sherborne School, Sherborne
Shernold School, Maidstone
Sherrardswood School, Welwyn
Shiplake College, Henley-on-Thames
Shoreham College, Shoreham-by-Sea
Shrewsbury House School, Surbiton
Shrewsbury School, Shrewsbury
Sibton Park, Folkestone
Silchester House School, Maidenhead
Slapton Pre-Preparatory School, Towcester
Smallwood Manor Preparatory School, Uttoxeter
Snaresbrook College Preparatory School, London
Solefield School, Sevenoaks
Solihull School, Solihull

Sompting Abbotts School, Sompting
Southdown Nursery, Steyning
Spratton Hall, Northampton
St Agnes PNEU School, Leeds
St Albans High School for Girls, St Albans
St Andrew's School, Eastbourne
St Andrew's School, Reading
St Andrew's School, Woking
St Andrew's Senior Girls' School, Harrow
St Aubyn's, Brighton
St Aubyns School, Brighton
St Bees School, St Bees
St Catherine's School, Guildford
St Christopher's School, Burnham-on-Sea
St Christopher's School, Hove
St Christopher's School, Epsom
St David's School, Purley
St Dunstan's Abbey Preparatory School, Plymouth
St Dunstan's Abbey School, Plymouth
St Dunstan's College, London
St Edmund's School, Hindhead
St Edmund's School Canterbury, Canterbury
St Edmunds Junior School, Canterbury
St Edward's School, Oxford
St Elphin's School, Matlock
St Francis Preparatory School, Drifield
St Francis School, Pewsey
St Gabriel's, Reading
St George's School, Ascot
St George's School, Windsor
St Helen & St Katharine, Abingdon
St Hilary's School, Alderley Edge
St Hilda's School, Wakefield
St Hilda's School, Whitby
St Hugh's School, Faringdon
St Hugh's School, Woodhall Spa
St Ives School, Haslemere
St James' School, Grimsby
St James's School, Malvern
St John's College School, Cambridge
St John's Northwood, Northwood
St John's School, Leatherhead
St John's-on-the-Hill, Chepstow
St Lawrence College Junior School, Ramsgate
St Margaret's School, Exeter
St Margaret's School, Bushey
St Margaret's School, Halstead
St Martin's Independent School, Crewkerne
St Martin's School, Northwood
St Martin's School, Bournemouth
St Mary's Calne, Calne
St Mary's Hall, Brighton
St Mary's Preparatory School, Tenbury Wells
St Mary's School, Gerrards Cross
St Mary's School, Wantage
St Michael's, Barnstaple
St Michael's School, Sevenoaks
St Neot's School, Hook
St Nicholas' School, Fleet
St Olave's School (Junior of St Peter's), York
St Paul's Cathedral School, London
St Paul's School, London
St Peter's School, Kettering

St Peter's School, York
St Petroc's School, Bude
St Swithun's School, Winchester
St Wilfrid's Junior School, Exeter
St Wilfrid's School, Exeter
St Wystan's School, Repton
St. Hilda's School, Harpenden
Stamford High School, Stamford
Stamford Junior School, Stamford
Stamford School, Stamford
Steephill Independent School, Longfield
Stepping Stones Nursery and Pre-Preparatory School, Marlborough
Stoke Brunswick, East Grinstead
Stoneygate School, Leicester
Stourbridge House School, Warminster
Stover School, Newton Abbot
Stowe School, Buckingham
Stubbington House, Ascot
Summer Fields, Oxford
Sunderland High School, Sunderland
Sunningdale School, Sunningdale
Sunnyside School, Worcester
Surbiton High School, Kingston-upon-Thames
Surbiton Preparatory School, Surbiton
Sussex House School, London
Sutton Valence Preparatory School, Maidstone
Sutton Valence School, Sutton Valence
Swanbourne House School, Milton Keynes
Talbot Heath, Bournemouth
Temple Grove, Uckfield
The Abbey, Woodbridge
The Abbey School, Tewkesbury
The Abbey School, Reading
The Acorn School, Nailsworth
The Atherley School, Southampton
The Blue Coat School, Birmingham
The Cathedral School, Lincoln
The Chorister School, Durham
The Croft Preparatory School, Stratford-upon-Avon
The Dormer House PNEU School, Moreton-in-Marsh
The Downs School, Wraxall
The Elms, Malvern
The Elvian School, Reading
The Godolphin School, Salisbury
The Hall School, London
The Hereford Cathedral Junior School, Hereford
The Jordans Nursery School, London
The Junior School, Wellingborough School, Wellingborough
The King's School, Macclesfield
The King's School, Gloucester
The King's School, Canterbury
The King's School, Worcester
The King's School, Chester
The King's School Ely, Ely
The Kingsley School, Leamington Spa
The Knoll School, Kidderminster
The Littlemead School, Chichester
The Manor Preparatory School, Abingdon
The Minster School, York
The Mullberry Bush Nursery, Halesworth
The New Beacon, Sevenoaks

The Old Hall School, Telford
The Old Malthouse, Swanage
The Old School, Beccles
The Peterborough School, Peterborough
The Pilgrims' School, Winchester
The Prebendal School, Chichester
The Royal School, Haslemere
The Royal School For Girls, Haslemere
The Royal Wolverhampton Junior School,
    Wolverhampton
The School of St Clare, Penzance
The Stroud School, Romsey
The Study School, New Malden
The Willow School, London
The Yarlet Schools, Stafford
Thomas's Kindergarten, London
Thomas's Preparatory School, London
Thomas's Preparatory School, London
Thorpe House School, Gerrards Cross
Tockington Manor School, Tockington
Tonbridge School, Tonbridge
Trevor Roberts School, London
Truro High School, Truro
Tudor Hall School, Banbury
Twyford School, Winchester
Upfield Preparatory School Ltd, Stroud
Upper Chine School, Shanklin
Uppingham School, Uppingham
Upton House School, Windsor
Victoria Park Preparatory School, Shipley
Vinehall School, Robertsbridge
Wakefield Independent School, Wakefield
Warminster School, Warminster
Warwick School, Warwick
Wellesley House School, Broadstairs
Wellington College, Crowthorne
Wellington School, Wellington
Wells Cathedral Junior School, Wells
Wells Cathedral School, Wells
West Buckland Preparatory School, Barnstaple
West End School, Harrogate
Westbourne House School, Chichester
Westbrook Hay Preparatory School, Hemel Hempstead
Westminster Abbey Choir School, London
Westminster School, London
Westminster Under School, London
Weston Favell Montessori Nursery School, Northampton
Westonbirt School, Tetbury
Wickham Court School, West Wickham
Widford Lodge, Chelmsford
Wilton House School, Battle
Winchester College, Winchester
Winchester House School, Brackley
Windlesham House School, Pulborough
Windrush Valley School, Chipping Norton
Wisbech Grammar School, Wisbech
Witham Hall, Bourne
Wolborough Hill School, Newton Abbot
Wood Dene School, Norwich
Woodbridge School, Woodbridge
Woodleigh School, Malton
Wrekin College, Telford
Wroxall Abbey School, Warwick

Wycombe Abbey School, High Wycombe
Wykeham House School, Fareham
Yateley Manor Preparatory School, Yateley
York College for Girls, York
York House School, Rickmansworth
Yorston Lodge School, Knutsford

CHURCH OF SCOTLAND

Butterstone School, Blairgowrie
The Glasgow Academy, Glasgow

EPISCOPALIAN

Glenalmond College, Perth
Hemdean House School, Reading

INTER-DENOMINATIONAL

Abacus College, Oxford
Abberley Hall, Worcester
Abbotsholme School, Uttoxeter
Aberlour House Preparatory School, Aberlour
Albemarle Independent College, London
Alder Bridge School, Reading
Alexanders International School, Woodbridge
Arbor Preparatory, Bury St Edmunds
Arnold School, Blackpool
Arts Educational Schools London, London
Ashdown School And Nursery, Jersey
Ashford School, Ashford
Ashgrove School, Bromley
Avalon Preparatory School, Wirral
Ayscoughfee Hall School, Spalding
Bablake Junior School, Coventry
Ballard School, New Milton
Bangor Grammar School, Bangor
Barnard Castle School, Barnard Castle
Basil Paterson College, Edinburgh
Bedford Modern School, Bedford
Bedford School Study Centre, Bedford
Beech House School, Rochdale
Bellerbys College, Mayfield, Wadhurst
Bentham Grammar School, Lancaster
Birkdale School, Sheffield
Bolton School (Boys' Division), Bolton
Boundary Oak School, Fareham
Bournemouth Collegiate Prep School, Poole
Bournemouth Collegiate School, Bournemouth
Bramdean School, Exeter
Briar School, Lowestoft
Bridge Lane Montessori School, London
Bristol Grammar School, Bristol
Brooklands School & Little Brooklands Nursery, Stafford
Bryony School, Gillingham
Buckholme Towers, Poole
Buckingham College School, Harrow
Buckland School, Watchet
Burgess Hill School for Girls, Burgess Hill
Cabin Hill School, Belfast
Cannock School, Orpington
Cargilfield, Edinburgh

Channing Junior School, London
Channing School, London
Charters-Ancaster School GPDST, Bexhill-on-Sea
Chase School, Whickham
Cheltenham Ladies' College, Cheltenham
Cherubs Pre – School, Lee-on-the-Solent
Chetwynde School, Barrow-in-Furness
City of London Freemen's School, Ashtead
Claires Court Schools, The College, Maidenhead
Clewborough House Preparatory School, Camberley
Cliff School, Wakefield
Cobham Hall, Gravesend
Cokethorpe School, Witney
Colchester High School, Colchester
Collingwood School, Wallington
Convent Preparatory School, Gravesend
Coworth-Flexlands School, Woking
Craigclowan Preparatory School, Perth
Craigholme School, Glasgow
Craigievar School, Sunderland
Crawfordton House School, Thornhill
Croftinloan School, Pitlochry
Crosfields School, Reading
Dauntsey's School, Devizes
Davenport Lodge School, Coventry
Dean Grange Preparatory School, Huntingdon
Drayton House School, Guildford
Dulwich Montessori Nursery School, London
Eastcliffe School, Newcastle upon Tyne
Eaton Square School
Elliott-Clarke School, Liverpool
Eltham College, London
Eylesden Court Preparatory School, Maidstone
Falcon Manor, Towcester
Fettes College, Edinburgh
Freddies (Reading) Limited, Reading
Froebel House School, Hull
Fulham Prep School (Pre-Prep), London
Garden House Boys' School, London
Garden House School, London
Gateways School, Leeds
GEMS Hampshire Schools, London
Gidea Park College, Romford
Giggleswick Junior School, Settle
Gosfield School, Halstead
Green Hill School, Evesham
Greycotes School GDST, Oxford
Grindon Hall Christian School, Sunderland
Grosvenor School, Nottingham
Hampton School, Hampton
Hanbury Prep School, Hanbury
Hawkesdown House School, London
Hereward House School, London
Hessle Mount School, Hessle
High Elms Manor School, Watford
High March School, Beaconsfield
Highfield School, London
Highfield School, Birkenhead
Hill House School, Doncaster
Holmewood House, Tunbridge Wells
Homefield School Senior & Preparatory, Christchurch
Howell's School, Llandaff GDST, Cardiff
Howsham Hall, York

Hutchesons' Grammar School, Galsgow
Joseph Rayner Independent School, Lancashire
Keil Junior School, Helensburgh
Keil School, Dumbarton
Kensington Prep School, London
Kew College, Richmond
King Edward VI High School for Girls, Birmingham
King Edward's Pre-Prep School, Bath
King's House School, Richmond
Kingsbury Hill House, Marlborough
Kingswood House School, Epsom
Ladymede, Aylesbury
Langdale Preparatory School, Blackpool
Lathallan School, Montrose
Leaden Hall School, Salisbury
Lincoln Minster School, Lincoln
Little Folk Montessori & Music Kindergarten, London
Lodge School, Purley
Longacre School, Guildford
Longridge Towers School, Berwick-upon-Tweed
Longwood School, Bushey
Lyonsdown School Trust Ltd, Barnet
Madingley Pre-Preparatory School, Cambridge
Maldon Court Preparatory School, Maldon
Manor House School, London
Manor Lodge School, Shenley
Merchiston Castle School, Edinburgh
Millfield Preparatory School, Glastonbury
Millfield School, Street
Moira House Girls School, Eastbourne
Moira House School, Eastbourne
Montessori Pavilion School, London
Morrison's Academy, Crieff
Mount Carmel School, Ormskirk
Mrs Radcliffe's Montessori School, York
New Park School, St Andrews
New West Preston Manor Nursery School, Littlehampton
Newell House School, Sherborne
Newlands School, Seaford
Northamptonshire Grammar School, Pitsford
Northfield School, Watford
Oakfield School, Woking
Oakhyrst Grange School, Caterham
Oaklands School, Loughton
Ockbrook School, Derby
Ormer House Preparatory School, Alderney
Orwell Park, Ipswich
Our Lady of Sion School, Worthing
Overstone Park School, Northampton
Oxford House School, Colchester
Paragon School, Prior Park College Junior, Bath
Penrhos College Junior School, Colwyn Bay
Pershore House School, Wirral
Playdays Nursery/School and Montessori College,
    London
Plymouth College Preparatory School, Plymouth
Polam Hall, Darlington
Polwhele House School, Truro
Port Regis Preparatory School, Shaftesbury
Portora Royal School, Enniskillen
Pownall Hall School, Wilmslow
Priory Preparatory School, Banstead
Queen Elizabeth's Grammar School, Blackburn

Queen Elizabeth's Hospital, Bristol
Queenswood, Hatfield
Ramillies Hall School, Cheadle
Rannoch School, Pitlochry
Rickmansworth PNEU School, Rickmansworth
Riverston School, London
Rockport School, Holywood
Rookesbury Park School, Portsmouth
Rose Hill School, Tunbridge Wells
Rydal Penrhos Senior School Girls' Division, Colwyn Bay
Scaitcliffe and Virginia Water Preparatory School, Egham
Scarborough College & Lisvane School, Scarborough
School of Jesus and Mary, Ipswich
Sevenoaks Preparatory School, Sevenoaks
Sevenoaks School, Sevenoaks
Shaftesbury Independent School, Purley
South Lee Preparatory School, Bury St Edmunds
Springfield Independent School, Ongar
St Albans School, St Albans
St Antony's Preparatory School, Sherborne
St Bede's Prep School, Eastbourne
St Bede's School, Hailsham
St Brandon's School, Clevedon
St David's College, West Wickham
St Denis and Cranley School, Edinburgh
St Dominic's Independent Junior School, Stoke-on-Trent
St George's School, Harpenden
St John's Preparatory School, Lichfield
St Joseph's In The Park, Hertford
St Margaret's School for Girls, Aberdeen
St Mary's Preparatory School, Melrose
St Michael's Preparatory School, Jersey
St Piran's School, Hayle
St Ursulas Convent School, Wigton
Stancliffe Hall, Matlock
Stockton House School, Fleet
Stonar School, Melksham
Stormont, Potters Bar
Stretton School, Norwich
TCS Tutorial College, Harrow
Terra Nova School, Holmes Chapel
Terrington Hall, York
Tettenhall College, Wolverhampton
The Albany College, London
The Buchan School, Castletown
The Cobham Montessori School, Cobham
The Drive School, Wolverhampton
The Falcons School for Boys, London
The Hall School, Wimbledon, London
The Hampshire Schools (Kensington Gardens), London
The High School of Glasgow, Glasgow
The Knightsbridge Kindergarten, London
The Larks, Oxted
The Leys School, Cambridge
The Mill School, Devizes
The Mount School, Mill Hill
The Park School, Bournemouth
The Perse School, Cambridge
The Perse School for Girls, Cambridge
The Study Preparatory School, Wimbledon
Thorngrove School, Newbury
Thornlow Preparatory School, Weymouth

Thornlow Senior School, Weymouth
Thorpe House School, Norwich
Tower College, Prescot
Tower House School, Paignton
Tring Park School for the Performing Arts, Tring
Trinity School, Teignmouth
Walthamstow Hall, Sevenoaks
Wellow House School, Newark
West Dene School, Purley
West Lodge Preparatory School, Sidcup
Westbourne Preparatory School, Wallasey
Westerleigh & St Leonards College, St Leonards-on-Sea
Westfield School, Newcastle upon Tyne
Westholme School, Blackburn
Westville House Preparatory School, Ilkley
White House School, Seaton
Whitford Hall & Dodderhill School, Droitwich
Willington School, London
Willoughby Hall School, London
Wimbledon Common Preparatory School, London
Wispers School for Girls, Haslemere
Woodcote House School, Windlesham
Woodside Park International School, London
Wycliffe College, Stonehouse
Wycliffe College (Special Needs), Stonehouse
Wycliffe Preparatory School, Stonehouse
Yarrells School, Poole

JEWISH

Akiva School, London
Beis Hamedrash Elyon, London
Beis Malka Girls School, London
Beis Rochel D'Satmar Girls School, London
Bnois Jerusalem School, London
Carmel College, Wallingford
Gateshead Jewish High School for Girls, Gateshead
Gateshead Jewish Primary School, Gateshead
Getters Talmud Torah, London
Hasmonean Preparatory School, London
Hubert Jewish High School for Girls, Salford
Immanuel College, Bushey
Kerem House, London
Kerem School, London
London Jewish Girls' High School, London
Lubavitch House School (Junior Boys), London
Lubavitch House Senior School for Girls, London
Manchester Jewish Grammar School, Prestwich
Mathilda Marks-Kennedy School, London
Mechinah Liyeshivah Zichron Moshe, London
Menorah Grammar School, Edgware
Naima Jewish Preparatory School, London
OYH Primary School, London
Pardes Grammar Boys' School, London
Side by Side Kids School, London
Talmud Torah Bobov Primary School, London
Talmud Torah Chinuch Norim, Salford
Talmud Torah Jewish School, London
Talmud Torah Machzikei Hadass, London
Talmud Torah Tiferes Shlomoh, London
Talmud Torah Torat Emet, London
Talmud Torah Yetev Lev, Salford
Tashbar of Edgware, Edgware

Tashbar School, Salford
Torah Academy, Hove
Yeshivah Ohr Torah School, Salford
Yesodey Hatorah Jewish School, London
Yetev Lev Day School for Boys, London

METHODIST

Ashdown Lodge, Apperley Bridge
Ashville College, Harrogate
Bronte House School, Bradford
Crowthorn School (NCH Action for Children), Bolton
Culford School, Bury St Edmunds
Edgehill College, Bideford
Farringtons School, Chislehurst
Kent College, Canterbury
Kent College Infant & Junior School, Canterbury
Kent College Pembury, Tunbridge Wells
Kingsley School, Bideford
Kingswood Preparatory School, Bath
Kingswood School, Bath
Queen's College, Taunton
Queen's College Junior, Pre-Prep & Nursery Schools, Taunton
Rydal Penrhos Preparatory School, Colwyn Bay
Rydal Penrhos School, Colwyn Bay
Shebbear College, Beaworthy
St Crispin's School, Leicester
The Leys School, Cambridge
Truro School, Truro
Truro School Preparatory School, Truro
Woodhouse Grove School, Apperley Bridge

MUSLIM

Abu Bakr Independent School, Walsall
Adam Primary School, London
Afifah High School For Girls, Manchester
Al Hijrah School, Birmingham
Al Huda Girls School, Birmingham
Al Karam Secondary School, Retford
Al Mumin Primary School, Bradford
Al-Burhan Grammar School, Birmingham
Al-Furqaan Preparatory School, Dewsbury
Al-Furqan Community College, Birmingham
Al-Khair School, Croydon
Al-Mizan Primary & London East Academy Secondary & Sixth Form, London
Al-Muntada Islamic School, London
Amina Hatun Islamic School, London
Andalusia Academy Bristol, Bristol
Azhar Academy, London
Balham Preparatory School, London
Birchfield Independent Girls School, Birmingham
Birmingham Muslim School, Birmingham
Bolton Muslim Girls School, Bolton
Brondesbury College For Boys, Brondesbury
Copsewood School, Coventry
Coventry Muslim School, Coventry
Crescent Community High School for Girls, Manchester
Crystal Gardens, Bradford
Darul Arqam Educational Institute, Leicester
Darul Hadis Latifiah, Bethnal Green

Darul Uloom Dawatul Imaan, Bradford
Date Valley School, Mitcham
Gloucestershire Islamic Secondary School For Girls, Gloucester
Hanifah Infants Small School, Longsight
Imam Muhammad Zakariya School, Preston
Imam Zakaria Academy, London
IQRA School, Oxford
Islamia Girls High School, Huddersfield
Islamia Girls' School, London
Islamic Shakhsiyah Foundation, Slough
Islamic Shakhsiyah Foundation, London
Islamiyah School, Blackburn
Jamahiriya School, London
Jamea Al Kauthar, Lancaster
Jameah Islameah, Crowborough
Jamia Al-Hudaa Residential College, Mapperley Park
Jamia Islamia Birmingham, Birmingham
Jamiah Madaniyah Primary School, London
Jamiatul Uloom Al-Islamia, Luton
Jamiatul Ummah School, London
Jamiatul-Ilm Wal-Huda UK School, Blackburn
King Fahad Academy, London
London East Academy, London
London Islamic School, London
Madinatul Uloom Al Islamiya School, Kidderminster
Madni Girls School, London
Madni Muslim Girls' High School, Dewsbury
Madrasatul Imam Muhammad Zakariya, Bolton
Manchester Islamic High School, Manchester
Markazul Uloom, Blackburn
Mazahirul Uloom School, London
New Horizon Community School, Leeds
Noor Ul Islam Primary School, London
Paradise Primary School, Dewsbury
Preston Muslim Girls Secondary School, Preston
Quwwatt Ul Islam Girls School, London
Rabia Girls School, Luton
Rawdha Tul Uloom, Blackburn
Rochdale Girls School, Rochdale
Tawhid Boys School, Tawhid Educational Trust, London
Tayyibah Girls School, London
Tiny Tots Pre- School, Leicester
TTTY School, London
Zakaria Muslim Girls High School, Batley

NON-DENOMINATIONAL

Abbey College, Manchester
Abbotsford Preparatory School, Manchester
Abbotsford School, Kenilworth
Abercorn School, London
Aberdeen Waldorf School, Aberdeen
Aberdour, Tadworth
Abinger Hammer Village School, Dorking
Acorn Independent College, Southall
ACS Cobham International School, Cobham
ACS Egham International School, Egham
ACS Hillingdon International School, Hillingdon
Akeley Wood Junior School, Milton Keynes
Akeley Wood School, Buckingham
Al-Sadiq and Al-Zahra Schools, London
Albyn School, Aberdeen

Alcuin School, Leeds
Alpha Preparatory School, Harrow
Altrincham Preparatory School, Altrincham
Amberley House School, Bristol
Amberley School, Bexhill-on-Sea
Annemount Nursery School, London
Arden College, Southport
Arley House PNEU School, Loughborough
Arley House School, East Leake
Arts Educational Schools London – Sixth Form, London
Arundale Preparatory School, Pulborough
Ashbourne Independent Sixth Form College, London
Ashbourne Middle School, London
Ashbrooke House, Weston-Super-Mare
Ashton House School, Isleworth
Aston House School, London
Astwell Preparatory School, Birmingham
Atherton House School, Liverpool
Atholl School, Pinner
Attenborough Preparatory School, Nottingham
Avenue House School, London
Babington House School, Chislehurst
Bablake School, Coventry
Badminton School, Bristol
Bairnswood Nursery School, Scarborough
Barbara Speake Stage School, London
Barbourne Preparatory School and Cygnet Nursery, Worcester
Basil Paterson Tutorial College, Edinburgh
Bassett House School, London
Bath Academy, Bath
Bath High School GPDST, Bath
Batley Grammar School, Batley
Battle Abbey School, Battle
Beaconhurst School, Stirling
Bedales School, Petersfield
Bedford High School for Girls, Bedford
Belfast Royal Academy, Belfast
Belhaven Hill, Dunbar
Bell Bedgebury International School, Cranbrook
Bellerbys College, Hove
Belmont (Mill Hill Junior School), London
Belmont (Mill Hill Preparatory School), London
Belmont Grosvenor School, Harrogate
Belmont House, Newton Mearns
Bembridge School, Ryde
Bickley Park School, Bromley
Bickley Parva School, Bromley
Birkdale School for Hearing Impaired Children, Southport
Birkenhead High School GDST, Wirral
Birkenhead School, Wirral
Bishop's Stortford College, Bishop's Stortford
Bishop's Stortford College Junior School, Bishop's Stortford
Bishopsgate School, Egham
Bishopstrow College, Warminster
Blackheath High School GDST, London
Blackheath Preparatory School, London
Bloomsbury College, London
Bolton School (Girls' Division), Bolton
Box Hill School, Dorking
Brabyns School, Stockport

Brackenfield School, Harrogate
Bradford Girls' Grammar School, Bradford
Bradford Grammar School, Bradford
Braeside School for Girls, Buckhurst Hill
Bramley School, Tadworth
Brampton College, London
Brantwood School, Sheffield
Branwood Preparatory School, Eccles
Breaside Preparatory School, Bromley
Bricklehurst Manor Preparatory, Wadhurst
Bridgewater School, Manchester
Brighton and Hove High School GDST, Brighton
Bristol Steiner School, Bristol
Broadhurst School, London
Broadmead Lower School, Bedford
Brockwood Park School, Bramdean
Brooke House College, Market Harborough
Brooke Priory School, Oakham
Broomham School, Hastings
Buckswood School, Hastings
Burwood Park School and College, Walton-on-Thames
Bury Grammar School Boys, Bury
Bury Grammar School Girls, Bury
Bury Lawn School, Flitwick
Bury Lawn School, Milton Keynes
Bute House Preparatory School for Girls, London
Buxlow Preparatory School, Wembley
Cambridge Centre for Sixth-form Studies, Cambridge
Cambridge Tutors College, Croydon
Cameron House School, London
Campbell College, Belfast
Canbury School, Kingston-upon-Thames
Canterbury Steiner School, Canterbury
CATS College Cambridge, Cambridge
CATS College Canterbury, Canterbury
CATS College London, London
Cedar School, Street
Central Newcastle High School GDST, Newcastle upon Tyne
Cheadle Hulme School, Cheadle
Chelsea Independent College, London
Cherwell College, Oxford
Cheshunt Pre-preparatory School, Coventry
Chetham's School of Music, Manchester
Chetwynd House School, Sutton Coldfield
Chiltern House School, Thame
Chinthurst School, Tadworth
Chiswick and Bedford Park Preparatory School, London
Churchers College Junior School, Liphook
Churchers College Senior School, Petersfield
City of London School, London
City of London School for Girls, London
Claires Court School, Maidenhead
Claires Court Schools, Ridgeway, Maidenhead
Clarendon Cottage School, Eccles
Cleve House School, Bristol
Clevedon House Preparatory School, Ilkley
Clevelands Preparatory School, Bolton
Clewborough House School, Frimley
Clifton Hall School, Edinburgh
Clifton High School, Bristol
Clifton Preparatory School, York
College Saint-Pierre, Leigh-on-Sea

Collingham Independent GCSE and Sixth Form College, London
Colston's Girls' School, Bristol
Concord College, Shrewsbury
Connaught House, London
Cooley Primary School, Sixmilecross
Copthill School, Stamford
Corfton Hill Educational Establishment, London
Craig-y-Nos School, Bishoptston
Cranbrook, Ilford
Cranbrook School, Cranbrook
Cransley School, Northwich
Croft House School, Hexham
Crown House School, High Wycombe
Croydon High School GDST, South Croydon
Culcheth Hall, Altrincham
d'Overbroeck's College, Oxford
Dagfa House School, Nottingham
Daintry Hall Preparatory School, Congleton
Dallington School, London
Dame Bradbury's School, Saffron Walden
Davies Laing and Dick, London
Davies's College, London
Delrow House, Watford
Devonshire House Preparatory School, London
Dodderhill School, Droitwich Spa
Dollar Academy, Dollar
Dolphin School, Reading
Dorchester Preparatory and Independent Schools, Dorchester
Downsend Girls' Preparatory School, Leatherhead
Downsend School, Leatherhead
Downsend School – Ashtead Lodge, Ashtead
Downsend School – Epsom Lodge, Epsom
Downsend School – Leatherhead Lodge, Leatherhead
Dragon School, Oxford
Drumley House School, Ayr
Duke of Kent School, Guildford
Dunedin School, Edinburgh
Dunhurst (Bedales Junior School), Petersfield
Dunottar School, Reigate
Durston House, London
Ealing College Upper School, London
Ealing Independent College, London
Ealing Montessori School, London
Eastbourne House School, Birmingham
Eastcourt Independent School, Ilford
Eaton House Belgravia, London
Eaton House The Manor Girls' School, London
Eaton House The Manor Nursery, London
Eaton House The Manor Pre-Preparatory, London
Eaton House The Manor Preparatory, London
Eaton House The Vale, London
Eccleston School, Birmingham
Eden Park School, Beckenham
Edgbaston High School for Girls, Birmingham
Edinburgh Academy Junior School, Edinburgh
Elliott Park School, Sheerness
Elm Green Preparatory School, Chelmsford
Elm Tree House, Cardiff
Elmfield Rudolf Steiner School, Stourbridge
Elmhurst School, South Croydon
Elmwood Montessori School, London

Emberhurst, Esher
Emscote House School and Nursery, Leamington Spa
Essendene Lodge School, Caterham
Fairfield Preparatory School, Loughborough
Fairfield Preparatory School, Saxmundham
Fairstead House School, Newmarket
Falkner House, London
Farleigh Further Education College (Frome), Frome
Farleigh Further Education College Swindon, Swindon
Farrowdale House Preparatory School, Oldham
Ferndale Preparatory School, Faringdon
Fine Arts College, London
Finton House School, London
Firth House Preparatory School, Littlehampton
Firwood Manor Prep School, Oldham
Forest Park School, Sale
Forest School, Altrincham
Fosse Way School, Leicester
Frensham Heights School, Farnham
Friars School, Ashford
Fulham Prep School (Prep Dept), London
Fyling Hall School, Whitby
Gad's Hill School, Rochester
Gask House School, Lanarkshire
Gateway School, Great Missenden
George Heriot's School, Edinburgh
George Watson's College, Edinburgh
Glaisdale School, Cheam
Glebe House School, Rochdale
Glen House Montessori School, Hebden Bridge
Glendower Preparatory School, London
Glenesk School, Leatherhead
Golders Hill School, London
Goodrington School, Hornchurch
Goodwyn School, London
Gordonstoun School, Elgin
Gower House School, Kinsbury
Grainger Grammar School, Newcastle upon Tyne
Gramercy Hall School, Torbay
Grange Park Preparatory School, London
Grantchester House, Esher
Grasscroft Independent School, Oldham
Great Houghton Preparatory School, Northampton
Greenacre School for Girls, Banstead
Greenbank Preparatory School, Cheadle
Greenfield School, Woking
Greenfields School, Forest Row
Greenhayes Pre-Preparatory School, West Wickham
Greenholme School, Nottingham
Grittleton House School, Chippenham
Grove Independent School, Milton Keynes
Haberdashers' Monmouth School For Girls, Monmouth
Haberdashers' Redcap School, Hereford
Haddon Dene School, Broadstairs
Hall Grove School, Bagshot
Hall School Wimbledon (Junior School), London
Hall School Wimbledon (Senior School), London
Halliford School, Shepperton
Hampstead Hill Pre-Preparatory & Nursery School, London
Hampton Court House, East Molesey
Handel House Preparatory School, Gainsborough
Harecroft Hall School, Seascale

Harenc School Trust, Sidcup
Haresfoot Senior School, Berkhamsted
Harpenden Preparatory School, Harpenden
Harrogate Tutorial College, Harrogate
Hartlebury School, Kidderminster
Harvington School, London
Hawley Place School, Camberley
Hazelhurst School For Girls, London
Heathcote School, Chelmsford
Heatherton House School, Amersham
Heathfield School, Pinner
Heathfield School, Kidderminster
Heathland College, Accrington
Heathside Preparatory School, Hampstead
Hendon Preparatory School, Hendon
Herington House School, Brentwood
Herries School, Maidenhead
Highclare School, Birmingham
Highfield Priory School, Preston
Highfield School, London
Highfield School, Maidenhead
Highfield School, East Grinstead
Highfields School, Newark
Hill House International Junior School, London
Hill House St Mary's School, Doncaster
Hillcrest Grammar School, Stockport
Hillside School, Malvern
Hilltop Small School, St Leonards-on-Sea
Hipperholme Grammar School, Halifax
Hoe Bridge School, Woking
Holly Park Montessori School, London
Hollygirt School, Nottingham
Holmwood House, Colchester
Homefield Preparatory School, Sutton
Homewood Pre-Preparatory School, St Albans
Hopelands School, Stonehouse
Horlers Pre-Preparatory School, Cambridge
Hornsby House School, London
Hounslow College, Feltham
Howe Green House School, Bishop's Stortford
Huddersfield Grammar School, Huddersfield
Hulme Hall Schools, Cheadle
Hulme Hall Schools (Junior School), Cheadle
Hunter Hall School, Penrith
Hunterhouse College, Belfast
Hurst Lodge School, Ascot
Hurtwood House, Dorking
Hurworth House School, Darlington
Hyland House, London
Hylton Kindergarten & Pre-preparatory School, Exeter
Ibstock Place School, Roehampton
Inchkeith School and Nursery, Dunfermline
Ingleside PNEU School, Cirencester
International College, Sherborne School, Sherborne
International Community School, London
International School of Aberdeen, Aberdeen
International School of London, London
International School of London in Surrey, Woking
Ipswich High School GDST, Ipswich
Jordanhill School, Glasgow
Justin Craig Education, Borehamwood
Kayes' College, Huddersfield
Keble Preparatory School, London

Kelvinside Academy, Glasgow
Kenley Montessori School, London
Kew Green Preparatory School, Richmond
Kimbolton School, Huntingdon
King Edward VI School, Southampton
King Edward VII and Queen Mary School,
   Lytham St Annes
King Edward's Junior School, Bath
King Edward's School, Bath, Bath
King Henry VIII School, Coventry
King's High School, Warwick, Warwick
Kings Monkton School, Cardiff
Kings Monkton School and College, Cardiff
Kingswood College Trust, Ormskirk
Kirkham Grammar School, Preston
Kirkstone House School, Bourne
Knightsbridge School, London
Ladbroke Square Montessori School, London
Lady Lane Park School, Bingley
Lancaster House School, Weston-Super-Mare
Langley Preparatory School & Nursery, Norwich
Langley School, Norwich
Lansdowne College, London
Latymer Prep School, London
Latymer Upper School, London
Le Herisson, London
Leckford Place School, Oxford
Leeds Girls' High School, Leeds
Leicester Montessori School, Leicester
Lewes Old Grammar School, Lewes
Lime House School, Carlisle
Lion House School, London
Little Acorns Montessori School, Bushey
Littlegarth School, Colchester
Locksley Preparatory School, West Bridgford
Lomond School, Helensburgh
London Montessori Centre Ltd, London
Long Close School, Slough
Longacre Preparatory School, Nottingham
Lord Wandsworth College, Hook
Loretto Junior School, Musselburgh
Loretto School, Musselburgh
Loughborough Grammar School, Loughborough
Loughborough High School, Loughborough
LVS Ascot, Ascot
Lycee Francais Charles de Gaulle, London
Lyndhurst House Preparatory School, London
Lyndhurst School, Camberley
Lynton Preparatory School, Scunthorpe
Lynton Preparatory School, Epsom
Macclesfield Preparatory School, Macclesfield
Maharishi School, Ormskirk
Maltman's Green School, Gerrards Cross
Manchester High School for Girls, Manchester
Mander Portman Woodward, Birmingham
Mander Portman Woodward, London
Manor House School, Ashby-de-la-Zouch
Maria Montessori School Hampstead, London
Marycourt School, Gosport
Mayfield Preparatory School, Alton
Mayville High School, Southsea
McCaffreys School, London
McKee School of Education, Dance & Drama, Liverpool

Meoncross School, Fareham
Merchant Taylors' Boys' Schools, Liverpool
Merchant Taylors' Girls' School, Liverpool
Methodist College, Belfast
Michael Hall (Steiner Waldorf School), Forest Row
Mill Hill School, London
Millfield Pre-Preparatory School, Glastonbury
Milton Keynes Preparatory School, Milton Keynes
Montessori School, Lavenham
Moor Allerton School, Manchester
Moorfield School, Ilkley
Moorlands School, Luton
Moorlands School, Leeds
Moreton Hall School, Oswestry
Mortarboard Nursery School, Bracknell
Mostyn House School, South Wirral
Motcombe Grange School, Shaftesbury
Mount School, Bromsgrove
Mount School, Huddersfield
Mountford House School, Nottingham
Nethercliffe School, Winchester
Netherleigh and Rossefield School, Bradford
Netherleigh School, Bradford
New College, Leamington Spa
New College and School, Cardiff
Newborough School, Liverpool
Newbridge Preparatory School, Wolverhampton
Newcastle School for Boys, Newcastle upon Tyne
Newcastle-under-Lyme School, Newcastle-under-Lyme
Newland House School, Twickenham
Newlands School, Seaford
Newlands School, Newcastle upon Tyne
Newton Prep, London
Norfolk House School, London
Norland Place School, London
Normanhurst School, London
North Bridge House Junior School, London
North Bridge House Lower Prep School, London
North Bridge House Nursery School, London
North Bridge House School Nursery and Prep, London
North Bridge House Senior School, London
North Cestrian Grammar School, Altrincham
North London Collegiate, Edgware
North London Rudolf Steiner School, Kings Langley
Northgate Preparatory, Rhyl
Northwood College, Northwood
Norwich High School for Girls GDST, Norwich
Notting Hill and Ealing High School GDST, London
Notting Hill Preparatory School, London
Nottingham High Junior School, Nottingham
Nottingham High School, Nottingham
Nottingham High School for Girls GDST, Nottingham
Oakfield Preparatory School, London
Oakleigh House School, Swansea
Oldham Hulme Kindergarten, Oldham
Orchard House School, London
Oswestry Junior School, Oswestry
Oswestry School, Oswestry
Overndale School, Old Sodbury
Oxford High School GDST, Oxford
Oxford International College, Oxford
Oxford International Study Centre, Oxford
Oxford Tutorial College, Oxford

Padworth College, Reading
Paint Pots Montessori School Hyde Park, Hyde Park Crescent
Palmers Green High School, London
Park School, Totnes
Park School for Girls, Ilford
Parkgate House School, London
Parkside Kindergarten and Preparatory School, Leighton Buzzard
Parkside School, Cobham
Pembridge Hall, London
Plymouth College, Plymouth
Polam School, Bedford
Portland Place School, London
Portsmouth High School GDST, Southsea
Primrose Independent School, London
Prior's Field School, Godalming
Priory Preparatory & Nursery School, Stamford
Prospect House School, Roehampton
Putney High School GDST, London
Queen Elizabeth Grammar School, Wakefield
Queen Mary School, Lytham
Queen Victoria School, Dunblane
Queen's Gate School, London
Queen's Park School, Oswestry
Quinton House School, Northampton
Radlett Preparatory School, Radlett
Rainbow Montessori Junior School, London
Rainbow Montessori Nursery School, London
Ramshill School, Petersfield
Raphael Independent School, Hornchurch
Ravenscourt Park Preparatory School, London
Ravenstone Day Nursery and Nursery School, Paddington
Ravenstone Preparatory School, London
Redehall Preparatory School, Horley
Redland High School for Girls, Bristol
Reigate Grammar School, Reigate
RGS The Grange, Worcester
RGS Worcester & The Alice Ottley School, Worcester
Ringwood Waldorf School, Ringwood
Ripley Court School, Woking
River House Montessori School, London
Robert Gordon's College, Aberdeen
Robina Advantage, Marchington
Rokeby School, Kingston-upon-Thames
Rolfe's Montessori School, London
Rookwood School, Andover
Rosebrae School, Elgin
Rosemead Preparatory School, London
Rosemeade School, Huddersfield
Rossholme School, East Brent
Rougemont School, Newport
Rowan Preparatory School, Esher
Royal Ballet School, London
Royal Belfast Academical Institution, Belfast
Royal Caledonian Schools, Watford
Royal Grammar School, Guildford
Royal Grammar School, Newcastle upon Tyne
Ruckleigh School, Solihull
Rudolf Steiner School, Kings Langley
Rudston Preparatory School, Rotherham
Rupert House, Henley-on-Thames

Rushmoor Independent School, Farnborough
Ruthin School, Ruthin
Saint Felix School, Southwold
Saint Martin's School, Solihull
Saint Michael's College, Tenbury Wells
Salcombe Preparatory School, London
Salterford House School, Nottingham
Sandbach School, Sandbach
Sandhurst School, Worthing
Sands School, Ashburton
Saville House School, Mansfield
Scarisbrick Hall School, Ormskirk
Sea View Private School, Kirkcaldy
Seaton House School, Sutton
Sheffield High School GDST, Sheffield
Shepherd's Bush Day Nursery, London
Sherborne House School, Eastleigh
Sherfield School, Hook
Shrewsbury High School GDST, Shrewsbury
Sir William Perkins's School, Chertsey
Slindon College, Arundel
Somerville School, London
South Devon Steiner School, Dartington
South Hampstead High School, London
South London Montessori School, London
Southfields School, Sale
Springfield School, Worcester
St Andrew's, Wantage
St Andrew's School, Bedford
St Anne's High School, Bishop Auckland
St Anne's Preparatory School, Chelmsford
St Bernard's Preparatory School, Newton Abbot
St Catherine's Preparatory School, Stockport
St Catherine's School, Camberley
St Cedd's School, Chelmsford
St Christopher School, Letchworth Garden City
St Christopher's, Wembley
St Christopher's School, Beckenham
St Christopher's School, Wembley
St Christopher's School, Norwich
St Clare's School, Porthcawl
St Clare's, Oxford, Oxford
St Colette's School, Cambridge
St Columba's School, Kilmacolm
St David's School, Ashford
St Edward's School, Reading
St Faith's at Ash School, Canterbury
St George's Preparatory School, Jersey
St George's School, Southwold
St George's School for Girls, Edinburgh
St Hilary's School, Godalming
St Hilda's School, Bushey
St Ia School, St Ives
St James Independent Junior School, Stockport
St James Independent School for Boys (Senior), Ashford
St James Independent Schools for Boys and Girls, London
St James Junior School, London
St James Senior Girls' School, London
St John's Preparatory School, Potters Bar
St John's Priory School, Banbury
St John's School, Sidmouth
St John's School, Porthcawl

St John's School, Billericay
St Johns Wood Pre-Preparatory School, London
St Joseph's School, Launceston
St Leonards – New Park, St Andrews
St Leonards School, St Andrews
St Martin's, London
St Martin's Preparatory School, Grimsby
St Mary's Music School, Edinburgh
St Mary's School, Henley-on-Thames
St Mary's School, Colchester
St Michael's School, Llanelli
St Nicholas Nursery School, Folkestone
St Nicholas Preparatory School, London
St Nicholas School, London
St Nicholas School, Harlow
St Olave's Preparatory School, London
St Peter & St Paul School, Chesterfield
St Peter's Nursery School, Burgess Hill
St Serf's School, Edinburgh
St Winifred's School, Southampton
Stafford Grammar School, Stafford
Staines Preparatory School, Staines
Stepping Stones Day Nursery School, Leeds
Stewart's Melville College, Edinburgh
Stockport Grammar School, Stockport
Stoke College, Sudbury
Stonelands School of Ballet & Theatre Arts, Hove
Stratford Preparatory School, Stratford-upon-Avon
Strathallan School, Perth
Streatham & Clapham High School, London
Streatham House School, Liverpool
Suffolk Country Courses, Bury St Edmunds
Sunny Bank Preparatory School, Burnley
Sunnymede School, Southport
Surrey College, Guildford
Sutton High School GDST, Sutton
Swan School for Boys, Salisbury
Syddal Park School, Stockport
Sydenham High School GDST, London
Sylvia Young Theatre School, London
TASIS The American School in England, Thorpe
Taunton Preparatory School, Taunton
Taunton School International, Taunton
Taunton School Senior, Taunton
Taverham Hall Preparatory School, Norwich
Tavistock & Summerhill School, Haywards Heath
Teesside High School, Eaglescliffe
The Abbey College, Malvern Wells
The Abbey School, Torquay
The American School in London, London
The Belvedere School GDST, Liverpool
The Cardiff Academy, Cardiff
The Carrdus School, Banbury
The Chelsea Nursery School, London
The Compass School, Haddington
The Dixie Grammar Junior School, Nuneaton
The Dixie Grammar School, Market Bosworth
The Dominie, London
The Duchy Grammar School, Truro
The Edinburgh Academy, Edinburgh
The Edinburgh Rudolf Steiner School, Edinburgh
The Falcons School for Girls, London
The Fold School, Hove

The Galloway Small School, Barnbarroch
The Glasgow Academy Dairsie, Glasgow
The Gleddings Preparatory School, Halifax
The Godolphin and Latymer School, London
The Grammar School at Leeds, Leeds
The Grange School, Northwich
The Grantham Preparatory School, Grantham
The Granville School, Sevenoaks
The Hawthorns School, Redhill
The Highlands School, Reading
The Hill Preparatory School, Westerham
The Hulme Grammar School for Girls, Oldham
The Hurlingham School, London
The International School of Choueifat, Chippenham
The Italia Conti Academy of Theatre Arts, London
The John Lyon School, Harrow
The Junior School, Bishop's Stortford College,
   Bishop's Stortford
The King Alfred School, London
The Ladies' College, Guernsey
The Little Folks Lab, Stevenage
The Mall School, Twickenham
The Manchester Grammar School, Manchester
The Mary Erskine School, Edinburgh
The Maynard School, Exeter
The Merlin School, London
The Montessori House, London
The Montessori House School, London
The Mulberry House School, London
The New Eccles Hall School, Norwich
The New Small School (Bath), Bath
The North London International School, London
The Old Vicarage School, Derby
The Oldham Hulme Grammar Schools, Oldham
The Phoenix School, London
The Purcell School, Bushey
The Queen's School, Chester
The Red Maids' School, Bristol
The Richard Pate School, Cheltenham
The Roche School, London
The Rowans School, London
The Royal High School, Bath, Bath
The Royal Masonic School for Girls, Rickmansworth
The Royal School Armagh, Armagh
The Royal School Dungannon, Dungannon
The Royal School, London
The Ryleys, Alderley Edge
The Small School, Bideford
The Village School, Hampstead
The White House Prep & Woodentops Kindergarten,
   London
Thetford Grammar School, Thetford
Toad Hall Montessori Nursery School, London
Toddlers and Mums Montessori, London
Tormead School, Guildford
Torwood House School, Redland
Tower Dene Preparatory School, Southport
Tower House, Barmouth
Tower House School, London
Town Close House Preparatory School, Norwich
Treffos School, Menai Bridge
Trent Fields Kindergarten, Nottingham
Trentvale Preparatory School, Keadby

Twycross House School, Atherstone
Unicorn School, Richmond
University College School, London
University College School Junior Branch, London
Upper Tooting Independent High School, London
Vernon Lodge Preparatory School, Brewood
Victoria College Belfast, Belfast
Victoria College Preparatory School, Jersey
Virginia Water Preparatory School, Virginia Water
Wakefield Girls' High School, Wakefield
Waldorf School of South West London, London
Wallop School, Weybridge
Waverley House PNEU School, Nottingham
Waverley School, Wokingham
Wellington School, Ayr
West House School, Birmingham
Westbourne School, Sheffield
Westbourne School, Cardiff
Western College Preparatory School, Plymouth
Westminster Preparatory School, Westcliff-on-Sea
Westward Preparatory School, Walton-on-Thames
Westwood, Bushey Heath
Wetherby School, London
Wheelgate House School, Newquay
White House School, Whitchurch
White House School, Stamford
Whitehall School, Huntingdon
Whitgift School, South Croydon
Whittingham School, London
William Hulme's Grammar School, Manchester
William Hulme's Preparatory Department, Manchester
Wimbledon High School GDST, London
Winbury School, Maidenhead
Windermere School, Windermere
Withington Girls' School, Manchester
Wolstanton Preparatory School, Newcastle-under-Lyme
Wolverhampton Grammar School, Wolverhampton
Woodford Prep & Nursery School, Stockport
Woodhill Preparatory School, Southampton
Woodlands School, Preston
Wychwood School, Oxford
Wylde Green College, Sutton Coldfield
Wynstones School, Gloucester
Yarm at Raventhorpe School, Darlington
Yehudi Menuhin School, Cobham
Young England Kindergarten, London

QUAKER

Ackworth School, Pontefract
Ayton School, Great Ayton
Bootham Junior School, York
Bootham School, York
Friends' School, Lisburn
Friends' School, Saffron Walden
Leighton Park School, Reading
Sibford School, Banbury
Sidcot School, Winscombe
The Hall Pre-Preparatory School Sidcot, Winscombe
The Mount School, York
Tregelles, York

ROMAN CATHOLIC

All Hallows, Shepton Mallet
Alton Convent School, Alton
Ampleforth College, York
Ashbourne, London
Austin Friars School, Carlisle
Austin Friars St Monica's School, Carlisle
Barlborough Hall School, Chesterfield
Barrow Hills School, Godalming
Beechwood Sacred Heart School, Tunbridge Wells
Besford Court School, Worcester
Bishop Challoner RC School, Bromley
Brigidine School Windsor, Windsor
Bury Catholic Preparatory School, Bury
Carleton House Preparatory School, Liverpool
Convent of Mercy, Guernsey
Convent Primary School, Rochdale
Crackley Hall School, Kenilworth
Cranmore School, Leatherhead
Donhead Prep School, London
Downside School, Bath
Farleigh School, Andover
Farnborough Hill, Farnborough
FCJ Primary School, Jersey
Fernhill School, Glasgow
Grace Dieu Manor School, Leicester
Holy Cross Convent, Gerrards Cross
Holy Cross Junior School, Portsmouth
Holy Cross Preparatory School, Kingston upon Thames
Holy Trinity College, Bromley
Ilford Ursuline High School, Ilford
Ilford Ursuline Preparatory School, Ilford
Kilgraston, Perth
La Sagesse Convent, Romsey
Laleham Lea School, Purley
Leweston School, Sherborne
Loreto Grammar School, Altrincham
Loreto Preparatory School, Altrincham
Loyola Preparatory School, Buckhurst Hill
Marist Convent Independent Day School For Girls, London
Marymount Convent School, Wallasey
Marymount International School, Kingston-upon-Thames
Moor Park School, Ludlow
More House School, London
Moreton Hall Preparatory School, Bury St Edmunds
Mount St Mary's College, Spinkhill
Mount St Mary's Convent School, Exeter
Mylnhurst Preparatory School & Nursery, Sheffield
New Hall School, Chelmsford
Notre Dame Preparatory School, Cobham
Notre Dame Preparatory School, Norwich
Notre Dame Senior School, Cobham
Oakhill College, Clitheroe
Oakwood School & Nursery, Purley
Our Lady's Abingdon Junior School, Abingdon
Our Lady's Abingdon School, Abingdon
Our Lady's Convent Preparatory School, Kettering
Our Lady's Convent School, Loughborough
Our Lady's Convent School, Cardiff
Our Lady's Preparatory School, Crowthorne
Princethorpe College, Rugby
Prior Park College, Bath

Prior Park Preparatory School, Cricklade
Priory School, Birmingham
Ratcliffe College, Leicester
Redcourt- St Anselms, Prenton
Rosecroft School Didsbury, Manchester
Runnymede St Edward's School, Liverpool
Rye St Antony School, Oxford
Sacred Heart R.C. Primary School, Wadhurst
Sacred Heart School, Swaffham
Salesian College, Farnborough
Sinclair House School, London
St Aloysius' College, Glasgow
St Ambrose College, Altrincham
St Ambrose Preparatory School, Altrincham
St Andrew's Preparatory School, Edenbridge
St Anne's Preparatory School, Sturry
St Anselm's College, Birkenhead
St Anthony's Montessori School, Sunderland
St Anthony's Preparatory School, London
St Anthonys School, Cinderford
St Augustine's Priory, London
St Bede's College, Manchester
St Bede's School, Stafford
St Bede's School, Stafford
St Benedict's Junior School, London
St Benedict's School, London
St Bernard's Preparatory School, Slough
St Brigid's School, Denbigh
St Catherine's School, Twickenham
St Christina's RC Preparatory School, London
St Clotilde's Senior School, Lechlade
St Columba's College, St Albans
St Dominic's Priory School, Stone
St Edmund's College, Ware
St Edmund's College and St Hugh's School, Ware
St Edward's College, Liverpool
St Edward's School Cheltenham, Cheltenham
St George's College, Weybridge
St George's College Junior School, Weybridge
St Gerard's School, Bangor
St John's Beaumont, Windsor
St John's College, Southsea
St John's Nursery School, Tadworth
St Joseph's College, Reading
St Joseph's College with The School of Jesus & Mar, Ipswich
St Joseph's Convent, Chesterfield
St Joseph's Convent School, London
St Joseph's Convent School, Broadstairs
St Joseph's Dominican Convent, Pulborough
St Joseph's Preparatory School, Wolverhampton
St Joseph's Preparatory School, Reading
St Joseph's Preparatory School, Stoke-on-Trent
St Joseph's School, Kenilworth
St Joseph's School, Nottingham
St Joseph's School, Park Hill, Burnley
St Leonards-Mayfield School, Mayfield
St Margaret's School, Midhurst
St Margaret's School, Edinburgh
St Margaret's Senior School Convent of Mercy, Midhurst
St Martha's Senior School, Barnet
St Martin's Ampleforth, York
St Mary's, Worcester

St Mary's College, Southampton
St Mary's College, Folkestone
St Mary's College, Liverpool
St Mary's Hall, Clitheroe
St Mary's Hare Park School, Romford
St Mary's Junior School, Cambridge
St Mary's School Hampstead, London
St Mary's School, Ascot, Ascot
St Mary's School, Cambridge, Cambridge
St Mary's School, Dorset, Shaftesbury
St Michaels School, Newbury
St Monica's School, Carlisle
St Philip's School, London
St Philomena's Preparatory School, Frinton-on-Sea
St Pius X Preparatory School, Preston
St Richard's, Bromyard
St Teresa's Catholic Independent & Nursery School, Princes Risborough
St Teresa's Preparatory School, Effingham
St Teresa's School, Dorking
St Thomas Garnet's School, Bournemouth
St Ursula's High School, Westbury-on-Trym
St Winefride's Convent School, Shrewsbury
Stella Maris Junior School, Stockport
Stonyhurst College, Clitheroe
Stoodley Knowle School, Torquay
The Abbey School, Westgate-on-Sea
The Marist Preparatory School, Ascot
The Marist Senior School, Ascot
The Oratory Preparatory School, Reading

The Oratory School, Reading
The Towers Convent School, Steyning
Thornton College Convent of Jesus and Mary, Milton Keynes
Upton Hall Convent School, Wirral
Ursuline College, Westgate-on-Sea
Ursuline Preparatory School, Brentwood
Ursuline Preparatory School, London
Virgo Fidelis, London
Vita Et Pax Preparatory School, London
Westminster Cathedral Choir School, London
Winterfold House, Kidderminster
Woldingham School, Woldingham
Worth School, Turners Hill

SEVENTH DAY ADVENTIST

Dudley House School, Grantham
Fletewood School, Plymouth
Newbold School, Bracknell
Stanborough School, Watford
The John Loughborough School, London

UNITED REFORMED CHURCH

Caterham School, Caterham
Silcoates School, Wakefield
Sunny Hill House School, Wakefield
The Firs School, Chester

Schools Registered with CReSTeD (Council for the Registration of Schools Teaching Dyslexic Pupils)

Registered charity number 1052103
Information provided by CReSTeD

CReSTeD (the Council for the Registration of Schools Teaching Dyslexic Pupils) produces a twice yearly register of schools that provide for dyslexic children. The aim is to help parents and those who advise them to choose a school that has been approved to published criteria. CReSTeD was established in 1989 – its main supporters are the British Dyslexia Association and Dyslexia Action. Schools wishing to be included in the Register are visited by a CReSTeD consultant whose report is considered by the CReSTeD Council before registration can be finalized.

Consulting the Register should enable parents to decide which schools they wish to approach for further information. Dyslexic students have a variety of difficulties and so have a wide range of special needs. An equally wide range of teaching approaches is necessary. CReSTeD has therefore grouped schools together under four broad categories, which are designed to help parents match their child's needs to an appropriate philosophy and provision.

The four categories of the schools are described below:

SPECIALIST PROVISION SCHOOLS – SP

The school is established primarily to teach pupils with dyslexia. The curriculum and timetable are designed to meet specific needs in a holistic, coordinated manner with a significant number of staff qualified in teaching SpLD pupils.

DYSLEXIA UNIT – DU

The school has a designated unit or centre that provides specialist tuition on a small group or individual basis, according to need. The unit or centre is an adequately resourced teaching area under the management of a senior specialist teacher, who coordinates the work of other specialist teachers and ensures ongoing liaison with all mainstream teachers. This senior specialist teacher will probably have head of department status, and will certainly have significant input into the curriculum design and delivery.

SPECIALIST CLASSES – SC

Schools where dyslexic pupils are taught in separate classes within the school for some lessons, most probably English and Mathematics. These are taught by teachers with qualifications in teaching dyslexic pupils. These teachers are deemed responsible for communicating with the pupils' other subject teachers.

WITHDRAWAL SYSTEM – WS

Schools where dyslexic pupils are withdrawn from appropriately selected lessons for specialist tuition from a teacher qualified in teaching dyslexic pupils. There is ongoing communication between mainstream and specialist teachers.

Note: **Qualified** means holding a BDA-recognized qualification in the teaching of dyslexic pupils.

The list below includes those schools registered with CReSTeD which are listed elsewhere in this Guide. For a full list of schools registered with CReSTeD, including specialist schools and maintained schools, contact CReSTeD on 01242 604852 or by email at admin@crested.org.uk, or by writing to The Administrator, CReSTeD, Greygarth, Littleworth, Winchcombe, Cheltenham GL54 5BT. Alternatively, visit the website at www.crested.org.uk.

SPECIALIST PROVISION SCHOOLS

Abingdon House School, London W8
Appleford School, Salisbury
Brown's School, Orpington
Calder House School, Bath
The Dominie, London SW11
East Court School, Ramsgate
Edington & Shapwick School, Bridgewater
Fairley House School, London SW1P
Frewen College, Rye
Knowl Hill School, Pirbright
Mark College, Highbridge
The Moat School, SW6
Moon Hall School, Dorking
More House School, Farnham
Northease Manor School, Lewes
Nunnykirk Centre for Dyslexia, Morpeth
The Old Rectory School, Ipswich
St David's College, Llandudno
Sunnydown School, Caterham
Trinity School, Rochester
The Unicorn School, Abingdon

DYSLEXIA UNIT

Avon House, Woodford Green
Barnardiston Hall Preparatory School, Havershill
Bethany School, Cranbrook
Bloxham School, Banbury
Bredon School, Tewkesbury
Centre Academy, Battersea SW11
Clayesmore Preparatory School, Blandford Forum
Clayesmore, Blandford Forum
Clifton College Preparatory School
Cobham Hall, Gravesend
Danes Hill School, Leatherhead
Ellesmere College, Ellesmere
Finborough School, Stowmarket
Fulneck School, Leeds
Grenville College, Bideford
Holmwood House, Colchester
Hordle Walhampton School, Lymington
King's Bruton and Hazlegrove, Bruton
Kingham Hill School, Chipping Norton
Kingswood College Trust, Ormskirk
Kingswood House School, Epsom
Lime House School, Carlisle

Malvern St James, Great Malvern
Mayville High School, Southsea
Merton House, Chester
Monkton Combe School, Bath
Mostyn House School, South Wirral
Moyles Court School, Ringwood
Newlands School, Seaford
Ramillies Hall School, Cheadle
Riddlesworth Hall, Diss
St Bees School, St Bees
St David's College, Llandudno
Sibford School, Banbury
Slindon College, Arundel
Stowford College, Sutton
Tettenhall College, Wolverhampton
Wycliffe, Stonehouse
Wycliffe Preparatory School, Stonehouse

SPECIALIST CLASSES

Bruern Abbey School, Chesterton
St Crispin's School, Leicester

WITHDRAWAL SYSTEM

Dover College, Dover
Kilgraston, Perth
King's School, Rochester
Milton Abbey School, Blandford Forum
The North London International School, N11
Our Lady's Convent School, Loughborough
Prior Park Preparatory School, Cricklade
Putney Park School, Putney
The Royal Wolverhampton School, Wolverhampton
Thames Christian College, London SW11
Woodleigh School, Malton
Ysgol Rhydygors, Carmarthen

Provision for English as a Foreign Language

This index is intended as a general guide only and is compiled upon the basis of information given to Gabbitas by schools. Parents should note that there are wide variations in provision and are advised to contact individual schools for further details.

Schools listed below with a 'U' have a dedicated English language unit or offer intensive initial tuition for students whose first language is not English. Schools with no 'U' displayed offer one-to-one English language tuition, or arrange this tuition, according to need, for students whose first language is not English.

Parents may also wish to refer to the list of International Study Centres on page 32.

ENGLAND

BEDFORDSHIRE

Acorn School, Bedford
Bedford High School for Girls, Bedford
Bedford School, Bedford
Bedford School Study Centre, Bedford   U

BERKSHIRE

The Abbey School, Reading
The Ark School, Reading
Bearwood College, Wokingham   U
Bradfield College, Reading   U
Brockhurst & Marlston House Pre-Preparatory School, Thatcham
Brockhurst and Marlston House Schools, Newbury
The Cedars School, Aldermaston
Cheam School, Newbury   U
Claires Court School, Maidenhead
Claires Court Schools, The College, Maidenhead
Claires Court Schools, Ridgeway, Maidenhead
Dolphin School, Reading
Eagle House, Sandhurst
Elstree School, Reading
Heathfield School, Ascot   U
Highfield School, Maidenhead
Holme Grange School, Wokingham

Horris Hill School, Newbury
Hurst Lodge School, Ascot
Lambrook, Bracknell
Langley Manor School, Slough
Luckley-Oakfield School, Wokingham
Ludgrove, Wokingham
LVS Ascot, Ascot
Newbury Hall International School, Newbury   U
The Oratory School, Reading   U
Padworth College, Reading   U
Papplewick School, Ascot
Queen Anne's School, Reading   U
St Gabriel's, Newbury
St George's School, Ascot
St John's Beaumont, Windsor   U
St Joseph's College, Reading
St Piran's Preparatory School, Maidenhead
Sunningdale School, Sunningdale
Upton House School, Windsor
Waverley School, Wokingham
Wellington College, Crowthorne
White House Preparatory School, Wokingham
Winbury School, Maidenhead

BRISTOL

Badminton School, Bristol
Bristol Grammar School, Bristol
Clifton College, Bristol   U
Clifton College Preparatory School, Bristol   U
The Downs School, Wraxall
Gracefield Preparatory School, Fishponds
Queen Elizabeth's Hospital, Clifton
The Red Maids' School, Westbury-on-Trym
St Ursula's High School, Westbury-on-Trym   U
Tockington Manor School, Tockington   U
Torwood House School, Redland

BUCKINGHAMSHIRE

Akeley Wood School, Buckingham
The Beacon School, Amersham
Bury Lawn School, Milton Keynes
Caldicott School, Farnham Royal
Godstowe Preparatory School, High Wycombe   U
Grove Independent School, Milton Keynes
High March School, Beaconsfield
Kingscote Pre-Preparatory School, Gerrards Cross
Ladymede, Aylesbury
Maltman's Green School, Gerrards Cross
Milton Keynes Preparatory School, Milton Keynes
Pipers Corner School, High Wycombe
St Mary's School, Gerrards Cross
St Teresa's Catholic Independent & Nursery School,
   Princes Risborough
Stowe School, Buckingham   U
Swanbourne House School, Milton Keynes
Thornton College Convent of Jesus and Mary,
   Milton Keynes
Wycombe Abbey School, High Wycombe

CAMBRIDGESHIRE

Bellerbys College & Embassy CES Cambridge,
   Cambridge   U
Cambridge Centre for Sixth-form Studies,
   Cambridge   U
CATS College Cambridge, Cambridge   U
Kimbolton School, Huntingdon
The King's School Ely, Ely   U
The Leys School, Cambridge   U
Madingley Pre-Preparatory School, Cambridge
MPW (Mander Portman Woodward), Cambridge   U
The Perse School, Cambridge
The Peterborough School, Peterborough   U
St John's College School, Cambridge
St Mary's School, Cambridge   U
Sancton Wood School, Cambridge
Whitehall School, Huntingdon
Wisbech Grammar School, Wisbech

CHANNEL ISLANDS

St George's Preparatory School, Jersey

CHESHIRE

Abbey Gate School, Chester
Beech Hall School, Macclesfield
Cransley School, Northwich
Culcheth Hall, Altrincham
The Firs School, Chester
Forest Park School, Sale
Greenbank Preparatory School, Cheadle
Hale Preparatory School, Altrincham   U
The King's School, Chester
Loreto Preparatory School, Altrincham
North Cestrian Grammar School, Altrincham
The Queen's School, Chester
The Ryleys, Alderley Edge
St Ambrose Preparatory School, Altrincham
Terra Nova School, Holmes Chapel
Wilmslow Preparatory School, Wilmslow

CORNWALL

Gems Bolitho School, Penzance   U
Highfields Private School, Redruth
St Piran's School, Hayle
Truro School, Truro

CUMBRIA

Casterton School, Kirkby Lonsdale
Chetwynde School, Barrow-in-Furness
Holme Park School, Kendal
Lime House School, Carlisle   U
St Bees School, St Bees   U
Sedbergh School, Sedbergh   U
Windermere School, Windermere   U

DERBYSHIRE

Derby Grammar School, Derby
Derby High School, Derby
Foremarke Hall, Derby
Mount St Mary's College, Spinkhill   U
Repton School, Derby   U
S. Anselm's School, Bakewell

DEVON

Blundell's School, Tiverton
Bramdean School, Exeter
Edgehill College, Bideford   U
Exeter Cathedral School, Exeter
Exeter Tutorial College, Exeter   U
Kelly College, Tavistock   U
King's School, Plymouth
Kingsley School, Bideford   U
The Maynard School, Exeter
Mount House School, Tavistock
Plymouth College, Plymouth   U
Plymouth College Prepratory School, Plymouth
Stover School, Newton Abbot   U
Shebbear College, Beaworthy   U
South Devon Steiner School, Dartington

Tower House School, Paignton
Trinity School, Teignmouth U
West Buckland School, Barnstaple U

DORSET

Bournemouth Collegiate School, Bournemouth U
Bryanston School, Blandford Forum
Clayesmore, Blandford Forum
Clayesmore Preparatory School, Blandford Forum
International College, Sherborne School, Sherborne
Knighton House, Blandford Forum
Leweston School, Sherborne
Milton Abbey School, Blandford Forum U
Port Regis Preparatory School, Shaftesbury U
St Mary's School, Dorset, Shaftesbury
Sherborne Girls, Sherborne U
Sherborne School, Sherborne
Talbot Heath, Bournemouth
Yarrells School, Poole

COUNTY DURHAM

Barnard Castle School, Barnard Castle
Durham High School For Girls, Durham
Durham School, Durham
Polam Hall, Darlington U

ESSEX

Avon House, Woodford Green
Bancroft's School, Woodford Green
Braeside School for Girls, Buckhurst Hill
Brentwood School, Brentwood U
Chigwell School, Chigwell U
College Saint-Pierre, Leigh-on-Sea
Elm Green Preparatory School, Chelmsford U
Felsted School, Felsted U
Friends' School, Saffron Walden U
Gosfield School, Halstead
Holmwood House, Colchester
New Hall School, Chelmsford U
Oaklands School, Loughton
Park School for Girls, Ilford
Raphael Independent School, Hornchurch
St John's School, Billericay
St Mary's School, Colchester
Thorpe Hall School, Southend-on-Sea
Woodlands Schools, Brentwood

GLOUCESTERSHIRE

The Acorn School, Nailsworth
Airthrie School, Cheltenham
Bredon School, Tewkesbury
Cheltenham College, Cheltenham U
Cheltenham College Junior School, Cheltenham
Cheltenham Ladies' College, Cheltenham
Dean Close Preparatory School, Cheltenham U
Dean Close School, Cheltenham U
Hatherop Castle School, Cirencester
The King's School, Gloucester

Rendcomb College, Cirencester
Rose Hill School, Wotton-under-Edge
St Edward's School Cheltenham, Cheltenham
The School of the Lion, Gloucester
Westonbirt School, Tetbury U
Wycliffe College, Stonehouse U
Wycliffe Preparatory School, Stonehouse U
Wynstones School, Gloucester

SOUTH GLOUCESTERSHIRE

Silverhill School, Winterbourne

HAMPSHIRE

Ballard School, New Milton
Bedales School, Petersfield
Boundary Oak School, Fareham
Brockwood Park School, Bramdean U
Daneshill School, Basingstoke
Dunhurst (Bedales Junior School), Petersfield
Durlston Court, New Milton
Forres Sandle Manor, Fordingbridge
Glenhurst School, Havant
The Gregg School, Southampton
Grey House Preparatory School, Hook
Hampshire Collegiate School, UCST, Romsey
Highfield School, Liphook
Hordle Walhampton School, Lymington
Lord Wandsworth College, Hook
Mayville High School, Southsea U
Portsmouth High School GDST, Southsea
Prince's Mead School, Winchester
Rookesbury Park School, Portsmouth
Rookwood School, Andover
St John's College, Southsea
St Mary's College, Southampton
St Neot's School, Hook
St Nicholas' School, Fleet
St Swithun's School, Winchester U
St Winifred's School, Southampton
Stockton House School, Fleet
Sherborne House School, Eastleigh
Sherfield School, Hook
Twyford School, Winchester
Winchester College, Winchester
Woodhill School, Chandler's Ford
Wykeham House School, Fareham
Yateley Manor Preparatory School, Yateley

HEREFORDSHIRE

Hereford Cathedral School, Hereford
Lucton School, Leominster
St Richard's, Bromyard

HERTFORDSHIRE

Aldwickbury School, Harpenden
Beechwood Park School, St Albans
Berkhamsted School, Berkhamsted U
Bishop's Stortford College, Bishop's Stortford

Bishop's Stortford College Junior School,
    Bishop's Stortford
Duncombe School, Hertford
Edge Grove, Aldenham Village
Francis House Preparatory School, Tring
Haileybury, Hertford
Haresfoot Preparatory School, Berkhamsted
High Elms Manor School, Watford
Howe Green House School, Bishop's Stortford
The Junior School, Bishop's Stortford College,
    Bishop's Stortford
Justin Craig Education, Borehamwood
The King's School, Harpenden
Lockers Park, Hemel Hempstead
Queenswood, Hatfield   U
Rickmansworth PNEU School, Rickmansworth
The Royal Masonic School for Girls, Rickmansworth
St Albans High School for Girls, St Albans
St Christopher School, Letchworth Garden City
St Edmund's College and St Hugh's School, Ware U
St Francis' College, Letchworth Garden City   U
St Hilda's School, Bushey
St Margaret's School, Bushey
Stanborough School, Watford   U
Sherrardswood School, Welwyn
Tring Park School for the Performing Arts, Tring
York House School, Rickmansworth

ISLE OF MAN

King William's College, Castletown

ISLE OF WIGHT

Ryde School, Ryde

KENT

Ashford School, Ashford
Beechwood Sacred Heart School, Tunbridge Wells U
Benenden School, Cranbrook
Bethany School, Cranbrook   U
Bishop Challoner RC School, Bromley
Bromley High School GDST, Bromley
CATS College Canterbury, Canterbury   U
Cobham Hall, Gravesend   U
Dover College, Dover   U
Dulwich Preparatory School, Cranbrook, Cranbrook
Farringtons School, Chislehurst   U
Fosse Bank School, Tonbridge
Harenc School Trust, Sidcup
Holmewood House, Tunbridge Wells
Junior King's Canterbury, Canterbury   U
Kent College, Canterbury   U
Kent College Infant & Junior School, Canterbury U
Kent College Pembury, Tunbridge Wells
King's Rochester, Rochester
Northbourne Park School, Deal   U
Rochester Independent College, Rochester   U
St Andrew's School, Rochester
St Christopher's School, Canterbury   U
St Edmund's School Canterbury, Canterbury

St Edmunds Junior School, Canterbury
St Lawrence College, Ramsgate   U
St Lawrence College Junior School, Ramsgate
St Michael's School, Sevenoaks
Steephill Independent School, Longfield
Sevenoaks School, Sevenoaks
Sutton Valence School, Sutton Valence
Tonbridge School, Tonbridge
Walthamstow Hall, Sevenoaks
West Lodge Preparatory School, Sidcup
Wickham Court School, West Wickham

LANCASHIRE

Beech House School, Rochdale
The Bennett House School, Chorley
Bolton School (Girls' Division), Bolton
Clevelands Preparatory School, Bolton
Farrowdale House Preparatory School, Oldham
Kingswood College Trust, Ormskirk
Kirkham Grammar School, Preston
Langdale Preparatory School, Blackpool
Moorland School, Clitheroe
Queen Elizabeth's Grammar School, Blackburn
Rossall School, Fleetwood   U
Rossall School International Study Centre,
    Fleetwood   U
St Anne's College Grammar School,
    Lytham St Annes   U
St Mary's Hall, Clitheroe   U
Stonyhurst College, Clitheroe   U

LEICESTERSHIRE

Brooke House College, Market Harborough   U
Grace Dieu Manor School, Leicester
Leicester Grammar School, Leicester   U
Loughborough High School, Loughborough
Our Lady's Convent School, Loughborough
Ratcliffe College, Leicester   U
St Crispin's School, Leicester

LINCOLNSHIRE

Copthill School, Stamford
Dudley House School, Grantham
The Grantham Preparatory School, Grantham
Kirkstone House School, Bourne
Stamford High School, Stamford
Stamford Junior School, Stamford
Stamford School, Stamford

NORTH EAST LINCOLNSHIRE

St James' School, Grimsby   U

NORTH LINCOLNSHIRE

Trentvale Preparatory School, Keadby

LONDON

Abercorn School, London
Albemarle Independent College, London   U
Arnold House School, London
Ashbourne Middle School, London
Aston House School, London
Avenue House School, London
Bales College, London
Barbara Speake Stage School, London
Belmont (Mill Hill Preparatory School), London
Blackheath High School GDST, London
Brampton College, London   U
Broomwood Hall School, London
Cameron House School, Chelsea
CATS College London, London   U
The Cavendish School, London
Channing School, London
Chelsea Independent College, London   U
City of London School, London
Colet Court, London
Collingham Independent GCSE and Sixth Form College, London
Connaught House, London
David Game College, London   U
Davies Laing and Dick, London   U
Devonshire House Preparatory School, London
Dolphin School (Including Noah's Ark Nursery School), London
Donhead Prep School, London
Duff Miller, London
Dulwich College, London
Dulwich College Preparatory School, London
Ealing Independent College, Ealing
East London Christian Choir School, London   U
Eaton House Belgravia, London
Eaton House The Manor Pre-Preparatory, London
Eaton House The Manor Preparatory, London
Eaton House The Vale, London
Eaton Square School, London
Eridge House Preparatory, London
The Falcons School for Girls, London
Falkner House, London
Finton House School, London
Francis Holland School, Sloane Square SW1, London
Gatehouse School, London
GEMS Hampshire School, London
Goodwyn School, London
Grangewood Independent School, London
Great Beginnings Montessori School, London
Hall School Wimbledon (Junior School), London
Hall School Wimbledon (Senior School), London
Hawkesdown House School, London
Heath House Preparatory School, London
Heathside Preparatory School, Hampstead
Hendon Preparatory School, Hendon   U
Hill House International Junior School, London   U
Holland Park Pre-Preparatory School, London
Holly Park Montessori School, London
Ibstock Place School, London
International Community School, London   U
International School of London, London   U
Islamia Girls' School, London
James Allen's Preparatory School, London

Kerem School, London
The King Alfred School, London
Knightsbridge School, London
Lansdowne College, London
Le Herisson, London
Lion House School, London
The Lloyd Williamson School, London
Lyndhurst House Preparatory School, London
Mander Portman Woodward, London   U
The Merlin School, London
Mill Hill School, London
The Mount School, London   U
The Mulberry House School, London
Norland Place School, London
North Bridge House Senior School, London
North Bridge House Upper Prep School, London
The North London International School, London
Northcote Lodge School, London
Oakfield Preparatory School, London
Orchard House School, London
Parkgate House School, London
Portland Place School, London   U
Primrose Independent School, London
Prospect House School, London
Putney High School GDST, London
Putney Park School, London
Queen's College Prep School, London
Queen's Gate School, London
Rainbow Montessori Junior School, London
Ravenscourt Park Preparatory School, Hammersmith
Ravenstone Day Nursery and Nursery School, London
Redcliffe School, London
River House Montessori School, London
Riverston School, London
The Roche School, London
The Rowans School, London
The Royal School, Hampstead, London
St Augustine's Priory, Ealing
St Benedict's School, Ealing
St James Junior School, London
St James Senior Girls' School, London
St Johns Wood Pre-Preparatory School, London
St Margaret's School, London
St Martin's, London
St Mary's School Hampstead, London
St Olave's Preparatory School, London
St Paul's Cathedral School, London
The Study Preparatory School, London
Southbank International School, Hampstead, London   U
Southbank International School, Kensington, London   U
Southbank International School, Westminster, London   U
Sylvia Young Theatre School, London
Thames Christian College, London   U
Thomas's Fulham, London
Thomas's Preparatory School, London   U
Tower House School, London
The Village School, London
Welsh School of London, London
Westminster School, Westminster
Westminster Tutors, London

Wetherby Preparatory School, London
The White House Prep & Woodentops Kindergarten,
   London
Willington School, London

GREATER MANCHESTER

Clarendon Cottage School, Eccles
St Bede's College, Manchester
Withington Girls' School, Manchester

MERSEYSIDE

Birkenhead School, Wirral
Kingsmead School, Wirral   U
Liverpool College, Liverpool
Merchant Taylors' Boys' Schools, Liverpool
Merchant Taylors' Girls' School, Liverpool
Runnymede St Edward's School, Liverpool
St Mary's College, Liverpool

MIDDLESEX

ACS Hillingdon International School, Hillingdon   U
Ashton House School, Isleworth
Buckingham College School, Harrow
Denmead School, Hampton
Halliford School, Shepperton
Hampton School, Hampton
Harrow School, Harrow on the Hill
Little Eden & Eden High SDA, Brentford
The Mall School, Twickenham
Northwood College, Northwood
St Catherine's School, Twickenham
St Christopher's School, Wembley
St Helen's College, Hillingdon
St Helen's School, Northwood
St Martin's School, Northwood
Staines Preparatory School, Staines
Twickenham Preparatory School, Hampton

NORFOLK

Beeston Hall School, Cromer
Gresham's School, Holt
Hethersett Old Hall School, Norwich   U
Langley School, Norwich   U
The New Eccles Hall School, Norwich   U
Norwich High School for Girls GDST, Norwich
Notre Dame Preparatory School, Norwich
Riddlesworth Hall, Diss   U
St Nicholas House Kindergarten & Prep School,
   North Walsham   U
Stretton School, Norwich
Taverham Hall Preparatory School, Norwich   U

NORTHAMPTONSHIRE

Bosworth Independent College, Northampton   U
Maidwell Hall School, Northampton
Northamptonshire Grammar School, Pitsford

Oundle School, Nr Peterborough
Quinton House School, Northampton
Spratton Hall, Northampton

NORTHUMBERLAND

Longridge Towers School, Berwick-upon-Tweed

NOTTINGHAMSHIRE

Dagfa House School, Nottingham
Greenholme School, Nottingham
Grosvenor School, Nottingham
Highfields School, Newark
Ranby House School, Retford
Saville House School, Mansfield
Trent College & The Elms, Nottingham
Wellow House School, Newark
Worksop College, Worksop

OXFORDSHIRE

Abacus College, Oxford   U
Abingdon Preparatory School, Abingdon
Abingdon School, Abingdon
Cherwell College, Oxford
Christ Church Cathedral School, Oxford
Cokethorpe School, Witney
Cothill House Preparatory School, Abingdon
Cranford House School, Wallingford
d'Overbroeck's College Oxford, Oxford   U
Dragon School, Oxford
Greene's Tutorial College, Oxford
Headington School, Oxford
IQRA School, Oxford   U
Leckford Place School, Oxford
The Manor Preparatory School, Abingdon
New College School, Oxford
The Oratory Preparatory School, Reading
Our Lady's Abingdon Junior School, Abingdon
Our Lady's Abingdon School, Abingdon
Oxford Tutorial College, Oxford   U
St Clare's, Oxford, Oxford   U
St Edward's School, Oxford
St Helen & St Katharine, Abingdon
St Hugh's School, Faringdon
St John's Priory School, Banbury
Shiplake College, Henley-on-Thames
Sibford School, Banbury   U
Summer Fields, Oxford
Tudor Hall School, Banbury
Wychwood School, Oxford

RUTLAND

Oakham School, Oakham
Uppingham School, Uppingham

SHROPSHIRE

Adcote School for Girls, Shrewsbury   U

Bedstone College, Bucknell
Castle House School, Newport   U
Concord College, Shrewsbury
Dower House School, Bridgnorth
Ellesmere College, Ellesmere   U
Kingsland Grange, Shrewsbury
Moor Park School, Ludlow
Moreton Hall School, Oswestry   U
Oswestry School, Oswestry   U
Packwood Haugh School, Shrewsbury
Prestfelde Preparatory School, Shrewsbury
St Winefride's Convent School, Shrewsbury
Shrewsbury High School GDST, Shrewsbury
Shrewsbury School, Shrewsbury
Wrekin College, Wellington

SOMERSET

All Hallows, Shepton Mallet
Bath Academy, Bath   U
Bruton School for Girls, Bruton   U
Chard School, Chard
Chilton Cantelo School, Yeovil
Downside School, Bath
Hazlegrove Preparatory School, Yeovil
King's College, Taunton
King's Hall, Taunton
Millfield Preparatory School, Glastonbury   U
Millfield School, Street   U
The Park School, Yeovil
Perrott Hill School, Crewkerne
Queen's College, Taunton   U
Queen's College Junior, Pre-Prep & Nursery Schools,
    Taunton
Taunton Preparatory School, Taunton   U
Taunton School International, Taunton   U
Taunton School Senior, Taunton   U
Wellington School, Wellington   U
Wells Cathedral School, Wells   U

BATH & NORTH EAST SOMERSET

Kingswood Preparatory School, Bath
Kingswood School, Bath   U
Prior Park College, Bath
The Royal High School, Bath, Bath

NORTH SOMERSET

Sidcot School, Winscombe   U

STAFFORDSHIRE

Abbots Bromley School for Girls, Abbots Bromley
Abbotsholme School, Uttoxeter
Brooklands School & Little Brooklands Nursery, Stafford
Chase Academy, Cannock   U
Denstone College, Uttoxeter
Lichfield Cathedral School, Lichfield
Newcastle-under-Lyme School, Newcastle-under-Lyme
St Dominic's Independent Junior School, Stoke-on-Trent
St Dominic's School, Stafford
St Joseph's Preparatory School, Stoke-on-Trent

STOCKTON-ON-TEES

Teesside High School, Eaglescliffe

SUFFOLK

The Abbey, Woodbridge
Alexanders International School, Woodbridge   U
Brandeston Hall, The Preparatory School for
    Framlingham College, Brandeston   U
Culford School, Bury St Edmunds
Fairstead House School, Newmarket
Felixstowe International College, Felixstowe   U
Framlingham College, Woodbridge
Ipswich School, Ipswich
Moreton Hall Preparatory School, Bury St Edmunds
Old Buckenham Hall School, Ipswich   U
Orwell Park, Ipswich
The Royal Hospital School, Ipswich   U
St Joseph's College, Ipswich   U
Saint Felix School, Southwold
Summerhill School, Leiston
Woodbridge School, Woodbridge   U

SURREY

Aberdour, Tadworth
ACS Cobham International School, Cobham   U
ACS Egham International School, Egham   U
Aldro School, Godalming
Amesbury, Hindhead
Barrow Hills School, Godalming
Box Hill School, Dorking   U
Bramley School, Tadworth
Broomfield House School, Richmond
Cambridge Tutors College, Croydon   U
Charterhouse, Godalming
Chinthurst School, Tadworth
City of London Freemen's School, Ashtead
Claremont Fan Court School, Esher
Collingwood School, Wallington
Cranleigh School, Cranleigh
Cranmore School, Leatherhead
Croydon High School GDST, South Croydon
Cumnor House School, South Croydon
Downsend School, Leatherhead
Downsend School - Epsom Lodge, Epsom
Epsom College, Epsom
Ewell Castle School, Epsom
Feltonfleet School, Cobham
Frensham Heights School, Farnham   U
Grantchester House, Esher
Greenacre School for Girls, Banstead
Hampton Court House, East Molesey
Hawley Place School, Camberley
The Hawthorns School, Redhill
Hoe Bridge School, Woking
Homefield Preparatory School, Sutton
Hurtwood House, Dorking   U
Kew College, Richmond
Kew Green Preparatory School, Richmond   U
King Edward's School Witley, Godalming   U
King's House School, Richmond

Kingston Grammar School, Kingston-upon-Thames
Kingswood House School, Epsom
Laleham Lea School, Purley
Longacre School, Guildford
Manor House School, Leatherhead
Marymount International School,
    Kingston-upon-Thames   U
New Life Christian School, Croydon
Notre Dame Preparatory School, Cobham
Old Palace of John Whitgift School, Croydon
Park Hill School, Kingston-upon-Thames
Prior's Field School, Godalming
Priory Preparatory School, Banstead
Redehall Preparatory School, Horley
Reigate St Mary's Preparatory and Choir School,
    Reigate
Ripley Court School, Woking
Royal Ballet School, Richmond
Royal Grammar School, Guildford
Royal Russell School, Croydon   U
The Royal School, Haslemere   U
St Catherine's School, Guildford
St David's School, Purley
St Hilary's School, Godalming
St James Independent School for Boys (Senior), Ashford
St John's School, Leatherhead   U
St Teresa's School, Dorking   U
The Study School, New Malden
Surbiton High School, Kingston-upon-Thames
Surbiton Preparatory School, Surbiton
Sutton High School GDST, Sutton
TASIS The American School in England, Thorpe   U
Trinity School, Croydon
Westbury House School, New Malden
Westward Preparatory School, Walton-on-Thames
Woodcote House School, Windlesham
Yehudi Menuhin School, Cobham   U

EAST SUSSEX

Ashdown House School, Forest Row
Battle Abbey School, Battle   U
Brighton College, Brighton   U
Brighton College Pre-preparatory School, Brighton
Brighton College Prep School, Brighton
Brighton Steiner School Limited, Brighton
Buckswood School, Hastings   U
Eastbourne College, Eastbourne
Greenfields School, Forest Row   U
Lancing College Preparatory School at Mowden, Hove
Michael Hall (Steiner Waldorf School), Forest Row   U
Moira House Girls School, Eastbourne   U
Moira House School, Eastbourne
Newlands School, Seaford   U
Roedean School, Brighton   U
St Andrew's School, Eastbourne   U
St Aubyns School, Brighton
St Bede's Prep School, Eastbourne
St Bede's School, Hailsham
St Leonards-Mayfield School, Mayfield   U
Stonelands School of Ballet & Theatre Arts, Hove
Vinehall School, Robertsbridge   U

WEST SUSSEX

Ardingly College, Haywards Heath
Ardingly College Junior School, Haywards Heath
Burgess Hill School for Girls, Burgess Hill
Cottesmore School, Pease Pottage
Dorset House School, Pulborough
Farlington School, Horsham   U
Great Ballard School, Chichester
Handcross Park School, Haywards Heath
Hurstpierpoint College, Hurstpierpoint
The Prebendal School, Chichester
Seaford College, Petworth
Slindon College, Arundel
The Towers Convent School, Steyning
Worth School, Turners Hill

TYNE AND WEAR

Central Newcastle High School GDST,
    Newcastle upon Tyne
Grindon Hall Christian School, Sunderland   U
The King's School, Tynemouth
Sunderland High School, Sunderland
Westfield School, Newcastle upon Tyne

WARWICKSHIRE

Arnold Lodge School, Leamington Spa
Bilton Grange, Rugby
The Kingsley School, Leamington Spa
Princethorpe College, Rugby
Rugby School, Rugby

WEST MIDLANDS

Al-Burhan Grammar School, Birmingham
Birchfield School, Wolverhampton
The Blue Coat School, Birmingham
Coventry Prep School, Coventry
Edgbaston High School for Girls, Birmingham
Eversfield Preparatory School, Solihull
Highclare School, Birmingham
Mander Portman Woodward, Birmingham
Priory School, Birmingham
St George's School, Edgbaston, Birmingham
Saint Martin's School, Solihull
Tettenhall College, Wolverhampton   U
Wolverhampton Grammar School, Wolverhampton

WILTSHIRE

Avondale School, Salisbury
Bishopstrow College, Warminster   U
Chafyn Grove School, Salisbury
Dauntsey's School, Devizes
The Godolphin School, Salisbury
Grittleton House School, Chippenham
Marlborough College, Marlborough
Norman Court Preparatory School, Salisbury
Pinewood School, Shrivenham
Prior Park Preparatory School, Cricklade

St Margaret's Preparatory School, Calne
St Mary's Calne, Calne
Salisbury Cathedral School, Salisbury
Sandroyd School, Salisbury
Stonar School, Melksham U
Warminster School, Warminster U

WORCESTERSHIRE

Abberley Hall, Worcester U
The Abbey College, Malvern Wells U
Bowbrook House School, Pershore
Bromsgrove Preparatory School, Bromsgrove U
Bromsgrove School, Bromsgrove U
The Downs, Malvern, Malvern
Green Hill School, Evesham
King's Hawford, Worcester
Malvern St James, Great Malvern U
Moffats School, Bewdley
St Mary's, Worcester
Saint Michael's College, Tenbury Wells U
Winterfold House, Kidderminster

EAST RIDING OF YORKSHIRE

Pocklington School, Pocklington

NORTH YORKSHIRE

Ampleforth College, York
Ashville College, Harrogate
Aysgarth Preparatory School, Bedale
Bootham School, York
Brackenfield School, Harrogate
Bramcote School, Scarborough
Fyling Hall School, Whitby
Giggleswick Junior School, Settle
Giggleswick School, Settle
Harrogate Ladies' College, Harrogate U
Harrogate Language Academy, Harrogate U

Harrogate Tutorial College, Harrogate U
Malsis School, Near Skipton
The Mount School, York U
Queen Ethelburga's College, York U
Queen Mary's School, Thirsk
Read School, Selby
Ripon Cathedral Choir School, Ripon
St Martin's Ampleforth, York
Scarborough College & Lisvane School, Scarborough
Terrington Hall, York
Woodleigh School, Malton

SOUTH YORKSHIRE

Ashdell Preparatory School, Sheffield
Sheffield High School GDST, Sheffield
Westbourne School, Sheffield

WEST YORKSHIRE

Ackworth School, Pontefract U
Batley Grammar School, Batley
Dale House School, Batley U
The Froebelian School, Leeds
Fulneck School, Leeds U
Gateways School, Leeds
Ghyll Royd School, Ilkley
The Gleddings Preparatory School, Halifax
Lady Lane Park School, Bingley
Moorlands School, Leeds
New Horizon Community School, Leeds
Queen Elizabeth Grammar School, Wakefield
The Rastrick Independent School, Brighouse
Rathbone Choices, Huddersfield
Richmond House School, Leeds
Rishworth School, Rishworth U
Wakefield Independent School, Wakefield
Woodhouse Grove School, Apperley Bridge U

NORTHERN IRELAND

COUNTY ANTRIM

Campbell College, Belfast U
Victoria College Belfast, Belfast

COUNTY ARMAGH

The Royal School Armagh, Armagh U

COUNTY DOWN

The Holywood Rudolf Steiner School, Holywood
Rockport School, Holywood

COUNTY TYRONE

The Royal School Dungannon, Dungannon U

SCOTLAND

ABERDEENSHIRE

Albyn School, Aberdeen
International School of Aberdeen, Aberdeen U
St Margaret's School for Girls, Aberdeen

SOUTH AYRSHIRE

Wellington School, Ayr

FIFE

St Leonards School, St Andrews

GLASGOW

Craigholme School, Pollockshields
Hutchesons' Grammar School, Glasgow
St Aloysius' College, Glasgow

LOTHIAN

Basil Paterson Tutorial College, Edinburgh	U
Belhaven Hill, Dunbar	U
Clifton Hall School, Edinburgh	
The Edinburgh Rudolf Steiner School, Edinburgh	U
Fettes College, Edinburgh	U
George Watson's College, Edinburgh	
Loretto Junior School, Musselburgh	U
Loretto School, Musselburgh	U
Merchiston Castle School, Edinburgh	U
St George's School for Girls, Edinburgh	U
St Serf's School, Edinburgh	

MORAYSHIRE

Gordonstoun School, Elgin	U

PERTH AND KINROSS

Craigclowan Preparatory School, Perth	
Glenalmond College, Perth	
Kilgraston, Perth	U
Morrison's Academy, Crieff	
Strathallan School, Perth	U

STIRLING

Beaconhurst School, Bridge of Allan

WALES

BRIDGEND

St Clare's School, Porthcawl

CARDIFF

The Cardiff Academy, Roath	
Howell's School, Llandaff GDST, Llandaff	
Kings Monkton School, Cardiff	
Westbourne School, Penarth	U

CARMARTHENSHIRE

Llandovery College, Llandovery	U
St Michael's School, Llanelli	

CONWY

St David's College, Llandudno

DENBIGHSHIRE

Howell's School, Denbigh	U
Ruthin School, Ruthin	U

GWYNEDD

Hillgrove School, Bangor

MONMOUTHSHIRE

Monmouth School, Monmouth	
St John's-on-the-Hill, Chepstow	

POWYS

Christ College, Brecon	U

SWANSEA

Craig-y-Nos School, Bishoptston

CONTINENTAL EUROPE

Chavagnes International College, Chavagnes-En-Paillers, France	
John F Kennedy International School, Saaren, Switzerland	U
King's College Madrid, Madrid, Spain	
Mougins School, France	U
St Columba's College, Dublin, Ireland	

Schools in Membership of the Constituent Associations of the Independent Schools Council

The schools listed below are all in membership of the Independent Schools Council in the UK. Please note that ISC-accredited special schools and overseas schools are not included. The constituent associations of the ISC include:

Association of Governing Bodies of Independent Schools (AGBIS)
The Girls' Schools Association (GSA)
The Headmasters' and Headmistresses' Conference (HMC)
The Independent Association of Prep Schools (IAPS)
The Independent Schools Association (ISA)
The Independent Schools' Bursars Association (ISBA)
The Society of Headmasters and Headmistresses of Independent Schools (SHMIS)

ENGLAND

BEDFORDSHIRE

Bedford High School for Girls, Bedford
Bedford Modern School, Bedford
Bedford Preparatory School, Bedford
Bedford School, Bedford
Dame Alice Harpur School, Bedford
Orchard School and Nursery, Bedford
Pilgrims Pre-Preparatory School, Bedford
Rushmoor School, Bedford
St Andrew's School, Bedford

BERKSHIRE

The Abbey School, Reading
Bearwood College, Wokingham
Bradfield College, Reading
Brigidine School Windsor, Windsor
Brockhurst and Marlston House Schools, Newbury
Cheam School, Newbury
Claires Court School, Maidenhead
Crosfields School, Reading
Dolphin School, Reading
Downe House, Thatcham
Eagle House, Sandhurst
Elstree School, Reading
The Elvian School, Reading
Eton College, Windsor
Eton End PNEU, Slough
Heathfield School, Ascot
Hemdean House School, Reading
Herries School, Maidenhead
Highfield School, Maidenhead
Holme Grange School, Wokingham

Horris Hill School, Newbury
Hurst Lodge School, Ascot
Lambrook, Bracknell
Leighton Park School, Reading
Luckley-Oakfield School, Wokingham
Ludgrove, Wokingham
The Marist Preparatory School, Ascot
The Marist Senior School, Ascot
The Oratory Preparatory School, Reading
The Oratory School, Reading
Padworth College, Reading
Pangbourne College, Pangbourne
Papplewick School, Ascot
Queen Anne's School, Reading
Reading Blue Coat School, Reading
Ridgeway School, Maidenhead
St Andrew's School, Reading
St Bernard's Preparatory School, Slough
St Edward's School, Reading
St Gabriel's School, Newbury
St George's School, Ascot
St George's School, Windsor
St John's Beaumont, Windsor
St Joseph's Convent School, Reading
St Mary's School, Ascot
St Piran's Preparatory School, Maidenhead
Sunningdale School, Sunningdale
Upton House School, Windsor
Waverley School, Wokingham
Wellington College, Crowthorne
White House Preparatory School, Wokingham
Winbury School, Maidenhead

BRISTOL

Badminton School, Bristol
Bristol Grammar School, Bristol
Clifton College, Bristol
Clifton College Preparatory School, Bristol
Clifton College Pre-Prep–Butcombe, Bristol
Clifton High School, Bristol
Colston's Collegiate School, Bristol
Colston's Girls' School, Bristol
Colston's Lower School, Bristol
The Downs School, Bristol
Fairfield School, Backwell
Queen Elizabeth's Hospital, Bristol
The Red Maids' School, Bristol
Redland High School, Bristol
St Ursula's High School, Bristol
Tockington Manor School, Bristol

BUCKINGHAMSHIRE

Ashfold School, Aylesbury
The Beacon School, Amersham
Caldicott School, Farnham Royal
Chesham Preparatory School, Chesham
Dair House School Trust Ltd, Farnham Royal
Davenies School, Beaconsfield
Gateway School, Great Missenden
Gayhurst School, Gerrards Cross
Godstowe Preparatory School, High Wycombe

Heatherton House School, Amersham
High March School, Beaconsfield
Kingscote Pre-Preparatory School, Gerrards Cross
Ladymede, Aylesbury
Maltman's Green School, Gerrards Cross
Milton Keynes Preparatory School, Milton Keynes
Pipers Corner School, High Wycombe
St Mary's School, Gerrards Cross
St Teresa's Catholic Independent & Nursery School,
    Princes Risborough
Stowe School, Buckingham
Swanbourne House School, Milton Keynes
Thornton College Convent of Jesus and Mary,
    Milton Keynes
Thorpe House School, Gerrards Cross
Wycombe Abbey School, High Wycombe

CAMBRIDGESHIRE

CATS Cambridge
Cambridge Centre for Sixth-form Studies, Cambridge
Kimbolton School, Huntingdon
Kings College, Cambridge
The King's School Ely, Ely
The Leys School, Cambridge
The Perse School, Cambridge
The Perse School for Girls, Cambridge
Peterborough High School, Peterborough
Sancton Wood School, Cambridge
St Faith's, Cambridge
St John's College School, Cambridge
St Mary's Junior School, Cambridge
St Mary's School, Cambridge
Whitehall School, Huntingdon
Wisbech Grammar School, Wisbech

CHANNEL ISLANDS

Elizabeth College, Guernsey
The Ladies' College, Guernsey
St Michael's Preparatory School, Jersey
Victoria College, Jersey
Victoria College Preparatory School, Jersey

CHESHIRE

Abbey Gate College, Chester
Abbey Gate School, Chester
Alderley Edge School for Girls, Alderley Edge
Beech Hall School, Macclesfield
Cransley School, Northwich
The Firs School, Chester
The Grange School, Northwich
Hammond School, Chester
The King's School, Chester
The King's School, Macclesfield
Loreto Preparatory School, Altrincham
Pownall Hall School, Wilmslow
The Queen's School, Chester
Ramillies Hall School, Cheadle
The Ryleys, Alderley Edge
Terra Nova School, Holmes Chapel
Wilmslow Preparatory School, Wilmslow

CORNWALL

Polwhele House School, Truro
Roselyon, Par
St Joseph's School, Launceston
St Piran's Preparatory School, Hayle
Truro High School, Truro
Truro School, Truro

COUNTY DURHAM

Barnard Castle School, Barnard Castle
The Chorister School, Durham
Durham High School For Girls, Durham
Durham School, Durham
Polam Hall, Darlington

CUMBRIA

Austin Friars St Monica's School, Carlisle
Chetwynde School, Barrow-in-Furness
Hunter Hall School, Penrith
Lime House School, Carlisle
St Bees School, St Bees
Sedbergh School, Sedbergh
Windermere St Anne's, Windermere

DERBYSHIRE

Derby Grammar School, Derby
Derby High School, Derby
Foremarke Hall School, Derby
Mount St Mary's College, Spinkhill
Ockbrook School, Derby
Repton School, Derby
St Anselm's School, Bakewell
St Peter and St Paul School, Chesterfield
St Wystan's School, Repton

DEVON

Blundell's Preparatory School, Tiverton
Blundell's School, Tiverton
Exeter Cathedral School, Exeter
Exeter School, Exeter
Kelly College, Tavistock
Kelly College Preparatory School, Tavistock
Kingsley School, Bideford
Manor House School, Honiton
The Maynard School, Exeter
Mount House School, Tavistock
Plymouth College, Plymouth
St Christopher's School, Totnes
St Dunstan's Abbey, Plymouth
St John's School, Sidmouth
St Margaret's School, Exeter
St Michael's, Barnstaple
St Peter's School, Exmouth
Shebbear College, Beaworthy
Stover School, Newton Abbot
Trinity School, Teignmouth
West Buckland School, Barnstaple

DORSET

Bryanston School, Blandford Forum
Canford School, Wimborne
Castle Court Preparatory School, Wimborne
Clayesmore Preparatory School, Blandford Forum
Clayesmore, Blandford Forum
Dumpton School, Wimborne
Hanford School, Blandford Forum
International College, Sherborne School, Sherborne
Knighton House, Blandford Forum
Leweston School, Sherbourne
The Park School, Bournemouth
Port Regis School, Shaftesbury
St Antony's Leweston Schools, Sherborne
St Mary's School, Shaftesbury
Sherborne Preparatory School, Sherborne
Sherborne School, Sherborne
Sherborne School for Girls, Sherborne
Sunninghill Preparatory School, Dorchester
Talbot Heath, Bournemouth
Thornlow Preparatory School, Weymouth
Uplands School, Poole
Wentworth College, Bournemouth
Yarrells School, Poole

ESSEX

Alleyn Court Preparatory School, Southend-on-Sea
Bancroft's School, Woodford Green
Braeside School for Girls, Buckhurst Hill
Brentwood School, Brentwood
Chigwell School, Chigwell
Colchester High School, Colchester
Coopersale Hall School, Epping
Crowstone Preparatory School, Westcliff-on-Sea
Dame Bradbury's School, Saffron Walden
Elm Green Preparatory School, Chelmsford
Felsted Preparatory School, Felsted
Felsted School, Felsted
Friends' School, Saffron Walden
Gidea Park College, Romford
Gosfield School, Halstead
Heathcote School, Chelmsford
Holmwood House, Colchester
Littlegarth School, Colchester
Loyola Preparatory School, Buckhurst Hill
Maldon Court Preparatory School, Maldon
New Hall School, Chelmsford
Oaklands School, Loughton
Park School for Girls, Ilford
St Anne's Preparatory School, Chelmsford
St Aubyn's School, Woodford Green
St Cedd's School, Chelmsford
St Hilda's School, Westcliff-on-Sea
St John's School, Billericay
St Margaret's School, Halstead
St Mary's School, Colchester
St Michael's School, Leigh-on-Sea
St Nicholas School, Harlow
St Philomena's Preparatory School, Frinton-on-Sea
Thorpe Hall School, Southend-on-Sea
Ursuline Preparatory School, Brentwood
Widford Lodge, Chelmsford

Woodford Green Preparatory School, Woodford Green
Woodlands Schools, Brentwood

GLOUCESTERSHIRE

Beaudesert Park School, Stroud
Berkhampstead School, Cheltenham
Bredon School, Tewkesbury
Cheltenham College, Cheltenham
Cheltenham College Junior School, Cheltenham
The Cheltenham Ladies' College, Cheltenham
Dean Close Preparatory School, Cheltenham
Dean Close School, Cheltenham
Hatherop Castle School, Cirencester
The King's School, Gloucester
Rendcomb College, Cirencester
The Richard Pate School, Cheltenham
Rose Hill School, Wotton-under-Edge
St Edward's School, Cheltenham
Westonbirt School, Tetbury
Wycliffe, Stonehouse
Wycliffe Preparatory School, Stonehouse

HAMPSHIRE

Alton Convent School, Alton
Ballard School, New Milton
Bedales School, Petersfield
Boundary Oak School, Fareham
Churchers College, Petersfield
Daneshill School, Basingstoke
Ditcham Park School, Petersfield
Dunhurst (Bedales Junior School), Petersfield
Durlston Court, New Milton
Farleigh School, Andover
Farnborough Hill, Farnborough
Forres Sandle Manor, Fordingbridge
The Gregg School, Southampton
Hampshire Collegiate School UCST, Romsey
Highfield School, Liphook
Hordle Walhampton School, Lymington
King Edward VI School, Southampton
Lord Wandsworth College, Hook
Mayville High School, Southsea
Moyles Court School, Ringwood
The Pilgrims' School, Winchester
The Portsmouth Grammar School, Portsmouth
Portsmouth High School GDST, Southsea
Prince's Mead School, Winchester
Rookesbury Park School, Portsmouth
Rookwood School, Andover
St John's College, Southsea
St Neot's School, Hook
St Nicholas' School, Fleet
St Swithun's School, Winchester
St Winifred's School, Southampton
Salesian College, Farnborough
Sherborne House School, Eastleigh
Sherfield School, Hook
Stanbridge Earls School, Romsey
The Stroud School, Romsey
Twyford School, Winchester
West Hill Park, Fareham

Winchester College, Winchester
Wykeham House School, Fareham
Yateley Manor Preparatory School, Yateley

HEREFORDSHIRE

The Hereford Cathedral Junior School, Hereford
The Hereford Cathedral School, Hereford
Lucton School, Leominster

HERTFORDSHIRE

Abbot's Hill School, Hemel Hempstead
Aldenham School, Elstree
Aldwickbury School, Harpenden
Beechwood Park School, St Albans
Berkhamsted Collegiate Preparatory School, Berkhamsted
Berkhamsted Collegiate School, Berkhamsted
Bishop's Stortford College, Bishop's Stortford
CKHR Immanuel College, Bushey
Edge Grove, Aldenham
Egerton Rothesay School, Berkhamsted
Francis House Preparatory School, Tring
Haberdashers' Aske's Boys' School, Elstree
Haberdashers' Aske's School for Girls, Elstree
Haileybury, Hertford
Haresfoot Preparatory School, Berkhamsted
Heath Mount School, Hertford
Howe Green House School, Bishop's Stortford
Immanuel College, Bushey
Kingshott School, Hitchin
Lochinver House School, Potters Bar
Lockers Park, Hemel Hempstead
Lyonsdown School, New Barnet
Manor Lodge School, Shenley
Northwood Preparatory School, Rickmansworth
The Princess Helena College, Hitchin
The Purcell School, Bushey
Queenswood, Hatfield
The Royal Masonic School for Girls, Rickmansworth
St Albans High School for Girls, St Albans
St Albans School, St Albans
St Christopher School, Letchworth
St Columba's College, St Albans
St Edmund's College and St Hugh's School, Ware
St Francis' College, Letchworth Garden City
St Hilda's School, Bushey
St Hilda's School, Harpenden
St Joseph's in the Park, Hertingfordbury
St Margaret's School, Bushey
Sherrardswood School, Welwyn
Stanborough School, Watford
Stormont, Potters Bar
Tring Park School for the Performing Arts, Tring
Westbrook Hay Preparatory School, Hemel Hempstead
York House School, Rickmansworth

ISLE OF MAN

The Buchan School, Castletown
King William's College, Castletown

ISLE OF WIGHT

Ryde School, Ryde

KENT

Ashford School, Ashford
Babington House School, Chislehurst
Beechwood Sacred Heart School, Tunbridge Wells
Benenden School, Cranbrook
Bethany School, Cranbrook
Bickley Park School, Bromley
Bronte School, Gravesend
Cobham Hall, Gravesend
Combe Bank School, Nr Sevenoaks
Derwent Lodge School for Girls, Tonbridge
Dover College, Dover
Dulwich Preparatory School, Cranbrook, Cranbrook
Farringtons School, Chislehurst
Fosse Bank School, Hildenborough
Gad's Hill School, Rochester
The Granville School, Sevenoaks
Harenc School Trust, Sidcup
Hilden Grange School, Tonbridge
Hilden Oaks School, Tonbridge
Holmewood House, Tunbridge Wells
Junior King's School, Canterbury
The Junior School, St Lawrence College, Ramsgate
Kent College, Canterbury
Kent College Infant & Junior School, Canterbury
Kent College Pembury, Tunbridge Wells
King's Preparatory School, Rochester
The King's School, Canterbury
King's School Rochester, Rochester
Lorenden Preparatory School, Faversham
Marlborough House School, Hawkhurst
The Mead School, Turnbridge Wells
The New Beacon, Sevenoaks
Northbourne Park School, Deal
Rochester Independent College, Rochester
Rose Hill School, Tunbridge Wells
Russell House School, Sevenoaks
Sackville School, Tonbridge
St Edmunds Junior School, Canterbury
St Edmund's School Canterbury, Canterbury
St Lawrence College, Ramsgate
St Michael's School, Sevenoaks
St Ronan's School, Hawkhurst
Sevenoaks Preparatory School, Sevenoaks
Sevenoaks School, Sevenoaks
Solefield School, Sevenoaks
Spring Grove School, Ashford
Steephill Independent School, Longfield
Sutton Valence Preparatory School, Maidstone
Sutton Valence School, Maidstone
Tonbridge School, Tonbridge
Walthamstow Hall, Sevenoaks
Wellesley House School, Broadstairs
Yardley Court, Tonbridge

LANCASHIRE

Arnold School, Blackpool
Highfield Priory School, Preston
The Hulme Grammar School for Girls, Oldham
King Edward VII and Queen Mary School, Lytham St Annes
Kirkham Grammar School, Preston
Moorland School, Clitheroe
The Oldham Hulme Grammar School, Oldham
Queen Elizabeth's Grammar School, Blackburn
Rossall Junior School, Fleetwood
Rossall School, Fleetwood
St Joseph's Convent School, Burnley
St Mary's Hall, Stonyhurst
St Pius X Preparatory School, Preston
Stonyhurst College, Clitheroe
Westholme School, Blackburn

LEICESTERSHIRE

Arley House PNEU School, Leicestershire
The Dixie Grammar School, Market Bosworth
Fairfield Preparatory School, Loughborough
Grace Dieu Manor School, Leicester
Leicester Grammar School, Leicester
Leicester High School For Girls, Leicester
Leicester Montessori Grammar School, Leicester
Loughborough Grammar School, Loughborough
Loughborough High School, Loughborough
Manor House School, Ashby-de-la-Zouch
Our Lady's Convent School, Loughborough
Ratcliffe College, Leicester

LINCOLNSHIRE

Ayscoughfee Hall School, Spalding
Copthill School, Stamford
Kirkstone House School, Bourne
Lincoln Minster School, Lincoln
St Hugh's School, Woodhall Spa
Stamford High School, Stamford
Stamford Junior School, Stamford
Stamford School, Stamford
Witham Hall, Bourne

NORTH EAST LINCOLNSHIRE

St James' School, Grimsby
St Martin's Preparatory School, Grimsby

LONDON

Abercorn School, NW8
Abingdon House School, W8
Alleyn's School, SE22
Arnold House School, NW8
Avenue House School, W13
Bassett House School, W10
Belmont (Mill Hill Preparatory School), NW7
Broomwood Hall Upper School, SW12
Bute House Preparatory School for Girls, W6
Cameron House School, SW3
The Cavendish School, NW1
Channing School, N6
City of London School, EC4V
City of London School for Girls, EC2Y

Colfe's School, SE12
Davies, Laing & Dick College, W1
Devonshire House Preparatory School, NW3
Donhead Prep School, SW19
Dulwich College, SE21
Dulwich College Preparatory School, SE21
Durston House, W5
Eaton House The Manor, SW4
Eaton House The Vale, SW7
Eaton Square School, SW1V
Eltham College, SE9
Emanuel School, SW11
The Falcons School for Boys, SW7
The Falcons School for Girls, W5
Fairley House School, SW1P
Falkner House, SW7
Finton House School, SW17
Forest School, E17
Francis Holland School, Regent's Park NW1
Francis Holland School, SW1W
Garden House School, SW3
Gatehouse School, E2
Glendower Preparatory School, SW7
The Godolphin and Latymer School, W6
Grange Park Preparatory School, N21
Grangewood Independent School, E7
The Hall School, NW3
Harvington School, W5
Hawkesdown House School, W8
Hereward House School, NW3
Herne Hill School, SE24
Highgate School, N6
Ibstock Place School, SW15
The Italia Conti Academy of Theatre Arts, EC1M
James Allen's Girls' School, SE22
James Allen's Preparatory School, SE22
Keble Preparatory School, N21
Kensington Prep School, SW6
The King Alfred School, NW11
King's College Junior School, SW19
King's College School, SW19
Knightsbridge School, SW1X
Latymer Prep School, W6
Latymer Upper School, W6
Lyndhurst House Preparatory School, NW3
Mander Portman Woodward, SW7
Mill Hill School, NW7
The Moat School, SW6
More House, SW1X
The Mount School, NW7
The Mulberry House School, NW2
Naima Jewish Preparatory School, NW6
Newton Prep School, SW8
Norland Place School, W11
Northcote Lodge School, SW11
The North London International School, N11
Notting Hill and Ealing High School GDST, W13
Oakfield Preparatory School, SE21
Orchard House School, W4
Palmers Green High School, N21
Pembridge Hall, W2
Portland Place School, W1B
Prospect House School, SW15

Putney High School GDST, SW15
Putney Park School, SW15
Queen's College, W1G
Queen's Gate School, SW7
Ravenscourt Park Preparatory School, W6
Redcliffe School, SW10
Riverston School, SE12
Rosemead Preparatory School, SE21
Royal Ballet School, WC2E
The Royal School, Hampstead, NW3
St Anthony's Preparatory School, NW3
St Benedict's School, W5
St Christina's RC Preparatory School, NW8
St Christopher's School, NW3
St Dunstan's College, SE6
St James Independent School for Boys and Girls, W14
St James Independent School for Girls (Juniors), W14
St James Independent School for Senior Girls, W14
St Margaret's School, NW3
St Mary's School Hampstead, NW3
St Olave's Preparatory School, SE9
St Paul's Cathedral School, EC4M
St Paul's Girls' School, W6
St Paul's Preparatory School, SW13
St Paul's School, SW13
South Hampstead High School, NW3
Southbank International School, Hampstead, NW3
Southbank International School, Kensington, W11
Southbank International School, Westminster, W1B
Streatham and Clapham High School, SW16
The Study Preparatory School, SW19
Sussex House School, SW1X
The Swaminarayan School, NW10
Sydenham High School GDST, SE26
Sylvia Young Theatre School, NW1
Tower House School, SW14
Trevor Roberts School, NW3
University College School, NW3
University College School Junior Branch, NW3
Ursuline Preparatory School, SW20
Virgo Fidelis, SE19
Vita Et Pax School, N14
Westminster Abbey Choir School, SW1P
Westminster Cathedral Choir School, SW1P
Westminster School, SW1P
Westminster Under School, SW1P
Wimbledon High School GDST, SW19
Woodside Park International School, N11

GREATER MANCHESTER

Abbey College, Manchester
Abbotsford Preparatory School, Manchester
Chetham's School of Music, Manchester
The Manchester Grammar School, Manchester
Manchester High School for Girls, Manchester
Moor Allerton School, Manchester
St Bede's College, Manchester
Withington Girls' School, Manchester

MERSEYSIDE

The Belvedere School GDST, Liverpool

Birkenhead High School GDST, Wirral
Birkenhead School, Wirral
Carleton House Preparatory School, Liverpool
Kingsmead School, Wirral
Liverpool College, Liverpool
Merchant Taylors' Girls' School, Liverpool
Prenton Preparatory School, Wirral
Redcourt-St Anselms, Prenton
Runnymede St Edward's School, Liverpool
St Mary's College, Liverpool
Sunnymede School, Southport
Tower College, Prescot

MIDDLESEX

ACS Hillingdon International School, Hillingdon
Alpha Preparatory School, Harrow
Ashton House School, Isleworth
Buckingham College School, Harrow
Denmead School, Hampton
Halliford School, Shepperton
Hampton School, Hampton
Harrow School, Harrow on the Hill
Heathfield School, Pinner
Innellan House School, Pinner
The John Lyon School, Harrow
The Lady Eleanor Holles School, Hampton
The Mall School, Twickenham
Merchant Taylors' School, Northwood
Newland House School, Twickenham
North London Collegiate, Edgware
Northwood College, Northwood
Orley Farm School, Harrow
Peterborough & St Margaret's School, Stanmore
Quainton Hall School, Harrow
Reddiford, Pinner
St Catherine's School, Twickenham
St Christopher's School, Wembley
St David's School, Ashford
St Helen's College, Hillingdon
St Helen's School, Northwood
St James Independent School for Boys (Senior), Twickenham
St John's Northwood, Northwood
St Martin's School, Northwood
Staines Preparatory School, Staines
Twickenham Preparatory School, Hampton

NORFOLK

Beeston Hall School, Cromer
Glebe House School, Hunstanton
Gresham's Preparatory School, Holt
Gresham's School, Holt
Hethersett Old Hall School, Norwich
Langley Preparatory School & Nursery, Norwich
Langley School, Norwich
The New Eccles Hall School, Norwich
Norwich High School for Girls GDST, Norwich
Norwich School, Norwich
Notre Dame Preparatory School, Norwich
Riddlesworth Hall, Diss
Sacred Heart Convent School, Swaffham

St Nicholas House Kindergarten & Prep School, North Walsham
Taverham Hall Preparatory School, Norwich
Thetford Grammar School, Thetford
Thorpe House School, Norwich
Town Close House Preparatory School, Norwich

NORTHAMPTONSHIRE

Beachborough School, Brackley
Great Houghton Preparatory School, Northampton
Laxton Junior School, Nr Peterborough
Maidwell Hall School, Northampton
Northampton High School, Northampton
Northamptonshire Grammar School, Pitsford
Oundle School, Nr Peterborough
St Peter's School, Kettering
Spratton Hall, Northampton
Wellingborough School, Wellingborough
Winchester House School, Brackley

NORTHUMBERLAND

Longridge Towers School, Berwick-upon-Tweed
Mowden Hall School, Stocksfield

NOTTINGHAMSHIRE

Dagfa House School, Nottingham
Grosvenor School, Nottingham
Highfields School, Newark
Hollygirt School, Nottingham
Nottingham High Junior School, Nottingham
Nottingham High School, Nottingham
Nottingham High School for Girls GDST, Nottingham
Plumtree School, Nottingham
Ranby House School, Retford
St Joseph's School, Nottingham
Salterford House School, Nottingham
Trent College, Nottingham
Wellow House School, Newark
Worksop College, Worksop

OXFORDSHIRE

Abingdon School, Abingdon
Bloxham School, Banbury
Bruern Abbey, Chesterton
The Carrdus School, Banbury
Chandlings Manor School, Oxford
Christ Church Cathedral School, Oxford
Cokethorpe School, Witney
Cothill House Preparatory School, Abingdon
Cranford House School, Wallingford
d'Overbroeck's College, Oxford
Dragon School, Oxford
Ferndale Preparatory School, Faringdon
Headington School, Oxford
Kingham Hill School, Chipping Norton
The Manor Preparatory School, Abingdon
Moulsford Preparatory School, Wallingford
New College School, Oxford

Our Lady's Convent Senior School, Abingdon
Oxford High School GDST, Oxford
Radley College, Abingdon
Rupert House, Henley-on-Thames
Rye St Antony School, Oxford
St Clare's, Oxford
St Edward's School, Oxford
St Hugh's School, Faringdon
The School of St Helen & St Katharine, Abingdon
Shiplake College, Henley-on-Thames
Sibford School, Banbury
Summer Fields, Oxford
Tudor Hall School, Banbury
Windrush Valley School, Chipping Norton
Wychwood School, Oxford

RUTLAND

Brooke Priory School, Oakham
Oakham School, Oakham
Uppingham School, Uppingham

SHROPSHIRE

Adcote School for Girls, Shrewsbury
Bedstone College, Bucknell
Castle House School, Newport
Concord College, Shrewsbury
Ellesmere College, Ellesmere
Moor Park School, Ludlow
Moreton Hall School, Oswestry
The Old Hall School, Telford
Oswestry School, Oswestry
Packwood Haugh School, Shrewsbury
Prestfelde Preparatory School, Shrewsbury
St Winefride's Convent School, Shrewsbury
Shrewsbury High School GDST, Shrewsbury
Shrewsbury School, Shrewsbury
Wrekin College, Telford

SOMERSET

All Hallows, Shepton Mallet
Bruton School for Girls, Bruton
Chilton Cantelo School, Yeovil
Downside School, Bath
King's College, Taunton
King's Hall, Taunton
King's Bruton and Hazlegrove, Bruton
Millfield Preparatory School, Glastonbury
Millfield School, Street
The Park School, Yeovil
Perrott Hill School, Crewkerne
Queen's College, Taunton
Queen's College Junior, Pre-Prep & Nursery Schools, Taunton
Taunton Preparatory School, Taunton
Taunton School, Taunton
Wellington School, Wellington
Wells Cathedral Junior School, Wells
Wells Cathedral School, Wells

BATH & NORTH EAST SOMERSET

King Edward's School, Bath
Kingswood Preparatory School, Bath
Kingswood School, Bath
Monkton Combe Junior School, Bath
Monkton Combe School, Bath
Paragon School, Bath
Prior Park College, Bath
The Royal High School, Bath

NORTH SOMERSET

Sidcot School, Winscombe

STAFFORDSHIRE

Abbots Bromley School for Girls, Abbots Bromley
Brooklands School, Stafford
Chase Academy, Cannock
Denstone College, Uttoxeter
Edenhurst School, Newcastle-under-Lyme
Lichfield Cathedral School, Lichfield
Maple Hayes School, Lichfield
Newcastle-under-Lyme School, Newcastle under Lyme
St Bede's School, Stafford
St Dominic's Priory School, Stone
St Dominic's School, Stafford
St Joseph's Preparatory School, Stoke-on-Trent
Stafford Grammar School, Stafford
Vernon Lodge Preparatory School, Brewood
Yarlet School, Stafford

STOCKTON-ON-TEES

Red House School, Norton
Teesside High School, Eaglescliffe

SUFFOLK

The Abbey, Woodbridge
Amberfield School, Ipswich
Barnardiston Hall Preparatory School, Haverhill
Brandeston Hall, The Prep School for Framlingham College, Brandeston
Culford School, Bury St Edmunds
Fairstead House School, Newmarket
Finborough School, Stowmarket
Framlingham College, Woodbridge
Framlingham College Preparatory School, Brandeston
Ipswich High School GDST, Ipswich
Ipswich Preparatory School, Ipswich
Ipswich School, Ipswich
Moreton Hall Preparatory School, Bury St Edmunds
Old Buckenham Hall School, Ipswich
Orwell Park, Ipswich
Royal Hospital School, Ipswich
Saint Felix School, Southwold
St Joseph's College, Ipswich
South Lee Preparatory School, Bury St Edmunds
Stoke College, Sudbury
Woodbridge School, Woodbridge

SURREY

Aberdour, Tadworth
ACS Cobham International School, Cobham
ACS Egham International School, Egham
Aldro School, Godalming
Amesbury, Hindhead
Barfield School, Farnham
Barrow Hills School, Godalming
Belmont School, Dorking
Bishopsgate School, Egham
Box Hill School, Dorking
Bramley School, Tadworth
Canbury School, Kingston upon Thames
Caterham Preparatory School, Caterham
Caterham School, Caterham
Charterhouse, Godalming
Chinthurst School, Tadworth
City of London Freemen's School, Ashtead
Claremont Fan Court School, Esher
Coworth-Flexlands School, Woking
Cranleigh Preparatory School, Cranleigh
Cranleigh School, Cranleigh
Cranmore School, Leatherhead
Cumnor House School, South Croydon
Danes Hill Preparatory School, Leatherhead
Duke of Kent School, Guildford
Dunottar School, Reigate
Edgeborough, Farnham
Epsom College, Epsom
Ewell Castle School, Epsom
Feltonfleet School, Cobham
Frensham Heights School, Farnham
Greenacre School for Girls, Banstead
Greenfield School, Woking
Guildford High School, Guildford
Hall Grove School, Bagshot
Halstead Preparatory School, Woking
Haslemere Preparatory School, Haslemere
Hawley Place School, Camberley
The Hawthorns School, Redhill
Homefield Preparatory School, Sutton
Hurtwood House, Dorking
King Edward's School Witley, Godalming
Kingston Grammar School, Kingston upon Thames
Kingswood House School, Epsom
Lanesborough, Guildford
Lingfield Notre Dame School, Lingfield
Longacre School, Guildford
Lyndhurst School, Camberley
Manor House School, Leatherhead
Marymount International School, Kingston upon Thames
Micklefield School, Reigate
Milbourne Lodge School, Esher
More House School, Farnham
Notre Dame Preparatory School, Cobham
Notre Dame Senior School, Cobham
Oakhyrst Grange School, Caterham
Parkside School, Cobham
Prior's Field School, Godalming
Priory Preparatory School, Banstead
Reed's School, Cobham
Reigate Grammar School, Reigate

Reigate St Mary's Preparatory and Choir School, Reigate
Ripley Court School, Woking
Rowan Preparatory School, Esher
Royal Grammar School, Guildford
The Royal School, Haslemere
Rydes Hill Preparatory School, Guildford
St Andrew's (Woking) School Trust, Woking
St Catherine's School, Guildford
St Christopher's School, Epsom
St David's School, Purley
St Edmund's School, Hindhead
St George's College, Weybridge
St George's College Junior School, Weybridge
St Hilary's School, Godalming
St Ives School, Haslemere
St John's School, Leatherhead
St Teresa's Preparatory School, Effingham
St Teresa's School, Dorking
Seaton House School, Sutton
Sir William Perkins's School, Chertsey
Surbiton High School, Kingston-upon-Thames
Surbiton Preparatory School, Surbiton
Sutton High School GDST, Sutton
Tormead School, Guildford
Westward Preparatory School, Walton-on-Thames
Woldingham School, Woldingham
Woodcote House School, Windlesham
Yehudi Menuhin School, Cobham

EAST SUSSEX

Ashdown House School, Forest Row
Battle Abbey School, Battle
Bricklehurst Manor Preparatory, Wadhurst
Brighton and Hove High School GDST, Brighton
Brighton College, Brighton
Brighton College Prep School, Brighton
Eastbourne College, Eastbourne
Frewen College, Rye
Greenfields School, Forest Row
Lewes Old Grammar School, Lewes
Newland School, Seaford
Northease Manor, Lewes
Roedean School, Brighton
St Andrew's School, Eastbourne
St Aubyns School, Brighton
St Bede's Prep School, Eastbourne
St Bede's School, Hailsham
St Leonards-Mayfield School, Mayfield
St Mary's Hall, Brighton
Sacred Heart School, Wadhurst
Skippers Hill Manor Preparatory School, Mayfield
Vinehall School, Robertsbridge

WEST SUSSEX

Ardingly College, Haywards Heath
Ardingly College Junior School, Haywards Heath
Arundale Preparatory School, Pulborough
Brambletye, East Grinstead
Broadwater Manor School, Worthing
Burgess Hill School for Girls, Burgess Hill

Christ's Hospital, Horsham
Copthorne Prep School, Copthorne
Cottesmore School, Pease Pottage
Cumnor House School, Haywards Heath
Dorset House School, Pulborough
Farlington School, Horsham
Fonthill Lodge, East Grinstead
Great Ballard School, Chichester
Great Walstead, Haywards Heath
Handcross Park School, Haywards Heath
Hurstpierpoint College, Hurstpierpoint
Lancing College, Lancing
Lavant House, Chichester
Oakwood School, Chichester
Our Lady of Sion School, Worthing
Pennthorpe School, Horsham
The Prebendal School, Chichester
St Margaret's School Convent of Mercy, Midhurst
Seaford College, Petworth
Shoreham College, Shoreham-by-Sea
Slindon College, Arundel
Sompting Abbotts School, Sompting
Stoke Brunswick, East Grinstead
The Towers Convent School, Steyning
Westbourne House School, Chichester
Windlesham House School, Pulborough
Worth School, Turners Hill

TYNE AND WEAR

Argyle House School, Sunderland
Central Newcastle High School GDST,
  Newcastle upon Tyne
Dame Allan's Boys School, Newcastle upon Tyne
Dame Allan's Girls School, Newcastle upon Tyne
The King's School, Tynemouth
Newcastle Preparatory School, Newcastle upon Tyne
Royal Grammar School, Newcastle upon Tyne
Sunderland High School, Sunderland
Westfield School, Newcastle upon Tyne

WARWICKSHIRE

Arnold Lodge School, Leamington Spa
Bilton Grange, Rugby
The Crescent School, Rugby
The King's High School for Girls, Warwick
The Kingsley School, Leamington Spa
Princethorpe College, Rugby
Rugby School, Rugby
Stratford Preparatory School, Stratford-upon-Avon
Warwick Preparatory School, Warwick
Warwick School, Warwick

WEST MIDLANDS

Bablake Junior School, Coventry
Bablake School, Coventry
The Blue Coat School, Birmingham
Coventry Prep School, Coventry
Crackley Hall School, Kenilworth
Davenport Lodge School, Coventry
Edgbaston High School for Girls, Birmingham
Elmhurst School for Dance, Birmingham

Eversfield Preparatory School, Solihull
Hallfield School, Birmingham
Highclare School, Birmingham
King Edward VI High School for Girls, Birmingham
King Edward's School, Birmingham
King Henry VIII School, Coventry
Mayfield Preparatory School, Walsall
Newbridge Preparatory School, Wolverhampton
Norfolk House School, Birmingham
Priory School, Birmingham
The Royal Wolverhampton Junior School,
  Wolverhampton
The Royal Wolverhampton School, Wolverhampton
Ruckleigh School, Solihull
St George's School, Edgbaston, Birmingham
Saint Martin's School, Solihull
Solihull School, Solihull
Tettenhall College, Wolverhampton
West House School, Birmingham
Wolverhampton Grammar School, Wolverhampton

WILTSHIRE

Appleford School, Salisbury
Chafyn Grove School, Salisbury
Dauntsey's School, Devizes
The Godolphin School, Salisbury
Heywood Preparatory School, Corsham
Leaden Hall School, Salisbury
Marlborough College, Marlborough
Norman Court, Salisbury
Pinewood School, Shrivenham
Prior Park Preparatory School, Cricklade
St Francis School, Pewsey
St Margaret's Preparatory School, Calne
St Mary's Calne, Calne
Salisbury Cathedral School, Salisbury
Sandroyd School, Salisbury
Stonar School, Melksham
Warminster School, Warminster

WORCESTERSHIRE

Abberley Hall, Worcester
The Alice Ottley School, Worcester
Bowbrook House School, Pershore
Bromsgrove Preparatory School, Bromsgrove
Bromsgrove School, Bromsgrove
Dodderhill School, Droitwich Spa
The Downs School, Malvern
The Elms, Malvern
Heathfield School, Kidderminster
Holy Trinity School, Kidderminster
King's Hawford, Worcester
The King's School, Worcester
The Knoll School, Kidderminster
Malvern College, Malvern
Moffats School, Bewdley
St James's School, Malvern
St Mary's Convent School, Worcester
Winterfold House, Kidderminster

EAST RIDING OF YORKSHIRE

Hull Collegiate School, Anlaby
Hymers College, Hull
Pocklington School, Pocklington

NORTH YORKSHIRE

Ampleforth College, York
Ashville College, Harrogate
Aysgarth Preparatory School, Bedale
Bootham School, York
Bramcote School, Scarborough
Clifton Preparatory School, York
Fyling Hall School, Whitby
Giggleswick School, Settle
Harrogate Ladies' College, Harrogate
Malsis School, Nr Skipton
The Minster School, York
The Mount School, York
Queen Ethelburga's College, York
Queen Margaret's School, York
Queen Mary's School, Thirsk
Read School, Selby
Ripon Cathedral Choir School, Ripon
St Martin's Ampleforth, York
St Olave's School (Junior of St Peter's), York
St Peter's School, York
Scarborough College & Lisvane School, Scarborough
Terrington Hall, York

SOUTH YORKSHIRE

Ashdell Preparatory School, Sheffield
Birkdale School, Sheffield

Brantwood School, Sheffield
Hill House School, Doncaster
Mylnhurst Preparatory School & Nursery, Sheffield
Rudston Preparatory School, Rotherham
Sheffield High School GDST, Sheffield
Westbourne School, Sheffield

WEST YORKSHIRE

Ackworth School, Pontefract
Batley Grammar School, Batley
Bradford Girls' Grammar School, Bradford
Bradford Grammar School, Bradford
Bronte House School, Bradford
Cliff School, Wakefield
Dale House School, Batley
The Froebelian School, Leeds
Fulneck School, Leeds
Gateways School, Leeds
The Gleddings Preparatory School, Halifax
The Grammar School at Leeds, Leeds
Hipperholme Grammar School, Halifax
Lady Lane Park School, Bingley
Moorfield School, Ilkley
Moorlands School, Leeds
Queen Elizabeth Grammar School, Wakefield
The Rastrick Independent School, Brighouse
Richmond House School, Leeds
Rishworth School, Rishworth
Silcoates School, Wakefield
Sunny Hill House School, Wakefield
Wakefield Girls' High School, Wakefield
Westville House Preparatory School, Ilkley
Woodhouse Grove School, Apperley Bridge

NORTHERN IRELAND

COUNTY ANTRIM

Belfast Royal Academy, Belfast
Campbell College, Belfast
Methodist College, Belfast
Royal Belfast Academical Institution, Belfast

COUNTY DOWN

Bangor Grammar School, Bangor
Rockport School, Holywood

COUNTY FERMANAGH

Portora Royal School, Enniskillen

COUNTY LONDONDERRY

Coleraine Academical Institution, Coleraine

COUNTY TYRONE

The Royal School Dungannon, Dungannon

SCOTLAND

ABERDEENSHIRE

Robert Gordon's College, Aberdeen
St Margaret's School for Girls, Aberdeen

ANGUS

High School of Dundee, Dundee
Lathallan School, Montrose

ARGYLL AND BUTE

Lomond School, Helensburgh

CLACKMANNANSHIRE

Dollar Academy, Dollar

FIFE

St Leonards School & VIth Form College, St Andrews

GLASGOW

Craigholme School, Glasgow
The Glasgow Academy, Glasgow
The High School of Glasgow, Glasgow
Hutchesons' Grammar School, Glasgow
Kelvinside Academy, Glasgow
St Aloysius Junior School, Glasgow

LOTHIAN

Belhaven Hill, Dunbar
Cargilfield, Edinburgh
Clifton Hall School, Edinburgh
The Edinburgh Academy, Edinburgh
Fettes College, Edinburgh
George Heriot's School, Edinburgh
George Watson's College, Edinburgh
Loretto School, Musselburgh
The Mary Erskine School, Edinburgh
Merchiston Castle School, Edinburgh
St George's School for Girls, Edinburgh
St Margaret's School, Edinburgh
Stewart's Melville College, Edinburgh

MORAYSHIRE

Gordonstoun School, Elgin

PERTH AND KINROSS

Ardvreck School, Crieff
Craigclowan Preparatory School, Perth
Glenalmond College, Perth
Kilgraston, Perth
Morrison's Academy, Crieff
Strathallan School, Perth

RENFREWSHIRE

St Columba's School, Kilmacolm

ROXBURGHSHIRE

St Mary's Preparatory School, Melrose

STIRLING

Beaconhurst School, Bridge of Allan

WALES

CARDIFF

The Cathedral School, Cardiff
Howell's School, Llandaff GDST, Cardiff
Kings Monkton School, Cardiff
St John's College, Old St Mellors
Westbourne School, Cardiff

CARMARTHENSHIRE

Llandovery College, Llandovery
St Michael's School, Llanelli

CONWY

Lyndon Preparatory School, Colwyn Bay
Rydal Penrhos Senior School, Colwyn Bay
St David's College, Llandudno

DENBIGHSHIRE

Howell's School, Denbigh
Ruthin School, Ruthin

GWYNEDD

St Gerard's School, Bangor

MONMOUTHSHIRE

Haberdashers' Monmouth School For Girls,
    Monmouth
Monmouth School, Monmouth
St John's-on-the-Hill, Chepstow

NEWPORT

Rougemont School, Newport

POWYS

Christ College, Brecon

Educational Associations and Useful Addresses

The Allied Schools
Cross House
38 High Street
Banbury
Oxon OX16 5ET
Tel: (01295) 256441
Fax: (01295) 275350
E-mail: z.foard@alliedschools.org.uk
Website: www.alliedschools.org.uk
General Manager: Michael Porter BA, MSc

The organization provides management, financial, helpline and other support services to member schools, as well as operating a communications network between school governors, heads, bursars and other staff for the exchange of information and ideas. The Allied Schools include:

Barnardiston Hall
Harrogate Ladies' College
St John's-on-the-hill, Chepstow
Westonbirt School

Canford School
Riddlesworth Hall
Stowe
Wrekin Old Hall Trust

The Association for the Education and Guardianship of International Students (AEGIS)
Tel/Fax: (01453) 755160
E-mail: secretary@aegisuk.net
Website: www.aegisuk.net
Secretary: Janet Bowman
Registered Charity No. 1111 384

The Association promotes best and legal practice in all areas of guardianship and the care of international students, under 18 years of age, at school or college in the United Kingdom. All members, including school members, are required to adhere to the AEGIS Code of Practice and undertake to follow guidelines on caring for international students. Guardianship organizations are admitted to membership after a successful accreditation inspection.

Association of Governing Bodies of Independent Schools (AGBIS)
3 Codicote Road
Welwyn
Hertfordshire AL6 9LY
Tel: (01438) 840730
Fax: (0560) 3432632
E-mail: gensec@agbis.org.uk
Website: www.agbis.org.uk
General Secretary: Stuart Westley, MA

The aim of the Association is to advance education in independent schools, to promote good governance and administration in independent schools and to encourage co-operation between their governing bodies. For details please contact the General Secretary.

Association of Heads of Independent Schools
St Nicholas School
Redfields House, Redfields Lane
Church Crookham
Fleet
Hampshire GU52 0RF
Honorary Secretary: Mrs A V Whatmough

Membership of AHIS is open to the Heads of girls' independent secondary schools and girls' co-educational junior independent schools which are accredited by the Independent Schools Council (see below).

Association of School and College Leaders (ASCL)
130 Regent Road
Leicester LE1 7PG
Tel: (0116) 299 1122
Fax: (0116) 299 1123
E-mail: info@ascl.org.uk
Website: www.ascl.org.uk
General Secretary: Dr J E Dunford

ASCL is the only professional association and trade union in Britain to speak exclusively for secondary school and college leaders, in both the independent and mainstream sectors.

The Association has nearly 15,000 members including heads, deputy heads, assistant heads, bursars and business managers and others with school/college responsibility.

ASCL has strong ties with the Headmasters' Conference and Girls' School Association and their members are automatically part of ASCL.

Benefits of ASCL membership include access to legal support and advice, a telephone hotline for guidance on urgent issues, personal support from regional field officers, regular publications and guidance on courses and conferences, and pension advice.

Association of Tutors
Sunnycroft
63 King Edward Road
Northampton NN1 5LY

Tel: (01604) 624171
Fax: (01604) 624718
Website: www.tutor.co.uk
Secretary: Dr D J Cornelius

The professional body for independent private tutors. Members provide advice and individual tuition to students at all levels of education. The tutoring may be supplementary to full course provision or may be on a full course basis.

Boarding Schools' Association (BSA)

Grosvenor Gardens House
35–37 Grosvenor Gardens
London SW1W 0BS
Tel: (020) 7798 1580
Fax: (020) 7798 1581
E-mail: bsa@boarding.org.uk
Website: www.boarding.org.uk
National Director: Hilary Moriarty

The BSA has the twin objectives of promoting boarding education and developing quality boarding through high standards of pastoral care and boarding facilities.

A school can join the BSA only if it is a member of one of the constituent associations of the Independent Schools Council or, for state-maintained boarding schools, a member of SBSA (the State Boarding Schools Association). These two bodies require member schools to be regularly inspected by the Independent Schools Inspectorate (ISA) or OFSTED. Parents and prospective pupils choosing a boarding school can therefore be assured that BSA member schools are committed to providing the best possible boarding environment for their pupils.

For further information about the BSA Professional Development Programme please contact:

Alex Thompson BSc (Hons) PGCE DipEd FCIPD MIFL
BSA Director of Training
Grosvenor Gardens House
35–37 Grosvenor Gardens
London SW1W 0BS
Tel: (01722) 790090

British Accreditation Council

The Chief Executive
44 Bedford Row
London WC1R 4LL
Tel: (020) 7447 2554
Fax: (020) 7447 2555
E-mail: info@the-bac.org
Website: www.the-bac.org

BAC is a registered charity organization which was established in 1984 to act as the national accrediting body for independent further and higher education. A college accredited by

BAC undergoes a thorough inspection every four years, which is followed up with an interim visit after two years. Accreditation means that a BAC college has achieved a satisfactory standard in the areas of *health and safety provision, administration and staffing, the management of quality, student welfare* and *teaching and learning*. BAC also attempts to take action to intercede for students if a conflict arises between the student and the accredited college.

At present BAC accredits over 230 colleges in the UK and more than 25 overseas in 11 different countries: the Czech Republic, France, Spain, Pakistan, United Arab Emirates, Bulgaria, Greece, India, Mauritius, Germany and Switzerland.

British Association for Early Childhood Education (Early Education)
111 City View House
463 Bethnal Green Road
London E2 9QY
Tel: (020) 7739 7594
Fax: (020) 7613 5330

A charitable association which advises on the care and education of young children from birth to 8 years. The Association also publishes booklets and organizes conferences for those interested in early childhood education.

British Dyslexia Association
Unit 8 Bracknell Beeches
Old Bracknell Lane
Bracknell RG12 7BW
Fax: (0118) 935 1927
E-mail: helpline@bdadyslexia.org.uk
Website: www.bdadyslexia.org.uk
(Helpline/Information Service 10am–4pm Monday–Friday (5pm–7pm) also Wednesdays.

Charity offering information and help to dyslexic people, their families, professionals and employees.

Children's Education Advisory Service
Trenchard Lines
Upavon
Pewsey
Wilts SN9 6BE
Tel: (01980) 618244
E-mail: enquiries@ceas.detsa.co.uk

To support Service families and entitled civilians in obtaining appropriate educational facilities for their children and to provide high quality, impartial advice on all aspects of education worldwide.

Choir Schools Association
Wolvesey
College Street
Winchester SO23 9ND
Tel: (01962) 890530
Fax: (01962) 869978
E-mail: info@choirschools.org.uk
Administrator: Susan Rees

An association of schools educating cathedral and collegiate boy and girl choristers. Membership comprises the following schools:

Bristol Cathedral School, Bristol
The Cathedral School, Llandaff
Chetham's School of Music, Manchester
The Chorister School, Durham
Christ Church Cathedral School, Oxford
Exeter Cathedral School, Exeter
Hereford Cathedral Junior School, Hereford
King's College School, Cambridge
King's Preparatory School, Rochester
The King's School, Ely
The King's School, Gloucester
The King's School, Worcester
Lanesborough, Guildford
Lichfield Cathedral School, Lichfield
Lincoln Minster School, Lincoln
Magdalen College School, Oxford
The Minster School, Southwell
The Minster School, York
New College School, Oxford
Norwich School, Norwich

The Pilgrim's School, Winchester
Polwhele House, Truro
The Prebendal School, Chichester
Reigate St Mary's Preparatory and Choir
   School, Reigate
Ripon Cathedral Choir School, Ripon
St Edmunds Junior School, Canterbury
St George's School, Windsor
St James's School, Grimsby
St John's College, Cardiff
St John's College School, Cambridge
St Mary's Music School, Edinburgh
St Paul's Cathedral School, London EC4
Salisbury Cathedral School, Salisbury
Wells Cathedral School, Wells
Westminster Abbey Choir School,
   London SW1
Westminster Cathedral Choir School,
   London SW1

Associate Members
Ampleforth College, Ampleforth, North Yorkshire
City of London School, EC4V
The King's School, Peterborough
The Oratory School, Reading
Portsmouth Grammar School, Portsmouth
Runnymede St Edward's School, Liverpool
Queen Elizabeth Grammar School, Wakefield
St Cedd's School, Chelmsford
St Edward's College, Liverpool
Warwick School, Warwick

Council for Independent Education (CIFE)
1 Knightsbridge Green
London SW1X 7NW
Tel: (020) 8767 8666
E-mail: enquiries@cife.org.uk
Website: www.cife.org.uk

CIFE, founded in 1973, is a professional association for independent colleges of further education which specialize in preparing students for GCSEs, A and AS levels and university entrance. In addition, some colleges offer English language tuition for students from abroad. The Association promotes good practice and adherence to strict standards of professional conduct and ethical propriety. Full membership is open to colleges which have been accredited either by the British Accreditation Council (BAC) or by the Independent Schools Council. All CIFE colleges, of which there are currently 17 spread throughout England, with concentrations in London, Oxford and Cambridge, have to abide by exacting codes of conduct and practice; and the character and presentation of their published exam results are subject to formal validation by the BACS. Further information and a list of colleges are available from the Secretary.

CReSTeD (Council for the Registration of Schools Teaching Dyslexic Pupils)
Registered Charity No: 1052103
Greygarth, Littleworth
Winchcombe
Cheltenham GL54 5BT
Tel: (01242) 604 852
E-mail: admin@crested.org.uk
Website: www.crested.org.uk
Chairman: Brendan Wignall

The CReSTeD Register is to help parents and those who advise them to choose schools for children with SpLD (dyslexia). Its main supporters are the British Dyslexia Association and Dyslexia Action who, with others, established CReSTeD to produce an authoritative list of schools, both maintained and independent, which have been through an established registration procedure, including a visit by the CReSTeD selected consultant.

Department for Children, Schools and Families
Sanctuary Buildings
Great Smith Street
London SW1P 3BT
Tel: (08700) 000 2288
Fax: (01928) 794 248
E-mail: info@dcsf.gsi.gov.uk
Website: www.dcsf.gov.uk

The Dyslexia Institute: National Training and Resources Centre
Park House, Wick Road
Egham
Surrey TW20 0HH

Tel: (01784) 222300
Fax: (01784) 222333
E-mail: info@dyslexiaaction.org.uk
Website: www.dyslexiaaction.org.uk
Registered Charity No. 268502

Dyslexia Action is a national charity and the UK's leading provider of services and support for people with dyslexia and literacy difficulties. We specialize in assessment, teaching and training. We also develop and distribute teaching materials and undertake research.

Dyslexia Action is committed to improving public policy and practice. We partner with schools, LEAs, colleges, universities, employers, voluntary sector organizations and government to improve the quality and quantity of help for people with dyslexia and specific learning difficulties.

Our services are available through our 26 centres and 160 teaching locations around the UK. Over half a million people benefit from our work each year.

Gabbitas Educational Consultants

Carrington House
126–130 Regent Street
London W1B 5EE
Tel: (020) 7734 0161
Fax: (020) 7437 1764
E-mail: market@gabbitas.co.uk
Website: www.gabbitas.co.uk

Gabbitas offers independent, expert advice on all stages of education and careers:

- choice of independent schools and colleges;
- educational assessment services for parents concerned about their child's progress at school;
- Sixth Form options – A and AS level, International Baccalaureate and vocational courses;
- university and degree choices and UCAS applications;
- alternatives to university;
- careers assessment and guidance;
- extensive guidance for overseas students transferring into the British system;
- specialist services, including guardianship, for overseas students attending UK boarding schools.

Gabbitas also provides a full range of services for schools, including the appointment of Heads and staff as well as consultancy on any aspects of school management and development.

The Girls' Day School Trust (GDST)

100 Rochester Row
London SW1P 1JP
Tel: (020) 7393 6666
Fax: (020) 7393 6789
E-mail: info@wes.gdst.net
Website: www.gdst.net

The GDST is a registered Charity (No. 306983).

The GDST is one of the largest, longest-established and most successful groups of indepen-dent schools in the UK, with 4,000 staff and 20,000 students. As a charity that owns and runs a family of 29 schools in England and Wales, it reinvests all its income for the benefit of the pupils. With a long history of pioneering innovation in the education of girls, the GDST now also educates boys in some of its schools; has two co-educational Sixth Form Colleges; and is developing a selective group of prep schools, some of which are co-educational.

The wide-ranging curricular and extra-curricular opportunities available in GDST schools encourage creativity, articulate self-expression and enterprise in students who are prepared to participate fully in the challenges of 21st-century life.

Schools

The Belvedere Academy, Liverpool
Birkenhead High School, Birkenhead
Blackheath High School, London SE3
Brighton and Hove High School, Sussex
Bromley High School, Kent
Central Newcastle High School,
    Newcastle upon Tyne
Croydon High School, Croydon
Great Houghton Prep School,
    Northampton
The Hamlets Prep School, Liverpool
Heathfield School, Pinner
Hilden Grange School, Tonbridge, Kent
Howell's School, Llandaff, Cardiff
Ipswich High School, Suffolk
Kensington Preparatory School,
    London SW6
Northampton High School,
    Northampton

Norwich High School for Girls, Norfolk
Notting Hill & Ealing High School,
    London W13
Nottingham High School for Girls,
    Nottingham
Oxford High School, Oxford
Portsmouth High School, Hampshire
Putney High School, London SW15
Royal High School, Bath
Sheffield High School, Sheffield
Shrewsbury High School, Shropshire
South Hampstead High School,
    London NW3
Streatham & Clapham High School,
    London SW16
Sutton High School, Surrey
Sydenham High School, London SE26
Wimbledon High School, London SW19

All GDST schools are non-denominational day schools, and The Royal High School, Bath, also takes boarders. The GDST's small group of prep schools – Great Houghton, The Hamlets, Hilden Grange and Kensington – prepare pupils for entry to other schools at 11 or 13. All other schools in the group offer an 'all-through' education, catering for pupils from ages 3 or 4 to 18, with thriving Sixth Forms and, in many cases, nursery classes too.

Howell's School in Cardiff and the Royal High School in Bath have a co-educational Sixth Form College and, in a new initiative, The Belvedere School in Liverpool transferred from the independent sector to Academy status and opened as The Belvedere Academy in September 2007.

The Girls' Schools Association (GSA)
130 Regent Road
Leicester LE1 7PG

Tel: (0116) 254 1619
Fax: (0116) 255 3792
E-mail: office@gsa.uk.com
President: Mrs Jill Berry
Executive Director: Ms Sheila Cooper

GSA is the professional association representing the heads of leading girls' independent schools. Its aims are to promote high standards of education for girls; to inform and influence national educational debate; raise awareness of the benefits of single-sex education for girls and to support members through the provision of a broad range of services. GSA also operates the MyDaughter website – www.mydaughter.co.uk – the first website dedicated to providing information, expert opinion and lively debate on all aspects of raising and educating happy and fulfilled girls.

The Headmasters' and Headmistresses' Conference (HMC)
12 The Point
Rockingham Road
Market Harborough
Leicestershire LE16 7QU
Tel: (01858) 469 059
Fax: (01858) 469 532
Membership Secretary: I Power
Secretary: G H Lucas

The Headmasters' and Headmistresses' Conference (HMC) represents the headteachers of some 250 leading independent schools in the United Kingdom and the Republic of Ireland.

IAPS (The Independent Association of Prep Schools)
11 Waterloo Place
Leamington Spa
Warwickshire CV32 5LA
Tel: (01926) 887833
Fax: (01926) 888014
E-mail: iaps@iaps.org.uk
Chief Executive: David Hanson

IAPS is the main professional association for Heads of independent preparatory and junior schools in the UK and overseas. There are some 600 schools whose Heads are in membership, accommodating over 130,000 children.

The Independent Schools Association (ISA)
1 Boys' British School
East Street
Saffron Walden
Essex CB10 1LS
Tel: (01799) 523619
Chief Executive: Neil Roskilly

There are approximately 300 schools in membership of ISA. These are all schools which have been accredited by the Independent Schools Council Inspection Service. This and the requirement that the school should be good of its kind are the criteria for membership. ISA represents schools with pupils throughout the age range. The majority of schools are day schools, but a significant number also have boarders. Membership of the Association enables Heads to receive support from the Association in a number of ways and enables pupils to take part in many events organized by ISA.

The Independent Schools' Bursars Association (ISBA)
Unit 11–12, Manor Farm
Cliddesden, Basingstoke
Hants RG25 2JB
Tel: (01256) 330369
Fax: (01256) 330376
E-mail: office@theisba.org.uk
Website: www.theisba.org.uk
General Secretary: Mr Jonathan Cook

The ISBA, with over 1,000 schools in membership, aims to support and advance financial and operational performance in schools. The Association deals with Ministers, civil servants, the media, the general public, a wide range of professional advisers and suppliers, and schools at a number of different levels including governors, heads and bursars. It works closely with the Independent Schools Council (ISC) and its other seven associations together with the Independent Schools Inspectorate (ISI) and the Boarding Schools Association (BSA). The ISBA's staff and Secretariat provide help and advice to schools, seek to keep ahead of regulatory change and promote the sharing of best practice.

The Independent Schools Careers Organisation (ISCO)
ISCO is the independent schools careers service from The Inspiring Futures Foundation.

ISCO c/o Inspiring Futures
St George's House
Knoll Road
Camberley
Surrey GU15 3SY
Tel: (01276) 687525
E-mail: helpline@inspiringfutures.org.uk
Websites: www.isco.org.uk; www.inspiringfutures.org.uk; www.myfuturewise.org.uk; www.expandinghorizons.info; www.careerscope.org.uk

ISCO, part of Inspiring Futures, is a not-for-profit organization established to help young people make informed decisions about higher education and career choices. It provides support to schools through its ISCO Membership and Information Service schemes and direct help and guidance to young people and their parents through the Futurewise scheme. This provides a range of career and higher education services, online and face-to-face, from enrolment to age 23. Services are delivered across the UK and internationally through a network of professionally qualified Regional Directors and Regional Advisers. Operations are supported centrally to ensure that up-to-date information is provided to members of the schemes through a range of resources, online services and the termly *Careerscope* magazine. The Expanding Horizons team organizes a range of unique development and career preparation opportunities for young people including InterActives, Insight courses and GAP year fairs.

Independent Schools Council (ISC)
St Vincent House
30 Orange Street
London WC2H 7HH
Tel: (020) 7766 7070
Fax: (020) 7766 7071
Chief Executive: David Lyscom

ISC is the umbrella body for the following associations:

The Association of Governing Bodies of Independent Schools (AGBIS), (COBIS)
The Girls' Schools Association (GSA)
The Headmasters' and Headmistresses' Conference (HMC)
The Independent Association of Prep Schools (IAPS)
The Independent Schools' Association (ISA)
The Independent Schools' Bursars Association (ISBA)
The Society of Headmasters and Headmistresses of Independent Schools (SHMIS), (COBIS)

The total membership of ISC comprises about 1,300 schools which are accredited by ISC and inspected on a six-year cycle by the Independent Schools Inspectorate (ISI) under arrangements agreed by the DCSF and OFSTED. ISC deals with matters of policy and other issues common to its members and when required speaks collectively on their behalf. It represents its members in discussions with the Department for Children, Schools and Families and with other organizations, and represents the collective view of members on independent education.

Independent Schools Examinations Board
The Pump House
16 Queen's Avenue
Christchurch BH23 1BZ
Tel: (01202) 487538
Fax: (01202) 473728
E-mail: enquiries@iseb.co.uk
Website: iseb.co.uk

Details of the Common Entrance examinations (see the section on Examinations and Qualifications) are available from the General Secretary at the address above.

The Round Square Schools
Braemar Lodge
Castle Hill, Hartley, Dartford
Kent DA3 7BH
Tel: (0147) 470 6927

Fax: (01737) 217133
E-mail: jane@roundsquare.org
Secretary: Mrs J Howson

An international group of schools which follow the principles of Kurt Hahn, founder of the Salem School in Germany and Gordonstoun in Scotland. There are now over 50 member schools in more than 12 countries: Australia, Canada, England, France, Germany, India, Japan, Kenya, Oman, Scotland, South Africa, Switzerland, Thailand and the United States. Member schools arrange regular exchange visits for pupils and undertake aid projects in India, Kenya, Eastern Europe and Thailand. All member schools uphold the five principles of outdoor adventure, community service, education for democracy, international understanding and environmental conservation. UK member schools are as follows:

Abbotsholme, Uttoxeter (Co-ed)
Box Hill, Dorking (Co-ed)
Cobham Hall, Gravesend (Girls)
Gordonstoun, Elgin (Co-ed)

Wellington College, Crowthorne
(Boys, Girls in Sixth Form)
Westfield, Newcastle upon Tyne (Girls)
Windermere St Anne's (Co-ed)

SATIPS
Professional Support and Training for Staff in Independent Schools
Cherry Trees, Stebbing
Great Dunmow
Essex CM6 3ST
Tel/Fax: (01371) 856823
E-mail: admin@satips.com
Website: www.satips.com
General Secretary: Andrew Davis
Administrator: Mrs P M Harrison

SATIPS – founded in 1952 – is a source of professional support and encouragement for staff in preparatory and other schools. We are now one of the foremost providers of subject-based and cross-curricular INSET courses for prep school and other staff. SATIPS is a registered charity. In 1993 the Society widened its appeal by changing its emphasis from purely preparatory school teachers to any school staff, especially those in independent schools. In particular, teachers who have pupils in Key Stages 1, 2 and 3 will find the membership of SATIPS useful: we are particularly interested in making contact with colleagues in the maintained sector. The Society publishes 19 Broadsheets each term in all subject areas and runs conferences (mostly one-day) at various venues during the year. We offer school and individual membership.

The Society of Headmasters and Headmistresses of Independent Schools (SHMIS)
12 The Point
Rockingham Road
Market Harborough
Leicestershire LE16 7QU
Tel: (01858) 433760
Fax: (01858) 461413

E-mail: gensec@shmis.org.uk
Website: www.shmis.org.uk
General Secretary: David Richardson

A society of some 105 schools, most of which are co-educational, day and boarding, and all of which educate children up to the age of 18.

Steiner Waldorf Schools Fellowship
Kidbrooke Park
Forest Row
East Sussex RH18 5JA
Tel: (01342) 822115
Fax: (01342) 826004
E-mail: info@swsf.org.uk
Website: www.steinerwaldorf.org.uk
Chairman: Christopher Clouder

The Steiner Waldorf Schools Fellowship represents the 32 autonomous Steiner Waldorf Schools and 45 Early Years Centres in the UK and Eire. There are now over 958 schools worldwide. Key characteristics of the education include: careful balance in the artistic, practical and intellectual content of the international Steiner Waldorf curriculum; co-educational from 3 to 19 years. Shared Steiner Waldorf curriculum for all pupils. GCSE and A Level examinations. A broad education based on Steiner's approach to the holistic nature of the human being. Co-operative school management – usually a variable parent payment scheme. Steiner Waldorf education is rapidly gaining in popularity all over the world.

Woodard Schools (The Woodard Corporation)
High Street
Abbots Bromley
Rugeley
Staffordshire WS15 3BW
Tel: (01283) 840120
E-mail: jillshorthose@woodard.co.uk
Website: www.woodard.co.uk

The Woodard Corporation has 48 schools throughout the country, including 22 Affiliated schools and two academies. All have an Anglican foundation and together they form the largest independent group of Church Schools in England and Wales. Member and associated schools are listed below.

Member Schools

Abbots Bromley School for Girls, Abbots Bromley
Ardingly College, Haywards Heath
Ardingly College Prep School, Haywards Heath
Ardingly College Pre-Prep School, Haywards Heath
Bloxham School, Banbury
The Cathedral School, Cardiff
Denstone College, Uttoxeter

Ellesmere College, Ellesmere
Hurstpierpoint College, Hassocks
Hurstpierpoint College Prep School,
   Hassocks
King's College, Taunton
King's Hall School, Taunton
The King's School, Tynemouth
Lancing College, Lancing
Lancing College Prep School at Mowden,
   Hove
Peterborough High School, Peterborough
Prestfelde School, Shrewsbury
Queen Mary's School, Thirsk
Ranby House School, Retford
Roch House Prep School, Abbots Bromley

Smallwood Manor Prep School, Uttoxeter
St James' School, Great Grimsby
St Margaret's School, Exeter
Worksop College, Worksop

Associated Schools (Independent)

Alderley Edge School for Girls, Alderley
   Edge
The Bolitho School, Penzance
Derby Grammar School, Derby
Derby High School, Derby
Exeter Cathedral School, Exeter
King's School, Rochester
St Mary's Prep School, Lincoln

Glossary of Abbreviations

ABRSM	Associated Board of the Royal Schools of Music
ADD	Attention Deficit Disorder
ADISR	Association des Directeurs d'Instituts de la Suisse Romande
AEB	Associated Examining Board
AGBIS	Association of Governing Bodies of Independent Schools
AHIS	Association of Heads of Independent Schools
ASCL	Association of School and College Leaders
AICE	Advanced International Certificate of Education
ANTC	Association of Nursery Training Colleges
ARCS	Accreditation, Review and Consultancy Service
AVDEP	Association Vaudoise des Ecoles Privees
BACIFHE	British Accreditation Council for Independent Further and Higher Education
BAGA	British Amateur Gymnastics Association
BAYS	British Association for the Advancement of Science
BHS	British Horse Society
BSA	Boarding Schools Association
CAE	Cambridge Certificate in Advanced English
CASE	Council for Advancement and Support of Education
CEE	Common Entrance Examination
CIFE	Council for Independent Further Education
COBIS	Council of British International Schools
CReSTeD	Council for the Registration of Schools Teaching Dyslexic Pupils
CSA	Choir Schools Association
DCSF	Department for Children, Schools and Families
ECIS	European Council for International Schools
EFL	English as a Foreign Language
ESL	English as a Second Language
ESOL	English for Speakers of Other Languages
EUK	English UK, language teaching association

FCE	Cambridge First Certificate in English
FOBISSEA	Federation of British International Schools in South-East Asia
FSEP	Federation Suisse des Ecoles Privees
GBA	Governing Bodies Association
GBGSA	Governing Bodies of Girls' Schools Association
GDST	Girls' Day School Trust
GSA	Girls' Schools Association
HAS	Head Teachers' Association of Scotland
HMC	Headmasters' and Headmistresses' Conference
IAPS	Independent Association of Prep Schools
IB	International Baccalaureate
IBO	International Baccalaureate Organisation
IBSCA	International Baccalaureate Schools and Colleges Association
IBTA	Independent Business Training Organisation
ICG	Independent Colleges Group
IGCSE	International General Certificate of Secondary Education
ISA	Independent Schools Association
ISBA	Independent Schools Bursars' Association
ISC	Independent Schools Council (formerly Independent Schools Joint Council or ISJC)
ISCIS	Independent Schools Council Information Service (formerly ISIS)
ISCO	Independent Schools Careers Organisation
ISI	Independent Schools Inspectorate
ISIS	Independent Schools Information Service
LAMDA	London Academy of Music and Dramatic Art
LISA	London International Schools Association
MSA	Middle States Association of Colleges and Schools (USA)
NABSS	National Association of British Schools in Spain
NAHT	National Association of Head Teachers
NAIS	National Association of Independent Schools
NE/SA	Near East/South Asia
NEAB	Northern Examinations and Assessment Board
NEASC	New England Association of Schools and Colleges
OFSTED	Office for Standards in Education
OUDLE	University of Oxford Delegacy of Local Examinations
PET	Cambridge Preliminary English Test
PSE	Personal and Social Education
RSA CLAIT	Computer Literacy and Information Technology
SATIPS	Society of Assistants Teaching in Preparatory Schools
SCIS	Scottish Council of Independent Schools
SGS	Scottish Girls' Schools
SHMIS	Society of Headmasters and Headmistresses of Independent Schools
SpLD	Specific Learning Difficulties
STABIS	State Boarding Schools Information Service
WJEC	Welsh Joint Education Committee

Abbreviations used to denote Special Needs provision are as follows:

Special needs support provided (independent mainstream schools)

Learning difficulties

CA Some children with special needs receive help from classroom assistants

RA There are currently very limited facilities for pupils with learning difficulties but reasonable adjustments can be made if necessary

SC Some children with special needs are taught in separate classes for specific subjects

SNU School has a dedicated Special Needs Unit, which provides specialist tuition on a one-to-one or small group basis by appropriately qualified teachers

WI There is no dedicated Special Needs Unit but some children with special needs are withdrawn individually from certain lessons for one-to-one tuition

Behavioural disorders/emotional and behavioural difficulties/challenging behaviour

CA Some children with behavioural problems receive help from classroom assistants

CO Trained counsellors available for pupils

RA There are currently very limited facilities for pupils with behavioural disorders but reasonable adjustments can be made if necessary

ST Behaviour management strategies identified in school's behaviour management policy

TS Staff trained in behaviour management available

Physical impairments/medical conditions

AT Adapted timetable for children with health problems

BL Materials can be provided in Braille

CA Some children receive help from classroom assistants

DS Signing by staff and pupils

HL Hearing loops available

IT Specialist IT provision available

RA There are currently very limited facilities for pupils with physical impairments or medical conditions but reasonable adjustments can be made if necessary

SL Stairlifts

SM Staff with medical training available

TW Accessible toilet and washing facilities

W School has wheelchair access (unspecified)

WA1 School is fully wheelchair accessible

WA2 Main teaching areas are wheelchair accessible

WA3   No permanent access for
       wheelchairs; temporary ramps
       available

Special needs

ADD	Attention Deficit Disorder
ADHD	Attention Deficit/Hyperactivity Disorder
ASD	Autistic Spectrum Disorder
ASP	Asperger's Syndrome
BESD	Behavioural, Emotional and Social Disorders
CB	Challenging Behaviour
CP	Cerebral Palsy
DOW	Down's Syndrome
DYC	Dyscalculia
DYP	Dyspraxia
DYS	Dyslexia
EPI	Epilepsy
HEA	Health Problems (eg heart defect, asthma)
HI	Hearing Impairment
IM	Impaired Mobility
MLD	Moderate Learning Difficulties
PMLD	Profound and Multiple Learning Difficulties
SLD	Severe Learning Difficulties
SP&LD	Speech and Language Difficulties
TOU	Tourette's Syndrome
VI	Visual Impairment
WU	Wheelchair User

Further Reading

Schools and Further Education

Schools for Special Needs 2011–12: The complete guide to special needs education in the United Kingdom
17th Edition: Gabbitas Educational Consultants and Kogan-Page
*The definitive guide to special needs education in the UK
£25.00   Paperback   ISBN 978 0 7494 6417 2   592 pages   2011

How to Pass Secondary School Selection Tests
Contains over 600 practice questions
Mike Bryon
*Ideal for 11+ common entrance & SATS
£8.99   Paperback   ISBN 978 0 7494 4217 0   224 pages   2004

Everything You Need to Know about Going to University
3rd Edition: Sally Longson
"comprehensive resource to help you make the right choices" – Mandy Telford, former National President, National Union of Students
£9.99   Paperback   ISBN 978 0 7494 3985 9   192 pages   2003

The Essential Guide to Paying for University
Effective funding strategies for parents and students
Catherine Dawson
£9.99   Paperback   ISBN 978 0 7494 5635 1   344 pages   2009

Educational Reference

British Qualifications
A complete guide to professional, vocational & academic qualifications in the United Kingdom
42nd Edition
"The single best one-volume reference on British educational awards in print" – *World Education News & Reviews*
£60.00   Paperback   ISBN 978 0 7494 6411 0   2012

British Vocational Qualifications
A directory of vocational qualifications available in the United Kingdom
12th Edition
"Splendid . . . Every imaginable accessible procedure is packed into its pages" – *New Statesman*
£40.00   Paperback   ISBN 978 0 7494 5881 2   408 pages   2010

Careers

The A–Z of Careers & Jobs
18th Edition: Susan Hodgson published in association with *The Times*
"The perfect starting point for students and school leavers" – *Education & Training*
£16.99   Paperback   ISBN 978 0 7494 6259 8   480 pages   2011

Also available:

Careers & Jobs in IT   David Yardley   £7.99   Paperback   ISBN 978 0 7494 4245 X
144 pages   2004
Careers & Jobs in the Police Service   Kim Clabby   £7.99
Paperback   ISBN 978 0 7494 4204 2   112 pages   2004
Careers & Jobs in Travel & Tourism   Verité Reily Collins   £7.99
Paperback ISBN 978 0 7494 4205 0   112 pages   2004

What Next after School?
All you need to know about work, travel & study
9th Edition: Elizabeth Holmes, published in association with *The Times*
"A wealth of practical information about the world of work, training and
higher-education" – *Evening Standard*
£8.99   Paperback   ISBN 978 0 7494 5972 7   472 pages   2010

What Next after University?
Work, travel, education & life with a degree
2nd Edition: Simon Kent, published in association with *The Times*
"Covers everything from basic work, travel and education options and graduate
recruitment tests to finding a home and personal finance" – *Girl About Town*
£8.99   Paperback   ISBN 978 0 7494 4251 4   320 pages   2004

Job Applications

Great Answers to Tough Interview Questions
8th Edition: Martin Yate
"The best book on job-hunting" – *Financial Times*
£9.99   Paperback   ISBN 978 0 7494 6352 6   296 pages   2011

Ultimate CV
Write the perfect CV and get that job
Martin Yate
*Over 100 samples of job-winning CVs
£9.99   Paperback   ISBN 0 978 0 7494 5327 5   2008

Ultimate Job Search Letters
Write the perfect letter and get that job
Martin Yate
£9.99   Paperback   ISBN 978 0 7494 5328 2   2008

Readymade Job Search Letters
Every type of letter for getting the job you want
4th Edition: Lynn Williams, published in association with *The Times*
"The first book I've seen which specifically deals with letters. . . . A really useful
resource" – *Phoenix Journal*, Keele University
£8.99   Paperback   ISBN 978 0 7494 5322 0   224 pages   2008

Readymade CVs
Sample CVs for every type of job
4th Edition: Lynn Williams, published in association with *The Times*
"A resource book offering several ways to design your CV for a multitude of needs" – *All About
Money Making*
£8.99   Paperback   ISBN 978 0 7494 5323 7   224 pages   2008

Property

The Complete Guide to Buying & Selling Property
How to get the best deal on your home
2nd Edition: Sarah O'Grady
Published in association with the *Daily Express*
"Valuable, no-nonsense information" – *Ideal Home*
£8.99   Paperback   ISBN 978 0 7494 4194 4   240 pages   2004

The Complete Guide to Renovating & Improving Your Property
2nd Edition: Liz Hodgkinson
"Focuses on major renovation work, from obtaining planning permission to employing and
managing contractors" – *What Mortgage*
£10.99   Paperback   ISBN 978 0 7494 4870 7   224 pages   2007

Also available:

The Complete Guide to Buying Property Abroad
7th Edition: Liz Hodgkinson
£12.99   Paperback   ISBN 978 0 7494 5240 7   320 pages 2008

The Complete Guide to Buying Property in France
4th Edition: Charles Davey
£10.99   Paperback   ISBN 978 0 7494 4646 8   304 pages   2006

The Complete Guide to Buying Property in Italy
Barbara McMahon
£9.99   Paperback   ISBN 978 0 4794 4151 7   224 pages   2004

The Complete Guide to Buying Property in Portugal
Colin Barrow
£9.99   Paperback   ISBN 978 0 7494 4303 0   240 pages   2005

The Complete Guide to Buying Property in Spain
Charles Davey
£9.99 Paperback   ISBN 978 0 7494 4056 5   208 pages   2004

Personal Finance

A Complete Guide to Family Finance
Essential advice on everything from student loans to inheritance tax
Roderick Millar: published in association with the *Daily Express*
*Comprehensive and practical advice on everything you need to know about saving, investing and insuring for the future
£12.99   Paperback   ISBN 978 0 7494 4203 3   368 pages   2004

How the Stock Market Works
A beginner's guide to investment
3rd Edition: Michael Becket and Yvette Essen
"Not just for investors, but for anyone who wishes to understand our financial system" – Neil Collins, City Editor, *Daily Telegraph*
£9.99   Paperback   ISBN 978 0 7494 5689 4   208 pages   2009

How to Write Your Will
19th Edition: Marlene Garsia
"A practical and easy-to-read guide" – *Pensions World*
£9.99   Paperback   ISBN 978 0 7494 5540 8   280 pages   2009

Relocation

Working Abroad
The complete guide to overseas employment
31st Edition: Jonathan Reuvid
"Anyone involved in working abroad will quickly come to look upon this as their bible" – *Personnel Today*
£12.99   Paperback   ISBN 978 0 7494 6111 9   320 pages   2010

Kogan Page publishes books on Business, Management, Marketing, HR, Training, Careers and Testing, Personal Finance, Property and more.

**Visit our website for our full online catalogue:
www.koganpage.com**

5.13

Main Index

D

E

I

M

Q

R

S

W

Y

Yardley Court Preparatory School, Tonbridge   101, 314, 329, 342, 359

Yardley Court, Tonbridge   395

Yarlet School, Stafford   136, 318, 333, 353, 398

The Yarlet Schools, Stafford   136, 333, 364

Yarm at Raventhorpe School, Darlington   88, 312, 373

Yarm School, Yarm   137, 318, 333, 359

Yarrells School, Poole   87, 312, 366, 383, 393

Yateley Manor Preparatory School, Yateley   94, 313, 364, 383, 394

Yehudi Menuhin School, Cobham   144, 319, 334, 339, 353, 373, 388, 399

Yeshivah Ohr Torah School, Salford   367

Yesodey Hatorah Jewish School, London N16   117, 348

Yesodey Hatorah Jewish School, London   367

Yetev Lev Day School for Boys, London N16   116, 342

Yetev Lev Day School for Boys, London   367

York College for Girls, York   364

York House School, Hertfordshire   97

York House School, Rickmansworth   329, 364, 384, 394

Yorston Lodge School, Knutsford   82, 364

Young England Kindergarten, London   373

Ysgol Rhydygors, Carmarthen   379

Z

Zakaria Muslim Girls High School, Batley   367